LIVING LEGACIES AT COLUMBIA

LIVING LEGACIES
AT COLUMBIA

—⅏—

EDITED BY WM. THEODORE de BARY

WITH JERRY KISSLINGER AND TOM MATHEWSON

A COLUMBIA UNIVERSITY PUBLICATION

Library of Congress Cataloging-in-Publication Data

Living legacies at Columbia / edited by Wm. Theodore de Bary; with Jerry
Kisslinger & Tom Mathewson.
    p. cm.
  Includes index.
  ISBN 0-231-13884-9 (alk. paper)
  1. Columbia University—Faculty—Biography. 2. Columbia University—Alumni
and alumnae—Biography. I. De Bary, William Theodore, 1919–
  LD1240.L58 2006
  378.747'1—dc22

2006000033

CONTENTS

CONTENTS

VII

PREFACE

—⁂—

Wm. Theodore de Bary

When I was invited to attend the first meeting of the 250th Anniversary Committee, I assumed that it was in the role of an old-timer, with a longer memory of things at Columbia than anyone else present. I was certainly not looking for more work to do. Having formally retired in 1989, I was already doing more volunteer work than anyone else who was off the payroll—teaching four regular courses and an extracurricular alumni colloquium, and still directing the Heyman Center for the Humanities, which I had set up in the early eighties. I also had three books in process.

But at that first meeting as the discussion got going of suitable projects for the 250th anniversary, I made the mistake of enthusiastically supporting the idea put forth by Eric Kandel that, in addition to having a new history of Columbia over the 250 years of its life, it would be good to have a series devoted to more recent times—to major figures or developments in the twentieth century that tend to become forgotten when those with firsthand memories depart the scene. (My earliest memories of the place, going back over seventy years, are not of the scientific giants Professor Kandel writes about in his Living Legacies essays, but of the almost forgotten giants of the gridiron at Baker Field in the late twenties—Ralph Hewitt, Ralph Furey, Hubie Schulze, and, a little later, the Rose Bowlers Cliff E. Montgomery and Al Barabas, none of whom appear in these pages.) When everyone else present agreed with the proposal, it was left to Fritz Stern—who, besides his successful career as an historian at Columbia, has made a second career of recruiting colleagues to take on difficult assignments—to suggest that I be asked to head the effort. At the time I thought I was just being asked to chair a subcommittee, but I ended up as editor of the series, which I named Living Legacies.

What was more crucial in getting things off the ground was the willingness of key people to take on the writing of the individual essays themselves. Here I had to rely on the loyalty and public-spiritedness of Columbians who agreed to pay tribute to their own teachers, mentors, or collegial associates. Fortunately it has been my privilege to work as provost and then director of the Heyman Center with many wonderful colleagues. They are the ones to whom I turned as editor of Living Legacies, because they have been a source of encouragement and inspiration to me over the years. They are the ones who made the Living Legacies project not just another extracurricular burden, but a source of genuine satisfaction with the very best that Columbia has had to offer. They represent the true Living Legacies at Columbia today.

Among those whose ready response made it possible to make a quick and lively start were many old friends whom I had known and worked with over the years: people like Jacques Barzun, Jack Beeson, Ronald Breslow, Eric Foner, Carl Hovde, James Kuhn, Ray Robinson, David Rosand, John Rosenberg, Wim Smit, John Van Doren, and Tom Vinciguerra—to name just a few who got on board early and encouraged me to think the project doable.

The next most crucial step was to identify a publication vehicle—that being altogether uncertain at the start. Here too I was fortunate in getting help from those in charge of *Columbia* magazine, the most logical venue for reaching the whole Columbia community. The enthusiasm of Kevin McManus and Patrick Queen was crucial in the early stage, and their dependable, competent, and timely help has since been matched by that of their successor, Jerry Kisslinger, who commissioned a number of the essays and orchestrated the publication of Living Legacies in book form. Susan Feagin, Columbia's executive vice president for development and alumni relations, proved highly supportive of the project. We were also fortunate that *Columbia College Today* editor Alex Sachare agreed to publish several essays with most direct relevance to College alumni and current *Columbia* editor Michael Shavelson lent a hand. Tom Mathewson, secretary of the University Senate, provided crucial late-stage editing on a number of essays. Paul Hond provided creative photo research, as did Heather Campbell, in the university's development and alumni relations office, who assisted in other aspects of managing the project. Our colleagues in University Publications—Sandy Kaufman, Junie Lee, and Margaret Ross Griffel— lent their design and editorial skills. Not to mention all that this involved for my late secretary Pam Stiles, who was already handling more things for me than the typical executive secretary and continued bravely to serve the Living Legacies project up to her death in October of 2005.

Finally I wish to acknowledge the support I have had in this project from my wife Fanny, who has been my help in everything I have done for more than sixty years— first through war and peace in World War II, then through the ups and downs of Columbia for more than fifty years, and even through war—and peace—at Columbia.

PART ONE

ARTS AND LETTERS

Lionel Trilling at Columbia

——✳——

Quentin Anderson

It is perhaps enough of an introduction to an essay on Lionel Trilling, already widely known by mid-century as a major literary and cultural critic on the New York scene, to say that his intellectual and scholarly preeminence was recognized by his being chosen as the first person to give the Thomas Jefferson Lecture at the Kennedy Center for the Arts in Washington when the lectureship was inaugurated in 1975. Trilling's eminence and personal distinction had, of course, long been recognized at Columbia and was confirmed when Trilling was chosen to give the first University Lecture in Low Library that same year.

At the time he wrote this essay, Quentin Anderson, who enjoyed a long and close association with Trilling in the English department of Columbia College, was the Julian Clarence Levy Professor of the Humanities Emeritus at Columbia and had served as the former chair of the Literature Humanities Colloquium. Anderson, who died in 2003, taught at Columbia for more than forty years and was the author of The American Henry James, The Imperial Self, *and* Making Americans: An Essay on Individualism and Money.

—*Wm. Theodore de Bary*

——✳——

L ionel Trilling joined the Department of English and Comparative Literature in 1932, a membership that proved lifelong. He had earlier written stories and reviews for the College paper, for a Jewish magazine called the *Menorah Journal,* and for the *New York Evening Post* and had taught at the University of Wisconsin and Hunter College. He married Diana Rubin in 1929, and their son, James, was born in 1948.

Trilling's senior colleagues in the department were uneasy about his continued presence ostensibly on the ground that "as a Freudian, a Marxist, and a Jew" he might not be happy at Columbia. The young teacher's response was a denial so firm and persuasive that it resulted in his retention—and a growing regard for his work. (He had no shred of Communist piety but no impulse to deny what many educated people shared—respect for the intelligence of Marx.)

The publication of *Matthew Arnold,* his Columbia dissertation, led President Butler "under his summer powers" to promote him to assistant professor. Diana Trilling described both episodes in "Lionel Trilling, a Jew at Columbia" in the March 1979 *Commentary.*

The Liberal Imagination (1950), his first volume of essays, enforces the demand Trilling made in all his work that we should look at the imaginative consequences of our politics and the political consequences of our use of the imagination. Liberal politics, he argued, while itself rooted in sentiment and concerned with asserting the importance of human emotion, also tended to deny the concrete reality and individuality of human feeling and imagination. The study of literature might help to correct this tendency. Trilling had found an understanding of the tie between moral principles and the imagination in the English novelist E. M. Forster, the subject of a book Trilling published in 1943. But the first full development of his views on the relations between politics and the imagination appears in *The Liberal Imagination,* which drove his views home and had an effect no less than national. Insofar as liberalism depends on a belief that the primary political reality is realized in individual human beings, could Americans be called "liberal" when we substituted abstract zeal for an awareness of our existing human situation? Trilling's most concise treatment of this contradiction comes from an introduction to his novel, *The Middle of the Journey:* "This negation [of the human situation] was one aspect of an ever more imperious and bitter refusal to consent to the conditioned nature of human existence."

The important preface to *The Liberal Imagination* also explores the tension between liberalism's conscious principles and its actual consequences for the imagination. The volume opens with essays on minor American writers and then moves with greater power and interest to a theme Trilling commanded, "Freud and Literature," and thereafter to the authority of the great essays of the 1940s and 1950s, "Manners, Morals and the Novel" and "Art and Fortune." Along the way current concerns are visited, as in the essay on *The Kinsey Report,* which deals with prevailing attitudes toward sexuality, and a study of current little magazines, including *Partisan Review.* All in all, the collection announced and established a new critical eminence among us and was an enormous success. (Though it was of greatest value, perhaps, to those whom it led to take a continuing interest in Trilling's works, many such readers eventually came to cherish his later works more.)

A COMEDY OF IDEAS

Trilling's only novel, *The Middle of the Journey* (1947), was reissued in 1975 with a twenty-five-page introduction and appeared once again in 1980 in the twelve-volume Uniform edition of the works of Lionel Trilling published posthumously by Harcourt Brace Jovanovich. This edition was supervised by Diana Trilling, who also selected the materials for *Speaking of Literature and Society*, a volume of hitherto uncollected essays and reviews, and for *The Last Decade*, which contains the essays of his last ten years.

The introduction Trilling added to the novel treated questions regarding a character called Gifford Maxim, who was based on Whittaker Chambers, a Columbia College student at the same time as Trilling. Chambers subsequently joined the Soviet espionage apparatus, and Trilling encountered him again when, after breaking with the Communist Party, Chambers sought to reestablish a public identity to make it harder for the party to assassinate him.

Trilling did not know when he published the novel that Whittaker Chambers would become a public figure in the Hiss-Chambers affair, in which Chambers accused Alger Hiss, who had been an important member of the State Department, of having been a Soviet agent. The novel's central characters, aside from Maxim and the narrator John Laskell, are a couple called Arthur and Nancy Croom, middle-class radicals and sympathizers with the Soviet Union. So close, apparently, was the resemblance between the Crooms as Trilling described them and Alger and Priscilla Hiss that many readers, including close friends of the Hisses, thought that Trilling had based the characters of the Crooms on them and had had prior knowledge of Chambers's connection to the Hisses. In fact, Trilling says in his introduction: "The name Hiss was unknown to me until some months after my novel had appeared."

Maxim's fear of assassination is important to the novel's portrayal of the "liberal imagination" because the Crooms do not believe the danger Maxim fears is real, and indeed are shocked by Maxim's belief that the Communist Party would be capable of such wickedness. One of the shrewdest of Trilling's devices is to find in this mistaken trustfulness an occasion for Laskell's discovery of the denials of reality associated with radical political convictions. There are still more central grounds for this discovery, including the unwillingness of the Crooms, the hero's hosts, to consider the fact of death—real indeed to their guest, who has recently recovered from a very dangerous illness.

Trilling's wife, Diana, a noted essayist and nonfiction writer, edited the authoritative posthumous edition of Trilling's works.

The novel constituted a grave and inclusive attack on the pieties of the middle-class radicalism of its time. It was not received with universal applause. The chief of the contemporary pieties it offended was the faith among Communist sympathizers that the world could be remade in accord with our personal demands. When John Laskell steps into Nancy Croom's flower bed of cosmos while trying to talk to her about death, Nancy says, "John, get out of my cosmos!" And while she thinks she is talking about flowers, we, like Laskell, realize that she is acting to cancel the reality of a friend's emotions if they interfere with her attempt to deny death through political hope.

Trilling notes that the English edition of his novel was better received. Perhaps the English of 1947 took it for granted that ideas had a clear relation to the intellectual groups and social classes that adopted them. An English identity was achieved *after* one had willy-nilly accepted the fact of one's social origin and the social milieu—perhaps a very different one—that one had come to occupy. It is harder for Americans, born more like gods of their own creation, to accept the idea of an intellectual milieu or a social class, except as something altogether foreign. Americans do not have much feeling for the social comedy of ideas.

THE MAJOR ESSAYS

The Opposing Self (1955) is titled for an observation Trilling attributes to Hegel, who had held that in the eighteenth century individuals came to oppose the self to the culture in which it had grown. This conception of the self was to be a central theme in Trilling's later work, particularly in his discussion of authenticity in *Sincerity and Authenticity*.

A Gathering of Fugitives (1956) prints the introductions Trilling had done for The Reader's Subscription, a book club headed by W. H. Auden, Jacques Barzun, and Trilling. *Sincerity and Authenticity* (1972) presents the lectures Trilling delivered as Charles Eliot Norton Professor at Harvard in 1970. Trilling had earlier edited an anthology called *The Experience of Literature*, published in 1967. The prefaces to the individual selections it contains comprise a volume in the Uniform edition. The present writer suggests that the original anthology, including Trilling's prefaces together with the works they deal with, makes an excellent introduction to the powers and interests of Trilling himself.

Beyond Culture (1965) contains powerful essays on Jane Austen's *Emma*, on Isaac Babel, on the modern view of pleasure, and on other topics. One of these, "On the Teaching of Modern Literature," is more often discussed than others nowadays because it is thought to have a particular importance for students of literature. This essay demands nothing less than full attention, and I can't attempt to give it that here, except to note that those whose lives are exclusively devoted to money and success find little sanction or excuse in its pages.

Of this book as a whole, Diana Trilling, the editor, notes, "A central enterprise of the volume is its search for a way out of the adversary culture which will not preclude a genuine experience of life. One such rescue from the tyrannies of contemporary cultural subversion Trilling finds in Freud's tragic acceptance of the biologically given." The speech Trilling addressed to the New York Psychoanalytic Society in 1955 gives the volume its title. It was the first occasion on which the members of the society were addressed by someone outside their number. It should be noted that Trilling collaborated with Steven Marcus to produce a one-volume version of Ernest Jones's three-volume biography of Freud.

Trilling also wrote a number of short stories, and Mrs. Trilling edited a volume of these for the Uniform edition, with a title drawn from the best known of them, "Of This Time, of That Place." The volume includes the often anthologized "The Other Margaret" as well as a number of stories bearing on Jewishness.

Trilling, who became an associate professor at Columbia in 1945, was made a full professor in 1948, and thereafter achieved the university's highest honor, becoming a University Professor in 1970. He was awarded a number of honorary degrees by American institutions including Harvard, Northwestern, Case Western Reserve, Brandeis and Yale; he also received Honorary Litt. D. degrees from the universities of Durham and Leicester in England. He held the Eastman Professorship at Oxford (1965) and was later appointed a Visiting Fellow at All Souls College, Oxford (1972–73). In 1951, Trilling became a member of the

National Institute of Arts and Letters and a Fellow of the Academy of Arts and Letters. In 1972 he received the first Thomas Jefferson Award in the Humanities. His lecture on that occasion was entitled "Mind in the Modern World."

Some people were convinced that Trilling was an anglophile. In fact he rejected the offer of a distinguished post in England. His American identity was precious to him, and it bore on his views on the citizen's duty.

In England, even more than in this country, it was commonly held in the 1950s that one must not name names when questioned by the government about some-one's Communist sympathy or affiliation. Trilling, on the contrary, held that it was not dishonorable for an American citizen to answer such questions. A number of his colleagues in the College, including good friends of his, differed sharply, according to Diana Trilling, but one can infer from the introduction to *The Middle of the Journey* that he never changed his view.

COLLEGE LOYALTIES

Early in their careers in the College, Trilling and Jacques Barzun taught the Senior Colloquium, and I was lucky enough to take the course with them in 1936–37. For me (and I am sure it was true of others also) the experience was unique and unforgettable. The College of those years had a splendid staff, and many students had occasion to rejoice as I did.

Trilling was to become a friend when I began teaching in the College in 1939, and it may be useful to note something I found characteristic in him. He took teaching very seriously. For him it was an occasion to judge, to offer praise, and to seek to see what powers the student had and how they were being employed. If they were being wasted or misapplied he made it his responsibility to try to help. When I became his colleague and friend I was on occasion privy to these efforts and to his sustained fidelity to the obligations of teaching.

In those years the College offered a three-year course in English literature from the earliest times to the end of the nineteenth century. Trilling taught the third year over a long period. The course embraced works of the Romantics and the Victorians, and one of Trilling's happiest achievements is the essay on Keats he published in *The Opposing Self*. Another figure by whom he set great store was Wordsworth, and there was an annual struggle with an often resistant group of juniors and seniors to win them to recognition of the poet's powers. Among the Victorians, the novels and tales of Henry James stood high for Trilling. His interest in the cultural office of the novel carried over to the twentieth century, as many of his essays attest.

*Lionel Trilling with
Quentin Anderson in
front of Lamb House in
Rye, England, where
Henry James lived
and wrote during the
last eighteen years of
his life*

One of the recollections of my colleague that stands out for me is how persist-
ently thoughtful he was about the ongoing affairs of the College wing of the
department. His heart was there. He taught graduate courses and supervised dissertations, but the College had his deepest loyalty.

The reader of this brief account of a remarkable man, whose abilities exceeded
those of any other I have ever encountered, might be excused for wondering how
he exhibited the powers I saw in him. I despair of conveying more than a suggestion of the fascination offered by a particular work. *Sincerity and Authenticity* consists
of six lectures delivered at Harvard in the spring of 1970. He traces the idea of sincerity through the 400 years of its employment in England and elsewhere and its
fascinating permutations from Rousseau and Diderot (in his *Rameau's Nephew*)
through Goethe and Hegel, to such amazing cultural landmarks as Conrad's *Heart of
Darkness.* Among other things, he teaches us what an extraordinary wealth of meaning is contained in the customary signature of our letters, "Sincerely yours." How
authenticity then arose as a standard and at what cost we learn in the lectures that
followed. The final lecture in the series concludes with extraordinary force. The
chapter is called "The Authentic Unconscious," and the term "unconscious," though
it had been Freud's, is not here used with reference to psychoanalysis but to a transformation in its meaning, which reaches its apogee in a shocking moment of the
1960s. Trilling quotes two British psychiatrists, David Cooper and R. D. Laing. In
an introduction to the English translation of Michel Foucault's *Histoire de la folie,*

Cooper had written: "What madness is is a form of vision that destroys itself by its own choice of oblivion in the face of existing forms of social tactics and strategy. Madness, for instance, is a matter of voicing the realization that I am (or you are) Christ."

Trilling characterizes Cooper's view as follows: "So far from being an illness, a deprivation of any kind, madness is health fully realized at last." He then quotes Laing as saying that "true sanity entails in one way or another the dissolution of the normal ego, that false self completely adjusted to our alienated social reality."

Trilling comments:

> Who that has had experience of our social reality will doubt its alienated condition? And who that has thought of his experience in the light of certain momentous speculations made over the last two centuries, of which a few have been touched on in these pages, will not be disposed to find some seed of cogency in a view that proposes an antinomian reversal of all accepted values, of all received realities?
>
> But who that has spoken, or tried to speak, with a psychotic friend will consent to betray the masked pain—his bewilderment and solitude—by making it the paradigm of liberation from the imprisoning falsehoods of an alienated social reality? Who that finds intelligible the sentences which describe madness (to use the word that cant prefers) in terms of transcendence and charisma will fail to penetrate to the great refusal of human connection that they express, the appalling belief that human existence is made authentic by the possession of a power, or the persuasion of its possession, which is not to be qualified or restricted by the coordinate existence of any fellow man? . . .
>
> Perhaps exactly because the thought is assented to so facilely, so without what used to be called seriousness, it might seem that no expression of disaffection from the social existence was ever so desperate as this eagerness to say that authenticity of personal being is achieved through an ultimate isolateness and through the power that this is presumed to bring. The falsities of an alienated social reality are rejected in favor of an upward psychopathic mobility to the point of divinity, each one of us a Christ—but with none of the inconveniences of undertaking to intercede, of being a sacrifice, of reasoning with rabbis, of making sermons, of having disciples, of going to weddings and to funerals, of beginning something and at a certain point remarking that it is finished.

The fierceness of this denunciation is unmatched in Trilling, but it conveys the passion he everywhere brought to considering the relation between emotions and ideas.

As I approach my conclusion I must not fail to remark that Trilling wished to speak for and to everyone, and not for a particular sect or party. He sought to do this by speaking on each occasion from the freedom of a judgment unconstrained by doctrine.

I am reminded of one of my happiest memories of him. John Thompson and I loved fly-fishing and taught Trilling to fish. One day a shout of pleasure from a neighboring pool greeted us. It was his celebration of his first ten-inch trout.

CHAPTER 2

Gilbert Highet and
Classics at Columbia

—⁂—

Robert Ball

This essay features one of the dominant figures in classical studies at Columbia in the nineteen forties, fifties, and sixties—Gilbert Highet. Highet, as I recall him from my undergraduate days, was not only a great classroom lecturer but a brilliant speaker at campus events, with a thespian gift for mimicry (he did a marvelous takeoff on the oratory of Adolf Hitler). He was, of course, also a major cosmopolitan figure who served as a regular cultural critic for radio station WQXR and was known, even more widely, as a world-class scholar. I myself had no chance to study with Highet (my colleague in Japanese studies Donald Keene did), but I held him in such awe from a distance that I was taken aback when the distinguished Oxford don and UNESCO pooh-bah Ronald Syme referred to him at an international meeting in the fifties simply as "young Highet." The other thing that sticks in my mind about Highet is his explanation for no longer going to the Faculty Club: "Every time I went there, I found myself appointed to another faculty committee!"

Robert Ball, a Ph.D. student of Highet in the sixties, is a professor of classics at the University of Hawaii. He has published two editions of Gilbert Highet's papers: The Classical Papers of Gilbert Highet *and* The Unpublished Lectures of Gilbert Highet.

—*Wm. Theodore de Bary*

—⁂—

Most eloquent among the sons of Scotland, educated at Glasgow and Oxford, you have for the last forty years enriched the world of classical letters with the richness of your scholarship. You have been at once a support and an ornament to humane learning in this, your adopted country. Generations of Columbia students can testify to the scope of your erudition and the precision of your wit. In nearly a score of books—

doctis, Iuppiter, et laboriosis [from Catullus 1, meaning "learned, Jupiter, and full of labor"]—you have charted the enduring forms and themes of literature, with a spirit as indefatigable as it is passionate. A Varro in learning, a Cicero in eloquence, you have not only defended the vitality and grace of the classical tradition, you have also embodied it.

So spoke President William McGill at the spring 1977 commencement in awarding Gilbert Highet the honorary degree of Doctor of Letters for his stellar achievements as a world-class educator. Indeed, during his long and warm association with Columbia, Highet became the most famous classical scholar in the United States, with a career that streaked through the sky like a blazing comet. Consummate teacher, author, and literary critic, he used the classroom, his publications, and the electronic media to bring the classical world to the specialist and the general public. For countless thousands who had never studied the classical languages, he breathed new life and meaning into the literary masterpieces bequeathed to posterity by the Greeks and Romans.

Before coming to Columbia in 1937, Highet had demonstrated his love for classics as a youthful prodigy and throughout his university studies. Born on June 22, 1906, in Glasgow, Scotland, to educated parents, he began learning Latin at the age of eleven, and soon afterward Greek, on special scholarships at Hillhead High School. By fourteen he could read Homer and Virgil with ease and for pleasure, and by sixteen he read Aeschylus's *Prometheus Bound* and also read and analyzed ten plays of Shakespeare. At Glasgow University (1925–28), he became the most well-known classicist in Scotland, where he earned a master's degree in Greek and Latin, and a diploma in ancient history and archaeology. He also received the Logan Memorial Medal and Prize (as most distinguished graduate) and the Snell Exhibition and Newlands Scholarship (entitling him to four years of study at Oxford). At Oxford's Balliol College (1929–32), he earned a B.A. in classics and received a number of prestigious awards—the Ferguson Scholarship, the Craven Scholarship, and the Jenkyns Exhibition. There he studied under three great teacher-scholars—Cyril Bailey, Maurice Bowra, and Gilbert Murray, who collectively provided him with outstanding role models for his own career. He taught at St. John's, Oxford (1933–37), as tutor and fellow—something that he regarded as one of the best experiences of his life—while studying for and obtaining a master's degree in classics. During this period he and his wife, Helen MacInnes, cotranslated from the German Otto Kiefer's *Sexual Life in Ancient Rome* and Gustav Mayer's *Friedrich Engels: A Biography.*

GILBERT HIGHET: POET IN A LANDSCAPE

Gilbert Highet loved and wrote poetry, having written his first poem at the age of sixteen after reading George Meredith's "Lucifer in Starlight." At Glasgow he composed poetry under the pseudonym of "Cyrano," and at Oxford he composed two verse-dramas, produced in the private theater of the poet laureate John Masefield. At Columbia he translated classical poetry into English, frequently in the meters of the original Greek or Latin, as he did in his translations of Catullus and Horace in *Poets in a Landscape*. During his American career, he published original poetry and translated classical poetry in *Harper's*, *Horizon*, *The New Yorker*, *The American Scholar*, and Columbia's own *Columbia Forum*. A romantic at heart, he published in *The American Scholar* the following poem—a self-composed epitaph—in which the poet pictures himself (not his persona) in his own special landscape:

OBIT

What shall we say about him in the papers?
Stepped out into the path of a speeding car
No. Not such a stupid end for a man of mind.
In Claremont Hospital after a long illness
Among his scholarly works the most important
He had continued yes yes yes no. No.
Suddenly, by a stroke, after a class
No. Not that either, although possible.
Yesterday on the third floor of the library
Among the immortals speaking silent Greek
That would be peaceful, yet perhaps too pat.
But no, the air is wrong, the place is wrong:
Where are the heights, the trees, the wind, the birds?
Write in the notice: on the slopes of—what?
Some insignificant hill, it doesn't matter,
But climbing, with the wind around him and
The sky above and his remembering head
Quite full of poetry and music, climbing
Together with his one true friend and love
Up through the stalwart trees to timberline—
After a life of effort, rest and sleep.

*Highet and his wife,
Helen MacInnes, a
best-selling novelist
who published twenty-
one books.*

Highet's defining moment (professionally) came in 1937, when Columbia hired him as a visiting associate on a one-year appointment. President Nicholas Murray Butler had originally (albeit unsuccessfully) attempted to recruit Maurice Bowra for the position, which carried with it an attractive salary. In declining the offer, Bowra allegedly informed Butler that he (Butler) would never be able to lure an Englishman to America but that he might well be able to lure a Scotsman for the money. When the Scotsman arrived at Columbia, he joined a classics faculty that included LaRue Van Hook, Wilbert Carr, Clinton Keyes, William Dinsmoor, and William Westermann. In 1938, within one year of accepting the temporary appointment, Highet became professor of Greek and Latin—a remarkable accomplishment for a man who was just turning thirty-two. Highet came to realize that during the 1930s American classical studies had suffered serious damage, partly brought on by the social and economic upheavals that followed World War I. In the painful aftermath of the Great Depression, classicists witnessed the onslaught of educational reform that banished Greek and Latin from the center of the liberal arts curriculum. Convinced that classics needed a fresh direction to survive this assault, he worked with Moses Hadas, then an untenured member of the faculty, on revitalizing the humanities program. In Humanities A, where Columbia's freshmen read the classical works in English translation, Highet kept his "pupils" on the edge of their seats in his early days on Morningside Heights.

WARTIME SERVICE

Highet's American career was just beginning to soar when he was called up to serve in the British Army at the outbreak of World War II. From 1941 to 1946 (on leave from Columbia) he served in the British Mission to the United States, in the British Intelligence Center in New York, and in the British Zone of occupied Berlin. Under Sir William Stephenson, the Canadian special operations executive, he carried out many missions, shrouded in mystery over the decades by the British Official Secrets Act. During the war he pioneered the art of preparing psychological profiles of Nazi leaders such as Hitler, Goebbels, Goering, and Himmler—based on his psychoanalysis of Roman emperors. With limited information about his German subjects, he succeeded in predicting their behavior under different circumstances, in documents regarded as highly significant in those days. As America armed herself for battle, he shuttled between New York and Washington and traveled to Canada and South America and Great Britain on military airplanes and ocean liners. On the shores of Lake Ontario, in a secret Canadian training facility, he prepared the first draft of the recently released volume, *The Secret History of British Intelligence in the Americas*. As a member of the British Army of Occupation, he entered the smoldering remains of Hitler's bunker and became responsible for helping to recover the gold reserves hidden by the Nazis. During the war he also completed his three-volume translation from the German of Werner Jaeger's *Paideia: The Ideals of Greek Culture*, still the classic model of the translator's art.

When Highet returned to the United States in the summer of 1946, he left his duties as a lieutenant colonel to take up those of a college professor. Although he had offers at the end of the war to pursue a more lucrative career, he turned them down to resume teaching at Columbia—a decision that he claimed he never regretted. He regarded the ex-soldiers who came in on the GI Bill as highly intelligent and remarked that in those postwar years he got from his students almost as much stimulus as he gave them. In full bloom as a teacher and scholar, he became Anthon Professor of the Latin Language and Literature in 1950 and an American citizen in 1951, committed to his adopted homeland. He continued to strengthen instruction in the humanities with his colleague Moses Hadas, who himself became professor of Greek and Latin in 1953, then Jay Professor of Greek in 1956. In the spring of 1953 Oxford University asked Highet to allow his name to be entered as a candidate for the Corpus Professorship of Latin, which would open at the end of that academic year. He wrote to President Grayson Kirk that although he had aspired to that position for many years, he would not permit his name to be submitted because Columbia had treated him so well. Devoted to Columbia and to the students whom he found so stimulating, Highet taught the Greek and Roman classics on a campus that featured an exceptional liberal arts professoriate. He belonged to a faculty that included such luminaries as Mark Van Doren, Lionel Trilling, and Jacques Barzun, who all helped enhance Columbia's reputation in the nation and the world.

A LEGENDARY TEACHER

When Gilbert Highet entered the classroom, one felt as though the curtain were going up on a Broadway play, with a living legend in the lead. He reminded students (not surprisingly) of a British Army officer—of the kind portrayed by Jack Hawkins in motion pictures—tall, erect, handsome, clean-shaven, and impeccably dressed. He consistently gave his audience a commanding performance, whether he spoke or sang or stood or walked, with a presence comparable to that of Laurence Olivier or John Houseman. With his Scottish-English burr and his riveting, rapid-fire delivery, he dazzled students with his dynamic lectures, brilliant in their organization and brimming with critical insights. The inspired anecdotes, the poignant pauses, and the sudden bursts of laughter formed part of a magnificent, comprehensible structure that gripped the heart and held one spellbound. He loved Virgil and taught the *Aeneid* (in the original Latin) every year to packed classes; he loved his "darling" Juvenal and the Roman satirists for exposing decadence and corruption. He detested Plato and Julius Caesar—the one, for outlining the principles of dictatorship; the other, for becoming the accomplished dictator who crushed the life out of the Roman Republic. Imitating a Roman soldier, he brandished a window pole; impersonating Marius at the gates of Rome, he crouched down, then sprang across the floor to battle his great rival Sulla. With his powerful and speculative mind, he gave his students an extraordinary intellectual experience, capped by a showmanship perhaps unparalleled in the American college classroom.

In his thirty-five years of teaching at Columbia, Highet never found anything as painful as the student riots that exploded on campus in 1968. During the late 1960s his classics colleagues included Coleman Benedict, Howard Porter, William Calder, James Coulter, and Steele Commager (not the historian but his son the Latinist). During those years of violent protest and agonizing reappraisal, Highet came to despise the student radicals, especially those who wanted to destroy Columbia during the Vietnam War. Although he had misgivings about America's involvement in

the conflict in Southeast Asia, he believed that the student activists had gone far beyond the motivation of an antiwar protest. When some threatened to burn down Butler Library tier by tier, he may have recalled the Dark Ages, when the forces of barbarism almost extinguished the Greek and Roman classics. Regarding the anarchists, whom he characterized as dirty and dizzy with drugs, he allegedly uttered his famous paraphrase of Matthew 7.6: "I shall not cast false pearls before real swine." He recalled a doctoral examination, interrupted by the rhythmic shouts from a protest rally, which reminded him of the "SIEG HEIL! SIEG HEIL! SIEG HEIL!" of a Hitler demonstration. When demonstrators blockaded the entrance to his building, he angrily told them that after teaching at Columbia for thirty years, he would be damned if he would leave through the window. He wrote to President Kirk, who resigned because of the riots, that he blamed him no more than he would blame the director of a museum if a gang of hoodlums began slashing the paintings.

Highet with his students. He was a hugely popular teacher on campus, dazzling students with his charismatic performances in class.

LABOR OF LOVE

Highet's complete bibliography, spanning a fifty-year period, consists of roughly a thousand items—a monumental achievement for a classicist. He authored twenty-one books, which (excluding the translations referred to a little earlier) fall into three categories—pedagogy, scholarly research, and essays of a general nature. (His wife, Helen MacInnes, published twenty-one books of her own as a best-selling novelist who became famous for her tales of intrigue and espionage set during and after World War II.) His articles demonstrate an extremely broad range of interests—from essays on the classical authors and the classical tradition to essays of a nonclassical and more general nature. His reviews of books about classical and contemporary literature enjoyed a large audience during the years that he held prestigious editorial appointments with several major publishers. As chief literary critic for *Harper's* magazine (1952–54), he reviewed new books every month in his own column, in a potpourri format, involving clusters of books on various themes. As chairman of the editorial advisory board of *Horizon* magazine (1958–77), he reviewed numerous books, including his critique of William Shirer's *The Rise and Fall of the Third Reich*. As a member of the board of judges of the Book-of-the-Month Club (1954–78), he wrote more than 400 book reviews, which appeared continuously in *Book-of-the-Month Club News*. Clifton "Kip" Fadiman, a fellow judge, regarded him as the most erudite member of the board, with a histrionic talent that would rescue their meetings from excessive sobriety.

Highet's books on pedagogy sprang from his seeing teaching and research as two complementary endeavors, each replenishing the other. His ideal teacher—a liberal educator in the best sense—will consistently and enthusiastically communicate to his or her students the genuine and permanent importance of the subject. Such a teacher will also engage in productive scholarly research, as a means of discovering new knowledge and demonstrating the importance of reevaluation and reinterpretation. While teaching at Oxford, he published *An Outline of Homer*, a student commentary on twenty-three passages from the *Iliad* and the *Odyssey* that form a microcosm of Homer's poetry. Before his departure from Oxford, he also completed *Beginning Latin*, a textbook divided into seventy-two lessons, displaying his talent for presenting difficult material clearly and crisply. *The Art of Teaching* (1950), on the methods of teaching, became an instant success—reprinted numerous times in English and translated into sixteen languages, from Arabic to Urdu. In it Highet describes the qualities of the good teacher, the methods to be used in class, and those used by some of the world's great teachers—Socrates, Plato, Aristotle, Jesus, and the Jesuits. *The Immortal Profession* (1976) consists of a series of essays on the joys of teaching and

Highet receiving an honorary degree from President William McGill in May 1977

learning—a retrospective of his earlier views but with special application to the college teacher. In it one also finds stimulating pieces on Gilbert Murray, Albert Schweitzer, and Jesus—not on Jesus's methods of teaching but his relation to the Twelve Apostles and other secret disciples.

In the area of scholarly research, Highet authored books with widespread appeal for the classical scholar and the educated layperson. *The Classical Tradition* (1949) examines Greek and Roman influences on Western literature from the fall of classical civilization through the nineteenth and twentieth centuries. This herculean feat reveals not only Highet's mastery of comparative literature but also (as the critic Edmund Wilson wrote) his ability to cover an enormous amount of literary material. *Juvenal the Satirist* (1954) considers the life, work, and influence of the Roman poet Juvenal, with its central contribution being a detailed literary analysis of each of his sixteen satires. This admirable study—the first of its kind for Juvenal's poetry—

reveals Highet's razor-sharp critical acumen and his vast knowledge of previous scholarship on the individual poems. *Poets in a Landscape* (1957), a pilgrimage through places associated with seven Roman poets, received the Italian government's ENIT Prize (*Ente Nazionale Italiano per il Turismo*). *The Anatomy of Satire* (1962), a study of satire under its three main forms (monologue, parody, and narrative), received the Award of Merit from the American Philological Association. *The Speeches in Vergil's Aeneid* (1972) analyzes all the speeches in the *Aeneid*—the speeches and their speakers, formal and informal speeches, and the speeches and their models. This exhaustive labor of love represents the culmination of Highet's experience with the *Aeneid*, which he came to believe gained immensely from its affinities with the *Iliad* and the *Odyssey*.

In his books of essays of a general nature, Highet published lectures connected with his radio program of the 1950s, *People, Places, and Books*. In 1952, on WQXR (the radio station of *The New York Times*) and under the auspices of Oxford University Press, he began to speak weekly on a variety of subjects in literature and the arts. By 1959, when the program ended, his talks were carried by more than 300 stations in the United States and Canada and by the British Broadcasting Company and Voice of America. His lectures, both educational and entertaining, exhibited a broad range of classical and nonclassical topics—from language and literature, to history and philosophy, to music and art. His eloquent voice captivated the public—whether he spoke about Horace and Apuleius, or Shakespeare and Dickens, or Washington and Jefferson, or Bach and Brahms, or Bosch and Bruegel. John Crosby, who wrote for *The New York Herald Tribune*, described the first season of these popular radio talks as scholarly and flavorsome and deserving of publication in book form. The critic Edmund Wilson consented to Highet's doing a broadcast about him on six humorous conditions, which included the recording on a silver spool and a case of Old Forester whiskey. Highet eventually revised a large number of the radio talks for Oxford, for publication in five volumes of essays, which stand as a lasting memorial to a program that charmed the nation. One may still savor his winning words in his *People, Places, and Books* (1953), *A Clerk of Oxenford* (1954), *Talents and Geniuses* (1957), *The Powers of Poetry* (1960), and *Explorations* (1971).

HUMANE SCHOLARSHIP

Although Gilbert Highet became famous for his books and lectures, he may seem somewhat out of place in today's world of literary criticism. In this age of post-structuralism, postmodernism, and postcolonialism, some may see him as a "liberal humanist," with an unwavering belief in the moral value of the literary classics. Indeed he was, in the sense that he believed in the universal value of the classics and that the great authors can provide the standards by which people may lead happy and productive lives. As scholars were shifting from the poet's personality to the poet's persona, he pursued his biographical approach to interpreting poetry—an integral part of his work on Juvenal's satires. Facing considerable criticism in this area, he defended his objection to the exploitation of the persona theory in a masterful article: "Masks and Faces in Satire," *Hermes* 102 (1974): 321–37. All in all, he presented his audience with a humane form of scholarship—free of the vacuous, jargon-filled kind of literary criticism plaguing some areas of current classical scholarship. He enabled his readers to experience (heaven forbid!) something called "literary appreciation," to travel through a world of truth and beauty, elegance and splendor, or just plain meaning. He would explore those aspects of great writing that make the classical authors worth reading, without burying the soul of a masterpiece beneath a technical theoretical superstructure. He would emphasize how the authors presented themselves (whether real or a persona) and how they expressed their innermost thoughts, with powerful imagery and quotable statements.

Although Highet rose to eminence in America's cultural pantheon, some classicists regarded him as a "popularizer," in the negative sense. Jealous perhaps of his outstanding achievements and his virtual celebrity status, they could not understand that he had done more than anyone to revitalize the study of Greek and Latin. A frequent focus of media attention in the United States and abroad, he became the most recognized and most talked-about classics teacher and classical scholar of his generation. A popularizer in the positive sense, he provided the classics establishment with something that it desperately needed (as it does today)—respectability with an audience of nonspecialists. The very antithesis of the stereotypical academician, he paraded the classical authors from the groves of academe into the public's living room with his incisive books, articles, and lectures. He invited his audience to a celebration of classical literature, on a journey in search of broad knowledge about classical civilization—a journey open to both specialists and nonspecialists. Every step of the way, he continuously referred to the literature, music, and art of later civilizations in order to emphasize the majesty, strength, and influence of the classical tradition. The journey came to an end on January 20, 1978; at his memorial service in St. Paul's Chapel on the ides of March, Columbia paid tribute to the most accomplished classicist of his time. There Alan Cameron, who succeeded him as Anthon Professor, remarked that never again would the profession see the entire field of classics through the perspective of one man's vision.

In 1954, the midpoint of Highet's long and extraordinary career at Morningside, Columbia celebrated the 200th anniversary of her founding. For that occasion Highet wrote "Her Sons—'Alert and Grateful,'" *Life* 36 (February 15, 1954): 126–31—an article in which he showed his respect and admiration for Columbia's students. He described her sons (in those days her daughters attended only Barnard) as diverse and talented individuals, molded by the faculty, by one another, and by the energy of New York City. For that occasion, too, he wrote *Man's Unconquerable Mind*, on the powers of knowledge and the intellect, and *The Migration of Ideas*, on the influence of great thoughts upon human affairs. He concluded the first of these books by praising the achievements of the world's great universities, in words that one may apply to the 250th anniversary that Columbia has just celebrated. After referring to the laboratory in which I. I. Rabi worked, he stated:

> Even to tread the floor of such a room, knowing no more than the outlines of the work done there, is to forget one's own petty self, to revere the ardors and efforts of the great thinkers and teachers who have helped to make our world, and to feel, like the majestic roll of

some vast river, the urgent march of the mind, imperfect but marvelous, unique in every individual and yet super-personal, the mysterious power which has brought us out of bestial savagery toward civilization and wisdom, and will take us further still. It is to dedicate oneself again to the purpose of the university, which is to acquire and to extend knowledge for the service of all mankind.

For bibliography, see Notes, page 654.

CHAPTER 3

Da Ponte, MacDowell, Moore, and Lang: Four Biographical Essays

—〰—

Jack Beeson

His versatile and flamboyant career at Columbia may have been more as a promoter of Italian liter-
ature than as an impresario of Italian opera, but Lorenzo Da Ponte's fame as a librettist for Mozart
is what interests the author of these essays on music at Columbia—the distinguished composer of
American opera and MacDowell Professor Emeritus of Music, Jack Beeson. Beeson's achievements
range over many musical genres: 122 works, including songs, choral pieces—"Everything," he says,
"except ballet." But of the total, it is his ten operas that have attracted the most attention, among them
Jonah, Hello Out There, The Sweet Bye and Bye, *and especially* Lizzie Borden, *recent-*
ly revived by the New York City Opera in a new production and televised on Live from Lincoln
Center.

Beeson studied under Béla Bartók before joining Columbia, where he has played a major role, not
only in the development of the music program and the School of the Arts during the latter half of the
twentieth century, but also as an active participant in the life of the Columbia community and one
much engaged as a citizen in the academic affairs of the university.

—*Wm. Theodore de Bary*

—〰—

A thousand years ago, more *and* less, music, together with its then-related subjects, astronomy, arithmetic, and geometry, formed the *quadrivium,* that part of the medieval curriculum that led to the Master of Arts. Music has long since had no such honorable place in universities and in the American university had no place at all until well into the nineteenth century. When it reappeared it had lost its connections with both astronomy and mathematics. In these interplanetary days the "music of the spheres" is but a poetic image; professors of music are more likely to visit departments of anthropology, computer science, history, and languages than mathematics. In fact, music departments lead somewhat sequestered lives, puzzles to administrators who try in vain to fit them into conventional patterns. Nevertheless, they are valuable public relations assets, for they train musicians who sometimes become successful performers and harbor composers who also become known to the larger public.

LORENZO DA PONTE

That Columbia professor best known to music lovers the world over was not a musician at all, but its first professor of Italian, Lorenzo Da Ponte, Mozart's librettist for *Le Nozze di Figaro* (1786), *Don Giovanni* (1787), and *Così Fan Tutte* (1790). His "Mozart period" had been over by a third of a century when he was appointed professor in 1825—at the age of seventy-six! He could have found no composer-collaborator at Columbia, for there was to be no Columbia professor of music until 1896.

Knowing that he was always the rewriter of preexisting material—as two of his Mozart libretti attest—one tends to think that he was also the reviser of his own life story. But however much one may be forced to suspend belief, the bare facts are these:

He was born Emanuele Conegliano in a Jewish ghetto near Venice in 1749. When he was fourteen, his widowed father remarried, this time to a Catholic, requiring the family to convert to Catholicism, whereupon Emanuele took the name of the officiating bishop. He eventually entered a seminary, mastered Hebrew and the classical languages (in which he wrote poetry), and soon was promoted to professor, then vice rector—all the while carrying on several love affairs.

He was ordained at age twenty-four and assigned to a church in Venice, where he caroused with the likes of Casanova and Gozzi for six years. Though he arranged entertainment for a brothel and got a married woman twice pregnant, among other forgivable unclerical escapades, the authorities found some of his poetry unforgivably seditious. He was brought to trial—in absentia, for he had already fled to Vienna—and banished.

In Vienna he acquired such a reputation as a poet and librettist that he was named Poet to the Court Theater of the Hapsburg Emperor. It was Mozart's landlady who introduced him to Da Ponte, who was known as Abbate Da Ponte (one who has studied for the priesthood) and not as an ordained priest. Of their collaboration we know little, for there was no occasion for Mozart's usual chatty and informative correspondence. Their three happy marriages of text and music, on amatory subjects chosen jointly and quickly, suggest a collaboration like no other.

In 1791 Mozart died, and Da Ponte was dismissed by the new emperor. He left for Trieste with a reigning soprano. After she had been reclaimed by her husband, Da Ponte proposed marriage to an Englishwoman whose Jewish parents were supposedly rich. Whether they actually married is not clear: he was still a priest, she had converted to the Church of England, and both were Jewish by birth. Nevertheless they were known as Mr.—later, Professor—and Mrs. Da Ponte, Anglicans.

On the advice of his chum Casanova, to whom he introduced Mrs. Da Ponte as his mistress for the sake of appearances, they moved to London, where for twelve years he wrote, play-doctored, libretto-doctored, translated, and ran a rare-book shop. Just before he was to be arrested for debt, he escaped to the United States.

Their ship, *The Columbia*, was a harbinger. The twenty years Da Ponte spent in the United States before he joined the College faculty were his usual combination of high living and misadventure. A chance meeting in a bookstore with the recent Columbia College alumnus Clement Clarke Moore led to private teaching and to meeting Moore's father, Benjamin, who was Bishop of the Anglican Church. (Benjamin was also president of Columbia College, and his son was a Columbia trustee.) But Da Ponte's distilleries and grocery stores failed. His cartage service between Sunbury, Pennsylvania, and Philadelphia was a success, but the former court poet found Sunbury dull.

At the suggestion of the younger Moore, he returned to New York City and opened a bookstore and a rooming house, both frequented by Columbia College students, who savored the sophisticated talk about the arts, the Mozart years, and the Italian cooking. It was not long before Moore, by that time the author of "'Twas the Night Before Christmas," suggested a professorship in Italian, and Da Ponte was forthwith appointed. The professorship added dignity to what he had already been doing since his move to New York City: teaching the Italian language and literature to private students (mostly young women) and in various schools. His continuing public lectures on Dante—and his efforts on behalf of other classic writers, such as Petrarch, Tasso, Ariosto, and Metastasio—made him the founder of Italian literature studies in the United States. His teaching at Columbia also met with great enthusiasm, but within a couple of years registration dwindled: in those days the study of modern languages had to be paid for in addition to regular tuition. His highly idiosyncratic ideas for improving matters were not accepted by the trustees—nor was his letter of resignation.

When he died, at nearly ninety and still a professor of Italian, and last rites were administered, it was thought best not to mention the vows he had once taken. He was buried with pomp in the Roman Catholic Cemetery on East Eleventh Street. But before a headstone could be put in place, the cemetery's contents were removed to another site. And so it is that the whereabouts of the librettist's remains were long as unknown as those of his composer, Mozart. In 1988 Columbia commemorated the sesquicentennial of his death and also transformed McMillin into the Kathryn Bache Miller Theatre. During a university lecture that was the first event in the nearly completed Miller Theatre, I offered the following thoughts:

> Da Ponte would certainly have applauded the University's rebuilding of its theater. He would have thought it a minor effort, though, for he, at the age of eighty-five, raised the funds, helped design, supervised the building of, and then comanaged the first theater in New York City intended only for opera performances. . . . He may have been the first Jewish-born professor in the College; he may have been the first Catholic priest to have been a professor. He was surely the first to have been one or the other—or both—and to have been thought an Anglican.

EDWARD MACDOWELL

In the year of Da Ponte's death, 1838, Lowell Mason, noted hymnodist and publisher of hymns, introduced music into American public schools in Boston. Almost immediately music worked itself up the academic ladder, appearing in the curricula of midwestern and women's colleges, then in graduate schools. Joining in the trend, Yale appointed a German, Gustave Stoeckel, instructor of vocal music in 1855 and promoted him to professor in 1890. Harvard named John Knowles Paine instructor in 1862 and professor in 1875, but not without opposition: it was said that the establishment of music led the eminent historian Francis Parkman to cry out, parodying Cato the Elder, at each meeting of the Harvard Corporation, *musica delenda est* (music must be destroyed), and to vote against funding it. Both Stoeckel and Paine were composers, but it is probable that their fame as performers was more persuasive to their appointers than their compositions.

Columbia's president, Seth Low, was not to be outdone by Yale and Harvard. Spurred on by a promised gift of $150,000 (nearly three million in today's dollars) for instruction in music, he sought advice from the Episcopal bishop and John

Edward MacDowell

Burgess, professor of political science and law. They quickly agreed that composition and the philosophy and history of music should be the subject matter of the new department, not the technical training more suitable to conservatories: that choice would not preclude a glee club, perhaps a student orchestra, and token instrumental study. (This dichotomy between what was thought to be proper to a university on the one hand and professional study—applied music—on the other has bedeviled the study of music ever since, except in those universities that have added schools of music or have formed alliances with conservatories.)

Having seemingly so simply settled the matter of what should be taught, the committee incongruously asked two pianists, William Mason (son of Lowell) and Ignace Jan Paderewski, who should lead the department. They recommended MacDowell, who had been composing and concertizing in Boston for eight years, making his living chiefly as a piano teacher. Their recommendation was strengthened by there having been a recent New York concert by the Boston Symphony Orchestra, during which MacDowell played his First Concerto and his *Indian Suite* was premiered. The concert had been rapturously received by the press and public.

Two days after the Morningside campus site was dedicated on May 2, 1896, MacDowell was appointed professor of music and the Department of Music was created, shortly thereafter empowered to offer undergraduate and graduate instruction. The news was received by the musical public and the university with enthusiasm, for MacDowell was thought to be the preeminent American composer and pianist.

A brief curriculum vitae outlines how MacDowell arrived at his preeminence. Born in New York to prosperous Scotch-Irish parents, he studied the piano from the age of eight. He progressed so rapidly that at the age of sixteen his mother removed him from school and took him to Paris for advanced study. Perhaps because of a misunderstanding about the age limit for entrance to the conservatory, at about this time his birth date was changed from 1860 to 1861. A memorial plaque at Columbia has the later date cast in bronze; the correct date was established 110 years later. (Draft-age men have discovered since how difficult it can be to reestablish a birth date.)

In Paris he began to compose and studied piano and theory assiduously. He had sketched for years, and a surreptitious caricature of one of his teachers so impressed the subject that he was offered three years of instruction in painting by an eminent École des Beaux-Arts faculty member. (MacDowell was later often to design the covers of his published works.) After a period of teenage indecision, inhibited by his weak spoken French and dissatisfaction with some of the instruction (shared by his classmate Debussy), mother and son left for Germany, the goal of almost every young composer of the time.

Settled down alone in Frankfort, MacDowell quickly made a strong impression as pianist and composer on the much sought-after Joachim Raff, who arranged for him to play his music for Franz Liszt. Liszt was so impressed by the young man's first piano concerto that he accepted its dedication and arranged for MacDowell's first publications. With such support, his music soon became widely known in Europe and was often performed in the United States by the virtuosa Teresa Carreño. Edward Grieg, with whom and with whose music MacDowell had much in common, was later pleased to become the dedicatee of two piano sonatas. After this European sojourn, MacDowell and his wife—at twenty-four he had married one of his American students—left for Boston in 1888, where they were to remain for the eight years before he left for Columbia.

The correspondence between President Low and the new professor, before as well as after his appointment, is fascinating. MacDowell, in his middle thirties, was both ignorant of and unencumbered by university ways. He outlined courses for undergraduate and graduate study intended for music specialists. He also designed courses for the general liberal arts student and argued for similar courses in the fine arts: "Our doctors, lawyers, literary and scientific men know but little of the arts except what comes to them through . . . social intercourse." (Courses in music and fine arts became part of the Core Curriculum half a century later.) He and Low agreed that Columbia should establish a School of the Arts, to include music, painting, and sculpture—and Low added architecture. (A building to house these, and theater arts, was promised in 1954 and not built. Columbia's School of the Arts, with theater arts but not architecture, came into existence in 1965.) They agreed that Columbia should also establish a school of music or affiliate with one. (The College formed an attachment with The Juilliard School in 1989.)

Had MacDowell been any better acquainted with the universities of his time, he would not so wholly have committed his boundless energy, imagination, and teaching abilities to such ambitious plans. He had, indeed, accepted the appointment with qualms: he suspected—correctly—that his performing and composing career would be relegated to summers, spent on the large farm his wife had just purchased in Peterboro, New Hampshire. He could willingly give up the concert career: though he enjoyed performing his own works, he suffered from stage fright and disliked playing conventional recitals and concerti. He had earlier given up concertizing for composing, which he considered his reason for existing.

During his eight years at Columbia, he wrote (mostly in the first four years) two excellent piano sonatas and short piano pieces, some songs to his own texts, as well as numerous choruses for the glee club and commencement fanfares. Clearly there was not the time necessary to conceive and carry out any more substantial orchestral works.

It must be conceded that MacDowell, the good citizen, took the time peripherally to "center the arts" elsewhere, in Jacques Barzun's phrase of 1954. As befitted his reputation, he was the first composer nominated for membership in the National Institute of Arts and Letters (1898) and then was instrumental in organizing the interrelated American Academy of Arts and Letters. He justified his efforts on behalf of the fledgling American Academy in Rome: "For years it has been my dream that the arts of painting, sculpture, and music should come into such contact that each and all should gain from their mutual companionship. . . . "

With the advantage of hindsight we know that he had but four post-Columbia years to live, some of them clouded by mental illness. We cannot know what other important mature works he might have written at the height of his powers between the ages of thirty-six and forty-four had he not accepted the professorship. Was it a "total mistake" as one of his early biographers wrote?

Having devised the curriculum, MacDowell proceeded for more than two years to teach all the classes. He was then given an assistant, and the faculty was later modestly increased as the curriculum enlarged and students flocked to his classes. Among them were Upton Sinclair and John Erskine, who wrote at length in reminiscences about the enduring impression their teacher had made as a person and musician.

It is painful to recount even briefly the dramatic falling out that took place in MacDowell's eighth and final year (1903–04). After President Low resigned to run for mayor of New York City, Nicholas Murray Butler was appointed. He had his own ideas about education in the arts, and when MacDowell returned from a sabbatical he found his music offerings—and those of fine arts—intermingled with the courses listed in the bulletin of Teachers College. Butler was unresponsive to his strong objections to this and other matters. MacDowell agreed to a frank "off-the-record" interview with *Spectator* reporters: within a few days six newspapers entered the fray. Both MacDowell and Butler published letters in *The New York Times* and elsewhere. MacDowell resigned. The trustees, appalled, accepted his letter of resignation (as of June 30, 1904) with a rebuke for his offenses against propriety.

During this unpleasantness, MacDowell sometimes seemed to lack his usual vivacity and resilience. Then, over the next two years, he lost his robust health, and, finally, his mind. The death certificate stated "Paresis (Dementia Paralytica)." Had his physician dared to write what was very likely tertiary syphilis, Columbia would have been spared the often-repeated accusation that it had been largely responsible for MacDowell's "depression," "nervous exhaustion," "brain fever," and death.

To aid the two MacDowells financially during his illness and to promote his music, at least three organizations were formed. The MacDowell Fund in New York included among its 400 members all the financial and artistic leaders of the city, among them Seth Low. MacDowell Clubs were established in sixty-six cities, and contributions were received from England and the continent.

Even in his late moments of lucidity, MacDowell often spoke of centering the arts on the New Hampshire farm. With the aid of the accumulating funds, the Edward MacDowell Association was formed to administer the property as the MacDowell Colony, a haven for the undisturbed work of composers, writers, painters, and sculptors. Months before his death there were two colonists in residence. Since then residencies have been enjoyed by more than 4,500 individuals—an enduring legacy of a farsighted man.

DOUGLAS MOORE

The North Fork of Long Island resembles the upper tail fin of a fish whose head is Brooklyn and Queens. Flat, fertile, and embayed, to the north are Long Island Sound and Connecticut—to the east, Peconic Bay. For 250 years immigrants from New England and their descendants sailed across the sound rather than trekking overland to distant New York City. Even Walt Whitman's central Long Island was far "up-island" (that is, upwind), though he taught school for a while on the North Fork, living at a crossroads known thereafter as Sodom's Corner.

In the first 1640 boatload of settlers from New Haven was Thomas Moore. His descendants were farmers and tradesmen. Douglas Moore (1893–1969) relished repeating the comment of a local historian who claimed that the Moores never had amounted to much because they had been too addicted to music and sex. But Douglas's father amounted to a great deal: the first to leave North Fork for the city, he founded the *Ladies' World* magazine, lived in a Stanford White house in Brooklyn, and built a shingle-style villa on Peconic Bay.

The father went along with his son's early passion for music because there were two much older brothers whom he expected to take over his magazine (later sold to Hearst). Given these comfortable circumstances, Douglas went off to prep school, Hotchkiss, where he made many friends, among them Archibald MacLeish ("Archie"), with whom he was later to collaborate, and who—much later—was to officiate at the Columbia memorial for his old friend in 1969.

Yale was proper after Hotchkiss in those days, and there Moore earned two degrees, the second in music. Going to New Haven was also symbolic, for it was from there that Thomas Moore had left nearly three centuries earlier.

Douglas Stuart Moore is remembered today not only for his thirty-six years at Columbia—he shaped the music department as chairman from 1940 to 1962 into what it largely still is today—but also as the founder and tireless supporter of several organizations that aid composers. The wider musical public knows him as a composer of operas, particularly *The Ballad of Baby Doe* and *The Devil and Daniel Webster*. It is always written of Moore that his seven operas are based on American subjects. And so they are, as are his several other theater pieces, two films, and even much instrumental music. But they are more specifically engendered: the subject matter is intimately related to his birthplace, Cutchogue, and its surrounding farmland, and to a long life of summers spent in his father's villa, Quawk's Nest, then next door to his own smaller shingled house, Salt Meadow. Almost all his music was composed in a secluded studio overlooking a tidal inlet.

Douglas Moore gave lasting shape to Columbia's music department in a university career spanning nearly four decades. He was also a prolific composer, producing operas, orchestral works, chamber pieces, art songs, and catchy tunes for sports and collegiate life that are still popular today.

If it is true that since Beethoven composers usually have chosen subjects for their operas, whether consciously or unconsciously, that are close to their preoccupations, Moore is a prime example. Most of his opera libretti deal with strong, protective husbands, often close to the earth—in *The Ballad of Baby Doe*, the powerful Horace Tabor literally digs for silver—and loving, often ailing, wives. In the above-mentioned operas there are two strong wives: one is ailing in her last scene; the other, Baby Doe, is indomitable, even as she freezes to death. In *The Devil and Daniel Webster*, the husband, a farmer, tries to better his family's lot by making a pact with the devil; he is supported loyally by his wife. The farmer-lawyer, Daniel Webster, wins his client's case against the devil by converting a jury of the worst blackguards in American history. *Giants in the Earth* (Pulitzer Prize, 1951), and *Carry Nation* carry on this Moore-ish tradition, although in the latter the traits switch genders: Carry chops up bars with a hatchet and her husband succumbs to alcoholism. Moore's one transatlantic foray, based on James's *The Wings of the Dove*, differs from the above in its English setting, but the heroine is mortally ill; and Moore knew about Americans abroad, for he lived among them for three years in France during the twenties.

Given the above relationships of life-as-opera and opera-as-life, it may be unnecessary to mention that Moore enjoyed tending a large vegetable garden near his studio and that his wife was beset with lingering, overlapping illnesses during their long marriage. But many singers who have impersonated the four gossips in *Baby Doe* would be surprised that the models for their roles—Sarah, Mary, Emily, and Effie— were Douglas's two daughters, wife, and sister-in-law. Moore's intimate collaborations with his librettists permitted these and other such semiprivate references.

From his earliest years he had the ability to write catchy, humorous songs. At Yale-Harvard games his "Goodnight, Harvard" is still bellowed. John Kander, who once introduced himself as Moore's illegitimate son—and this writer as Moore's legitimate son—can be talked into performing "Naomi, My Restaurant Queen" and others of Moore's Yale and World War II navy songs.

His ability to write pop songs and later a dozen "art songs" had something, but not much, to do with composing operas and hardly anything to do with his writing a number of orchestral works and a decent amount of chamber music. That necessary craft, developed in a personal way, he was slow in developing.

He revered his main composition teacher at Yale but later had to unlearn much else learned there. Mustered out of the navy in 1919 in Paris, he stayed on to join those of his contemporaries who were arriving to study with the already-fabled Nadia Boulanger. She and Moore did not get on: she was becoming accustomed to Americans with limited craft, but she was not sympathetic to what he wanted to write; and he was not enamored of the composers she favored. He decamped to the Schola Cantorum to study composition with Vincent D'Indy and organ with Tournemire. D'Indy was a profound influence, in part because he was a composer of operas and sometimes based instrumental works on popular and folk melodies. One sometimes catches whiffs of his harmonic progressions even in Moore's later works.

Leaving Paris for home, Moore accepted the position of curator of music and organist at the Cleveland Museum. He took advantage of the presence at the Cleveland Institute of the Swiss composer Ernest Bloch for further study. On the side he took several acting roles in the Cleveland Playhouse, then in its heyday. His passion for the theater had been thwarted at Yale, where that Hoosier upperclassman, Cole Porter, was favored as lyricist and show-composer. (Later Moore was to provide incidental music for two Shakespearean plays on Broadway; later still he added a stage to the huge living room at Salt Meadow, suitable for charades and family theatricals, the first of which he had written and composed at about the age of seven.)

In 1926 he was offered a teaching post at Columbia but through the back door of Barnard College, so to speak, a subterfuge used occasionally by Columbia to acquire composers. He became one of the five faculty members of the Barnard-Columbia music department. There were but two classrooms, a number of books, scores, and pianola rolls and no librarian. It was said that the shorter professors used Bach Gesellschaft volumes as chair-heighteners. Moore climbed the academic ladder rapidly and succeeded Daniel Gregory Mason as chairman in 1940. (Mason, by the way, was the grandson and nephew respectively of the two Masons earlier mentioned.) In that year Yale tempted its by then well-known alumnus with a deanship. President Butler countered by alerting Moore to an expected large legacy "for the aid and encouragement of musicians," composers particularly, not to be used for educational purposes. Moore turned down the Yale offer and then, after the will was probated, engineered the resignations of the self-interested members of the advisory committee of the Alice M. Ditson Fund and their replacement by others more likely to carry out the implications of the will.

In this maneuver, he showed two qualities that served him well both at Columbia and in the numerous other organizations he served and often led—and sometimes had helped to establish: great charm and velvet-gloved toughness. He sweet-talked Butler into dismissing a professor he thought poised to set up a rival music department. When John D. Rockefeller Jr. invited Butler and Moore to move the music department to Lincoln Center, then in the planning stage, Moore refused on the grounds that Music Humanities and other liberal arts students couldn't be expected to attend classes by subway. It is an action MacDowell would have approved. When William Schuman, president of The Juilliard School, learned that his school had been second choice, he was aghast. So was Rockefeller.

In addition to being charming and tough, Moore was also thoroughly knowledgeable about and in love with music. Accordingly he was a Great Teacher (the award of 1960), a fair-minded critic and music juror, and the author of two books intended for Music Humanities students and other laymen. In his day, chairmen were appointed "at the pleasure of the Trustees," and he pleased them for twenty-two years until his retirement in 1962. By that time he had accomplished much of what MacDowell had envisaged in 1896.

Moore was a more fervent spokesman for the music of others than he was for his own because, I think, of a certain musical modesty that bordered on insecurity. His early interest in Americana was bolstered by the strong encouragement of Vachel Lindsay. Later he was to move amiably among sophisticated composers of all kinds, some of whom, as usual, looked askance at one who insisted on writing operas and may not have recognized in his conservative music the "modesty, grace, and sound construction" noted by Virgil Thomson.

He was also a better protector of other composers' rights than of his own. He neglected to ask formally for the operatic rights to his friend Philip Barry's play *White Wings*; heirs and lawyers held up its premiere for fifteen years. When his friend Stephen Vincent Benét suggested his short story *The Devil and Daniel Webster* as an opera subject, the two worked out the libretto together. The dramaturgy was chiefly the composer's. Foolishly, there was no written agreement. Benét published the almost unchanged libretto as a play that was to be performed hundreds of times and then filmed—starring Walter Huston and with a score by another composer— all without credit and royalties to Moore.

When such unpleasantness occurred or an unkind review was let into the house, Moore was never outwardly angry. He simply adopted, as his allusively literary family called it, his Eeyore manner.

PAUL HENRY LANG

Sometime in 1932 an acquaintance of Moore insisted that he meet Paul Henry Lang, a tall, dark, and handsome Hungarian in his early thirties then teaching at Wells College. Moore invited him to lunch at the Faculty Club. According to Moore's account it was a long, animated lunch hour. One can assume that these two good, digressive talkers covered their separate and common interests and that Moore was piecing together in his head the outlines of Lang's curriculum vitae: born in 1901; studied music at the Budapest Academy with Zoltán Kodály—with Béla Bartók as his adviser; orchestral bassoonist and vocal coach at the Opera (Moore would have perked up at the mention of a coachee, Maria Jeritza, one of his favorite sopranos at the Metropolitan Opera); to Germany to study musicology, history, and literature; to Paris for more of the same; wrote a dissertation there but could not meet the requirement of its publication because his father had lost money under the Horthy regime; emigrated to the United States; another dissertation at Cornell on the literary history of French opera (Moore would have enjoyed pointing out that Otto Kinkeldey, the musicologist at Cornell, had been a MacDowell student at Columbia); taught at Vassar and Wellesley; and—oh, yes!— while in Paris had been on an Olympic rowing team.

Then, according to Moore's recollection, the two walked toward Broadway until Moore arrived outside Journalism (which then housed Music) and they went their separate ways. On a sudden impulse he turned, shouted to Lang to wait, ran after

him, and asked, "Would you like to teach at Columbia?" When he said, "Yes, of
course," Moore went immediately to Mr. Mason (under his chairmanship first names
were not commonly used) and shared with him his plan to add a musicologist to the
staff. Mason demurred: there was no need, for there was already a year of music history and music literature courses, symphony, and chamber music; besides, there was
no money for another salary. (The department had been somewhat somnolent since
MacDowell had left; his successor had added little and subtracted some; his successor, Mason, occasionally requested no increase in the annual budget and refused to
answer correspondence concerning a summer session.)

   Although Moore was too much the gentleman to tell me so, it may be that Mason
was also put off by Lang's name (then spelled Láng, with an accent). His writings
include encoded anti-Semitism. When I asked Lang toward the end of his life if he
were Jewish, he answered, "Well, no, I'm a Catholic, though I don't often go to Mass.
In the thirties there was an influx of Central European refugee musicologists, and I
was naturally thought to be one of them, though I'd been here for a decade." That

he was telling the truth—if anyone still cares—was already proved at his christening: Paul Maria Henry Ferdinand László Láng. Whatever the objections of Mason, Moore went to the Carnegie Foundation and arranged for a grant to cover the first two years of Lang's salary.

Lang's mentor at Cornell, Kinkeldey, was the first professor of musicology in the United States. Lang immediately began to teach the subject at Columbia—he was among the first in the United States to do so—though he was not recognized with the same title until 1941.

Laymen see the word *musicology* most often in CD booklets. The discipline was a mid-nineteenth-century German and Austrian conflation of all studies in music except composition and performance. It made its way here by way of returning Americans who had done their graduate study abroad (as had Kinkeldey) or by way of immigrants (such as Lang). For a while, there were turf battles with the reigning composers. Once it was established, there were other turf battles as the all-too-encompassing discipline divided into specialties: historical musicology, ethnomusicology, the speculative aspects of theory and aesthetics, and (as of today) of whatnot. By the time these later battles were joined, Lang's position had become so impregnable that he rarely seemed embattled. In any case, he was tolerant, and when he had to give ground, he could take pleasure in his decided streak of masochism.

That high ground he achieved in part (with the eventual collaboration of at least three colleagues at a time) by training innumerable graduate students who were then to find important far-flung teaching positions.

In addition, the restless, energetic, and ambitious Lang became the editor of *The Musical Quarterly* in 1945 and remained so until 1973. He could not accomplish the impossible: make a profit from a learned journal for its publisher, G. Schirmer. But he was proud never to have run a budget deficit.

When Virgil Thomson unexpectedly gave up his post as chief music critic on the high-minded *Herald Tribune*, its owners realized that no second Virgil Thomson existed and turned to a professor who wrote fluently and interestingly and who was happily married with four children. For almost ten years (1954–63), Lang enjoyed covering concerts and opera and writing Sunday articles (both later the substance of published books). In those days, review copy had to be submitted for the next day's morning edition—and for Lang there was a long commute home.

These nonuniversity activities—not to speak of service on behalf of musicological and learned societies and assembling a groundbreaking series of books on music for the publisher W. W. Norton—exacted a price that his students and colleagues were paying. He might have disregarded that debt with his usual insouciance, but he was deeply offended when the university's president at important functions introduced him as the chief critic of the *Trib*. When he decided to quit the post, the *Trib's* owners offered to add the whole of his Columbia salary to his critic's salary if he would remain. He resigned. He was not the only one of my seniors to say, ruefully, that universities are insecure in judging the qualities of their professors: therefore, reputations within the university are made on the basis of outside accomplishments.

Lang once confided that he preferred cabinetmaking to practicing music history, "particularly now that steam-shovel musicology has become the thing." True, he was not always to be believed, but his favorite phrase, *se non è vero, è ben trovato* (if it's not true, it's nicely invented) was disarming. The Langs changed houses often, and in each there was something to be improved. One of the more impressive was a converted early poured-concrete structure built by Horace Greeley. In it was a study that could be compared only to the library of an English country house. It was full of his handiwork, including double-height bookcases. In the basement of each house were innumerable bottles of identified hardware, like three-by-five cards awaiting some new scholarly undertaking.

My first acquaintance with Lang was by way of reading his *Music in Western Civilization* as a student at the Eastman School of Music shortly after its 1941 publication. I had never read anything like it, nor have I since. It read like a 1,000-page essay, placing music in the context of the other arts, philosophy, and history; it was at once magisterial and intimate. I was disturbed, though, by the regretful tone that suffused his discussion of the twentieth-century musical scene—which I was preparing to enter.

When I met Lang himself in the fall of 1944, he was delighted that I had come to New York City to study with his friend Bartók. In friendly fashion he cautioned, "Don't put any currency in Bartók's hand at the end of a lesson: some Hungarians are uncomfortable with money, and he has no talent at all for making it." At that time Lang was feuding with Howard Hanson, the director of the Eastman School, about the Ph.D. in composition; in addition, the heads of theory in the two institutions were feuding about the proper way to teach the subject. Accordingly, when I was invited to join the Columbia department the following year, it was thought that I, fresh out of the enemy camp, should be indoctrinated in Columbia ways by attending Lang's Proseminar in Musicology. It was exhilarating to experience his book brought to life: he improvised brilliantly on themes from an overflowing mind. There were inventive speculations that could be followed by alert students. That he loved the sound of music was obvious when he played recordings, even when he fumbled at the keyboard. He had a habit of suddenly asking difficult questions. When nobody could answer, he would call on me (or on William Bergsma, an Eastman composer friend who occasionally audited for the fun of it). I remember one such exchange: "What are the dates of Giovanni Pergolesi?" When nobody knew, he called on me. "1710–36," I answered. (What twenty-four-year-old composer would not remember the dates of a composer who had written so well and so much in just twenty-six years?) There was then yet another opportunity to castigate his students for not spending enough time reading and listening and for not living up, even, to schools-of-music standards.

Late in life he was to write the impressive *George Frideric Handel* and to look forward to preparing a new edition of *Music in Western Civilization*. Much later, deteriorating eyesight permitted him only to add an occasional essay and many record reviews to the several hundred he had already amassed.

In 1997, six years after his death, his 1941 magnum opus was reprinted unaltered. The perspicacious foreword by Leon Botstein includes the following tribute: "The passage of time has not diminished its virtuosity and stature as a tour de force . . . [It] would be a good place to begin the debate that increasingly occupies scholars and listeners alike concerning the future of the classical and serious music tradition in the United States and Europe."

CHAPTER 4

The Many Lives of Moses Hadas

—╲ℳ╱—

Rachel Hadas

*Moses Hadas was one of my instructors in the junior-year Colloquium on Important Books, the cel-
ebrated honors course of John Erskine in which Hadas was teamed with Raymond Weaver of
Herman Melville fame. A distinguished classicist himself, Hadas was also the epitome of the great
teacher, whose personal engagement with undergraduates made him a father figure for students in the
undergraduate humanities program and whose intellectual adventurousness led him to join in the first
Oriental Colloquium (attended by such Columbians as the critic Norman Podhoretz, the poet John
Hollander, and John Rosenberg, the authority on Carlyle and Ruskin).*

    *A special feature of our essay on Moses Hadas is that it is written by his daughter Rachel, a crit-
ic, translator, and essayist as well as a noted poet, who includes in her account of her father charming reminiscences of her childhood on Morningside Heights and her impressions of the Columbia community. Rachel Hadas was a fellow at the New York Public Library Center for Scholars and Writers
from 2000 to 2001. Since 2002, she has been Board of Governors Professor of English at Rutgers-
Newark. Her most recent book of poems is* Laws *(Zoo Press, 2004). Two more books are forthcoming:* The River of Forgetfulness, *poems, 2006; and* Classics, *essays, 2007.*

                                                  —*Wm. Theodore de Bary*

—╲ℳ╱—

In the 1930s, the decade in which my father, Moses Hadas, began his long career
in the Department of Classics at Columbia, the discipline of classical philology
was still strongly influenced by German and British models. Whether the student was reading Homer, Sophocles, or (A. E. Housman's specialty) Manilius,

expertise in textual criticism and in grammar was paramount; interpretation and appreciation of the text were secondary. If a student happened to enjoy the poetry of Homer or the tragedians, well and good; but such enjoyment was not the point of the exercise. The possible benefits of a literary critical approach, let alone of teaching texts in translation for students who knew no Greek or Latin, were by and large sternly ignored.

In the last half-century, a dramatic cultural shift has clearly occurred in the teaching of classics in American universities. So pervasive has been this change that it's all too easy to take it for granted. A detailed account of Columbia's Literature Humanities and Contemporary Civilization courses such as *Great Books* by David Denby virtually ignores the shift, focusing instead on what might be labeled the Anti–Dead White Male reaction against the teaching of Western masterpieces that arose in the politically conscious seventies and eighties. It's worth pondering, then, that had it not been for teachers like Moses Hadas (1900–1966), generations of students who knew no Greek and Latin and did not major in classics might never have had the opportunity to read translations of epic or tragedy in the first place.

Hadas's former Columbia colleague William M. Calder III notes: "That Sophocles is almost as well known as Shakespeare to so many Americans educated after 1945 is largely due to Hadas."

How did this quiet revolution come about? Hadas was reticent about his own career. But an early experience, to which he often referred to illustrate the importance of teaching the classics in translation, is fully narrated in an unpublished and undated typescript of a talk entitled "On Teaching Classics in Translation"; it was evidently delivered to, as the writer puts it, "colleagues in other branches of literary study." (He adds mischievously, "It is a delicious experience to emerge from the academic limbo to which so many of us have been relegated and to say, reproachfully, 'We always tried to tell you that we are indispensable.'")

Here is Hadas's account: "I am so far a renegade from the principles of my own teachers as to believe that the teaching of ancient books in translation, even of the Bible, is a good thing. In the early years of my own teaching I had simultaneously a course in Euripides, with four students, and one in Greek tragedy in translation, with twenty. At the end of the term I decided that it was useless to set the Hellenists the usual examination, for I had heard them perform daily, so I asked them the questions on Euripides which I was putting to my tragedy class; I had after all not limited my exegesis to metrics and grammar. I learned a useful lesson when I found that what the English readers had received was more meaningful and more likely to endure than what the Hellenists had learned. I still teach Euripides, and other authors, in

With Jacques Barzun (right) at a picnic in 1939

Greek, for that is the prime obligation of my profession; but I have regarded it as no less an obligation to multiply the beneficiaries of the legacy by teaching the ancients in translation."

From this point on, Hadas never looked back but enthusiastically taught texts in translation. And not only taught them—translated them.

TRANSLATING FOR A NEW GENERATION

Hadas, in a way that seems to me characteristically self-effacing, fails to mention in the above anecdote that he himself did an enormous amount to multiply not just the beneficiaries of the legacy but also the legacy itself, by his numerous translations. Both as a teacher and as a translator of the classics, Hadas prized clarity above all. He saw that each generation needs its own versions, and in "On Teaching Classics in Translation" he has penetrating things to say about the perils of Victorian renderings of Greek tragedy that give students the misleading impression that Aeschylus or Euripides were Old Testament prophets. He once commented: "It's a little too much to expect a student to pick up a Victorian translation of the *Iliad*. He's got two strikes against him if he does. No, let each age put down the classics in its own language, just so long as they keep the spirit of the original." Hadas's own way of remaining faithful to the spirit of his beloved Euripides, for example, was to efface himself, presenting a plain if formal prose text in place of the flowery and fanciful spirit of an earlier translator like Gilbert Murray. Below is Murray's rendering of a choral strophe followed by the heroine's opening lines in Euripides' *Medea* and then a translation of the same passage by Hadas and his Euripides cotranslator, John McLean. The contrast speaks eloquently for itself.

TWO TRANSLATIONS

Chorus
I heard a song, but it comes no more.
Where the tears ran over:
A keen cry but tired, tired:
A woman's cry for her heart's desired,
For a traitor's kiss and a lost lover.
But a prayer, methinks, yet riseth sore
To God, to Faith, God's ancient daughter—
The Faith that over sundering seas
Drew her to Hellas, and the breeze
Of midnight shivered, and the door
Closed of the salt unsounded water.

Medea
Women of Corinth, I am come to show
My face, lest ye despise me. For I know
Some heads stand high and fail not,
even at night
Alone—far less like this, in all
men's sight . . .

> *Gilbert Murray*
> *The Medea of Euripides*
> (New York: Oxford University Press, 1912)

Chorus
I hear a cry of grief and deep sorrow. In piercing accents of misery she proclaims her woes, her ill-starred marriage and her love betrayed. The victim of grievous wrongs, she calls on the daughter of Zeus, even Themis, Lady of Vows, who led her through the night by difficult straits across the briny sea to Hellas.

Medea
Women of Corinth, do not criticize me, I come forth from the palace. Well I know that snobbery is a common charge, that may be levelled against recluse and busy man alike . . .

> *Moses Hadas and John McLean*
> *The Plays of Euripides* (New York: Dial Press, 1936)

Old Wine, New Bottles is the title of one of Hadas's many books. Even a partial list of the remarkable variety of wines Hadas rebottled includes works from Hebrew and German as well as Greek and Latin; the astonishing range speaks to Hadas's cultural reach, which encompassed European historiography, biblical scholarship, and much else as well as classical philology. Thus in addition to such classics as Euripides, Aristophanes, and Plutarch (as well as the Hellenistic romance writers Longus and Heliodorus) among the Greeks and Caesar, Cicero, Tacitus, and Seneca among the Romans, Hadas also translated from German the Swiss historian Jacob Burckhardt and scholarly works by Walter Otto, Karl Vietor, and Elias Bickerman. Then there was the other branch of his expertise, expressed in translations of medieval Hebrew poems and fables. His last book, posthumously published in 1967 and reissued in 2001 by David R. Godine, is entitled *Fables of a Jewish Aesop*.

TRANSMITTING THE CLASSICAL LEGACY

Moses Hadas was raised in Atlanta in an Orthodox household by Yiddish-speaking parents and trained as a rabbi (he graduated from The Jewish Theological Seminary in 1926 and completed his doctorate in classics in 1930); later in life he continued to fulfill the rabbinical function of performing wedding ceremonies, specializing in marriages, like his own second one, between Jews and Gentiles. Thus not only in his teaching, translating, and scholarship but also in his own life, Hadas was a bridge builder who crossed his own bridges; a mapper of cultures who especially enjoyed seeing where traditions converged. His linguistic talent (Yiddish, German, Hebrew, Greek, Latin, French, Italian, and add later some Spanish, Dutch, Modern Greek, and Hebrew as he experienced it spoken in Israel) was mirrored by a remarkable cultural fluency. Hadas's bookplate, designed for him early in his career, neatly illustrates what would now be called multiculturalism: it depicts a menorah for Judaism, Athena's owl for Hellenism, and Roman fasces. Throughout his career, most notably in his 1959 study *Hellenistic Culture: Fusion and Diffusion*, Hadas traced connections between these worlds—an undertaking that has now become far more fashionable than it was in his day, in the field of classics as in other areas of the humanities and social sciences, but one that even today few scholars are fully equipped to undertake.

Thus although Hadas was praised by his colleague Jacques Barzun as belonging "to that ancient time when scholars loved to teach, knew how to write, and developed personalities without effort," his distinctively multicultural interests and identity make him look, from my perspective now in 2001, more like a man ahead of his time. Hadas was also ahead of his time in his populist instinct. A crucial—perhaps the crucial—theme of his career was the urge to transmit the classical legacy, in the widest sense of the term, to as wide an audience as possible—certainly an audience outside the classrooms of Columbia College. Thus mid-century technology allowed him to reach a television audience; he spoke about the classical legacy on Channel 13 and traveled to Israel with Eric Sevareid in 1965 for a program about the Shrine of the Book. And in 1963, in a pilot program conducted under the auspices of the Ford Foundation, Hadas delivered lectures on classical civilization by telephone to several Southern black colleges, including Grambling State University. (Partial tapes and transcripts of these lectures survive; it is a chapter of

At the 1962 Yule Log Ceremony, reading "A Visit from Saint Nicholas"

his career worth reexploring and more surprising than the fact that Hadas corresponded with Robert Graves about Greek mythology and with Mary Renault about the way Euripides' Medea hisses her s's.)

As his supple use of media shows, Hadas welcomed technology as a means to his humanistic ends. A wry comment in an unpublished 1959 talk entitled "Science and Education" gives a clue as to what his opinion of e-mail might have been: "I . . . like the gadgets that technology produces; a tape recorder is a very handy thing on which to dictate a harangue against gadgets." But he continues on a more serious note: "The real issue . . . is not between science on the one side and the humanities on the other, but between one approach to both science and humanities and another. Humanity is more important than either science or the humanities separately."

LIVING MANY LIVES

Translator, scholar, builder of cultural bridges, charismatic teacher with a restless sense of his mission—Moses Hadas was all these things. And if it seems paradoxical that so dynamic a figure is now less remembered and celebrated than his slightly younger Columbia colleague Lionel Trilling, part of the reason lies in an elusive quality in Hadas's temperament, a reticence inseparable from, indeed inextricably linked to, the very modesty and versatility I have already mentioned. At a recent (and rare) Hadas family reunion, my sister Beth commented in exasperation that the Hadas family motto ought to be "Don't ask, don't tell." She had a point. In Hadas's rather short life he managed to play a striking number of successive roles, to undergo a number of fundamental changes. His work as teacher and scholar was a constant, but this work was performed by, at different times, an Orthodox Jew and— as he once described himself to some proselytizing Jehovah's Witnesses—a godless person (he seems to have broken with Orthodox practice well before 1945, the year he remarried). He was a Southerner by upbringing and accent ("He sounds like Jimmy Carter!" gasped one of my Rutgers students some years ago upon hearing a tape of him reading *The Apology*—in translation, of course), then a New Yorker. He was a rabbi, then a professor; then, like many academics in his generation, an O.S.S. operative who, more unusually, took an active interest in Greek politics after the war; and then a professor again, not to mention a talking head on TV and a telelecturer. He was a scholar at home in three ancient languages who was also a Groucho Marx fan. He was a husband and father to two very different families in succession. Three of his four children have had careers in the academy or the humanities; the youngest of the four, I was born when he was forty-eight.

It's as if it were possible, just barely, to live all these lives but only if no time was wasted talking about them. Or writing about them—for much of Hadas's personality, let alone his experience, remains outside the scope of his written work. However regrettable, this omission is consistent. In transmitting the classical heritage, Hadas prized clarity; accordingly, a quality of transparency prevents his books from becoming personal documents in the sense many of Trilling's books are. Given the life he led, did my father never feel ambivalence, nostalgia, divided loyalties, regret? Don't ask, don't tell.

One thing I do know he felt was exhaustion. By the time I was finishing high school, he would lie down as soon as he returned from teaching, so that he and I read Cicero's *De Senectute* together horizontally. *On Old Age*—how apt it sounds. When I was sixteen, he naturally seemed old to me, but he was only sixty-five. He was never too tired, though, to teach. He could translate any Latin poem at sight; late in his life he taught me the Greek alphabet (though he refused to transliterate the word *fuck*, spelled in Greek letters, when I came across it in an e. e. cummings poem) and a little German; and I'm aware these interchanges only scratch the surface of what he knew. He always praised my poetic efforts, moreover. Two of my books have titles that pay tribute to him in ways I was unconscious of at the time I chose them: *Pass It On* and *The Double Legacy*.

A PUZZLE OF CONTRADICTIONS

The legacy Hadas left us is at once substantial and elusive. In looking over tributes from his Columbia colleagues, some of whom knew my father for longer than
I did, I find myself identifying pieces of the puzzle of a temperament that had its
contradictions. For example, Hadas was simultaneously extroverted and reticent.
How would this combination play out in the classroom? Gilbert Highet's eulogy
supplies at least part of an answer:

> Well before his career came to an end he had the pleasure of teaching
> the sons of some of his earlier pupils. They found him just as charming
> and just as stimulating as their fathers had found him. He really knew a
> great deal more by that time; but he did not let it show because it might
> inhibit them. He would rather efface himself (in part at least) than seem
> mentally distant or pedantically erudite, and risk cutting down a young
> mind. That is rather difficult. It can be done only by a man who is fun-
> damentally wise, learned, and warm-hearted.

And, I would add, by a teacher whose mode is essentially dialogic. My father
needed his students to complete his thought, to earn for themselves what he had to
give them. In this connection there is a most germane passage in "On Teaching
Classics in Translation"—germane for what it shows us about Hadas in the classroom, as well as relevant to anyone who has ever tried to teach literature.

> The first rule, especially hard for teachers fresh from graduate school to
> apply, is to teach the book, not about the book. It is easier to lecture
> about the time and place of a book, the culture that produced it, the
> special historical or linguistic problems involved in it. It is harder, but
> more to our purpose, to face the book as a masterpiece and to help the
> student understand why it is a masterpiece. The great audiences which
> the book commanded over great stretches of time found it meaningful
> without scholarly subsidia. This must involve a degree of superficiality,
> but it also encourages freshness. Professional philosophers and philolo-
> gians who take a year for *The Republic* are outraged that we despatch it
> in a week. If the students' reading is superficial, any honest scholar will
> admit that his is also, and *The Republic* was not intended as a preserve for
> professors. If you dodge the book and conceal your fecklessness by loud

noises in the outworks, the whole enterprise becomes fraudulent. There are crambooks from which your students can get all the knowledge you purvey with their bare feet on a table. I emphasize this point because I find it needs to be impressed on all instructors in our Humanities course, and not least myself. I would cheerfully undertake an hour's discourse on any author included in my history of literature courses without preparation; I would not dare to enter a Humanities class without first trying to recover the excitement of a first unprofessional reading.

Clearly, Hadas drew encouragement and energy from his students' response to his own excitement. It was not preparing "an hour's discourse" that so exhausted him at the end of his life; it was being up for the give-and-take, the call and response. He needed his students as much as they needed him. It is not enough to say he was wise and warm-hearted; rather, he was by temperament that kind of teacher.

THE SHAPE OF THE MIND

Another eulogy of Hadas by a Columbia colleague, Herbert Deane, admirably captures some of the contradictions of a complex nature: "By turns he could be puckish, irreverent, idealistic, outrageous, and serious, even impassioned. He was

Hadas with Gilbert Highet in 1956

an exquisitely refined person, and yet he was also capable of an almost Rabelaisian earthiness. Although he had an unusual capacity for indignation in the presence of injustice, hypocrisy, or shoddiness, he was never self-righteous or condemnatory. All these different aspects of Moses Hadas's personality lived together in a harmonious whole."

But now, more than thirty years after my father's death, I find I cannot follow Deane quite all the way to his conclusion when he courageously touches on an aspect of his colleague's character that some clearly found disconcerting. Deane honestly notes Hadas's appetite for admiration: "He knew that his students felt affection as well as respect for him, and he enjoyed their devotion, as he enjoyed the praise of his written teaching when it came, as it so often did, from discriminating men whom he admired. In this innocent joy in the love and praise that he inspired, he sometimes startled some of us who think that we have escaped the danger of vanity by coyly pretending that we do not care about the reactions of our students or our peers."

So far so good. But then Deane continues: "But Moses could enjoy the affection and admiration that came to him because in the last analysis he did not need them; his relations with his family and his close friends were so deeply satisfying that he had no temptation to seek substitute gratifications in his activities as a scholar or teacher."

This seems wrong, for Hadas did indeed need the affection and admiration that came to him and that he certainly earned. I would amend Deane's conclusion: In the last analysis, Hadas's life was his work. True, he was a loving if weary father whose death when I was seventeen shook me for many years but whose life influenced mine in innumerable ways. True, too, he was beloved by many people during his lifetime. But regarded as a teacher and writer, Hadas remains, as his favorite Stoic writers might have pointed out, far more durable than the driven human being who worked so incessantly and productively all his life.

In yet another affectionate collegial comment on this complicated man's career, William Calder notes that Hadas "died shortly after his retirement from Columbia. There was nothing to live for." So much for those friends and family Deane evokes. The truth, as I now see it, is that my father knew how to work but not how to rest. Rest turned out to amount to death; but death was not a cessation. Three of my father's children and hundreds of his students continue working in the ever-broadening field of the humanities. Countless other people read his books, particularly his translations. The same transparency that makes much of his written work impersonal also makes much of it accessible and durable. In *Agricola*, Tacitus's eulogy of his

A Hadas family portrait, circa 1957. Clockwise from left: the author, Rachel Hadas; her mother, Elizabeth Chamberlayne; her sister, Beth; and Butterscotch, the cat.

father-in-law, is a passage my mother, a Latin teacher, marked for me after the death of her husband and my father:

"*Ut vultus hominum, ita simulacra vultus imbecilla ac mortalia sunt, forma mentis aeterna, quam tenere et exprimere non per alienam materiam et artem, sed tuis ipse moribus possis*": "Just as men's faces are frail and perishable, so are likenesses of their faces, but the shape of the mind is an eternal thing, one which you cannot hold on to and express through an artistic medium or skill, but by your own manner of life." At seventeen, I found these words consoling, and I still do. Not that I think my father is a perfect role model in all respects, even if I commanded the body of knowledge that was his. But the best way to honor our beloved dead is not by idolatry but by our own conduct. The human mind was Moses Hadas's constant theme, and he honored it as long as he worked, which was as long as he lived.

CHAPTER 5

Brander Matthews and Theater Studies at Columbia

—ɱ—

Howard Stein

Drama as a performing art and education as a gentlemanly pursuit had long thrived separately in New York City before Brander Matthews's natural interest in the two won out over his father's ambition for his son: to succeed to the "profession of a millionaire," well enough off so that he would be free to consider a political career. But when his father lost most of his fortune, Matthews was forced to earn his own living working as a lawyer in his father's business. As Columbia's and America's luck had it, soon after the son's graduation from Columbia College (1871) and Law School (1873), the young Matthews had recovered enough from his father's financial ruin to pursue his own talent for playwriting and eventually to move into theater reviewing and literary criticism. Today the Brander Matthews Chair in Dramatic Literature at Columbia—occupied by Martin Meisel and formerly by Joseph Wood Krutch, Eric Bentley, and Robert Brustein—honors Matthews's legacy.

The story of how Matthews went on to teach English literature at Columbia and then to become the first professor of dramatic literature in America is also the story of New York City as the hub of American theater and literary criticism in the late nineteenth century. It is told here by Howard Stein, former chair of the Oscar Hammerstein II Center for Theater Studies and professor of theater at Columbia, author of A Time to Speak *(Harcourt Brace, 1974), and now a member of the Society of Senior Scholars in Columbia's Heyman Center for the Humanities.*

—Wm. Theodore de Bary

—ɱ—

B rander Matthews was the first professor of dramatic literature in the United States, a quintessential pioneer. At the time of his death in 1929, an anonymous commentator in *Commonweal* wrote, "Today, the colleges are redolent of drama, experimental and otherwise. Not a few of the initiates forget that what they are attempting would probably never have been possible but for the witty, somewhat old-fashioned sage who really talked to the United States from his pulpit on Morningside Heights."

Clayton Hamilton, writing in *The New York Times*, made Matthews's contribution and legacy even more specific: "Until Matthews occupied the first chair in any American university specifically dedicated to the study of drama, drama had been regarded as a department of literature, like the essay or the novel, or the short story. He was the first to teach that drama was a separate area and could be studied not in the library but only in the theater. He was the first to teach that Shakespeare must be judged as a practical competitor with George M. Cohan for the applause and the money of the multitudes, instead of being judged as a literary competitor of such a poet as John Milton."

Obviously, Matthews was a challenge to some of his colleagues. Recalling the voices of those detractors, George C. D. Odell, one of Matthews's champions, stated that "when Matthews first described Shakespeare as primarily a writer of plays, certain academic critics met him with something like derisive rebuke; today [1939] no one would dream of editing a Shakespeare play without some reference to the stage history and its dramatic quality." Odell's comments are echoed today by as eminent an academic figure as Northrop Frye, who, in *Northrop Frye on Shakespeare*, maintains, "With Shakespeare the actable and theatrical are always what come first; the poetry, however unforgettable, is functional to the play; it doesn't get away on its own." Matthews's book on Shakespeare is *Shakspere as a Playwright* (1913).

Matthews became a pioneer partly because he was also a maverick—untrained for an academic career or for university teaching. His father was among the richest men in America, a Wall Street tycoon who trained his only son "for the profession of a millionaire, with no need for business but with an eye to the possibility of a political career." But, as John Lennon reminds us, "Life is what happens while you are busy making other plans." In 1873, the year Brander graduated from Columbia Law School, his father lost most of his fortune. Brander was obliged to seek a second profession. He joined his father's business as a lawyer and worked there for a few years making his own living and catching material for *His Father's Son*, a novel he was to write many years later.

Matthews's bookplate

From his earliest years, Matthews was intent upon a playwriting career. Before his father's financial ruin, he had written drama reviews and play scripts, especially translations from the French. His first script was an adaptation of a French farce that played for one night only at the Indianapolis Academy of Music in 1871. Another adaptation of a French play, *Frank Wylde*, was published in 1873; though never staged professionally, it became a favorite of the Comedy Club of New York and was often performed by amateur actors. During the next twenty years, he wrote (frequently with a collaborator) six plays that were produced in New York, two of which were performed all over the country—*A Gold Mine* (1887) and *On Probation* (1889)—both cowritten with collaborator George H. Jessop. Neither work established Matthews as a playwright of any significance, which was a major disappointment to him. As writer Lawrence J. Oliver has pointed out, "His playwriting legacy today seems confined to Theodore Dreiser's novel, *Sister Carrie*, in which Carrie gets turned on to the theater in a great awakening while attending a performance of *A Gold Mine*."

THE LITERARY LIFE

Although he would have preferred that his second profession be that of a playwright, in reality it was that of a "literary fellow." He wrote theater and book reviews, articles on European (particularly French) and American drama, and many sketches and short stories for various magazines, including *Appleton's Journal, The Atlantic, The Critic, The Galaxy, Harper's Magazine, Lippincott's Magazine, The Nation, Puck, Scribner's Monthly,* and *Saturday Review,* all prestigious periodicals of his day. He also wrote significant literary criticism. His *French Dramatists of the Nineteenth Century* (1881) was the first scholarly examination in French or English of the emergence of romantic drama in France. Very well received, the book went through five editions in Matthews's lifetime and remains today a valuable example of that century's scholarship. *Pen and Ink: Papers on Subjects of More or Less Importance* (1888) reflects his growing interest in fiction and poetry. Collaborating with fellow drama critic Laurence Hutton, he edited *Actors and Actresses of Great Britain and the United States, from the Days of David Garrick to the Present* (1886), a five-volume work blending biography, criticism, and anecdote, calculated to make theater more familiar and appealing to American audiences. His literary enterprise created friendships and acquaintances with some of the most distinguished writers and personalities of his time—Matthew Arnold and Rudyard Kipling in England; Constant Coquelin in France; and Bret Harte, William Dean Howells, Henry James (Sr. and Jr.), Theodore Roosevelt, and

Mark Twain in America. Yet despite this literary success, he yearned to be a play-wright to the very end of the century because "what had the power to excite me was the theater; and its allurements were immediate and genuine."

One of those immediate allurements was Ada Smith, who first appeared on an American stage in 1868, when Matthews was a sixteen-year-old sophomore in Columbia College. The daughter of a London physician, she was a dancer and an actress who performed under the name of Ada Harland in Lydia Thompson's British burlesque troupe.

Thompson's company comprised five performers, a troupe dubbed "British Blondes." Since Ada was a brunette, she inspired the following comment in *Spirit of the Times* on October 3, 1868: "Ada Harland is one of the most graceful dancers we have seen in a long time, and we were several times on the verge of applause, but she has dark hair—alas! that it should be so. It obscures her merit." The same report describes the company: "It is remarkably free from vulgarity and coarseness of mien and gesture. Thompson has captivated her audiences, men and women, by her delightful deviltry." Whether Matthews was in the audience at any specific time between 1868 and 1873 is not a matter of record, but that he was captivated by and then subsequently married Ada Harland is a fact recorded in his autobiography, *These Many Years*, published in 1917. Ada retired from acting altogether when they mar-ried (just before he graduated from the Law School), and her obituary makes no mention of her career with Lydia Thompson.

By the spring of 1891, at the age of thirty-nine, with degrees from Columbia College (1871) and Columbia Law School (1873), married with a daughter, finan-cially solvent as a result of his mother's modest legacy and a productive literary career, Matthews had recovered from his father's bankruptcy and even had a slight commercial success with *A Gold Mine*. His reputation as a man of letters both here and abroad was considerable and positive, which filled him with pride but not wealth. That reputation encouraged a representative from the Department of English at Columbia to pay him a call, one with a mission that was to have far-reach-ing effects and that thrust Brander Matthews into a third profession.

THE ART OF TEACHING

H. H. Boyesen startled Matthews by inviting him to take the place of Professor Thomas Price, who would be absent from Columbia the following winter. Matthews was thrown quite off balance, and even though he was aroused and flattered, he declined the invitation, admitting to Boyesen that he was totally ignorant of academia and teaching: "Not only have I had no experience in teaching, but I have never been called upon to consider its principles or to bestow on it even cursory attention. I have never even conversed about the principles and practice of education. All that I really know is that teaching is truly an art, and therefore I should have to acquire it somehow—and probably at the expense of my earliest classes."

At the same time, his critical impulse received a severe dose of muscle memory: He recalled being a student in Professor Thomas Lounsbury's History of English Literature class, in which they were introduced to none of the actual writings of any of the authors nor was any hint dropped that the students might benefit by reading them for themselves. Instead, the students had been required to procure a manual of English Literature and to recite from its pages the names of the writers, the titles of the books, and the dates of publication. The manual illustrated admirably the definition of history as "an arid region abounding in dates."

Boyesen was neither discouraged by Matthews's recollection of this earlier experience nor disturbed by his confession of ignorance and incompetence. He quickly offered Matthews not only an unconventional remedy but also an unparalleled freedom in an academic community: He suggested that Matthews choose his own three courses, to be open to seniors in Columbia College and to such graduate students as might be present.

Matthews eventually agreed and gravitated immediately to those subjects he knew best: American Literature, Modern Fiction, and English Versification. None of these courses had been taught before at Columbia; indeed it is unlikely that any of the three was offered in any college catalogue at the time. Boyesen was, nevertheless, happy with the arrangement, and Matthews was free to learn the art of teaching.

He approached his new task as a serious scholar might. "The art of teaching," he maintained, "requires the instructor to guide his student to work independently to discover principles for himself, and in time to acquire the power of principles to the manifold situations which may confront him." His course in English versification, for example, was not intended to create verse makers but to tempt the students into various kinds of verse making, "not with any absurd hope of developing them into poets but mainly because metrical composition is an excellent discipline for prose writing." Thus began his academic journey.

As Oscar J. Campbell noted in his chapter on the English department in *A History of the Faculty of Philosophy: Columbia University*, a volume edited by Jacques Barzun, "The addition of Matthews's three courses to the English curriculum greatly expanded its scope for all time, and marked the initiation of the department's

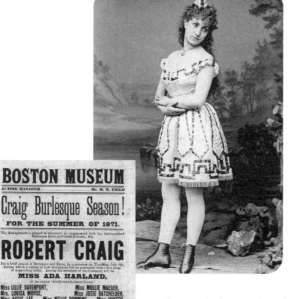

Matthews was a soph-
omore at Columbia
when Ada Smith (left)
first danced in New
York with Lydia
Thompson's British
burlesque troupe under
the name Ada
Harland. (She later
formed her own group,
featured in the poster
above.) The two mar-
ried in 1873, shortly
before Matthews grad-
uated from Columbia
Law School.

tending to deal as much with the immediate as with the remote in literature." (Matthews was always a little suspicious of the term *contemporary*,
for he claimed that the word was three-fourths temporary.) His first
year was so successful that President Seth Low and the trustees established a new professorship in literature especially for him. Matthews
responded by adding to his schedule a course on nineteenth-century
French playwrights, a course that absolutely did not exist on any campus in the United States. That developed into one entitled Modern
Drama, which has had a long and distinguished history at the university.

For the next six years, Matthews devoted himself to refining his four courses, and
in 1899, President Nicholas Murray Butler and the administration advanced the
1892 professorship in literature to the unique chair: Professor of Dramatic
Literature. Matthews continued his academic role until 1924, when he retired. He
died five years later, having already buried his wife and daughter.

A LEADING FORCE IN CRITICISM

A special legacy of Matthews's teaching was the prolific progress in the areas of
literary and theatrical reviewing and criticism. One of his students, Stark Young,
became the regular reviewer for *The New Republic*, a post he maintained until he
retired in 1947 (with one year out in the mid-twenties to write for *The New York*

Times). Another student, Ludwig Lewisohn, started a tradition of consequence by becoming the theater reviewer/critic for *The Nation* in 1919 and continuing until 1924. John Gassner upon leaving Columbia College reviewed for a variety of publications and then became the "play reader" for the Theater Guild Productions. From 1925 until he died in 1967, Gassner was a distinguished theater historian, critic, and scholar (he joined the Columbia faculty in the 1940s). Joseph Wood Krutch, a graduate student in the Department of English and Comparative Literature during Matthews's tenure, began writing theater reviews for *The Nation* in 1924 and continued in that position until 1951. Krutch joined the Columbia faculty in 1937 and assumed the Brander Matthews Chair in 1939, the year that Odell retired (after having occupied the chair since 1924). When Krutch left Columbia and New York for the Arizona desert in 1952, Eric Bentley accepted the chair and at the same time began his career of reviewing for *The New Republic*. Thereafter Robert Brustein joined the faculty in 1957, and in 1959 began writing for *The New Republic* himself; he has been writing the theatrical reviews for that magazine ever since.

Continuing that tradition is one of Brustein's students, Michael Feingold, who first studied with Brustein as an undergraduate and then followed him to the Yale School of Drama, when Brustein became its dean in 1966. Feingold began his reviewing by writing for the *Columbia Daily Spectator* in 1964 and has been a major drama critic for *The Village Voice* for the last thirty years. Such was the legacy of Matthews as teacher.

The distinguished array of professors who have taught courses or proseminars in modern drama at Columbia reads like a "Who's Who in Dramatic Literature": Brander Matthews; George Odell; Joseph Wood Krutch; Eric Bentley; Maurice Valency; Robert Brustein; Bernard Beckerman; Martin Meisel, the current Brander Matthews Professor of Dramatic Literature; and Austin Quigley, the present dean of Columbia College. When in 1947, twenty-three years after Matthews's retirement, the rating of English departments by the Association of American Colleges and Universities was announced, the unanimous choice for first place went to the Department of English and Comparative Literature at Columbia University—a decision that reflected in no small part the offerings in dramatic literature and the faculty.

This all started with the imaginative appointment of Brander Matthews in 1891.

Another spectacular legacy that Matthews left to Columbia is the Brander Matthews Collection. It was originally named the Brander Matthews Museum, a term Matthews appropriated from a nineteenth-century contribution to art—Museum: a home for the Muses. The museum was to be a teaching tool because he believed that the great dramatic poets prepared their plays to be performed by actors in a theater and before an audience. They had to take into account the method of the actor, the size and circumstances of the theater, and the feelings and prejudices of the audience. Matthews stated his own position clearly: "One cannot rightly estimate the dramas of Sophocles, Shakespeare, and of Molière unless we inform ourselves as fully as may be in regard to all the conditions they accepted freely, and in accordance with which they wrought out their masterpieces. For its proper understanding, it needs a gallery and a museum. Such a museum . . . would stand in the same relation to the arts of drama as the Avery Library of Columbia University stands to the arts of the architect, the decorator, and the landscape artist."

Matthews, an obsessive theatergoer and collector, began collecting in 1865 at age thirteen and apparently never threw anything away. He tirelessly and compulsively collected theatrical artifacts, which he then willed to Columbia with a modest maintenance stipend. That collection consists of ten models of theaters, twenty-nine stage sets from various periods of theater history from ancient to modern, photographs, manuscripts, posters, 300 tribal and theatrical masks from all over the world, more than 400 puppets—ranging from shadow puppets from Thailand and South India to Japanese puppets, Sicilian marionettes, and French Punch and Judy figures to oversize puppets of Oedipus and Jocasta, created by puppet maker Remo Bufano for the stage designer Robert Edmund Jones. The museum resided first on the sixth floor of Philosophy Hall and later on the fourth floor of Low Library; the bulk of the collection is now housed in the Rare Book and Manuscript Library on the sixth floor of Butler Library.

In addition to creating the museum as a repository for physical artifacts about the theater, Matthews published under the museum's name twenty-two small books on the theater between 1914 and 1922, two of which were reissued in 1956—*Papers on Acting* and *Papers on Playmaking*.

AN AMERICAN SPIRIT

Matthews's passion for the theater and Columbia was matched by his passion for New York City and America. Although born in New Orleans, he was moved to New York at the age of eight, and thereafter his love for the city never wavered. George Odell accounts for Matthews's passion: "The most devoted New Yorkers hail from other parts of the country. Matthews's father was from New Orleans, his mother from Virginia. The passionate lovers of the city, Matthews held, are seldom native sons." He wrote three books of sketches and short stories, all concentrating on the

*Matthews (right) and
British actor George
Arliss at Columbia's
1919 commencement
ceremony, during
which Arliss received
an honorary degree*

workings of New York: *Vignettes of Manhattan, Studies in Local Color,* and *Vistas of New York;* his three novels are all set in New York, and the city is the ground on which the characters play out their destinies: *His Father's Son, A Confident Tomorrow,* and *The Action and the Word.* He worked, spoke, and wrote with a desire to establish New York City as the hub of literary America. Indeed, he convinced William Dean Howells to move from Boston to New York; he organized and supported all sorts of organizations that would help nurture New York's role in America's literary development. He was a founder of the Authors' Club, which he claimed offered "the opportunity to rub elbows and to develop a solidarity among the men of letters in New York"; he helped found the American Copyright League, which enhanced the solidarity of American writers and especially those in New York. He was an original member of the National Institute of Arts and Letters (1898), an organization based in New York City; and in 1904, a central group from that organization formed the American Academy of Arts and Letters, also based in New York. Matthews was elected and acted as its chancellor from 1922 to 1924.

Many university people to this day think of George Pierce Baker at Harvard as the force within the university that brought drama from the page to the stage. The fact is that Baker started his good work many years after Matthews had begun his on Morningside Heights, while Baker in the Boston area was at a distance from the center of the theater's glamour, energy, and enterprise. Baker, for his part, was interested in training playwrights, while Matthews made his position clear with respect to that activity by quoting Dumas fils: "A man or a woman may become a painter, a sculptor, even a musician, by study—but not a playwright. . . . It is a freak of nature, which has constructed the vision such as to enable him or her to see things in a certain way." Matthews's mission was thus different from Baker's, and his New York was the one place whereby he could expose his students to the dynamics of the drama and thereby help them fulfill themselves with their own talent and craft.

Matthews's devotion to America was every bit as great as his devotion to New York City. From his early writings about James Fenimore Cooper, Mark Twain, and William Dean Howells, his work continued to reflect the sterling virtues that he identified with the American character: ethical standards, honesty and integrity, a fierce democratic spirit, a deep sense of humanity and compassion, and an equally fierce patriotism. In 1906 he gave the Phi Beta Kappa address, a speech entitled "American Character," a response to those European detractors of Americans—of their provincialism, their preoccupation with money, and their cultural poverty. His American Literature course, first offered in 1891, culminated in Matthews's publishing in 1896 *An Introduction to the Study of American Literature*, a volume that sold over 250,000 copies in the twenty-five years following its initial publication. His colleague William P. Trent organized and edited *The Cambridge History of American Literature*, a multivolume project that required decades to complete and used Matthews's *Introduction* as its basis. Subsequently, Matthews's contribution to American studies was summed up in a book by Lawrence J. Oliver, published in 1992, entitled *Brander Matthews, Theodore Roosevelt, and the Politics of American Literature, 1880–1920*. Oliver describes an article in *American Quarterly* by Eric Cheyfitz in which Cheyfitz argues that F. O. Matthiessen's book *American Renaissance*, frequently looked upon as single-handedly establishing American literature in the academy, was really not the origin but a culmination of a movement initiated in the nineteenth century to nationalize and professionalize American literature. *American Renaissance*, as Cheyfitz puts it, was thus a "classically corporate project." Oliver goes on to make his point:

> If we accept Cheyfitz' metaphor, "classically corporate project," then the Columbia professor [Matthews] who in the 1890s authored such essays as "American Literature" and "The Literary Independence of the United States," lobbied for American spelling and the Copyright Act of 1891, developed one of the first college courses on American writers, and produced a textbook on American literature that eventually sold over a quarter of a million copies, deserves recognition as a leading member of the board during the "corporation's" formative years.

An 1898 note from friend Mark Twain. Matthews's acclaim as a literary figure extended beyond New York to Paris and London, and his friends and correspondents included some of the most distinguished writers and personalities of the time, including Matthew Arnold, Rudyard Kipling, William Dean Howells, and Henry James.

During the last decade, scholars have found renewed interest in Matthews. Besides the volume mentioned above, Lawrence J. Oliver has also published *The Letters of Theodore Roosevelt and Brander Matthews* (1995). Joseph Kissane, while working on the plays of George Kelly, published an article in *Theater History Studies*, "Brandered by Matthews: The 1924 Pulitzer Prize" (1999). And Susanna Ashton, a professor of English at Clemson University, features a chapter on Matthews in her upcoming book *In Partnership—Literary Collaborators in America, 1870–1920*.

Although the bust of Brander Matthews was an appropriate likeness, and the portrait that hangs in the seminar room of the Department of English presents him as the maverick that he was, the most accurate description of the man that we have was made by Lloyd Morris many years ago. According to Oscar J. Campbell, Morris gave the following account of Matthews's periodic entrances on the stage of the Columbia campus to join his departmental colleagues at Morningside Heights: "Twice each week a burnished coupe, drawn by fat old horses and piloted by a fat old coachman, set down in their midst an aging Cyrenaic, urbane, dryly malicious, often mocking figure, who was—like the gilded statue of Alma Mater—a distinctive campus landmark."

CHAPTER 6

Joseph Wood Krutch as Cultural Critic, Drama Critic, and Nature Writer

—⚏—

John Margolis, Howard Stein, and Gerald Green

Joseph Wood Krutch, Brander Matthews Professor of Dramatic Literature at Columbia (1937–52), was a popular teacher on campus and also one of America's most visible men of letters. Like a number of other figures at the university, he was widely influential because he wrote not only for the academic world but also for an intelligent audience wherever it was to be found.

Krutch's work falls into three groups. First, in The Modern Temper *(1929) and other books, he commented on the general intellectual atmosphere of the modern age as he saw it. His fine biographies,* Samuel Johnson *and* Henry David Thoreau, *are in a sense part of this work, for in them he portrayed the spirit of those earlier periods through the lens of the individual lives. Second, he had a long career in theatrical criticism both in the classroom and as drama reviewer for a number of journals. Finally, he became in his later years perhaps the country's most familiar voice writing about the world of nature and what was happening to it as population increased and urban sprawl consumed more of the landscape.*

In 1996 The Friends of the Heyman Center for the Humanities held a symposium on Krutch's work, and presented here are three of the papers given on that occasion. John Margolis of Northwestern University, author of Joseph Wood Krutch, A Writer's Life, *discusses him as a cultural commentator. Howard Stein, professor emeritus of theater arts at Columbia, writes about his dramatic criticism. Gerald Green, a pioneer innovator of early television, produced a noted series of films featuring Krutch as a commentator about the natural world and discusses him in that role.*

—Carl Hovde
Professor Emeritus of American Literature and Former Dean of Columbia College

Joseph Wood Krutch as
Cultural Critic

John Margolis

Though he may well be remembered most for his remarkable nature writing, it was as a cultural critic that Joseph Wood Krutch gained his earliest recognition. Even as an undergraduate, Krutch understood that if he were to be more than a journalist, a mere dispassionate reporter of the passing scene, he needed to be a cultural commentator: he must assume a special angle of vision and offer a perspective that was, at least in part, contrary to the times. As editor of the University of Tennessee literary magazine, Krutch was eager in his monthly editorial essays to attract readership and to make his mark. Thus, eschewing such hackneyed topics as school spirit, he boldly addressed himself to rather more controversial matters such as liberal education and the prohibition of alcoholic beverages.

In one such essay—and with some apparent pride—Krutch noted that "the ideas presented in this essay do not fall in with the spirit of the times." This studied distancing of himself from his era would characterize much of his social commentary in the decades to follow. In his undergraduate apprentice pieces, as in the writing to follow, Krutch the cultural critic was Krutch the dissenter—the observer of the parade of contemporary life who asked quizzically, and sometimes stridently, whether the emperor was in fact wearing clothes.

In 1924, after he completed his graduate study here at Columbia, Krutch joined the editorial board of *The Nation* and, as the author of unsigned editorials in that weekly, had the opportunity to practice further the craft of cultural commentary he had begun as an undergraduate in Knoxville. However, the anonymous editorial column was hardly an ideal genre for a young writer eager to make a reputation. Thus it was surely with eagerness that not long after becoming an editor of *The Nation*, Krutch accepted the assignment to travel to Dayton, Tennessee, to serve as *The Nation's* correspondent on the Scopes trial there during the sweltering summer of 1925.

This son of Knoxville—who now enjoyed the urbanity of his Columbia Ph.D. and his Greenwich Village walk-up—was proud to announce in his dispatches that his standards were different from those of his fellow Tennesseans. "There is no state of the Union, no country of the world, which does not have communities as simple-minded as this one," he wrote from Dayton. "If Tennessee has become the laughing stock of the world it is not because she has her villages which are a half-century behind world thought but rather because among her sons who know better there is scarcely one who has the courage to stand up for what he thinks and knows." Krutch was happy to count himself as one of those few.

For Krutch, the Scopes trial was a symptom of "the vast gulf which lies between the two halves of our population"—benighted provincials and educated, sophisticated urbanites. In his dispatches from Dayton, as in much of his other cultural commentary in the twenties, Krutch aligned himself squarely with the latter. However, it was not primarily as a cultural commentator that Krutch gained recognition in the early years of his professional literary career. The Scopes trial had been a one-time opportunity for him, and his editorials in *The Nation* were unsigned.

Instead, he was, early on, best known as a book reviewer and drama critic; and in that capacity Krutch read scores of books and attended hundreds of plays. Whatever the artistic merit of those works—lucky if merely uneven—his reviewing fed his cultural commentary, as it gave him an opportunity to take a measure of the intellectual currents of the era. And he drew upon what he read and saw to inform the crafting of his most durable single work of cultural commentary, *The Modern Temper*, where Krutch offered a powerful—though selective—description of the drift of contemporary thought.

In the initial essay in that collection, which, like most of the others, was first published in *The Atlantic Monthly*, Krutch compared the development of civilization to that of a child. "It is one of Freud's quaint conceits that the child in the mother's womb is the happiest of living creatures," he began." Even as an infant, the child finds the world generally compliant to his needs and wants. Soon, however, the child discovers with enraged surprise that there are wills other than his own and physical circumstances that cannot be surmounted by any human will. Only after the passage of many years does he become aware of the full extent of his predicament in the midst of a world which is in very few respects what he would wish it to be."

Thus too, Krutch suggested, with civilization: "As civilization grows older, it too has more and more facts thrust upon its consciousness and is compelled to abandon one after another, quite as the child does, certain illusions which have been dear to it."

In the series of essays that followed, Krutch described the dilemma of modern man bereft of the comforts of poetry, mythology, and religion, and left only—in Krutch's view—with the sterile knowledge of nature.

Humanism, he suggested, was inevitably and unalterably opposed to the natural impulses, as revealed by science, that have made the human animal possible. If humanism had been rendered impotent by science, science itself offered no solace to the human spirit: "The most important part of our lives—our sensations, emotions, desires, and aspirations— takes place in a universe of illusions which science can attenuate or destroy, but which it is powerless to enrich." Love, in this modern era, "has been deprived of its value." The power of tragedy too was diminished. "The death of tragedy," he wrote, "is, like the death of love, one of those emotional fatalities as the result of which the human as distinguished from the natural world grows more and more a desert."

In his essays on the modern temper, Krutch was not only describing—but also in some measure creating—the intellectual currents of the time. His book was a best-seller when it appeared in 1929, and Krutch was much in demand as a lecturer. And his book, still in print today, became a canonical text for the understanding of what passed for the advanced thinking of his era.

But especially as one looks back on Krutch's career as a whole, it is difficult to escape the feeling that *The Modern Temper* was as much a dazzling intellectual and literary performance by a young writer on the make as it was a confession of Krutch's deepest feelings. In the heady days of the late twenties, just on the eve of the Depression, there was literary capital to be made by nay-saying in an era of optimism. Krutch's fundamental conservatism is no doubt implicit in his nostalgia for traditional values that he asserted modernism left enfeebled. But in *The Modern Temper* he luxuriated in his despair, resigned to his exquisite anguish.

In the thirties, however, Krutch's resignation was replaced by a spirit of resistance in his cultural commentary. Rather than climbing giddily onto the bandwagon of advanced thought, Krutch demurred from the leftist enthusiasms of his *Nation* colleagues and—now writing with unmistakable conviction—published a series of essays in *Harper's* and *The Nation* that were collected in a small volume, *Was Europe a Success?*

Having traveled to the Soviet Union in the late twenties, he was deeply skeptical of the enthusiasm of many of his fellow intellectuals for the Soviet experiment; and the political hurly-burly of the thirties, with its impassioned Marxism, left Krutch distinctly cold. He wrote that in the early thirties he felt much as a cultivated Greek or Roman must have felt in the early days of Christianity when he "discovered with amazement that his most intimate friends were turning, one by one, to the strange new delusion. . . . I, too," he said, "have now witnessed the process of conversion. I too have now found myself faced with friends whose mental processes have come, overnight, to be quite incomprehensible and to whose vocabularies have suddenly been added words obviously rich with meanings which elude all my efforts to comprehend them."

To his rhetorical question, Krutch responded that—warts and all—Europe was a success and was not to be readily exchanged for a mess of revolutionary porridge. He insisted "upon the right to value some things which have no bearing upon either production or distribution" and he rejected the claims of the economist who "proclaims—in too familiar an accent—thou shalt have no other God but me."

For Krutch, the term "Europe" usefully summarized "the whole complex of institutions, traditions, and standards of value" too readily dismissed by the Marxist. He said, "Humanity as Europe knows it cannot be imagined apart from the social order which Europe has created, the sensibilities which European art has developed, and the realm of thought which European philosophy has set in order."

Krutch acknowledged that the average Russian was better off in the thirties than he had been under the tzar, but he noted that America had never had a tzar. And he insisted that there was little reason, even in the midst of an economic depression, to hope that a postrevolutionary America—divorced from its European roots—would be a better place. "It is odd," Krutch noted, "that the only government which claims to have the good of its citizens at heart should also be the only one (except for fascist Italy and Nazi Germany) which finds it necessary to prevent them from escaping its jurisdiction. Surely," he concluded in the epigrammatic way that characterized his writing, "it is an odd Utopia which finds it necessary to lock its citizens in every night."

Not long after the publication of his commentaries on the political enthusiasms of the thirties, Krutch left the editorial board of *The Nation* and took his position on the Columbia faculty in 1937. His writing now was not that of the periodical journalist but rather that of the university professor. And it was not until he retired from Columbia to Tucson in 1952 that Krutch once again turned his hand seriously to cultural commentary. But in his intense engagement during his Columbia years with the lives and works of Samuel Johnson and Henry David Thoreau—two men about whom he wrote masterful critical biographies—Krutch found confirmation of perspectives that would powerfully inform the two decades of social commentary that, along with his nature writing, would distinguish the final phase of his career.

Krutch noted that Johnson, like Krutch himself in his essays on Communism, "genuinely believed that the current was running so strongly in one direction that someone ought to say what could be said against the prevailing tendency." And Johnson brought to his observations a quality that could be said to distinguish much of Krutch's social commentary as well: common sense. "Common sense,"

Krutch explained in his book on Johnson, "was the acceptance of certain current assumptions, traditions, and standards of value which are never called into question because so to question any of them might be to necessitate a revision of government, society, and private conduct, more thoroughgoing than anyone liked to contemplate." It was just such common sense that so clearly characterized Krutch's later social commentary.

In a similar fashion, from Thoreau Krutch gained confirmation of his temperamental apoliticism, of his conviction that man had freedom of choice and was not a victim of determinism—and, of course, that the natural world was charged with far more human meaning than Krutch had allowed in *The Modern Temper.*

Many of these convictions came together in his book *The Measure of Man,* which received the 1954 National Book Award for nonfiction. The book was conceived as a reassessment of the modern temper Krutch had described twenty-five years before; and it was, in the end, Krutch's repudiation of the anguished defeatism that marked the earlier study. Now informed by his patient observations of the nonhuman natural world of plants and animals, Krutch insisted that two of man's distinctive human characteristics were his ability freely to choose one thing over another and his capacity to create and act upon values.

The social sciences, he insisted, took at best a partial measure of man. "The methods employed for the study of man," he said, "have been for the most part those originally devised for the study of machines or the study of rats, and are capable, therefore, of detecting and measuring only those characteristics which the three have in common." Human consciousness may not lend itself to quantification in the laboratory or examination by questionnaire, but the commonsense evidence of experience shows it to be "the one thing which incontrovertibly is," Krutch insisted. "To refuse to concern ourselves with it is to make the most monstrous error that could possibly be made."

As with much of the social commentary that would follow in Krutch's Tucson years, *The Measure of Man* was less an effort to affirm a fully formulated set of principles or convictions than it was an effort to examine critically many widely held but too rarely questioned assumptions. He looked not to convert his readers, but rather to challenge them.

Looking back in the fifties on his earlier career and thinking of *The Modern Temper,* for which he was best known, Krutch commented:

> I thought I was an intellectual because of the number of things I did not
> believe. Only very slowly did I come to realize that what was really

characteristic of myself and my age was not that we did not believe anything but that we believed very firmly in a number of things which are not really so. We believed, for example, in the exclusive importance of the material, the measurable, and the controllable. We had no doubts about what science "proves" and we took it for granted that whatever science did not prove was certainly false. . . . The trouble was not that we were skeptical but that we were not skeptical enough.

As a public thinker and an essayist in the fifties and sixties, Krutch exhibited this skepticism as he examined a variety of developments in contemporary life and thought. His goal was not, as earlier, to establish himself as an advanced thinker, as a spokesman for the latest intellectual fashions. Instead, from his desert home in Tucson, he cast a skeptical eye upon the passing scene and recorded his observations in familiar essays.

As a regular columnist in the *Saturday Review* and *The American Scholar* and as a contributor to many other periodicals, Krutch addressed himself to a wide variety of topics—aptly summarized by the title of a popular 1959 collection, *Human Nature and the Human Condition*. He considered topics as various as our infatuation with progress and its handmaiden technology; the shallowness of our values and the tawdriness of our man-made surroundings; the environmental dangers of pollution, overpopulation, and diminishing resources; the modesty of our aspirations (as seen, for example, in such institutions as schools and churches); the responsibility of the intellectual; and the spiritually paralyzing and artistically pernicious influence of modernism. Many of these essays were collected in two volumes. The title of his *American Scholar* column—"If you don't mind my saying so . . ."—became the title of one of his two collections of these cultural commentaries. The other was *And Even If You Do*. Both titles suggest the engaging, sometimes tentative, generally modest approach Krutch brought to his reflections.

In such earlier commentary as *The Modern Temper* or his essays on Communism Krutch had ambitiously endeavored to address himself expansively to major intellectual currents of the time. Now—perhaps conditioned by his new interest in nature and his years of patient observation of the most mundane of natural phenomena—he addressed the particular rather than the general.

"Even a casual reading of newspapers and magazines will keep you constantly supplied with new occasions for pet indignations," he remarked. And the inspiration for his scores of essays during these two decades was as likely to be an article in *TV Guide* as a treatise in some scholarly journal—as likely a friend's casual remark as the pronouncement of some noted public figure. As in his nature writing, where he found unexpected implications in familiar but unexamined natural phenomena, Krutch in his later social commentary addressed himself to random, quotidian specimens of contemporary life and asked us to join him in examining their implications.

Though the sweeping, self-assured, ex cathedra judgment of his earlier cultural commentary was replaced by a familiar and personal tone and though he now wrote easily in the first person, Krutch no more now than before offered final answers to the questions he raised. His role was that of a gadfly, a doubter and questioner, rather than an advocate for this or that point of view. He was less interested in persuading his readers to accept some novel ideology than in stimulating them to measure, as he had, the current fashions in thought, taste, and behavior against an implicit standard of common sense.

Having himself set aside, earlier in his career, the dictates of common sense to make a stunning literary effect, the older—not to say wiser—Krutch, writing his cultural commentary from Tucson, became a widely heard voice of common sense—an avuncular figure, who mused on the passing scene and quietly remarked, "If you don't mind my saying so . . ."

The many readers of his widely published essays minded not at all.

Joseph Wood Krutch: A Rare Critic

Howard Stein

When Columbia president Nicholas Murray Butler told the English department during the academic year 1936–37 that he would like to see a new faculty member appointed who might represent the man of letters rather than the specialist scholar then holding most appointments, Mark Van Doren, a member of the committee charged with nominating such a person, suggested Joseph Wood Krutch.

Krutch's association with Columbia started in 1915. Soon after arriving to undertake graduate studies in English, he befriended his classmate Van Doren, whose brother Carl was already a faculty member of that department. Carl Van Doren became Krutch's master's thesis supervisor, and Mark, upon receiving his Ph.D. in 1920, joined the faculty at about the same time that Carl added to his Columbia duties the position of literary editor of *The Nation* magazine. Carl reduced his Columbia teaching to part-time and hired Mark to work on the editorial board of *The Nation.* This Columbia family added both men's wives to the editorial board of *The Nation* as well and recruited another Columbia graduate, Ludwig Lewisohn, as drama critic in 1919. When Lewisohn resigned in 1924, the board added Krutch to the editorial staff; one of his duties was to take Lewisohn's place as drama critic. That was in the same year that Krutch received his own Ph.D. and had his dissertation published as *Comedy and Conscience After the Restoration.*

Thus, for the next thirteen years (1924–37), Krutch had precious little connection to Columbia. He was busy establishing himself as a man of letters, and his duties at *The Nation* played no small part in that enterprise. Therefore, when the department acted on President Butler's suggestion and appointed Krutch, he diligently maintained his connection with *The Nation,* reducing his tasks to those of the weekly drama reviewer. Krutch began his Columbia duties in September 1937 and within a few years was elevated to the Brander Matthews Chair of Dramatic Literature, a position he held until his retirement in 1952 from both Columbia and *The Nation.*

He brought to his two courses at Columbia—English Drama from Dryden to Sheridan: 1660–1800 and Modern Drama (from Ibsen to the present, with emphasis on American drama)—the excitement and rigors of almost daily theatergoing. In 1928, for example, 280 plays opened on Broadway; although that number dwindled during Krutch's years as a professor, the average number of openings annually was still about 100.

His classes were filled with entertainment, wit, and information as well as critical insights. To describe the atmosphere of seventeenth-century London under Charles II, he told us about the actress Nell Gwynn, one of the first professional actresses in the English theater and one of the king's mistresses, who, while riding in the king's carriage, was assumed by an angry mob to be one of the king's Catholic concubines. When pelted with stones, she leaned out of the carriage and cried, "Nay, nay, my good people—I'm the Protestant whore."

He once described Eugene O'Neill to us, a playwright whom he enthusiastically admired, by saying, "He was a man of genius without talent." His sentences, his anecdotes, and his performances were not only unforgettable but arousing, with the result that his courses began to overflow with both graduate and undergraduate students. He told us about his animated conversations with O'Neill and then reported to us that he had told O'Neill that his students considered him their favorite American playwright and Ibsen their favorite European. O'Neill responded, "Tsk, tsk, I wish it were Strindberg."

Krutch talked about these conversations and about his discomfort with the latest Broadway potboiler. But the classes were never enough for us. We ran to the newsstand to get *The Nation*, to see if we already knew what he was going to say or to read what he had not dared tell us. His criticism was always intelligent, informed, corrective, insightful, and substantial. For all the right reasons, his fellow critics asked him to be president of the New York Drama Critics' Circle in the 1940–41 Broadway season.

Although most critics can be discussed in the context of their evaluating instruments, which usually reduce to taste, Krutch can best be examined in the context of his vision of the human predicament. In his biography of Krutch, John Margolis concludes that Krutch "had no procrustean critical bed upon which to force plays for analysis. . . . Krutch had various notions about the theater, but no grand critical system which consistently informed his writing." His "grand critical system," however, can be recognized in his uncertain romance with the universe; he was preoccupied with man's relationship to nature, which dictated his critical responses to his theatrical experiences. Early in his career he established what criticism should be: "an attempt to penetrate into the soul of a work and to discover what the author meant, how sincerely and passionately he meant it, and finally how true and important is his meaning."

The first two standards are an examination of the text or the performance, but the final test, the critical test, is what the critic thinks important to the human experience. How true and important indeed is the author's meaning to the living of a human life? Krutch applied this third standard in one of his very first theater reviews for *The Nation*, in 1924, when he wrote about *Desire Under the Elms*, in which he judged that O'Neill was "interested in an aspect of the eternal tragedy of man and his passions, the eternal struggle between aspirations and frustrations. . . . He set himself a task which was different in kind not degree from that which the contemporary playwright commonly undertakes."

For O'Neill, Krutch's criticism was also different in kind rather than degree. During the period in which O'Neill was writing and Krutch was criticizing, the prevailing American aesthetic was established in 1917 by the statement announcing the Pulitzer Prize for drama, the most coveted prize for American playwrights: "a prize to be given annually for the best original play to be performed in New York, which shall best represent the educational value and the power of the stage in raising the standard of good morals, good taste, and good manners." The contemporaneous European aesthetic was not that different. In 1919 in *The Changing Drama*, Archibald Henderson articulated what he believed was taking place throughout the Western world in dramatic writing: "The prime function of the dramatist of today is to bring man to the consciousness of his responsibility and to incite him to constructive measures for social reform." In neither statement was there any mention of art, poetry, or vision.

O'Neill spoke for his subject as well as Krutch's when he declared in 1930, "The playwright today must dig at the roots of the sickness of today as he feels it—the death of the old God and the failure of science and materialism to give any satisfying new one for the surviving primitive religious instinct to find a meaning for life in, and to comfort one's fears of death." Krutch told us that O'Neill told him in conversation, "Most modern plays are concerned with the relationship between man and man, but that does not interest me at all. I am interested only in the relationship between man and God." The difference is indeed dramatic. In 1948, Krutch told our class, "The meaning and unity of O'Neill's work lies not in a controlling intellectual idea and certainly not in a 'message,' but merely in the fact that each play is an experience of extraordinary intensity. . . ."

Such an aesthetic and such a vision would have seemed unlikely for a youngster fresh from Knoxville, Tennessee, who had lived a rather ordinary middle-class existence prior to his journey to New York City in 1915 to compete with apparently sophisticated classmates in the graduate program at Columbia. However, young Krutch had already had an experience of consequence while an undergraduate at the University of Tennessee that gave him courage if not comfort in his new unfamiliar surroundings. While chancing on *Man and Superman* by George Bernard Shaw, Krutch discovered in his first reading that "Anyone allowed to get into print could say such mischievously pertinent things." He later acknowledged that play as "the light which broke upon me on my way to Damascus." His observations of his own society inspired him to choose Restoration drama for his dissertation subject, which to his mind reflected the society of the twenties in the United States as much as that of England 1660–1725.

Krutch was indeed tuned in to his time, as *The Modern Temper* attests. Despite the cynicism and social upheaval he analyzed in that volume, Krutch was aware of an even more fundamental predicament of the human being, whose life was always at the mercy of a nature that doomed the aspirations, wishes, hopes, and dreams of the human spirit to frustration. The tragedy for Krutch came with the battle of those passions. He was impatient with the universe—although not at all with O'Neill—in his review of a revival in 1926 of *Beyond the Horizon*, which had been O'Neill's first play and the first of three to win a Pulitzer Prize. Krutch wrote: "Divesting himself of every trace of faith in the permanent value of love and presenting it as merely one of the subtlest of those traps by which nature snares man, O'Neill turns a play which might have been merely ironic into an indictment not only of chance or fate but of that whole universe which sets itself up against man's desires and conquers them."

That tragic sense of life informed Krutch's existence all the way to Arizona, where he observed the nature of nature and never lost his humility nor his wonder at the power of natural beauty. For O'Neill, his plays reflected his preoccupation with the relationship of man to God; for Krutch, his writing and his life reflected his preoccupation with the relationship between man and nature.

One would assume that such a vision would lead its victim to a despair packed with gloom and doom. Not so with Krutch. Tragedy was not a matter of an unhappy ending, but instead the best reflection of the human spirit in its confrontation with the mysterious forces ultimately controlling human experiences. The human spirit had dimensions to be honored and respected, to be received with joy, hilarity, mirth, and admiration. In Krutch's *The Measure of Man*, he articulates the minimal requirements with which nature has endowed the human species: the capacity to be at least sometimes a thinking animal, the ability sometimes to exercise some sort of will and choice, and the power of making individual value judgments. These minimal requirements leapt from a man with a comic spirit as well as a tragic sense of life.

Krutch lived a life based on a description with which he captured the essence of Samuel Johnson: "He was a pessimist with an enormous zest for living." While O'Neill illuminated Krutch's pessimistic side, S. N. Behrman illuminated his comic spirit. When Krutch reviewed Behrman's *The Second Man*, he poured light onto how comedy is created. "The theme was the Comic Spirit itself and the hero a man forced to make the decision between the heroic and the merely intelligent which must be made before comedy really begins. Follow the emotions and you may reach ecstasy, but if you cannot do that, then listen to the dictates of common sense and there is a good chance that you will be comfortable—even, God willing—witty besides."

Behrman's plays, for Krutch, one after the other, extended the playwright's demonstration of the comic solution to the problem of civilized living. He placed him on the same level as he did O'Neill. "Mr. Behrman pays the penalty of seeming a little dry and hard to those pseudo-sophisticates who adore their tear-behind-the-smile because they insist upon eating their cake and having it too. Just as they giggle when they find themselves unable to sustain the level of O'Neill's exaltation— unable, that is to say, to accept the logic of his demand that life be consistently interpreted in terms of the highest feeling possible to it—so, too, they are equally

One of the most popular lecturers in the university, Krutch brought to campus the latest news from Broadway, where he was an inveterate and influential reviewer for more than twenty years.

though less consciously baffled by Behrman's persistent anti-heroism. Comedy and tragedy alike are essentially aristocratic; only the forms in between are popular."

This elitist response might have offended both Krutch's colleagues in the New York Drama Critics' Circle and his audience, but Krutch was never given over to meanness of spirit or to nasty, self-indulgent criticism. Margolis notes that "Krutch assumed no license to make the review merely an excuse for writing an essay in which he could display his own brilliance." Nor did Krutch take pleasure in being negative or disapproving of a playwright's work. In responding to George S. Kaufman's plays, Krutch took considerable exception to their standard of excellence; but his most severe critical comment was tempered: "Once when he was asked why he did not write consistent satire instead of mere popular entertainment with half-satiric flavor, Kaufman is said to have replied, 'Satire is what closes Saturday night.' The remark is first-rate Broadway, and has been accepted as a genuine explanation, but I venture to say that it is not, at best, more than witty rationalization. Mr. Kaufman does not consistently write satire chiefly because he has never taken the trouble to consider what such satire would be."

It was Shaw's wit and intelligence that captivated Krutch while he was still an adolescent, and it was the era's wit and decadence that captivated Krutch as a graduate student concentrating on Restoration literature. Wit and tolerance are forms of beauty just as the passion and exaltation of the tragic hero are and as such their own excuse for being. Comedy compensates for the lack of ecstasy by the cultivation of that grace and wit which no one can be too sophisticated to achieve: "Just as the tragic writer endows all his characters with his own gift of poetry, so Mr. Behrman endows all his with his own gift for the phrase which lays bare to the mind a meaning which emotion has been unable to entangle."

Krutch's American writer of tragedy, O'Neill, did suffer from a severely limited language. By his own admission, O'Neill recognized that his gift was cursed with only "a touch of the poet." Krutch's favorite American comedy playwright, Behrman, similarly did not always succeed. In his review of *Meteor*, Krutch wrote, ". . . a comedy-drama in which the playwright fumbled the intended effect for the very reason that he had, apparently, not thought the situation through to the point where it could be stated in purely intellectual terms." Krutch recognized limitations and weaknesses in his most admired playwrights, but he never let those weaknesses detract from the strength of their work. He responded to their strengths and carried their weaknesses on his back like a burden, the fate of a civilized human being.

Krutch's enthusiasm for and belief in the comic spirit emanated from his faith in human intelligence and reason: "Comedy first deflates man's aspirations and pretensions, accepting the inevitable failure of his attempt to live by his passions or up to his enthusiasms. But when it has done this, it demonstrates what is still left to him—his intelligence, his wit, his tolerance and his grace—and then finally it imagines with what charm he could live if he were freed, not merely from the stern necessities of the struggle for physical existence, but also from the perverse and unexpected quixoticisms of his heart."

The result of cultivating such a perspective is explained in alternative terms by Carl Hovde: "Common sense of Krutch's kind is a poised alertness of the balanced mind, which can in turn move to the emotional extreme of proper tragedy, or to the restoration of order by comedy's departure from and return to the freshened values of the proper social order. However rare the playwright's capacity to do both at the highest level, the audience's capacity to enjoy both is the mark of a flexible and civilized mind." I would add that Krutch's gifts derived from what D. H. Lawrence called "an intelligent heart" and what Albert Camus deemed "a compassionate mind: the mark of an integrated human being, having cooperated with nature."

In the Desert with Joseph Wood Krutch

—〰—

Gerald Green

Our helicopter bobbed and hovered over the blackened crater of a dead volcano in the Sea of Cortez and descended into a lava cave dotted with startling yellow flowers.

The pilot, a moonlighting San Diego policeman, eased us to the rocky floor and called out, "Basement, gents. Snakes, scorpions, and Gila monsters."

This expedition was part of an NBC documentary series on nature, conservation, and the environment. Our guide and writer was Joseph Wood Krutch, whom I had induced to try educational television. The program was based on his book *Forgotten Peninsula*. This was Baja California, a savage, hot, seemingly barren place that had earned his admiration. He called Baja "an example of how much bad roads can do for a country."

Whenever we filmed a sequence—a stream, a mountain range, a canyon, a rare tree, or an elusive bird—I would challenge my former teacher to supply an appropriate literary quote. After all, Krutch had lived many lives. He had written superb books, taught appreciative students, achieved eminence as critic, biographer, philosopher, and essayist, and in these last years of his productive life he had become a lover of lizards and a confidant of coyotes.

His years on Morningside Heights behind him, he had changed appearance markedly. Now he was suntanned and leathery and relaxed, a different man. Clearly the sandy wastes of the Southwest had worked some magic on the renowned academic, who had battled colds and headaches in New York too long. Now he exhibited an energy rarely in evidence on the Columbia campus. The dusty stacks of a university library were no competition for his new life in the healing sun. And instead of writing critiques of plays and books, he extolled the courage of the kangaroo rat and walked for hours amid stands of giant saguaro.

The pilot tried to help him through the aircraft's narrow exit, but Krutch, often afflicted with a tremor, insisted on climbing out unaided, as if to say, "It's my desert, and it will treat me kindly."

Our cameraman, a surly Alabaman (he had noted Krutch's Tennessee drawl and respected him), followed him around the crater floor. "This is what I do best in films," Krutch said. "I wander about sunstruck and stare at succulents." He suggested that his new occupation should be Inspector of Wildflowers. Krutch identified a barrel cactus, a dune primrose, a host of butterflies. He was at peace with the gods of the Sonora. His happiness pleased Mrs. Krutch, who watched his every move, fearful he would get too much sun. "How about an appropriate quote for your visit to Hades?" I insisted. "We can't let the audience forget that you're a literary man."

He paused. "Virgil would be suitable. You recall he went into hell with Aeneas."

The pilot smiled. "I love to hear the professor talk," he said innocently. "Even though I don't understand him."

"*Facilis descensus Avernus,*" Krutch said. We looked like a class of C-minus freshmen. He went on: "Virgil says it's easy getting into hell, but adds, '*Hoc opus labor est*'—which means getting out may present a problem."

"Not with a helicopter," said the pilot. He had joined our seminar as easily as if he had just registered for an adult education class.

Krutch's wife, Marcelle, was amused by the cast of characters. She told me that now that her husband was free of classrooms, examinations, term papers, and faculty meetings, he had become outgoing, almost exuberant, one of the boys.

"I never saw such a change in Joe," Marcelle said. "He was always shy. He didn't mingle with students. He kept his distance. But out here he is forever trading stories with cowboys, desert rats, tourists, and Indians."

The word "belletrist" flitted through my head. Was Krutch our national belletrist of wildcats and cacti? Or had he simply moved his literary style to another world? Who but Krutch would enter a volcano and quote Virgil? His new colleagues— cowhands and Pueblo Indians—delighted him. But did they understand him? No matter. He had long wearied of political cant and literary feuds. He had grown uneasy with the stubborn wrongheadedness of the Left and the unforgiving, vengeful Right, and most of all the modernist writers, who like naughty children demanded that their "private lunacies become public necessities." I could see why he preferred the company of horned toads.

Fortunately, his scholarly attainments and his astonishing memory endowed him with a wondrous talent for combining the works of nature and the humanist canon. Krutch on mountains:

> In the legends of the saints and prophets, either a desert or a mountain is pretty sure to figure. It is usually in the middle of one, or on the top of one, that the vision comes or the test is met.
>
> To give their message to the world they came down or came out, but it is almost invariably in a solitude either high or dry, that it is first revealed. Moses and Zoroaster climbed up. Buddha sat down. Muhammad fled.

In his later years, Krutch became "a lover of lizards and a confidant of coyotes."

This is vintage Krutch, a summation of great religions—terse, witty, clearly stated. Buddha sat down. Muhammad fled.

Watching him commune with manta rays rising in a cascade from the Sea of Cortez or laughing as a jackrabbit fled from our Jeep, or observing the acrobatics of a hummingbird spinning around that botanical comedian, the boojum tree, I had to remind myself that this was a man who had abandoned the written word for nature's daily drama.

He still enjoyed theatrical and academic gossip, old anecdotes about his contemporaries, amusing marginalia. But these had assumed a supporting role in his cosmos. Once, while on a lunch break in the desert, he recalled being witness to a historic battle between two theatrical heavyweights. "I forget the play, but it was by Lillian Hellman," he said, "and it starred Tallulah Bankhead. George Jean Nathan and I were invited to an opening night party. The four of us took a taxi. This was the era of those comfortable cabs with jump seats. Hellman and Bankhead took the rear seats. Nathan and I sat in front of them.

"We hadn't been under way a minute when Bankhead said to Hellman, 'That's the last time I act in one of your goddamned plays.' Miss Hellman responded by slamming her purse against the actress's jaw. Bankhead took the blow stoically, but Nathan and I were made of weaker stuff. The cab stopped at a red light, and without a word he and I each seized a door and exited into the night—silent, abashed, flustered."

"And you concluded?" I asked.

"I decided that no self-respecting Gila monster would have behaved in that manner."

He told the story while we prepared our sleeping bags. Night fell on Havasupai Canyon. Marcelle, loyal wife, companion, and audience, said, "Joe makes up some of these stories."

She was gray-haired, pretty, vigorous. And she guarded his health like the nurse she had trained to be. She was a French Basque who had come to America in her youth and was a fine source of malapropism. "You go to sleep, Joe," she said, gently placing a blanket on him. "Close your eyes, and I'll put something over on you."

Literary friends back east often puzzled over his new interests. Whom did he talk to? What did the mountain lion and the chuckwalla lizard say to one another? Or to him?

"Read *The Rubáiyát*," he counseled. "'The Lion and the Lizard keep the Court where Jamshyd gloried and drank deep.'"

He was taunting us. Fifteen years ago, after he had moved to the desert, in an essay entitled "What Is Modernism?" he made clear why he had no heart for new literary modes.

Taking a minority position, he shocked establishment intellectuals, fashionable critics, and "in" writers with the judgment that he found modern novels "full of violence, perversity, and nihilism."

Film and theater were just as bad. He quoted Susan Sontag's review of a motion picture called *Flaming Creatures*. She had called it a work of "voluptuousness, sexual frenzy, romantic love, and vampirism."

This awesome modern critic went on to describe a final scene in which "the chorale of flutish shrieks and screams accompany the group rape of a bosomy woman, rape happily converting itself into an orgy."

Such claptrap revolted him, particularly the conclusion that the trashy film was "a triumphant example of an aesthetic vision of the world—and such a vision is perhaps always, at its core, epicene."

Krutch pointed out that Sontag "does not explain why an aesthetic vision must be epicene (i.e., homosexual), a question no one else seems to have asked."

He concluded: "In the atmosphere of the present moment, the boldest position a creative or critical writer could take would be one championing not only morality but gentility and bourgeois respectability."

How dare he advocate decency! Those who rejected Krutch's call for a humane society—in place of violence and nihilism—should not have been surprised. In 1929, in *The Modern Temper,* Krutch had looked at Communism and found it destructive, a system whose "hopes are no hopes in which we may have any part." Thus he had been out of step with two of the defining codes of modernism—erotica and Bolshevism. At the risk of being called an old fogey, he had rejected Communism in 1929. Forty years later, he was offended by the depravity and brutality in literature. And the arbiters dismissed him. Is it any wonder that Krutch, who dared raise the banners of civilized behavior and honest discourse, would come to prefer the company of buzzards to the ways of modern man?

He posed the question: "What can any reasonable man choose to do except escape either life or literature—if he can?"

He took his own advice. The desert became his fief, a place of riotous sunsets and multicolored mountains, sudden angry storms, odd forms of life, a place of courage and beauty and intriguing scarcity.

One hot morning I saw him in conversation at the Tucson Desert Museum. That institution, of which he had become secretary, was zoo, botanical garden, research center, and the heart of the conservation movement in Arizona. He was as proud of this position as of any honorary degree or literary prize. He was talking to a dark, stocky man. Krutch and his companion both wore matching straw sombreros and were studying the man's opened palm.

Marcelle explained, "The friend he's talking to is Cactus John, the chief gardener. Joe spends hours with him studying desert plants."

Krutch introduced Cactus John to us as if he were presenting a Nobel laureate. The Indian gardener showed me his calloused hand. It was dotted with minuscule black seeds—the seeds of the giant saguaro. Krutch had written: "The disproportion of the acorn and the oak is not nearly so great. After two or three years a seedling is only a few millimeters high; after ten years, less than an inch. . . . If anyone ever planted a saguaro for the sake of future generations, he was carrying such faith and such concern to fantastic limits."

"People said he was out of step with the modern world, that he was old-fashioned," Marcelle said later. "But he was an honest westerner. He liked Indians. He loved the Havasupai. They live next to a beautiful waterfall in a canyon. Once Joe asked the Havasupai chief if they still did war dances."

"What did the chief say?" I asked.

"He said they didn't do much dancing, but they might if Joe and his friends tied a white man to a stake."

We laughed. The story could be told without worries about political correctness. The Indians knew he was a friend, whose love included the Native Americans—the people of Crazy Horse, Chief Joseph, and Geronimo. He appreciated their bonds with the burning land. Like Krutch, they were not ashamed of the pathetic fallacy. Yes, Badger was brave. Coyote was cunning. Raven, a thief.

He summed up his affection for the desert as grounded in "the acute awareness of a natural phenomenon of the living world . . . the thing most likely to open the door to that joy we cannot analyze."

He was not an emotional or demonstrative man. But I recall the end of a tiring day, when after a six-hour search, we came upon the rare caterpillar cactus (or creeping devil), a forest of spiny horizontal trunks suggesting Martian reptiles, each twisting log sending out a single pink flower. He had opened his arms gratefully as if seeking to embrace this corner of God's private garden.

He was no preacher or missionary. But he made an eloquent case for the preservation of the natural world. And his voice was heard.

Krutch wrote, "The sense that nature is the most beautiful of all spectacles and something of which man is a part; that she is a source of health and joy which inevitably dries up when man is alienated from her; these are the ultimate reasons why it seems desperately important that the works of nature should not disappear to be replaced by the works of man alone."

As was his custom, he reached into the world of literature to emphasize his feelings:

> There was a time when meadow, grove, and stream,
> The earth, and every common sight,
> To me did seem
> Apparelled in celestial light,
> The glory and the freshness of a dream. . . .

He said rather sadly, "When the moment of happiness passed, it was not because the glory had faded, but only because Wordsworth's own sight had grown dim."

Krutch's own mind never dimmed. The biographer of Poe, Thoreau, and Samuel Johnson had assuredly lived many lives. He was a humane and eloquent voice who could evoke poets and playwrights, then effortlessly present us with nature writing that is still quoted by conservationists and anyone who has been thrilled by a soaring eagle or the ingenuity of a cactus wren. The desert, he told us, was part of man's world and deserved preservation. As he once whispered to the first frogs of spring, "We're in this together."

CHAPTER 7

John Dewey on Morningside Heights

Sidney Hook and Isaac Levi

As a major twentieth-century philosopher John Dewey had, and still has, a worldwide following. Many volumes have been written about his philosophical contributions and more are still to come. We focus here on Dewey's role on Morningside Heights, as a teacher in Philosophy Hall and a leader in a distinguished philosophy department.

Our first essay is taken from a tribute written by one of Dewey's best-known students, Sidney Hook (1902–1989), who in his 1987 autobiography Out of Step: An Unquiet Life in the 20th Century gives this intimate account of his own relation to Dewey, conveying his qualities as a teacher, mentor, and person. Before coming to do graduate work at Columbia, Hook had already been challenged by two leading philosophers at City College, Harry Overstreet and Morris Cohen; at Columbia he encountered such major figures as Frederick J. E. Woodbridge and William Pepperell Montague. It is in this distinguished setting that Hook assesses Dewey.

Hook went on to his own outstanding career as a political philosopher at New York University and a public intellectual, first as a Marxist and then, after his break with the Communist Party in 1933, as a trenchant and redoubtable critic of Communism.

Complementing Hook's personal view of Dewey we have Isaac Levi's overview of Dewey's work as a successor to Charles Peirce and William James in the American pragmatist tradition and as a broad thinker whose holistic vision was borne out by students pursuing many different lines of inquiry, including Justus Buchler in metaphysics, Charles Frankel and Sidney Hook in political and social thought, Ernest Nagel in logic and scientific method, and Stephen Rockefeller in the philosophy of religion. Levi thus locates Dewey both as the central figure in philosophical studies at Columbia and in the larger spectrum of twentieth-century American philosophy.

Professor Levi himself has contributed to studies in the philosophy of science, epistemology, probability and induction, rational choice, social choice, value conflict, theories of belief change, and the philosophy of Charles Peirce. He came to Columbia in 1970 from Case Western Reserve University.

A member of the National Academy of Arts and Sciences, he is the author, most recently, of Mild Contraction: Evaluating Loss of Information Due to Loss of Belief *(2004), and of* Gambling with Truth *(1967),* The Enterprise of Knowledge *(1980),* Decisions and Revisions *(1984),* Hard Choices: Decision Making Under Unresolved Conflict *(1986),* The Fixation of Belief and Its Undoing *(1991),* For the Sake of the Argument: Ramsey Test Conditionals, Inductive Inference and Nonmonotonic Reasoning *(1996), and* The Covenant of Reason *(1997). He has also been an editor of the* Journal of Philosophy.

—*Wm. Theodore de Bary*

My Memories of John Dewey

—ᴍ—

Sidney Hook

I have related my memories of John Dewey in many places and on many occasions. Sometimes I suspect that these reveal more things about me than about him. This seems unavoidable because, among other reasons, Dewey was and remains one of the most controversial figures of his age, despite the mildness of his manner, the softness of his speech, and his kindly disposition. When I got to know him well—which was after my student days—we fought in so many causes together that he himself and the ideas he stood for became one of the central "causes" in my life. In some quarters this earned me the sobriquet "Dewey's bulldog," because of my efforts to clarify his views and to defend them against the misunderstandings of critics and sometimes the misstatements of fancied disciples.

In this chapter I shall write of my experiences and observations as a graduate student at Columbia from 1923 through 1927.

—ᴍ—

I had first heard of John Dewey when I was a high school student. Casual references were made to him as an educator. That didn't mean very much to me at the time and for some years to come. As a young socialist, I was almost automatically an advocate of progressive education or of anything that would break the educational lockstep. My own educational experiences, looking back, were devastating confirmations of Dewey's criticisms of conventional education. Elementary school was a period of prolonged boredom, and high school was a succession of nightmares and persecutions.

My familiarity with Dewey's writings began at the College of the City of New York. I had enrolled in an elective course in social philosophy with Professor Harry Overstreet, who was a great admirer of Dewey's and spoke of him with awe and bated breath. The text of the course was Dewey's *Reconstruction in Philosophy*, which we read closely. Before I graduated, and in connection with courses in education, I read some of Dewey's *Democracy and Education* and was much impressed with its philosophy of education, without grasping at that time its general significance.

What did impress me about *Reconstruction in Philosophy*, and later other writings of Dewey, was the brilliant application of the principles of historical materialism, as I understood them then as an avowed young Marxist, to philosophical thought, especially Greek thought. Most Marxist writers, including Marx and Engels themselves, made pronouncements about the influence of the mode of economic production on the development of cultural and philosophical systems of thought, but Dewey, without regarding himself as a Marxist or invoking its approach, tried to show in detail how social stratification and class struggles got expressed in the metaphysical dualism of the time and in the dominant conceptions of matter and form, body and soul, theory and practice, truth, reason, and experience. However, even at that time I was not an orthodox Marxist. Although politically sympathetic to all of the social revolutionary programs of Marxism, and in complete agreement with Dewey's commitment to far-reaching social reforms, I had a much more traditional view of philosophy as an autonomous discipline concerned with perennial problems whose solution was the goal of philosophical inquiry and knowledge.

A student wandering into a class given by John Dewey at Columbia University and not knowing who was delivering the lecture would have found him singularly unimpressive, but to those of us enrolled in his courses, he was already a national institution with an international reputation—indeed the only professional philosopher whose occasional pronouncements on public and political affairs made news. In that period he was indisputably the intellectual leader of the liberal community in the United States, and even his academic colleagues at Columbia and elsewhere who did not share his philosophical persuasion acknowledged his eminence as a kind of intellectual tribune of progressive causes.

As a teacher Dewey seemed to me to violate his own pedagogical principles. He made no attempt to motivate or arouse the interest of his auditors, to relate problems to their own experiences, to use graphic, concrete illustration in order to give point to abstract and abstruse positions. He rarely provoked a lively participation and response from students, in the absence of which it is difficult to determine whether genuine learning or even comprehension has taken place. Dewey presupposed that he was talking to colleagues and paid his students the supreme intellectual compliment of treating them as his professional equals. Indeed, if the background and preparation of his students were anywhere near what he assumed, he would have been completely justified in his indifference to pedagogical methods. For on the graduate level students are or should be considered junior colleagues, but when they are not, especially when they have not been required to master the introductory courses, a teacher has an obligation to communicate effectively. Dewey never talked down to his classes, but it would have helped had he made it easier to listen.

Dewey spoke in a husky monotone, and although there was a sheet of notes on the desk at which he was usually seated, he never seemed to consult it. He folded it into many creases as he slowly spoke. Occasionally he would read from a book to which he was making a critical reference. His discourse was far from fluent. There were pauses and sometimes long lapses as he gazed out of the window or above the heads of his audience. It was as if he were considering and reconsidering every point until it was tuned to the right degree of qualification. I believe it was Ernest Nagel who first observed that Dewey in the classroom was the ideal type of a man thinking. His listeners sometimes feared that, because of his long pauses, Dewey had lost the thread of his thought, but if they wrote down and then reread what Dewey had actually said, they would find it amazingly coherent. At the time, however, because of the absence of fluency or variation of tone in his speech—except for an occasional and apparently arbitrary emphasis upon a particle word like *and* or *of*, which woke many of his auditors with a start—the closely argued character of his analysis was not always apparent.

Every experienced teacher knows that, because of the vicissitudes of life he or she sometimes must face a class without being properly prepared. This is not always educationally disastrous. Some individuals have a gift for improvisation, and a skillful teacher can always stimulate fruitful discussion. Dewey never came to a class unprepared, and there were plenty of family crises in his life. Rarely did he miss a class. There was an exemplary conscientiousness about every educational task he undertook, all the more impressive because it was so constant. His posthumous papers reveal draft upon draft of lectures and essays.

Despite the distracting extrinsic features of Dewey's teaching, the high seriousness of his concentration, unrelieved by any irrelevant humor, affected us in the same way it did his colleagues. Dewey seemed to exemplify not only man thinking, but nature itself thinking.

—⁓—

John Dewey (back row center, with black bow tie) at the University of Chicago in the 1890s. To his right is his lifelong friend and fellow pragmatist George Herbert Mead.

During the first year of my study with Dewey—the course may have been Types of Logical Theory—I constituted myself, so to speak, as the official opposition. I did the apparently unprecedented thing of interrupting him from time to time with questions that reflected the metaphysical and logical standpoints, as I understood them, of [Bertrand] Russell and [Morris] Cohen. This annoyed some of my fellow students, whom I awoke out of their somnolent drowse. Others informed me after class, with some acerbity, that they had paid good money to hear John Dewey speak, not to hear me ask him questions. But Dewey showed not the slightest annoyance or impatience. Before the year was out, there were others too who had questions. All I remember about these questions is that, whenever they caught him up on a terminological inconsistency or on a purely dialectical difficulty, he would smile and with a twinkle in his eye resolve it with an easy dexterity. Years later I asked him whether he had resented my persistent questioning, which must sometimes have interrupted his trend of thought. "No," he replied, "it was obvious to me that you were eager to find out and struggling to come to grips with a position unfamiliar to you." He had easily divined the quarter from which my questions had come.

Nothing Dewey said in class convinced me of the validity of his general position. It was only at the end of the year, when I sat down to write a definitive refutation of pragmatism, that I discovered to my astonishment, as I developed my argument, that I was coming out in the wrong place. Instead of refuting Dewey's views, I was *confirming* them! They involved judgments of perception, nature of theories, and the ultimately existential character of the laws of logic. My point of departure was Peirce's fallibilism and his theory of leading principles, to which I had been introduced in CCNY days by Morris Cohen. I was intellectually distressed by this outcome, and the first thing I did was to repair to Cohen to find out what was wrong with the way the argument was coming out. He shrugged off my complaint that he had not done justice to Dewey's views about the nature of being "practical"— Dewey made the practical synonymous with the "experimental" and not with the "useful"—and that in some respects he had not sharply enough differentiated Dewey's theories of meaning and truth from those of James. After he read the draft of my article, to my astonishment, Cohen said: "What you have written is true enough. If that's pragmatism, I'm a pragmatist. But it isn't Dewey." I then went to see Dewey, whose office I had been reluctant to visit until then because of my critical role in his class, and said in effect: "I started out to criticize your positions, but I seem to have come to the conclusion that they can very well be squared with Peirce's arguments, his rejection of Cartesian dualism, and his doctrine of leading principles. I think something is wrong, for instead of refuting your views, here I am confirming them." I can still remember his grin as he took the paper and suggested that I return later. When I did, he handed the paper back to me with the smiling observation: "I don't see anything wrong with it."

Subsequently I was to come to the conclusion that Dewey rarely found anything wrong with the position of anyone who was moving philosophically in his direction. At the time it was clear to me that, although kindly and amused, Dewey was really pleased with my development.

—⚏—

During those years at Columbia, we graduate students never socialized with our professors. What we got to know about them was largely hearsay or inferred from public prints, reviews, association meetings, and sometimes news stories. Dewey, and especially F. J. E. Woodbridge, dominated the department at Columbia. Too much so. The degree of their agreement and difference on key issues was the subject of much speculation and debate among us, something that could have easily been ascertained had they and the other members of the department talked back to each other in joint meetings with us. Only William Pepperell Montague would occasionally in his classes venture on indirect criticisms of the views of his colleagues.

—⚏—

The primary difficulty with the teaching of philosophy at Columbia when I was a student was that it was insufficiently systematic. Woodbridge was a thinker of deep insight, thoroughly steeped in the history of philosophy, who was convinced that epistemology was a mistake. He was always asking "simple" questions that had, he insisted, "simple answers," but it required considerable philosophical sophistication to understand the meaning of the questions and preternatural powers of intuition to grasp the "right" answers—which we did by guessing. Dewey at the time was challenging the confusion between cosmic and ethical issues central to the Greek classical tradition in philosophy and the mistaken theories of experience on which the whole of the modern philosophy of empiricism rested. Long before Wittgenstein, he denied that there was any philosophical knowledge and dissolved questions like the existence of the external world, the traditional mind-body problem, etc., by showing that on their own assumptions they were insoluble or question begging. This approach, as well as that of Woodbridge, would have been stimulating and challenging to students already well trained in the analysis of the traditional problem, but to the miscellany of theological students, social workers, teachers, seekers of wisdom, beauty, or social salvation that in those days constituted a considerable part of the classes in philosophy, Dewey and Woodbridge were obscure. Their junior colleagues, some of whom were just as mystified by them, could not dissipate the obscurity.

But to return to the teaching scene. I doubt that the teaching staff got much philosophical stimulation or challenge from those taught, except in a few small seminars. There was not enough intellectual feedback. Woodbridge enjoyed asking questions that stumped his class but didn't fancy getting questions in return. Montague was always wary of the philosophical quarter from which a dissenting query came. The younger men were suspicious when questions were asked of them that someone was trying to catch them out. Everyone except Dewey and Montague seemed to me to be trying to understand why the philosophers of the past said the odd things they did, not whether what was said was true or even formally valid. In later days the pendulum may have swung to the other extreme, and the historical dimensions of philosophical problems were not sufficiently appreciated when linguistic analysis became the rage. No one who was genuinely interested in philosophy was discouraged. If he caught fire, it was from an outside source, usually from something read. A few of us kept abreast of the professional periodicals, which in perspective seemed more exciting than those today, possibly because the issues discussed seemed larger and not so specialized.

Dewey was the soul of kindliness to questioners whenever they were bold enough to interrupt him, which they did with greater frequency as the course wore on. He never put any student down. If a question was obscure or made no apparent sense, he would find an intimation of relevant significance in it that encouraged some students to take themselves more seriously as thinkers than was warranted. As a rule I have discovered that students seem to resent classmates who ask questions more than their teachers do.

In my own case, I recall an act of extraordinary kindness on Dewey's part, which was all the more surprising to me since at the time I had little contact with him. During that period, to qualify as a doctoral student, one had to pass a preliminary oral examination of two hours on four philosophers, two ancient and medieval and two modern. I selected Plato, Plotinus, Schopenhauer, and Charles Peirce. We were required to hand in questions or extended topics on each of them, which would indicate the area and range of our interests, although the faculty could question us about anything if it chose. Usually I am in good form with interlocutors, but for the first hour and a half I was conscious that I was not doing well. I tangled with Montague on Plato, who was nettled by my rejection of the subsistence doctrine of universals to which he subscribed. I answered inadequately a question from Woodbridge on the relation between Plotinus and Christian theology because I had concentrated on some of the more difficult points in the *Enneads*. (The course on Plotinus was the first one I took at Columbia with Irwin Edman whom, I fear, I terrified because I had read the same secondary sources he consulted. Neither of us knew Greek.)

By the time Dewey began the questioning on Peirce, I was rather rattled. Dewey began in words that I still recall, at least in part. "I wish I could take the time to read all the questions Mr. Hook has submitted on Peirce's doctrines. They reveal a thoroughgoing grasp and mastery not only of Peirce's doctrines but of their revolutionary impact on traditional philosophy," and he went on in this vein for a minute or two before he put his own questions. It restored my nerve, and I finished with fine rhetorical flourishes about Pierce's seminal ideas that I owed to Cohen. I am confident that Dewey would have done the same thing for any other student in the same position.

I began publishing while a graduate student, and reactions from Harvard and elsewhere were favorable. By the time I faced the department at the final examination in defense of my dissertation, "The Metaphysics of Pragmatism," which I had stitched together out of the articles I had published, everything went smoothly.

Although at the time the world seemed in turmoil, looking back from where we are today, and despite the hurried quality of our student days, Columbia during those golden years seemed an island of peace and calm and yet of intense intellectual excitement. We were filled with hope and a tremendous expectation that great things were in the offing, that the ideas we were debating would play a role. Memories of the First World War and the inglorious postwar years in America, when the worst cultural excesses in American history had occurred, were receding. We sensed the presence of intellectual giants on the campus—not only Dewey, but Robinson and Bead (who had been in recent residence), Mitchell, Boas, and others.

———

All great visions in philosophy are based on simple ideas, but Dewey's philosophic vision was revolutionary in its outlook and conclusion: It denied that there was any such thing as philosophical knowledge, denied that we ever have immediate or certain truths of fact, even of sense perception, denied that we ever learn from experience, ours or others', unless we bring ideas to that experience. On the other hand, he opened up a view of the world in which human beings did not regard themselves as slaves of fate, history, or necessity, or lose themselves in the fantasies of magical idealism, but became aware of genuine possibilities and novelties and their own responsibilities, however limited. Although he repudiated philosophy in the grand manner, he restored the conception of philosophy as a quest for wisdom. Every distinctive philosophical doctrine of Dewey's could be derived from this approach. He wrestled to the end of his days with a multitude of technical details and difficulties that in the eyes of his critics confront this bold reconstruction of the philosophical enterprise.

———

It is not relevant to his philosophy, but I must say something about Dewey as a human being. He was world famous when I first got to know him, but he didn't seem to know it. He was the soul of kindness and decency in all things to everyone, the only great man whose stature did not diminish as one came closer to him. In fact it was difficult to remain in his presence for long without feeling uncomfortable. He seemed too good to be true.

———

There is no doubt that he encouraged too many people in their thinking and their writing. He would justify himself by saying that one could never know what would come of the effort.

There was an air of abstraction about Dewey that made his sensitivity to others surprising. It was as if he had an intuitive sense of a person's authentic, unspoken need. Anyone who thought he was a softie, however, would be brought up short. He had the canniness of a Vermont farmer and a dry wit that was always signaled by a chuckle and a grin that would light up his face.

When I was still a student at Columbia, he invited me to his home for Sunday dinner. His daughters, son, and daughter-in-law were there, and it seemed to me a rather formal affair. It was my first visit, and I was naturally nervous. When I rang the bell, he himself came to the door. The first thing he did when I had shed my hat and overcoat was to point out the bathroom. I had no experience with dinners as elaborate as this seemed to me and don't remember whether I talked too much or too little. I wasn't sure what all the knives and forks were for, and my lack of ease must have been quite apparent. At the end of the meal, when the nuts were passed around, I took only one lest I be considered greedy. "Sidney," remarked Dewey, "you remind me of the man who kept a bee."

— ⚬ —

The character of John Dewey became more manifest to a wider public in its quiet heroism and unfailing goodness during the thirties and forties, both in defending the heritage of American democracy and in resisting the advance of totalitarian thought and practice. At a time when age and achievement had earned him the right to retire from active political life, he devoted all his energies and most his husbanded hours of leisure in the fight for freedom, from which many younger colleagues turned away.

John Dewey and Intelligent Problem Solving

— ⚬ —

Isaac Levi

John Dewey came to Columbia in 1904 as professor of philosophy. He retired to become professor emeritus in 1930 and remained active in that capacity at Columbia for the next decade. He died in 1952.

Prior to Columbia, Dewey had established his reputation as an academic philosopher at the University of Michigan and the University of Chicago. During the ten years he was at Chicago, he became actively involved in directing the famous Chicago Laboratory School. It was there that he began to develop a philosophy of education as integral to his philosophical outlook.

His years at Columbia witnessed an outpouring of books on moral philosophy, metaphysics, logic understood as the method of inquiry, philosophy of education, ethics, art, political philosophy, and philosophy of religion. These writings and his personal contacts with colleagues and graduate students at Columbia established his reputation as the preeminent American philosopher prior to World War II.

This reputation was enhanced by his role as a *philosophe engagé*. The most famous of his public roles was his chairmanship in 1937 of the commission that investigated the assassination of Leon Trotsky.

Dewey saw the philosophical relevance of his work in educational reform as deriving from his concern, central to his political philosophy, to promote a genuine social democracy. Democracy requires trust by the members of society in the judgment of their fellows. To achieve genuine democracy, it becomes urgent to develop citizens who can exercise their intelligence in addressing the problems they may face as individuals and as participants in social institutions. Dewey's educational philosophy focused on identifying ways and means for educating such citizens. He pursued this project in a close association with Teachers College throughout his Columbia career.

A bust of John Dewey by sculptor Jacob Epstein

Dewey is taken to be the third member of the trio of classic American pragmatists that also included Charles Peirce and William James. These authors shared in common a respect for approaching questions in logic and theory of knowledge by focusing on their relevance to problem-solving inquiry. Both Peirce and Dewey made this focus the pivot of their philosophical projects. Dewey's ambition, however, had greater scope than Peirce's. Where Peirce tended to restrict his methodological reflections to scientific inquiry, Dewey thought that the "belief-doubt" model of inquiry developed by Peirce for scientific inquiry could be extended further to moral conflicts and to problems of aesthetics.

Intimation of Dewey's vision of problem-solving inquiry as a holistic process appears in 1896 in his famous paper, "The Reflex Arc Concept in Psychology" (*Psychological Review* 3, 357–70), and near the end of his career in his 1949 collaboration with Arthur F. Bentley, *Knowing and the Known*. The 1896 paper was also recognized at the time to be a forceful critique of the then influential views of the psychologist Wilhelm Wundt and a first intimation of Dewey's eventual break with idealism and subsequent emergence as one of the leading figures of American pragmatism. His *Logic* (1938) undertakes a more fine-grained analysis of the process of problem solving and the relation between science and common sense. *Art as*

Experience (1934) extends Dewey's vision of problem-solving inquiry to the work of creative artists and critics. His naturalistic metaphysics is articulated in *Experience and Nature* (1925). And his ethical views are expressed in *Ethics* (1908, coauthored with James Tufts) and in *Human Nature and Conduct* (1922).

—⁂—

"Give a dog a bad name and hang him." Human nature has been the dog of the professional moralists and consequences accord with the proverb.

Dewey was a self-described "naturalist." However, his naturalism is a moral rather than a metaphysical thesis. For metaphysical naturalists, humans are "nothing but" physical mechanisms or biological organisms. For Dewey, our goals, values, and aspirations are situated in a biological and social "matrix" and are to be best understood as responses to problems and challenges that emerge in that environment. The difference between our adaptive responses and those of other organisms derives from our capacity to use "intelligence" to confront these challenges—an intelligence that Dewey did not try to "reduce" to physical or neurophysiological process.

His concern was with how intelligence can be utilized to respond to the moral and political problems thrown up by our environment (an environment that includes social as well as physical and biological factors). His naturalism is best understood as an opposition to theological and other supernaturalisms that ground values in transcendental authorities, as well as to other authoritarianisms that take a relativistic or skeptical view of morality. All such views resist intelligent efforts to resolve our moral conflicts through inquiry by refusing to identify the problems that occasion the conflicts as arising within the biological and social matrix. In this sense, they "separate morals from human nature."

Morality, in Dewey's view, should not focus on how we ought to overcome the devil—the "Old Nick" that is the dog of human nature. To think of morality as the struggle to resist temptation is to take for granted that the issue as to what is to be resisted has been settled. For example, to regard pro-choice advocates (or right-to-life advocates, for that matter) as morally crippled is to presuppose that the moral acceptability or unacceptability of abortion has been settled in such a manner that only the morally or psychologically defective can fail to understand. Sometimes the issue has been settled in a manner that renders additional investigation pointless. In that case, therapy and not inquiry may be the best option. But all too often this is not the case. To charge that one's opponent is morally defective in the case of abortion is to nip the opportunity for inquiry in the bud. Dewey urged us not to confuse conflicts calling for inquiry with conflicts calling for therapy in this way. He advocated efforts to identify genuine problems that occasion the conflicts we face and to use intelligence to resolve them. He sought to persuade parties to such conflicts to avoid judging their opponents to be guilty of "unnatural acts." They should recognize that perhaps there is a problem that neither side has solved satisfactorily and that requires further investigation.

However, recognition of the presence of a problem warranting inquiry rather than persuasion, therapy, or some form of coercion is not enough. According to Dewey, a method for settling disputes outside the natural sciences ought to call for carefully controlled empirical investigation whenever feasible. And when such inquiry is not feasible, acknowledgment of ignorance rather than wishful thinking should be encouraged.

Dewey's advice is surely relevant to current controversies such as whether sexual abstinence is a better method of reducing the spread of AIDS than the use of condoms. Dewey would have insisted that this question should be settled by looking at the available data and without appeal to the moral preconceptions of any party to the dispute.

John Dewey sought to extend the use of intelligence in problem-solving inquiries in the sciences, not only to moral and political problems and to efforts to create and critically assess works of art, but to the understanding of religiosity as well. Such efforts can only proceed without interference from the dogmas of organized religion, and they take on new urgency in the light of recent governmental and political efforts to promote the influence of "faith-based" organizations as organs of public policy. The very same emphasis on moral inquiry rather than on an appeal to fundamental values undercuts the charge of moral relativism or skepticism that has been wrongly equated with secularism by the new pope, Pope Benedict XVI, and other religious conservatives. In this light, John Dewey's message meant for an audience more than a half-century ago takes on a new urgency and relevance for our time.

—⁓—

After the Second World War, interest in Dewey's philosophy began to wane. Thanks to the influence of the members of the Vienna Circle and their associates in Central Europe who had fled from Nazism, Dewey's ideas were taken to be of some interest as "methodology," but not acceptable as an account of the objective aspects of science, mathematics, and logic that the logical empiricists considered to be integral to the "logical analysis" of language. Like Dewey, many philosophers prominently associated with this general point of view from Russell to Carnap, Popper,

Ernest Nagel (left) and Sidney Morgenbesser (right)

and Hempel saw an appeal to science and logic as a refuge from the ideological and political excesses of the Nazis, Fascists, and Stalinists that were salient threats to civilization in the period between the two World Wars. They admired scientific inquiry for its lack of sensitivity to historical, social, moral, and aesthetic context.

Dewey, by way of contrast, insisted that scientific methods did take such contextual factors into account when relevant and urged the application of scientific methods of inquiries in such domains. In the late publication *Knowing and the Known*, Dewey vigorously rebutted the charge that his reliance on context lacked "objectivity."

Dewey, like James and Peirce, recognized the importance of keeping relevant contextual features under critical control. Some of the sensitivity to context neglected by the logical empiricists was restored through the influence of Wittgenstein and the Oxford ordinary language philosophers. The Harvard philosopher W. V. Quine acknowledged affinity with some of Dewey's ideas. Nonetheless, with the ascendancy of analytic philosophy in the United States after the Second World War, there was little appreciation among leading philosophers of the scope of Dewey's philosophical interests and the centrality of the belief-doubt model of inquiry to his thought. Some notable exceptions were Dewey's students Justus Buchler, Charles Frankel, Sidney Hook, Ernest Nagel, Morton White, and Nagel's student Patrick Suppes as well as prominent admirers such as Sidney Morgenbesser and Israel Scheffler.

Thanks to the presence of Buchler, Frankel, Nagel, and Morgenbesser in the Columbia philosophy department, the influence of Dewey's thought remained strong at Columbia after his departure.

At the present moment, several influential and important authors have revived interest in the work of John Dewey. Richard Rorty is preoccupied with Dewey's indifference to Truth and his antifoundationalism; Alan Ryan addresses Dewey's political philosophy; and Stephen Rockefeller focuses in an excellent monograph on Dewey's ongoing concern with religiosity. But none of these accounts shows how each of these problems is integrated into Dewey's overarching concern with problem-solving inquiry. An exception to this pattern is Jennifer Welchman's reconstruction of the development of Dewey's ethical views

Dewey was a systematic philosopher surveying the full range of human experience. As such, there is something in Dewey to engage the attention of all reflective people—even those who resist his views. This circumstance undoubtedly fuels the tendency to offer partial accounts of his philosophy. But his originality is often underestimated because of a failure to recognize the extent of his own ambition to provide a vision of human experience that makes central the importance of intelligently conducted inquiry aimed at coping with human problems.

The revival of interest in Dewey mentioned above has been accompanied by a substantial amount of scholarship devoted to Dewey's work. His papers and books have been collected in comprehensive and authoritative editions under the editorial supervision of Jo Ann Boydston and Larry Hickman that are readily available. We can look forward to more extensive probing of Dewey's ideas in the future based on deeper understanding of Dewey's ambitions than we currently have.

CHAPTER 8

The Many Lives of
Paul Oskar Kristeller

—⚊—

John Monfasani

Paul Oskar Kristeller's towering stature as a scholar of the Renaissance stems from his precocious interest in the study of classical and medieval philosophy as a young German-Jewish lad in Berlin. Philosophy was his passport to escape from the dangers of Nazism and, later, Italian Fascism. Kristeller's wanderings in diaspora took him eventually to the United States, New York, and a new home at Columbia, where he was to serve as Frederick J. E. Woodbridge Professor of Philosophy until his retirement in 1973.

It was no doubt also his intense dedication to scholarship, compounded by his own bitter experience of political persecution, that led him to become in his later years at Columbia such an uncompromising opponent of ideological pressures from the left. Indeed, his sometimes curmudgeonly outspokenness on such issues (similar to that of his Philosophy Hall colleague Gilbert Highet) irritated some on campus who considered his attitude unbecoming in an "ivory tower" philosopher.

John Monfasani, a student of Kristeller's in these same years, received his B.A. from Fordham University in 1965 and his Ph.D. from Columbia in 1973. His dissertation on the Renaissance figure George of Trebizond, under the direction of Kristeller and Eugene F. Rice, won the John Nicholas Brown Best First Book Prize of the Medieval Academy of America in 1980. Three volumes of his collected articles have appeared with Variorum. He is presently professor of history at SUNY/Albany and executive director of the Renaissance Society of America.

—*Wm. Theodore de Bary*

—⚊—

Perhaps "The Many Personae of Paul Oskar Kristeller" or even "The Many University Departments of P. O. K." would be better titles. An active participant in Columbia's intellectual life for sixty years, in instructional positions from 1939 to 1976 and as a prodigious scholar until his death in 1999, Kristeller served as a reader of doctoral dissertations in philosophy (his home department), history, art history, religion, political science, Greek and Latin, English, Italian, French, and even Chinese. But Kristeller's talents extended beyond the academic, as his university career in Germany in the 1920s and 1930s shows.

During the summer semester of 1926 at Marburg, Kristeller attended for the first time a seminar of Martin Heidegger. Soon he was also playing the piano at evenings in Heidegger's home. That same term he and two fellow students of Heidegger's, Hans-Georg Gadamer and Karl Löwith, formed a trio that performed in various venues. Kristeller left Marburg for Heidelberg the next semester to take his doctorate in ancient philosophy with a dissertation on Plotinus under Ernst Hoffmann. When he subsequently worked under Werner Jaeger, Eduard Norden, Ulrich von Wilamowitz, Paul Maas, and others in Berlin to gain his Prussian State School Licence in classical philology, he would often play the piano in Norden's home. After passing the Staatsexam at the beginning of 1931 with a thesis in Latin on Pericles' first speech in Thucydides,[1] Kristeller returned to Heidegger (who was now at Freiburg, called there to succeed Husserl in the chair of philosophy) to write his *Habilitationschrift* (the major second dissertation needed for a university career in Germany) on the Italian Renaissance philosopher Marsilio Ficino—and of course resumed playing the piano regularly in Heidegger's home. Even in the strained circumstances of his Italian years in the mid- and late 1930s, he still practiced daily on the piano at the Scuola Normale Superiore in Pisa.[2] In his interview for Columbia's Oral History Project, he remarked, "I must say that in my younger years music played such an important role in my life that there were moments when I was not doing well in my studies, that I played with the idea of becoming a professional musician."[3] Only in the late 1940s, about a decade after coming to America, when the press of scholarly projects demanded all his time, did he give up daily piano practice and eventually stop playing altogether.[4]

Kristeller also wrote poems, some of which he sent as gifts to friends. Another illustrious German expatriate, Felix Gilbert, recalled Kristeller in his student days as a rather dreamy type strolling along the Neckar River in Heidelberg.[5] To those of us who knew the latter-day Kristeller—gray-haired, large in girth, the prototypical old-fashioned German professor—photographs of him in the 1920s and 1930s, wonderfully tall and svelte, came as a shock.[6] "In his youth, when it most matters, he looked as glamorous as a movie star," went one tribute to Kristeller near the end of his life.[7] Edith Lind Lewinnek Kristeller, whom Paul married in New York in 1940 and lost in 1992, once said that the contemplative, serious Paul never seemed aware of the fact that he was the heartthrob of many girls of their set in Germany in the 1920s and 1930s.[8] Imagining the young Kristeller in Weimar Germany as a sort of Schroeder intent on playing his piano surrounded by multiple Lucys may be far-fetched, but not completely.

Kristeller was born into a prosperous Jewish family in Berlin on May 22, 1905. His father, Oskar Gräfenberg, died the day before; his mother, Agnes Magnus, married the Jewish businessman Heinrich Kristeller in 1911; in 1919 Paul officially took his stepfather's name. Kristeller saw his promising academic career in Germany come to an end with Hitler's accession to power in 1933, and by 1934 he had moved to Italy. His work on Marsilio Ficino had caught the eye of the Fascist intellectual Giovanni Gentile, who appointed Kristeller instructor in German at the Scuola Normale Superiore in Pisa in 1935 and protected him against German demands for his removal. But in August 1938 Mussolini issued his racial laws. As a Jew without Italian citizenship, Kristeller had six months to leave the country. He and his friends wrote numerous letters to England and America, but in the end it was the church historian Roland Bainton at Yale who arranged for a nonpaying position teaching a seminar at Yale on Plotinus in the spring term of 1939.[9] That position proved to be sufficient justification to wrest a nonquota visa from immigration officials—but not before the American consular officer in Naples made Kristeller take a literacy test, just to be safe.

Kristeller disembarked in New York harbor on February 23, 1939, and went straight up to New Haven.[10] But at the end of the spring term he still had to find a new job. He traveled that spring and summer to various cities and institutions on the East Coast, but the one offer that materialized was from Columbia's philosophy department.

Kristeller did not have the most auspicious of starts on Morningside Heights. He arrived in the summer of 1939 with a one-year contract as an instructor. His salary was so small that he survived only because of a supplementary grant from the Oberländer Trust and because Giuseppe Prezzolini of the Italian department gave him a room to live in on one of the upper stories of Columbia's Casa Italiana on Amsterdam Avenue. Though he moved out after a year, Kristeller kept his office in Casa Italiana for as long as he taught at Columbia. It was touch and go for a while, and Kristeller lived on one-year contracts until 1948, when the threat of an offer from Haverford College provoked the department into voting him tenure. He became full professor in 1956 and the Frederick J. E. Woodbridge Professor of Philosophy in 1968.

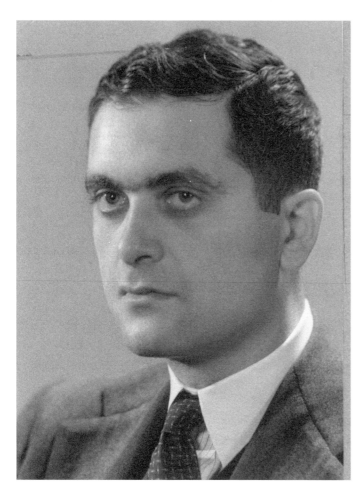

Kristeller at about twenty years old in Berlin

By then Kristeller was an academic superstar. Interestingly, however, most of his famous work in Renaissance studies can be traced back to the 1930s and 1940s, when he was a nobody trying to survive.[11] His masterful *Supplementum Ficinianum* (1937) and *The Philosophy of Marsilio Ficino* of 1943 marked him as the leading authority in the world on the most influential Platonic philosopher of the Renaissance. The *Supplementum* astounds even today for the quality and richness of its textual and bibliographical discoveries; the *Philosophy* not only effectively captured for the first time the underlying principles of Ficino's philosophy, but also showed how and why Ficino coined the term "Platonic love." In the 1930s and 1940s Kristeller also published an extraordinary series of seminal articles, none more influential than "Humanism and Scholasticism in the Italian Renaissance" (1945), which argued that humanism was no philosophy at all, but a "characteristic phase in what may be called the rhetorical tradition in Western culture"; and as for Scholasticism, i.e., the Aristotelianism of the medieval universities, far from being crushed, it flourished in Renaissance Italy. Kristeller was massively changing how we think of the Renaissance. Almost in passing, he also wrote a major article showing how the modern concept of the arts emerged between the Renaissance and the eighteenth century.[12]

In the 1930s, while working on Marsilio Ficino, Kristeller realized that an enormous number of manuscripts of other Renaissance authors had gone unnoticed. So he began to take methodical notes, which he showed to Fritz Saxl, the director of London's Warburg Institute, in 1945. Thus was born *Iter Italicum* (*A Voyage to Italy*).

The publication of the first volume in 1963 transformed Renaissance scholarship;
with the publication of volume 6, in 1992, nearly fifty years after his meeting with
Saxl, Kristeller had described more than 200,000 manuscripts and completed one
of the greatest single-handed bibliographical projects ever.

From his first months in America Kristeller became a peripatetic speaker, first
simply out of a need to establish contacts and supplement his income but eventually because he was in such demand. Rare was the research trip in which he did not
also give several guest lectures. The most significant of these were the Martin
Classical Lectures at Oberlin College in 1955, where he laid out his views on the
main contours of Renaissance intellectual history. These were published that same
year as *The Classics and Renaissance Thought* and became the core of a highly successful paperback in 1961 in the Harper Torchbooks series: *Renaissance Thought: The
Classic, Scholastic and Humanistic Strains*. A whole series of paperbacks followed.
Kristeller had the knack of combining highly technical scholarship and popular
presentation. He used to complain in class about commentators who became
opaque at the very point where their subject became difficult. He wrote pellucid
prose in five languages (English, French, German, Italian, and Latin).

The paperbacks preserve only a fraction of Kristeller's articles. Even the four volumes of his *Studies in Renaissance Thought and Letters*, though each runs well over 600
pages, do not encompass the full range of his articles. The first of the *Studies*
appeared in 1956 and contained twenty-five significant articles from the 1930s and
1940s; the last came out in 1996, gathering together articles and notices from the
1950s through the 1980s but still leaving out much from that period and including
nothing from the 1990s. Kristeller's bibliography, in fact, consists of some 700
entries, many of which are massive and can well stand by themselves as the work
of a lifetime.[13]

Kristeller's interest in Renaissance Aristotelianism was further stimulated at
Columbia by two colleagues in the philosophy department: the legendary John
Herman Randall Jr. and Ernest A. Moody. By 1939 Randall had already made
Aristotelianism at the University of Padua a special interest. Moody, a Columbia
Ph.D. with a published dissertation on late medieval Scholastic logic, had been
hired along with Kristeller in 1939. Kristeller's collaboration with both colleagues
bore fruit in teaching as well as in scholarship. In his second year at Columbia,
1940–41, he team-taught a course on medieval and Renaissance philosophy with
Randall, Moody, and others. The department also asked Moody and Kristeller to
develop a new course on research techniques for studying the unedited sources of
medieval and Renaissance philosophy. They began teaching the course together in

1941–42. After Moody left Columbia in 1951, Kristeller taught the course alone. It became sui generis, combining paleographical, codicological, and editorial instruction with detailed guidance on manuscript collections, sage advice on texts, authors, and problems, and a nice dollop of anecdotes and Kristellerisms (e.g., concerning Giovanni Mercati, the great Vatican scholar and paleographer: "If Mercati pronounces on a hand, in my view the burden of proof is for anyone to prove otherwise."). Kristeller published most of his year-long courses, and the one in research techniques was no exception. Close attention to the introductions to each manuscript collection in *Iter Italicum* will provide both the flavor and benefit of a large component of the course. The seminar paper that came out of the course invariably became the start of, or a key component in, a Columbia dissertation. Having completed it, one felt that one had just been shown how to be a scholar. Kristeller would end the course with an ominous admonition: "Henceforth I shall help you in direct proportion as you will help scholarship."

The dictum had a nice scientific ring to it and must have satisfied Kristeller's sense of the right order of things, but its implication that he would refuse some queries was totally false. I never knew Kristeller not to help a student or colleague who asked for help, and many told how as total strangers they approached him on a scholarly problem and received more detailed advice than they could have ever imagined. Some years ago, quite by chance, I came across the typescript of an edition of a Renaissance author presented by a well-known scholar whose control of Latin was less than stellar. To my amazement it was immediately obvious that Kristeller, in his prime and burdened with enormous commitments, had himself typed hundreds of these pages, patiently and silently reediting the text without taking any credit. One wonders how many other similar acts of charity remain to be discovered.[14]

Randall especially cooperated with Kristeller in team-teaching graduate seminars in philosophy. Over the years they led seminars together on Renaissance philosophy, Plato, Aristotle, Descartes, Spinoza, Leibniz, Kant, and recent continental philosophy. Kristeller also gave graduate seminars by himself on the same authors as well as on Plotinus and Hegel and taught graduate seminars in philosophy with other colleagues, such as Horace Friess and James Gutmann. Kristeller's two year-long lecture courses, Ancient Greek Philosophy after Aristotle and Renaissance Philosophy, are both available in print, the former as *Greek Philosophers of the Hellenistic Age* (1993), the latter as *Eight Philosophers of the Italian Renaissance* (1964).

Kristeller once mentioned in class that he discovered philosophy at age fourteen, reading Plato and, under the influence of his high school teacher Ernst Hoffmann,

*Kristeller continued
to publish at an
astounding rate
through the early
1990s.*

also Kant. At the university, he became much interested in existentialism, studying
with Karl Jaspers and Martin Heidegger. He took courses from the neo-Kantian
Heinrich Rickert and from Edmund Husserl, the founder of phenomenology. He
also became friendly with the neo-Kantian Ernst Cassirer and, of course, continued
his association with Hoffmann, under whom he wrote his thesis at Heidelberg,
attempting, as he explained in a memoir, "an existentialist interpretation of
Plotinus."[15] His philosophical sympathies always remained with Kant. It was probably Kantian ethics that also gave him a special appreciation of the Stoics, just as
his study of Plotinus gave him an abiding interest in ancient philosophy between
Plato and Plotinus and prepared him well for his study of Ficino.

Given the centrality of philosophy to Kristeller's private as well as his professional life, his rejection of an offer from Harvard University in 1965 was almost predictable. Harvard's history department made the offer, but the philosophy department declined to make it a joint appointment. As Kristeller explained in his Columbia Oral History interview, "My whole work at Columbia involved the entire history of philosophy, including classical antiquity and early modern thought down to Hegel. And all this would have disappeared from my work as a teacher and it would have impoverished me. . . . I am only a historian of philosophy, but my universe circles around Plato and Kant, not about Feudalism and the Reformation, nor about Dante and Shakespeare."[16]

The 1960s brought Kristeller the honor and prestige he had long deserved but also two shocks: the assassination of John Kennedy in 1963 and the student revolt of 1968. A liberal in American terms, he had twice voted for Adlai Stevenson against Columbia's former president Dwight Eisenhower, and he had voted for Kennedy. The assassination, of course, affected everyone who was above the age of reason. But I have been told by those who knew him at the time that it disturbed Kristeller terribly. Having known political violence firsthand in Europe in the 1920s and 1930s, he had believed America to be different. As he must have sensed, the assassination would be just the beginning of a decade of violence.

The student revolt of 1968 on the Columbia campus set him against not only the radical students who occupied the buildings and shut down the campus, but also colleagues who supported the student radicals or lacked the courage to condemn their actions. It took years for the scars to heal. He himself refused to be bullied. He held classes in his apartment and took to carrying his umbrella as a last line of defense against threats of violence. The illiberalism of the radical Left on campus was no more justified in his eyes than that of the Nazis at Germany universities a few decades earlier. Kristeller declared, "I did not back down to the SS; I will not back down to the SDS."[17]

Through the 1970s, 1980s, and early 1990s, Kristeller continued to publish at an astounding rate, with the increased leisure provided by retirement and the aid of a series of skilled assistants funded from various sources compensating nicely for the physical infirmities and declining energy of old age. In 1984, at age seventy-eight, he became the oldest person ever to receive a MacArthur Foundation Fellowship. Only in the very last year or so, did he sometimes seem to remember yesteryear more clearly than yesterday.[18] But what a run he had! In his retirement he produced the last four of the six volumes of *Iter Italicum;* the last three of the four volumes of *Studies in the Renaissance;* and a whole string of separate studies, such as *Medieval Aspects of Renaissance Learning* (1974), *Philosophy and Rhetoric from Antiquity to the Renaissance* (Part Five of his *Renaissance Thought and Its Sources,* 1979), *Marsilio Ficino and His Work after Five Hundred Years* (1987), and the already mentioned book on Hellenistic philosophers.

Already the recipient of many awards, honorary degrees, and memberships in the leading national academies, Kristeller in his last years also received the honor of no less than six Festschriften in his name from 1975 to 1987. Indeed, a group of German scholars has recently published what we may count as the seventh Festschrift, though strictly speaking delay has made it a memorial volume. Spontaneously and independently, scholars in different countries and age cohorts have simply banded together to express the debt they felt to one of the great scholars of the twentieth century. Rightly therefore, on the occasion of his ninetieth birthday on May 23, 1995, when Columbia University presented Kristeller with the Nicholas Murray Butler Medal in Gold, Professor Eugene F. Rice Jr. noted that when the Renaissance Society of America purchased its first computer, the staff named it P. O. K., since until then Paul Oskar Kristeller had been the Society's best retrieval system. With two index fingers banging away at the typewriter faster than most eyes could follow and a mind of extraordinary retentiveness, Kristeller did indeed rival the wondrous capabilities of the computer. Kristeller also had the gift to get it right the first time in almost all instances when he committed his ideas to paper. His scholarly genius can never be duplicated by a computer, but its products happily remain for us in books. His generosity, devotion to principle, and dry wit, alas, we can only memorialize.

CHAPTER 9

Making Art History at Columbia: Meyer Schapiro and Rudolf Wittkower

—w—

David Rosand

*When the first University Professorships were established at Columbia, they were limited to three—
a highly exclusive and selective group: Lionel Trilling, Jacques Barzun, and Meyer Schapiro. These
men were obvious choices at the time, distinguished not only by their exceptional scholarly attainments, but also by two other shared features: they were home-bred New Yorkers and graduates of
Columbia College and the Columbia Graduate Faculties. Trilling is the subject of one Living Legacies
essay; and Barzun, another, while Barzun himself has given us an account of the history department.*

*Meanwhile, David Rosand contributed this account of art history at Columbia, featuring the
third, Schapiro, to which he adds a vignette of Rudolf Wittkower. Both were teachers of Rosand's as
well as leaders in the establishment of art history as one of Columbia's most distinguished departments.
A third major figure in the ascendancy of art history is Rosand himself, who, like Schapiro, earned
his bachelor's and doctoral degrees at Columbia. He has produced work that ranges from Renaissance
painting and poetry to graphic arts and modern art, as shown in the publications* Titian *(1978),*
The Meaning of the Mark: Leonardo and Titian *(1988),* Painting in Sixteenth-
Century Venice: Titian, Veronese, Tintoretto *(1982, rev. 1997),* Robert Motherwell
on Paper *(1997), and* The Invention of Painting in America *(2004). His most recent books
are* Myths of Venice: The Figuration of a State *(2001) and* Drawing Acts: Studies in
Graphic Expression and Representation *(2002).*

*Rosand's administrative service to the university has also been noteworthy through two terms
as chair of the Department of Art History and Archaeology, as chair of Art Humanities in the
College, and as chair of the Society of Fellows in the Humanities. His contribution as a teacher*

was recognized by the Great Teacher Award conferred on him by the Society of Columbia Graduates
in 1997. With other colleagues, he was also a recipient of the Alexander Hamilton Medal, for distin-
guished service to the Core Curriculum.

—Wm. Theodore de Bary

—⁓—

Art history came relatively late to Columbia, long after it had been established as an academic field at other major universities and colleges in
America. Shortly after his appointment as president of the university in
1902, Nicholas Murray Butler submitted to the trustees a "Report on the
Organization of Instruction in the Fine Arts," in which he deplored that "at present
Columbia University makes no pretense of representing the art element in life and
in civilization. References to it are cursory and inadequate, and this extremely
important and significant branch of culture is, to all intents and purposes, unrecog-
nized by us."

It was only in 1921 that art history became part of the liberal arts curriculum of
Columbia College, thanks to a bequest of $100,000 from the estate of the art col-
lector Hugo Reisinger for the establishment of a professorship in fine arts.
Appointed the first assistant professor of fine arts was one Butler Murray Jr. (the
intriguing similarity of his name to that of Columbia's president and its possible role
in his appointment have remained a matter of speculation). Dominating serious
scholarship in the field at Columbia, however, was William Bell Dinsmoor, known
for his pioneering work on ancient Greek architecture. A professor in the School of
Architecture and head of the Avery Architectural Library, the greatest collection of
its kind in this country, Dinsmoor designed a program in archaeology that drew
upon the faculties of the Departments of Greek and Latin, Semitic Languages, and
Chinese and Japanese as well as the recently established Department of Fine Arts
(renamed Art History and Archaeology in 1960).

Although a strong bias toward classical art and archaeology continued to mark the
curriculum, the program in art history expanded with new faculty appointments at
Barnard as well as Columbia. Medieval art was taught by Ernest DeWald—who was
to leave for Princeton after a few years—and by Charles Rufus Morey of Princeton,
who crossed the Hudson to offer courses on Morningside Heights. Instruction in
Asian art was given by a curator at the Metropolitan Museum, thus initiating a pattern of adjunct appointments by which Columbia took advantage of the resources of
museums in New York. Marion Lawrence, a specialist in early Christian art, was

appointed to the Barnard faculty in 1929 and served as chair for many decades. The 1930s saw the arrival of a number of distinguished scholars whose careers were to add new distinction to its programs in art history: Millard Meiss, whose work transformed the understanding of early Renaissance painting; Margarete Bieber, an authority on Greek and Roman sculpture; and, at Barnard, Julius S. Held, who was to become the leading interpreter of Rubens and Rembrandt.

REDEFINING A DISCIPLINE: MEYER SCHAPIRO (1904–1996)

From the very beginning of its official establishment, one name defined the special character of art history at Columbia: Meyer Schapiro. An undergraduate in Columbia College when the department was created, he received the first Ph.D. in the field awarded by Columbia, became a member of the faculty in 1928, and remained at Columbia beyond his retirement in 1973 as University Professor emeritus. Schapiro came to personify art history at Columbia and to stand for a particularly American approach to the study of art, one founded on a deep intellectual engagement with its European elders but particularly shaped by an equally profound response to developments in modern art.

Born in Lithuania in 1904, Schapiro came to America with his family when he was three; he grew up in the Brownsville section of Brooklyn, attended Boys High School, and in 1920, at the age of sixteen, entered Columbia College. His course of studies included Latin, modern languages, ancient and modern literature, anthropology, philosophy, mathematics, and art history, demonstrating an intellectual range that was to inform and characterize his work throughout his career. As much as he appreciatively recalled "a largely friendly faculty with some inspiring teachers," the talented youth from Brooklyn especially "enjoyed the great libraries in which I loved to browse, the opportunities of learning in new fields," as well as "the companionship of congenial, like-minded students with strong intellectual and artistic interests and readiness for conversation, whether serious or playful." As an undergraduate he continued to draw and paint, at the National Academy of Design. At Columbia he discovered the new literature of modernism as he confirmed his commitment to the visual modernism of Matisse and Picasso—and perhaps especially Cézanne, who was to be the subject of one of his first and most influential books (*Paul Cézanne*, Abrams, 1952). Schapiro obviously stood out as a remarkable student.

In the *Menorah Journal* of 1927, in an essay bearing the now embarrassing (but telling) title of "Jewish Students I Have Known," Mark Van Doren, then a young member of the faculty, recalled Schapiro, who in the alphabetic anonymity of the reminiscence is referred to as "student C": "C's face is as clear in my eye now as if he were not, as he is, four thousand miles east of New York, clambering up no doubt to some rose window in a French or English cathedral that he may quench his thirst for details in thirteenth-century design." "C's face was passionate," the description continues, ". . . it was positively beautiful. C glowed—in his thick curly black hair, in his eager white cheeks, and in his darkly rolling eyes. He too knew everything, but what he knew best was the history of art. I never saw any of his own paintings, but I have sat hypnotized while he roamed my office and poured into my ears a bibliography of, say, Byzantine sculpture. I recall a very clear exposition he gave one day of certain modern theories concerning the spread of early cultures through the migration of symbols; he described the symbols, and he made as if to tell me all the places on Earth where they might still be seen. That I could not stay to hear was not because I was unwilling; I had another appointment—to which he conducted me, still talking. I heard now and then that his instructors often resented his knowledge, which they felt was intruded without cause during class discussions. I am sure, however, that this was the best of causes—a passion to know and make known. The passion of a pitcher to spill its contents, the passion of a river to flow and, if the sun shines, to sparkle."

Schapiro graduated from the College in 1924 and continued his graduate studies at Columbia—having been rejected by Princeton. His classes with Franz Boas and John Dewey, he confessed, meant more to him than any in art history, a discipline that lacked the intellectual rigor and challenge he found in other areas of study. His dissertation, "The Romanesque Sculpture of Moissac," was defended in 1929, and parts of it were published in two issues of *The Art Bulletin* in 1931. Such publication, however, was evidently not considered sufficient to meet the formal requirements for the degree: "printing and deposit with the Librarian of the University of seventy-five copies." In 1935 Dinsmoor interceded, and Schapiro was finally awarded his Ph.D.—a situation that has confused a generation of younger scholars currently writing their own dissertations on Meyer Schapiro.

On a Carnegie Corporation fellowship, Schapiro traveled widely in Europe and the Near East in 1926 and 1927. Voraciously taking in a vast range of art while doing research for his thesis, he was preparing the foundations for the larger vision of his subsequent work. He was also leaving behind a trail of legendary anecdotes that continued to be recounted long after by those who met the brilliant young graduate student.

Works of art and pages from Schapiro's travel notebook of 1926–27

At Villa I Tatti outside Florence, he visited the redoubtable Bernard Berenson, who recorded the occasion with undisguised sarcasm: "Yesterday a very handsome youth named M. Schapiro sent up his card on which was written Columbia University. . . . It turned out he had been sent by Creswell [the Islamicist K. A. C. Creswell] whom he had seen in Cairo and Riefstahl [Rudolf Meyer Riefstahl, also an Islamicist] whom he had seen in Constantinople. He is acquainted with the entire personnel of the arts and the entire literature: he has worked years and years on Coptic art and as many again on the local school of Azerbaijan; decades he has spent in Spain and Southern France, and as for the remotest corners of Byzantine and Cappadocian art, he has explored, delved, and assimilated it all. I put him to the test by showing him my jade libation cup and my little bronze candlestick, and he praised them and discoursed about them as sweetly as Solomon did about the hyssop in the wall." Whatever his appreciation of the young Schapiro's learning and eloquence, the grand connoisseur—and fellow Lithuanian Jew (by then twice converted)—was obviously less sympathetic to such passion than was Van Doren.

Schapiro in 1978

Self-Portrait,
Brussels, 1923, Meyer
Schapiro, conté
crayon

The source of another, more legendary recollection of the young scholar is the Abbey of Silos in northern Spain, whose art, in both sculpture and manuscript painting, was the subject of one of Schapiro's most ambitious and provocative studies, "From Mozarabic to Romanesque in Silos" (1939). The French art critic Jean Leymarie, a friend of Schapiro, tells of visiting the monastery in the years following World War II and hearing an elder monk recall the impression made by the traveling Jewish student: "His face was so radiant and he explained the meaning of the sculpture in the cloister with such eloquence that we thought we had some idea of what our Lord must have been like."

Upon his return to New York and appointment to the faculty, Schapiro added significant new dimensions to the program at Columbia and opened new perspectives on the field at large. With his critical commitment to modern art, Schapiro effectively redefined the responsibilities and ambitions of the discipline. In the winter session of 1934–35, for example, he was offering both a course on "manuscript painting, drawing, ornament, and calligraphy from late antiquity to the thirteenth century in Europe and the Near East" and a seminar in contemporary art, the syllabus of which was organized around the following topics: "(a) functionalist and postfunctionalist architecture, (b) the content of modern painting, (c) painting and cinema, (d) sociology of modern art, (e) contemporary philosophy of art in relation to contemporary art." Early in his career he also developed the course that was to become the intellectual core of the graduate program in art history at Columbia, Introduction to the Literature, Theories, and Methods of Art History.

On the undergraduate level, Schapiro brought the study of art history into the Core Curriculum of the College, before the creation of Art Humanities, through his contribution to the revised, seventh edition of *An Introduction to Contemporary Civilization in the West* (1928), a chapter, "Art in the Contemporary World." In it he adumbrated the complex vision of modernism that he would further refine in the course of the next decade—especially in critical response to the formalist values of the recently established Museum of Modern Art. His was a vision that recognized the dialectic tension between the assertion of artistic freedom and the constraints of social and economic life. Schapiro's liberal Marxism combined with his own artistic instincts to yield a particularly profound awareness of that tension and its creative potential. He knew that "individuality is a social fact." Nonetheless, "Art has its own conditions which distinguish it from other activities," as he declared to a professional audience at the First American Artists' Congress in 1936. "It operates with its own special materials and according to general psychological laws."

The larger aim of Schapiro's project might be termed the reclamation of the artist, whether medieval or modern, in and from history. From the beginning, his method involved effectively reconstructing the creative process, through close and sympathetic stylistic description. From the expressive qualities of the work of art, discovered in accordance with those "general psychological laws," there emerged a persona of its creator. Behind the style, Schapiro sought and found the artist. In the marginal figures of jongleurs at Silos, he saw affirmation of "the self-consciousness of an independent artistic virtuosity," and he delighted in discovering and sharing the inventive fantasy of Hiberno-Saxon monks of the seventh and eighth centuries. He rescued this art from its neglect in an art historiography founded on traditional Western aesthetic values, based ultimately upon some sense of a "classical" (i.e., Greco-Roman) norm.

It seems perfectly logical that Schapiro's focus should have been on those periods in the history of art when the basic elements of picture-making were subjected to the most fundamental pressures and reevaluation: In Hiberno-Saxon and Romanesque painting, as in impressionism and cubism, the picture plane itself is viewed as a dynamic field of conflicting energies and ambiguous relationships, the resolution of which resides in the very act of painting—and in the act of interpretation. As an artist himself, Schapiro was sensitive to the marks on the surface—the "special materials" of art—to the qualities of their making and of their expression, their "physiognomic" character, as he phrased it. Eventually, he formulated essential aspects of this analytical experience in a now-classic essay, "On Some Problems in the Semiotics of Visual Art: Field and Vehicle in Image-Signs" (1969), whose rather intimidating title only hints at its fundamental presentation of a pictorial semiotics.

As Schapiro demonstrated consistently by example, especially in lecturing, where his own enthusiastic engagement was so much in evidence, the best criticism reenacts creation. Those who attended his public lectures on Picasso in 1980 will recall the ebullient choreography of his re-creation of that painter's *Three Dancers*. Through his imaginative projections, his students were led into the scriptorium, the workshop, and the studio; they learned about artistic creation through his reenactment.

It was that special sympathy with the creative act that made him particularly welcome in the artists' world. Throughout his career, Schapiro moved between the Columbia campus on Morningside Heights and his home in Greenwich Village, between the university and the city at large. The shuttling was cultural as well as geographic. No academic or critic was more respected by the artists themselves—I recall Barnett Newman and Saul Steinberg, among others, as faithful auditors in Schapiro's class on abstract art in the early 1960s. Part of the Schapiro legend involved his privileged position among them—guiding the young Robert Motherwell, who had come to Columbia to study with him; persuading Willem de

ON MEYER SCHAPIRO

A complete listing of Meyer Schapiro's published works (to 1995) will be found in *Meyer Schapiro: The Bibliography*, compiled by Lillian Milgram Schapiro (New York: George Braziller, 1995). Posthumous publications are *Words, Script, and Pictures: Semiotics of Visual Language* (1996), *Impressionism: Reflections and Perceptions* (1997), *Worldview in Painting—Art and Society: Selected Papers* (1999), *The Unity of Picasso's Art* (2000), all by Braziller; and *Meyer Schapiro: His Painting, Drawing, and Sculpture* (New York: Abrams, 2000).

Two periodicals have devoted special issues to Schapiro: *Social Research* (Spring 1978) and *Oxford Art Journal* 17, no. 1 (1994). The fullest biographical account is by Helen Epstein, "Meyer Schapiro: A Passion to Know and Make Known," *ArtNews* (May 1983 and Summer 1983); Schapiro's achievement is reviewed by David Rosand in the *Encyclopedia of Aesthetics*, edited by Michael Kelly (New York: Oxford University Press, 1998).

Kooning that his canvas *Woman I* was indeed finished; inspiring a younger generation of artists like Alan Kaprow and Sol LeWitt. Through Schapiro, students in art
history at Columbia felt they gained some special access to the creative world of
the studio. It seems only fitting that the endowed professorship established to
honor Meyer Schapiro should have been funded primarily through the sale of an
album of prints contributed by twelve contemporary artists, among them Jasper
Johns, Roy Lichtenstein, and Robert Motherwell.

In concluding a retrospective account of the history of art at Columbia, Julius
Held offered "a salute to one who not only brought honor to art history at
Columbia, but has been an inspiration to all people who study and love art: Meyer
Schapiro." Indeed, no name was more intimately and significantly connected with
the development of the discipline of art history at Columbia or has had a greater
impact on the field in this country, an impact that reached well beyond the halls of
the academy to shape the critical response to art in the broadest sense.

BUILDING A DEPARTMENT: RUDOLF WITTKOWER
(1901–1971)

During the two decades of William Bell Dinsmoor's leadership (1934–54), the
department expanded its programs in several ways. For the Core Curriculum it
developed Masterpieces of Fine Arts, the course that has come to be known as Art
Humanities. It expanded the range of its curriculum to include courses in African
and oceanic art; inspired by Franz Boas in the Department of Anthropology, this
pioneering effort to include so-called primitive art was led by Paul Wingert. And
yet the department was hardly collegial, and upon Dinsmoor's retirement, internal
tensions frustrated the effort to select a successor. The university administration
stepped in, appointing an outsider, Albert Hofstadter from philosophy, as acting
chairman. During his term (1955–57), Hofstadter oversaw further significant additions to the faculty, most notably Otto Brendel, who brought new critical perspectives to the study of classical art. Hofstadter's most significant achievement, however, was the appointment of a new chairman from abroad. In 1957, Rudolf
Wittkower assumed that position, and the department embarked on a period of
growth that was to lead it to its current preeminence in the field.

Wittkower came to Columbia from London where he had been Durning
Lawrence Professor at University College, having left Hitler's Germany for England
in 1933. Born in Berlin in 1901, Wittkower had studied first at the University of

Munich and then at the University of Berlin, where he received his Ph.D. in 1923. For the following decade he served as research fellow at the Bibliotheca Hertziana in Rome, and it was there that the major concerns of his own research took shape, above all, the art of Michelangelo and that of Gianlorenzo Bernini, the giant of baroque art and architecture—and the artist with whom Wittkower was to become most closely identified. In 1931 he coauthored the two-volume corpus of Bernini drawings, pioneering in a field that had been neglected by contemporary art history, or, worse, rejected as unworthy of serious study. (He recalled that Bernard Berenson, on being shown photographs of drawings by Bernini, confessed to feeling physically ill.)

In England, Wittkower turned his attention to the more theoretical aspects of Renaissance architecture. His research culminated with the publication in 1949 of his most broadly influential book, *Architectural Principles in the Age of Humanism.* Wittkower set out to dispel the Ruskinian notion that this art, inspired by the classical forms of pagan antiquity, was essentially profane and unfit for a truly Christian culture. Denying that Renaissance architects were indulging in mere formalism, he insisted on the symbolical values of this art and demonstrated the meaning of its forms. The section on the principles of Palladio's architecture opened entirely new prospects on the understanding of harmonic proportion in architecture. Wittkower explored the significance of musical theory for architecture, the ways in which a building could deliberately declare its consonance with the larger Pythagorean order of the universe. Not only did his studies restore the fullest cultural resonance to the architecture of the Renaissance, but they proved an inspiration to a generation of architects in the twentieth century. The triumphal monument of Wittkower's work on baroque art was his contribution to the Pelican History of Art series, the volume *Art and Architecture in Italy 1600–1750* (1958). In this magisterial and beautifully written study, Wittkower organized for the first time an incredible range of art-historical material—painting, sculpture, and architecture. Shaping his complex subject with critical intelligence and methodological awareness, he effectively returned the Italian baroque to the history of art.

When Wittkower left London for Morningside Heights in 1956, he had already experienced the American university scene, having taught as a visiting professor at Columbia the previous year and at Harvard in the summers of 1954 and 1955. Howard Hibbard, who was eventually to join him at Columbia, was a graduate student in those seminars, and, in the obituary notice in *The Burlington Magazine* of 1972, he recalled that experience: "I shall never forget my first impression of that awesome figure, who immediately proved to be so gentle, so generous, and so kind. . . . [His students] were profoundly and permanently influenced by the seriousness, range, and enthusiasm of his scholarship. But it must be said that Wittkower too was impressed by his new students—perhaps our combination of enthusiastic naïveté and admiration was a novelty."

Wittkower recognized the potential of this American enthusiasm. His new appointment offered the kind of major challenge that inspired his best talents; he saw the opportunity to build. He had warned the dean of the Graduate Faculties at Columbia that his appointment would cost the university dearly; during his tenure the department's annual budget reportedly rose from $50,000 to more than $600,000. The faculty already boasted a number of major scholars—most notably Otto Brendel, Julius Held, and, above all, Meyer Schapiro—but Wittkower expanded its range, inviting Edith Porada to develop the program in ancient Near Eastern art and archaeology and bringing in a younger generation of outstanding scholars— including Robert Branner in medieval architecture, Howard Hibbard in baroque art and architecture, and Theodore Reff in modern art. At Wittkower's retirement in

1969 the programs of the department encompassed the world—from Europe and the Americas to Africa and Asia, from the ancient Near East to the contemporary scene in New York.

In addition to new appointments, Wittkower invited a series of distinguished visitors to enrich the offerings, and he created seminars in cooperation with museum curators and collectors to assure that Columbia students had the opportunity to study works of art firsthand. There was no aspect of the study of art that did not find its place within the generous curricular arena envisioned by Wittkower. Beyond the curriculum, he created an Advisory Council, a group of friends from the New York art world dedicated to supporting the goals and programs of the department. Typically, that support came from projects that involved students and contributed to their education: a series of loan exhibitions prepared in graduate seminars, the catalogues written by students. The aim was to raise funds for scholarships to enable students to travel. Wittkower wanted his students to know their art in situ.

ON RUDOLF WITTKOWER

Papers commemorating the twentieth anniversary of Wittkower's retirement from Columbia were published in *Source: Notes in the History of Art* 8–9 (1989). On that occasion, the department and the Istituto della Enciclopedia Italiana published a full bibliography: *The Writings of Rudolf Wittkower*, edited by Donald M. Reynolds—which also reprints Howard Hibbard's moving obituary notice in *The Burlington Magazine* 114 (1972): 173–77. A further memoir by David Rosand was published in the *Proceedings of the British Academy* 90 (1995).

ON THE DEPARTMENT

William Bell Dinsmoor, "The Department of Fine Arts and Archaeology," in *History of the Faculty of Philosophy, Columbia University* (New York: Columbia University Press, 1957), and Julius S. Held, "History of Art at Columbia," in *The Early Years of Art History in the United States: Notes and Essays on Departments, Teaching, and Scholars*, edited by Craig Hugh Smyth and Peter M. Lukehart (Princeton: Department of Art and Archaeology, Princeton University, 1993).

Colleagues and students remember Wittkower as a genial and generous giant. He encouraged the intellectually ambitious student to test new fields and try new methods; he was prepared to offer the less secure student ideas and topics that he knew would yield genuinely interesting and even important results. Any measure of his contribution to art history must inevitably take into account the scholarship that he fostered, that is, the achievements of his students and his younger colleagues. His effect was at once inspiring and catalytic.

Wittkower's rare wisdom was never more apparent than in the spring of

Wittkower's students often noted their teacher's resemblance to Bernini's portrait bust of Cardinal Scipione Borghese.

1968, when the campus was in turmoil. Several prominent members of the faculty, distinguished scholars who remembered the university violence of their own earlier careers in Germany, could view Columbia's student rebellion only with dismay as a repetition of that past. Although he had shared their pilgrimage, Wittkower maintained a clearer and more objective vision and remained calm. He thus offered an important ethical example as well as very definite political acumen. Marshaling peers like Otto Brendel and Meyer Schapiro, he managed to turn a time of crisis into a shared moment of self-reflection. The events of 1968 only confirmed Wittkower's benevolence as a leader. By bringing conflicting generations together, he enabled his department, which only fourteen years earlier had been severely splintered, to remain, not just intact, but truly collegial.

CHAPTER 10

The "Conscience of Columbia": Remembering Marjorie Hope Nicolson, Scholar and Teacher

—ᴍ—

Andrea Walton

As the first female full professor at any Ivy League university and chair of a major department at Columbia as well as the first woman president of the national Phi Beta Kappa, Marjorie Nicolson clearly qualifies as a trailblazer for women in academia. But even while she stood firmly for women's equality, its ultimate value for her rested not on attaining any personal rank or power, but on the opportunity to serve the higher goals of true learning. She could turn down any number of academic deanships but was satisfied to serve as chair of the English department at Columbia because to her it represented a genuine community of the best in learning and teaching.

Thus, when Andrea Walton presents Marjorie Nicolson not as the champion of some political or social cause, but (in the words of Edward Tayler) as the "conscience of Columbia," she invokes an educational or communitarian ideal, a higher conception of humanistic scholarship and classical liberal education. This Nicolson recognized in such worthy Columbia predecessors as the critic George Woodberry, the drama critic Brander Matthews, and the literary critic and musician John Erskine, who founded the Great Books honors course. Carrying on their "living legacy" in the humanities, she presided over what has been called the golden age of the Columbia English department. To qualify as the "conscience" of such a tradition, Nicolson had to demonstrate her own unexcelled dedication to the highest standards of a scholarship in the service of the common good, not just the recognition of spectacular individual achievement. This shared excellence of a true teaching company is what Marjorie Nicolson stood for and we prize most of all as a living legacy at Columbia.

Andrea Walton is associate professor of education at the School of Education at Indiana University, Bloomington. She received her Ph.D. at Columbia in 1995 in history and education.

Professor Walton has written extensively on women in higher education and philanthropy and has published a study of Marjorie Nicolson, "'Scholar,' 'Lady,' 'Best Man in the English Department'?" in the History of Education Quarterly *40 (Summer 2000).*

—*Wm. Theodore de Bary*

——ᘯᘯ——

I f we are to try for Professor Nicolson we must begin without delay . . . we fear that she will not keep on declining presidencies unless we can make her the offer she so abundantly merits." Department chair Ernest Hunter Wright was sure he had found a suitable candidate for a senior position in English at Columbia. Marjorie Hope Nicolson, a respected scholar-teacher, known internationally for her writings on Milton, Donne, and the literary imagination, was then a full professor and dean at Smith College. "We still believe we can secure her if we approach her first," Wright assured the Columbia administration, "because we think she will prefer a life of scholarship to one of administration."[1]

This assessment was right. In fact, Nicolson declined a number of prestigious offers—including a chance to become Smith's first woman president—before joining the faculty of Columbia in 1941. Her arrival at Morningside Heights made her the first woman to hold a full professorship at one of the Ivies. But the forty-seven-year-old Nicolson saw her appointment at Columbia less as a milestone for women than as the crowning glory of an already deeply satisfying and rewarding career.

Indeed, Nicolson's career had been impressive. She had advanced rapidly and distinguished herself as a highly productive and original scholar. A 1914 graduate of the University of Michigan, she earned her master's degree in philosophy from her alma mater in 1918 and her Ph.D. in literature from Yale in 1920. During the 1920s, Nicolson achieved the rank of associate professor, edited two collections of poetry, published a textbook, and contributed to various Modern Language Association (MLA) publications. An early recipient of a Guggenheim Fellowship, she had earned an enviable reputation for her pioneering studies of science and literature by the 1930s.[2] Before joining Columbia, she had already held the vice presidency of the MLA and soon thereafter was elected the first woman president of Phi Beta Kappa. During her Columbia years additional high-profile honors and awards would enhance her stature in the literary profession and among her Columbia colleagues. She received the British Academy's Rose Crawshay Prize in 1947, for *Newton Demands the Muse*, became a member of the American Philosophical Society, was awarded

Columbia's bicentennial silver medallion, and held the William Peterfield Trent Chair at Columbia.

Nicolson defies easy categorization. She was neither a "feminist"—a label she equated with belligerence and militancy—nor unmindful of the unique burdens borne by women academics: "She has no wife—no *alter ego* to take over the social and domestic duties."[3] By her own admission, Nicolson savored the financial independence and personal freedoms gained by the "woman movement." Smoking, drinking, driving (she dubbed her car "Calvin" after President Coolidge because "he did not choose to run"), and sporting a short-cropped haircut were tangible signs of freedom to her, but these paled before the "romance" of scholarship. Nicolson revered her doctorate as the true symbol of her intellectual emancipation.[4] Believing in meritocracy and the intrinsic rewards of erudition, she negotiated the narrow path of acceptance in the profession and avoided the pitfalls that thwarted the career aspirations of many talented women. Her frame of reference was not the political cause of women's social advancement but rather an intellectual commitment to free inquiry and the university ideal. Known by her doctoral students as an inspiring scholar—the "Fourth Fate, the Fourth Grace, and the Tenth Muse"—to her colleagues she was the voice of clarity in a confusing time of burgeoning enrollments, a synthetic thinker who embraced the unity of science and art, and an articulate spokesperson for the "rights and privileges" of faculty life—in all, the "Conscience of the University."[5]

—⁂—

Marjorie Hope Nicolson was born in Yonkers, New York, on February 18, 1894, to Lissie Hope Morris Nicolson, a British-born nurse, and Charles Butler Nicolson, a Canadian lawyer-turned-journalist. She spent most of her childhood in Canada. From there to Columbia she followed a straight and purposeful course: undergraduate years at Michigan, doctoral work at Yale, postdoctoral studies abroad and at Johns Hopkins, and teaching at Minnesota, Goucher, and Smith. Each of these stints contributed significantly to shaping her academic ambitions, her understanding of what it meant to be a scholar-teacher, and her perspectives on the status of women in education. At Michigan, Nicolson's interest in the classics and philosophy led her to work closely with Robert Mark Wenley. A pragmatic man, Wenley was frank in his appraisal of Nicolson's career possibilities. Cigar and Scotch whiskey in hand, he listened carefully to Nicolson's plans for an academic career before offering his advice. "Until you can drink this and smoke this, you'll ne'er be a philosopher," he told her.[6] With that Wenley steered Nicolson toward literature, a field that was more open to women, and he recommended Yale. But Nicolson found Yale a hostile environment for women, in sharp contrast to Michigan. Years later, Nicolson could still vividly recall a brusk encounter with Professor Chauncey Brewster Tinker, who slammed a door in her face, and the "pedagogical misogyny" of the Shakespearean scholar Tucker Brooke.[7] But the indefatigable "Miss Nicki," as generations of students and colleagues fondly called her, was not deterred by overt hostility toward a bright woman; on the contrary, such affronts steeled her determination to excel. In 1920, she completed her Ph.D. after two years and became the first woman to receive the coveted $500 John Addison Porter Prize for the year's outstanding dissertation.[8]

Degree in hand, Nicolson began her career at the University of Minnesota but soon left for a position at Goucher, the women's college near Baltimore, primarily to live near her parents. Her father, who had joined the editorial staff of the *Baltimore Sun* a few years earlier, was in poor health. But after coeducational university life, Nicolson found Goucher provincial. "I was intellectually lonely," she later recalled.[9] Nicolson found her milieu at nearby Johns Hopkins, where she began informal post-graduate study in philosophy with A. O. Lovejoy, the influential historian of ideas, and Edwin Greenlaw, a noted scholar of sixteenth-century history. To characterize this apprenticeship, she elaborated on a well-known contemporary image of the ideal liberal education that featured the celebrated nineteenth-century educator Mark Hopkins. It was, she said, "Mark-Hopkins-Lovejoy-and-Greenlaw at one end of a log and us at the other."[10]

In 1927, Nicolson joined the faculty of Smith College. Within two years, she was promoted to a full professorship and soon became dean, a position she held for twelve years and viewed as integral to her growth as an educator. Foremost, the years working alongside President William A. Neilson reinforced Nicolson's appreciation of the liberating power of a liberal arts education. As she once said, "Never was there a college which came as close to Academe, the Ideal of what a college should be, as Smith in his best years."[11] It was also at Smith that Nicolson, anchoring her views in personal experience and a deep attachment to academic tradition, began to crystallize her perspective on women's status in the academy. Although some women professors at Smith—Nicolson sometimes called them the "ardent feminists"—advocated hiring more women faculty as a matter of principle, Nicolson believed that maintaining a mixed teaching staff was "sound and intelligent" policy—for the well-being of students (men and women alike) and for institutional prestige.[12] From her vantage point, the advancement of women as a group was a misguided priority, at odds with scholarly and academic standards and common sense.[13]

Nicolson's stance disappointed those Smith students, faculty, alumnae, and parents who wanted the dean of Smith College to be a champion for the academic advancement of women. At the same time, the challenges that intellectual women encountered throughout the ages intrigued Nicolson, as did the question of women's academic potential. In fact, she addressed these subjects repeatedly during her Smith years. On one hand, her scholarship, notably, her *Conway Letters* (1930), and her Smith College seminar on science and imagination demonstrated her long-standing but diverted interests in philosophy and a remarkable attentiveness to female intellectuality and imagination (a subject virtually ignored by the emerging history of science). On the other hand, Nicolson asserted that women need not imitate men; they should carry their scholarship "lightly," so as to retain their feminine virtues.[14] The challenge was to be a

Despite her illustrious career, Nicolson remains a relatively unexplored figure.

scholar and a lady. In Nicolson's view, many women were "overconscientious" and "pedants and plodders" who, unlike men, became "bogged down in petty details."[15] Further, while women could be "competent teachers," they could not easily become scholars, because of their "feminine temperament" and the "social feeling" that connects them to others, especially family: "It is the rare woman—an older generation would have called her 'an unnatural' woman—who can continue her work unmindful or oblivious of want in her family."[16]

Nicolson was not oblivious to the challenges that academic women faced. In "The Rights and Privileges Pertaining Thereto . . . ," a speech delivered at the University of Michigan's centennial celebrations in 1937, she contrasted the openness of the World War I years for academic women with the backlash that followed—a phenomenon that she described poignantly as the "shades of the prison house" closing on the "emancipated" women of her generation.[17] But these lines, often quoted by historians, are best considered within the broader context of

A. O. Lovejoy, the historian of ideas at Johns Hopkins University, had a great influence on Nicolson.

Nicolson's career. Rarely did she address the subject of gender bias so directly. Equally important, she forged her highly regarded career while generally standing apart from women's groups and women's issues. Indeed, rather than emphasize the challenges she had overcome, Nicolson made light of her achievements, portraying herself as a cross between Eve and the woman preacher whom Dr. Samuel Johnson compared to a dog walking on its hind legs: "[She] doesn't do it well, but attracts attention because [she] does it at all."[18] And, finally, it is worth noting that in the late 1930s, when she wrote "Rights and Privileges Pertaining Thereto," her own career was taking off. The author of three books and thirty-three articles, Nicolson had reached a crossroads.

Her 1941 appointment at Columbia represented an auspicious fit between her long-standing career aspirations and Columbia's pressing departmental needs. Still, Ernest Hunter Wright did not have an easy task securing trustee approval for this new faculty hire. Nicolson would not consider coming to Columbia unless she retained her professorial rank, and the Columbia trustees, reflecting a long-standing hostility to the advancement of faculty women, were reluctant to grant Nicolson a full professorship. Indeed, before Nicolson, Columbia had struggled in the mid-1930s with the case of another woman, Ruth Benedict, the acting chair of Anthropology, whose junior rank belied her international standing and who was passed over in the naming of Franz Boas's successor.[19] Although the outcome in Benedict's case was a disappointment for women's supporters, the possibility of a senior appointment for a female scholar at Columbia had begun to seem less remote. In fact, in the mid-1930s at least one Columbia administrator had admitted candidly (though privately) that "the universities will have to come to it," and that it was "[not] bad policy to take the bull by the horns and accept the necessity."[20]

By the spring of 1940, Wright had finally won President Nicholas Murray Butler's full support and gained the approval of Columbia's trustees. In accepting, an enthusiastic Nicolson wrote, "I am particularly touched by the fact that both of them [the department and the administration] have been willing to disregard my inferior sex! Personally I have always found my masculine colleagues ready to forgive what was no fault of mine." She added, invoking a familiar Miltonic allusion, "But I think it extraordinarily liberal of Columbia to be willing to face the world in their refusal to quote again: 'He for God only; she for God in him'!"[21]

If Columbia had acted boldly in appointing a woman to a full professorship, there was, in fact, little risk associated with the choice of Nicolson, a woman who believed in the equalizing qualities of intellectual life and embraced academic tradition. "I'm inclined to feel that I ought to pay Columbia for the privilege of teaching here," she once wrote to Secretary Frank Fackenthal.[22] Indeed, Nicolson found the Columbia English department a congenial intellectual niche. The humanistic approach to literature that Nicolson valued had been cultivated earlier by Columbia's "gentleman" scholars, including literary critic George Woodberry, drama critic Brander Matthews, literary historian Ashley Thorndike, and literary scholar John Erskine. In the early 1940s, this tradition continued in the careers of a number of English professors at Columbia whose reputations as scholar-teachers and whose essays, poetry, novels, and criticism were known to an audience beyond the university gates: notably Joseph Wood Krutch, who served as drama critic for *The Nation*; Mark Van Doren, who won a Pulitzer Prize in 1939 for his *Collected Poems*; and Lionel Trilling, who gained prominence as a critic and public intellectual.

More than many of these new colleagues, Nicolson's ambition, intellectual roots, and sensibilities were strictly in the academy and professional organizations such as the MLA and Phi Beta Kappa. Nicolson characteristically favored the canon over contemporary writing, British and continental history and literature over American, the clarity and precision of the Baconian method over then-popular currents of modernism and subjectivism, and detective stories and crossword puzzles over psychological and "women's" novels. Even if several of her Columbia colleagues were intellectually drawn to cultural and political criticism, debates about American literature or the New Criticism, modernism, myth, or Freudian interpretations and the like, the department was in general agreement about what constitutes "good" literature and a liberal education.[23] Self-described as a "conservative and traditionalist," in the Ruskinian sense, Nicolson joined and amplified that consensus.[24] Her orientation as a teacher-scholar expressed a brand of intellectualism and humanism that had characterized the history of the Columbia department. She had absorbed these educational ideals through her study of Milton and the classics, and her association with men like Wenley, Lovejoy, Greenlaw, and Neilson.

Nicolson was a Columbia professor at a pivotal time in world events and the academy's history. If war posed one set of challenges to universities in the United States, the post–World War II years posed another. The influx of students into colleges and universities across the nation created particular challenges to humanities departments, where traditionally classes were small and writing skills were emphasized. As chair of Columbia's English department, Nicolson struggled to maintain intellectual standards and a coherent curriculum against the mounting pressures of burgeoning enrollments and professionalizing trends within scholarship itself. Earlier, as dean at Smith, Nicolson had defended the merits of a liberal arts curriculum and tried to elevate academic standards in the difficult financial and political climate of the 1930s; now in the 1940s, Nicolson became a Cassandra-like critic of trends within the academy, warning colleagues about the danger of intense professionalization. Like Robert Hutchins and Mortimer Adler at Chicago and Mark Van Doren and Jacques Barzun at Columbia, she ardently defended the place of the humanities in a curriculum that she believed was increasingly dominated by world politics, scientific methods, and utilitarian and positivist principles. "Social scientists must believe that poetry, essays, and drama are as legitimate expressions of the spirit of man as the works of John Stuart Mill, Adam Smith—or even Karl Marx," she wrote. "Novelists and poets, as well as sociologists, have done much to correct abuses in slums and prisons. . . . We have one common end: the search for Truth."[25] Nicolson called the attention of the American professoriate to "an artificial and serious distinction between *research and scholarship* on the one hand, and *teaching and education* on the other." She recognized a "deep-rooted academic feeling for 'specialization' and 'departmentalism'" that had become a veritable "curse."[26]

At Columbia, Nicolson expanded her reputation as a productive and original scholar. She published seven books between 1946 and 1962, served on the editorial boards of the *Journal of the History of Ideas* and *The American Scholar*, and lectured extensively. Her work on science and literature was praised in leading journals for its eloquence and bold interpretations. Her award-winning *Newton Demands the Muse* (1946), her first book after joining Columbia's faculty, showed how Isaac Newton's popular *Opticks* (1704) "gave color back to poetry from which it had almost fled during the period of Cartesianism."[27] In *The Breaking of the Circle* (1950) Nicolson provocatively analyzed the influence of science on seventeenth-century poets, especially John Donne. And, in 1959, Nicolson's *Mountain Gloom and Mountain Glory* offered a nuanced interpretation of images of mountains as a lens to reveal the shifting eighteenth-century sensibilities that led to romanticism.[28] Still, Nicolson's approach was not without its critics, who saw in it a stark "intellectualism" that failed to situate literature within its economic, cultural, and social context.

Nicolson (center) with unidentified woman (right) and department secretary Adele Mendelson (left), to whom she dedicated her prize-winning book Newton Demands the Muse

Ironically, although Nicolson had come to Columbia with the aim of focusing on research, she found herself accepting various leadership roles. She represented the faculty of philosophy on the University Council from 1946 to 1950 and succeeded Oscar James Campbell as the English department's chair in 1954.[29] Perhaps no other Columbia school or program experienced the influx of students after World War II as dramatically as the English department.[30] Nicolson was proud of the department's academic standing and credited her department secretary and longtime friend Adele Borgo Mendelson for its reputation for efficiency. The two women became legendary among professors and students in their service to Columbia and epitomized what many nostalgically have referred to as the "golden age" of Columbia's English department.[31]

Nicolson neither presented herself as a female role model, nor was she inclined, by nature or principle, to take affirmative steps on behalf of women students or female junior colleagues for the sake of advancing women in the academy.[32] In fact, she might be "far harder on women," as one former student recalled: "So much sternness because so much hope."[33] Indeed, Nicolson was gratified by teaching, developed several close and lasting friendships with students, and was proud of the women scholars she trained, among them Aileen Ward, Helen Randall, Rosemond Tuve, and Gretchen Finney. Nicolson's colleagues admired her firm yet humane decision making, her loyalty, and her willingness to criticize policies that she felt jeopardized the university's educational integrity.[34] It was Nicolson's abiding respect for scholarly excellence that led her, as a member of an ad hoc committee reviewing the fine arts department in 1954, to ask why the world-renowned scholar Margarete Bieber, a German refugee, had attained only an associate professorship at Columbia. Nicolson's recommendations concerning salaries and promotions were also principled. As the department's highest-paid member in the early 1950s, she volunteered, though she was a single woman supporting four relatives, to take a salary cut so that junior scholars and secretaries could earn a living wage. Beyond that, she advised President Butler to offer any salary increase or perks necessary to retain one world-class scholar.[35] In all, it was beliefs and practices like these that earned Nicolson the title "Conscience of Columbia" and led Columbia men to call her admiringly the "best man in the English department."[36]

How did Nicolson remember her professional life? She grew despondent as she retraced her career, from her years at Michigan to her appointment, after her Columbia retirement in 1962, at the Institute for Advanced Study in Princeton. She believed that the humanistic world view so central to her professional life had disappeared. She had revered the university as an ideal transcending American culture and gender, an egalitarian intellectual meeting place. But changes in the broader culture of post–World War II America had transformed the university. For her, the harmony between science and art and the bridge between tradition and modernity that had been fundamental to her research had vanished. By her own account, Nicolson now found herself "wandering between two worlds." One was academe, as she had known it up through her "early period" at Columbia. The other she described as "phantasmagoria," evoking Charlie Chaplin's film *Modern Times*. "We mechanically feed them in [students], patterning our educational institutions upon technological factories," she observed.[37] She sadly concluded that professors of her "ilk" had vanished from campuses and that academic life had "degenerated."[38]

Today, despite her illustrious career, Nicolson remains a relatively unexplored figure. Nicolson broke new ground in literary scholarship and was an eloquent defender of the humanities and university ideals, but her contributions have been obscured not only by gender biases in historical writing but also by the shifting intellectual currents within her field. Equally important, Nicolson's career has received scant attention from historians of academic women, save for passing references to the "Rights and Privileges" speech. The oversight has been unfortunate because Nicolson's story extends our understanding of how academic women have negotiated the challenges they encountered in the male-dominated academy. But beyond that, her career reminds us that the history of academic women entails more than women's fight for access to the academy—a common theme of recent historical accounts. It is also the story of what attracted women to an academic career and how women scholars helped to shape the institutions where they taught. Nicolson not only devoted herself to the life of the mind and therein found personal success and satisfaction, but also provided leadership in promoting ideals that are central to university life.

CHAPTER 11

Learning a Pedagogy of Love: Thomas Merton

--~w~--

Martha S. Jones

At the convocation held in St. Paul's Chapel in May 2002 for graduate students in arts and sciences who would receive their degrees at commencement the next day, Martha S. Jones, a candidate for the Ph.D. in history, was asked to represent her fellow graduates as a principal speaker. She chose to talk about her experience as a student reliving, in her own way and time, the life of Thomas Merton, which she had read about in his spiritual autobiography, The Seven Storey Mountain. *From this account of his dedication to the religious life, she found much in his experience that resembled her own.*

Somewhat in contrast to our other Living Legacies essays, here is a young student of history, at the start of her career, reflecting on the thoughts of the young poet and monk at the start of his, sixty years earlier. Jones recalls a legacy of student life on Morningside Heights that carries on its own intellectual tradition, and in this personal account she shows how Merton's writings gave added meaning and perspective to her own career as a student in the same halls and haunts he knew.

Jones is currently an assistant professor at the University of Michigan, in the Department of History and in the Center for Afroamerican and African Studies. She is completing a book entitled "All Bound Up Together": The "Woman Question" in African-American Public Culture, 1830–1900, *an examination of the emergence of African-American women into public life during the nineteenth century.*

—Wm. Theodore de Bary

--~w~--

The day I arrived at Columbia was a memorable one, and I can still recall it vividly. It was a warm August afternoon, the kind of day when the campus is brimming with life. Students were taking advantage of the break in the academic calendar, many of them clad in swimwear and sprawled out on blankets.

Children were running up and down, transforming College Walk into a playground. I even remember a young woman whom I took to be a harried graduate student. You know the look. She emerged from the shadows of Butler Library with a heavy satchel tipping her to one side, her left arm loaded with books.

I had ridden the subway up from the Lower East Side, having escaped for the afternoon from my hectic law practice. By the time I arrived at 116th Street, I felt, as I often did in those days, bone tired. That summer I was marking my tenth year in the field of public-interest law. My work as an advocate for people with mental illness and people with HIV and AIDS required that I spend my days litigating cases in some of the city's grittiest courthouses. I believed I was fighting the good fight—saving a client's home or helping a dying mother plan for her children's future. Day in and day out, the *fight* was what had given my life deep meaning. But on that day I was walking away from all that and into the world of the university. As I stepped out in front of Low Library from the shade of the linden trees that usher you onto campus, I took in the scene, inhaled deeply, and knew something momentous was about to begin.

I had as much trepidation as I did anything else. I steeled myself as I climbed the steps of Low Library, silently invoking some of those who had walked the same path before me. There was my paternal grandfather, David Dallas Jones, who had come to Columbia as a young man to do his graduate work. There was my mother, Suzanne Y. Jones, a member of the inaugural cohort of Charles H. Revson Fellows on the Future of New York, who had studied here in 1979 and 1980 while caring for three high-spirited teenagers. As I imagined the journeys of graduates past, my mind turned to the experience of Thomas Merton, the poet, philosopher, and Trappist monk who had attended Columbia in the 1930s. Earlier that summer I had read his autobiography, *The Seven Storey Mountain*. In it Merton recounts how he had arrived in Morningside Heights as a young man who was somewhat adrift. By the time he left the university, he had discovered his spirituality (he was converted to Roman Catholicism at Corpus Christi Church on 121st Street), constructed an intellectual life, and filled his world with lasting friendships and an enduring sense of community. Merton's years at Columbia had been transformative, giving his life both a vocation and deep meaning.

When he later reflected on his time here, Merton wrote: "The thing I always liked best about Columbia was the sense that the university was, on the whole, glad to turn me loose in its library, its classrooms, and among its distinguished faculty, and let me make what I liked out of it all." But Merton knew that to be "turned loose" was a double-edged sword. At Columbia there are no easy answers for graduate students, no prescribed paths, and very little hand-holding. Each of us is left to make his or her own meanings out of the experience.

Merton was also mindful that, as he put it, "the least of the work of learning is done in classrooms." It was frequently in informal, often unplanned spaces that our moments of greatest insight came into being—in a diner sipping a bottomless cup of coffee, in a meeting planning a student event, or during a chance encounter in the library; during a conversation that extended long after a professor's office hours had expired, or in the early hours of the evening when things in the lab had quieted down. In these encounters that are not accounted for by residence units or

Martha S. Jones speaking on Thomas Merton to her fellow graduates at the GSAS Commencement Convocation in May 2002

credit hours, in these "scores of incidents, remarks, and happenings, that took place all over the campus and sometimes far from it," we experienced what Merton explained were for him "small bursts of light that pointed out his way in the dark" of his own identity.

Often what we ultimately take away from an experience such as graduate school is something that, at the outset, we did not even know we wanted or needed. This was certainly true for Merton, who could not have imagined that what awaited him on the other side of his studies was a lifetime of cloistered contemplation; he had aspired to be a writer of popular novels. And this has also been true for me. I arrived at Columbia seeking a historian's training, but I discovered my core, my essence, my insight, and it was about love. Now, back on that August afternoon when I first climbed the Low Library steps, you could not have told me that love was either what I wanted or what I needed. But I would have admitted to a type of longing that I think Merton also felt—a longing to find a new ethic, a philosophy of life, an essence that would better equip me for all that might lie ahead. And today I can confess that the most enduring facets of my Columbia experience have been the opportunities I have had to get and give love and to begin to see its transformative power at work in my life, in all of our lives.

The question that I want to ask you all to consider today is to what extent can our lives in a university community—as teachers, scholars, colleagues, and public figures—be lived through an ethic of love? Merton is instructive here because his vantage point as a cloistered thinker reminds us that love is far more than romantic happenstance. It is instead the highest expression of our humanity. He wrote: "Love is in fact an intensification of life, a completeness, a fullness, a wholeness of life. We do not live merely in order to vegetate through our days until we die. Nor do we live merely in order to take part in the routines of work and amusement that go on around us. . . . Life is not a straight horizontal line between two points, birth and death. Life reaches its high point of value and meaning when . . . the person transcends himself or herself in . . . communion with another. It is for this that we came into the world—this communion and self-transcendence. We do not become fully human until we give ourselves to each other in love."

Surely few of us chose doctoral study during the 1990s, of all times, because it was the ordinary or the obvious choice. We have all been asked to defend this decision—perhaps by a family member who believed we could be equally happy following a more "practical" path or at social gatherings, with the question, "But what are you going to do with that?" I suspect that the majority of us chose doctoral study because we were driven, we were drawn, we were called to do that which we loved and to do it well, even in the face of our loved ones' gentle skepticism. We are among the very people whom Merton had in mind when he imagined those most capable of love. We already know that life is not a straight path, because we have stumbled and struggled to come to this moment. And we know that life is not lived only in the realm of the routine, that, in its fullest, life is lived in those extraordinary moments when we come together—as teachers and learners, as thinkers and doers—to become more than we might ever be alone.

Many of us look forward to becoming teachers in our everyday lives—in classrooms and in labs, in public culture, and in communities. Educator Paolo Freire insists that a good teacher must include lovingness in his or her arsenal, and Freire would agree with Merton, I think, that an ethic of communion and self-transcendence can permit us, as teachers and students together, to accomplish radical objectives. But Freire goes further, urging us to adopt what he terms "armed love." For him, the challenge for the teacher, who is also a learner, is to be both "joyful and rigorous . . . to be serious, scientific, physical, and emotional." It is, he argues, impossible to teach without the courage to love, without the courage to try a thousand times before giving up. It is impossible to teach without a forged, invented, and well-thought-out capacity to love.

Freire's urgency is fueled, in part, by his deep interest in seeing that students experience the best learning possible, and for him love is essential to this end. But he is as deeply concerned with our survival, as teachers, in environments that are sometimes hostile, always demanding, and that invariably ask us to commit 100 percent, even as we are being continually subjected to the scrutiny of the tenure track. This can be a debilitating existence, and many of us have already witnessed those among us who bemoan their lot in the life of the academy, working tirelessly while never certain that promotion to tenure is within reach. If we recall Merton's admonition, it should be no surprise that such a narrow drive toward tenure is demoralizing. Life is not lived in a straight path between two points—birth and death—or, for us, between landing a faculty appointment and being awarded tenure. Life's meanings, its deep meanings, will not come in the routine pursuit of such an end. They will come instead in those extraordinary moments when we encounter, respond to, and work in communion with others.

How might we carry this ideal of love from the realm of the abstract into our lived experience? Legal scholar Derrick Bell offers the notion of "ethical ambition" in an effort to help us imagine how to put love into action. In his recent reflections on his career in the academy, Bell locates a space in which integrity and ambition might coexist—not to produce dissonance, but to manufacture a unique type of success that respects our core values and ethical convictions. For Bell, this means respecting our passions, mustering the courage to take risks, having the humility to see our mistakes, and relying on family, friends, and colleagues for the resources to weather difficult times. Bell's vision requires, above all else, that we challenge ourselves to be uncompromising, but not about the vagaries of any given moment. Instead, we must be uncompromising in our commitment to our own ethical view, and we must have the courage to speak that conviction and invite others to join us in it.

In my life it was my own grandmother, Susie Williams Jones, who put the fine point on my worldview. Having spent her adult life living and working on the campus of a small historically black college, she, too, offered an approach to daily life that was guided by an intimate sense of the ethical. She wrote: "It has always seemed important to me to give all I have to the things at hand—that the daily routines and the small happenings by the way are not means or paths to great undertakings, but are ends within themselves. Serving a meal, making a bed, bathing a child, preparing a paper for a club meeting, visiting a friend—daily routines have helped me to find myself." Rather than shunning the ordinary, we might embrace the routines of daily life with an ethic of self-transcendence that will allow us to realize our fullest humanity.

This challenge requires that we contemplate not only our relationships with students, but also our relationships with peers—in faculty meetings and through committee assignments, in conferences and through writing groups, in the university

Senate and through peer review. What would it mean, as we traverse these spaces, to replace an ethic of cynicism, a narrative of overwhelmedness, or a worldview of petty competition, with a spirit of communion and self-transcendence? As I implore you to do, I challenge myself to strive for the greatest meaning in a culture that already offers us so many opportunities to know love.

When I returned to College Walk this week, it had been nearly nine months since I was at Columbia. I found myself sometimes alone, at other times with a friend, wandering from building to building, office to office, greeting many of the people who worked so hard to make our accomplishments possible. These days I take my daily walk in another place, at the University of Michigan, on what we call "The Diag." There I am steeled, not through the invocation of those who walked there before me, but by my own experience, and by the relationships I forged at Columbia. Every moment of communion and self-transcendence, every moment of love, both given and received, has strengthened and emboldened me. I take those moments with me, and I strive to replicate them again and again. This is why I get up in the morning, and it is what I bring to my classroom and even the most challenging of faculty meetings. This is why I stand before you this afternoon. This is how I make meaning out of my life. I leave here with so very much more than I ever hoped for—I have learned the pedagogy of love.

PART TWO

THE SCIENCES

CHAPTER 12

Edmund Beecher Wilson: America's First Cell Biologist

—⁓—

Qais Al-Awqati

In his Living Legacies essay on Thomas Hunt Morgan and the origins of biology, Eric Kandel notes the importance of Edmund Beecher Wilson to Morgan's work. When Morgan arrived on campus, Kandel says, "he came under the influence of his long-term friend and colleague, the zoology department's chairman, Edmund Wilson, one of the eminent cytologists of his time and a founder of the field of cell biology. Wilson convinced Morgan that the key to understanding development—how one cell, the egg, gives rise to the animal—is to understand heredity, since it provides the means by which the egg and the sperm carry the properties of individuals from one generation to another."

In the present essay on Wilson, Qais Al-Awqati, M.D., Robert F. Loeb Professor of Medicine and professor of physiology and cellular biophysics in the College of Physicians and Surgeons, fills out the picture of Wilson as a giant in his own right; as the chair of the department who, in his pioneering work on cell biology, set the direction for a whole new field; and as a teacher in Columbia College trained a generation of brilliant scholars, many of whom went on to work with Morgan. Wilson may be thought of as one of the first cell biologists, in the modern sense of the phrase, who used microscopy to answer what we now call molecular questions. Al-Awqati was born and raised in Baghdad, Iraq, where he obtained his medical degree. He completed his training at Johns Hopkins and Harvard. His research focuses on the mechanism by which cells control the location of ion-transporting proteins.

—Wm. Theodore de Bary

—⁓—

When Seth Low became president of Columbia College in 1890, it marked the beginning of some of the most dramatic changes in the institution's history—from the move to Morningside Heights in 1897 to a major restructuring and expansion of the existing faculties and schools.

Low also placed a new emphasis on scientific research at Columbia and served as a guiding influence in establishing the zoology department in 1891 as well as the new School of Pure Science a year later. The new dean of the School was Henry Fairfield Osborn, who had recently recruited to the zoology department a thirty-five-year-old biologist from Bryn Mawr named Edmund Beecher Wilson.

Wilson would eventually lead the department and become one of the most influential cell biologists of all time. His own research and leadership paved the way for the groundbreaking work of future Nobel Prize winners Thomas Hunt Morgan and Hermann Muller and elevated the department of zoology at Columbia to a position of international prominence.

Wilson was born in Geneva, Illinois, in 1856. He later wrote of his childhood: "It would not be easy to imagine a happier environment for a boy who somehow managed to combine a passion for natural history with an almost equal love for music."

At the age of sixteen Wilson taught for a year at a country school. The following summer he reached a decision that would change the course of his life. Inspired by conversations with his cousin Sam Clarke, who was a student at Antioch College, Wilson decided to "try for a college education and a life devoted to biology." He enrolled at Antioch but one year later followed in Clarke's footsteps and transferred to Yale. He was offered a position there when he graduated, but his cousin was giving him glowing reports about graduate study at Johns Hopkins, so he applied there and obtained a fellowship to study biology. Wilson carried out most of his graduate work at Johns Hopkins under the tutelage of William Keith Brooks. About Brooks, he wrote: "From him I learned how closely biological problems are bound up with philosophical considerations. . . . He taught me to think about the phenomena of life instead of merely trying to record and classify them." After Wilson obtained

his Ph.D. in 1881, he decided to study in Europe for a year. With a loan from his brother, he sailed for England, where he met some of the most important British scientists at that time, such as Thomas Henry Huxley, Adam Sedgwick, W. H. Caldwell, and William Bateson.

While studying at Johns Hopkins, Wilson had heard of the Zoological Station in Naples. The station had been established by a group of European institutions to investigate critical problems in phylogeny and evolution. German biologists, the dominant force in research at the time, flocked to Naples, and its director, Anton Dohrn, was an important figure in the field. Wilson desperately wanted to do research at the Zoological Station but could not afford the dues of renting a table in the laboratory. Eventually Clarke, by now a professor at Williams College, came up with the solution: Williams College would rent a table, and Clarke and Wilson would split the time if Wilson would teach Clarke's courses at Williams during his absence.

In Naples the sun and scenery of southern Italy had its customary effect on a "northern" scholar, driving him, as it did Goethe 100 years earlier, into lyrical flights. Wilson wrote, "That first year in Naples—it was not quite a year—was the most wonderful year of my life. I despair of conveying any notion of what it meant to me, and still means as I look back upon it through the haze of fifty years. It was a rich combination of serious effort, new friendships, incomparable beauty of scenery, a strange and piquant civilization, a new and charming language, new vistas of scientific work opening before me; in short a realization of my wildest, most unreal dreams."

He completed his agreement with Williams College on his return, and after a year of teaching at MIT he was appointed in 1885 as the first chairman of the biology department at Bryn Mawr. He stayed there for six years before he received the offer from Columbia and eventually helped Bryn Mawr recruit his replacement, Thomas Hunt Morgan, a man ten years younger, who had also studied at Johns Hopkins. (Wilson would eventually recruit Morgan to Columbia.)

Columbia allowed Wilson to travel in Europe for a year before he assumed his teaching duties, and that year was a *Wanderjahr* spent in Naples and in Munich, a year that changed his research program from investigations of phylogeny and evolutionary biology to cell biology and experimental embryology. This was in no small part due to the influence of Theodor Boveri in Munich, who became Wilson's closest friend. Boveri, an amateur musician and painter, was a brilliant experimentalist who later demonstrated that each individual chromosome conferred hereditary properties on daughter cells. Wilson said, "The best thing that he gave me was at the Café Heck, where we used to dine together, drinking wonderful Bavarian beer, playing billiards, and talking endlessly about all manner of things." On Wilson's return to New York, he began spending his summers at the newly established Marine Biological Laboratory in Woods Hole, Massachusetts, where he met his future wife, Anne Kidder. He then settled into a life of research and teaching that lasted forty years.

Wilson left few notes describing his life and times. He was described as "a quiet gentleman" even in his obituary in the *Herald Tribune*. But the warm feelings expressed in the many memoirs by his colleagues and students attest to his gift for friendship.

CELL BIOLOGY AND DEVELOPMENT IN THE LATE 1800s

The last quarter of the nineteenth century saw the widespread acceptance of the cell theory or the notion that all living things are composed of cells. Evolution provided the other major foundation for biology, and many researchers asked questions about how organisms and their parts become adapted to their environments and what causes homologies, or similarities in parts, across species. Since Darwin, researchers had often focused on vertebrates and asked about their evolutionary past and relationships to other species. This is especially interesting, obviously, because it is about the origins of humans. When the German popularizer of evolutionary theory Ernst Haeckel stated that individual organisms pass through the same stages in their development as species did in their evolutionary past (or the so-called biogenetic law according to which "ontogeny recapitulates phylogeny"), some saw this as a key research tool. Now they could learn about the evolutionary origin of vertebrates by studying individual development through embryology. Haeckel held that the first important stage of individual development is when the embryo forms three germ layers, namely the ectoderm, mesoderm, and endoderm. At this point, it is called a *gastrula*, and Haeckel hypothesized that the earliest stage of evolution of vertebrates was a *gastrea* just like this embryonic stage.

While some biologists, especially in Germany, found this an enticing interpretation, Wilson launched one of the most effective challenges. His studies of cell lineage, in which he traced what happens to every cell as the egg divides into two, then four, eight, and more cells up to the gastrula stage, showed serious inconsistencies in what Wilson and many of his American contemporaries saw as Haeckel's speculative and unwarranted hypothesis. These cell lineage studies, carried out by Wilson and his colleagues largely at the Marine Biological Laboratory, established our basic understanding of cell division. Wilson saw these early divisions as products of both heredity and adaptation to surrounding conditions. As he put it, "The form of cell division is determined by two factors. The first factor is the inherited tendency of the cell to pursue a definite course, a tendency that we may assume exists by virtue of a corresponding molecular or protoplasmic structure. The second factor is the influence upon the cell of other cells in the colony. When the second factor is removed or modified, the first is correspondingly modified, and a complete readjustment takes place." This was written in 1892, but one could not ask for a more modern view of cellular development.

Two biologists from Columbia, Wilson and Thomas Hunt Morgan, and Wilson's friend Boveri provided major contributions on which modern genetics and cell

biology are based. Wilson pointed to "two fundamental questions which still remain in their essence without an adequate answer though metamorphosed. . . . The first of these is whether the embryo exists preformed or predelineated in the egg from the beginning or whether it is formed anew, step by step in each generation. The second question is that of mechanism versus vitalism—whether development is capable of a mechanical or physico-chemical explanation or whether it involves specific vital forces that are without analogy in the non-living world." The second he felt had been decided in favor of mechanism and physico-chemical explanation. The first remained.

If preformation occurs, then the form must be there in the fertilized egg cell since that is the beginning of every organism. Where was it? Wilson carried out meticulous studies of the egg from its very beginning. By the 1890s, he used important technical refinements in optical microscopy, staining, and tissue sectioning, which put him in a position to perform incisive experiments to carry out careful observations of just what happens at each step of development. His beautiful drawings and clear, eloquent writing helped to convince others. His friend Boveri, to whom Wilson dedicated his most important book, also contributed to interpreting the role of the nucleus and chromosomes. Boveri demonstrated that when the

Seth Low, Columbia's twelfth president, set the stage for a new generation of progressive research in the biological sciences when he oversaw the creation of a zoology department in 1891.

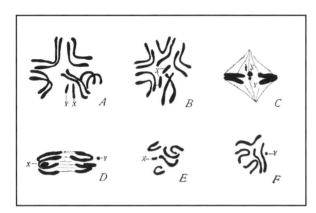

nuclei of one species of sea urchin were transplanted into cell fragments of another, the resulting embryos followed the characteristics of the species from which the nucleus was taken. Morgan translated this paper into English but doubted that the experiments were correct. He himself failed to reproduce the results. Because he had found that removal of a part of the cytoplasm of a fertilized egg resulted in an imperfect embryo, he thought that the cytoplasm controlled development. However, Boveri came back with even more extensive results confirming his view of the primacy of the nucleus. He later extended these studies in a series of celebrated experiments in which sea urchin eggs were fertilized with two sperms: he found that after two cleavages, each of the separated blastomeres had different numbers of chromosomes, and each had different anomalies—leading him to conclude that the chromosomes, located in the nucleus, were the agent of heredity. Wilson agreed, concluding in a remarkably prescient comment that "chromatin is . . . nuclein, which analysis shows . . . to be composed of a nucleic acid, a complex organic acid rich in phosphorus. And thus we reach the remarkable conclusion that inheritance may perhaps be affected by the physical transmission of a particular chemical compound from parent to offspring." This was written in 1895, five years before the rediscovery of Mendel's laws.

Several investigators attempted to determine the role of chromosomes in sex determination. The initial findings were somewhat confusing, largely due to the use of different organisms and staining procedures. Thomas Montgomery was the first to propose that chromosomes play the most important role in determining what sex an individual organism will be. In 1902, Clarence Erwin McClung, a professor at the

University of Kansas and a former student of Wilson's, identified a body in grasshopper nuclei that he called an "accessory chromosome" because he found it in only half of the sperm cells. He concluded that it had to do with sex determination, since male grasshoppers had one more chromosome than the females. In 1902, a student of McClung's named W. S. Sutton enrolled as a graduate student at Columbia and worked with Wilson, studying chromosomes and their role in heredity.

Thomas Hunt Morgan

Wilson performed his own important studies on the role of chromosomes in sex determination between 1905 and 1912. He counted and identified the chromosomes of sperm cells before and after the reduction division. Wilson and a former student of Morgan's named Nettie Stevens (then at Bryn Mawr) simultaneously but independently performed the definitive studies that demonstrated the role of chromosomes in sex determination. Wilson found that in two insects the female has one more chromosome than the male, while Stevens found that the male has a smaller Y chromosome in one half of the sperm while a larger chromosome went to the other half. The type found by Stevens (XX for females and XY for males) was much more frequent than the type found by Wilson (XX for females and XO for males). These findings form the basis for our modern view of sex determination and formed the beginning of our general chromosomal understanding of heredity. Wilson's paper was submitted ten days before Stevens's and was published two months before in *The Journal of Experimental Zoology*. But Wilson added a footnote stating that he was aware of Stevens's studies ("now in the course of publication . . . by whose kind permission I am able to refer to her results") and described them briefly. He also concluded that "McClung's hypothesis may, in the end, prove to be well founded."

Morgan, in contrast, did not accept this conclusion; he argued that a French scientist Cuenot had demonstrated that a mouse mutant in hair color (now called agouti) failed to give pure yellow-colored mice on repeated crossbreeding with black mice, "demonstrating" the lack of Mendelian inheritance. (Studies in the past decade have shown, however, that the reason is that mice homozygous at the lethal yellow agouti locus die in utero at the preimplantation stage, which explains the absence of purebred yellow mice). By 1911, however, Morgan discovered that eye

Hermann Muller, who studied under Wilson, went on to win a Nobel Prize in 1946 for the discovery that X-rays cause mutations. Of Wilson he wrote, "His students meant very much to him, and he took his responsibilities in connection to them very seriously."

color, body color, wing shape, and sex in the fruit fly all segregated together with the X chromosome, and hence he was forced to agree with the Mendelian nature of chromosomal inheritance, against which he had fought for over a decade.

Wilson and Morgan also rapidly extended their findings to human genetic diseases when each separately concluded that color blindness in the published pedigrees follows Mendelian inheritance. Morgan stated that color blindness "follows the same scheme as does white eyes in my flies," and Wilson referred to the same conclusion in an equally brief note. This apparently was the first definite specification of the linkage of a characteristic in man with the sex chromosome.

Despite their differences of biological interpretations at times, these two Columbia professors were neither competitive nor antagonistic in their personal interactions. Nothing could be further from the truth; they were intimate friends at every level. According to developmental biologist Ross Granville Harrison, "Wilhelm Ostwald in his interesting book on great men of science classified them according to their talents as romantics and classics. . . . To the romantic, ideas come thick and fast; they must find quick expression. His first care is to get a problem off his hands to make room for the next. The classic is more concerned with the perfection of his product, with setting his ideas in proper relation to each other and to the main body of science. His impulse is to work over his subject so exhaustively and perfectly that no contemporary is able to improve upon it. . . . It is the romantic that revolutionizes, while the classic builds from the ground up. Wilson is a striking example of the classic, and it is interesting to note that for many years his nearest colleague and closest friend (Morgan) was an equally distinguished romantic."

Wilson wrote *The Cell in Inheritance and Development* as a set of lecture notes for his first course in cell biology when he came to Columbia. It went through three editions, the last published in 1927. The field was undergoing such rapid change that much of the information was outdated by publication time, but the textbook was enormously influential nonetheless. In each section, he surveyed the field and identified the major questions in clear and muscular prose; he was also admirably fair in setting the historical context. But most significantly, his arguments for or against a hypothesis were clear and commanding. When the evidence itself was unclear, Wilson suggested his own interpretations, most of which turned out to be correct when later studies provided more decisive results. He left no doubt where he stood on unresolved questions, an approach that gave the text the wonderful flavor of a conversation with an agile mind. By concentrating a large part of the book on the role of the cell as an agent of heredity, he provided a focus for a field that was full of disparate information and random descriptions. Its reception as a signal contribution helped shift the balance of power away from the German investigators. The last edition received a highly unusual honor—the Elliott Medal from the U.S. National Academy of Sciences—the first and only time a textbook was so honored.

WILSON THE TEACHER

Some scientists may say that they want only to uncover the secrets of nature, but the added glory of influence on the thoughts and works of their peers must be an added bonus. (Skeptics might call it the driving force behind their commitment to work.) Yet such influence is difficult to measure. In their own publications, scientists generally refer only to the most recent work of others, and papers published just five years ago often seem to disappear into a realm of quiet obscurity. But the influence that teachers have on their young (or not so young) students has a far longer "time constant" than most publications. One hears it at celebrations and Festschrifts of retiring scientists. Wilson makes a superb case study of this influence. He took his teaching responsibilities seriously, and the comments published by his students stress his personal involvement and the care he took in preparing his lectures. He supervised the teaching throughout his department and had a tremendous influence in shaping the thinking of a generation of influential biologists.

Hermann Muller, who went on to win the Nobel Prize for discovering the role of X-rays in causing mutations, reflected this influence in a memoir of his days as a student:

> The excitement of the advances in chromosomal theory made by Wilson from 1905 to 1910 communicated itself through the Department of Zoology at Columbia. This helps to explain why it was that most of the first batch of youngsters who became *Drosophila* workers with Morgan had been undergraduates in Columbia College in the latter part of this period and others came through by the same route afterwards. Lured on by their first course in biology, where they were molded by William Sedgwick and Wilson's text and by the teaching of Gary Calkins and James McGregor, both former students of Wilson's, some of them had the privilege of taking in their sophomore year Wilson's thrilling one-semester course on heredity and the chromosomes, variation and evolution. They usually took Wilson's superb course on cytology, with its unequalled laboratory training and demonstrations, in their third or fourth year after entering as freshmen. After this stimulating and thoroughly systematic preparation, their embarking upon the adventure of the fascinating new work on chromosomal heredity in *Drosophila* that had just been opened up by Morgan (1910 and 1911) was the logical continuation, now grown more specific in its direction, of the quest to which they had already become dedicated, calling for the ways of thinking, the knowledge and to some extent even the technique acquired during their previous years of training. And the striking similarity in the attitude of all of them toward the new problems was in no small measure a reflection of the degree to which this common training has been driven home. Thus it is likely that only these *Drosophila* workers, of the earlier years, fully realize to what an extent modern genetics traces its descent through Wilson.

Alfred Henry Sturtevant similarly noted that "no small part of the success of the undertaking (Morgan's *Drosophila* work) was due also to Wilson's unfailing support and appreciation of the work—a matter of importance partly because he was the head of the department."

At Woods Hole, "Wilson played the role of elder brother," wrote Frank R. Lillie, the embryologist who would go on to become president of the Marine Biological Laboratory. Lillie was thrilled by Wilson's remark to him in 1891: "I believe I am going to destroy the germ layer theory of development." To an eager student of twenty-one engaged in his first investigation, there was something sacrosanct about this theory, in which he had been indoctrinated as an undergraduate student; this remark taught him the difference between scientific theory and dogma.

Wilson also played a large role in recommending younger scientists for positions in other institutions. The most famous, Morgan, took Wilson's place at Bryn Mawr and then was recruited by Wilson to Columbia. Marcella O'Grady, who graduated from MIT in biology under Wilson's tutelage, was then recruited by him to Bryn Mawr. She later chaired the biology department at Vassar College. On Wilson's recommendation, she went on a European tour, where she worked with Boveri. They rapidly established a solid working relationship that evolved into a romantic attachment. They were married within the year and had a fruitful working collaboration that lasted many years. On his untimely death she returned to the United States, where she became the chair of biology at Albertus Magnus College in New Haven. There she translated her husband's book on the chromosome theory of cancer, which focused attention on the origin of cancer as a problem of cellular proliferation, a precursor of the view that we still hold today.

Wilson said he owed to music "some of the greatest pleasures of my life." Above with his beloved cello.

WILSON'S LOVE FOR MUSIC

It seems that everybody in Wilson's family played an instrument. His father played the violin and cello, his mother and sister played the piano (as did both of his aunts), and his brother Charles was a violinist. Wilson began by taking singing lessons, and although he did not have a good singing voice, he says that these lessons left him "with an inveterate habit of reading all of music in do re mi language." He learned to play the flute, but when he went to Johns Hopkins, he developed a lifelong passion for playing the cello. He wrote, "I was too old to take up so difficult an instrument with any hope of mastering it." But he eventually became an accomplished cellist and reveled in playing quartets in Bryn Mawr, Philadelphia, and New York. His friend Anton Dohrn, the director of the Zoological Station, was also "music mad"; he introduced him to the musical society of Berlin, where he came to know Joseph Joachim and the brothers Robert and Felix Mendelssohn, who "between them owned a whole quartet of fine Stradivari fiddles." He wrote, "Music has always seemed to me to be the most mysterious of fine arts, a language sui generis and one that cannot really be translated into words." He also said, "I have always loved music, and to it I owe some of the greatest pleasures of my life." Another of his greatest pleasures was watching his daughter, Nancy, develop into a fine professional cellist.

CELL BIOLOGY AND DEVELOPMENTAL BIOLOGY, THEN AND NOW

Wilson's books are peppered with terms such as "cellular biology," and he may have been the first to use it. The title of his magnum opus, however, was *The Cell in Development and Inheritance*. The two fields of cell and developmental biology started as one, led by Wilson and Boveri with the aim of providing a cellular basis for the mechanisms of inheritance.

Wilson is credited with being the first American cell biologist; indeed, the American Society for Cell Biology awards an E. B. Wilson medal every year to a distinguished cell biologist. But his contributions are best described in Gilbert's *Developmental Biology*, the standard textbook in the field. He remains an ancestor to both fields. Cell biology diverged from the study of development when the new methods of cell culture—the electron microscope, radioisotopes, and the ultracentrifuge—were developed. These new technologies allowed its practitioners to concentrate more on the biochemical basis of the components of the cell and the function of the proteins in complex cellular events such as the biogenesis of organelles, cell division, and cell-to-cell interaction. Developmental biology and embryology concentrated on the original problems of morphogenesis, induction, and patterning, helped by the ease of manipulation of some large embryos and fueled by the remarkable advances in genetics of model organisms such as fruit flies, worms, zebra fish, and now the mouse. But it is remarkable how much overlap there has always been between the two fields, and it continues to increase, as a brief perusal of the major journals of each field would show. Yeast genetics, which played an important role in cell biology and developmental biology, is becoming increasingly focused on the function of individual proteins in the context of a multicomponent signal transduction pathway. Thus the future of the two fields harkens back to their origins. The revolution produced by the discovery of DNA and the development of methods of its manipulation has affected every field of biology.

Now that we are in the "post-genome" era, it is pretty clear that the problems of cell and developmental biology need to be addressed with a new perspective. DNA encouraged biologists to think reductively, but cell and developmental biology have shown that the problems of real cells and organisms are produced by complex systems of interaction. These new views of complexity bring us back to the Wilsonian ideal, where the unit of heredity is the cell. Perhaps this is the reason why science historian Jane Maienschein, in discussing the future of biological research in its second century in an essay entitled "Old Wine in New Bottles," found that Wilson's agenda of research is the same as that of today's biologists, whose study of evolution, inheritance, and development is solidly based on understanding the structure and function of cells.

For bibliography, see Notes, pages 657–658.

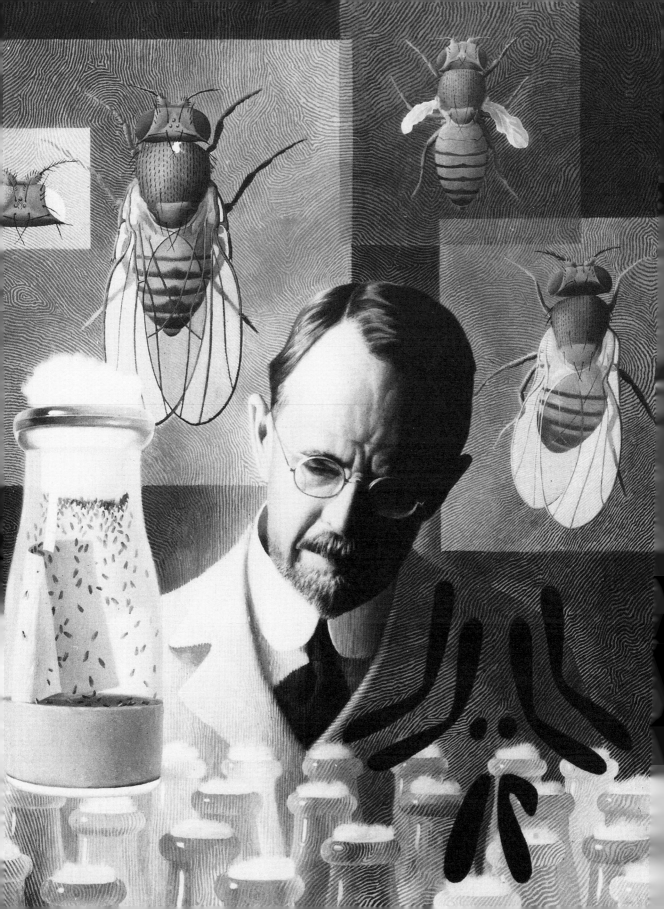

CHAPTER 13

Biology at Columbia

—⁓—

Eric Kandel and Darcy B. Kelley

These three essays on biology at Columbia inaugurated the Living Legacies *series in Columbia magazine back in 1999. All three were written by Eric Kandel, M.D., the third coauthored with Darcy Kelley, Ph.D.*

Eric R. Kandel, a senior investigator at the Howard Hughes Medical Institute, has held the highest academic rank at Columbia, that of University Professor, since 1983. In 2004 Kandel was named Fred Kavli Professor and director, Kavli Institute for Brain Sciences. A graduate of Harvard College and the New York University School of Medicine, Kandel trained in neurobiology at the National Institutes of Health and in psychiatry at the Harvard Medical School. He held appointments at Harvard and NYU before coming to Columbia in 1974. He joined the faculty of the College of Physicians and Surgeons as professor of physiology and psychiatry and as founding director of the Center for Neurobiology and Behavior. Together with James H. Schwartz and Thomas Jessell of the Center for Neurobiology and Behavior, Kandel has coauthored Principles of Neural Science, *now in its fourth edition, generally considered the standard textbook in the field.*

Kandel's research has opened up the molecular biological study of memory storage and delineated a genetic switch whereby short-term memory is converted to long-term memory. In recognition of his accomplishments, Kandel has received honorary degrees from fifteen universities. He has been elected to the U.S. National Academy of Sciences as well as to the National Academies of Germany, France, Greece, and Austria. He also has been recognized by a number of major scientific awards, including the Albert Lasker Basic Medical Research Award, the Harvey Prize and the Wolf Prize in Medicine and Biology of Israel, the Gairdner Award of Canada, the Dr. A. H. Heineken Prize for Medicine of the Netherlands, and the National Medal of Science.

In 2000, Kandel was awarded the Nobel Prize in physiology or medicine for his discoveries of the molecular mechanisms of memory storage. Using the nervous system of a sea slug as an experimental model, he has demonstrated that changes in synaptic function are essential for learning and memory. He discovered that short-term memory is the result of protein phosphorylation at synapses that results in the strengthening of preexisting synaptic connections. Long-term memory, he found, requires gene expression, new protein synthesis, and the growth of new synaptic connections.

Dr. Darcy B. Kelley is professor of biological sciences at Columbia and codirector of the university's doctoral program in neurobiology and behavior, a joint initiative between neurobiologists on the Morningside and Health Sciences campuses. After earning her undergraduate degree from Barnard, she received her Ph.D. from The Rockefeller University and served on the faculty there and at Princeton before coming to Columbia in 1982.

Known for her commitment to bringing together research and teaching in both the classroom and laboratory, Professor Kelley is the author of more than 100 scientific articles. Her research uses the South African clawed frog, Xenopus laevis, *to study the neurobiology of social communication, with the goal of determining how one brain communicates with another and to study sexual differentiation, the hormone-directed developmental program that leads to male and female phenotypes. Darcy Kelley and her colleagues at Columbia University have pioneered a new Core course in science for all entering Columbia College students: Frontiers of Science. She is the editor of the* Journal of Neurobiology *and was elected a fellow of the American Association for the Advancement of Science in 1989. Dr. Kelley currently holds an HHMI Professor's Award from the Howard Hughes Medical Institute. She was the 2003 Forbes Lecturer for the Grass Foundation at the Marine Biological Laboratory. Dr. Kelley is a trustee of the Marine Biological Laboratory and consultant to the Hughes, Sloan, and Wenner-Gren Foundations.*

—*Wm. Theodore de Bary*

Thomas Hunt Morgan at Columbia University

Eric Kandel

The student of the humanities as well as the intelligent public looks at the history of human thought as a history of abstract ideas. . . . It is true that minds like those of Plato, Thomas Aquinas, Spinoza, Descartes, Hegel and Kant have exercised a strong influence upon the progress of thinking in all spheres, even upon the actual course of historical events. The scientist who looks beyond his specialized work is as fully aware of these historical facts as the humanist. But he is also aware that abstract thinking, remote from, and even antagonistic to the study of nature, leads easily into dogma, taboos and fettering of free thinking because it does not carry its own corrective, the recourse to factual evidence. The scientist, therefore, with all respect for the many facets of the human mind, is more impressed by the revolutions in thinking brought about by great factual discoveries, which by their very nature lead to generalizations which change at once the outlook of many, if not all, lines of thought. Such events are rare. In modern history three are most conspicuous: the explanation of the movements of the celestial bodies by Kepler, Copernicus and Newton; Galileo's experiments inaugurating the age of inductive science; and Darwin's establishment of the theory of evolution on the basis of an overwhelming body of facts. All of them at once evoked the wrath of the vested interests of the mind; all conquered within a generation or two all fields of intellectual endeavor and changed the basic aspects of practically every science, natural or humanistic.

. . . The rise and development of genetics to mature age is another instance of an all-comprising and all-affecting generalization based upon an overwhelming body of integrated facts, . . . [and] will rank in the history of science with such other great events as mentioned, . . . The basic tenets of genetics have already influenced decisively all parts of biology after what has been only a short span in the history of science; and further that beyond this, many other fields of science have fallen under the spell and we have every reason to believe that genetics is bound to remain in a pivotal position in the future.

—Richard B. Goldschmidt, *The Impact of Genetics Upon Science* (1950)

When future historians turn to examine the major intellectual accomplishments of the twentieth century, they will undoubtedly give a special place to the extraordinary achievements in biology, achievements that have revolutionized our understanding of life's processes and of disease. Important intimations of what was to happen in biology were already apparent in the second half of the nineteenth century. Darwin had delineated the evolution of animal species; Mendel had discovered some basic rules about inheritance; and Weissman, Roux, Driesch, de Vries, and other embryologists were beginning to decipher how an organism develops from a single cell. What was lacking at the end of the nineteenth century, however, was an overarching sense of how these bold advances were related to one another.

The insight that unified these three fields—heredity, evolution, and development—and set biology on the course toward its current success came only at the beginning of the twentieth century. It derived from the discovery that the gene, localized to specific positions on the chromosome, was at once the unit of Mendelian heredity, the driving force for Darwinian evolution, and the control switch for development. This remarkable discovery can be traced directly to one person and to one institution: Thomas Hunt Morgan and Columbia University. Much as Darwin's insights into the evolution of animal species first gave coherence to nineteenth-century biology as a descriptive science, Morgan's findings about genes and their location on chromosomes helped transform biology into an experimental science.

Even more important, Morgan's discoveries made it possible to address a series of questions regarding the function and structure of genes. What is their chemical nature? How do genes duplicate themselves? What goes wrong when genes mutate? How do genes provide the basis for understanding genetic disease? How do genes determine the properties of cells, the development of organisms, and the course of evolution? Answers to some of these questions came directly from Morgan and his students, while other advances were the work of scientists touched by his broader influence. In every case, the discoveries made by these pioneering researchers set the agenda for biology in the twentieth century.

For example, George Beadle, who trained with Morgan and with Morgan's student Alfred H. Sturtevant, joined Edward L. Tatum to examine how genes determine the properties of the cell. In addressing this problem, they discovered that genes control the synthesis of the cell's proteins, many of which are enzymes. Then Oswald T. Avery, another graduate of Columbia, teamed with Maclyn McCarty and Colin MacLeod at the Rockefeller Institute for Medical Research to show that the transforming genetic material is made of DNA. Theodosius Dobzhansky, a postdoctoral fellow of Morgan's, related genetic mutations to evolutionary change. Hermann J. Muller, another Morgan student, discovered that X-irradiation dramatically increases the rate at which mutations occur, an advance that focused attention on the role of environmentally induced and inherited gene mutations in important diseases ranging from cancer to Huntington's disease and schizophrenia. Joshua Lederberg, an academic grandchild of Morgan, discovered transduction—the ability of viruses to carry exogenous genes into a bacterial cell—the first step on the road to genetic engineering. James D. Watson and Francis Crick next showed that DNA has a double helical conformation, a chemical conformation that immediately led to an understanding of how DNA and genes are replicated. Edward B. Lewis, another academic grandchild of Morgan, used genetics to probe development and found that a special set of genes determines the organization of the body plan. Thus, biology at the beginning of the twenty-first century represents, in good part, the molecular realization of the ideas and way of thinking introduced at the beginning of the twentieth century by Thomas Hunt Morgan at Columbia University.

MORGAN AND THE MECHANISMS OF
MENDELIAN HEREDITY

Thomas Hunt Morgan was born in Kentucky in 1866 to a distinguished southern family whose members included Francis Scott Key. Morgan was trained as a developmental biologist, receiving his Ph.D. in 1890 from The Johns Hopkins University for work on the development of sea spiders, a specialized group of invertebrate animals, and in 1891 he accepted a teaching post at Bryn Mawr College.

In 1904 Columbia University announced the establishment of a new chair in experimental zoology and offered it to Morgan. Arriving on campus, he came under the influence of his long-time friend and colleague, the zoology department's chairman, Edwin Wilson, one of the eminent cytologists of his time and a founder of the field of cell biology. Wilson convinced Morgan that the key to understanding development—how one cell, the egg, gives rise to the animal—is to understand heredity, since it provides the means by which the egg and the sperm carry the properties of individuals from one generation to another.

Later findings proved Wilson correct, and we now know that the human genome consists of forty-six chromosomes, arranged in twenty-two pairs of autosomes (not linked to sex), and one pair of sex chromosomes (two X chromosomes in females, one X and one Y chromosome in males). The 100,000 genes in our genome are arranged along the chromosomes in precise order, with each being uniquely identifiable by its location at a characteristic position (*locus*) on a specific chromosome. The two copies of a gene at corresponding loci on each pair of chromosomes are known as *alleles*.

The modern concepts of heredity and the existence of alternative (*allelic*) forms of genes had been discovered in 1865 by Gregor Mendel, a teacher and monk of the Augustinian monastery in Brno, then part of the Austro-Hungarian empire. Mendel carried out breeding experiments with plants, especially garden peas, and identified hereditary traits in them. These traits, later called *factors*, were found by Mendel to account for such features as whether peas were wrinkled or smooth and for the differences between dominant and recessive alleles; he did not know, however, where these traits were located or what they were. Mendel's findings were published in the *Proceedings of the Natural Science Society of Brno* in 1866, only to be ignored until the turn of the century. His work was rediscovered in 1900, just before Morgan arrived at Columbia.

In taking up his own inquiries, Morgan turned from Mendel's plants to the study of animals but soon found that the rats and mice he was using reproduced so slowly as to be impractical for studying heredity. His search for a more suitable organism led him to *Drosophila melanogaster*, known as the fruit fly because it feeds on decaying fruit. Drosophila is small, about 3 mm long, and easy to raise in the laboratory—a thousand can be collected in a one-quart glass milk bottle. Moreover, it is fertile all year long and very prolific, producing a new generation every twelve days, or thirty generations per year. Not only are male and female offspring easy to distinguish, but embryonic development occurs outside the body, making it a simple matter to study the effects of mutations on development. Finally, Drosophila has only four pairs of chromosomes.

Morgan began working seriously with Drosophila in 1907, with the intention of breeding many generations of flies and perhaps producing one that looked different from the rest. In short, he hoped to find an occasional fly that had undergone a mutation, sudden change in body form, a phenomenon that had recently been discovered in plants by the Dutch biologist Hugo de Vries. But despite much effort and the breeding of successive generations, Morgan initially failed to detect a single mutation. "Two years work wasted," he lamented to one visitor to his laboratory. "I have been breeding those flies for all that time and I've got nothing out of it." (R. G. Harrison, "Embryology and Its Relations")

YEAR OF DISCOVERY

But Morgan persisted, and in April 1910 he suddenly had a breakthrough. In one of his bottles filled with Drosophila was a male fly with white eyes rather than the normal red eyes. Morgan realized the implications of this immediately; the birth of this single spontaneous mutant—*this one male fly with white eyes*—allowed him to begin addressing some key questions in heredity: How did this white eye color originate? What determines eye color?

As the next step, Morgan bred this white-eyed (mutant) male to a red-eyed (wild-type) virgin sister and found that white-colored eyes are inherited in a special way. In the first generation of brother-sister mating, labeled F1, there were only red-eyed offsprings, suggesting that red eye color is *dominant* and that white eye color is *recessive*. To prove this idea Morgan carried out brother-sister matings with the next generation (F2) and found that the offspring followed the expected Mendelian ratio for a recessive trait: three red-eyed flies to every one white-eyed fly. With these experiments Morgan started a tradition, which continues to this day, whereby he named the gene "white" by the result of its mutation. But then came a surprise. He had expected there would be an equal number of males and females with white eyes, but it turned out that all the female flies had red eyes; only males had white eyes, and, even more, only some of them displayed the trait. Morgan realized that white eye color is not only recessive but is also linked in some way to sex. The subsequent appearance of two other spontaneous mutations (rudimentary wings and yellow body color) also linked to sex further suggested to Morgan that these three genes might be carried on the same chromosome and that this chromosome is the sex chromosome.

By 1910, it was already known that chromosomes occur in pairs and that Drosophila had four pairs of chromosomes. Several decades earlier, these thread-shaped structures had been seen under a microscope to be located in the nucleus, but nobody knew their function. Morgan later was to describe them in the following terms:

Thomas Hunt Morgan at Columbia, 1917

> The egg of every species of animal or plant carries a definite number of bodies called chromosomes. The sperm carries the same number. Consequently, when the sperm unites with the egg, the fertilized egg will contain the double number of chromosomes. For each chromosome contributed by the sperm there is a corresponding chromosome contributed by the egg, i.e., there are two chromosomes of each kind, which together constitute a pair. (T. H. Morgan et al., *The Mechanism of Mendelian Heredity*)

When Morgan turned to examining the fruit fly's chromosomes under the microscope, he immediately appreciated that not all four pairs of chromosomes were always identical. In particular, whereas female flies had two identical-looking X chromosomes, in the male the X chromosome was paired with a Y chromosome, which looks different and is never present in the female.

Morgan deduced that a male must inherit the X chromosome from his mother and Y from his father, and he immediately spotted a correlation between these sex-linked chromosomes and the segregation of the factors determining eye color. When the mother was homozygous and had two copies of the gene for red eyes, the male offspring invariably had red eyes, even if the father had white eyes. But when the mother had white eyes, the male offspring did too, even if the father's eyes were red. In contrast, a female fly gets one X chromosome from each parent, and if one passed along an X chromosome with a gene for red eyes, the offspring had red eyes because the color is dominant over white. Only when both parents gave her an X chromosome with a gene for white eyes did she display the recessive trait. From these observations, Morgan concluded that the allele-producing eye color must lie on the X chromosome that governs sex. This provided the first correlation between a specific trait and a specific chromosome.

Morgan's initial paper on fruit flies, entitled "Sex-Limited Inheritance in Drosophila," was published in *Science* in July 1910. In this and in a subsequent paper published in *Science* in 1911, Morgan outlined his three major findings: (1) that genes must reside on chromosomes; (2) that each gene must reside on a particular chromosome; and (3) that the trait for eye color must reside on the sex chromosome, with the eye-color locus (or white gene) missing on the Y chromosome and red being dominant on the X chromosome.

These findings formed the heart of Morgan's most important idea: the *chromosomal theory of heredity*. He proposed that each chromosome contains a collection of small units called *genes* (a term he adopted from the Danish physiologist Wilhelm Johannsen who had lectured at Columbia in 1909), with different genes having specific locations along specific chromosomes. Once this idea formed in his mind, Morgan sensed that the experimental power of the fly would allow him to understand heredity.

A focus on chromosomes and their morphology was not what Morgan had in mind when he started to work on flies. In fact, until he saw the white-eyed mutant and appreciated that its defect acted as if it were part of the X chromosome, he had been skeptical about Mendel's theory of heredity and Mendel's factors. Now that he had seen the possibility that these factors might have a physical reality as genes on chromosomes, Morgan began to view the Mendelian theory in a new light.

A LEGACY OF ACCOMPLISHMENT

As early as 1911, Morgan had redirected his research in an attempt to provide additional information about the chromosome theory of heredity, and before long he achieved another major conceptual breakthrough. Since chromosomes are contiguous assemblages of genes, those traits (mutations in some of the genes) mapping to one particular chromosome naturally tended to segregate together. But on occasion Morgan noted that these "linked" traits would separate, even while other traits on the same chromosome showed little or even no detectable linkage.

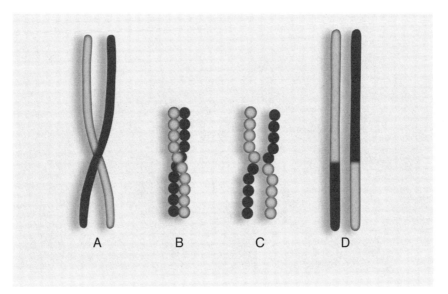

A B C D

A representation of chromosome recombination, in which paired chromosomes exchange or "crossover." Where black and white rods cross in A, they fuse and unite as shown in D. Details of crossing over are shown in B and C. Morgan's intuition into this process was a step toward creating the first chromosome map, achieved by his student A. H. Sturtevant.

From this evidence, Morgan inferred the process of *chromosome recombination:* he postulated that the two paired chromosomes could "exchange" or "crossover" between each other, and he further proposed that the frequency of recombination is a function of the distance between genes on the chromosome. The nearer two relevant genes lie on a chromosome, the greater their chance of being inherited together, while the farther away they are from each other, the more chance of their being separated by the process of crossing over. In short, Morgan suggested that the strength of linkage between genes depended on the distance between them on the chromosome.

On the basis of these observations, Alfred Henry Sturtevant, then an undergraduate at Columbia College who was working with Morgan, recognized that the variations in the strength of linkage could be used as a means of mapping genes on chromosomes by determining their relative spatial distances apart. As Sturtevant himself later recalled:

> I suddenly realized that the variations in the strength of linkage already attributed by Morgan to difference in the spatial separation of the gene offered the possibility of determining sequence in the linear dimensions of a chromosome. I went home and spent most of the night (to the neglect of my undergraduate homework) in producing the first chromosome map. (A. H. Sturtevant, unpublished interview with G. E. Allen)

A 1918 party in honor of A. H. Sturtevant held in the Chart Room of Schermerhorn Hall. Attending are, clock-wise from far left: E. G. Anderson, A. Weinstein, S. C. Dellinger, C. B. Bridges, the "honored guest," a dummy of Pithecanthropus, H. J. Muller, T. H. Morgan, F. Lutz (barely visible on the extreme right), O. L. Mohr, A. F. Huettner, A. H. Sturtevant, and F. Schrader.

The *Morgan* is now the unit of measurement of distances along all chromosomes in fly, mouse, and humans.

A year after Morgan had spotted the white-eyed fly, Sturtevant drew up the first genetic map for the sex-linked genes. A sufficient number of mutations had by then been observed to allow him to express the strength of linkage in units of distance on a chromosome. In fact, the order and spacing that Sturtevant worked out in 1911 are essentially those found on modern maps of the Drosophila X chromosome. The profound insight that genes are aligned on the chromosome like beads on a string with specific distances between them eventually produced a conceptual basis for hunting for disease genes through linkage analysis and for mapping whole genomes, such as the human genome. All this was accomplished by a nineteen-year-old Columbia third-year undergraduate by simply skipping one night's homework! Morgan, who was not given to overstatement, later was to call the realization that genes could be precisely mapped in relation to one another on the chromosome as "one of the most amazing developments in the history of biology." (I. Shine and S. Wrobel, *Thomas Hunt Morgan: Pioneer of Genetics*)

By correlating breeding results with cytological observations of chromosomes under the microscope, Morgan's group rapidly transformed the abstract idea of Mendel's hypothetical factors into the physical reality of particular genes located at specific loci along the length of the chromosome. Initially their maps were quite abstract, since they were based only on the relative positions of genes to one another on the chromosome, as determined by linkage analysis—the sort of map now called a *recombination* map. But two decades later Calvin Bridges succeeded in developing a second independent map—*a physical one*—showing the exact physical location of a gene on a chromosome. He accomplished this by exploiting an unanticipated advantage of Drosophila, which in its larval stages has chromosomes in its salivary glands that Theophilus Painter discovered to be multistranded and gigantic, much larger than the chromosomes of the other cells of the body. These giant chromosomes show a pattern of bands or stripes that divide each chromosome into physical subregions, and Bridges was ultimately able to recognize 1,024 invariant bands on the X chromosome. The development of physical maps proved especially valuable because they allowed a visual presentation of the sequence of genes on the chromosome—a sequence that can only be inferred from the abstract recombination map.

By 1913 Sturtevant contributed yet another major breakthrough with his insight into the existence of different allelic forms, which he saw as alternative states (alleles) of the same gene at the same locus. Research on the white-eyed gene clearly revealed that a gene could mutate from one allele to another—from red to white. In some rare instances, a red allele was observed to mutate to a different allele, then to a third, and eventually a fourth, with each new allele corresponding to a different eye color. But every time a gene gave rise to a new allele, the mutant form was perpetuated in the offspring and remained unchanged unless—again, in very rare cases—a new mutation occurred in one of the offspring. Thus, Morgan's group was able to show that alleles are remarkably stable!

The low frequency of spontaneous mutation and the perpetuation of mutations that did occur indicated that genetic material is constant. The observation was soon confirmed in many other organisms, from Drosophila to man and from bacteria to yeast, offering proof both of inheritance and of the capacity for mutation to allow for evolutionary change in spite of the general constancy of genetic material.

These seminal findings were summarized in 1915 by Morgan and his three Columbia students, Sturtevant, Bridges, and Hermann J. Muller, in *The Mechanism of Mendelian Heredity*, a book that proved to be of historic importance. To begin with, it set forth the physical basis for the new science of genetics. On top of that, the experimental discipline outlined in its pages provided the first experimental basis for modern biology, transforming it from a descriptive science that relied heavily on morphology. Anatomy, the queen of the biological sciences from the time of the Renaissance to the beginning of the twentieth century, was now replaced by genetics as biology itself emerged as an exact, rigorous, quantitative experimental science

*Calvin Bridges in the
Fly Room, circa 1920*

that could exist on an equal footing with physics and chemistry.

In recognition of his work on chromosomes, Morgan was awarded the Nobel Prize in physiology or medicine in 1933. He shared the prize money with Bridges and Sturtevant. The Nobel Prize recognized Morgan's two fundamental scientific contributions: the development of the chromosome theory of heredity, a theory of the gene that proved to be the driving biological concept of the twentieth century, and the creation of a new biology based on a rigorous experimental method.

THE COLUMBIA ENVIRONMENT: THE FLY ROOM

Morgan also made a third contribution, a sociological one that helped introduce at Columbia and into American science as a whole a set of sweeping institutional changes. Until the start of the twentieth century, the leading American research universities—Harvard, Johns Hopkins, Columbia, and Chicago—had all been inspired by the model of the German research university, in which the *Geheimrat*, the great scientific leader, ordered the hierarchy of his subordinates. Morgan, however, based laboratory governance on democratic principles of merit rather than seniority. If one were to ask scientists around the world what is unique about America, they point to the university and to this day foreign scientists are amazed that students working in a laboratory call professors by their first names.

Morgan surrounded himself with a brilliant group of undergraduate and graduate students. Together they set up the Drosophila laboratory in Schermerhorn Hall, Room 613, known worldwide as the *Fly Room*. In retrospect, the Fly Room seems surprisingly small, measuring only 16 x 23 feet and containing eight desks. Yet, it housed a stream of Columbia students as well as foreign visitors and soon received wide recognition, not only for the remarkable quality and clarity of its science, but also for the democratic nature of its social interaction. Morgan encouraged the free exchange of ideas in an atmosphere that was at once friendly, yet self-critical.

The atmosphere in the Fly Room was described by Sturtevant, one of the youngest in the group. He wrote:

> This group worked as a unit. Each carried on his own experiments, but each knew exactly what the others were doing, and each new result was freely discussed. There was little attention paid to priority or to the source of new ideas or new interpretations. What mattered was to get ahead with the work. There was much to be done; there were many new ideas to be tested, and many new experimental techniques to be developed. There can have been few times and places in scientific laboratories with such an atmosphere of excitement and with such a record of sustained enthusiasm. This was due in part to Morgan's own attitude, compounded with enthusiasm combined with a strong critical sense, generosity, open-mindedness, and a remarkable sense of humor.
> (A. H. Sturtevant, *Thomas Hunt Morgan: Biographical Memoirs*)

Although this idyllic view was not shared by all,[1] the Fly Room nevertheless characterized science at its best and continues to provide a prototype for how research should be done, at Columbia and elsewhere. In terms of the work conducted there, the science that began at Columbia spread to laboratories all over the world as Morgan, the members of his group, and the scientists they trained helped to shape the course of biology during the decades that followed. Of the people who worked with Morgan directly or who worked with one of his students, five went on to win their own Nobel Prize: Muller, Beadle, Lederberg, and Lewis. Another student, Dobzhansky, went on to place evolution into a modern biological context. Impelled by their achievements, the center of influence in biology shifted from Europe to the United States, making the twentieth century an American century in biology.

At the same time, the open, critical, yet fully democratic and egalitarian atmosphere that was evident in the Fly Room soon came to characterize the distinctively American atmosphere of university research—an especially significant development as American graduate education increasingly became the model for graduate education throughout the world.

I have benefited from the comments on this essay by Garland Allen, Norman Horowitz, Tom Jessell, Joshua Lederberg, E. B. Lewis, Robert Merton, Gary Struhl, Andrew Tomlinson, and Harriet Zuckerman. For bibliography, see Notes, page 658.

An American Century of Biology

Eric Kandel

From both a geographic and sociological perspective, the biology of the nineteenth century was much like that of previous eras. The major ideas emanated from Europe, stimulated by experiments carried out at the great British and Continental universities. The three major biological insights that dominated the thinking of biologists at the end of the nineteenth century—the insights into evolution, heredity, and development—all reflected Europe's continued preeminence in biology.

But the unifying principle underlying these three areas of inquiry was not to be discovered by the biologists of the Old World, but by the biologists of the new. Morgan's discovery that the gene was the unit of Mendel's inheritance, that it was the fuel for Darwin's evolution, and that it served as the control switch for development inaugurated an American century in biology that accompanied the emergence of the American research university and with it the assumption of American leadership in all areas of science. Much as Thomas Hunt Morgan at Columbia was defining and localizing the gene and thereby founding the twentieth-century science of genetics, American physicists were measuring the speed of light and the charge on the electron, and American engineers were putting an aircraft in the sky.

The influence of Morgan's work at Columbia set the agenda for the decades to come, helping the American university system to establish, through its combination of teaching and research, the model for modern scientific work. Not only was

Morgan the first native-born American to be awarded the Nobel Prize in medicine or physiology; the honor he received in 1933 for his pioneering discoveries at Columbia opened a floodgate. Over the next sixty years, some fifty Nobel Prizes in physiology or medicine were awarded to Americans, including several who had worked directly with Morgan or with one of his students.

The following profiles highlight the accomplishments of a core group of scientists responsible for carrying Morgan's legacy into the present.

X-RAY MUTAGENESIS: HERMANN J. MULLER

One of the great strengths of genetics is its ability to identify new mutations and to study their effects on an animal during development, behavior, or learning. This endeavor requires more than the spontaneous appearance of an occasional mutation, as Morgan had to rely on, but the ability to generate many mutations, almost at will. Credit for developing the first method of inducing controlled evolution goes to Hermann Joseph Muller, one of Morgan's early students at Columbia. In 1926, Muller obtained the startling result that by bombarding flies with X-rays he could produce several hundred fly mutants in one day, as compared to the 400 spontaneous viable mutations that Morgan and his group had observed in working with twenty million flies during twenty years of *Drosophila* research. For his work on X-ray mutagenesis, Muller was awarded the Nobel Prize in 1946.

Among his other accomplishments, Muller also had the remarkable foresight to recognize as early as 1921 that microorganisms and, specifically, bacterial viruses (*phages*) offered the next step in efforts to understand the molecular nature of the gene. It was his presence at Indiana University in the late 1940s that drew James Watson there for graduate study—though Watson ended up working with former Columbia faculty member and Nobel laureate Salvador Luria, who provided the introduction to bacterial viruses that inspired the younger scientist in his collaboration with Francis Crick to solve the chemical structure of genes.

ONE GENE, ONE ENZYME: GEORGE BEADLE

Once the ability to mutate genes at will was at hand, geneticists were in a postion to study how a single gene controls the function of the cell. Taking the lead in this effort was Morgan's last postdoctoral student, George Beadle, who together with Edward L. Tatum realized in the 1940s that genes directed the manufacture of specific proteins. They subsequently introduced the concept of one gene = one enzyme.

Beadle initially focused on the genes that control eye pigment formation in the *Drosophila*, working with Boris Ephrussi in Paris to reveal that eye color is produced by a stepwise series of chemical reactions, each of which appears to be controlled by a certain gene. Recognizing that Drosophila was not the ideal organism for trying to dissect multistep processes, he subsequently teamed up with Tatum and turned to a simpler, single organism, the bread mold *Neurospora*. Using Muller's method of inducing mutations with X-rays, Beadle and Tatum analyzed the metabolic variations that came from these mutations and found that when a specific gene was active, the cell could synthesize a given substance; when the gene was altered or eliminated by mutation, however, the particular metabolic step at which that enzyme operated was defective, and the whole biosynthetic pathway would be slowed or brought to a stop. Their conclusion that enzymes controlled the specific stages of multistep metabolic pathways provided direct support for an idea expressed at the beginning of the twentieth century by Scottish physician Archibald Garrod. Beadle and Tatum's hypothesis has since been refined as the one-gene–one-polypeptide hypothesis, but at mid-century it represented a startling breakthrough in physiological genetics, winning the two—along with Joshua Lederberg—a Nobel Prize in 1958.

GENES AND THE BODY PLAN: E. B. LEWIS

The discovery that genetics could be used to analyze a biological pathway prompted an awareness that some of the most interesting pathways were related to development, raising important new questions about the way genes control developmental programs and the plan of the body. Among the leaders in exploring this new area of inquiry was Edward B. Lewis, one of Alfred Sturtevant's students and thus an heir to the intellectual legacy of Thomas Hunt Morgan and Calvin Bridges.

Beginning in 1946, Lewis brought renewed attention to the study of homeotic mutations, which had been identified in 1915 by Calvin Bridges, one of Morgan's early students. The subjects of Bridges's research included a fly that had undergone a mutation to produce an extra set of wings in place of a pair of balancers (small, winglike appendages). Bridges called the mutation "homeotic," because it changed one body part into another. This transformation—along with another homeotic mutation in a gene called *Antennapedia*—that caused legs to sprout from a fly's head where antennae would normally be—was interesting because it suggested the existence of control genes responsible for directing the development of large parts of the body.

In his work spanning five decades, Lewis built up the insight that genes control body territories, encoding the information necessary to set up each segment. His discoveries included the observation that a mutation to the members of a gene family known as the *Bithorax*-complex had led to the duplication of an entire body segment in *Drosophila*, thereby producing the extra pair of wings. He subsequently found that genes were arranged in the same order on the chromosomes as the body segments they controlled—a correspondence that has proved to be remarkably conserved throughout evolution. Lewis further demonstrated that each part of the body is specified by different sets of active Bithorax genes, paving the way to an awareness that a combinatorial code defines developmental pathways. Gary Struhl, now at Columbia, subsequently split the complex to show that the individual components also work in physical isolation from one another.

Hermann J. Muller

Lewis's work, together with large-scale screens of Drosophila larvae by Eric Wieschaus and Christiane Nüsslein-Volhard, transformed development into a molecular science. For this achievement, the three were awarded the Nobel Prize in 1995.

A NEW EVOLUTIONARY SYNTHESIS: THEODOSIUS DOBZHANSKY

It was Morgan's postdoctoral fellow, Theodosius Dobzhansky, who first appreciated what the new genetics meant for the theory of evolution set forth in *On the Origin of Species* in 1859. Darwin, whose book had been published seven years before Mendel's report on his work with peas, spelled out two major ideas: that all organisms have descended from a common ancestor by gradual, continuous modifications (*evolution*) and that the principal mechanism of evolution is the natural selection of heritable variations. However, because he worked in the absence of information about genes and mutations, Darwin lacked any mechanism for explaining how variants are generated or how they persist through selection and subsequent inheritance. He theorized that environmental factors such as stress and deprivation may have generated variations that are considered adaptive and that,

George Beadle (left)

E. B. Lewis (right)

once generated, these variations could be passed on through heredity. He also presumed that natural selection would be uniform and gradual in its effects.

In light of Morgan's discoveries, the notion about the gradualness of evolution—
long a point of contention—became even more controversial. Morgan found not
continuity and gradualism in his mutations, but a level of discontinuity that he initially interpreted as a challenge to Darwin's ideas. Moreover, biologists defined a
species as a form that differed in morphology from another species, and such mor-
phological differences required major discontinuous changes.

The crucial insight offered by Dobzhansky in collaboration with Ernst Mayr was
that, although a trait such as eye color could be changed by a single mutation, the
majority of mutations were more gentle, or passive; over the long haul, a species
would acquire a great many genetic changes, allowing for graded variations in
appearance (*phenotype*) between individuals. During hard times, evolution would
select for the more favorable variants, and the less favorable would be lost.

In short, genes and their various *allelic* forms could be seen as fueling the engine of
evolution. This view reflected an influential modern synthesis in evolutionary
thought first described by Dobzhansky in his classic 1937 study, *Genetics and the Origin
of Species*. His accomplishment in the book was to bring together the contributions of
genetics, systematics, and paleontology, forging them into a neo-Darwinian theory
that reconciled Darwin's original theory with the new field of genetics.

Theodosius Dobzhansky (left)

Joshua Lederberg (right)

SEX AND GENES IN BACTERIA: JOSHUA LEDERBERG

In 1944, when Joshua Lederberg was a twenty-year-old student at Columbia, he imagined that two bacteria could mate by fusing and pooling their entire genetic resources. Using a variety of genetic crosses in a highly creative way, he went on to show that this actually occurred and that bacteria exchanged chromosomes. He further observed that bacteria had a linear chromosome that could be mapped, establishing them as having genetics comparable to that of higher organisms.

Working with Ed Tatum, Lederberg demonstrated that the exchange of genes that sometimes took place in bacteria achieved the mix that is the evolutionary function of sex in higher organisms. Proof of such genetic recombination—which Lederberg termed *conjugation*—had been sought before but with no success. In 1951, Lederberg and Norton Zinder, his graduate student at the University of Wisconsin, discovered a second process, *transduction*, whereby phage particles were shown to be capable of carrying a few genes from a host into another target cell. Transduction offered the possibility of deliberately inserting known genes into a target cell, where they would function as part of that cell's chromosome. For this work, Lederberg received the 1958 Nobel Prize, sharing the award with Tatum and Beadle—an association that confirmed his place as yet another of Thomas Hunt Morgan's intellectual heirs.

The discovery of transduction marked the beginning of genetic engineering, an idea and a methodology that have carried biology to the present. Recombinant DNA has once again revitalized the field, making it possible to clone genes, to read their sequence, to appreciate similarities between genes in different contexts, and to manipulate genes in model organisms ranging from flies to mice. These advances in molecular biology have had far-reaching consequences for understanding biological processes, including the biology of the brain and of the mental processes that the brain mediates. In addition, genetic engineering has introduced the concept of molecular medicine, with its promise of diagnosing diseases at the level of DNA— a crucial first step toward the goal of one day being able to replace defective genes with normally functioning ones.

I have benefited from the comments on this essay by Garland Allen, Norman Horowitz, Joshua Lederberg, E. B. Lewis, and Andrew Tomlinson. For bibliography, see Notes, page 659.

Genetics, Biology, and the Mysteries of the Mind at the Cusp of the Twenty-first Century

—⁓—

Eric Kandel and Darcy B. Kelley

An age or culture is characterized less by the extent of its knowledge than by the nature of the questions it puts forward.

—François Jacob, *The Logic of Life* (1981)

When Thomas Hunt Morgan started his work on Drosophila at the beginning of the twentieth century, the problems of heredity, development, and evolution were complete mysteries. How does like beget like? How does a single cell, the egg, divide and differentiate to give rise to a complex organism —a whole person? How does a group of organisms evolve to give rise to a new species? These were the major questions that confronted biology in the year 1900.

Morgan and his students at Columbia pioneered the modern discipline of genetics and then went on to harness its power to address each of these questions. As a result, we now understand heredity, development, and evolution in principle, even if we do not yet have all the details.

With the approach of the new millennium, what challenges remain for genetics? In a broader sense, what mysteries remain for biology in the twenty-first century?

Perhaps the last great remaining mystery for modern biology, and, in fact for all of science, is to understand the biological basis of mental experience. How do we sense the world around us, how do we remember that perception, and how do we color it with emotion? Because of the continuing fascination the brain holds for us, biologists predict that such studies will be, for the twenty-first century, what the exploration of the gene was for the twentieth century and what investigations of the cell were for the nineteenth century. When Morgan developed genetics at Columbia, his goal was to determine how genes control development. One hundred years later, we ask: can genetics also contribute to an understanding of mind?

An effective approach to mind/brain studies must obviously reach beyond genetics to direct observation of mental activity in humans and other primates. Such a wide-ranging initiative, known as molecular cognition, is now underway at Columbia. This effort is combining the techniques and insights of genetics and molecular biology with those of cognitive psychology to continue and extend the tradition of accomplishment that is the enduring legacy of Thomas Hunt Morgan, his students, and his colleagues at the university.

COGNITIVE BIOLOGY: WHAT IS THE MIND AND WHERE IS IT LOCATED?

Cognitive psychologists and biologists have come to share a belief that what we call "mind" is the range of functions carried out by a physical organ, the brain. Thus, the workings of the brain underlie not only relatively simple mental acts such as the motor behaviors of walking, running, or hitting a tennis ball, but also elaborate emotional and cognitive behaviors such as feeling, learning, thinking, or composing a symphony. As a corollary, the disorders that characterize neurotic and psychotic illness can be seen as specific disturbances of brain function.

Viewed in this way, the scientific challenge posed by the mind becomes that of understanding how the brain produces its mental functions, a subject we can now approach using the tools of modern biology. Of course, understanding how the brain gives rise to mental activity still poses an enormous scientific challenge: creating a larger unification of thought to demystify the mind. There is nevertheless a sense of optimism in the air—driven by the gradual convergence during the past decade of neural science (the science of the brain) and cognitive psychology (the science of the mind).

The central principle for understanding how mental functions relate to brain functions derives from the finding that the functions of mind have a *distributed representation* in the brain: various mental functions are mediated not by single brain regions, but by distributed sets of different regions connected in very specific ways. Each region analyzes a particular component of a mental process (parallel processing), with some sending the processed information on to other brain regions (serial processing). This awareness that most mental faculties are made possible by the serial and parallel interconnections of multiple brain regions has given rise to the related insight that almost all mental operations are divisible into subfunctions.

This insight is quite counterintuitive. Most of us have the sense that we store and recall our knowledge of representations of the people and objects we encounter—and of the events that occur in our environment—as unified images that can be evoked by appropriate sensory reminder cues or even by the imagination alone. Our knowledge about our grandmother, for example, seems to be stored in a single representation as "grandmother," one that is equally accessible whether we see her, hear her voice, or simply think about her. But we now know that this belief is not supported by the facts and that knowledge of people, objects, and events, far from being stored as single images, is instead subdivided into distinct categories.

This remarkable insight first emerged from an examination of the fragmented nature of mental deficits following damage to different brain regions. Damage to a particular part of the cerebral cortex (a brain region essential for higher cognition) can block the ability to name a person—for example, one's grandmother—without interfering with the ability to recognize her. A lesion to a different cortical area will destroy the ability to recognize grandmothers and other friends and relations, but not inanimate objects.

The details of this subdivision of mental processes are best understood for visual perception. The brain does not simply replicate the external world like a kind of three-dimensional photograph; rather, the brain's representation of the world is an abstraction—and, even more surprising, the brain builds up this image of the outside world only after first breaking it down into its constituent parts. In scanning a visual scene, the brain analyzes the form of objects as distinct from their movements and apart from their color, all before reconstituting the full image again according to the brain's own rules. Each component is processed in a different region, explaining why—as in the case of recognizing one's grandmother—individuals with lesions to a certain part of the brain might have no difficulty in visual reception per se, even though their visual recognition or visual knowledge might be severely impaired.

It was Sigmund Freud who first proposed at the end of the nineteenth century that defects in visual perception might be caused not by a sensory deficit of the eye or its nerve, but by a cortical deficit that affects the brain's ability to combine components of the visual impression into a meaningful pattern. Freud called these defects *agnosias*, or loss of knowledge. A striking kind of agnosia is the inability to recognize faces, or *prosopagnosia*. Patients suffering from it can identify a face as a face, name its parts, and even recognize specific emotions expressed by it, but they are unable to identify a particular face as belonging to a specific person—such as our grandmother.

Perhaps the most astonishing example of the combinatory structure of mental processes is the finding that our very sense of ourselves as a *self*—a coherent being—depends on neural connections between the two hemispheres of the cerebral cortex. In some epileptic patients the fiber tract connecting the two hemispheres, the corpus callosum, is severed to prevent seizures from spreading from one side of the brain to the other. As a result, each hemisphere carries an independent awareness of the self—for example, each responds to tactile stimuli applied to the opposite hand, but not to stimuli applied to the same-side hand. When identical objects are placed in both hands of such patients, the object in the left cannot be compared with the one in the right hand, because the two hemispheres are no longer in communication with each other. Even more dramatic, in most of these patients the right hemisphere cannot understand language that is well understood by the isolated left hemisphere. As a result, conflicting commands can be given selectively to each side of the brain!

The brain accomplishes its remarkable computational feats—the initial deconstruction and the subsequent reconstruction, or binding together, of perceptions and other mental phenomena—because the nerve cells that form its many components are wired together in very precise ways. Yet, equally remarkable, this wiring is not immutable. Connections between nerve cells can be altered by learning. We remember events because the structure and function of connections within the brain can be modified through experience. Thus, if you remember anything tomorrow about this essay that you have read today, it is because your brain has been altered by this particular reading experience.

MOLECULAR COGNITION: BRIDGING GENES TO MIND

A major factor behind Thomas Hunt Morgan's success in relating genes to chromosomes, and then in showing how both are connected to the organism's overt characteristics, was his decision to use the fruit fly as the subject for his experiments.

But most biologists believe that for processes as complex as the functioning of the brain, no single organism will suffice—there is no Drosophila to serve as a model organism for molecular cognition. So, in addition to studying simple organisms such as worms, flies, and snails, we will also need to study mice and monkeys and ultimately to examine the human mind directly.

Of the more complex animals, the mouse has a long history as a subject for the study of behavioral genetics. At the turn of the century, "waltzing" strains of mice produced by spontaneous mutations made popular household pets. These spontaneous mutations, changes in the DNA, were induced by events in the mouse's environment such as natural radiation. It was, however, the pioneering work in the late 1940s by L. C. Dunn, then chairman of Columbia's zoology department who as an undergraduate had been inspired by Morgan's writings, that introduced the study of spontaneous mutations as a new technique for understanding vertebrate development. Determining exactly which genes were affected by spontaneous mutations was very difficult in mice, so scientists initially turned to flies and worms, where methods for gene discovery are much easier. In the 1980s, a revolutionary technical breakthrough allowed researchers to replace any mouse gene at will with altered or nonfunctional versions (the latter are often called "knockouts"), which could in turn be transmitted to the mouse's offspring. The new knockout methodology catapulted mice to the forefront of genetics. The opportunity to modify the genome of mice has given rise to important questions about the role of genetics in solving the remaining problems that confront biology and more specifically about the role that genetics can play in helping to address the problems of the mind.

Several of the first gene knockouts in mice were achieved at Columbia by Elizabeth Robertson working with Argiris Efstratiadis and Steven Goff on studies of development and cancer biology. Influenced by their efforts, Eric Kandel used these and other knockout mice to examine how specific genes affect neuronal communication in the brain on the one hand and learning and memory storage on the other.

Like humans, mice have two memory systems: an *implicit* system that stores information about how to do things (perceptual and motor strategies) and an *explicit* one that stores information about the things themselves (facts or events involving places, objects, and other living things). The explicit memory system is located in the medial temporal lobe of the cerebral cortex, and its focus is a specific brain region, the hippocampus. Lesions of the hippocampus disrupt memories of space. Kandel and his colleagues found that altering the expression of certain genes in the hippocampus interferes with changes in the signaling between neurons—signaling that is crucial for memory storage, especially memory of place. Moreover, mice carry in

Eric R. Kandel

their hippocampus an internal representation of space—a kind of cognitive map—and Kandel and his colleagues at Columbia together with Susumu Tonegawa and his colleagues at MIT found that genes that block the storage of spatial memory do so by interfering with the normal stability of the animal's internal representation. In this way, the use of mouse knockouts has provided a preliminary understanding of how connections between nerve cells change as a result of experience (learning) and how these changes are maintained in memory.

It soon became clear that genetics could be used to study not only what an animal *knows* and *remembers*—its cognitive capabilities—but also what it feels—its emotional or *affective* sensibilities. The latter includes aggression and mood, which provide the focus of René Hen's studies of genetically modified mice. Many of the drugs used to treat disorders of mood and emotion in humans act via a brain chemical called serotonin or via the different kinds of proteins that this neurotransmitter binds on the surfaces of brain cells. Hen knocked out a number of the proteins through which serotonin acts, one at a time, in each case revealing specific effects on the mouse's behavior. He is currently identifying the serotonin receptors that mediate the antidepressant effects of drugs such as Prozac.

Richard Axel has used molecular cloning to open up the study of smell, one of our most elaborate senses. Humans are able to perceive perhaps 10,000 different odors, all of which tap into our mental processes and our memory storage in complex ways.

Until recently it has been difficult to study smell because we knew nothing about the molecules that detect smells (receptors)—not even how many there are. Does smell work like vision, in which we perceive the richness of the visual word using three receptors for colors and mixing their outputs? Or is olfaction more elaborate?

Axel succeeded in identifying the olfactory receptors and found that there are not three or four, but 1,000; fully one percent of all human genes are devoted to the perception of odors. He demonstrated that the molecular decoding of smells begins at the olfactory periphery, in the sensitive tissue lining the nasal cavity, and that any olfactory neuron expresses only one receptor. Each olfactory neuron in the nose sends a projection to a particular spot in the brain, with all the members of one olfactory receptor class converging on a few specific sites in the first olfactory way station (*glomeruli*). As the brain "reads" the activity of individual glomeruli we construct a world of smells.

Yet another Columbia scientist, Thomas Jessell, uses genetics to establish how the neurons of the brain develop their specific identities and how they form the correct connections essential for all brain functions. How is an entire neural circuit for a behavior, a complete reflex from sensory input to motor response, constructed? Jessell's research has shown that neurons that wire up to each other to form a particular circuit all share a common master regulatory factor, one that may be responsible for coordinating their patterns of genetic activity and permit the formation of specific connections between them.

GENES AND THE HUMAN BRAIN

Human beings are far from ideal as experimental organisms for the study of genetics, but they provide fertile ground for exploring cognition. One reason for this, of course, is that they are the organisms whose cognition we ultimately hope to understand. In addition, not only do humans have remarkable cognitive capabilities, but they are also verbally insightful, making it easy to test them for a variety of cognitive skills.

Despite experimental limitations, we have learned a great deal recently about human genes, thanks to the introduction of DNA markers, which facilitate gene mapping. Once mapped onto different chromosome regions, the genes can be cloned and identified—a key thrust of the ongoing Human Genome Initiative. We can identify genes that contribute to cognition and other higher mental functions and may gain insight into the genetic factors that influence the attributes of person-

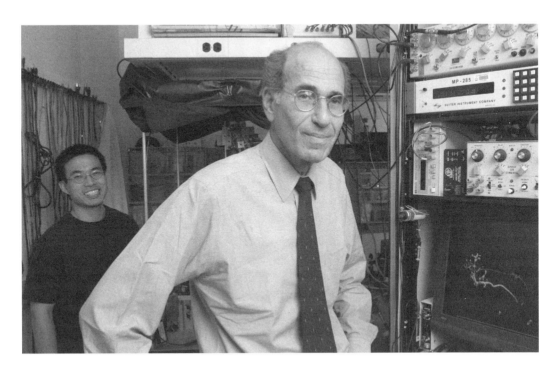

Richard Axel in his laboratory. To Axel's left is a student, Allan Wong.

ality and intelligence, a possibility that is exciting and at the same time daunting. It is a prospect that raises ethical issues for the university and for society as a whole, difficult ethical questions that must be faced with each new advance in molecular biology.

One of the most instructive examples to date of how genes affect human behavior has come from an analysis of Huntington's disease, a degenerative disease of the nervous system and the first complex human behavioral abnormality to be traced to a single gene. This important feat of genetic detective work has been spearheaded by Columbia's Nancy Wexler and her colleagues throughout the world. Huntington's disease affects both men and women with a frequency of about five per 100,000. Over the long course of the disease, neurons in the basal ganglia, a region of the brain involved in regulating voluntary movement and aspects of cognitive function, misfunction and then die. Huntington's is characterized by incessant, rapid, jerky movements and cognitive impairment (hence, its old name, Saint Vitus's dance, and its common name, Huntington's chorea) and also by changes in memory and emotion. Everyone who inherits even one copy of the gene gets the disease; it strikes people in their late forties and early fifties, after they have married and had children, and progresses ruthlessly toward death.

Thomas Jessell

Wexler and her colleagues identified the Huntington's disease gene on chromosome 4. This gene encodes a large protein called *Huntingtin;* we don't know yet what the normal protein does. The mutated form of the Huntingtin gene revealed a fascinating feature now known to be shared with some other degenerative diseases of the brain: it encodes a protein containing a repeated stretch of one particular amino acid, glutamine. In individuals with the disease, the stretch is abnormally long, and this DNA repeat (CAG for glutamine) kills certain nerve cells in ways that are not yet understood. The use of mouse models of Huntington's promises to reveal key links between the gene, its effects on nerve cells, and the behavioral impact—both emotional and cognitive—of this devastating disease.

Even at this early stage in the study of human genes, research findings are beginning to reveal the scope of the issues that lie ahead. Long-held distinctions between the effects of genes (nature) and the environment (nurture) can be viewed in new ways. Both genetics and environmental factors may influence the same biological substrates; accumulating evidence suggests, for example, that the adverse impact of environmental stressors can be reversed by pharmacological manipulations. Researchers have discovered that learning gives rise to long-term memory, leading to changes in the expression of genes and structural alteration of the brain—in short, that the activity of genes themselves can be influenced by environmental factors.

Genetic studies of personality and mood suggest, for example, that natural variations among personality traits and pathological mood disorders actually lie along a continuum, effectively blurring any distinction between normal and abnormal. We have long recognized that some of the most creative members of our species are subject to extremes of temperament. Genetic knowledge provides us not only with a molecular explanation for various behaviors, but also with the realization that we all carry vulnerabilities to disorders of gene function, disorders that contribute to cancer or psychiatric breakdowns. An understanding of these molecular mechanisms promises to bring new cures for the diseases, along with new challenges on issues involving individual accountability and freedom. Future advances in understanding the biological basis of thought and mood will have significant repercussions for our medical and legal systems.

COGNITIVE NEUROSCIENCE OF HUMAN AND NONHUMAN PRIMATES

Millions of items . . . present to my senses which never properly enter my experience. Why? Because they have no interest for me. My experience is what I agree to attend to. . . . Everyone knows what attention is. It is taking possession by the mind in clear and vivid form of one out of what seem several simultaneous objects or trains of thought. Focalization, concentration of consciousness are of its essence. It implies withdrawal from some things in order to deal effectively with others.
—William James, *Principles of Psychology* (1890)

What we would ultimately like to understand are elements of consciousness—and, if we are to come to grips with the biological underpinnings of consciousness, we will have to look beyond the gene to brain systems that have evolved over the centuries in primates. One approach to exploring consciousness has been to examine the biological basis of selective attention, a component of conscious awareness, via a rigorous analysis of complex behavior in intact, awake, behaving primates as they carry out highly controlled perceptual or motor tasks. Monkeys have proven to be a valuable subject for such research, especially since studies with humans performing similar tasks while undergoing brain imaging have shown strong similarities in the elementary mechanisms of perception and movement control.

Initial hints about the physiological substrate of selective attention date back to the nineteenth century and the work of the English neurophysiologist David

Ferrier. In 1876, Ferrier described what happened when an electrical stimulus was applied to the prefrontal cortex of a rhesus monkey: "The eyes open widely, the pupils dilate, and head and eyes turn towards the opposite side." In short, the monkey behaved in a way consistent with shifting attention to a new location in space. But it was not for another hundred years, in the 1970s, that neurophysiologists started to investigate systematically the neural basis of selective attention. They found that neurons in the prefrontal cerebral cortex were activated when monkeys moved their eyes to look at visual stimuli (overt attention), while neurons in the parietal cortex were instead activated when monkeys shifted attention to a new location, even if their eyes didn't move (covert attention). The response of visual neurons is affected by attention in a way that suggests that the area of visual space driving their neurons (receptive fields) "shrinks" to focus on attended stimuli. In research now under way at Columbia, Vincent Ferrera is studying how spatial attention and feature-selective attention are integrated in the prefrontal cortex of monkeys. In the process, he is developing computational models to link cellular and behavioral correlates of attention.

Technology now allows us to visualize the activity of millions of neurons in specific regions of the human cortex while engaging in solving complex problems via PET (positron emission tomography) and functional NMR (nuclear magnetic resonance). At Columbia, these brain imaging methods are being applied by Yaakov Stern and Lynn Cooper to study normal implicit and explicit memory storage, by Richard Mayeux and Scott Small to examine changes in memory storage during aging, and by John Mann to examine changes in brain activity associated with depression.

Other research builds on the finding that attention and emotion not only color our memories, but are integral to their creation, providing the contextual cues later used to bind the fragments together into recollected wholes. In this vein, Janet Metcalfe and Walter Mischel are exploring a monitoring-and-control system for human explicit memories that generates a "feeling-of-knowing." Their analysis focuses on the way the control system assesses incoming events and adjusts the attention or effort assigned to them on the basis of novelty: little energy goes to old and already well-known events, but considerably more attention is devoted to novel events.

In the long run, we hope to be able to study similar tasks in monkeys and humans and then carry out intervention experiments in monkeys in order to distinguish brain activity patterns that are actually responsible for (or cause) components of conscious experience. But because of the brain's extraordinary complexity and the sheer number of nerve cells it contains—a million-million—we will never be able to achieve a complete understanding of its information processing functions without some sort of a computational theory, just as we cannot comprehend how a computer works without concepts such as an operating system and data structure. Columbia's Ning Qian has been applying the techniques of mathematical analyses and computer simulations to his investigations of how a population of cells with realistic physiological properties could act in concert to solve perceptual problems such as depth perception and motion detection. In the process, he, like his colleagues in a range of scientific disciplines throughout the university, is laying the essential groundwork for advances still to come.

COLUMBIA AND THE MIND/BRAIN INITIATIVE

The scope and complexity of initiatives now under way at Columbia highlight the formidable challenges posed by mind/brain studies, which have now been taken up by the university's combined neuroscience and cognitive psychology faculty, including scientists on the Health Sciences and Morningside Heights campuses. The product of their shared commitment is the new Mind/Brain Initiative, launched with the enthusiastic endorsement of President George Rupp and representing the most extensive and far-reaching collaboration to date between these two units of the university. This effort builds on the university's well-established base in molecular neural science, which was recognized by the Howard Hughes Medical Institute when it selected Columbia as the site of one of four national centers for neuroscience in 1984. The mission of the Mind/Brain Initiative is to focus the strengths of psychology and neural science at Columbia on mental processes, including perception, action, memory, thought, emotion, attention, consciousness, and self-awareness.

Such an ambitious undertaking will have consequences for many areas of academic life at the university. To begin with, the importance of neurobiological insights into the human brain will most likely lead to a merger between the disciplines of psychology and neurobiology. Psychology will continue to provide the detailed analysis of mental processes, but biology will provide the tools to discover how these mental processes are generated. From cellular recordings of the primate cortex on the one hand to the imaging of human brain activity on the other, we will be able to determine how the brain reconstructs the most complex memories and the role of emotion and attention in re-creating the composite whole. In a corollary development, psychiatry and neurology will come together as two aspects of a new science of brain function, with disorders of mind being perceived as a distinctive set of disorders of the brain, much along the lines of other neurological disorders.

A focus on understanding the biology of mind will also have a profound effect on the computational sciences. Studies of artificial intelligence and of pattern recognition by computers have made us realize that the brain recognizes movement, form, and color using strategies that no existing computer begins to approach. Simply to look out into the world and recognize a face or enjoy a landscape entails an amazing computational achievement, one that is much more difficult than the ones required for solving logic problems or playing chess. Understanding how the brain sees, hears, thinks, and feels will have a major and instantaneous impact on the design of computers and robots alike.

In the field of education, the Mind/Brain Initiative will inspire a new level of empirical investigation into the kinds of questions that generations of students have assumed are purely philosophical, answerable only by introspection and logic: What aspects of the mind are innate? How does experience interact with the mind's innate organization? How do we perceive the world, learn about each other, and remember what we experience? The biological investigation of mental activity might even serve as an intellectual bridge in Columbia's Core Curriculum, forging a new synthesis between the humanities, which have traditionally been concerned with the place of the individual in society, and the biological and physical sciences, with their traditional focus on nature and the universe. Understanding the biology of the mind would thus come to represent not only a scientific goal of great promise, but also one of the ultimate aspirations of humanistic scholarship, part of the continuous attempt of each generation of scholars to understand human thought and human action in new and more complex terms.

On a broad societal level, many of the most pressing problems that confront us today—addiction, aggression, and war, to name just three—revolve around the biological nature of human behavior. Our understanding of how humans bond to one another, whether in the mother-child interaction or larger group cohesion, can also be enriched by understanding the underlying biology. Without question, these issues are on the distant horizon, but most neural scientists believe they will be within reach during the next century. Work undertaken today will allow the biology of mind to have a major impact on sociology and on social psychology.

GENETICS IN PERSPECTIVE: COLUMBIA'S CONTRIBUTION TO MODERN THOUGHT

In honor of the university's 250th anniversary, we have looked both backwards and forwards, focusing on genetics to illustrate how biology has matured as a science during the twentieth century and to highlight the distinctive role Columbia has

René Hen

played at key points in this process. As we approach the twenty-first century, it is clear that genetics in particular and biology in general will exert an even greater influence on modern thought.

Already the pace of achievement is breathtaking. First in 1996, we had the complete genome of yeast, all 6,000 genes of a single organism possessing a nucleus. Then, in 1999, the first genome was obtained for a multicellular organism, the 17,000 genes of the worm *C. elegans*. And most important by 2003 we were in possession of all of the genes that make up the human genome (as well as the 20,000 genes of the fly genome). We have in hand, for the first time, the equivalent in biology of a periodic table. We know all the genetic elements that make up life in all of its forms.

As a result, the very nature of biology—including human biology—will change dramatically. These developments will challenge all aspects of the university, raising ethical, political, social, and scientific issues in biology, medicine, philosophy, psychology, and religion. We shall have tasted once again from the tree of knowledge, and we shall be confronted with all the benefits and challenges that this exposure entails. The true challenge for a great university such as ours is to savor that knowledge and to debate its consequences for the betterment of society.

We have benefited from comments on this essay by Thomas Jessell. For bibliography, see Notes, page 659.

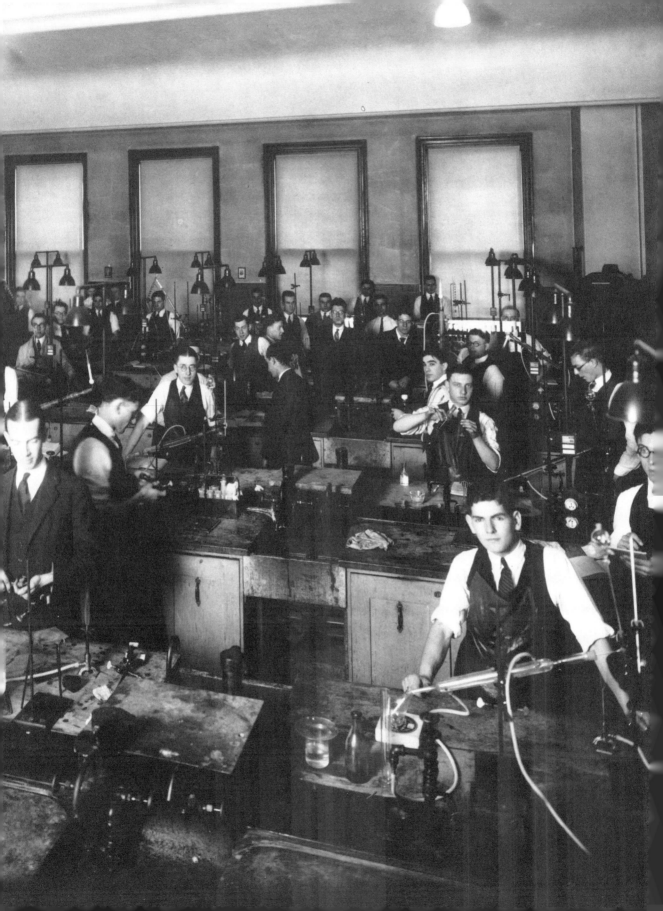

CHAPTER 14

Chemistry at Columbia

—⚏—

Leonard W. Fine and Ronald Breslow

Chemistry as a subject of intellectual inquiry has been a part of Columbia almost from its beginnings with the appointment in 1784 of Samuel Latham Mitchill as a professor of an astounding array of subjects: "Natural History, Chemistry, Agriculture and other Arts Depending on Theory." Much later, when the university established itself on Morningside Heights at the turn of the twentieth century, Chemistry, by then a full-fledged department in its own right, moved into brand-new Havemeyer Hall, the bastion at the northwest corner of campus. Chemistry is still in Havemeyer, a symbol of the discipline's centrality at Columbia.

Chemistry under the dynamic leadership of Charles Frederick Chandler (1836–1925) quickly became the fountainhead of major developments in new fields of engineering, medicine, and pharmacy, serving also as a training ground for scientists and technicians in the burgeoning world of industrial laboratories. Indeed Chandler was a key figure not only in the rise of his department to national leadership but also in the founding and growth of the Columbia Graduate Faculties as a whole.

In his own department Chandler has been succeeded by a long line of distinguished scholars, including the Nobel Prize–winners Irving Langmuir and Harold Urey. Filling in this account are Ronald Breslow and Leonard Fine, two current members of the department. University Professor Breslow's many awards include the National Medal of Science and the Priestley Medal; he is a member of the National Academy of Science and the American Academy of Arts and Sciences and a past president of the American Chemical Society. Professor Fine has been the department's director of undergraduate studies in chemistry since 1982. Both men have won Great Teacher Awards at Columbia.

—Wm. Theodore de Bary

—⚏—

October 1864. A lot had happened since he had left Massachusetts to study chemistry in Göttingen with Friedrich Wöhler. Inorganic chemistry and analysis interested him, and his Ph.D. thesis described the properties of some minerals crystallizing in the rock formations in Wöhler's basement. He met many of the young and future leaders of European chemistry before returning to take a position as an instructor at Union College in upstate New York at no salary. A janitor's job provided subsistence. And now after half a dozen years in Schenectady he had landed at Columbia College in the City of New York.

So begins the most important chapter in the history of chemistry in America. It belongs to Charles Frederick Chandler. From his new home, a low brick building housing the School of Mines, would spring nothing less than chemistry at Columbia. The classrooms and laboratories within would provide scientific education and training in the Central Science on a par with the classics of the curriculum on which Columbia had been founded a century earlier. By the end of his long career, Chandler was internationally recognized for his role in the early development of modern chemistry in America. Here is an account of this essential contribution, along with those of several other Columbia professors, including Samuel Latham Mitchill, Marston T. Bogert, Irving Langmuir, Louis Hammett, Victor LaMer, and Harold Urey.

CHARLES FREDERICK CHANDLER AND HIS STUDENTS

In the genealogy of chemistry, there are two main roots: one derives from Antoine Lavoisier in France; the other derives from Friedrich Wöhler in Germany and Charles Frederick Chandler in the New World. Chandler was twenty-seven years old in 1864 when he joined Columbia as professor of analytical chemistry. He pursued his career here until his retirement in 1910 and death in 1925. Many students came to work with Chandler and with the faculty he attracted to Columbia. They took their newly won Ph.D. degrees with them as they migrated to other colleges and the first American universities, helping to extend and establish teaching laboratories as Chandler had done at Columbia. Some became Columbia professors.

During the half-century of his career, in addition to his significant contributions to the development of engineering, medicine, and pharmacy, Chandler is credited with industrializing and professionalizing the discipline of chemistry. For the first time, industry began to hire scientists from universities to do research in laboratories as diverse as those of General Electric and the American Sugar Refining Company. Training became an important part of education. The number and kinds of jobs

Not yet thirty years old, Charles Frederick Chandler, in center with book, is surrounded by his first Columbia chemistry students. The equipment suggests the mix of engineers and chemists in the group. The year is 1866.

available to scientists and technologists expanded greatly, in turn altering the curriculum of the college in significant ways. World War I changed things forever as faculty began solving problems for the military and the war effort, especially in chemistry. This relationship laid the groundwork for the lead role played by Columbia faculty in World War II, most notably in the Manhattan Project, in nuclear fission and the making of the atomic bomb, and in the development of synthetic materials and explosives.

Chandler also played important professional roles outside Columbia. He was the first chemist in the New York City Department of Health and for several years served as president of its board. Working closely with William Havemeyer, three-term mayor of New York, Chandler put into place rules that cleaned up the unhealthy and often revolting problems produced by slaughterhouse waste and inadequate sewage treatment. He was also a founder of the American Chemical Society, which is now the largest scientific society in the world, and served twice as its president.

Chandler took special pride in the role he played in establishing Columbia as a force in graduate education. In 1875, the first doctoral degree in chemistry at Columbia—the fourth in America—was awarded to Elwyn Waller, a Chandler student who was then appointed instructor in qualitative analysis. Prior to that time, all American Ph.D.'s had been European educated. When Chandler retired in 1910, Columbia was the leading institution of higher learning for the study of chemistry

Harold Urey in November of 1931 with Ph.D. student Donald MacGillavry (left) observing an electric discharge through hydrogen gas concentrated in deuterium. The experiment proved the existence of deuterium and brought Urey the 1934 Nobel Prize in chemistry.

in America. By the time of his death in 1925, the Columbia department rivaled the great schools of chemistry in Europe from which Chandler and his generation of chemists had arisen. Between 1898 and 1938 Columbia graduated the lion's share of Ph.D.'s in chemistry, each year more than any other American institution. On Chandler's death, Henry Clapp Sherman, then chairman of the department, noted that of the 160 chemistry Ph.D.'s granted since the move to Morningside, 40 percent of the recipients had gone into teaching and academic research. The other 60 percent formed the first legion of industrial chemists. Since then, the number of Ph.D. degrees in chemistry has increased by an order of magnitude. The result is a disproportionately large Columbia influence on chemistry in America.

Chandler's most famous student was Irving Langmuir. After graduating with the class of 1903, Langmuir studied for his Ph.D. with Walther Nernst (1920 Nobel laureate in chemistry) in Berlin. By the time he returned, as an instructor at Stevens Institute of Technology, the General Electric Company had built laboratories in Schenectady, New York, to develop the inventions of Edison and Steinmetz—especially the electric light bulb. Langmuir was hired away from Stevens in the summer of 1909 and stayed in Schenectady for the next forty-eight years. A gifted theoretician and experimentalist, he opened the field of surface science, for which he was recognized with the 1932 Nobel Prize in chemistry. His name will be forever linked to the study of liquid films, monolayers, surfaces and catalysis, the early application of the new quantum theory to chemistry, and the development of the modern tungsten filament electric light bulb, which is still widely used today.

Irving Langmuir behaved like an academician in industry, enlisting a small army of Ph.D.'s to work on the problems that filled the pages of fifty-four research notebooks. He was widely acknowledged as a great lecturer, with a style that was fast-paced, emphatic, and filled with the intensity of his topic. He spent considerable time at Columbia during his long career, teaching courses, working with graduate students, and collaborating with Victor LaMer and Harold Urey in chemistry and Isidor Rabi in physics. Langmuir's theory of electron-pair bonds gained wide acceptance for its originality and the value it added to current thinking about the structure and reactivity of molecules. He was always concerned about clear thinking and spoke of the other kind as "pathological science," pointing out the sources of errors and misconceptions of both the scientific kind and the human kind in some of the most famous works of the day.

Chandler's last and longest-lived student was Michael Heidelberger, who became professor of biochemistry at Columbia. Reminiscing at the sesquicentennial birthday party for Chandler on December 6, 1986, the ninety-seven-year-old Heidelberger recalled the mutual warmth and respect between Chandler and "his boys."

The Chandler Laboratories building (attached to Havemeyer Hall) was the gift of Ellen Harris and her brother John, a Chandler student (School of Mines, Class of 1884). Struck in his name and awarded to him on his retirement, the Chandler Medal has since been given forty-one times. In thirteen cases (so far), the recipient has gone on to win the Nobel Prize.

MITCHILL AND RENWICK

Chandler was not the first Columbia chemist. When the institution began as King's College in 1754, the curriculum was classical; no science was taught that first year, and in all likelihood the word *chemistry* was never mentioned. There was also no mention of chemistry in the titles of the first science professors at King's College—David Treadwell in mathematics and natural philosophy, and James Smith in medicine.

In 1784, after a hiatus for the Revolutionary War, the College was renamed Columbia, and the trustees allocated funds for the appointment of Samuel Latham Mitchill as "Professor of Natural History, Chemistry, Agriculture, and other Arts Depending on Theory." Mitchill published 175 scientific papers and treatises during his career. He was familiar with Antoine Lavoisier's work in Europe and Benjamin Franklin's experiments in Philadelphia, and he met with Joseph Priestley when he came to America. While a member of the faculty, Mitchill served in the New York State Legislature and eventually went to Washington, first as a United States congressman and then as a senator.

Bridging the end of the Mitchill era (1814) and the beginning of the Chandler era half a century later, James Renwick brought engineering and practical training in chemistry to the burgeoning College and made evident the need for a new and expanded campus. He graduated from Columbia College in 1807, received an M.A.

in 1810, and in 1817 at age twenty-seven became a trustee of the College, sharing with Alexander Hamilton the honor of being the youngest Columbia trustee. Renwick entered his father's business, but when it failed he accepted a professorship at Columbia in 1820, a position he held for thirty-three years. In 1841 he published *First Principles of Chemistry*, the authoritative textbook of the day. His students were required to purchase it, but he refunded his royalties to them, establishing a precedent not since widely practiced.

By the time Columbia had completed the move to larger quarters at Fourth Avenue and Forty-ninth Street in 1846, Renwick's professorship had been split in two, one in chemistry and one in physics. Charles Joy of Union College was appointed to the chemistry professorship in 1857. Joy induced the trustees to put up money for subscriptions to scientific journals and periodicals and to establish a scientific library. He required his students to have competence in French and German, and they worked in the laboratory all hours of the night and day, much like graduate students today. But most important, Joy doubled the size of the department by convincing the trustees of the need for still another appointment in chemistry. His choice was Charles Frederick Chandler, whom he had already hired once, at Union College.

CHEMISTRY ON MORNINGSIDE HEIGHTS

In 1897 Columbia moved to Morningside Heights and the chemistry department moved into its own building—brand-new Havemeyer Hall, the fourth building to be completed on the Morningside campus (after Fayerweather, Schermerhorn, and Engineering). The family of Frederick Christian Havemeyer of the class of 1825, who founded the American Sugar Refining Company, responded to a brilliantly conceived solicitation letter from Chandler and gave $450,000 in 1896. Completed late in 1897—a record in construction time that modern builders of chemistry laboratories can only stand in awe of—Havemeyer Hall is a fireproof, six-story building roughly 80 by 200 feet, made of red, overburned brick and trimmed with Indiana limestone.

Since the move to Havemeyer there have been 129 professors in the Columbia chemistry department. Marston T. Bogert was the first professor of organic chemistry. In a career that spanned half a century (1897–1954), he produced more than 500 scientific papers, mainly on medicines and vitamins, of which more than 250 were original contributions to the field, published in collaboration with candidates for the Ph.D. In 1897, as an undergraduate enrolled in the organic chemistry class taught by Professor Charles Edward Colby, Bogert had to take over the course at the start of the term when Colby suddenly died.

Henry Clapp Sherman took his Ph.D. in 1897 with Marston Bogert. An analytical chemist, he did memorable work in food chemistry and nutrition, anticipating the discovery of vitamins and hormones and establishing the essential role of amino acids. Sherman continued the study of the chemical properties of enzymes and their biological activity until his retirement. This life's work, starting with his supervision of the Ph.D. thesis of Victor K. LaMer, opened the field of nutrition to quantitative study. During World War I, Sherman's early work on bioassay methods for vitamins attracted considerable attention, and he left Columbia during World War II to serve as chief of the Bureau of Human Nutrition at the Department of Agriculture. Henry Sherman published more than 200 original research papers and several monographs and textbooks. In an argument with the distinguished German chemist Richard Willstätter, he proved that the digestive enzymes are proteins.

John Maurice Nelson received his Ph.D. under the supervision of Marston Bogert in 1907 and took up a faculty position in organic chemistry alongside his mentor. Nelson was probably the first to consider the electron theory of valence as applied to covalent bonds. He was the first to state that the removal of electrons corresponded to oxidation and the addition of electrons to reduction. Nelson was also the first to study the kinetics of enzyme inhibition, before it was identified as

The faculty in chemistry on the steps of Havemeyer Hall in 1910, the year Chandler retired from Columbia. Seated, left to right: Tucker, Morgan, Bogert, Chandler, Pellew, and Sherman.

such. He made significant contributions to understanding the action of copper proteins and the mechanism whereby "browning" in exposed tissue occurs in nature. Nelson, fondly known to the undergraduates as "Pop," is said to have been an excellent lecturer in the undergraduate organic course for premedical students, but his unique course for first-year graduate students on the theories of organic chemistry was especially influential.

John L. R. Morgan (Ph.D. Leipzig, 1895; Columbia faculty member, 1897–1935) was the first professor of physical chemistry, the field that combines physics with chemistry and concentrates on quantitative measurements and theories. He published the first American textbook on the subject, *The Elements of Physical Chemistry* (1898). Joining Morgan in that field in the 1920s were Louis Hammett, Victor LaMer, and Harold Urey. Hammett opened the field of physical organic chemistry with the publication in 1940 of his book of that title. It was the first of several editions, in many languages, and became as famous to a generation of organic chemists as his fundamental work on structure/reactivity relationships and acidities. Among Hammett's many awards was the National Medal of Science. Victor LaMer became famous for his pioneering studies of the properties of electrolyte solutions and colloid chemistry. Hammett and LaMer both enjoyed long Columbia careers.

Harold Urey won the 1934 Nobel Prize in chemistry. His discovery of deuterium was quickly recognized for its value to the theory and practice of modern chemistry, particularly in delineating pathways in chemical and biological reactions, especially metabolism. Indeed, Urey's work set the stage for the use of isotopes to solve many important problems in chemistry, physics, and biology. Twice he shared major prizes, including a $7,600 award from the Carnegie Foundation with a young I. I. Rabi and his Nobel Prize with two junior colleagues in chemistry.

Urey went on to be a pioneer in many important areas of chemistry, but unfortunately he moved to the University of Chicago in 1945 and later to the University of California at San Diego, after heading up the Manhattan Project in World War II.

Joseph Mayer, Ralph Halford, Benjamin Dailey, George Kimball, Richard Dodson, T. Ivan Taylor, Jack Miller, and George Fraenkel joined the Columbia physical chemists in the following decades. Mayer's wife, Maria Geoppert Mayer, was a Columbia faculty member and later won a Nobel Prize for the shell theory of nuclei. Halford, Dailey, Taylor, and Fraenkel moved the department strongly toward new instrumental methods and technologies—especially in spectroscopy—that were rapidly changing the face of chemistry after World War II.

Louis Hammett receives the National Medal of Science from President Lyndon Johnson in 1967.

For a brief moment in history, the simultaneous departures of William Doering, Robert Elderfield, and David Curtin left the department deficient in organic chemistry. The addition of Cheves Walling (1952) and Gilbert Stork (1953), along with some younger people, helped Columbia extend the department's reputation as a leading center for research in organic chemistry.

THE CHEMISTRY DEPARTMENT TODAY

The Columbia chemistry department today has twenty-six faculty members, three with emeritus status. They are Bruce Berne, Ronald Breslow, Louis Brus, Virginia Cornish, Benjamin Dailey (emeritus), Samuel Danishefsky, Kenneth Eisenthal, Leonard Fine, George Flynn, Richard Friesner, George Fraenkel (emeritus), Brian Gibney, Thomas Katz, Laura Kaufman, Tristan Lambert, James Leighton, Ann McDermott, Koji Nakanishi, Jack Norton, Colin Nuckolls, Gerard Parkin, Philip Pechukas, David Reichman, Dalibor Sames, Scott Snyder, Gilbert Stork (emeritus), Nicholas Turro, and James Valentini. In contrast to the pattern in previous times, only one of them has a Columbia Ph.D., but two of the three women faculty graduated from Columbia College before taking their Ph.D. degrees elsewhere.

CHANDLER MEDALISTS 1910 TO THE PRESENT

1910 Charles Frederick Chandler	1943 Willard Henry Dow
1914 Leo Hendrik Baekeland	1948 Marston Taylor Bogert
1916 William Fredrick Hildebrand	and Henry Clapp Sherman
1920 Willis Rodney Whitney	1951 Milton C. Whitaker
1921 Sir Frederick Gowland Hopkins*	1954 Willard Frank Libby* and
1922 Edward Fahs Smith	Harry Linn Fisher
1923 Robert Eckles Swain*	1955 Vincent Du Vigneaud*
1925 Edward Calvin Kendall*	1957 William Hale Charch
1926 Samuel Wilson Parr	1958 Arthur Clay Cope
1927 Moses Gomberg	1964 Henry Taube*
1928 John Arthur Wilson	1966 Joseph Edward Mayer
1929 Irving Langmuir*	1968 Louis Plack Hammett
1931 James Bryant Conant	1970 Paul John Flory*
1932 George Oliver Curme Jr.	1973 Herbert Charles Brown*
1934 Jacob Goodale Lipman*	1976 Kai Siegbahn*
1936 William Francis Giauque*	1978 Joseph Chatt
1937 John Howard Northrop	1980 Frank H. Westheimer
1939 Thomas Hamilton Chilton	1983 Rudolph A. Marcus*
1942 Robert R. Williams and Roger	1986 Mildred Cohn
John Williams	1991 Howard E. Simmons
	1999 Harry B. Gray
	2005 Richard Zare

Asterisks indicate the thirteen who went on to win Nobel Prizes.

Collectively, the members of the faculty are part of the legacy of Charles Frederick Chandler and the house of chemistry that he built at Columbia. Eight are members of the U.S. National Academy of Science—a very large fraction of the twenty senior members of the department—and twelve are members of the American Academy of Arts and Sciences. Ten have won Sloan Fellowships. There are winners of the Wolf Prize, of the U.S. National Medal of Science, and of the Robert A. Welch Prize. Other awards to the current members number well over 100 and include some for outstanding teaching. Chandler would be pleased!

AND TOMORROW

Although the chemistry department is today quite strong, the path has not always been smooth. Some truly outstanding tenured chemists have left Columbia for what they perceived to be greener pastures in other leading chemistry departments, albeit thus making room for some of the current members. Some left in part because they were unhappy with the laboratory space in Havemeyer (now 108 years old but completely renovated twenty years ago) and Chandler (seventy-five years old and under extensive renovation). Some were attracted by stronger research support from their new institutions. Recently, Columbia has made commitments to increase modern research space and support of the sciences and can look forward to an even stronger chemistry department as it begins its second 250-year run. This will be the subject for another report on the 300th anniversary, perhaps with different authors.

CHAPTER 15

I. I. Rabi: Physics and Science at Columbia, in America, and Worldwide

—⁓⁓—

Samuel Devons

I. I. Rabi was for decades such a ubiquitous presence on the Columbia campus that Columbians who saw him making his way from Pupin to a meeting in Low Library or to lunch at the Faculty House would not perhaps have recognized in this white-haired gentleman the scientific giant who had been a dominant figure in the development of modern physics. To recall Rabi's role at Columbia and in the world at large we have Professor Emeritus of Physics Samuel Devons. Many who have attended commencement ceremonies at Columbia would recognize Devons easily in his resplendent ceremonial robes as the mace-bearer leading academic processions. His crimson robes are those of Cambridge University in England, whence Devons came to Columbia in 1960, soon to become chair of the physics department from 1963 to 1967.

More recently, in retirement Devons has been the spark plug of a new organization, Emeritus Professors in Columbia (EPIC, for short), that carries on a lively intellectual program for emeriti at Faculty House. The readiness and historical command with which he produced this essay on Rabi testify to his remarkable vitality in retirement and continuing responsiveness to calls for service to the university.

—*Wm. Theodore de Bary*

—⁓⁓—

A familiar problem in history is where to begin. Here our story conjoins the life of an institution with the life of an individual: the former spans two and a half centuries; the latter, a single century—the twentieth. The history of the institution provides a fiducial context for the lives of individuals, but since this is one of many narratives of many unique voices who collectively—with their academic progeny—define, indeed are, the institution, it is on the life of the individual that we focus.

A connecting thread between our individual—I. I. Rabi—and the institution of which he was a part—Columbia University—is from time to time provided by a much larger context: the evolution over the centuries of science in America. Here it should be remarked that the history of Columbia spans the whole history of American science, and the lifetime of Rabi covers the overwhelmingly greater part of its growth.

A SEMINAL PUBLIC SCIENTIST

Benjamin Franklin's autobiography tells us that when "Abbe" Jean-Antoine Nollet (1700–1770), authority on science in the court of Louis XV, "demonstrator" of electrical phenomena to all ranks including the queen and the Dauphin at Versailles, and known to a far wider audience as "Preceptor to the Children of France," first had his attention drawn to the writings on electricity of one Ben Franklin of Philadelphia, he refused to believe them. Not only did this panjandrum of science disbelieve the recorded phenomena and their interpretation, which he must have readily perceived as a threat to his own authority and scientific stature, but he denied the very existence of their author. How could an American, living on the perimeter of the untamed wilderness, far removed from European culture, have occasion or opportunity for such arcane philosophy? No! He and his alleged discovery were phantasms, cacodemons invented by Nollet's enemies to torment him (and there was no shortage of enemies in the court of Louis XV).

However, Franklin was real enough; his experiments were soon repeated, and his ideas spread widely. His "principles" soon led to the sensational demonstration of the electrical nature of lightning. His name, and "Franklinism," became known to most and familiar to many—statesmen and philosophers, ladies of the court, and scullery maids alike.

With such a glorious and dramatic demonstration of American colonial prowess in electrical science, one might have expected the field to have flourished and spread. However, there was but one Franklin, and American science was destined to be—for a couple of centuries—more the spontaneous efflorescence of individual genius than a widespread cultural phenomenon. However, Franklinism was perhaps a portent of the future. The invention of the lightning conductor to protect buildings was the first practical use of electrical "science"; and the exploitation of Franklin's scientific reputation enhanced the stature of science in the world of politics and diplomacy. Minister Turgot's characterization of Franklin as he "seized the fire from heaven and the scepter from the tyrant's hand" links together, ineluctably, his services to science and democracy.

It is unlikely that the Reverend Samuel Johnson, when he sat down in 1754 to educate his eight students in the liberal arts and sciences at King's College, the predecessor of Columbia, paid much attention to the seminal discoveries in electricity in Philadelphia. Not that Franklin and Johnson were unknown to each other. Franklin knew, and was impressed by, Johnson's work on ethics, had translated the Latin into English, and had tried to secure him as rector for his Philadelphia Academy. Nor were the sciences then ignored or even neglected. The liberal arts inherited from the medieval universities had their quota of these in the quadrivium: geometry, astronomy, arithmetic, and music. And the appointment in 1757 to King's College of the first professor of mathematics and natural philosophy— Daniel Treadwell—showed a more up-to-date concern. But all this referred to a borrowed culture, distant in time and space, with little ingredient of domestic product. And so it would remain for the first century and a half of Columbia's history.

SCIENTIFIC AWAKENINGS

During the rapid growth of the United States in the nineteenth century—extension of boundaries, agrarian and urban growth, emergent institutions and industries, and rapidly developing political structure—it would have been remarkable indeed if there had been no expression of scientific interest and activity. Outstanding examples of nineteenth-century American scientists were many: Joseph Henry (1797–1878), upstate New York, electromagnetism and telegraphy; Lewis Morris Rutherfurd (1816–1892), Columbia University, optics and astrophysics; Josiah Willard Gibbs (1839–1903), Yale, physics, chemistry, and thermodynamics; Henry Rowland (1848–1901), Johns Hopkins, optics and experimental physics; Albert Abraham Michelson (1852–1931), U.S. Naval Academy, the first American winner of the Nobel Prize for physics (1907). By the end of the century there was a significant growth of science in industry, especially the new electrical science, and opportunities therein attracted outstanding minds from abroad (Alexander Graham Bell and Nikola Tesla, among others).

Serbian immigrant and Columbia College graduate Michael Pupin would make significant contributions to long-range telegraphy and telephony—and a sizable

Rabi organized a Sunday study group of fellow graduate students in the mid-1920s to grapple with quantum mechanics, rapidly emerging in Europe but still little known in the United States. From left to right: S. C. Wang, Ralph de Kronig, Myron Schwarzchild, Mark Zemansky, and Rabi.

fortune. He attributed his success in part to a fortunate encounter with classical academics/mechanics. Inspired by this experience, he preached the study and promotion of "pure science," which he called the "goose that laid the golden egg." He was for many years professor of electrical engineering at Columbia, and when he died, he bequeathed the residue of his estate to "pure science"—as fostered by the newly completed physics building (1927), subsequently named Pupin Laboratory in his honor.

Pupin Laboratory eventually became I. I. Rabi's scientific home, the locus of virtually all his and his collaborators' scientific discoveries. In 1977, Columbia celebrated fifty years of Pupin Laboratory and fifty years of Rabi at Columbia. By then the two had become inextricably associated.

Rabi's Pupin was one of the earliest powerful and fertile American schools of physics. But it wasn't the first U.S. academic research center to match and embellish the traditions of the great research centers of Europe. That distinction surely belongs to Thomas Hunt Morgan (1866–1945) and his colleagues, working in what later became famous as the "Fly Room" in Columbia's Schermerhorn Hall. From this emerged the highly successful American school of genetics of Morgan, H. J. Muller and others.

Morgan's work was not overlooked in Europe. In an early review of its striking progress, Dutch geneticist Hugo De Vries (as I recall), in a review of the subject, refers to Columbia as a great "sleeping bear on Morningside Hill" that had "stirred and awakened itself" with quite astounding results.

In 1927, at the time of a dramatic breakaway in Europe from the "classical" notions of more than two centuries, Rabi, after a preliminary undergraduate education at Cornell, began his life's work at Columbia.

RABI AND THE NEW PHYSICS

Rabi's Jewish parents came to America from Central Europe in search of a better life, free from bigotry and the menace of persecution. Rabi's path from the crowded, indigent, immigrant life of New York's Lower East Side to its institutes of higher learning lay through the streets and public schools there and later in Brownsville, across the water in Brooklyn.

The education the schools provided may have been minimal, but for the resourceful and the independently minded the opportunities to learn were many. And Rabi found and exploited them. Local schools were run by the "wonderful tough Irish" from whom "you could get trouble if you looked for it," but they "created an atmosphere in which you could learn" if you wanted to.

He discovered the local public library (Carnegie), which "opened a universe" to him, and began a period of omnivorous reading. He began alphabetically on the library shelf with "A," and the new world of astronomy; the Copernican system especially, was a veritable epiphany of scientific enlightenment. There were equally profound lessons to be learned outside the library. As far as frugal resources allowed, Rabi immersed himself in a variety of activities at home—in the miracle and mystery of radio, in the variegated manifestations of nature evidenced through gardening, and in some down-to-earth photography.

Rabi, like many young immigrants of his day, lived in two worlds: one that he was leaving, that of the traditional customs and beliefs of his parents' home; the other that he was vigorously exploring for himself, of the artifacts, phenomena, and people outside. He recalls an amusing and characteristic effort to bring the two worlds together. On the occasion of his bar mitzvah, he addressed the gathering of family and friends on the subject, "How an Electric Light Works" in Yiddish.

Already in Rabi's school years, science was becoming central to his outlook. His early resolve to determine his own future was manifest in his decision to continue his education not at Boy's High School "where all the smart Jewish boys went," nor at a yeshiva, as his parents suggested, but at the Manual Training School in Brooklyn. However, science was not his only concern: he shared the characteristic immigrant determination to become a "good American." In his school-leaving Regents examination in 1916, Rabi placed first in history.

As he moved from Brooklyn's Manual Training School to the arena of frontline science, Rabi was again determined to find his own way, by trial and error if necessary. Of the opportunities available, he chose Cornell "with a sense of freedom and novelty," enrolling initially as a student of electrical engineering. Later he was attracted to and challenged by a course in analytical chemistry, which seemed to bring him closer to what he felt intuitively to be the intimate or ultimate structure of matter. At this time, the relationship between physics and chemistry was undergoing drastic change with respect to the study of the constitution of matter, which textbooks of the period would have reflected. For several years, then, Rabi was a chemist in embryo, actually discovering that the part of chemistry that really interested him was called physics. (How far was the distinction one of conventional definition?)

Despite a glowing testimonial from chemistry professor A. N. Brown, Rabi was not awarded a fellowship that would have enabled him to stay on at Cornell to study physics. Influenced in part by his future wife, Helen Newmark, Rabi decided in 1923 to become a graduate student at Columbia. He obtained a paying job as part-time tutor in physics at City College, New York: sixteen classroom hours of teaching a week with a stipend of $800 per annum. For the next two years, Rabi combined the demands of teaching at City College with his doctoral studies and research at Columbia. Additionally, he undertook the task of teaching himself (with a few fellow graduate students) the "new" physics—quantum mechanics—that was emerging with breathtaking speed and vigor in Europe but in which no American professors at Columbia were able to provide instruction or guidance.

Rabi accomplished everything in his own characteristic style. His instructional duties at City College were somewhat relaxed, and he managed to keep the demands of Columbia's graduate physics courses to a minimum. For his own research—the magnetic properties of crystalline Tutton salts, a topic inspired by English visitor W. L. Bragg's seminar—he developed an ingenious experimental procedure that obviated much of the tedious routine preparation and measurement of a more conventional approach.

Incidentally, Rabi's experimental approach came serendipitously from his reading of classical literature—in much the same way Pupin's inspiration came suddenly from J. L. Lagrange's *Mécanique analytique* (1788), which he had, some forty years earlier, picked up by chance from a secondhand bookstall on the banks of the Seine in Paris. In Rabi's case the work in question was J. C. Maxwell's *Treatise on Electricity and*

Magnetism of 1873. These are two examples of Pasteur's famous maxim that fortune favors the prepared mind.

Rabi devoted his Sundays to self-education. He organized a group to study the new physics with fellow graduate students Francis Bitter, Ralph de Kronig, S. C. Wang, and Mark Zemansky (all of whom became notable physicists). They met weekly, spent the day together talking, arguing, devouring and digesting the latest European journals, learning, and eating. Such was their devotion and infectious enthusiasm that in due course they were joined in their marathon sessions by some professors from New York University. (Not surprisingly, when Rabi later met his counterparts at leading German universities, he found that, notwithstanding his own lack of formal instruction by the great "masters," he was better prepared for research than were 95 percent of the German students.)

For Rabi and his fellow students it did not suffice to study, follow, and understand the work of others. The real test of understanding was to solve a problem of their own. They chose the application of Erwin Schrödinger's wave-mechanical equation to the symmetrical top. The mathematics was formidable, but serendipity once again came to the rescue, this time in the work of nineteenth-century mathematician C. G. J. Jacobi. De Kronig and Rabi's work on the quantum mechanics of the symmetrical top was accepted for publication in the February 1927 *American Physical Review*.

In July 1926, Rabi had completed work for a Ph.D. and successfully submitted his thesis for publication in the *Physical Review*. The following day he and Helen Newmark were married. In May 1927, he was awarded a Barnard Fellowship ($1,500 a year for two years), enabling him to do what he had set his mind on— complete his scientific apprenticeship in Europe.

In June 1927, Rabi resigned his appointment at City College, and in July he embarked for Europe. His destination was uncertain; he had no formal plans. Unannounced, he arrived in Zurich, hoping to meet and work with Schrödinger. But Schrödinger was just leaving Zurich to succeed Max Planck in Berlin. So Rabi changed course for Munich, home of pioneer of quantum mechanics and celebrated teacher Arnold Sommerfeld—a thoroughly European professor with an academic style not entirely to Rabi's taste.

A side trip to an annual British Association meeting in Leeds, England, provided Rabi with an opportunity to see and hear many of the greats, especially Peter Debye and the already renowned young Werner Heisenberg. He joined Helen Rabi in London, and they traveled to what was rapidly becoming the physicist's "shrine"—the Niels Bohr Institute in Copenhagen. Rabi may have been mystified and awed in the Bohr presence, but this was no basis for a lengthy association. In any case, Bohr had arranged for Rabi to go to Hamburg to work with Wolfgang Pauli (1900–1958), whose reputation as an acerbic theoretical physicist and a sharp critic was second to none.

After a few weeks in Copenhagen, the Rabis settled in Hamburg. Pauli's piercing arguments did not faze Rabi; he probably enjoyed the test of his mettle. And in Hamburg, it turned out, there was another attraction, the eminent experimental physicist Otto Stern (1888–1969), whose personal style and modus operandi Rabi would find most congenial and whose influence would have a profound effect on his future.

TICKLING A MOLECULAR BEAM

Stern had recently (1921–23) completed and published his already celebrated molecular-beam experiment demonstrating the phenomenon of "spatial quantization." The "Stern-Gerlach" effect was utterly perplexing from a "classical" viewpoint but a "natural" outcome of the quantum mechanical principles. This was the kind of issue that Rabi and his fellow students had sought to understand at the Sunday seminars at Columbia. Now here he was—by accident—at the very source, the fountainhead, of the latest in science. Stern's laboratory—which was composed of a group of some half-dozen students and associates, quite substantial in those days—became more than a distraction from Rabi's arranged program of theoretical work with Pauli. In true Rabi spirit, it was not enough to watch, listen, and learn passively; he wanted to get his hands on the business.

In the canonical Stern-Gerlach experiment, the streaming (sodium) atoms are deflected in their path by the influences of a nonuniform magnetic field. Rabi argued—by analogy to the passage of light through a prism—that if the atomic beam were to pass at a glancing angle into a uniform magnetic field, then this deflection would be different for different effective magnetic moments (that is, different orientations of the atom's axis). In mentioning this idea to Stern, the prompt and generous response was "Why not try the experiment here?"

Ironically, Rabi had come to Europe to learn theoretical physics. Now he was being invited to mount his own experimental project. Quite an honor, especially for a visiting American—and an irresistible opportunity to try a new variant of the Stern-Gerlach experiment in Stern's own laboratory. In 1928, the equipment was made ready with much help from a fellow visitor to Stern's laboratory, John Taylor from

"It's fun to be a physicist. . . ." reads the inscription on this photograph, doctored to show Rabi frying wieners on the cyclotron in the basement of Pupin. Rabi was famously informal throughout his working life, and he often whistled popular tunes or carved a piece of wood as he went from lab to lab.

Scotland. The experiment was completed successfully, and the work was published in *Zeitschrift für Physik* in German and, in a shorter version, *Nature*. The strenuous exertions as self-taught students at Columbia had reaped a good harvest in Germany.

In Hamburg Rabi heard quite casually an echo of the old theme: American science and physics were, at best, marginal. Browsing in the departmental library, he went to look at the latest happenings at home as reported in the *Physical Review*. The current monthly numbers were nowhere in sight. On inquiring at the librarian's desk, he was told that the Hamburg library had arranged to have the individual numbers of the journal collected and sent to Germany as a single package to economize on postage. In any event, he was assured, the delay was not important because "not much of great significance is published in the *Physical Review*."

Rabi's own success in Hamburg assured him that this attitude would soon be proved false. Numerous encounters with fellow students, visitors from America bent on similar paths of enlightenment, confirmed this view. They demonstrated that American physicists (or at least those who visited Germany) were a match, or more, for their German counterparts. And in Hamburg, the style of the Americans—their informality, lack of strict and regular hours, uninhibited expression of joy, anguish, or frustration in their work—had attracted attention and comment that "the American work method was, apparently, successful"; it might even be emulated.

After the experimental success in Hamburg, Rabi turned his attention to what was, ostensibly, his primary goal—enlightenment in theoretical physics. This took him early in 1928, again unannounced, to see Heisenberg in Leipzig. Heisenberg was preparing to leave Leipzig for an extended lecture tour in America, and the visit lasted just long enough for Rabi to make himself known and, apparently, to make a good impression, as subsequent events revealed.

Pauli had left Hamburg for a chair in Zurich. So Rabi went to Zurich once again in March 1929. There he found quite a galaxy of physicists, both European and American, attracted no doubt by Pauli's presence. They included Paul Dirac from Cambridge, Walter Heitler from Germany, Fritz London, Leo Szilard and Eugene Wigner from Berlin, John von Neumann from Göttingen, and Wheeler Loomis, J. Robert Oppenheimer, and John Slater from the United States.

Nearing the end of his European *Wanderjahre*, Rabi was enjoying the exhilarating air of the Swiss Alps and the stimulating society in Zurich. Heisenberg, meanwhile, was away in the United States, helping to shape Rabi's life in a most dramatic way. On a visit to Columbia, Heisenberg met George Pegram, chairman of physics, who had, in 1929, written to the leading theoretical physicists soliciting suggestions for a suitable professional appointment at Columbia. Heisenberg pointed out that Columbia already had an eminently suitable candidate of its own: I. I. Rabi.

Immediately Rabi received a cable offering him a lectureship at $3,000 per annum. He accepted promptly, and on August 1, 1929, he set sail for the United States and Columbia. Although the appointment was, implicitly, as a theoretical physicist, Rabi had already tasted the pleasures of experimentation both at Columbia and in Hamburg. When Pegram encouraged him to "at least direct some experimental work," Rabi began to actively contemplate such possibilities. In later years, Rabi lightly evaded the classification theoretical or experimental and declared himself "just a plain home-grown physicist."

Rabi devoted his first year at Columbia as lecturer exclusively to a strenuous effort to bring the graduate-student instruction up to date—to distribute some of the European bounty he had brought back in his lectures on quantum and statistical mechanics. Plans for experimentation were latent, nursed but not neglected.

In the 1920s, in Hamburg and elsewhere, the frontier of physics was in the atom and the new world of quantum mechanics that its study begot. But a new frontier lay ahead: the terra incognita of the atomic nucleus. To Rabi, on the threshold of his physics odyssey, the notion of combining the sophistication of quantum mechanics with the unexplored territory of the nucleus would have been irresistible. The molecular beam technique seemed to have possibilities far beyond the limited explorations in Stern's laboratory—and it held a greater appeal for Rabi than the high-energy, atom-smashing attack on the nucleus that was soon to emerge. Rabi found it more appealing and more sophisticated to gently tickle a beam of molecules. In any event, the material resources for the molecular beam technique were more practically realizable than the high-energy accelerator alternative. Rabi did not relish the task of coaxing from a departmental chairman or dean even the relatively modest funds needed for molecular beam equipment.

UREY'S BENEFICENCE

Again, fortune smiled—this time, in his association with an institution in which the university spirit of a "community of scholars" at times prevailed. Among Rabi's colleagues was the brilliant professor of chemistry Harold Urey (1893–1981), who demonstrated (working in Pupin Laboratory) the existence of a heavy isotope of hydrogen of mass 2 (deuterium). In recognition of this achievement, for which he won the Nobel Prize in 1934, Urey received an award from the Carnegie Foundation of about $8,000 to assist his research. Urey had no immediate need of this munificence, and in the course of a not-infrequent lunchtime meeting with his colleague Rabi, Urey asked if he could use some part for his research. For Rabi this never-to-be-forgotten act of generosity made possible the realization of his experimental plans, which he now began in earnest and which, for the next decade or so, flourished like the proverbial bay tree.

All that is possible here is to indicate a few salient features of the original Stern-Gerlach demonstration of quantum-mechanical atomic behavior. In the original experiments, magnetic forces acted directly on the atomic electrons. Optical spectroscopy, pushed to the limits of refinement, could show that atomic nuclei possess quantum-mechanical angular momentum and associated mechanical properties. The coupling between nuclear and atomic components indicated that proper understanding of those properties and experimental investigation of atomic interactions could reveal precise information about the nucleus—even though nuclear magnetic moments were some three orders of magnitude smaller than those of the electron.

Shortly after Rabi returned to Columbia, he set up a joint seminar with Gregory Breit (1899–1981), his colleague at New York University, to explore and discuss atomic-nuclear phenomena. One of the early fruits of this enterprise was their seminal theoretical paper (1931) exploring the variety of atomic-nuclear behavior in magnetic fields over a wide range of strengths. In the experimental molecular-beam

technique subsequently developed, a first separation would spread out the individual discrete quantum-mechanical component states, and then they could be individually subjected to known mechanical forces. Finally, the resulting beams could be recorded and analyzed.

For the next few years in the mid-1930s, Rabi and his growing group of disciples and coworkers were intensely absorbed in studying atomic-nuclear-molecular beams of their own creation. They were beginning to determine atomic-nucleus properties at a surprisingly vigorous rate. The brisk pace was essentially self-determined because they were not threatened by any immediate competition. The course of events in Germany had all but destroyed the Hamburg group. Otto Stern—Rabi's own mentor—was now a refugee from Nazi barbarity, living and working in Pittsburgh.

As Rabi and his colleagues refined their experimental techniques, and as the new results accrued, so did intuitive insights into the paradoxical quantum-mechanical features. One intriguing possibility was to go beyond observing the quantum-mechanical transitions incidental to the atomic passage through the various magnetic fields—to actively induce such transitions by imposing a (radio-frequency) oscillating field in addition to the (static) magnetic ones. A visit to the molecular-beam laboratory in 1937 by C. J. Gorter of Groningen precipitated active exploration of such techniques. Gorter had already attempted unsuccessfully to detect such transitions, not in the refined context of molecular beam experimentation, but more simply in aggregate bulk matter.

Within days of Gorter's visit, work was begun to modify a molecular-beam apparatus to test out the new so-called NMR (nuclear magnetic resonance) technique. Within a few months, there were lively celebrations by the team of Rabi, Sidney Millman, Jerrold Zacharias, and Polykarp Kusch, with all students and research associates joining in the festivities. A new chapter in atomic-molecular spectroscopy had been opened—one of extraordinary precision and refinement.

Prior to the success of NMR, physicists had tended to view the changes taking place in the space-quantified orientations of electrons in nuclei in terms of the arcane quantum mechanics of such dynamics. But soon a more general viewpoint prevailed: a "spectroscopic" transition between two quantum-mechanical states with the absorption of a quantum of the corresponding electromagnetic radiation of correct ("resonant") frequency.

In contrast to the time-honored optical spectroscopy (of visible light), the new NMR frequencies were one hundred million times smaller—and the two quantum-mechanical energy states were now separated by the correspondingly smaller energy. A new range of phenomena was now accessible to exploration and measurement with unprecedented exactness and sensitivity.

Rabi was elated—not least because he had helped demonstrate, with éclat, that American physicists had now come of age and were of full stature alongside those of Europe. Who now would trivialize the contents of the *Physical Review*? And Rabi himself, after a decade of intense work, had fully vindicated the trust and confidence of Stern, Heisenberg, Pegram, and Urey. He had realized the aspirations of Pupin at Columbia. American physics had found its leadership, and Rabi and Columbia were prominent at its center.

COLUMBIA'S RADIATION LAB

The power of the new sophisticated technique soon demonstrated itself in its application not simply to atoms but to cases in which fundamental principles were tested. To do so, physicists turned to the simplest system in which the particulars were considered well known. In atomic nuclear physics, this meant the hydrogen atomic system—one electron and one proton—or one heavy-hydrogen atom, where complexity would least obscure principle.

The Second World War diverted most scientific efforts from these lines of investigation. However, there were some quite remarkable early discoveries. Only seven

LIVING LEGACIES AT COLUMBIA

224

years earlier in Pupin, Urey had demonstrated the existence of the heavy hydrogen isotope "D." Now with the powerful NMR technique, Rabi and his colleagues determined the shape of the D nucleus and its surprising departure from sphericity (the "electrical quadruple moment"). What could be a more apt recognition of Urey's magnanimity of 1934? Again it was a clear example of the rapid ascent to prominence of American basic research in physics. For Rabi personally, there was a sense of religiosity ("nearer to God") in these deepening investigations, perhaps complementing the traditions of his early home and youth.

In the late 1930s there were dark clouds over Europe. For American scientists, there were also messengers who related the dire news—eminent refugee scientists who had escaped from Europe. Enrico Fermi came to Columbia, H. A. Bethe to Cornell, Felix Bloch to Stanford, George Gamow to Washington, D.C., and Rabi's mentor from Hamburg, Otto Stern, was in Pittsburgh. By 1940, the sweep of the Nazi blitzkrieg over Western Europe and the perilous, isolated position of England fully revealed in the Battle of Britain had begun to stir U.S. support, particularly among scientists. Developments in aerial, sea, and submarine capability revealed that the Second World War would be far more technological than previous wars. There was a clear appeal to the brains and skills of scientists as well as to their sympathies. The events in Europe were also a warning of what might befall the United States if it were swept into war ill prepared.

The sympathy of many U.S. scientists, who now included a significant proportion of refugees from Nazi Fascism, was undoubtedly with Great Britain and what remained of its allies. In principle, the industrial-technological might and scientific expertise of America were of formidable potential if they could be put to use—in the spirit of Churchill's plea, "Give us the tools and we'll finish the job." By 1941, there was a major political response: "Lend-Lease," an agreement that while remaining technically neutral, the United States would lease military equipment to Britain and provide other aid.

However, months earlier, the scientific community faced the problem of how best to bring its potency to bear. The crisis brought forth the latent power of American science—and the leadership to direct it. Rabi, though newly arrived at the forefront of American (and world) science, took up the challenge, and in the two or three succeeding war years he emerged as a foremost statesman of science. This was quite a different sort of "scientific" leadership from that which the neophyte American scientist wandering through Europe had yearned for. However, it was a leadership that in the near future would be sorely needed.

Rabi's—and Pupin's—wartime transformation was swift and effective. In November 1940, Rabi closed down his molecular-beam laboratory in Pupin and

Dwight D. Eisenhower, then president of Columbia, throws the switch in 1950 to start the synchrocyclotron at Columbia's Nevis Laboratories. From left: Hideki Yukawa, visiting professor; John Dunning, dean of engineering; an admiral from the Office of Naval Research (the sponsor of the construction of the cyclotron at Nevis); Rabi; and Eisenhower.

transferred his energies to radar development. With equal dispatch, he toured the country, coaxing his fellow physicists to join the new radar laboratory located at MIT (the "Rad Lab"). Rabi's talents, personal charm, and persuasiveness—as well as his scientific stature and integrity—were of inestimable value in the rapid establishment of "Rad Lab" and its role in the development of radar and other technologies as powerful tools in the military armory.

From late 1940 to 1945, Rabi was formally associate director and director of research, but his energies and influence extended far beyond the immediate scientific and technical realms. Formerly, his aim was, in his phrase, "to get closer to God"; now it was to close in on the Devil himself, to destroy Nazism and all its works.

To this end, the scientific community needed close, effective cooperation with the U.S. military. However, in view of their differing traditions, it was inevitable that there would be confrontations. It was not in Rabi's nature or in that of many scientists to simply serve the military as a hired technical aide. He could not accept the idea expressed by some higher military echelons that "scientists should be on tap, not on top." Rabi's aim was partnership with the military, the sharing of goals, and in his sphere, Rad Lab and radar, he was eminently successful. In his words, "When we got to know one another, when they (the military, specifically the Navy) learned we were trying to help them and that we respected them, when they discovered that we didn't want any of the glory, we came to be friends, with mutual respect."

Cooperation with the military was outstandingly successful. At the end of 1941 there were only a handful of scientists and little data on radar to work with. Within a couple of years, however, the few radar novices had grown to a mighty force of several thousand. In cooperation with the Armed Forces and industry, they designed, tested, set up for manufacture, and by war's end there were some 20,000 "3cm" radar systems in service. The technology was indispensable. In fact, military operations of any significant scale without radar had become unthinkable.

At the same time, Rabi's molecular-beam laboratory redirected its efforts entirely from atomic-magnetism to radar-magnetrons—the generators of microwave radiation at the heart of radar equipment. Stalwarts from the former molecular-beam laboratory—J. M. B. Kellogg, Sidney Millman, and Polykarp Kusch—were the mainspring of the work, a modern version of plowshares to swords. This auxiliary radiation laboratory, the Columbia Radiation Laboratory, supplied some invaluable basic scientific support for the main radiation laboratories at MIT. The Columbia Radiation Laboratory continued in existence at the war's end. Fittingly enough, its research work resulted in a fundamental reassessment of the basic science of electromagnetism—atomic quantum physics: the same electromagnetism that provided the basis for the sophisticated, elaborate technology represented by radar.

There were many major discoveries, such as the anomalous magnetic moment of the electron by Polykarp Kusch (with H. Foley) in 1947, who received the Nobel Prize in 1955; the fine-structure of the hydrogen spectrum by Willis E. Lamb (with R. C. Retherford) in 1947 (Nobel Prize in 1955); and microwave molecular spectroscopy, leading to the maser and laser, by C. Townes et al. in 1953 (Nobel Prize in 1964). By the mid-1950s, American physics was, in general, leading the world—and Columbia-Pupin was at the forefront.

SKEPTICISM ABOUT THE BOMB

In 1939–40, Columbia was already the locale of seminal activity that expanded into the awesome development of the atomic bomb. Enrico Fermi had escaped to Columbia from Mussolini's Italy; he, together with Urey, John Dunning, and visitor Leo Szilard, provided the inspiration and moving spirits in this effort. (Einstein was briefly but crucially drawn into the struggle.) After a couple of years, the project moved to Chicago, but the first federal government money—some $10,000 to find suitable graphite for Fermi's uranium assembly—was a grant made to Columbia.

Rabi was not directly involved in this historic enterprise, but he was far more than an interested spectator and critic. He was skeptical about the atomic bomb's contribution to the war effort and uneasy about the moral implications of such a weapon of mass and indiscriminate destruction. He also still had essential work to do at Rad Lab.

By 1943, when the United States had committed itself to the atomic bomb, Rabi had matured into an experienced authority on scientific-military-government cooperation. He also had a good rapport with J. Robert Oppenheimer (1904–1967), begun when they had met as fellow Americans in Leipzig in 1929. Oppenheimer was a theoretical physicist from California, newly chosen to be scientific director of the Manhattan Project, and Rabi provided fatherly advice on broad policy matters to his somewhat younger, less-seasoned colleague and friend. Officially, Rabi was throughout a senior consultant to the director. Though a not-infrequent visitor, he withstood efforts to draw him closer into the Los Alamos enterprise.

Rabi was eyewitness to the climactic and terrifying test at Alamogordo, the first atomic explosion, about which he wrote, "A new thing has been born, a new control, a new understanding of man, which man has acquired over nature. That was the scientific opening of the Atomic Age." It was an awesome responsibility for science, conferring a new sense of power and maturity. It also meant a loss of innocence, of childlike curiosity as a basis of scientific endeavor.

Alamogordo 1945 was a unique moment in human history. Locally, it marked a watershed for American science, as scientists who had flocked to enlist in the war effort now returned to take up abruptly where they left off years ago. For some who had participated in the enormous changes in science, the return proved not so simple. Rabi's wartime experience had shown him that stature, influence, and authority—at least over one's own activities—were necessary conditions for effective research and self-satisfaction. He eschewed the need to tangle with red tape endlessly. Spontaneity was his style, and it was possible in an academic setting if he could be manager of his own "show," chairman, for example, of his own department. And this he negotiated with a Columbia administration anxious to welcome him back.

Rabi's immediate task was to rebuild the thriving molecular-beam group. He and his coworkers John Nafe and Edward Nelson resumed the program with a simple hydrogen system with new sensitive and precise techniques. This work, together with Kusch's and Lamb's spectacular discoveries, led to the famous Shelter Island Conference of 1947, an elite gathering of some two dozen of the foremost physicists in the United States to review the fundamental implications of the new measurements and discoveries. American—and Columbian—physics was now not only of worldwide status: it was at its very center. This was, in essence, the climax of Rabi's postwar scientific efforts.

Within a few years, Rabi discovered the drawbacks inherent in his privileged position as department chairman. His authority and independence were counterbal-

Physicists Niels Bohr, James Franck, Albert Einstein, and Rabi, circa 1950. Although Rabi never worked with Einstein, he admired him greatly and was honored to discover that both Enrico Fermi and Einstein had signed the successful recommendation to award Rabi the 1944 Nobel Prize for physics.

anced by the responsibility of having to deal with the problems of others. In 1949 he confessed, "I found that I did not like to run people, to be responsible. The actual details of running the department, the nuts and bolts of it, were not to my taste." He left the decisions to a nominating committee and departed for Europe, passing the baton to Polykarp Kusch.

The period of Rabi's chairmanship had been one of strenuous rebuilding in a very competitive postwar situation. Topflight physicists had become celebrities to be sought and wooed. Rabi left his stamp of quality and style and a reputation of no-compromise standards for Columbia physics. What mattered was not so much who entered (as students) but who left with the Columbia imprimatur. Rabi referred to this as the mousetrap principle: easy to get in but not so easy to get out—alive!

He was willing to admit on trial anyone with a genuine interest in physics who was willing to work hard, with minimal a priori evidence of the ability to succeed. This policy may have been unpopular in some student circles, but it was vindicated in its wide influence on American academic physics. Many Columbia physics Ph.D.'s—those who had passed through the test of fire—were eagerly sought after to fill starting academic roles at other universities. And many were conspicuously successful in spreading Rabi's ideals and standards.

INSTITUTION BUILDING: NEVIS, BROOKHAVEN, AND CERN

Rabi had lasting influence on American science in other areas. Wartime experience had shown forcibly how science could operate on the grand scale. Rabi translated this possibility to the postwar academic scene and suggested academic cooperation of an unprecedented scale. There were like-minded colleagues in the Ivy League sister universities, but individually they were more used to viewing each other in a competitive rather than a cooperative spirit. But Rabi's diplomatic skills and the high esteem in which he was held were more than a match for the difficulties encountered. The first, exploratory discussion between representatives of nine participating universities took place early in 1946. By the end of the year, a site had been chosen on Long Island, N.Y., and in early 1947, in a formal contract between the group—Associated Universities, Inc.—and the Atomic Energy Commission, the Brookhaven National Laboratory was born. It has now passed its fiftieth year of operation.

To build up and maintain a viable, first-class academic department, Rabi was inevitably concerned with the attractiveness of its facilities. High-energy equipment at Columbia itself seemed essential, though it was hardly feasible within the confines of the Morningside Heights campus. The Nevis estate, some twenty miles north up the Hudson River Valley, was enticingly spacious and soon became the site for Columbia's Nevis Cyclotron Laboratory.

From about 1950 to 1970, the Nevis estate was the base for a most vigorous and successful research program, particularly in "meson" (intermediate) physics, a stage in the development of very large-scale high-energy physics. Within a decade or two, high-energy physics had outstripped the scale of any university or local research facility, finally becoming international and then global in scale. And in these developments, Rabi played a key role.

Inspired by Brookhaven, and in the context of his participation as U.S. delegate to the 5th General Assembly of UNESCO in Florence, Italy, in 1950, Rabi evoked the possibility of a similar European collaboration in a joint laboratory—one beyond the resources of any single country. The European scientists first reacted with ambivalence, even hostility. But with characteristic diplomatic skill, tact, and persuasiveness, Rabi coaxed several leading European scientists to themselves advocate the proposal, with UNESCO sponsorship, and to explore its realization without material support from the United States. Within a little less than two years, in February 1952, representatives from eleven European countries agreed formally to establish at Geneva the CERN (Conseil Européen pour la Recherche Nucléaire) Laboratory. At that meeting, they sent Rabi their greetings, informing him of the "official birth of the project you fathered in Florence. . . . Mother and child are doing well. . . ."

The twenty-three cosignatories included Heisenberg (Germany), Niels Bohr (Denmark), Pierre Auger (UNESCO France), Hannes Alfen (Sweden), and Eduardo Amaldi (Italy). Some twenty-five years later, a vigorous flourishing CERN could be held up as a supreme example of international cooperation in science. And Rabi's reputation as a statesman of science had become legendary. Indeed, when Columbia celebrated "Fifty Years of Pupin Laboratory and Fifty Years of Rabi:

1927–1977," CERN's director, John B. Adams, sent a message sadly regretting his inability to join the gathering in person, declaring that, had he been able to do so, he would have begun, without any implied impiety, with the words "Our Father who art in Columbia. . . ."

In all these efforts to promote the development of science, Rabi was affirming his conviction that cooperation in science provided incomparable opportunities to foster cooperation more widely. He may well have had in mind the sage advice of Ben Franklin: "Don't expect to do good and to get the credit for so doing." (At least not at the same time!)

In 1948, Dwight D. Eisenhower resigned his military position to become Columbia's fourteenth president. At their first meeting, congratulating Rabi on his recent Nobel Prize for physics (1944), Eisenhower added that he was always happy to see "one of Columbia's employees honored." The remark, it is recorded, drew from Rabi a measured response: "Mr. President, the faculty are not *employees* of the University—they are the University." This was, apparently, the beginning of some twenty years of friendship. To Eisenhower, Rabi represented science and its excellence at Columbia. At times, he expressed his anxiety that Rabi might yield to the many temptations to move elsewhere. But Rabi, virtually born and bred a New Yorker, regarded himself as part of Columbia and never seriously entertained leaving.

When, in 1953, Eisenhower left Columbia for the U.S. presidency, Rabi was already influential on the Washington and the international scene. In 1957, faced with the monumental scientific questions posed by the Atomic Age and spurred by the sudden appearance of the Soviet Sputnik, Eisenhower created (or re-created in new form) the office of Special Assistant to the President for Science and Technology (SAPST). Associated with this, and chaired by the special assistant, was the new Presidential Science Advisory Committee (PSAC). At the 1977 Columbia presentations, James Killian (first holder of the SAPST, then president of MIT) and the current incumbent, Frank Press (subsequently president of the National Academy of Sciences), paid tribute to Rabi. And a message from President Jimmy Carter expressed his pride "that both my scientific advisor and my secretary of defense [Harold Brown] were Rabi's pupils—influenced and guided in their college years by him."

Earlier, in 1953, Eisenhower, in an address to the United Nations in which he solemnly appraised the grave problems facing the world in the Age of Atomic Powers, raised the possibility of an international Atomic Energy Agency. It would help steer some of the growing, menacing stockpile of fissionable material away from warlike to peaceful purposes, "to open up a new channel for peaceful discussions . . . to shake off the inertia imposed by fear . . . to make a positive progress toward peace."

These words fell on many receptive ears. To Rabi, they confirmed his growing faith in science as, inter alia, a peaceful ambassador for international cooperation. As the then-chairman of the general advisory committee of the U.S. Atomic Energy Commission (AEC), he responded to an invitation from the chairman of the AEC for proposals to translate Eisenhower's plea into some form of action.

Early in 1954, Rabi suggested an international conference on "The Peaceful Uses of Atomic Energy." At first he met (as usual) with lukewarm response from some European colleagues. But familiarity with such initial circumspection and Eisenhower's own enthusiasm led him to persist in his efforts to persuade.

By year's end, Rabi had won a broad consensus. On December 4, 1954, the General Assembly of the UN unanimously adopted a resolution to sponsor "a technical conference of governments . . . under the auspices of the United Nations, to explore the means of developing the peaceful uses of atomic energy through international cooperation." UN Secretary-General Dag Hammarskjöld formed an advisory committee of scientists in January 1955. Rabi was the U.S. representative on this committee.

The unquestionable success of the first such conference (Geneva, August 1955) vindicated Rabi's judgment and his optimism. There were 3,000 participants from seventy-three countries (from both sides of the Iron Curtain). There was surprisingly high praise from the Russian delegate, physicist Vladimir Veksler, who called the meeting "not only the first truly great international conference in the field of physics. . . . It has opened up splendid perspectives for the peaceful utilization of atomic energy."

There were successors to the 1955 conference—in 1958, 1964, and 1971. Its success undoubtedly enhanced Rabi's political status—and effectiveness—in the 1957 deliberations leading to the creation of the PSAC, not to mention Eisenhower's rapport with Rabi and his esteem of scientists. Witness his flattering comment on the PSAC: "This bunch of scientists was one of the few groups I encountered (in Washington) who seemed there to help the country and not themselves." He confided that some of the most invigorating times he had while president were his meetings with them.

COLUMBIA'S FIRST UNIVERSITY PROFESSOR

In 1964, the new title University Professor was established at Columbia and Rabi was, appropriately enough, the first to be so designated. Rabi's counsel was sought

on an ever-widening range of government, academic, scientific, and industrial matters. Innumerable public honors and awards rested lightly on his shoulders. Perhaps
his most cherished acclaim was one not known publicly: the fact that his nomination for the 1944 Nobel Prize for physics was signed by Einstein and Fermi.

Science for Rabi remained a deeply personal affair. His home was in New York,
and his life work, laboratory, and office were in Pupin, a stone's throw away, as it had
been for more than half a century. Rabi continued to grace both the laboratory and
the tea room to greet students, faculty colleagues, and friends, and to appear at the
weekly colloquium. He was indomitable and seemingly timeless. Indeed, Rabi confessed that if he could choose where and how to leave this world, it would be to
"pass out peacefully" in a physics colloquium, adding that he hoped this would not
be interpreted as criticism of the colloquium speakers or censure of its committee.

Rabi's influence was most often and most deeply appreciated in his personal interactions. His dominant characteristic was his informality, expressed by unfeigned
candor, announced by a friendly smile or sometimes a not-unfriendly frown. He recognized formal structures and authorities as necessary, albeit of limited value; he tol-
erated and at times exploited them, but he rarely relished them. This informal
atmosphere infused all Rabi's works, in teaching, research, in politics.

Rabi's teaching style was not, by formal standards, outstanding. So it was especially gratifying to him, and perhaps affirmed his faith in American institutions,
when in 1981 the American Association of Physics Teachers awarded him (at the age
of eighty-three!) its Oersted Medal for distinction in teaching physics, citing "his
persuasive influence on American physics, through his own work, and through the
contributions of his many students."

"Wisdom is to be judged by its children." This truth is illustrated by the "Rabi
Tree," a tree-chart of scores of prominent scientists Rabi influenced, published in a
volume presented to him by the New York Academy of Sciences on his seventieth
birthday.

PERSONAL, RESPONSIBLE SCIENCE

Before World War II, science was a much smaller enterprise than it is today.
Physics, in particular, had hardly attained the rank of a profession outside academe.
In the time-compressed, breathless pace of war, however, potential leaders matured
at an accelerated rate. Comparatively young scientists became, at the peak rather
than the end of their careers, the new statesmen and elders of science. And
American science especially had acquired its leaders, Rabi preeminent among them.

In the postwar renaissance of science, the task of the new leadership was not only

to promote and develop science per se, but to guide its utilization and to guard against its misuse. "Nature," Francis Bacon had written more than three centuries earlier, "must in order to be commanded, first be obeyed." Mankind has developed vast skill in "obeying" nature. Ahead lay the much more daunting—at times terrifying—task of commanding. This would demand as much wisdom as knowledge. In Rabi's words, "Wisdom makes itself manifest in the application of knowledge to human needs. In a world that has amassed armaments sufficient to destroy if not all mankind then all fruits of human civilization many times over, survival must be ranked high among the human needs."

The tremendous experiences of World War II held many lessons. The immense power of science was driven home with a vengeance. Its primary drive may lie in the human yearning for knowledge and understanding, but its manifestations transform human labors and appetites. The exigencies of war magnified its potential—economic, technological, and social—to the point that science (cum technology?) might almost seem to be self-determining, to contain within itself the criteria for its own development. The more relaxed and contemplative postwar atmosphere permitted that the issues be examined more critically. And where else than at the university?

I. I. Rabi was a Nobel Prize–winning physicist, an internationally renowned statesman of science, and a beloved figure on Morningside Heights for more than a half century.

Some of the postwar developments—of better and bigger science—led one to circumspection. Rabi himself played a key role in the development of mega-science, involving cooperation too vast to be enveloped in an academic milieu. Science developed its own, and in its own, institutions. Rabi himself could not wholeheartedly follow. He had helped open the door into this future but did not pass through. His science was too personal, too rooted in academe to be transposed to the giant arenas of "big" science.

Rabi had collected some of his writings under the rubric "Science: The Center of Culture." Perhaps a more mellow phrase would have placed it *at* the center of culture—in the university, which was for Rabi a "repository of the past, a teacher and critic of the present, and through its science, an architect of the future." For Rabi science had a function in the university that transcended the "demands" of science itself. Perhaps it was here that the authentic and fundamental character of science—its essential contribution to the essential wisdom of our culture—was to be felt.

From time to time in preparing this tribute to Rabi, I have asked myself, "How would Rabi have reacted to this celebration of Columbia's 250th anniversary?" I recall that many years earlier, I was contemplating some explorations in the history of physics and happened to mention them to Rabi. His prompt reaction, albeit with some feigned expression of surprise, was "What? History of Science? At Columbia, in science, we don't study history, we make it!" Making science, was, to Rabi, making history—an essential part of our cultural history. Rabi's culture was a wide and generous one that included knowledge of and respect for the past, full participation in the present, and contributions (through science) to its future. Science was at the center of his culture. And he was fond of drawing contrasts between contemporary political history and the time of the founders of the country—a time when the spirit and ideals of the republic had roots closer to those of science and reason and practices based on honest labor and experience. Franklin epitomized this character. He was Rabi's hero, "my ideal man . . . the figure in American history most worthy of emulation . . . by scientists and nonscientists alike . . . everywhere."

For both Rabi and Franklin, science represented not only a power to alleviate life's burdens but also a sort of ideal with which to inspire more mundane affairs—even to transcend them. The ubiquity of its principles, their infinite expression in detailed actuality, and the endless subtleties and surprises (the lifeblood of science for its devotees) were awe-inspiring. Not for them the hubris of achievement, but the humility of what lay beyond, unaccomplished. "Knowledge is proud that it knows so much, wisdom is humble that it knows no more."

Humility could be evoked and expressed no less by the primitive "natural philosophy" of Franklin's day than by the sophisticated physics of Rabi's. For both men, it

A standing ovation for Rabi after he teaches his last class. He was a beloved figure on campus, a familiar presence in the graduate school tea room, and an inveterate attendee at the weekly colloquiums of the physics department. He once said that he would like to leave the world quietly during one of the colloquiums—as long as it was understood that he meant no disrespect to the speaker or the topic under discussion.

was the counterpart of the elation elicited by a spell of intense concentration on and mastery of science's subtleties. Thus Franklin, after a couple of years of (almost) total immersion in the mysteries of electricity (1750-style), could claim: "If no other use is found for Electricity, this much is certain: it makes a vain man humble." To which Rabi would have added "Amen!"

The Reverend Samuel Johnson and his eight students in 1754, Ben Franklin with his kite on the banks of the river Schuylkill, Columbia today with its many thousands, and Rabi's Pupin with its sophisticated subtleties and exquisite instruments, are worlds apart. Yet all are embraced by the transcendental natural laws, of which humble humans can discern a glimmer—guided by Franklin's principles of truth, honesty, and integrity. And both Franklin and Rabi could—each with his own interpretation—endorse the motto chosen for Columbia by the Reverend Johnson: *"In lumine tuo videbimus lumen"* ("In Thy light shall we see light." Psalm 36:9).

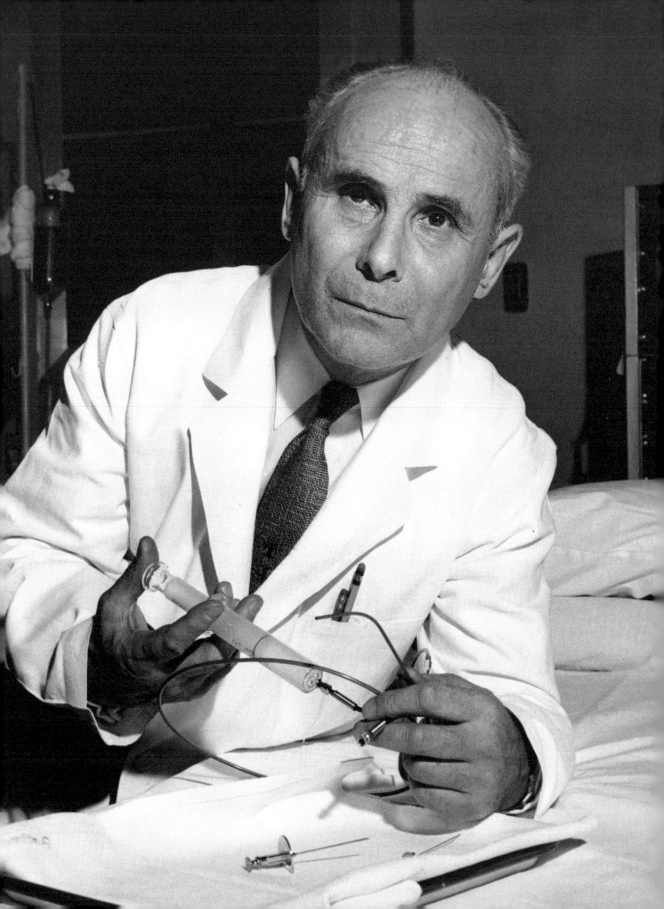

CHAPTER 16

Cournand and Richards and the Bellevue Hospital Cardiopulmonary Laboratory

—⟋⟋⟍—

Yale Enson and Mary Dickinson Chamberlin

From their eminence and celebrity as Nobel Prize–winners in medicine, one might expect an account of André Frédéric Cournand and Dickinson Richards to deal only with their remarkable achievements as research scientists working away in their laboratories. This essay by Yale Enson and Mary Dickinson Chamberlin, however, is a story of brilliant scholars and researchers, inspired by humanistic as well as scientific traditions, who contributed to the humanitarian service of Columbia's College of Physicians and Surgeons in the hospitals of New York.

Yale Enson is professor emeritus of clinical medicine and special lecturer in pulmonary medicine at the College of Physicians and Surgeons. He became a research fellow under Cournand in Columbia's Cardiopulmonary Laboratory at Bellevue Hospital in 1959—the last fellow for whom Cournand assumed direct responsibility. His own research has centered on the physiology of the pulmonary system, in which he has made substantial contributions to the study of arterial hypertension and the management of patients with circulatory complications of respiratory disease. He is a member of the American Physiologic Society and American Society for Clinical Investigation.

In contrast to André Cournand, who left rich documentation concerning his own early history and family background, Dickinson Richards left little. Mary Dickinson Chamberlin, M.D., proved to be the key to unlocking the personal history of her grandfather. A graduate of Cornell and of the University of Vermont Medical Center, she is currently a house officer in the Fletcher Allen Health Care Medical Center at the University of Vermont.

—Wm. Theodore de Bary

—⟋⟋⟍—

W e stand on the shoulders of giants to see even farther. For the contemporary cardiologist and pulmonologist these shoulders belong to Dickinson Woodruff Richards Jr. and André Frédéric Cournand, Nobel Prize–winners in medicine and physiology (together with Werner Forssmann of Germany) in 1956. But beyond this distinction, these physicians—each of whom partook of life in Columbia University for more than fifty years—merit celebration for elevating the empiricism of cardiology and pulmonology of the pre–World War II era to the level of hard science.

THE EARLY YEARS

André Frédéric Cournand (1895–1988) was born in Paris. His father, who held numerous patents in dental technology, was the source of the son's interest in medicine. Cournand was educated at the Lycée Condorcet but withdrew from the final year for private tutoring in philosophy. He received the *baccalauréat* in 1912. The following year he enrolled in the Faculté des Sciences and entered the Faculté de Médecine in 1914. With the outbreak of World War I, he enlisted in the army and served in the trenches near the German army as an auxiliary battalion surgeon (a rank created for medical students because of the high mortality rate among battalion surgeons). His duties involved searching for the wounded in no-man's-land, rendering first aid on the spot, and then supervising their evacuation. He was assigned initially to an infantry battalion engaged in the bloody trench warfare on the Chemin des Dames front. Early in 1918 he was transferred to Soissons, where mobile warfare produced equally severe casualties. Ultimately Cournand was awarded the Croix de Guerre with three bronze stars. His experience with the wounded in shock convinced him that a technique to deliver therapy directly into the heart might substantially reduce mortality, and it continued to influence his thinking twenty years later. His battlefield experiences were also the likely source of Cournand's willingness to undertake the risk of scientific challenges and to face crises with confidence and humor.

Cournand resumed his medical studies in 1919 and served as a house officer in the Hôpitaux de Paris, primarily at the Hôpital Laennec and the Hôpital Necker. During this period he also participated actively in the enthralling, vital cultural life of Paris of the 1920s. He was close to the Princess Marie Bonaparte and the French circle of Freudian psychoanalysts; the artists Yves Tanguy, Jacques Villon, Jacques Lipschitz, Max Ernst, Robert Delaunay, and Max Jacob; and the composers Darius Milhaud, Igor Stravinsky, and Edgar Varèse. By 1930, Cournand was qualified to enter private practice but first sought further training in pulmonary medicine under James Alexander Miller, director of the renowned Columbia Chest Service at Bellevue Hospital. During this residency, Dr. Miller suggested that Cournand participate in some studies of pulmonary physiology Dr. Richards was conducting there. Cournand leaped at the proposal, believing that the opportunity in this country for a career combining full-time research, teaching, and patient care would be more satisfying than private practice in France. He settled his affairs in Paris and, in January 1933, presented himself at Richards's laboratory, where, in Cournand's words, Richards "introduced me to all the techniques he had mastered in his early investigations and to sound and

Dickinson Richards

precise physiologic method and thinking. To the demanding taskmaster, to the scientific investigator, I owe more than I can tell."

Dickinson Woodruff Richards Jr. (1895–1973) was born in Orange, New Jersey. There were three generations of physicians in his mother's family, many with connections to the College of Physicians and Surgeons and/or Bellevue Hospital. He attended the Hotchkiss School in Lakeville, Connecticut, and, in 1917, received his bachelor's degree from Yale, where he excelled in Greek, the humanities, mathematics, and natural sciences. He served overseas as an artillery lieutenant in the army after graduation and began his medical education after the war, following a discussion with his uncle, Adrian Lambert, Professor of Surgery and Attending, First (Columbia) Surgical Service at Bellevue Hospital. Richards received the M.A. in physiology in 1922 and the M.D. in 1923 from the College of Physicians and Surgeons. He served as a house officer at The Presbyterian Hospital (1923–27) and took a postdoctoral fellowship (1927–28) under Nobel laureate Sir Henry Dale, whose laboratory at the National Institute for Medical Research, London, focused at the time on humoral agents responsible for circulatory control.

Back in New York, Richards was appointed to the Columbia faculty and initiated studies of blood oxygenation and carbon dioxide elimination as well as some aspects of circulatory physiology. A technique central to these studies involved measuring the volume of blood flowing through the lung each minute by what was known as the indirect Fick method, the only technique available at the time for use in human subjects. It was to an investigation of this method that Cournand was recruited.

By the time they met, both men had a clear understanding of their intellectual and scientific roots. Richards, the classicist, looked to the intellectual freedom and empiricism of fifth-century B.C. Greece as manifest in the writings of Hippocrates, which emphasized a wholly objective description of experience. He regarded Johannes Müller and Carl Ludwig, founders of the German school of experimental physiology, as his scientific progenitors (as did Dale, who traced his own roots, via Ernest Starling and William Bayliss, to Ludwig). Cournand, French to the core, regarded the rational and humanistic morality of René Descartes and Blaise Pascal as his guiding light, while Claude Bernard was his patron saint of experimental circulatory physiology. How many of Cournand's fellows still own copies of Bernard's *Introduction to the Study of Experimental Medicine!*

When Richards and Cournand began their collaboration, cardiology and pulmonology were dominated by the stethoscope, the electrocardiogram, and the necropsy suite, which defined normal and abnormal structure but gave precious little information about quantifiable disturbances in function. From the outset, therefore, these two were ideally positioned in a field lacking verifiable hypotheses (and methodologies) capable of explaining the functional disturbances encountered in lung diseases and in an environment (the First Medical Service and Chest Service at Bellevue Hospital, both under the aegis of Columbia University) rich in clinical material and diagnostic expertise.

A pattern of progress in their investigations persisted throughout the careers of these two researchers: functional descriptions in normal subjects and patients, elaboration of hypotheses concerning mechanisms, and experimental verification of hypotheses. Richards and Cournand began with studies of lung function, which they then extended to the heart and to the interaction of heart and lung. Their work resulted not only in methodologic and therapeutic advances but also in the production of new generations of investigators who continued and disseminated the work internationally. In the course of these efforts Cournand and Richards established the Cardiopulmonary Laboratory, the first clinical investigative unit of its kind.

LUNG STUDIES

Richards had been heavily influenced in his thinking by the celebrated Harvard physiologist Lawrence J. Henderson, and he took as the point of departure for his own studies Henderson's precept that the lungs, heart, and circulation constituted a single system whose function was to extract oxygen from the atmosphere and transport it to the various tissues to support their activities. It was clear to him that the key to a precise definition of this functional unit was an accurate measurement of blood flow through the lungs. The classic technique available for this assessment in humans at the time was the indirect Fick technique. The direct technique from which it evolved was developed during the nineteenth century for studies in animals. This benchmark method involved measuring oxygen consumption and mixed venous (i.e., right heart) and arterial blood oxygen contents so that flow could be calculated as the formula presented below.

$$\text{Pulmonary Blood Flow} = \frac{O_2 \text{ consumption}}{\text{arterial} - \text{mixed venous } O_2 \text{ difference}}$$

Because mixed venous blood was thought to be too dangerous to obtain in humans, researchers up to this point had used a modification that substituted carbon dioxide for oxygen in the above equation. This indirect method assumed equilibrium between carbon dioxide in the alveolar air and that in the mixed venous blood. Researchers measured carbon dioxide in a rebreathing bag system and arterial carbon dioxide content in samples obtained by direct arterial puncture. This method was used commonly and uncritically by others.

At the outset, Cournand and Richards made an effort to validate and improve the rebreathing method for estimating mixed venous carbon dioxide content and to apply it to individuals with lung disease. Their efforts, however, were only partially successful, for while they were ultimately able to define the "steady state" conditions (later adopted internationally) necessary for accurate measurements of flow, they ultimately demonstrated the inadequacy of the indirect Fick technique—a development that led inevitably to the development of cardiac catheterization, as discussed below. These studies, however, did indicate the value of a gentleman's three-piece suit: blood specimens obtained at Bellevue were immediately tucked into a vest pocket (to maintain them close to body temperature) and moved to the Medical Center for analysis.

An Army Air Forces mechanical respirator developed to maintain blood oxygenation during high-altitude flight. The efficacy of its design was evaluated in the Cardiopulmonary Laboratory.

Early in their collaboration Cournand and Richards successfully developed techniques that permitted the estimation of the volume of air in the lungs at the end of a complete inspiration ("the vital capacity") and at the end of a complete expiration ("residual volume"), using the elimination of nitrogen from the lungs during oxygen breathing (the "open circuit method") to calculate this "residual volume." The sum of the vital capacity and the residual volume defined the total lung capacity. Such assessments were obtained first in normal subjects, then repeated in patients with emphysema. In the first group nitrogen was eliminated within two minutes. The far slower rate of elimination of nitrogen in emphysema constituted the first demonstration of the maldistribution of respiratory gas in the lungs caused by airway obstruction. This observation had important implications for the study of ventilation-perfusion relationships, pulmonary arterial hypertension, and pulmonary heart disease, all future topics of concern for Cournand and Richards.

Within five years Cournand and Richards had sufficiently defined methods for describing lung function to permit them to evaluate mechanical respirators developed by the Army Air Forces to deliver oxygen to pilots flying at high altitude. They conducted these assessments in normal individuals, and the instrumentation was subsequently adapted for use in patients with respiratory failure due to heart failure, central nervous system depression, and neuromuscular disease (this being the era of rampant poliomyelitis). By the end of the 1940s they had described a fairly modern classification of pulmonary insufficiency, established standard methods of assessment, and published normal values of pulmonary function tests. They next turned their attention to abnormalities encountered in diffuse diseases of the lung parenchyma, and they described a novel disturbance of blood oxygenation (alveolar-capillary block with diffusion abnormality) stemming from such diseases.

Subsequent investigations conducted by Cournand and Richards and other members of the laboratory applied increasingly complex mathematical formulations to examine in greater detail the impact of pulmonary disease on respiratory gas exchange within the capillary blood phase in diseases involving the alveolar spaces. They also examined hemoglobin abnormalities and anemias as a source of changes of oxygen concentration in the blood. Finally, at the time of Cournand's retirement, a new technique that permitted quantitative descriptions of lung anatomy was developed.

HEART STUDIES

By 1936 it was clear to Cournand and Richards that the indirect Fick technique was inadequate for measuring pulmonary blood flow, especially in patients with chronic lung disease. Uniform equilibration between mixed venous blood carbon dioxide and alveolar concentration of the gas did not exist; furthermore, even in normal subjects, small shifts in the level of ventilation destroyed the "steady state" conditions required for accuracy. To measure pulmonary blood flow accurately, it would be necessary to sample mixed venous blood by the direct Fick technique. Cournand and Richards were aware of Werner Forssmann's report of catheterizing his own heart in 1929 and of subsequent pioneering work by European radiologists who injected contrast material into the right atrium for diagnostic purposes. Despite the opposition of many renowned cardiologists of the time, over the next four years Cournand worked to demonstrate the feasibility and safety of catheterizing the right heart, first in dogs, then in a chimpanzee, and, finally, in humans.

In this present age of interventional cardiology, it is difficult to realize the magnitude of the opposition to catheterizing the human heart—this in spite of the fact that catheters had been employed successfully in a variety of animals to measure blood flow since the previous century and that the necessary preliminary work had been accomplished in animals and human cadavers. Richard Riley, a senior member of the laboratory in the 1940s, describes important pragmatic considerations that helped Cournand and Richards to overcome this antagonism. With war looming on the horizon, the Office of Scientific Research and Development had a paramount interest in studies of the management of traumatic shock, for which measurement of blood flow was a necessity. He adds that, despite the disparaging things Richards had to say about tradition-bound medical priesthoods, his own status within that priesthood apparently gave him the privilege that others, including Cournand himself, lacked. Riley concludes that "these practical considerations in no way detract from Richards's inspired recognition. . . . He had the right intuition and he seized the moment." It is also important to remember that the inception of the work far antedated the concerns of ethics committees, patients' rights, and informed consent.

Early examinations in human subjects employed ureteral catheters used by urologic surgeons. Cournand and Richards reported more systematic comparisons of normal subjects and those with cardiac disease shortly thereafter. This later work provided an initial description of the hemodynamic abnormalities encountered in heart disease. Moreover, it demonstrated the safety, painlessness, feasibility, and diagnostic value of cardiac catheterization. Mixed venous blood was now available for measurement of pulmonary blood flow.

At this stage of development, intravascular pressure levels were measured with low-frequency water manometers that afforded only mean measurements of intra-cardiac pressures. Within a few years, however, technology evolved that permitted continuous recording of intravascular pressures. A special indwelling needle for sampling arterial blood and recording blood pressure was designed (the Cournand needle). The high-frequency Hamilton manometer that permitted accurate display of phasic intravascular blood pressure contours replaced the water manometer.

A description of a procedure in the catheterization room at Bellevue Hospital during this period may be of interest. The early fluoroscopes used to guide passage of the catheter did not couple the X-ray tube (below the table) to the above-table luminescent screen. Imagine one postdoctoral fellow manipulating the screen to follow the catheter tip while his wife (also a fellow) lay on the floor under the table moving the X-ray tube to follow the screen. Once the catheter was in place, all lights in the room were turned off, and the Hamilton manometer (which focused a light on sensitive paper to record the pressure contour) was attached to the catheter and manipulated in absolute darkness so that its light output could be captured with a handheld mirror and adjusted to strike the paper. Researchers then could record intravascular pressures and obtain samples for measuring blood flow. Not an easy procedure.

In all the early procedures, the catheter tip was positioned in the right atrium. It was feared that attempts to catheterize the pulmonary artery might be excessively dangerous. Indeed, catheterization of that vessel was fortuitous. The momentum of flowing blood, however, tends to carry a catheter along its direction of flow, and on several occasions in 1944 Cournand noted that the right atrial catheter suddenly appeared in the pulmonary artery at a time when no manipulations were being made. The catheters were permitted to remain in that position for prolonged periods without side effects or complications. As a consequence catheterization of this vessel became a routine feature of hemodynamic evaluations.

World War II interfered, for a time, with further development and wider application of the catheterization technique. Under the auspices of the Office of Scientific Research and Development, the laboratory undertook studies of the physiologic disturbances encountered in traumatic and hemorrhagic shock. This work established the therapeutic value of blood volume expansion with Dextran in patients with shock.

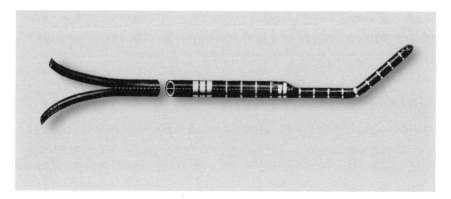

*An early form of car-
diac catheter employed
in the mid-1940s*

At the end of the war, in 1945, Richards became director of the First (Columbia) Medical Service at Bellevue. His educational, clinical, and administrative responsibilities precluded hands-on efforts in the laboratory, but he continued to participate actively in planning projects and protocols and evaluating results. Cournand was responsible for administrative and educational direction of the laboratory as well as direction of the diagnostic and research protocols.

An explosion of scientific and technical activity accompanied the conclusion of the war: in short order electronic advances achieved during the war were applied to pressure transducers and carrier amplifiers that permitted continuous pressure contour recording. Cardiac catheters fabricated from extruded nylon were designed to Cournand's specifications. The new technology of modern cardiac catheterization generated important new biomedical industrial activity. Within five years of the end of the war, Cournand, Richards, and other members of the laboratory had published systematic descriptions of the hemodynamic abnormalities encountered in congenital heart disease and in pulmonary heart disease and of the hemodynamic response, in patients with heart failure, to the administration of digoxin. In short order the same investigators followed these reports with detailed examinations of rheumatic valvular disease and of pericardial restrictive disease. Major consequences of these latter reports included innovations in patient management and criteria for selection of candidates for cardiac surgery. They provided currently employed normal and abnormal hemodynamic values and were the impetus for further studies of important side effects of heart failure. The work done in Cournand and Richards's laboratory had established modern diagnostic cardiology and paved the way for the development of interventive cardiology and radiology.

By the 1960s members of the Laboratory had developed additional techniques to examine detailed aspects of cardiac function. They employed radioisotopes for the noninvasive evaluation of right ventricular ejection rates, pulmonary blood flow, and pulmonary blood volume. Fiber-optic techniques were applied to cardiac catheters and permitted detection of blood flow through abnormal communications between the left-sided and right-sided chambers of the heart.

THE PULMONARY CIRCULATION

At the end of World War II it was generally held that the pulmonary vessels, by virtue of their scant smooth muscle endowment, were incapable of vasomotion (that is, functional change in caliber and hence in flow-resistive properties). Pulmonary hypertension in patients with chronic airway obstruction was thought to be the irreversible consequence of accompanying inflammatory changes. In 1946, however, Swedish physiologists reported that a decrease in inspired oxygen concentration evoked pulmonary arterial vasoconstriction in the cat. Recognizing that disease imposed a similar hypoxic stimulus on the pulmonary vessels in humans and that this deficiency of oxygen might serve as the link between lung disease and the development of pulmonary arterial hypertension, Cournand identified such vasoconstrictive properties in normal human subjects within a matter of months. He then initiated a systematic descriptive study of chronic airway obstruction and hypoxemia, which demonstrated a close relationship between the severity of hypoxemia and the level of pulmonary hypertension as well as the amelioration of hypertension with relief of hypoxemia during treatment.

Because an acute hypoxic stimulus was considered too hazardous to use in such patients, members of the laboratory employed an alternative experimental approach to confirm the role of hypoxia as the source of vasoconstriction. Acetylcholine, a selective pulmonary vasodilator in normal subjects under hypoxic conditions (selective because the agent is rapidly destroyed by circulating cholinesterase before it arrives in the left heart), was infused directly into the pulmonary artery of patients with chronic airway obstruction. A significant fall in pulmonary artery pressure resulted, confirming the functional nature of pulmonary hypertension in these patients. Equally important, the results indicated that hypoxic vasoconstriction diverts blood flow away from the least ventilated regions of the lung toward better-ventilated areas, thus defending blood oxygenation in the presence of disease.

After Richards and Cournand retired, other members of the laboratory extended these observations to consider the impact of respiratory acidosis on pulmonary artery pressure. They confirmed that increasing acidosis and hypoxemia were interacting factors that determined the level of pulmonary hypertension in chronic airway obstruction, in the obesity hypoventilation syndrome, in neuromuscular dis-

Bellevue Hospital, bell-wether of the New York City Hospital System, as it appeared in 1939

ease, and in the presence of respiratory muscle fatigue. They reported advances in understanding of pulmonary circulation from an important educational podium over a period of thirty years, demonstrating sustained leadership of the laboratory in this field.

THE CARDIOPULMONARY LABORATORY

From the late 1940s on, the laboratory's publications and distinguished reputation brought a host of fellowship applicants. As these physicians left Bellevue Hospital they assumed leadership positions in cardiologic and pulmonary centers across this country and Europe, disseminating the concepts Cournand and Richards had developed and contributing to the primacy of the laboratory. A stellar cadre of senior investigators also coalesced in the laboratory. William Briscoe provided detailed descriptions of the matching of abnormal lung ventilation and pulmonary blood flow as well as its consequences with respect to respiratory gas exchange. Harry Fritts Jr. studied the apportionment of blood flow between normal areas of the lung and sites of inflammatory or neoplastic abnormalities; he also examined the separate oxygen consumptions of these regions. Domingo Gomez, a renowned biomathematician, author of the first modern treatise on hemodynamics in the 1930s, and president-in-exile of Cuba in the aftermath of the Castro revolution,

Harry W. Fritts Jr. at the time of his accession to the directorship of the Cardiopulmonary Laboratory

elaborated physico-mathematical models of pulmonary function in health and disease. Réjane Harvey and M. Irené Ferrer examined the factors responsible for vasomotor control of the pulmonary circulation and the genesis of right heart disease caused by chronic lung disease, developing along the way many of the modern methods for managing chronic bronchitis and emphysema. Richard Riley investigated oxygen diffusion within the lungs and in the pulmonary microcirculation.

In the late 1950s Richards was an august personage in the laboratory. His rather taciturn and, in the eyes of young postdocs, austere demeanor was probably due to modesty, almost to the point of shyness. His warmth, kindness, and moral strength were most evident at the bedside with house officers and patients. He was not, however, without an understated, wry sense of humor. He had given the house staff permission to use his office as a library; when he announced one day, regretfully, that it was necessary to place a lock on his dial telephone because he had noted abuse of its availability, particularly with respect to calls to Paris, it was apparent to all that he was referring to Cournand rather than to the house officers. After winning the Nobel Prize, Richards immediately turned his efforts toward persuading the city administration to modernize the antiquated physical plant at Bellevue Hospital. Subsequently, he was generous with his time in support of the construction of the new hospital.

Cournand was equally endowed with gravitas. He was shorter, stocky, physically vigorous, and enthusiastically volatile under appropriate stimulation. He and Gomez (who, although Cuban, had been educated in Paris) would argue vociferously in the hall outside their offices, ranging from politics to the arts to science, and swinging from French to English and back. All members of the laboratory met in conference around a long table on Saturday mornings when clinical cases, work-in-progress, or physiologic topics were discussed. After Cournand had remarked on a paper he had read recently, one junior fellow remarked that his comments seemed paranoid. Cournand rose in a flash, ran down the table and confronted the young man nose-to-nose. "Correct! And by the end of your fellowship, Doctor, you will also have a yellow streak of paranoia down your back eighteen inches wide!" His kindness and scientific curiosity were unbounded. When the same fellow noted a phenomenon related to the reflection of light by flowing blood that could not be explained, Cournand arranged for him to confer with the eminent physicist Richard Garwin. The solution was not forthcoming, but became apparent at a cocktail party attended by all members of the laboratory the following Christmas, when Briscoe suggested that the phenomenon resembled the Rayleigh effect, which causes the sky to appear blue. He was correct. Apparently he could not refrain from discussing scientific problems, even under social circumstances.

Cournand and Richards provided an intellectually rich and nourishing environment for the members of the laboratory. One rubbed neurons with the best and the brightest on a daily basis. Eminent physiologists from all over the world visited each time they came to this country for a meeting or vacation. The urge to work, to understand, to "measure up" was generated from within and involved all. When time for retirement came, Charles Ragan, an eminent rheumatologist, succeeded Richards as director of the First Medical Service, while Harry Fritts Jr. a leading member of the cadre of senior investigators in the laboratory, succeeded Cournand as director. Research, education, and patient care continued undiminished under this new regime. However, in 1968 the city administration decided that three universities (Columbia, Cornell, and New York University) providing patient care at Bellevue Hospital was redundant and requested that Columbia and Cornell provide care at other components of the city hospital system. Accordingly, the First Medical Service moved to The Harlem Hospital Center. The Cardiopulmonary Laboratory closed its doors; its members dispersed.

POSTRETIREMENT

After retirement, both Cournand and Richards continued their intellectual pursuits as well as their activities within the university. Richards devoted himself to a variety of scholarly interests. As historian he edited (with Alfred Fishman) *A*

History of the Circulation and published insightful essays on William Harvey and Hippocrates. He celebrated his devotion to Greek classicism, to social criticism, and to cardiopulmonary physiology in a volume entitled *Medical Priesthoods and Other Essays*. He also helped organize interdisciplinary projects as a member (with Cournand and David Truman of the Administrative Committee of Columbia University) of the Institute for the Study of Science in Human Affairs and directed a program in the history of biomedical sciences at the College of Physicians and Surgeons. In a tribute to Richards, Cournand concluded that his colleague's postretirement concerns reflected qualities that characterized his entire professional life, "the sensitive yet very effective clinician, the dispassionate analytical philosopher, and the humanist of warmth and great moral strength."

For a number of years after retirement Cournand worked to acquaint American readers with the doctrines of Gaston Berger, which advanced a method of planning for the future (*Prospective Approach to the Future*) by placing preferred futures as the driving force for planning. He translated a number of Berger's works into English and published them as *Shaping the Future*. He also introduced into the medical school curriculum a course on the relationship between medicine and society, which he regarded as an opportunity to disseminate prospective ideas and methods. Another concern during retirement was to develop the principles of an ethical code for the scientist. At meetings of the Frensham Pond group (scholars, sociologists, philosophers, and educators brought together by the Bernard van Leer Foundation), he developed a close association with the social scientists Robert Merton and Harriet Zuckerman and was stimulated to articulate his own experiences as a scientist. Subsequently he and Zuckerman published "The Code of the Scientist and Its Relationship to Ethics in Science" in the journal *Science*. Finally, Cournand considered his own life as a scientist and its aftermath in a biography entitled *From Roots . . . to Late Budding*. He became preoccupied with the question "What is a scientific investigator?" The papers he wrote during these final years reflect his abiding concern with scientific responsibility.

L'ENVOI

The Nobel Prizes, and the recognition and encomiums stemming from them, memorialize an innovation. But these honors may tacitly scant the sum of achievement over the course of a professional life that in the most profound sense reflects the true value of that life. Cournand and Richards produced a technological innovation that resulted in a paradigmatic shift in diagnosis of diseases of the heart and lungs. The substance of their contribution, however, was the creation of modern cardiopulmonary medicine both technologically and conceptually. Henderson was correct: the heart, lungs, and circulation really are a single functional unit; here are its normal values, this is how it works, and these are the manifestations of malfunction. The framework they evolved for understanding normal and abnormal cardiopulmonary function was disseminated on a lasting and international basis and had a profound impact on patient management, on medical education, and on the biomedical industry. We truly do stand on the shoulders of giants.

We have benefited from comments on this essay by Peter R. B. Caldwell.

CHAPTER 17

Virginia Apgar:
Savior of New Lives

—※—

Marion Hunt

Infants today all over the world share in a legacy from Dr. Virginia Apgar that is a "living" one in a very special and exact sense: the enhancement of their survival rate by the tests she devised for their immediate care at the moment of birth. This is the method for evaluating the viability of newborns by five easily observed signs: respiration, heart rate, color, reflex irritability, and muscle tone. Known as the Apgar score, this test not only became the best predictor of infant survival in the first month of life, but also ushered in "a new era of interventive care for the very young." In fact, Apgar is credited with a pivotal role in reducing infant mortality by 75 percent from 1952 to 2002. One of only three women to graduate from Columbia's College of Physicians and Surgeons in the class of 1933, Apgar went on to become a leading anesthesiologist and neonatologist, heading a research team in the swift and specialized care of fragile newborns at the critical juncture between new life and possible sudden death. After twenty years of academic service at P&S, she capped her professional life by serving at the national level with the March of Dimes Foundation, as director of its birth defects division.

For drawing our attention to Apgar's extraordinary contributions to the health services and medical profession we have Marion Hunt to thank as an historian of social welfare and of medicine in particular. Dr. Hunt has been the primary consultant for Changing the Face of Medicine, *a major exhibit at the National Library of Medicine on the history of women physicians. With Dr. Ruth Fischbach, professor of bioethics and director of the Center for Bioethics at Columbia University, she organized the Virginia Apgar Symposium in 2002 at the College of Physicians and Surgeons. Hunt wrote the biographical essay on Apgar included in an award-winning publication honoring the fiftieth anniversary of the Apgar score. Her biographical essays on distinguished women physicians have appeared in the* Dictionary of American Biography *and* Notable American Women.

—*Wm. Theodore de Bary*

—⁓⁓—

Every baby born in a modern hospital anywhere in the world is looked at through the eyes of Virginia Apgar . . .

In 1949 Virginia Apgar, M.D., became the first woman to attain the rank of full professor at Columbia University's College of Physicians and Surgeons, an achievement all the more impressive in an era of pervasive prejudice against women physicians. A few years later Apgar developed the famous test for evaluating the condition of newborns, which bears her name. In 1959 she left her alma mater to become vice president of medical affairs at the National Foundation–March of Dimes, devoting the rest of her career to overseeing research and innovative prevention programs to save babies from birth defects, premature birth, and low birth weight. Equally important, she was a superb educator and advocate, who helped the American public understand that babies so afflicted were not just private family tragedies but an important national health problem.

Her most remarkable legacy lives on in the simple, accurate, and noninvasive test still used in the first moments of millions of babies' lives. At a medical meeting in 1952, Apgar presented her "new method of evaluating newborns," which used five easily observed signs: respiration, heart rate, color, reflex irritability, and muscle tone. In the first strenuous moments of life, each baby was given a number indicating the quality of the baby's response: 0, 1, or 2. An overall score of 7 to 10 indicated a newborn in good condition, 4 to 6 a moderately depressed infant, and 0 to 3 a severely depressed baby in need of immediate resuscitation. Medical personnel gave Apgar scores at one and five minutes after birth. In 1953, Apgar published a paper on the score's value as a predictor of survival that has become a classic text in the history of medicine.

Despite many advances in medical technology since then, the Apgar score has stood the test of time. In 2002 the *New England Journal of Medicine* published a lead article to mark the fiftieth anniversary of her pathbreaking paper. Based on a study of 150,000 births, Dr. Brian Casey concluded that the Apgar score remains the best predictor of infant survival in the first month: "If only one test is to be used . . . it should be the Apgar score." He credited Virginia Apgar with a pivotal role in the "tremendous improvement" in infant mortality rates since 1952, a 75 percent drop from 20 per 1,000 to 5 per 1,000.

How did Apgar attain her remarkable success? One crucial element was her gift for keen clinical observation; another was her farsighted approach to emerging frontiers in medicine. Pragmatic flexibility, high intelligence, and boundless energy were also essential. She gave a revealing retrospective view of her career: "I've been lucky all my life. True, I did not achieve everything for which I aimed, but these failures probably constitute less than 10 percent of the opportunities presented." Most important of all was her ability to overcome obstacles and make the best of every opportunity.

CHANGING THE CULTURE OF THE DELIVERY ROOM

Virginia Apgar's scoring system was a crucial step in changing the tradition of inattention and fatalism that had characterized the treatment of frail and premature newborns. Because little or nothing was done for these babies, neonatologists have called the decades between 1920 and 1950 "the hands-off years." Apgar's work marked a new era of interventive care for the very young.

Dr. William A. Silverman, a Columbia pediatrician and former director of the Neonatal Intensive Care Unit at Babies Hospital, described Apgar's shock on seeing the established practice of letting marginally viable neonates expire without any efforts at resuscitation: "She lost no time in launching a vigorous campaign to change the culture of the delivery room." According to Silverman, Apgar saved babies by "her enthusiastic teaching of mandatory resuscitation." As he recalled, she was "a very effective teacher who taught activism by example."

According to Dr. Selma Calmes, herself a leading anesthesiologist, "Dr. Apgar entered obstetrical anesthesia at the right time and in the right place." In 1949, when she began to specialize in this field, there was a shortage of obstetrical anesthesiologists and concern about the high rate of maternal mortality. The doctors at Columbia's Sloane Hospital for Women wanted to solve both these problems, and they made important improvements in delivery-room care.

Because of her innovative measurement of a complex clinical phenomenon, Apgar has been called "the founding parent of modern clinimetrics." The Apgar score heralded the development of both modern obstetrical anesthesia and neonatology. It showed doctors the practical value of paying close attention to the baby as the second patient in the delivery room.

The flash of insight leading to Apgar's innovation came in answer to a student's lunchtime question: how could the health of newborns be assessed? As a practicing anesthetist, Apgar's daily work involved close observation of newborns, and this experience—rather than any abstract theorizing—informed her response. An enthusiastic teacher, she immediately jotted down on a napkin a five-point list of what a doctor could immediately observe: heart rate, respiratory effort, muscle tone, reflex irritability, and color. Apgar then returned to the delivery room to test her idea.

Apgar presented her findings in a 1953 research paper, which frankly described the many confused and confusing ideas about infant resuscitation: "Seldom have there been such imaginative ideas, such enthusiasms and dislikes, and such unscientific observations and study about one clinical picture." Apgar's remedy was the simple, objective test that bears her name.

The Apgar score's impact was immediate and widespread. Dr. Harold Fox, a past chairman of Columbia's Department of Obstetrics and Gynecology, has noted, "Rarely in medicine has a simple clinical assessment been so universally accepted and applied." This swift acceptance was evidence both of the test's effectiveness and of a basic change in the culture of medicine. Silverman associates the change with a postwar "wave of optimism" in the wake of another major therapeutic victory—the discovery of antibiotics.

EARLY PROMISE FULFILLED

From childhood, Virginia Apgar had shown keen intelligence and extraordinary energy. Born in 1909 in Westfield, New Jersey, she was the younger of two surviving children of Charles and Helen Apgar. Apgar described her family as "people who never sat down," a trait she inherited.

Virginia shared her father's interests in music and, later, in science. She chose the violin as her instrument. Despite her busy career, playing chamber music was a lifelong avocation. An excellent student, she was active in athletics; her only failing grade in high school was in home economics. The 1924 Westfield High School yearbook noted, "The industry of the bee is second only to that of Virginia." A zoology and chemistry major at Mount Holyoke College, she also played on seven varsity teams. In recommending her for a biology fellowship, Professor Christianna Smith wrote: "It is seldom that one finds a student so thoroughly immersed in her subject and with such a wide knowledge of it." Since her family's financial resources were limited, Apgar took part-time jobs waiting on tables and catching cats for the biology laboratory.

Just before the stock market crash in 1929, she entered the Columbia College of Physicians and Surgeons, one of three women in a group of sixty-nine. Apgar graduated at the top of her class in 1933. Despite financial aid, at the end of four years,

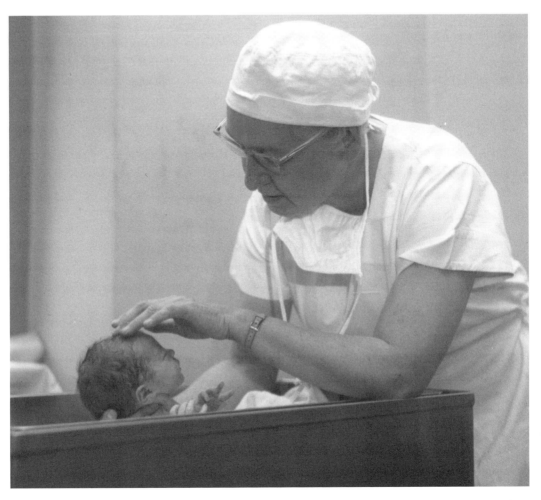

Dr. Apgar at work in the delivery room

the new Dr. Apgar was $4,000 in debt—then an enormous sum. Yet harsh econom-
ic circumstances never dampened her enthusiasm for learning or her personal
warmth. Dr. Vera Joseph, one of the rare women of color then enrolled at the medical school, vividly recalled Virginia Apgar's kindness almost seventy years later: "In
her keen, perceptive way, she recognized my need for assurance . . . she would
pause for a cheerful greeting, a reassuring hug, or a conversation."

Apgar won a coveted surgical internship at Presbyterian Hospital. However,
after two years of hard work, Dr. Alan Whipple, the chief of surgery, told her he
doubted a woman surgeon could make a living during the Depression. Pointing out
that improvements in anesthesia could lead to better surgical outcomes, Whipple
encouraged her to enter the new field of anesthesiology. Dismayed though she was

at giving up her ambition to be a surgeon, Virginia Apgar made the first of many positive adaptations to the barriers that confronted her: she turned to an uncertain, less prestigious field and helped develop it into a full-fledged medical specialty.

Nurses had been the first professional group to administer anesthesia, as subordinates to surgeons. Bringing doctors into the operating room to manage anesthesia would inevitably bring change to surgeons' traditional dominance. Apgar's own training reflected this evolution. During 1936 and early 1937, she worked alongside the nurse-anesthetists at Presbyterian Hospital to master the techniques then known. Her previous experience as a surgical intern gave her a distinct advantage, and she also sought the best available preparation. Apgar went to the University of Wisconsin School of Medicine—then the only medical school offering a training program in anesthesiology—for a six-month residency with Dr. Ralph Waters. Apgar was the only woman to enroll that year. She spent six additional months at Bellevue working with Dr. Emery Rovenstine, another key figure in the development of anesthesiology. In 1938, at the age of twenty-nine, Virginia Apgar was appointed the first director of the new division of anesthesiology at Presbyterian Hospital. The next year, she became the second woman to receive board certification from the American Society of Anesthetists.

Over the next decade, Apgar worked tirelessly to build the new division. At the same time, she was also caring for an ever-increasing number of patients—at first entirely on her own. During these years, she recruited young doctors for the evolving specialty. Often Apgar had to persuade reluctant surgeons to accept anesthesiologists as peers and to pay them fairly. Among her additional responsibilities as division head were organizing a residency program and designing medical school courses. In 1938, she instituted the first formal training in anesthesia for third- and fourth-year medical students. Apgar's efforts were "hands on" in every dimension. When she discovered the hospital had no call rooms available for her two new anesthesiology residents, Apgar paid the cost of their housing.

These were the crucial years when anesthesiology struggled to gain the status of a fully recognized medical specialty. Gradually, the number of nurse-anesthetists decreased, and the number of doctors completing residencies in anesthesiology increased. The war proved a turning point. Not only were new anesthetics developed, but surgeons realized that doctors who could manage pain on the battlefield would be invaluable in the operating room. And in the postwar years, a national baby boom increased the need for well-trained anesthesiologists in hospitals across the country.

Transformation of the once mostly feminine field of anesthesia would have an unexpected outcome for Virginia Apgar. In 1949 a young man, Dr. Emanuel Papper, was named to head the anesthesiology division, now a department, which she had developed and led for ten years. Both to soften this blow and to recognize her achievements, Apgar was promoted to full professor the same year. Rather than dwelling on her disappointment at not having been appointed head of the department she had founded and led, she returned to the delivery room as attending anesthesiologist at the Sloane Hospital. In this position, which combined the strands of her experience, training, and research interests, Apgar would make the discoveries that were to shape the development of neonatal medicine.

APGAR AFTER THE APGAR SCORE

Between 1952 and 1959, Apgar turned more of her attention to research on newborns and recruited younger colleagues to help her in this task. The most important of these was Dr. L. Stanley James, a pediatrician who had come from New Zealand to serve as chief resident at Bellevue Hospital for a year. Hearing Apgar speak enthusiastically about her work with newborns had a profound impact on him. Despite the skepticism of Dr. Emmett Holt, then chief of pediatrics, who told him that neonatal medicine was not a "real field" like cardiology, James changed his professional plans and spent the rest of his life as a faculty member at P&S. In 1972, he was appointed head of the Neonatal Intensive Care Unit at Presbyterian Hospital.

From 1955 to 1959, James worked with Apgar's team as a research assistant in neonatal physiology, helping her find new ways to measure pH, blood gases, and levels of anesthetics in newborns. Through a series of elegant studies using such innovative techniques as catheterization of the umbilical vessels, Apgar and her associates made important findings about neonatal physiology, correlating the Apgar score with the specific physical condition of infants and, importantly, with the effects of maternal anesthesia.

When residents observed that infants whose mothers had been anesthetized with cyclopropane showed more depressed vital signs, Apgar's reaction was swift and unequivocal: "There goes my favorite gas." To ensure safer deliveries, she and her colleagues became pioneers in developing regional anesthesia. Dr. Richard Clark has noted "the happy confluence at Columbia-Presbyterian Medical Center of several individuals who produced an explosion of teaching, research, and clinical development in the late 1950s; they propelled American obstetrical anesthesia

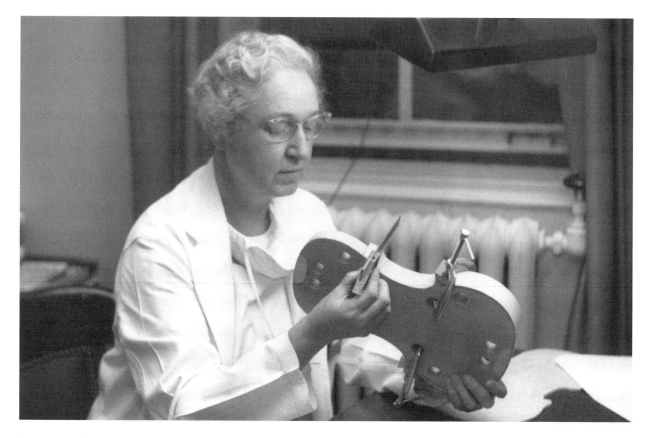

A conversation with a patient, instrument builder Carleen Hutchins, led to one of Apgar's many avocations.

to the preeminent position it holds today." In addition to Apgar and James, this group included Duncan Holaday, Frank Moya, Bradley Smith, Sol Schneider, Hisayo Morishima, and Miecyzslaw Finster.

In 1955, Apgar published a paper entitled "The Role of the Anesthesiologist in Reducing Neonatal Mortality." Since pediatricians were seldom available to care for newborns in the delivery room, Apgar pointed out that "the anesthesiologist is the logical person to observe and treat the infant." The last sentence of her paper was a call to action: "In no field of patient care is there more hope for improvement of mortality figures than in the newborn period." Three years later, she and her associates published a study of 15,000 births proving that her scoring system was an accurate predictor of the need for resuscitation. Increasingly, Apgar focused attention not only on normal infants with depressed vital signs but also on infants with special problems. As the pioneer neonatologist Dr. Murdina Desmond noted, "A significant step forward came with the realization that improvement in neonatal mortality must take place at the fault line between obstetric and pediatric responsibility . . . At Virginia Apgar's urging, infants were given a screening physical in the delivery room to detect congenital abnormalities."

The Apgar team's clinical research showed how fragile newborns could benefit from swift and specialized care. Drs. Apgar and James shared their findings in the most practical way, distributing informational pamphlets and showing films on infant resuscitation at dozens of medical meetings across the country. As doctors' understanding of this procedure increased, there was major improvement in the quality of infant resuscitation and, as a result, the newborn survival rate rose.

In the 1960s, the team's findings provided the basis for establishing neonatal intensive care units (known as NICUs) within pediatric hospitals where doctors and nurses could provide round-the-clock care. Such units reflected a major change in the treatment of newborns. The distinguished pediatrician Mary Ellen Avery has recalled that for an intern in the 1950s, "the newborn nurseries were the least stressful of all the services." With the development of NICUs across the country, the treatment of neonates became far more demanding, "hands on," and effective.

Apgar exhorted doctors who cared for newborns, "Time is of the utmost importance. Delay is damaging to the infant. Act promptly, accurately, and gently." As neonatal care was fast becoming more aggressive and invasive, this last word had special significance. It reflected Apgar's compassion for her small patients—a quality that had long been at the center of her clinical work. She routinely visited patients the night before surgery to reassure them about the procedures they were about to undergo. One parent gratefully remembered how Apgar carried a child who was afraid of elevators up nine flights of stairs to surgery.

Apgar's busy research schedule never interfered with her commitment to teaching. A former student, Dr. Leonard Brand, recalled: "No one ever fell asleep in Dr. Apgar's classes." The rapid pace of her speech and her clear enthusiasm for her subject engaged their attention. Dr. Henry Metzger vividly remembers Apgar's quick reactions in the delivery room—a place where, as he says, "things tend to happen very fast." Her rosy cheeks, energetic pace, and sturdy frame are still fresh in his mind. In spite of her senior status and white hair, medical students found Virginia Apgar youthful. Since relatively few anesthesiology textbooks were then available, her style of instruction was vivid, direct, informal, and sometimes personal. She used simple tools: an old skeleton and a battered pelvis.

Students' affection was clear in the 1957 yearbook dedication, which praised "her friendship, gaiety, interest in student activities, her devotion to her profession, and her alacrity and rapid stream of conversation."

A NEW ROLE WITH THE MARCH OF DIMES

By the end of the 1950s, Apgar had taught at Columbia for twenty years and had attended some 17,000 deliveries. She was ready for change and a new challenge, which came during a well-deserved sabbatical at Johns Hopkins. Her intention was to study statistics, obtain a master's degree in public health, and then return to Columbia. But a course with Dr. Victor McKusick, known as "the father of medical genetics," sparked her interest in congenital defects.

As a result of this new interest, Apgar decided to take a position as director of the birth defects division at the National Foundation–March of Dimes. Between 1955 and 1960, vital statistics had failed to show a continuing decrease in infant mortality. Analysis indicated that the major cause was an increased number of premature births, a problem that persists to this day. With the death of John and Jacqueline Kennedy's infant son Patrick in August of 1963, premature birth became a front page news story. A poignant photograph showed the president standing helplessly over his infant son's incubator as the baby struggled to survive respiratory distress syndrome.

In the next decades, both the federal government and the March of Dimes provided generous funding for research on neonatal mortality and morbidity. As a result, respiratory distress syndrome today has a mortality rate of less than 15 percent. Virginia Apgar's activism was an important part of this campaign. She took on her new job with what peers called "missionary zeal" and spent the next fifteen years working for the March of Dimes in a range of high positions. In each, she proved a highly effective fund-raiser, speaker, and advocate. As a colleague noted, Apgar "took birth defects from a secret closet and put them firmly on the map."

In addition, she continued to study the causes of birth defects, returning to take McKusick's famous summer course in genetics a second time. Despite her age and expertise, this decision was not surprising. As her colleague Stanley James recalled, "Learning was the focal point of her life." And when McKusick needed additional funding to continue the course, Apgar arranged for the March of Dimes to provide it. This commitment continues today: McKusick's genetics course remains the Foundation's longest-standing grant recipient.

Parents of babies with birth defects appreciated Apgar's warm and frank approach to the challenges they faced. Apgar's ceaseless travels and numerous talks increased the public's understanding of birth defects. A 1963 headline stated simply: "Her name is a lifeline for newborns." She savored the constant traveling: "After all those years under an anesthetist's sheet, I'm really seeing the world for the first time."

Virginia Apgar was so devoted to the cause of infant health that even during the last year of her life (when her own health was failing) she traveled 83,000 miles and visited three continents. Because of her extraordinary energy and drive, Apgar's death in 1974 at the age of sixty-five came as a great shock to colleagues and friends.

Apgar's "Great American" postal stamp, issued in 1994

AVOCATIONS AND ACCOLADES

Apgar enjoyed gardening, stamp collecting, fishing, baseball, and golf, and she wanted to get a pilot's license. But music making was at the center of her avocational life. She was a member of three orchestras and frequently took part in chamber music recitals with friends. A preoperative chat with Carleen Hutchins, a patient who was a distinguished instrument builder, led to fifteen years of collaboration. Working together between midnight and 2 a.m., she and Apgar crafted a quartet of stringed instruments meant to be played as an ensemble: violin, mezzo violin, cello, and viola. This joint venture included purloining a curly maple bench from a Harkness Pavilion phone booth to complete one of the instruments. They carefully replaced it with a similar but less desirable piece of wood.

This quartet of instruments would become a unique part of the Apgar legacy. In 1995, Drs. Joseph Butterfield and Nicholas Cunningham led a successful campaign to acquire them for the College of Physicians and Surgeons. Medical students and doctors play them on gala occasions—such as the 2002 Virginia Apgar Symposium at P&S. At this event, her collaborator Carleen Hutchins (then aged ninety-two) recalled, "Dr. Apgar possessed high intelligence and good hands; best of all, she was willing to follow directions—not always the case with highly intelligent people."

During her professional life, Apgar received many laurels, beginning with the American Society of Anesthesiology's Distinguished Service Award in 1961. In 1973, the year before her death, she received numerous honors. Cornell University

Medical College awarded her the first professorship devoted to the subspecialty of congenital disorders; she became the first woman to win the P&S Alumni Association's Gold Medal for distinguished service; the American Society of Anesthesiologists gave her its highest honor (the Ralph M. Waters award, named for her initial teacher in the field); and *The Ladies' Home Journal* voted her Woman of the Year in Science and Research. These last two awards, one from an elite medical society and the other from a popular magazine, reflected the breadth of Virginia Apgar's influence. In 1974 the American Academy of Pediatrics, noting that "she had influenced pediatrics as have few physicians," established the Virginia Apgar Award in the field of perinatal medicine.

But the recognition she would most have enjoyed came in 1994, some twenty years after her death. Following a long campaign by her admirer Dr. Joseph Butterfield, a postal stamp bearing her portrait was issued in the "Great Americans" series. The first-day-of-issue ceremony took place at the 1994 meeting of the American Academy of Pediatrics. Four pediatricians played her favorite chamber music on the instruments she had helped to craft—a perfect way to honor the physician who had once described a healthy baby's cry as "the sweetest music."

Recognition of her achievements continues to this day. In 1995, Apgar was elected to the National Women's Hall of Fame. In 2002, Dr. Margaret Wood, the first woman to head the Department of Anesthesiology at P&S, established the Virginia Apgar Scholars Program to support medical students who want to remain in academic medicine.

Long before her death, Apgar had become a legendary figure in American medicine. Yet this immensely practical, utterly unpretentious physician would never have wanted to be put on a pedestal. Friends and colleagues still recall her forthrightness and warmth. Virginia Apgar's sense of priorities was key to her professional success. Pioneering in a new specialty at a time when women physicians were marginalized, she overcame obstacles and pursued her goals. While exclusion from some male-only professional gatherings annoyed her, she kept these feelings private and maintained a clear focus on her work.

The most extraordinary aspect of Apgar's career is her impact on medical specialties other than her own—especially pediatrics and obstetrics. Dr. Julius Richmond, U.S. surgeon general in the late 1970s, credited her with having "done more to improve the health of mothers, babies, and unborn infants than anyone else in the twentieth century." But it was her close friend and collaborator Stanley James who summed up Apgar's remarkable legacy most succinctly: "We are remembered by the way our work is continued." Since the test she designed is used to evaluate millions of babies born every year in hospitals all over the world, Virginia Apgar's work is continued at a truly remarkable rate.

CHAPTER 18

Beyond Typhoid Mary: The Origins of Public Health at Columbia and in the City

———ɯ———

David Rosner

Few events could better illustrate early twentieth-century developments at Columbia than the founding of the School of Public Health. Formally established only in 1922, this school was the product of both Columbia's early history and the new needs of New York City at that time. It would not have come about were it not for the professional resources of the renowned College of Physicians and Surgeons (dating back to 1767) and if Columbia had not already been well poised, by its longstanding commitment to serve as "Columbia University in the City of New York," to fill the emerging needs of a bursting city.

Here to explain how this phase in Columbia's history arose from the confluence of increasing public needs with the services of a major medical center in an urban setting is David Rosner, director of the Center for the History and Ethics of Public Health at Columbia's Mailman School of Public Health and professor of history and socioeconomic sciences. A graduate of the City College of New York with a Ph.D. in the history of science from Harvard, Rosner, before coming to Columbia, served as university distinguished professor of history at the City University of New York. He is the author of A Once Charitable Enterprise *(1982) and, with Gerald Markowitz,* Deceit and Denial: The Deadly Politics of Industrial Pollution *(2002).*

—Wm. Theodore de Bary

———ɯ———

Crowded, unsanitary living conditions, such as those at Baxter Street Court circa 1890, contributed to New York's public health crisis.

In 1908, just as New York was emerging from a severe economic depression, Columbia's College of Physicians and Surgeons (P&S) organized a series of lectures featuring some of the nation's foremost engineers, public health officials, statisticians, and social welfare activists. Microbiologist William Sedgwick, from the Massachusetts Institute of Technology; William Park, the director of the New York City Department of Health's Bureau of Laboratories; Hermann Biggs, chief medical officer for the city's Department of Health; and Frederick Hoffman, vice president and chief statistician of the Prudential Life Insurance Company, were among the luminaries who came to the Fifty-ninth Street home of the college. Week after week the speakers told the audience of young physicians and their teachers of the enormous strides that public health had made in the preceding decades and of the even greater possibilities that lay ahead. What was needed for future advances was to train professionals in the art and science of disease prevention.

The series introduced students and faculty alike to the various disciplines that had, over the course of the previous four decades, transformed the health experiences of New York's population. For much of the nineteenth century, public health had been largely an engineering enterprise as the city built the Croton Reservoir System and massive aqueducts to move water from Westchester County and the Catskills to Manhattan. While smallpox outbreaks had largely been contained by mass inoculation campaigns, the extension of the water supply into poor neighborhoods limited the occurrence of water-borne diseases like cholera and typhoid. The draining of swamps in Queens and the Bronx was leading to declines in outbreaks of mosquito-borne diseases such as yellow fever.

Engineers had also built a massive sewer system, an extensive subway and transportation system, and new housing with better ventilation for the poor living in the city's teeming tenements. Regular garbage pickups had begun. All of these improvements to the city's infrastructure had led to dramatic declines in mortality rates from infectious disease.

However, engineering as a means of improving the city's health seemed to have reached its limit. This new generation of administrators, engineers, and scientists argued the need for more targeted methods for eliminating outbreaks of diseases transmitted person-to-person. They maintained that a merging of traditional environmental controls with the new science of bacteriology could make horrifying epidemics a thing of the past.

Sanitary engineering had cleaned up broad swaths of the city. Now medically trained health professionals could identify local sources of disease and infected individuals whose treatment or isolation would further reduce the spread of disease. "It is sincerely to be hoped that this beginning will lead to some permanent organization upon the lines of Sanitary Science and Public Health," Dean Samuel W. Lambert said of the lecture series in the 1909 P&S annual report, adding that a "special committee [has] outlined the possibilities for funding such a permanent department in connection with Columbia University."

The grand possibilities of the new merging of sanitary science and medicine had just been illustrated neatly, in 1907, through the city's experience with Mary Mallon, a cook for some of New York's elite families, who would become known as "Typhoid Mary." Mary Mallon was a "healthy" typhoid carrier, whom George Soper, an 1899 graduate of Columbia's School of Mines program in engineering, had identified as the source of an outbreak of typhoid among some wealthy New Yorkers vacationing at their summer cottage in Oyster Bay, Long Island.

Soper had been called in as an engineer to track the sources of pollution that led to the outbreak of this disease, usually caused by drinking water contaminated with human feces. After detailed inspections of the water supply, the oysters regularly harvested in the bay nearby, the sewer system, and other possible sources of contamination, Soper concluded that the problem was not caused by leaks or cross-contamination of sewage and drinking water. Rather the problem, he argued, was that Mary, as a cook in the house, had been passing bacteria into the food that she prepared for the family.

Using the newly developed epidemiological techniques and laboratories of the New York City Department of Health, Soper helped establish the effectiveness of the new advances in staining, microscopy, and bacteriology as tools in stemming the spread of infectious disease. Although Mary exhibited no symptoms of typhoid, she was forcibly taken by the Department of Health and placed in isolation on North Brother Island, the city's isolation hospital in the East River. Except for one brief interlude, she remained on the island for the rest of her life, nearly thirty years. Soper believed he was the first to use the laboratory in tracking down the source of an epidemic caused by a healthy typhoid carrier.

Such detective work showcased recent advances in bacteriology, histology, and hygiene. During the lectures, Norman Ditman, an instructor in pathology at Columbia's medical school, argued that between 20,000 and 25,000 lives had been saved by the recent advances in public health, and Herman Biggs, the director of New York's Department of Health, made the claim that in large measure, "public health is purchasable," meaning that the public's willingness to invest in a variety of public health activities, laboratories, vaccination campaigns, and the like could determine how long New York's population would live and how free from the ravages of infectious diseases they would remain.

THE UNSANITARY CONDITION OF THE CITY

The need for the inclusion of public health into some aspect of the training of physicians was clear. For many at those lectures in 1908 it was not difficult to remember the experience of mid-nineteenth-century New Yorkers, many of whom died of rampant outbreaks of infectious diseases such as cholera, typhoid, smallpox, and yellow fever. Nor was it difficult to recall the suffering of children who died of diphtheria, whooping cough, and a host of other intestinal or pulmonary diseases. Tuberculosis was a chronic and continual reminder of the dangers that attended city life.

By the mid-nineteenth century, New York had among the worst health statistics in the nation. Vital statistics gathered by the city showed that while one out of every forty-four people died in 1863 in Boston and one of forty-four that year in Philadelphia, New York's rate was one in thirty-six. Even when compared with European centers such as London and Liverpool, New York seemed strangely unhealthy. Mortality data highlighted the city's apparent decline.

The city that Columbia's medical school served had emerged as the national commercial hub, the nation's foremost center of trade, industry, finance, and communication. Yet, the poverty, illness, and crowding of the city appeared frightening. Infections and a host of intestinal diseases in the young and old alike accompanied the growth in poverty, population, and immigration. High death rates and pestilence now marked "with shame the great City of New York," remarked the authors of *Sanitary Condition of the City: Report of the Council of Hygiene and Public Health of the Citizens' Association of New York*, the 1866 document that spurred the creation that year of what became the city's Department of Health.

In this report, some of New York's leading physicians, including many from Columbia, documented the "shame" of the city. Valentine Mott, professor of surgery at P&S; surgery faculty member Willard Parker, known as the "father of vascular surgery"; John Griscom, author of *Sanitary Condition of the Laboring Population of New York*, a famous 1845 study; and Stephen Smith, soon to head New York's new Metropolitan Board of Health and in 1872 organizer of the American Public Health Association, all bemoaned the "pestilential diseases" that laid bare "the impotence of the existing sanitary system." The physicians noted that outbreaks of disease

Through the Little Mothers' League, new mothers and older daughters learned basic hygiene and child-care skills, circa 1910.

paralyzed the commercial and political life of the community: "The people are panic-stricken [and] the interests of commerce suffer by the insensible and certain loss of millions." It was clear that "the relation of the health and vigorous life of a people to the state, or to commercial prosperity, requires no discussion." Disease—the effects of which could be measured in dollars and cents—was a liability in the developing commercial capital.

Conquering disease was essential for reestablishing order in a city that appeared to many to be in the process of dissolution. Most frightening was the close connection between disease, moral decay, and the draft riots that in 1863 led to the city's occupation by federal troops returning from the Battle of Gettysburg. "The mobs that held fearful sway in our city during the memorable outbreak of violence in the month of July, 1863, were gathered in the overcrowded and neglected quarters of the city," the physicians reminded the reader in the 1866 report on sanitary conditions. The "closely packed houses where the mobs originated seemed to be literally hives of sickness and vice."

Written as it was by both medical and lay people, public health physicians and moral leaders, the 1866 report incorporated moralistic as well as scientific language, reflecting the contemporary understanding of illness as a sign of depravity or sin. Calling themselves "health missionaries," the authors wrote,

> Lewd but pale and sickly young women, scarcely decent in their ragged attire, were impudent and scattered everywhere in the crowd. But what numbers are made hideous by self-neglect and infirmity! . . . To walk the streets as we walked them, in those hours of conflagration and riot, was like witnessing the day of judgment, with every wicked thing revealed, every sin and sorrow blazingly glared upon, every hidden abomination laid before hell's expectant fire. . . . Here disease in its most loathsome form propagates itself.

New York streets were "very filthy" with accumulations of manure from the horses that traversed the area, dead dogs, cats, and rats, household and vegetable refuse that in winter accumulated to depths of three feet or more, the 1866 report also noted. "Garbage boxes," rarely emptied, overflowed with offal, animal carcasses, and household waste. "Pools" of stagnant water collected in the carcasses of dead animals and over sewer drains that were generally clogged.

These descriptions provided a vivid understanding of the intimate relationship between social and economic forces that created a slum and ill health throughout the city. The observation that housing, politics, morals, and health were all intertwined underscored the combined missions of public health activities for the next half-century. "Disease, debasement, and pauperism . . . are found closely allied" and "seriously endanger the sanitary safety of all other classes," the authors of the report concluded.

AN IMPROVED ENVIRONMENT

In the decade after the Civil War, epidemics of typhus, yellow fever, cholera, and other diseases swept through the tenements and slums of the city with fearsome impact. The city responded by creating a permanent institution, the Department of Health, as a part of New York's attempt to regulate conditions that caused disease. Housing, meat, and milk inspection, garbage collection and street cleaning, water distribution, and sewerage services would all be organized through a health department that sought to control the environment. Soon, this department would become a model for other cities throughout the nation, employing the latest scientific advances in bacteriology.

By the turn of the twentieth century, New York would emerge as preeminent in the field. Older sanitarians' notions of the cause of disease as residing in filth and immorality would slowly be supplemented with newer, more scientific views that disease was caused by specific pathogens, bacteria associated with particular diseases. The isolation of diseased individuals, the vaccination of potential victims of infection, and the laboratory analysis of milk supplies slowly gained a place alongside the more traditional sanitarian focus of the public health department. The advent of the bacteriological revolution had by the end of the century provided a common ground for clinical medicine and public health. Street cleaning, the provision of pure water supplies, and the treatment of bacterial disease were all essential for the control of infections and the elimination of epidemics.

With the revolution in bacteriology that followed the discoveries of Louis Pasteur, Joseph Lister, and Robert Koch in the mid-nineteenth century, a new faith in laboratory science emerged not only among physicians but also among public health workers. "Bacteriology . . . became an ideological marker, sharply differentiating the 'old' public health, the province of untrained amateurs, from the 'new' public health, which belonged to scientifically trained professionals," points out public health historian Elizabeth Fee, author of *Disease and Discovery: A History of the Johns Hopkins School of Hygiene and Public Health, 1916–1939* (1987). A revolution in ideology overtook the field in the 1880s, as William Sedgwick, one of the first to speak at the 1908 lecture series at Columbia's medical school, would remember: "Before 1880 we knew nothing; after 1890 we knew it all; it was a glorious ten years." A new model was gaining greater acceptance: A bacillus made people sick and diseases like tuberculosis were caused by germs. Dirty, crowded public spaces or unclean homes with moist, warm, and stagnant air were seen as the conduits for disease.

By 1906, it had become apparent that some sort of alliance between medicine and public health was necessary and that P&S was the perfect place for the new practitioners in both disciplines to forge a common ground.

NEW HEALTH ISSUES EMERGE

In the early years of the new century, the very successes of the reforms had led to the emergence of changing patterns of death in the city. Diseases of "old age," the very welcome result of improved urban health, began to replace dying children and epidemics as a major concern. Cancer, heart disease, and pneumonia were claiming larger numbers of the elderly. The data showed "in an unmistakable manner

Haven Emerson

the success of public sanitary administration which has heretofore directed its efforts almost entirely against infectious diseases," according to the 1912 annual report of the New York City Department of Health. On the other hand, the report "point[ed] with equal clearness toward the field in which public hygiene must [focus] in the future, namely, the reduction of mortality from the diseases of middle and old age." What techniques could be employed to address these new challenges? Were the traditional tools of environmental cleanup or the newer techniques of vaccination and medical interventions adequate?

No longer would public health be limited to environmental engineering and food inspection. In future years, on the one hand, public health would find itself coming into conflict with providers of medical care as prevention of disease through inoculation and vaccination, prenatal and well-baby care, factory inspection, and occupational disease prevention as well as treatment of communicable diseases such as syphilis and gonorrhea would force those in the field to venture into areas previously the preserve of the clinician. On the other hand, it would lead to a greater coherence and sympathy with medical science.

At Columbia, Dr. Walter Bensel of the medical school gave "the first regular course of instruction on the important subject of public health and sanitation," according to Dean Lambert in the 1911 P&S annual report. One of the school's projects then was a milk station peopled by P&S personnel that guaranteed the bacterial safety of milk provided to the city's schoolchildren. By 1916, Dean Lambert noted that "the proposed development of a School of Hygiene and Sanitary Science" was delayed by a lack of funds. The hope was that with the anticipated early 1920s opening of the new campus at 168th Street there would be space for the new school.

However, the 168th Street campus did not open until 1928, and by 1922 the urgent need for providing some sort of public health education to the health officers of the city, the students at P&S, and faculty at other schools had led to the opening of the Department of Public Health Administration as a unit of P&S. This collaboration was made possible with the help of a modest endowment from Joseph DeLamar, a Dutch sea captain who made his fortune in this country in mining and chemicals and who left his wealth to Columbia (as well as to Harvard and Johns Hopkins).

Dr. Haven Emerson, on the medical school faculty from 1902 to 1914 and former commissioner of health for the city, took over as head of the newly created department during its first year and led it for nearly two decades, until 1940. The author of numerous classics, including eight editions of *Communicable Diseases of Man*, Emerson expanded the scope of the department, and by the 1930s it had emerged as a school, teaching courses in epidemiology, public health administration, and the use of mass inoculation in the prevention of disease outbreaks.

In its first few years, the new "school within a school" organized courses on preventable disease and public health administration for fourth-year medical students and graduate nurses at Teachers College. New courses were added on communicable and occupational diseases, mental health, administration of public and private agencies, infant health service, prenatal supervision, and health examination of preschoolers, among others.

Initially, the new public health program was "devoted to the education of the lay public in matters of preventive medicine and particularly in matters of diet and the use of food," as Dean William Darrach reported in 1923. But it soon grew, becoming today Columbia's Mailman School, one of the nation's leading schools of public health.

CHAPTER 19

Maurice Ewing and the Lamont-Doherty Earth Observatory

—⁓∭⁓—

Laurence Lippsett

Maurice Ewing explored the depths of Earth's oceans in the course of revolutionizing the study of geology and oceanography. As the founder of the Lamont Geological Observatory (now known as the Lamont-Doherty Earth Observatory), he not only launched many geological expeditions but indeed set research vessels sailing from Piermont, New York, to range the seas like their predecessor clipper ships from the same launching site. At Lamont-Doherty in Palisades, New York, Ewing also established a major suburban campus as a base for earth and environmental studies at Columbia.

Ewing's grave lies on a mountainside overlooking the scene of his major scientific achievements, near a monument to another great American, the continental explorer General John C. Fremont. To give Ewing's achievements new life for us, we turned to Laurence Lippsett, at the time of writing a science editor at the Woods Hole Oceanographic Institution.

—Wm. Theodore de Bary

—⁓∭⁓—

B y the end of World War II, physicists and chemists, including many at Columbia University, had penetrated the molecular and subatomic worlds, revealing the fundamental structures and forces that compose matter and set it in motion. Similarly, biologists spearheaded by Columbia's Thomas Hunt Morgan had identified the gene, launching sweeping breakthroughs in the study of heredity, evolution, the development of complex organisms, and a wide range of other biological processes.

Maurice Ewing in 1949, taking a rare nap aboard the Atlantis.
He waged a personal battle against sleep to keep from wasting precious ship time.

But of the larger world—our home planet, Earth—we knew relatively little. The earth sciences languished in a state approaching astronomy before Copernicus and Galileo. No one knew what created the oceans, continents, mountains, islands, and volcanoes. The prevailing theory at the time—that the earth's surface was rigid and relatively permanent—was about as off-base as an earth-centered solar system.

In 1915, the German scientist Alfred Wegener had proposed that the continents were once connected but had separated and drifted apart. But Wegener had neither an underlying mechanism to explain the scenario nor the convincing evidence to support it, and his continental drift theory was declared scientific heresy.

Locked into the idea that the earth's surface was fixed and immobile, geology before the war "was not a study of processes except on a lilliputian scale; it was a historical science with causes left out," wrote H. E. LeGrand, a University of Melbourne science historian, in his book *Drifting Continents and Shifting Theories: The Modern Revolution in Geology and Scientific Change.* "The caricatured academic geologist was an elderly professor mumbling an interminable catalogue of the common fossils of the Carboniferous, occasionally stirring a cloud of dust as he produced a specimen."

Geologists were landlocked—not only conceptually but literally. Most people at the time nourished a comfortable notion that the globe had been largely explored. World maps had been filled in with details—mountains, rivers, lakes, deserts, and jungles—but all these were framed by a featureless blue border. Scientists and everyone else overlooked 70 percent of the planet that was covered by a vast, formidable, opaque barrier—the oceans.

"Geologists could not apply traditional field methods to the seafloors," LeGrand wrote. "There was also an unstated presumption that there were no problems or data unique to the ocean floors. Any general theory which could cope with the continents could surely be extended sight unseen to the seafloor. Why do underwater what could be done more easily and more cheaply on land?"

Thus, in 1946, virtually anything that wasn't terra firma was terra incognita.

But that same year, a brilliant, entrepreneurial, relentlessly driven young professor named William Maurice Ewing came to Columbia with little patience for traditional geologists. "Annoying fellows," he called them, "who spend their time poking around trying to explain this or that little detail. I keep wanting to say, 'Why don't you try to see what's making it all happen?'"

Answering that question with traditional explorations limited to Earth's small dry fraction, he said, was "like trying to describe a football after being given a look at a piece of the lacing." To pursue a radically different approach—to study earth processes on a Brobdingnagian scale—Ewing immersed himself and his colleagues in unprecedented explorations of the intimidating oceans. And, for the first time, he forcibly applied the disciplines of physics and chemistry to the study of geology.

Such was his impact that in two decades the methods he introduced, the instruments he built, the students he trained, the scientists and ships he marshaled, and the institution he created—now called Lamont-Doherty Earth Observatory—essentially launched whole new scientific fields and revolutionized our understanding of our planet almost as dramatically as Copernicus did centuries before.

He went by his middle name (pronounced "Morris"), but anyone who knew him just called him "Doc."

ROOTS AND RHYTHMS

Born in 1906, Ewing was the eldest surviving child of a large family that led a happy but hardscrabble existence on a farm in the Texas panhandle.

At sixteen, he won a scholarship to Rice Institute (now Rice University) in Houston, where he earned a Ph.D. in physics. To support himself, he tutored classmates and worked in an all-night drugstore, somehow finding time to play first trombone in the marching band throughout graduate school. During summers, he worked in grain elevators and for oil prospecting companies. His lifelong habit of working all day, every day, was already entrenched.

In 1930, he became a professor of physics at Lehigh University, zealous to do research. In those Depression-era days before government-sponsored research, he improvised physics experiments. He used magnetic measurements to look for buried apparatus. When local quarries were blasting, he recorded the seismic waves they generated. Ewing's summer jobs had made him familiar with emerging techniques employed by oil companies to reveal the thickness, composition, and contours of buried rock strata (and the oil hidden within them) by studying seismic waves traveling through and reflecting off rock layers.

Wrangling some dynamite of his own, Ewing concocted further rudimentary experiments. He spent weekends setting off explosions in the wilds of New Jersey, using sound energy to explore subsurface geology. He analyzed seismic waves traveling across "a solid interface between a gas and liquid"—the frozen surface of a nearby lake.

Ewing's modest but singular research attracted the attention of two geologists, Professor Richard Field of Princeton and Major William Bowie of the U.S. Coastal and Geodetic Survey. One snowy November day in 1934, they showed up at Lehigh to ask Ewing whether the seismic measurements he was pioneering on land could be adapted to investigate the geology of a completely unknown landscape—the seafloor. Ewing had already proposed the same thing to several oil companies, asking them to "support a modest program of research."

"This proposal received no support whatever," Ewing wrote in 1955. "I was told that work out in the ocean could not possibly be of interest to the shareholder and could not rightfully receive one nickel of the shareholder's money."

Bowie and Field encouraged Ewing to seek a grant from the Geological Society of America (GSA). "If they had asked me to put seismic equipment on the moon instead of the bottom of the ocean I'd have agreed, I was so desperate for a chance to do research," Ewing told his biographer, William Wertenbaker, in his book *The Floor of the Sea*.

In fact, decades later Ewing and Columbia colleagues did put such equipment on the moon aboard *Apollo* flights. But in 1936, with a $2,000 grant from the GSA, Ewing and a handful of students—none of them geologists—began to work on experiments that no one had ever imagined, let alone performed. As in New Jersey, they would use sound energy—explosions—to generate seismic waves to probe the seafloor.

"Geophysics as a science didn't really exist at the time," says J. Lamar Worzel, who was one of Ewing's undergraduate students in 1937. He followed Ewing to Columbia to earn his Ph.D. and later was a professor of geophysics at Columbia until 1972. "Commercially available geophysical instruments certainly didn't exist at the time."

So Ewing and his students designed and built them all themselves. It was the Depression, and so the group begged, borrowed, and bartered to get whatever they needed. They jury-rigged equipment, using fruit salad cans, drinking glasses from diners, and electric motors from toy trains. They detonated their explosives with caps from toy pistols. They sneaked into Lehigh's machine shop to work all night, slept in fields to save money, and washed photographic records in bathtubs. They gladly accepted castoffs and converted them into breakthroughs. Out of a surplus navy artillery shell, for example, they fashioned a device to test equipment at the high pressure they expected on the seafloor. They had only two precious weeks of ship time each summer to conduct experiments, as guests on Woods Hole Oceanographic Institution's *Atlantis*—the first, and at that time only, U.S.-dedicated oceanographic research vessel.

"We did everything we could to improve our instruments and methods during the year, then had one brief chance to see if they worked," Worzel says.

The landlubber's scourge, seasickness, would not deter them. Ewing's ability to overcome it "was largely from fury," he told Wertenbaker. "Seasickness is like a toothache, you know—you don't notice it if your house is burning. This was the chance of my life."

INVENTING A SCIENTIFIC DISCIPLINE

Their first year's experiments were hopelessly distorted because the rolling ship couldn't avoid tugging on a line of explosives and recorders laid on the seafloor—a difficult seagoing maneuver never previously attempted. The next summer, they instead devised a system to retrieve their instruments from the seafloor by attaching them to buoyant gasoline-filled hoses, blocks of salt, and weights. When the salt dissolved, the weights were released, and the instruments floated to the surface. That worked well, but high seafloor pressure caused the detonators to misfire.

To do research no one else had attempted, Ewing and his students had to design and build many of their instruments from scratch. This deep-sea camera, held by Ewing (right) and a crew member, was sealed with inner tubes and used coffee cans for reflectors.

J. Lamar Worzel (left) and Ewing in 1938. Worzel holds a large balloon filled with TNT; Ewing examines the first ocean seis-mometer. They would later monitor the seismic waves from undersea explosions to probe the seafloor.

Ewing could not stomach wasting any precious ship time, so while they waited for their turn to do experiments, they put together the first deep-sea camera, housed in a glass test tube about eight inches in diameter and four feet long, affectionately called the "Pyrex Penis." Its watertight seal was made from inner tubes, its reflectors out of coffee cans.

The following year, only one of their seismic instruments worked. By sheer accident, it contained a battery that operated at cold seafloor temperatures. Another brand of battery used in all the other instruments did not. Both had worked fine at the surface.

"We were physicists and engineers, using our wits and flying by the seats of our pants to bring these sciences to bear on the study of the Earth, working out the methods as we went along," Worzel says. "Most physicists and geologists thought our exploratory efforts were bastardizations of each of their sciences."

Then came World War II, and suddenly the Navy was extremely interested in the work of Ewing and colleagues. They remained at Woods Hole throughout the war, applying their nascent techniques to reveal for the first time how sound is transmitted through the oceans. The navy immediately put that knowledge to good use in antisubmarine and mining operations, and Ewing's team went on to design new apparatus that saved ships, submarines, and lives.

They discovered, for example, that sound waves transmitted down into the ocean would bend and split in two directions, some horizontally and some vertically, creating a "shadow zone" in between, where submarines could escape detection from sonar. Deeper down, they found that sound waves bounced off a layer in the ocean where water temperatures dropped sharply (the colder water was denser). Farther down was another sound-reflecting layer. These two layers created a kind of channel, with a floor and a ceiling. Sound caught in this channel bounced off the floor and ceiling and proceeded without losing energy throughout the world's oceans, carrying thousands of miles.

This fundamental property of the oceans, now called the SOFAR (sound fixing and range) channel, was wholly unexpected and led to the navy's SOSUS (Sound Surveillance System) array of underwater hydrophones to monitor great expanses of the ocean. (Today scientists use it to monitor marine mammals, seafloor volcanoes and earthquakes, and global ocean temperatures.)

As the war ended, Columbia offered Ewing a professorship to expand the beachhead he had established in geophysics. In 1946, he and a handful of graduate students established an academic base for their young science in hastily refurbished rooms in Schermerhorn Hall, outfitted with desks and equipment from government surplus lists. In one room, a trapdoor led to a small space hollowed out of Manhattan's bedrock, where they intended to install seismic equipment to observe earthquakes. Ewing hired Angelo Ludas, a veteran of the Manhattan Project at Columbia, to establish and run a machine shop to translate into metal and wires all their instrumental visions.

In early 1947, Ewing undertook a Sigma Xi lecture tour with the official purpose of finding bright students to work in oceanography. But "actually he was scouting for a group of technicians from wealthy families to whom he could offer adventure instead of pay," says Marie Tharp, one of the few women geologists at that time, who came to Columbia in 1948. After one Ewing talk at the University of Iowa, a bright-eyed junior named Bruce Heezen introduced himself, and Ewing immediately invited him on an expedition he was planning for that summer. Ewing's pursuit of knowledge was contagious: Heezen signed up, earned his Ph.D. under Ewing in 1957, and later became a Columbia professor. He and Tharp spent the next thirty years on a quest to map the seafloor.

THE FIRST EYE-OPENING CRUISE

Ewing had been granted use of the *Atlantis* for two months in the summer of 1947. "I felt an obligation, with an expedition entrusted to me for two months, to get data of every conceivable kind," Ewing told Wertenbaker. He took underwater cameras, dredges to collect seafloor samples, and a seismic array to explore subseafloor rock layers. Rather than stop the ship to take measurements, Ewing tried an unprecedented technique to get the most data as quickly as possible. As the *Atlantis* continued sailing, it towed hydrophones to receive reflected sound generated by explosives that crew members pitched overboard at precise intervals.

He also took an echo sounder to reveal the seafloor's contour. Of particular interest was a broad but vague rise in the middle of the Atlantic Ocean seafloor, which had been hinted at by nineteenth-century depth soundings that used long ropes and lead weights.

Ewing took along a sediment corer—a narrow metal cylinder that could be lowered on a line to the seafloor to collect a "plug" of sediment. Until that cruise, scientists' prevailing view was that the seafloor was stable, featureless, and uniform—a basket that caught the gentle, steady rain of particles that sank from the ocean surface, mostly remnants of dead microscopic marine plants and animals. Thus, anywhere one looked in the ocean, one would find the same constantly accumulating column of sediment, which represented the whole of geologic time.

In 1947 that theory was literally blasted out of the water by the jumbled sediments that Ewing and company observed in the first core they retrieved. When a young Woods Hole scientist, David Ericson, subsequently examined preserved plankton shells in the sediments, he found that sediments with modern plankton lay directly atop sediments with forty-million-year-old shells. It was obvious that great unknown processes were at work, transporting sediments and disrupting the way they were deposited on the ocean bottom.

The other instruments also produced surprises. It was like going for the first time into a dark attic with a proper flashlight—unexpected discoveries were inevitable. The echo sounder suggested that huge tracts of the seafloor were almost impossibly flat—the so-called abyssal plains. But then near the ocean's middle, the floor precipitously rose thousands of feet high. Dredges scraping the seafloor brought up basalt, a relatively fresh volcanic rock that is rare on land—not granite, the stuff of which continents were made. The seismic arrays indicated that the seafloor's crust was inexplicably thin—only about three miles thick, compared with the more than twenty for continents. The seafloor was clearly much more complicated than had been imagined.

Maurice Ewing in 1948

A NEW RESEARCH INSTITUTE IS BORN AT COLUMBIA

The 1947 cruise raised so many profound questions that the research exploded, and by the summer of 1948, Columbia's geophysicists already needed more space. "We even went so far as to design a new building for ourselves between Schermerhorn and Columbia's powerhouse," Worzel says. "About then, Ewing had received an offer to establish a geophysics research group at the Massachusetts Institute of Technology and to bring all his students there. MIT offered us a former estate near New Bedford to house our operations."

Ewing toured the grounds with his graduate students. He talked with Dwight D. Eisenhower, then Columbia's president, and Paul Kerr, chairman of the geology department. They countered MIT's proposal by offering an estate about to be donated to Columbia by Florence Lamont, the widow of financier Thomas Lamont. It was fifteen miles north of Columbia, across the Hudson River in Palisades, New York. Kerr promised to raise $200,000 to establish a new research institution. Ewing and his students debated between Columbia and MIT and then voted unanimously to stay at Columbia. Kerr kept his promise, and he and Eisenhower persuaded mining companies to provide funding to establish Columbia's Lamont Geological Observatory.

"Without Kerr's effort, Lamont never would have gotten off the ground," Worzel says. "In late December of 1948, Columbia received the deed for the property. The estate had 125 acres—actually more like 135 acres, but we had to give up ten acres that lay across the New Jersey state line. Robert Moses, New York's infamous road, bridge, and parks builder, wanted the ten acres for his new Palisades Interstate Park system. Columbia wanted to close West 116th Street across its campus from Broadway to Amsterdam Avenue. They struck a deal."

Not long after, Ewing and his merry band were installing seismometers in the estate's root cellar and abandoned indoor swimming pool, thrilled that they would no longer have to contend with confounding vibrations from subways and trucks on Broadway. They converted estate bedrooms into offices, the greenhouse into a machine shop. They moved into cottages formerly used by the estate's chauffeur and groundskeeper, creating a village of scientific homesteaders.

Spread beneath splendid chandeliers in a former dining room was an embryonic sediment core collection, overseen by Ericson, who followed Ewing and the scientific action. The kitchen, with its gas line, running water, and drains, naturally suited a budding corps of Columbia geochemists, led by Professor J. Laurence Kulp. Much the way Ewing was applying physics to study geology, the geochemists were poised to unleash modern postwar chemistry techniques and equipment to study the history and causes of climate change on Earth, to chart the ocean's circulation, and to confront a host of environmental problems.

In 1949, Columbia also established a station in Bermuda to continue research on the SOFAR channel. When the U.S. Navy submarine *Scorpion* mysteriously sank, the station helped pinpoint the disabled vessel. The station also located very precisely where test missiles (equipped with sound sources that exploded in the SOFAR channel) landed, helping the Navy assess missile accuracy. (When Columbia discontinued classified military research in the late 1960s, Ewing, Worzel, and others continued to operate the station as an independent nonprofit entity.)

The Columbia geophysicists had peeked through the veil obscuring the seafloor, but to see it fully, they needed better tools. As always, they designed and built what they needed.

"Ludas, the machine shop head, had that 'can-do' spirit," Worzel says, "and probably was the most naturally mechanically knowledgeable person I've ever met in my life. We worked together for the next twenty-five years, and there was no end to the things we built."

With Frank Press, Ewing designed new instruments that took advantage of a type of seismic wave that most scientists had overlooked or ignored. These were surface waves (usually generated by the shaking caused by earthquakes or underground nuclear weapons tests) that traveled along Earth's surface, rather than through its body. Ewing had remembered his early experiments tracking seismic waves across a frozen lake, and he exploited newfound understandings of sound transmission through the oceans. He and Press developed modern seismometers to reveal Earth's crustal skin in greater detail. In 1957–58, these Press-Ewing instruments were deployed in 125 locations to establish the World-Wide Standardized Seismograph Network—the first global earthquake-monitoring system.

To comprehend the seafloor fully, the Columbia geologists knew they would have to collect cores from all over the ocean. Existing coring systems were expensive and took a full day to lower to the seafloor and retrieve—for one core. Lamont scientists created the economical and efficient Ewing Piston Corer and a winch system that could get a core in a few hours. It "brings up samples of the ocean floor just as a housewife cores an apple," Ewing said.

Similarly, existing echo sounders would not produce sufficient detail to capture the subtleties and textures of the seafloor's intriguing topography, so Ewing assigned Bernard Luskin the task of building a more capable instrument. He invented the precision depth recorder (PDR), which gathered continuous profiles of seafloor topography in unprecedented detail.

THE FINAL NECESSARY PIECE

Established on land, the observatory needed just one thing more. Frustrated by having to beg and borrow limited, intermittent ship time, Ewing and company craved the freedom to conduct a boundless smorgasbord of experiments over a seemingly infinite ocean on a full-time, dedicated presence at sea—their own ship. In one desperate move, they got one.

She was originally christened *Hussar*—a 202-foot, three-masted schooner with teak decks and a wrought-iron hull built in 1923 in Copenhagen for the investment banker E. F. Hutton. Below deck, she was luxuriously appointed, with a Louis XV bedroom, an Edwardian sitting room with a marble-rimmed fireplace and Oriental rugs, a dining salon with stained-glass windows, and bathrooms with gold faucets. In 1934 she was bought by Georg Ungar Vetlesen, a shipping magnate, who renamed her *Vema* after the first two letters of his family name and his wife's name, Maud. Like all oceangoing yachts in this country, she passed to government ownership during World War II, at first patrolling coastal waters for the Coast Guard. Later she underwent a drastic conversion to a floating barracks and training ship for the U.S. Merchant Marine, losing her gold faucets and other amenities. After the war, she lay abandoned and aground on mud off Staten Island for several years, until she was salvaged by a Nova Scotian captain for use as a charter vessel.

Worzel found her in a yachting magazine ad during a last-minute search to replace another ship that had suddenly become unavailable. He chartered the *Vema* for $20,000 and, almost as an afterthought, suggested adding an option to buy her for an additional $80,000.

After her maiden research cruise, Ewing and company wanted to buy her, but on the last day of the charter, which expired at midnight, Ewing told Worzel that he could not raise the additional $80,000. Worzel argued that Lamont would never again get such a good ship so cheaply.

Ewing decided to call Joseph Campbell, Columbia's treasurer at the time. When his secretary said Campbell was gone for the afternoon, Ewing called Campbell's home and got his wife, who said that her husband was playing golf. He then persuaded Campbell's wife to drive to the golf course.

An hour later, Campbell called Ewing, who told the treasurer that the budding observatory had to have the ship. Ewing guaranteed that it would make Columbia proud and that somehow he would raise $80,000 to pay Columbia back. It was after 3:00 p.m.—too late in the day to secure Columbia funds. Campbell agreed to put up his own money temporarily to buy the *Vema* before the midnight deadline. He asked Ewing to let him break the news to the Columbia trustees.

Shortly after 5:00 p.m., still in his golf clothes, according to Worzel, Campbell bought the *Vema*. He immediately covered Columbia's new ship with an insurance policy. When Ewing returned to Lamont, the phone was ringing. It was an irate Columbia trustee, whose insurance company had been contacted to insure the ship. (The Navy eventually reimbursed Columbia for the ship.)

"Columbia garnered a great deal of pride and the Navy got more than its money's worth, because no research vessel collected more data from more parts of the unexplored ocean as efficiently as *Vema*," says Dennis Hayes, professor of earth and environmental sciences at Columbia and former department chair, who studied with Ewing and earned his Ph.D. in 1966.

To captain the *Vema*, Ewing hired a hard-nosed, old-school Nova Scotian seaman named Henry Kohler. He was as expert and canny about running a ship as Ludas was about running a machine shop. And like Ludas, Kohler saw obstacles as challenges and enlisted for the long haul in a scientific crusade. Kohler and the *Vema* retired together in 1981, after the two completed more than one million miles of oceanographic research—the first ship ever to achieve that mark.

Soon the pieces and people were in place. Columbia's geophysics and geochemistry programs comprised more than a dozen faculty members, who were highly active researchers, as well as scores of scientists and technicians supported by government research grants and scores more graduate students—many of whom became scientific pioneers, because their field was as young as they were.

In 1955 Ewing wrote, "I believe that we have built up here a unique team of scientists, unique in the diversity of techniques which it can bear on problems and in the fundamental importance of the problems in which the group is interested.

"I believe that this integrated group of scientists, this group of facilities, which includes the ship, the chemical laboratory, the collection of sediment cores, and the great seismograph station, constitutes a facility comparable with the greatest cyclotron or the greatest telescope, and it is unique. It is as though there was just one cyclotron in the world and we had control of it, or just one big telescope in the world, and we had control of it."

GO FORTH AND COLLECT DATA

The new institution was called an observatory for good reason. Its mission was to venture the world's oceans, make observations, and accumulate the volume of data necessary to reveal the earth.

Ewing set the tone and pace. The light burned late in his office every night. He waged a personal daily battle against wasteful sleep, often scribbling furiously in little books just to keep himself awake. He cut short the only vacation he ever took after two days—because it unnerved him so much. James Heirtzler, newly hired by Ewing to run a nascent program to study the seafloor's magnetic properties, recalled the first three times Ewing called him in for meetings: The first two were on Sundays; the third was on Christmas Day.

"From Ewing emanated the Lamont personality: a spartan life of hard work and dedication; a career driven by an intense need to explore; and a certain attitude of not giving in to the idea that you couldn't go someplace or do something, in the quest for clues to understand the earth," says Arnold Gordon, professor of earth and environmental sciences at Columbia and former department chair, who earned his Ph.D. at Columbia in 1965. "Along with every other graduate student, I fell into the Lamont style of working weekends and late into the night, driven by the quest to know, to divulge something new."

Under her bowsprit, the *Vema* had a huge, determined-looking eagle, which well represented Lamont's indomitable spirit. (Today it hangs in the front hall of

Lamont's Geoscience Building.) Never forgetting the days when ship time was precious, Ewing drove his research vessels as relentlessly as he did his students and himself.

In these early days of oceanography, ships of other great oceanographic institutions did not venture very far from their homeports and territorial waters, Hayes says. But from the start, the *Vema* circled the globe 320 days a year, embarking on nearly boundless missions to explore every ocean. So did Lamont's second ship, the *Robert D. Conrad*, a new research vessel built by the navy and given to the observatory to operate in 1962. The *Conrad* became the second ship in history to log more than one million miles of oceanographic research. For a time, Lamont also staffed and supervised geophysical research in the southern oceans surrounding Antarctica aboard the *Eltanin*, owned by the National Science Foundation. To get measurements from the ice-covered Arctic Ocean, where ships could not go, Lamont stationed scientists and instruments for months on drifting ice floes.

When a scientist from a rival institution chided Ewing that Columbia didn't have a proper port, Ewing replied matter-of-factly, "You don't collect much data when your ship is in port, tied to the dock."

"Ewing expected scientists to use the ship every minute of every day," Hayes says. "From the time we left port, the watches started, the equipment went into the water and was turned on and kept running until we got to another port. It was unusual on a thirty-day, port-to-port cruise to have as much as six hours without data." As they cruised, Columbia's ships continuously collected magnetic, gravity, seismic, and seafloor topography data.

The ships had standing orders to stop once or twice every day to collect a wide range of samples from wherever they happened to be. To do that, crews had learned how to lower two instrument-laden wires simultaneously from rolling ships to the seafloor. The instruments sampled seawater, detected currents, photographed the bottom, measured seafloor heat flow, and of course, collected sediment cores. Ewing's dictum was "a core a day." In 1948, some 100 deep-sea cores existed. By 1956, Lamont had collected 1,195. (Today the core lab holds nearly 19,000—a library of the seafloor available to the scientific community.)

"This strategy saved a lot of time, but it could be risky and had to be carried out with skill and care," says John Diebold, who started in Lamont's machine shop, served as a shipboard technician, earned his Ph.D. from Columbia in 1980, and is now Lamont's marine science coordinator. "It was routine on Lamont ships but was absolutely unheard of on ships operated by other oceanographic institutions."

"Quite unlike anyone else, we were collecting all that data all the time," Hayes says.

The work wasn't without danger. In 1954, while trying to secure fuel drums that had broken free on deck in heavy seas off Cape Hatteras, Ewing, his brother John, First Mate Charles Wilkie, and Second Mate Mike Brown were swept overboard by a huge wave. Somehow, the *Vema*'s captain turned the ship around and rescued John Ewing. Meanwhile, Brown had floated a fuel drum toward Ewing, and the two held on. The *Vema* approached again, and someone threw a rope. Ewing could not grab it because he had taken a blow to the neck, and his left side was paralyzed. Brown seized it and was pulled to the ship, hauling the drum and Ewing with him. The ship rolled so severely, its rails reached the sea. Brown snatched a rail and was rolled upward with the ship. The ship rolled back down, and someone reached under Ewing's armpits and swept him aboard. First Mate Wilkie was never found. Ewing walked with a limp from then on, but the incident in no way slowed him down or curtailed his time at sea.

In 1961, chief scientist John Hennion was killed in an explosives accident, the only such fatality through all the years of using explosives for their work. The acci-

Marie Tharp in Lamont Hall. One of few female geologists at the time, she spent nearly thirty years at Lamont mapping the world's vast hidden seafloor, which she likened to piecing together "a fascinating jigsaw puzzle."

dent precipitated the development of safer airgun technology to create sound waves in water by John Ewing and Lamont technicians.

ASSEMBLING A NEW PICTURE OF EARTH, PIECE BY PIECE

Each datum collected by Columbia scientists from one part of the ocean was like a dot in a pointillist painting or a tiny piece in the massive planetary jigsaw puzzle. Analyzing thousands of depth readings collected between 1947 and 1952, Tharp created six profiles across the Atlantic seafloor. Put together, they revealed a line of mountainous ridges, rising miles high and running north to south down the middle of the ocean. The ridges had a continuous V-shaped rift at their crests.

At the same time, Heezen and Tharp constructed maps locating earthquake occurrences in the oceans. Superimposing one map on the other, they found that the earthquake epicenters lined up within the rift valley.

Continuing on from one sounding and one earthquake to the next and then from one ocean to the next, Heezen, Tharp, and Ewing discovered that the mid-ocean ridge system extended throughout the world's oceans for 40,000 miles, encircling the globe like the seams on a baseball. Never before seen or imagined, it was the largest geological feature on Earth.

After Heezen gave a presentation on mid-ocean ridges in 1957, the eminent Princeton geologist Harry Hess stood up and said, "Young man, you have shaken the foundations of geology!"

The ridges served as borders separating the face of the earth into sections, or plates. At the edges of some oceans, however, particularly in the Pacific Ocean, Hess and others had discovered trenches plunging miles below the seafloor. Hess assembled the emerging assortment of geological clues to fashion a comprehensive theory, coined "seafloor spreading" by another researcher, Robert Dietz.

Earth's crust lies atop a hot interior region called the mantle, and as Hess explained it, hot buoyant magma from the mantle emerges in volcanic eruptions at the mid-ocean ridges—hence the fresh basalt and earthquakes. The magma cools and solidifies upon hitting cold seawater to create the volcanic subsea mountain chain as well as new ocean floor crust, which spreads outward from both sides of the ridges.

Over millions of years, the ocean crust moves outward, becomes denser as it cools, and begins to sink back into the mantle, forming deep trenches that also serve as plate borders. The thick, permanent continents simply rode atop a conveyor propelled by a thin sliver of impermanent seafloor that was created at the ridges and recycled in the trenches. The continents drifted apart, as Africa and South America did to form the intervening Atlantic Ocean, or collided, as India did with Asia to uplift the Himalayas.

Hess called his paper "an essay in geopoetry"—an elegant image to ponder but unsubstantiated by data. The new data had raised provocative questions that only more data could answer. But by the middle 1960s, all those years of relentless and systematic global data collecting by Lamont scientists had added up.

"It was clearly payoff time," Hayes says. "We alone were sitting on the mother lode [of data] with all the tools needed to mine it."

Ewing's compulsive core collecting proved the value of knitting together disparate clues from various locations. Among the first mysteries solved was the one inherent in that first core in 1947—why recent sediment lay directly on ancient sediment.

A series of cores was collected from the Hudson Canyon—a vast submarine canyon as remarkable as the Grand Canyon on land—which emerges from the mouth of the Hudson River, bites deeply into the continental shelf, and extends all the way to the flat abyssal plains hundreds of miles off the coast. Other cores were taken on the Grand Banks off Newfoundland, where several undersea transatlantic telegraph cables were mysteriously severed during a 1929 earthquake. Another core from the deep Puerto Rico Trench curiously contained the shells of a microscopic plant that lives in coastal waters.

The pattern that emerged from these series of cores all pointed to a phenomenon called turbidity currents. These are torrential underwater currents of water and sediments, set into roiling motion by a landslide on the slope or by an undersea earthquake. They thunder through the oceans with enormous speed and force and carry huge loads of material great distances until the currents lose momentum and the material at their front edges settles meekly into a flat plain. Turbidity currents in the ocean explain how canyons were cut, cables were broken, sediments were transported, abyssal plains were formed, and how offshore oil deposits (ultimately formed when organic matter is buried by sediments) were created.

With the discovery, earth scientists could factor out disruptions in the sequence of sediments and reconstruct Earth's history. Columbia geochemists then radio-carbon-dated preserved planktonic shells in various sedimentary layers, providing a way to establish the timing of events thousands of years in the past.

The cores also contained evidence that Earth's magnetic field had reversed several times in the past, with the north and south poles exchanging places. The sediments preserved a signature of the field that existed when they were made. Columbia professors Neil Opdyke and James Hays, along with graduate students

Billy Glass and John Foster, embarked on a mission to identify a record of Earth's magnetic reversals in the cores—to provide a geological calendar extending millions of years into the past.

Jim Heirtzler and Walter C. Pitman III analyzed data of seafloor magnetic properties collected aboard the *Eltanin*. In 1966, they found a striped pattern of rocks, parallel to a South Pacific mid-ocean ridge and extending hundreds of miles on either side of it. Rocks imprinted when Earth's magnetic field was in one position alternated with rocks imprinted when the field was reversed. The pattern was astonishingly symmetrical on either side of the ridge. The mirror image could be created only if new seafloor—created at the ridge crest and quenched there with the prevailing magnetic signature—then spread outward in both directions.

At most labs at the time, data were controlled by individual scientists who collected them. But at Lamont, all data collected were institutional data, available to everyone.

Opdyke says that Pitman sat "in the next office to me and what he knew, I knew within a day." Opdyke realized instantly that the timetable of magnetic reversals extending down inches in the sediment cores he was working on could be used to verify the record of magnetic reversals that Pitman and Heirtzler saw extending laterally over hundreds of miles of seafloor.

A young graduate student named Lynn Sykes, now Higgins Professor of Earth and Environmental Sciences at Columbia, also soon heard about Pitman and Heirtzler's so-called magic profile and began to apply data that were newly emerging from the recently established worldwide seismograph network. The network was largely funded by the Department of Defense, which was eager to apply the new science of seismology to monitor Soviet underground nuclear weapons tests. Today the expanded modern descendant of this original system provides the means to verify a Comprehensive Test Ban Treaty—a goal toward which Sykes and Paul Richards, the Mellon Professor of Natural Sciences, have devoted much of their research careers.

But as a graduate student in the early 1960s, Sykes examined the influx of seismic data streaming into Lamont to locate earthquakes near mid-ocean ridges. He proved that earthquakes occurred along recently discovered large seafloor faults, called transform faults. These ran perpendicularly between (and connected) parallel ridge segments. The earthquakes revealed friction and motion along transform faults— whose cause was best explained by new seafloor spreading outward from the ridges.

Sykes, along with Columbia professor Jack Oliver and graduate student Bryan Isacks, precisely located earthquakes in Pacific trenches. The earthquakes marked out the passages of one oceanic plate plunging down and thrusting under another plate—a process that was soon named "subduction."

The mass of accumulated, diverse evidence was overwhelming and convincing. The old frame of reference that Earth's surface was fixed and rigid was discarded. A new dynamic framework—plate tectonics—swept in. And, as Ewing and company at Lamont had averred, most of the action occurred in the oceans.

In just about two decades, Columbia scientists had dissected the planet and reassembled it in a revolutionary new way. The earth, and the study of it, were never the same.

CHAPTER 20

Edwin Howard Armstrong:
Pioneer of the Airwaves

———✺———

Yannis Tsividis

Perhaps few who look across the Hudson toward the Palisades at Alpine, New Jersey, or who from the Palisades Parkway see a giant antenna rising to the sky with its red warning lights recognize in this tower a stolid, surviving monument to the engineering genius of Major Edwin Armstrong, professor of electrical engineering at Columbia from 1934 to 1954. Not many more perhaps, even of those millions around the world with FM receivers in their homes or cars, think of each set as enduring testimony to the brilliant discoveries of this towering figure in electronics. And not many at all of those who pass by Columbia's Philosophy Hall or The Thinker *who ponders before it would think of the basement of Philosophy as the original site of Armstrong's experiments (except for those fledgling trials performed earlier in the attic of his Yonkers home).*

Here we recall both the triumphs and profound disappointments of this tragic figure in the annals of technology. Telling the story is Yannis Tsividis, Charles Batchelor Professor of Electrical Engineering in Columbia's Fu Foundation School of Engineering. Tsividis received his bachelor's degree from the University of Minnesota in 1972 and his Ph.D. from the University of California, Berkeley, in 1976. He has taught at Berkeley, MIT, and the National Technical University of Athens, Greece. For his distinguished scholarship and teaching he has won many awards, including the Great Teacher Award of the Society of Columbia Graduates in 1991 and Columbia's Presidential Award for Outstanding Teaching in 2003. His latest book is Operation and Modeling of the MOS Transistor, *2nd ed. (Oxford University Press, 1999).*

—Wm. Theodore de Bary

Armstrong atop RCA's 115-foot north tower, which stood on the roof of the twenty-one-story Aeolian Hall in midtown Manhattan.

The chief object of science is to explain nature. The chief object of engineering and technology is, or should be, to put nature to work for us. Much of the technology that has transformed modern life is based on the work of unusually creative people, many of whom remain relatively unknown. One striking example is Edwin Howard Armstrong, who spent his adult life at Columbia, first as a student and then as a faculty member. His should be a household name next to Edison's, and the reasons that this is not so—and Armstrong's life in general—tell a sad but fascinating story.

In contrast to many inventors (Edison included), Armstrong had a distinctly analytical mind. Instead of working by trial and error, he would proceed methodically toward identifying the root cause of a problem in order to find a path toward a solution. He placed his physical intuition above everything else and in fact mistrusted results based only on mathematics; he knew well that those are only as good as the assumptions behind them, which do not always correctly model the physical world. He delighted in plunging into areas that others had pronounced hopeless, and he did so with single-minded determination. He was one of those rare individuals who, with a master stroke, came up with ideas that resulted in quantum leaps in technology—and not just once, but three times. His work has made FM radio possible and is responsible for the circuit architecture in practically every modern radio and television set, and many cellular phones.

Why, then, have so many people never heard of Armstrong? The answer is ironic: Armstrong was all substance and no style. He could not play public relations games and was naive enough to underestimate the power of those whose interests were threatened by his inventions. At the same time, he refused to compromise. In the end, he fell victim to the very stubbornness that made possible his spectacular technical successes.

THE DAWN OF THE WIRELESS AGE

Edwin Howard Armstrong was born in Chelsea, New York City, in 1890. Shy as a child, perhaps because of a tic left by a bout of rheumatic fever, he often played alone. At fourteen, after his family had moved to Yonkers, he became fascinated by the stories of great scientists and inventors, in particular those of Michael Faraday and Guglielmo Marconi. He resolved that he, too, would be an inventor. Like many boys his age at the beginning of the century, he became fascinated with the new art of wireless and began building crystal sets—the simple receivers that marked the beginning of the wireless age. Back then Morse code was the only thing one could listen to, and to make out the faint signals one had to wear headphones in a quiet room. He resolved to find a way to increase the volume of those signals and to pick them up from the greatest possible distance.

Armstrong finished high school and was admitted to Columbia's Department of Electrical Engineering in 1909. He plunged into the study of electricity with a determination that was to characterize him for the rest of his life. He never took things for granted; he wanted to know why things were as his professors were telling him, and he often questioned their assertions with a self-confidence sometimes mistaken for arrogance. He valued and credited great minds—but he had no patience for those without substance who posed as great scientists and inventors. His passion to search and expose the truth angered many people.

Though his work made FM possible, Armstrong is not a household name.

As a junior at Columbia, Armstrong came to know well Professor Michael I. Pupin, a founding member of the Department of Electrical Engineering. Pupin was an important inventor himself, having contributed, among other things, to making long distance telephony possible. Pupin became Armstrong's mentor and supporter and made available to him his lab in the basement of Philosophy Hall. This was to become the main testing ground of Armstrong's creative ideas for the rest of his life. Pupin, with some of his colleagues, was also instrumental in defending Armstrong in front of an irate faculty who objected to the ways of the young student.

REGENERATION

At about the time these events were taking place, another inventor, Lee De Forest, was making waves. A graduate of Yale University, he had expanded on Fleming's electron tube by adding a third electrode and forming what he called the "audion"—the triode tube, as it later came to be called. De Forest had tried to apply his tube in radio reception but had achieved only a small improvement—radio signals still came in as faintly as before, requiring one to press the headphones tightly on one's ears in order to barely hear them. Armstrong studied the audion for several

Armstrong with his new wife, Marion MacInnis, on the beach in Florida with the first portable radio—an early "boombox"— Armstrong's wedding present to his bride.

years, performed extensive measurements, understood and explained its operation (a feat that had eluded the audion's inventor himself), and set out to find a way to use it to truly amplify radio signals. The idea hit him while on summer vacation in 1912, just before his senior year at Columbia: he would pass the signals through an audion circuit and feed them back to the input of the circuit in such a way as to make them reinforce themselves. He expected that this "positive feedback" would result in regeneration and great amplification—in fact, by a factor of thousands.

As soon as he returned from vacation, Armstrong tried his idea in his attic. His sister recounts how Armstrong burst into her room late in the night, dancing around and screaming, "I've done it!" Loud signals, clearly heard across the room, were emanating from the headphones left on his bench. What is more, Armstrong discovered that, when the positive feedback was sufficiently increased, the circuit became an "oscillator," and was able to transmit its own signal. Thus, in one masterstroke, a sensitive "regenerative" receiver and an effective electronic transmitter had been born.

The beaming student tried to patent his invention. His father, worried that this sort of extracurricular activity would interfere with his son's progress toward graduation, refused to give him the money. Armstrong had to borrow from relatives and friends and even had to sell his beloved red motorcycle—a high school graduation gift that he had been using to commute between Yonkers and Columbia. He applied for a patent in 1913, and this patent was issued the following year. Soon radios based on Armstrong's invention began to appear. Radio communication had finally become practical.

Armstrong graduated with a degree in electrical engineering in 1913 and was offered a position of assistant the same year. He hung a huge antenna between Philosophy, Havemeyer, and Schermerhorn Halls and was able to demonstrate to an amazed Pupin reception of signals from as far away as Honolulu. More demonstrations followed, including one to a visiting group of engineers from American Marconi. This group included David Sarnoff, who was to become Armstrong's friend and, later, his nemesis.

One of Armstrong's demonstrations was held in the course of a conference held by the the Institute of Radio Engineers (IRE) at Columbia. De Forest was in the audience. The two had never met, and the occasion marked the first time De Forest had heard his audion truly amplify. It also marked the beginning of his animosity toward Armstrong, which would only intensify in the years ahead.

Soon after Armstrong's success, De Forest began claiming that the idea of regeneration was his. He had observed a "howling" in his amplifiers; this, in hindsight, was the result of accidental positive feedback. Although he had never mentioned feedback at that time, never took advantage of it, and in fact tried to suppress its effects in his amplifiers, he now filed patent applications that resulted in interference proceedings with Armstrong's patents. In the meantime, Armstrong was publishing technical papers explaining correctly for the first time how De Forest's audion actually worked.

A battle ensued, too long and too complicated to present here. It began shortly after the end of World War I and continued for many years. Repeatedly during this battle it was shown beyond doubt that Armstrong was the true inventor of the regenerative circuit. Several faculty members of the Department of Electrical Engineering testified in court, and several graduates of Columbia Law School represented Armstrong. Repeatedly it became apparent that, when pressed in the course of court proceedings, De Forest did not understand how his own audion worked. An embarrassed De Forest escalated the legal battles, now backed by AT&T, which had purchased his patents, including the ones in interference with Armstrong's. The courts decided in favor of Armstrong several times, with these outcomes followed by reversals. In 1934 the Supreme Court, unable to understand scientific facts, found in favor of De Forest on the basis of a language detail.

The absurdity of the courts' decision was plainly evident to the technical community. The IRE had earlier given Armstrong its Medal of Honor for the discovery of the regenerative circuit. Now, a disheartened Armstrong attempted to return the medal during an IRE convention. They refused to accept it and gave him a standing ovation. In 1941, the Franklin Institute gave Armstrong the Franklin Medal for the regenerative circuit, and in 1942 the American Institute of Electrical Engineers awarded him the Edison Medal. He was similarly honored in Europe.

THE SUPERHETERODYNE RECEIVER

Armstrong had not been technically idle during his long battle with De Forest. During World War I, while stationed in France, he scored his second major success, which would change the face of radio once again. He applied the concept of heterodyning (mixing the signals of two different frequencies to produce a signal of a third frequency, equal to the sum or difference of the first two), to the reception of high-frequency radio signals. The result, which he termed the "superheterodyne receiver," was of such high performance that it eventually superseded all previous approaches, including his own regenerative receiver. Armstrong had outdone himself, as well as several other inventors who were working on related approaches at about the same time. Today, practically all modern radio and TV receivers, as well as many types of cellular phones and other communications devices, use the superheterodyne approach.

Armstrong rose to the rank of major, and the French government gave him access to the Eiffel Tower for his experiments and named him a Chevalier de la Légion d'Honneur. He filed for a patent for his superheterodyne circuit in 1918, and the patent was issued two years later. He sold this patent, as well as one for another invention—the super-regenerative receiver—and by 1923 he was a millionaire. Now an assistant professor at Columbia, he decided to accept no salary from the university. In this way, he could avoid administrative work and even teaching and could devote his energies to research—and to his legal battles. At about the same time, he married Marion MacInnis, Sarnoff's former secretary—a woman with plenty of understanding for her driven husband. She would be his companion for the next thirty years.

FM RADIO

It is amazing that while Armstrong was fighting his endless legal battles with De Forest, he had the energy to be working at the same time on another idea—FM radio. This was the result of a long study he had initiated with Pupin: to combat the problem of static in AM radio, the established technique at the time.

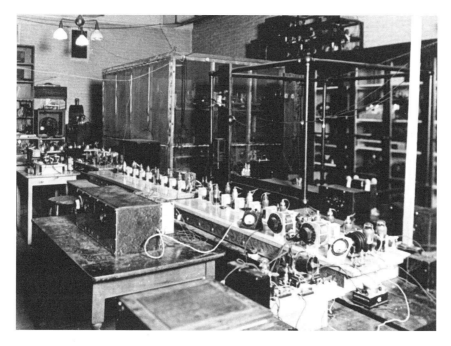

The Marcellus Hartley Laboratory in the basement of Philosophy Hall, where most of Armstrong's work took place. It was in this room that Armstrong created a receiver and a radio transmitter that resulted in FM—"staticless" radio.

AM, or amplitude modulation, is the technique of varying the amplitude, or strength, of a radio signal in accordance with the voice or music being transmitted. A radio receiving this signal is sensitive to such amplitude variations but is also sensitive to other disturbances related to amplitude, notably static due to thunderstorms, electrical machinery, and so on. The technical wisdom of the time held that nothing could be done about this. "Static, like the poor, will always be with us," a well-known engineer had pronounced. But Armstrong was unfazed. He believed that if, instead, one varied not the amplitude but the frequency of the signal being transmitted, the receiver could be designed so that it would respond to frequency changes rather than to amplitude changes—and would thus be oblivious to static. This is FM, or frequency modulation.

Others had considered FM before Armstrong, but the verdict was that it offered no advantages over AM. When a mathematical analysis by AT&T scientist John Carson was quoted as conclusive proof of this, the technical community committed the kind of logical error that, unfortunately, continues to be quite common. Someone proves a statement based on certain assumptions; others forget those assumptions and remember only the conclusions. People then tend to apply such conclusions to all cases, even ones that do not satisfy the original assumptions. This is what had happened here, and it was tantamount to a prejudice against FM.

General Ferrie, head of French military communications, pins the insignia of a Chevalier de la Légion d'Honneur on Armstrong in 1919.

The assumption under which FM has no advantages over AM is that its spectrum would occupy a narrow band of frequencies, a property considered at the time to be desirable for keeping noise low. Armstrong, in a brilliant moment of lateral thinking, decided to challenge that wisdom, and set out to find out what would happen if he used instead a wide band of frequencies for his FM signal. After years of painstaking experiments, with equipment spread over several tables in Philosophy Hall and involving as many as a hundred electron tubes, he was able to prove that wideband FM made possible a drastic reduction of noise and static (a hundred-fold, or even more). Since everyone else had followed the common wisdom that "wideband is bad," Armstrong was free to pursue FM by himself. By 1934, he had filed a series of patents relating to his latest brainchild.

Now a full professor, Armstrong was ready for a demonstration. During an IRE conference in 1935, he described FM radio and then turned on his receiver in front of the audience. An FM transmission from a friend's house in Yonkers came in totally free of static and, thanks to the wide audio spectrum being used, with a fidelity never heard before. A stunned audience listened to a live music performance transmitted with remarkable clarity and to a series of sounds, such as a glass of water being poured·or a piece of paper being torn—which would have been unrecognizable over AM radio.

The results of the demonstration were the opposite of what one would expect. As Sarnoff put it, he was expecting an evolution in the AM system that would reduce static; instead, Armstrong had come up with a revolution. FM radio was so much better than AM that the whole established order of things was threatened. Thousands of AM transmitters and millions of AM radios could become obsolete. The established broadcasting networks, their investments, and their markets, were in jeopardy. In addition, FM could interfere with the industry's up-and-coming big new sensation: television broadcasting, at the time being readied for the market by RCA under Sarnoff's leadership. Thus, ten days after Armstrong's demonstration of FM, the public was reading RCA's extensive public releases concerning the upcoming marvel of television—with no word about FM.

Not even De Forest's legal battles had prepared Armstrong for what was coming. This time he was up against too much and too many. To him, things were clear: since FM was proved beyond doubt to be immensely superior to AM, the public had the right to its benefits. He bet everything on this logic and decided to go it alone against corporate interests and lobbying efforts. Sarnoff asked him to remove his equipment from the top of the Empire State Building, to which he had given him access initially for his FM experiments. Various reports on the state of the art in communications ignored FM completely, including the Federal Communications Commission's annual report to Congress. The view was propagated that the public is not interested in high fidelity and would not pay for it. But Armstrong was convinced that FM radio would succeed. The only thing that could temporarily slow it down was, in his words, "those intangible forces so frequently set in motion by men, and the origin of which lies in vested interests, habits, customs, and legislation."

Yet Armstrong had not realized what he was up against. The FCC was successfully lobbied to turn down his request for an experimental FM station license. When he threatened to take his development of FM overseas, he got the license and a tiny FM band. The first FM station began broadcasting from Alpine, New Jersey, in 1939. The tiny "Yankee Network" in New England adopted FM and began spreading it. In 1940 RCA made Armstrong an offer to buy a license from him. He refused, insisting that they should pay royalties as other companies were doing and under the same terms. But RCA had been doing its own FM radio development in the meantime, and they and other companies were soon selling FM radios, ignoring Armstrong's patents. At the end of World War II, the FCC moved FM's existing band to higher frequencies "for FM's own good," and drastically reduced the maximum power allowed to an FM transmitter. The result was instant obsolescence of all existing FM transmitters and receivers as well as a greatly limited coverage.

But Armstrong would not give up. With the help of a few sympathetic senators, he carried the fight into Congress. In 1948 Armstrong charged RCA and NBC with infringement. An army of corporate lawyers began precourt proceedings, which were to last for several years. Armstrong was interrogated endlessly during these proceedings about irrelevant details, from his income tax and the size of the rooms in which he gave speeches to why he used Columbia letterhead for some of his communications and whether he had a formal agreement with the university. It took years to get these pre-court proceedings to the point that Sarnoff was called in as a witness.

Armstrong was now deteriorating quickly. He had predicted that "they will stall this along until I am dead or broke." His fortune had been depleted on legal fees, and his health was worsening. Nearing breakdown, saddened beyond hope, he became obsessed and desperate. On Thanksgiving night, 1953, he quarreled with his wife, and she left to live with her relatives.

On the night of January 31, 1954, Armstrong put on his overcoat, scarf, gloves, and hat, opened his window, and jumped out, falling ten stories to his death.

A note was found on his desk, written to his wife, talking about his deep grief for having hurt her and how his battles had broken him. "God keep you and the Lord have mercy on my soul," the note ended.

EPILOGUE

One month before his death, Armstrong had filed twenty-one infringement suits. His wife, Marion, carried on the battle, and by the mid-sixties had won two and settled all others successfully. Dana Raymond, a young lawyer who had been at her husband's side ever since graduating from Columbia Law School, was instrumental in these efforts.

In 1955, the Union Nationale des Télécommunications in Geneva added Armstrong's name to the list of such great men of electricity and telecommunications as André-Marie Ampère, Alexander Graham Bell, Michael Faraday, Carl Friedrich Gauss, Heinrich Rudolph Hertz, William Thomson Kelvin, Guglielmo Marchese Marconi, James Clerk Maxwell, Samuel F. B. Morse, Michael Pupin, and Nikola Tesla. A U.S. postal stamp was issued in his honor in 1983. He was inducted posthumously to the Consumer Electronics Association Hall of Fame in 2000, "in recognition of his contributions and pioneering spirit that have laid the foundation for consumer electronics."

Armstrong was the victim of a world in which, as he eloquently put it, "men substitute words for realities, and then talk about the words." Next time you turn on your FM radio or your cellular phone, think of that—and of him.

Much of the information in this article has been obtained from the excellent books by Lawrence Lessing, Man of High Fidelity: Edwin Howard Armstrong *(1991), and by Tom Lewis,* Empire of the Air: The Men Who Made Radio *(1991) as well as from the 1991 documentary by Ken Burns,* Empire of the Air, The Men Who Made Radio. *All are very highly recommended. The author would like to thank Kenneth K. Goldstein, Jeanne Hammond (Armstrong's niece), and Dana Raymond for their comments on the manuscript. For bibliography, see Notes, page 659.*

PART THREE

LAW AND SOCIETY

CHAPTER 21

Paul F. Lazarsfeld's Scholarly Journey

———✵———

Jonathan R. Cole

I am a transmitter, not a creator," Confucius once said of his own relation to tradition. Nevertheless, his readers for more than two millennia have seen Confucius otherwise—as both a transmitter and re-creator of tradition. Much the same could be said of Paul Lazarsfeld, as both a bearer to New York of Old World scholarship and a renewer of sociology in America.

The product of a strong socialist environment in early twentieth-century Vienna, Lazarsfeld turned his first efforts at the University of Vienna to scholarly studies of Marienthal, a nearby working-class suburb suffering severe unemployment. These studies attracted the attention of Robert S. Lynd, the Columbia sociologist whose study Middletown had broken new ground for an American sociology. When Lazarsfeld fled as a refugee from Fascist Austria, he joined a major movement of émigré scholars to the United States, transplanting mature European learning in the sciences and humanities to new and fertile American soil.

Lazarsfeld's early training in mathematics marked his contribution to the development at Columbia of a major center of quantitative research and eventually of the Bureau of Applied Social Research. As Jonathan R. Cole tells the story, Lazarsfeld stimulated an array of new initiatives in mathematical sociology, mass communications, market research, and sociological presentation as a literary form in itself.

In the process Lazarsfeld and Robert K. Merton, whose own work complemented Lazarsfeld's, attracted a distinguished company of sociologists to Columbia and led their collaborative enterprise. Cole's essay includes a substantial list of colleagues who have contributed to the large legacy left by these giants.

Jonathan Cole is one direct heir to that legacy as a student of both Lazarsfeld and Merton and subsequently as the Quetelet Professor of Sociology. In 2003, after his fourteen-year stint as provost and dean of faculties at Columbia, he resumed scholarship and teaching as the John Mitchell Mason Professor of the University. His scholarly contributions include Peer Review in the National

Science Foundation (*1978 and 1981, coauthored*); Fair Science: Women in the Scientific Community (*1979*); The Wages of Writing: Per Word, Per Piece, or Perhaps (*1986, coauthored*); The Outer Circle: Women in the Scientific Community (*1991, coeditor and author*); *and* The Research University in a Time of Discontent (*coeditor and author, 1994*).

—*Wm. Theodore de Bary*

More than a century has now passed since the birth in Vienna of Paul Lazarsfeld (1901–1976), who became one of the giants of American social science during his lifetime.[1] Almost thirty years after his death his intellectual influence in the social sciences remains formidable.

THE EARLY YEARS IN VIENNA

Paul Lazarsfeld was born well before the First World War, but his early years were influenced by that war and its aftermath. Raised in a middle-class, highly educated, but hardly affluent Viennese family, Lazarsfeld followed his parents' lead as an active participant in the young socialist movement that was concerned with, among other things, problems of massive unemployment and the need for social reform. Hans Zeisel, Lazarsfeld's lifelong friend and colleague, reflected nostalgically on those days: "For a brief moment in history, the humanist ideals of democratic socialism attained reality in the city of Vienna and gave new dignity and pride to the working class and the intellectuals who had won it."[2] Lazarsfeld tells us in his own wonderfully informative memoir that he tried during those years to combine "the ideas of the German youth movement with socialist propaganda among my colleagues."[3] By age eighteen, when he entered the university, he had become "too old" to be a *revolté*, so he became an amateur "educator," who worked at socialist youth camps and as a tutor in high schools (*Gymnasia*) to children of working-class parents.[4]

Lazarsfeld was trained as an applied mathematician and said his main influences were Ernst Mach, Henri Poincaré, and Albert Einstein—all scientists and philosophers of science. As a student at the University of Vienna, he became more interested in social psychology. He taught courses in the subject, while continuing his tutoring in the *Gymnasium*.

Foreshadowing an interest that would run throughout his career, Lazarsfeld created an empirical social research center in 1925 connected to Karl Bühler's center in Vienna. At the same time, Lazarsfeld continued to teach at the university and to encourage students to use data collected at the center in their dissertation research. In 1930, at the tender age of twenty-nine, Lazarsfeld was working with Hans Zeisel and Marie Jahoda on the now-famous study of the working poor in a village south of Vienna, Marienthal, whose population was almost entirely unemployed. The Marienthal study brought Lazarsfeld to the attention of the Rockefeller Foundation, whose Paris representative offered him a traveling fellowship to the United States for the academic year beginning in September 1933. At Columbia, fortuitously, he met sociologist Robert Lynd, who connected the Marienthal project to his and Helen Lynd's famous Middletown study. Lynd would prove to be instrumental in bringing Lazarsfeld to Columbia.

I dwell on these biographical facts because they are part of the larger story of the most important intellectual migration in the twentieth century, and quite certainly the most significant migration of rare intellectual talent working in or aspiring to positions at universities. This story, particularly the scale of the migration as well as its impact on the university systems of the United States, Germany, and other European countries, is perhaps less widely known to many younger scholars and scientists than it ought to be.

THE INTELLECTUAL MIGRATION

The intellectual exodus was, of course, almost entirely attributable to the rise to power of Hitler and the Nazis in January 1933 and the rapid purging of "Jewish science" from German universities and the civil service. In the wake of these purges came other successful Fascist movements in other nations. Lazarsfeld informs us that after the Conservative Party came to power in Austria in 1934, it "overthrew the constitution, outlawed the Socialist Party, and established an Italian-type Fascism."[5] Lazarsfeld's position in the *Gymnasium* was eliminated, and most of his family in Vienna was imprisoned. That "brief moment in history" alluded to by Hans Zeisel had come to a dramatic end.

In the early decades of the twentieth century, German universities were a mecca for physical science. Germans dominated the early Nobel Prizes in chemistry and physics. While American universities were already producing extraordinary research in genetics during the first two decades of the twentieth century (the work biologists like Thomas Hunt Morgan at Columbia), the physical sciences and their practical industrial applications were preeminent in European, particularly German, universities. We tend to forget that American research universities were young and rather sleepy institutions even in science at the beginning of the twentieth century. Hitler changed all of this within a few months during 1933.

Roughly one quarter of its pre-1933 physics community was lost to Germany as a result of the passage of the Law for the Restoration of the Career Civil Service. This purged Socialists and non-Aryans (meaning anyone whose ancestry was at least one-quarter Jewish) from their civil service jobs, including all positions in universities and the prestigious Kaiser Wilhelm institutes. Among those lost to the great German physics community were Nobel laureates Einstein, Schrödinger, Stern, Bloch, Born, Wigner, Bethe, Herzberg, Hess, and Debye; mathematicians Richard Courant and Herman Weyl (among others); and some physicists who later turned to the biological sciences, such as Max Delbrück and the great Leo Szilard. These scientists were exceptionally talented, with world-class originality and academic experience; they were of priceless value to any academic community.

Lazarsfeld was, of course, not alone among humanists and social scientists in taking up residency in the United States. Desperate to leave Europe in 1938, Theodor W. Adorno, for one, took a job in New Jersey working on the radio research projects of none other than Paul Lazarsfeld. Humanists such as Erwin Panofsky, Leo Spitzer, and Erich Auerbach also left. Harry Levin tells us that after 1933, psychoanalysis was classified as "Jewish science" and was banned from the Leipzig Congress on Psychology. Psychoanalytic literature was burned, and members of the psychoanalytic community in Berlin scattered to countries that would protect them. Even the elderly and ill Sigmund Freud and his daughter Anna Freud were forced to leave Vienna in 1938.[6]

Germany's unfathomable loss of talent was America's unfathomable gain. The German university system has still not fully overcome the devastation caused by the intrusion of National Socialist politics in the early 1930s. The migration of people like Lazarsfeld and the other scientists, when combined with the growing number of very talented American scientists, set the stage for the "takeoff" of the American research university that occurred after World War II. By 1945, many of the immigrant scientists had earned their stripes as active participants in the Manhattan Project and in other parts of the American war effort.

The presence of these talented foreigners also led to significant departures for the fields that they entered in American universities. They were at once "insiders" and "outsiders," providing new disciplines first with their European perspectives and later with their perspectives as newly assimilated American scholars and scientists who were becoming leaders in their fields. These scholars also had access to a growing number of exceptionally talented students. Paul Lazarsfeld, trained as an applied mathematician, had already published on social issues, but once in the United States he was able to expand his own "effective scope" to include multiple disciplines—not the least of which was sociology—and become a pioneer in developing modern empirical social science methods. By his own admission, Paul knew little about American sociology when he arrived in the United States. In summary, these immigrant intellectuals suffered a loss of place, they also experienced a new freedom, enabling them to infuse enormous energy into new disciplines in the American research university.

In the two decades that followed the European migration, a new intellectual chemistry was born in the United States by mixing two groups of socially mobile scientists and scholars. The "horizontally" mobile European scholars often merged their efforts with "vertically" mobile American scholars benefiting from a new openness to talent in American society regardless of religious or economic origins. These encounters often led to extremely fruitful cases of "outbreeding." An example is the collaborative relationship that took hold between Paul Lazarsfeld and Robert K. Merton. Lazarsfeld, who came from a bourgeois background despite his family's socialist leanings, seemed very American in his entrepreneurial efforts to link the American university with industry—and to develop applied social research that would fall squarely into what today we would call "Pasteur's quadrant" (research motivated by both curiosity and a particular mission). Merton, who came from a Jewish background and grew up in a poor section of Philadelphia, was an exemplar of the extraordinarily talented and intellectually curious youngster who now had genuine opportunities in American academe. They may have seemed like an "odd couple," as Merton says in his essay on working with Lazarsfeld, but through selective affinities and their desire to "make new disciplines," they became part of the new chemistry that propelled American universities to greater distinction.[7]

Immigrant scholars often feel that they straddle two worlds without being fully embraced by either. Lazarsfeld perceived himself as such a marginal person—not fully accepted by the American academy because he was a Jewish foreigner with a noticeable accent who studied seemingly lowbrow topics, such as why people listened to certain radio shows or why they bought Maxwell House coffee—marketing research done in collaboration with captains of industry.[8] Most indicators of acceptance, except for the crucial one of self-identity, would suggest that his status was anything but marginal. Within two decades of taking up his position at Columbia in 1940, Lazarsfeld was recognized as one of America's leading social scientists, whose pathbreaking work in the United States led to his election as president of the American Sociological Association as well as his election to the

U.S. National Academy of Sciences—a very rare distinction for a sociologist in those days. He also maintained a very significant following in Europe, especially in France (Paul was a true Francophile) and, in 1972, became the first American sociologist to receive an honorary degree from the Sorbonne.

Waiting to receive another honorary degree (from the University of Chicago) late in his career, Lazarsfeld met Anna Freud, who was also being honored that day. "Are you the little Paulie Lazarsfeld I used to know in Vienna?" Freud asked. "Well, we have come a long way, haven't we?"[9]

LAZARSFELD'S SCHOLARLY CONTRIBUTIONS— PAST AND PRESENT

Paul Lazarsfeld was an enormously energetic man who was both curious and relentless. His ideas seemed to spring forth from continual conversation—with colleagues in many fields, with leaders in industry, and with his students. He was essentially an intellectual innovator and leader who thrived on collaboration and often actively crossed boundaries to build interdisciplinary research groups. He also was persuaded that he could convince any bright student or colleague to work on his problems—those he thought were of fundamental interest. In fact, one measure of Lazarsfeld's and Merton's influence is the array of their students who pursued such paths. Both men exerted a powerful gravitational pull on students: some had no interest in trying to escape; others suffered in continual efforts to break free.

There is widespread agreement among Lazarsfeld's students[10] and colleagues[11] about his most basic scholarly and institutional contributions. Lazarsfeld transformed "public opinion polling methods into survey research, that is, into the analytical use of sample surveys to draw inferences about causal relations that affect the actions of individuals . . ." He pioneered "in the use of survey panel methods, that is, the further transformation of public opinion polling beyond cross-sectional surveys into panels involving two or more interviews of the same sample (or 'panel')."[12] These methods allowed him to study changes in the attitudes and behavior of individuals over time in a more precise way than had been done before. He simply created the field of mass communications research, partly through his early collaborations with Frank Stanton at CBS on radio research. His "two-step flow" model of influence, describing how personal relationships mediate mass communications and their influence on attitudes and behavior, is still used today. Lazarsfeld's studies demonstrated that mass media affect action in an indirect way—mediated by the opinion leaders who use the mass media for their own purposes as well as by social context—and they played a major role in the development of the market-research industry.

Lazarsfeld's work on voting behavior was the scholarly precursor to election polling and public opinion surveys and analysis that are commonplace today.[13] He "was one of the 'founders' of modern mathematical sociology" through his work on latent structure analysis and through his teaching, which sought to go beyond the positivistic thinking and behaviorism of the day and to explore unobservable ideas. In a conversation with his assistant John Shelton Reed, Lazarsfeld said "he'd had only four original ideas in his life. When asked what they were, he listed the elaboration scheme, panel analysis, latent structure analysis, and . . . contextual analysis. . . . Lazarsfeld said that everything he had done had been a matter of working out the implications of those four ideas. . . . No false modesty, though," Reed tells us. "After saying that, he added, 'But that's four more than most people, and three more than it takes to make a reputation.'"[14]

What are the common themes of Lazarsfeld's work? In studying action, he perceived that "a given situation normally gives birth to several types of response." This is what he found in his earliest work on unemployment in Marienthal—the loss of work can reinforce or destroy the nuclear family. For Lazarsfeld, the "story" lies in understanding why responses vary. Such understanding requires specification, which sometimes comes only from further qualitative analysis or the study of what Lazarsfeld called "deviant cases," the ones that seem to run counter to one's predictions or theory. His analysis of the multiple effects of certain causes, which we see in his earliest work, later finds more formal expression in his famous "elaboration scheme," which examines two-variable relationships in light of third variables that either precede the first two or intervene in time between them, and his interest in "contextual effects." He wrestled with problems of causation, never entirely successfully, in trying to understand how attitudes influence behavior and why attitudes change.

It was not, of course, without careful thought that Lazarsfeld titled one of his most important collections of papers "The Language of Social Research." What did he mean by "language"? For Lazarsfeld methodology was not the same as technology, although the two were often confused. The tools of research, the technology represented in statistical methods used by data analysts, are the products of methodology. Methodology emerges from a set of general intellectual attitudes and orientations rather than from a set of rules or principles.[15] Close attention to the meaning of words and concepts and their explication is part of the job of the methodologist—as much as it is for the literary critic.

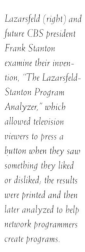

Lazarsfeld (right) and future CBS president Frank Stanton examine their invention, "The Lazarsfeld-Stanton Program Analyzer," which allowed television viewers to press a button when they saw something they liked or disliked; the results were printed and then later analyzed to help network programmers create programs.

For Lazarsfeld, methodology is almost a literary form since it depends on in-depth analysis of language and translation of it into more formal methods of data collection and analysis. He was determined to understand the language of variables and the relationships between concepts and indicators; he strove to produce a systematic underpinning for these relationships in the form of mathematics, yet he always was interested in what mathematics cannot do and what requires qualitative or historical inquiries instead. Titles of papers such as "The Art of Asking Why" suggest that the role of the methodologist is to clarify and organize, to formalize the language used to uncover the determinants of action. Both Lazarsfeld and Merton were very much aware that, as Columbia's Charles Tilly put it, "No one . . . can pursue empirical social research effectively without deploying and testing two interdependent bodies of theory simultaneously: a theory embodying explanations of the phenomenon under investigation, and another theory embodying explanations of the evidence concerning the phenomenon."[16]

Many commentators on Paul Lazarsfeld's work have debated whether he was, in Isaiah Berlin's famous distinction, a fox or a hedgehog—that is, a man of many ideas or of one big idea. His papers, books, monographs, and Bureau reports covered a broad range of topical interests. But whether he was studying mass communication or voting behavior or something else, there was always a methodological problem lingering close to the surface. *The Academic Mind*, about the erosion of civil liberties and academic freedom on American college campuses during the Cold War, was also an effort to develop new methods for understanding the influence of social networks, contextual variables, and group properties on attitudes and on action.

The influence of Paul Lazarsfeld is only partially reflected in his published work, as significant as that has been in Europe and the United States. His influence can be found as well in his intellectual progeny—the substantial number of exceptionally gifted and creative students that he taught and who were his protégés. For about fifteen years in the 1950s and 1960s, Lazarsfeld and Merton had an enormous impact on the field through the students they had trained. Merton, reflecting on his collaboration with Lazarsfeld, recalled the words of the nineteenth-century French mining engineer and self-taught sociologist Frédéric Le Play: "The most important thing to come out of the mine, he wrote, is the miner. In much the same spirit, it can be said that the most important thing to come out of Columbia sociology back then were the students."[17] Lazarsfeld insisted that we start with an interesting question or idea rather than with an existing data set and that we focus on how to gather data to test the idea within the context of theory—an approach that became a model for organizing an inquiry. He wanted his students to be able "to tell a story." Indeed, for some of their students, who had come to associate Merton with theory and Lazarsfeld with empirical method, it seemed ironic that Lazarsfeld was always asking how our ideas fit with theory, while Merton was always enjoining us to focus on how we might empirically test our theoretical ideas.

Paul's intellectual heirs, to their credit, did not become mannerist imitators, but exceptionally creative scholars, in many ways different from him. Thus, Paul's pattern of intellectual influence can be traced to more recent sociologists and other social scientists through *their* own students. The majority of his "discoveries," like those of any extraordinary scientist, are used today by social scientists without direct attribution—they have undergone the inevitable process that Merton called "obliteration through incorporation."

Even so, I should not minimize the large, continuing, and direct impact of some of Lazarsfeld's work on contemporary social science. Having been present at the birth of using citation analysis to measure scientific impact, I compared Lazarsfeld's citation rate in the years 2000 to 2004 to those of the current president and president-elect of the American Sociological Association, two other members of the ASA council, and the chairman of a major sociology department. Over the five-year period for which I collected data (in May 2004) from the Science Citation Index, Lazarsfeld had a total of 374 citations[18] of his work; the average number received by the comparative group was 408, with a range in the group from 138 to 681 citations. If we examine the previous five-year period, 1995–99, Lazarsfeld had 444 citations compared with an average of 275 for the comparative group of five stars. In short, considering the half-life of citations, which in sociology is probably about a decade, and despite the fact that Paul died in 1976, he holds his own quite well even today against leading sociologists in the field. In fact, his most cited work continues to be *The People's Choice*, first published in 1944. His influence has spread to many different fields and is felt today as much by students in the discipline of "communications" and in social psychology as in sociology.

INSIDE THE BUREAU AND THE DEPARTMENT OF SOCIOLOGY: PERSONAL REFLECTIONS

Many commentators have noted Paul's obsession with creating social science research organizations—his "babies." With the Columbia University Bureau of Applied Social Research (and before that, similar organizations in Vienna and at the University of Newark), Lazarsfeld produced the prototype of the university-based social research organization, a model for many other research centers, both in the United States and abroad.[19]

Even the Columbia Bureau, which offered on-site training for graduate and post-doctoral students, was not in itself a school of empirical research that would grant degrees. Lazarsfeld was attempting to reshape the way knowledge is generated in the social sciences. Quite unlike Merton, he envisioned collaborative projects involving senior colleagues, graduate students, and technical staff as the basic unit of creation—an approach much closer to laboratory science than to the social sciences of his day. A high proportion of Lazarsfeld's published and unpublished work, as I've noted, was collaborative. At a time when women were rarely found among the professoriate (but were numerous among sociology graduate students), Paul had many women collaborators at the Bureau.[20]

The Department of Sociology at Columbia, with its satellite Bureau of Applied Social Research, was a truly remarkable place during the three decades from 1940 to 1970. It attracted a distinguished group of faculty in addition to Merton and Lazarsfeld, including Allen Barton, Bernard Barber, Daniel Bell, Peter Blau, Theodore Caplow, James S. Coleman, Kingsley Davis, Sigmund Diamond, Amitai Etzioni, William J. Goode, Herbert Hyman, Mirra Komarovsky, Juan Linz, Seymour Martin Lipset, Robert Lynd, Robert MacIver, C. Wright Mills, Immanuel Wallerstein, Morris Zelditch, and Harriet Zuckerman. Some of these scholars eventually populated the leading departments of American sociology for decades.

But Lazarsfeld and Merton were unquestionably the intellectual core of the department. When I arrived as a graduate student in 1964, there was excitement there, with the framework of "theories of the middle range" providing sociological studies with results of high theoretical and empirical quality comparable to the best developments in economics, anthropology, political science, social psychology, and history. Students were taught to give their empirical work a narrative shape not unlike the plot of a mystery (a genre Merton and Lazarsfeld both loved), with a high value placed on surprising or counterintuitive conclusions resulting from an unusual perspective on the problem at hand.

Robert K. Merton, Lazarsfeld's collaborator for thirty-five years

There was little emphasis on statistical tests of significance or statistical models, a problem that led appropriately to substantial criticism of this approach. Nor was much of Lazarsfeld's earlier work deeply concerned with "sociological variables." Much of his survey research had a distinctly individualistic and even social-psychological bent to it—mirroring Lazarsfeld's own training. Much of this way of "doing sociology" was taught through example or as part of "apprenticeships" rather than by formula or direct instruction. Its best examples (not easily reproduced) were the papers of Lazarsfeld and Merton.

The famous thirty-five-year "collaboration" between Lazarsfeld and Merton was, in fact, a curious one. There can be no doubt from their collective testimony that each influenced the other enormously, but that mutual influence is not evident in their formal collaborations. Their total joint output was six papers, none of them seminal and only two of them significant, by my reckoning: the paper "Friendship as a Social Process" and their coedited volume *Continuities in Social Research: Studies in the Scope and Method of "The American Soldier."*

The paper on friendship has an unusual structure. It was really two essays, one by Merton, on sociological propositions about friendship patterns in two small communities, and the second by Lazarsfeld, an attempt to formalize these propositions in order to sharpen the focus of analysis. Merton of course acknowledged the unusual format in a ten-page epilogue that he calls an effort by "the guinea pig who was subjected to this experiment in continuity to report to the experimenter, and to other observers, what benefits, if any, have been gained from the harrowing experience."[21] The result is an extremely interesting paper in which Lazarsfeld uses his famous sixteen-fold-turnover table to specify the concepts and to map the sequences and the various effects over time of the ideas Merton had offered in his section.

At the end of the day, these two giants provided students with an exceptionally rich environment, complementing each other in several ways. The most obvious was the emphasis on theory or methods within the overall framework of middle-range theorizing and hypothesis testing. But the other dimensions were of equal importance. We could see two totally different styles of research lead to extraordinary results. Merton, the most influential proponent of structural-functional analysis (in its "modern form"), was interested in describing patterns of behavior, along with their positive, negative, and unanticipated consequences and the mechanisms that sustain the prevailing pattern in a state of conflict or stasis. He was a great lecturer who could work magic in the classroom and a careful and precise editor of a student's manuscript. Lazarsfeld was principally interested in studying action and causal relationships and pushed students to move from fuzzy ideas to precise conceptualization and measurement. He was far more at home in a seminar room in more casual conversation than in the lecture hall, believed in the collaborative enterprise, and never lost sight of "the story to be told," or the idea to be tested.[22] Both men moved from problem to measurement and then back to the problem. While both appreciated technology, they were never driven by it. This was a rare combination for those who could study in a serious way with both. Some of these students were Peter Blau, James S. Coleman, Elihu Katz, Seymour Martin Lipset, Peter H. Rossi, and Alice Rossi, all former presidents of the American Sociological Association, plus others such as Allen Barton, Stephen Cole, Anthony Obershall, David Sills, and John Shelton Reed.

The department ethos placed great value on original ideas—whether theoretical or methodological. It was a difficult place to work because the standards were high, and there was an implicit hierarchy among the faculty and among the students and a sense of competition for position. It was infused with infectious intellectual energy, as well as conflict. The overwhelming majority of students felt part of an intellectual mission with exceptional leaders, who were rigorous and extremely demanding—to the point where many of the brightest dropped out of the graduate program, believing incorrectly that they could not meet their mentors' standards. Nonetheless, the ambiance made us proud to be sociologists at a time when the discipline was often the subject of scorn in magazines like *The New Yorker* for the excessive jargon and poor writing of its practitioners. Much of the empirical work was done at the Bureau on a shoestring in a dingy, mildewy environment, where graduate students, researchers, and professors worked till all hours of the night. The university did little to support the Bureau, but there was a sense of richness in the exploration of ideas together as part of a community.

CHAPTER 22

Two Centuries of "Columbian" Constitutionalism

—⁀⁀—

Michael C. Dorf

In general the Living Legacies series pays attention to great Columbians of recent vintage—usually twentieth-century figures—and has left it to Stand Columbia, Robert McCaughey's history, to treat others no longer within living memory. Michael Dorf breaks out of this mold with his conviction that the whole development of constitutionalism in the United States derives from the contributions of Alexander Hamilton, to which one can trace "a distinctly Columbian approach to constitutionalism." Though Hamilton never served on the Court himself, it was nine Supreme Court justices from Columbia who successfully embodied what Dorf calls this "Columbian vision" of a "strong central government fostering a national economy while the federal judiciary protects individuals against the threat of majoritarian tyranny." This judicial line began with John Jay (1789–95), the first chief justice of the Court, and continues today with Ruth Bader Ginsburg (1994–present). Thus, Dorf concludes, "the story of Columbia's justices is in a real sense the story of American constitutionalism."

One might suspect such strong claims for a distinctive Columbia role of these proportions to come from an excess of native loyalty and zeal in an alumnus. Dorf, however, hails from Harvard, with bachelor's and law degrees, both magna cum laude. His perspective must include the contending, if not competing, claims to a major role in American constitutionalism. Dorf has served as law clerk to Supreme Court Justice Anthony M. Kennedy and has published numerous articles on the Supreme Court and constitutionalism in the law reviews of Columbia, Harvard, Stanford, and many others. His current areas of teaching and research are constitutional law, constitutional theory, and civil procedure.

—Wm. Theodore de Bary

—⁀⁀—

Alexander Hamilton, who studied at King's College from 1773 to 1774, devised the arguments most closely associated with American constitutionalism.

The nine justices with strong Columbia ties are John Jay, H. Brockholst Livingston, Samuel Blatchford, Charles Evans Hughes, Benjamin Nathan Cardozo, Harlan Fiske Stone, Stanley Reed, William O. Douglas, and Ruth Bader Ginsburg.

In assessing the collective contribution of the Columbia justices, two salient facts stand out. First, the Columbians were broadly engaged in public life. Their careers as justices followed, and, in two cases, interrupted, their extraordinary accomplishments in other fields. Second, to a remarkable degree, one can trace a distinctly Columbian approach to constitutionalism. As against what might be understood as a Jeffersonian commitment to a nation of yeoman farmers, the Columbian vision—traceable to Ur-Columbian Alexander Hamilton, who studied at KIng's College from 1773 to 1774—celebrates America as a mercantile republic in which a strong central government fosters the national economy while the federal judiciary protects individuals against the threat of majoritarian tyranny.

First, consider the richly varied career paths of some of the Columbian justices.

Before taking the oath as the first chief justice of the United States, John Jay had a distinguished record of service to the young nation. He was a delegate in both the First and Second Continental Congresses, and was elected president of the latter in 1779. He coauthored the *Federalist Papers* with fellow Columbian Hamilton and Virginia's James Madison. He was instrumental in negotiating the Treaty of Paris in 1783, and even while serving on the Court, he continued in a diplomatic capacity, negotiating the eponymous Jay Treaty in 1794. Jay resigned from the Court in 1795, becoming governor of New York. Although Chief Justice John Marshall is generally credited with building the Supreme Court into the institution it became, Jay's leadership in its early years was vital because, among other things, he lent his considerable prestige to the Court.

Jay's model of broad engagement in public affairs was carried forward, especially by the twentieth-century justices. Charles Evans Hughes, like Jay before him, served as governor of New York. He was first appointed to the Court as an associate justice by President Taft in 1910. Hughes resigned from the Court to run for president in 1916. He won the Republican nomination but lost the general election. Also like Jay, Hughes served his country in international matters, as secretary of state from 1921 to 1925, and then as a delegate to the Permanent Court of Arbitration and on the Permanent Court of International Justice. Hughes was reappointed to the Supreme Court, this time as chief justice, in 1930. He served in that capacity until 1941.

Although Benjamin Nathan Cardozo wrote important opinions as a justice of the Supreme Court, like his Columbia forebears, he is equally if not better known for his other contributions. Cardozo served as an associate justice of the Supreme Court for only six years. His well-deserved reputation as one of the greatest common-law judges in American history stems from his fifteen years as a judge, the last six as chief judge, of the New York Court of Appeals, the highest court of the state. His opinions in the 1916 case of *MacPherson v. Buick Motor Co.* and the 1928 case of *Palsgraf v. Long Island Railroad*, concerning respectively, the duties owed by product manufacturers to their foreseeable users, and legal causation, permanently reshaped tort law. His 1921 book, *The Nature of the Judicial Process*, traced a middle path between the formalism of previous generations and the thoroughgoing skepticism of some of his contemporaries in the legal realist movement. It remains the single best exposition of how a judge's decisions are constrained but not fully determined by law.

Following the Columbia pattern, Harlan Fiske Stone was also a Renaissance man of the law. For a quarter of a century, Stone simultaneously maintained an active private practice of law while serving as a professor and later dean of Columbia Law School. His moonlighting did not undermine his effectiveness. The "Stone-Agers," as Columbia graduates from the period of Stone's deanship fondly call themselves, report that Stone was personally acquainted with every student to pass through the law school during his tenure. President Coolidge appointed Stone attorney general of the United States in 1924 and associate justice of the Supreme Court the following year. In 1941, President Roosevelt elevated Stone to the position of chief justice, in which he served until his death in 1946.

William O. Douglas was yet another Columbia polymath. As a law professor at Columbia and Yale, Douglas specialized in business subjects, which led to his appointment by President Roosevelt to the Securities and Exchange Commission, which he chaired from 1937 through 1939. As a justice, Douglas was best known for consistently championing the causes of underdogs, especially in civil rights cases. He served as an associate justice from 1939 through 1975, the longest tenure in the Court's history.

Like Stone and Douglas, Ruth Bader Ginsburg was a prominent legal academic before taking her seat on the bench. As a professor at Rutgers and Columbia, Ginsburg combined an interest in the technicalities of civil procedure with a trailblazing litigation clinic. In the latter capacity, she argued a series of cases establishing that the Constitution's "equal protection clause" prohibits most forms of sex discrimination. Ginsburg's ingenious strategy relied on claims by men that official distinctions based on sex unfairly stereotyped both men and women. Ginsburg was appointed to the U.S. Court of Appeals for the District of Columbia Circuit in 1980 and became the second female justice of the Supreme Court in 1993. As a justice,

John Jay, Chief Justice 1789–95

H. Brockholst Livingston, Associate Justice 1807–23

Samuel Blatchford, Associate Justice 1882–93

Ginsburg is best known for her careful opinions in cases presenting technical questions of "lawyer's law" and her powerful opinion in the 1996 case of *United States v. Virginia* invalidating the Virginia Military Institute's all-male admissions policy.

These brief biographical sketches of six Columbian justices show them to be important, sometimes towering, figures in the law and beyond. But what of my second claim—that there is a distinctly "Columbian" approach to constitutionalism? I cannot in this short space provide anything like a comprehensive proof of the point, but I do think I can make it plausible. I begin with a Columbian patron saint who did not serve on the Supreme Court, Alexander Hamilton, for it was Hamilton who devised the arguments that we associate most closely with American constitutionalism in general, just as (I shall shortly argue) it was Stone who devised the argument that we associate most closely with modern American constitutionalism.

The two most enduring precedents of American constitutional law are *Marbury v. Madison*, decided in 1803, and *McCulloch v. Maryland*, decided in 1819. These cases respectively establish the power of judicial review and set forth a method for construing the Constitution broadly, as a flexible charter. They are widely understood as Chief Justice John Marshall's legacy, simultaneously building the young nation and the Court's role in the national government. Yet the central arguments of each case were clearly anticipated by Hamilton.

Marshall's argument for judicial review in *Marbury* proceeds syllogistically. (1) "It is emphatically the province and duty of the judicial department to say what the law is." (2) Because "the Constitution is superior to any ordinary act of the legislature," when the former conflicts with the latter, "the Constitution, and not such ordinary act, must govern the case to which they both apply." (3) And therefore the judiciary has the power to invalidate acts of Congress as unconstitutional.

Marshall's syllogism has become canonical. Yet it is only a peculiarity of our precedent-based legal system that we do not credit the syllogism to Hamilton. In *Federalist* No. 78, he wrote:

"The interpretation of the laws is the proper and peculiar province of the courts. A constitution is, in fact, and must be regarded by the judges, as a fundamental law. It therefore belongs to them to ascertain its meaning. . . . If there should happen to be an irreconcilable variance between the [Constitution and a statute], that which has the superior obligation and validity ought, of course, to be preferred; or, in other words, the Constitution ought to be preferred to the statute. . . ."

In *Marbury*, Marshall simply restated Hamilton's argument.

The same is true of *McCulloch*. At issue was the constitutionality of a federal statute creating the (second) Bank of the United States. Congress's enumerated powers include, among others, the power to tax, to spend, to coin money, and to regulate interstate and foreign commerce. The power to create a national bank is not expressly provided, and the Tenth Amendment reserves "powers not delegated to the United States . . . to the States." At the same time, the last clause of Article I, Section 8, states that Congress may "make all Laws which shall be necessary and proper for carrying" out the expressly enumerated powers. The question posed in *McCulloch* was whether chartering a bank was necessary and proper to Congress's other powers or whether, on the contrary, it was reserved to the states.

Marshall's opinion in *McCulloch* upheld the bank for two principal reasons. First, he argued that it is in the nature of a constitution to serve only as the frame of government, with details to be filled in through experience. "We must never forget that it is a constitution we are expounding," he famously declared. Second, Marshall thought that "necessary" as used in the necessary-and-proper clause, referred to "such powers as are suitable and fitted to the object" rather than just those that are "absolutely indispensable." The clause was meant "to enlarge, not to diminish the powers vested in the government." Thus, Marshall concluded: "Let the end be legitimate, let it be within the scope of the Constitution, and all means which are appropriate, which are plainly adapted to that end, which are not prohibited, but consist with the letter and spirit of the Constitution, are constitutional."

Like the argument in *Marbury*, Marshall's argument in *McCulloch* is a standard of the constitutional canon. Yet also like the argument in *Marbury*, it was fully anticipated by Hamilton. The validity of the (first) Bank of the United States had been hotly debated within the Washington administration, where Hamilton was secretary of the treasury. His argument, which prevailed, prefigured Marshall's.

In a 1791 opinion letter to the president, Hamilton began where Marshall would later conclude. He wrote "that every power vested in a Government . . . includes by force of the term, a right to employ all the means requisite, and fairly applicable to the attainment of the ends of such power; and which are not precluded by restrictions and exceptions specified in the constitution. . . ." So too did Hamilton's argument about the meaning of the necessary-and-proper clause prefigure Marshall's. Hamilton wrote that to adopt the narrow interpretation of the clause "would be to depart from its obvious and popular sense, and to give it a restrictive operation. . . . It would be to give it the same force as if the word absolutely or indispensably had been prefixed to it."

Judicial review and flexible, purposive interpretation—our Hamiltonian, and thus Columbian, legacy—are the twin pillars of our constitutional edifice. It is thus not surprising that our most heated constitutional controversies have concerned their scope. For example, after *Marbury v. Madison*, the Supreme Court did not invalidate another act of Congress until its infamous 1856 decision in *Dred Scott v. Sandford*. And it was the Court's willingness to use its power of judicial review aggressively from the 1890s through the 1930s to invalidate progressive and then New Deal legislation that prompted the Court-packing crisis.

During that crisis, the leadership of another Columbian, Chief Justice Hughes, was critical in maintaining the Court's ability to function as an independent, coequal branch of government.

In deciding cases, Hughes attempted to steer a moderate course. He refused to go along with the most conservative of his colleagues who viewed the Constitution as an engine of laissez-faire. For example, as an associate justice, Hughes dissented in the 1915 case of *Coppage v. Kansas*, in which the majority invalidated a Kansas statute that prohibited labor contracts in which employees, as a condition of keeping their jobs, were required to promise not to join a union. He acknowledged the importance of freedom of contract but thought that the Kansas act was a reasonable restriction of that freedom.

However, as chief justice, Hughes sometimes voted against the New Deal. He wrote the majority opinion in the 1935 case of *Schechter Poultry Corp. v. United States*, the famous "sick chicken" decision. There the Court invalidated a provision of the National Industrial Recovery Act that gave the president unilateral authority to convert a trade group's private rules into federal law. The Court ruled (among other things) that the act exceeded the scope of Congress's power to regulate interstate commerce, because it regulated intrastate activities that had only an "indirect" effect on interstate commerce.

Yet only two years later, in *NLRB v. Jones & Laughlin Steel Corp.*, Chief Justice Hughes wrote the Court's decision upholding the National Labor Relations Act against the

charge that manufacturing—as distinguished from transportation and trade—is not interstate commerce. Although his opinion cited *Schechter Poultry* as authority for congressional power over manufacturing, in time, *Jones & Laughlin* came to be understood as a repudiation of *Schechter Poultry's* distinction between direct and indirect effects on interstate commerce.

Jones & Laughlin was decided just two weeks after *West Coast Hotel Co. v. Parrish,* another landmark opinion authored by Hughes. In *West Coast Hotel,* the Court abandoned a line of cases that had read the due process clauses of the Fifth and Fourteenth amendments as providing expansive protection for freedom of contract and the right of property.

Together, *West Coast Hotel* and *Jones & Laughlin* mark what is commonly known as the "switch in time that saved nine." And because Hughes, along with Justice Owen Roberts, had been a "swing vote," siding with the liberals in some cases and with the conservatives in others, he has sometimes been portrayed as having succumbed to political pressure. But careful scrutiny belies this picture.

As his dissent in *Coppage* illustrates, Hughes had long resisted reading the Constitution as a laissez-faire charter. And although *Jones & Laughlin* was a reversal from *Schechter Poultry,* it is worth noting that *Schechter Poultry* itself was a unanimous decision, garnering the votes of liberals such as Cardozo as well as the conservatives and swing justices. The anomaly that warrants explaining is *Schechter Poultry,* not *Jones & Laughlin.*

To the extent that 1937 marked a real switch, the best explanation is probably the one given by Hughes himself in *West Coast Hotel.* At the end of the opinion, Hughes remarked that, besides matters of technical legal doctrine, "[t]here is an additional and compelling consideration which recent economic experience has

Charles Evans Hughes, Associate Justice 1910–16, Chief Justice 1930–41

Harlan Fiske Stone, Associate Justice 1925–41, Chief Justice 1941–46

Benjamin Nathan Cardozo, Associate Justice 1932–38

Stanley Forman Reed,
Associate Justice
1938–57

William O. Douglas,
Associate Justice
1939–75

Ruth Bader Ginsburg,
Associate Justice
1994–present

brought into a strong light. . . . We may take judicial notice of the unparalleled demands for relief which arose during the recent period of depression and still continue to an alarming extent despite the degree of economic recovery which has been achieved." True to his Hamiltonian legacy, Chief Justice Hughes was willing to read Congress's powers broadly to achieve the great aims of the nation.

If the modern understanding of the Constitution was conceived in 1937, it was fully born the following year. For while the 1937 cases established the proposition that Congress and the states would be granted substantial deference in regulating the economy, there remained the question of when the courts could properly overrule decisions taken by democratic means. Stone foreshadowed the answer in a famous footnote to the Court's otherwise obscure 1938 decision in *United States v. Carolene Products Co.*

Writing for the Court, Justice Stone explained that the general principle of deference should not apply in three categories of cases: (1) laws infringing upon specific constitutional provisions such as those enumerated in the Bill of Rights; (2) "legislation which restricts those political processes which can ordinarily be expected to bring about repeal of undesirable legislation"; and (3) laws directed at religious, national, racial, or other "discrete and insular minorities."

The transformation of the Supreme Court from an institution that principally protected the wealthy to one that championed the rights of the voiceless would not be completed until long after Stone's death in 1941, but it is no exaggeration to call his brief footnote in *Carolene Products* a blueprint for the next era of constitutional law. In it, Stone foretold (1) the extension of most of the provisions of the Bill of Rights, which previously had only been applied to the federal government, to state governments as well; (2) the one-person-one-vote jurisprudence that would result in wholesale reapportionment of state legislatures; and (3) the long-overdue effort to disentrench American apartheid through landmark decisions such as *Brown v. Board of Education* in 1954.

The last three decades of constitutional law have been a struggle over the boundaries of judicial review bequeathed to us by Hughes, Stone, and the New Deal Court. Conservatives have lately shown less deference to Congress, invalidating, since 1995, provisions of the Brady Handgun Act, the Religious Freedom Restoration Act, the Gun Free School Zones Act, the Age Discrimination in Employment Act, the Violence Against Women Act, and the Americans with Disabilities Act. With one exception, each of these decisions has been by the same 5–4 margin. Justice Ginsburg has voted with the dissenters, affirming a broad principle of deference to Congress—in her view, the same broad principle that can be traced all the way back to the Marshall Court's adoption of Hamilton's reasoning in *McCulloch v. Maryland*.

At the same time, the Court continues to struggle over the meaning of the discrete-and-insular-minorities prong of Justice Stone's footnote. Justice Ginsburg believes that the constitutional principle of equal protection focuses on patterns of subordination. She would uphold most government programs of affirmative action for traditionally subordinated groups. Accordingly, Justice Ginsburg has dissented from the Court's decisions striking down race-conscious measures under what she regards as a misguided principle of color blindness. Meanwhile, she has persuaded her colleagues that when it reinforces gender stereotypes, sex discrimination offends the Constitution even though women are neither insular nor a minority.

What influence future Columbian justices will have on the course of constitutional law cannot be known. To this point, however, we can say that the story of Columbian justices in a real sense is the story of American constitutionalism.

From Muskogee to Morningside Heights: Political Scientist Charles V. Hamilton

—⁓ɯ⁓—

Wilbur C. Rich

People who have known Charles V. Hamilton at Columbia think of him as a fine scholar, teacher, public-spirited citizen of the university, and true gentleman. They know him also as a black man who, in words and deeds, has fought for racial equality. But whether they think of him as a black activist depends on what one means by activism. To some people "activism" means being political in the partisan mode, highly visible and vocal—ruffling feathers and dramatizing one's cause. That is not Charles Hamilton. However, if public scholarship and especially inspirational teaching may be counted as true leadership and genuine public service, Hamilton may be considered an activist of the first order.

To tell his story we have Wilbur C. Rich, a former student of Hamilton's at Tuskegee and a junior colleague at Columbia. Rich received his Ph.D. in political science at the University of Illinois and taught there as well as at the universities of Michigan and Wisconsin before taking up his present professorship at Wellesley College. He is the author of The Politics of Urban Personnel Policy: Reformers, Politicians, and Bureaucrats *(1982);* Coleman Young and Detroit Politics: From Social Activist to Power Broker *(1989); and* Black Mayors and School Politics: The Failure of Reform in Detroit, Gary, and Newark *(1996). He has also edited three books:* The Politics of Minority Coalitions *(1996);* The Economics and Politics of Sports Facilities *(2000); and, with James R. Bowers,* Governing Middle-Sized Cities: Studies in Mayoral Leadership *(2000). His latest work is a coedited volume with Jeffrey R. Henig entitled* Mayors in the Middle: Politics, Race, and Mayoral Control of Urban Schools *(2004).*

—Wm. Theodore de Bary

—⁓ɯ⁓—

Political scientists often classify themselves as either empiricists or interpretative analysts. The career of Charles V. Hamilton reflects both traditions. His search for meaning within politics is found in his teaching, writing, and speeches. He was a teenager when the publication of Gunnar Myrdal's *An American Dilemma: The Negro Problem in Modern Democracy* (1944) spotlighted the country's racial issues and when President Harry Truman integrated the military (1948), in which Hamilton served for a year. A chronicler of the Civil Rights Movement, he was a young adult at the time of *Brown v. Board of Education* (1954) and the Montgomery Bus Boycott (1955–56). He lived through the Jim Crow era and witnessed the political transformation that made possible the election of black officials in the South. Watching the unfolding of civil rights history informed and enriched his scholarship as he created a role for himself as an intellectual amongst activists.

STIRRING UP TUSKEGEE

I first met Charles Vernon Hamilton when I was a student at Tuskegee Institute (now Tuskegee University) in Alabama. It was immediately obvious that Hamilton was different from the other professors. Not a Southerner, he did not sound like the rest of the Tuskegee faculty. Students in the dormitories would imitate his charismatic cadences, precise grammar, and impressive diction. He did not behave like most of the faculty, either.

Born in Muskogee, Oklahoma, in 1929, Hamilton had attended Roosevelt University, considered a hotbed of Chicago radicalism when he graduated in 1951. In contrast, in the 1950s Tuskegee Institute was still governed by the conservative ideas of the late Booker T. Washington, who had founded the college in 1881, and his approach to politics permeated the campus culture. Washington stressed economic preparation, rather than protest, as the means of promoting the social mobility of black people. But unlike most Tuskegee professors, who always seemed so deferential toward the school's traditions, Hamilton was not afraid to discuss the Civil Rights Movement or other controversial issues in class.

Fresh from participating in the Montgomery Bus Boycott, I had no idea what I wanted to do with my life. I was hoping that my courses at Tuskegee would teach me how to facilitate the making of a racially integrated America. However, in 1958, the year Hamilton arrived, most students still rarely left the self-contained campus of this black college, where they were protected from the highly segregated, potentially life-threatening surrounding community.

As civil disobedience grew in the South, it was not uncommon for worried parents to write to students warning them to stay away from protests and "just get your education." Thus, when Hamilton joined the faculty, students at Tuskegee had had little involvement in the types of civil rights actions that had begun to flourish in other places. Some time later, when Tuskegee Institute students held their first civil rights demonstration, against segregation in downtown Tuskegee, it was not surprising that people pointed to Hamilton's influence.

When Martin Luther King Jr. visited Tuskegee in the late 1950s, school administrators, fearful of reprisals from the white community, would not permit him to appear on campus, so he spoke at a local church instead. Sitting in the audience, I realized that Hamilton was the only Tuskegee professor in attendance. At a time when many people (both black and white) saw King as an outsider whose methods of nonviolent protest would only stir up more trouble for black people, Hamilton stood on stage with King and even had his photograph taken with him.

Hamilton quickly gained a reputation for teaching American government courses with a sense of urgency and skepticism. His lectures often contradicted the glowing textbook references to American democracy and the nation's venerated political institutions. He would point out, for instance, that while espousing the ideals of freedom and democracy, most of the country's founders were slave owners. He would note that the Supreme Court had ruled on *Brown v. Board of Education* four years earlier, yet Southern schools were still not desegregated. He would remind students of the signs all around them that read "White Only" and "Colored Only," signs that would not come down until 1964.

Always challenging his students to raise their own questions about commonly accepted ideas, Hamilton encouraged us to debate the issues of the day. But whenever anyone made a comment off the top of his head, Hamilton would shoot back, "Show me your data." Unsupported statements were not acceptable for political scientists, he would tell us.

One hot topic was the efficacy of Martin Luther King's nonviolent confrontational approach versus the legalistic tactics of Roy Wilkins and the National Association for the Advancement of Colored People. Hamilton had received his law degree from Loyola University in 1954, but he had always wanted to be a college professor and play an active role in the Southern Civil Rights Movement. Thus, he was drawn to Tuskegee since his wife, Dona Cooper Hamilton, was the daughter of a professor of veterinary medicine there. Hamilton's legal training allowed him to appreciate Roy Wilkins's view that to bring about real change, you had to have the law on your side. Hamilton realized, though, that this was a slow process, and he believed that King's protests were a necessary element as well.

Martin Luther King Jr. (center) inspired Hamilton and his students by leading protests such as the successful 1955–56 Montgomery Bus Boycott against segregated seating.

With the Civil Rights Movement a perfect backdrop for his lectures, Hamilton helped us understand the importance of both approaches in overcoming Jim Crow. However, as he became a model for young people aching to be on the front lines of the struggle, his colleagues and school administrators grew increasingly uncomfortable.

In 1960, when Tuskegee refused to renew his contract, Hamilton walked into a lecture with the termination letter in his shirt pocket. Students saw this as an act of defiance. Although he later told me that he had not been as confident as he acted, his unapologetic expression of his ideas, both inside and outside the classroom, left a lasting impression on me and his other students.

AFTER *BLACK POWER*: THE COLUMBIA YEARS

Hamilton's brief years at Tuskegee had given him the opportunity to gain a better understanding of the civil rights challenges faced by black Americans in the rural South. He went on to receive his Ph.D. in political science at the University of Chicago and to teach at Rutgers University in New Brunswick, New Jersey

(1963–64), Lincoln University in Pennsylvania (1964–67), and Roosevelt University in Chicago (1967–69). His students had the privilege of listening to him as he outlined his preliminary thinking about the future of American democracy, ideas that would find their way onto many a printed page.

In 1969, Hamilton arrived at Columbia University as a Ford Foundation–funded professor in urban political science and became one of the first African Americans to hold an academic chair at an Ivy League university. It was the height of the turbulent 1960s, and the nation was reeling from assassinations, demonstrations, and riots. These currents were felt with particular force at Columbia.

Hamilton was at the peak of his fame as the intellectual half of the "Black Power Duo." The activist half was Stokely Carmichael (later known as Kwame Ture), a former leader of the Student Nonviolent Coordinating Committee, self-professed Black Nationalist, and nascent Pan-Africanist. In a brilliant stroke, Hamilton had teamed up with Carmichael, a folk hero and icon for his generation, to write what would be Hamilton's most famous book, *Black Power: The Politics of Liberation in America* (1967).

Black Power became the manifesto of the black solidarity movement. The popularity of this book had transformed Hamilton into a highly visible public intellectual. Across the country, white Americans wanted to know what black people thought, what they wanted, and how they planned to get it. The book signaled a shift in thinking among black intellectuals: They knew that the triumphal days of the Civil Rights Movement were coming to an end and that they needed to consider the next step. With its theme of self-determination, *Black Power* allowed the intellectual community to focus more clearly on the future of black people in America. The book became a best seller and was translated into several languages.

During the 1970s, as New York City experienced a fiscal crisis and underwent a demographic transformation that saw increases in its minority population, city politicians looked to Hamilton for advice. In the 1977 New York mayoral election, candidates competed for his endorsement even though he lived in New Rochelle.

Named the Wallace S. Sayre Professor of Government at Columbia in 1971, Hamilton taught American government, urban politics, and minority politics. A very popular teacher, he drew large numbers of students to his courses. In 1973 Hamilton recruited me as a junior faculty member. During the seven years I spent at Columbia, I taught undergraduate courses in political science and Contemporary Civilization. More important, I had a second opportunity to learn from Hamilton, whom I had not seen since our Tuskegee days thirteen years earlier.

Not only did I come to call him "Chuck," but I also got a chance to watch him teach both undergraduate and graduate students. He once told me that when he first started at Columbia, every course he taught had the word *black* in the title. However, since his expertise was far broader than protest politics, he soon began to teach graduate courses on public policy and undergraduate courses on American government. Despite his busy schedule, Hamilton was always approachable. The hallway outside his office at the southwest end of the School of International Affairs building was often filled with students discussing city administration, presidential politics, and changes in the black leadership class.

He and I had many lively political discussions as well. I remember his explaining his theory of the connection between welfare and "functional anonymity"—that one unintended consequence of the welfare system was that it made black people less willing to confront social and political inequities for fear that speaking up would cost them their invisibility and thus put an end to their benefits.

Columbia University's political science department was divided into four sections: theory, comparative politics, international relations, and American politics. For years Hamilton led the American section, consisting of a fascinating team of scholars that included Demetrios (Jim) Caraley, Alan Westin, Robert Shapiro, and Ira Katznelson. When Hamilton and Caraley were interested in starting a master's program in public administration, they enlisted me to draft the initial proposal for the program. It was adopted and established in the School of International Affairs (now the School of International and Public Affairs).

During my time at Columbia, Hamilton assumed leadership of the Metropolitan Applied Research Center (MARC) from the retiring director, Kenneth Clark. Hamilton also served three years (1983–86) as a consultant to the Ford Foundation. Among the many honors and awards he has received, are the Columbia University Mark Van Doren Award for Excellence in undergraduate teaching (1982) and the Great Teacher Award from the Society of Columbia Graduates (1986). In 1993 he was elected a fellow in the American Academy of Arts and Sciences. When the Chicago *Sun-Times* listed the leading scholars in America in 1995, Hamilton was one of four Columbia professors included.

CONTROVERSIAL ENCOUNTERS

One of Hamilton's best-received books, *Adam Clayton Powell, Jr. The Political Biography of an American Dilemma* (1991), demonstrated his skills as a political analyst and historian. The first African American to represent New York in the U.S.

Hamilton's Black Power *coauthor, Stokely Carmichael (a.k.a. Kwame Ture) (left), and fellow activist H. Rap Brown (right) talked to reporters outside Hamilton Hall, one of five Columbia University buildings occupied by students in April 1968.*

Congress (in 1945), Powell was known for his flamboyant antics, which were legendary in Harlem and in the halls of Congress. Hamilton went behind the legend to discover a man with incredible rhetorical talent and legislative skills, yet one who squandered opportunities to accomplish more.

For instance, Hamilton noted that as chairman of the Education and Labor Committee, Powell would attach the so-called "Powell Amendment" to any bill that came before him. Stating that unless states desegregated they would be denied federal funds, this amendment was a symbolic gesture that demonstrated his power to affect public policy.

Like Powell, Hamilton has never been a man to shy away from controversy. He speaks his mind to the powerful and the powerless. He spoke his mind at Tuskegee Institute and at every other institution where he taught. In 1970 Hamilton was among a group of scholars invited to the White House. Apparently President Richard Nixon had read Hamilton's work and wanted to hear more about solutions to the race problem. In what was supposed to be an off-the-record discussion, as Hamilton later recalled, he urged Nixon "to back off the Black Panthers, to stop shooting them."

A few months later, in a speech in St. Louis, Nixon said that he had met with Charles Hamilton, from "the University of Columbia," and that Hamilton had assured him that black people in the United States were better off than those anywhere else in the world, American racial problems notwithstanding. "Those words had never crossed my lips," Hamilton said. He got his chance to respond to Nixon when a group of scholars published a set of essays in a book entitled *What Nixon Is Doing to Us* (Harper & Row, 1973).

Another example of his outspokenness came in a speech at a 1976 Democratic National Committee meeting, in which Hamilton suggested that it would be acceptable for presidential candidates to soft-pedal the race issue as long as they dealt firmly and unequivocally with issues that affected the black community once they were elected. No matter how sympathetic candidates were to black causes, Hamilton argued, they could do nothing to help African Americans if they alienated their mostly conservative electoral base and never took office. This statement, reflecting Hamilton's pragmatism about electoral politics, was not well received by some black activists. However, Hamilton saw his role as explaining the difference between electoral and protest politics.

This speech also provided a preview of his thinking regarding the possibility of "deracialized politics." Just as he had done in *Black Power*, Hamilton anticipated the shift in white attitudes toward race, this time concerning the increasing significance of black elected officials. He advised black politicians to deracialize their campaign rhetoric if they wanted to compete in predominantly white cities. He reasoned that since there were a limited number of predominantly black cities and congressional districts, a change in tactics was indicated if black politicians wanted to be competitive in mixed districts and statewide elections.

At the time, recommending downplaying the race issue in any way and for any purpose was considered heretical. The deracialization thesis was debated vigorously at the 1976 and 1977 annual meetings of the National Conference of Black Political Scientists. However, the idea was vintage Hamiltonian thinking, typically pragmatic. His essay on the topic appeared in *The First World*, a small journal, under the title "Deracialization: Examination of a Political Strategy." This essay caused quite a controversy among black political scientists and was one of the central issues in an anthology entitled *Race, Politics, and Governance in the United States* (1996).

Perhaps Hamilton's most controversial decision was to attend a conference with aides of the Republican President-elect Ronald Reagan. Hamilton, Percy Sutton, former borough president of Manhattan, and Harvard political science professor Martin Kilson were invited as the only black Democrats at the 1980 meeting sponsored by the Institute for Contemporary Studies. This meeting caused a stir in the black intellectual community as some colleagues considered meeting with Republicans an act of party disloyalty. Hamilton saw it as an opportunity to engage in dialogue with emerging black conservatives who would eventually play a more visible role in American politics.

Hamilton was one of the first black social scientists to visit South Africa during the apartheid era, in 1979. His travels to the garrison state left an indelible impression on him. He became a member of the Council on Foreign Relations and continued to pursue his interest in the political and economic development of the African continent. In 1997 Charles V. Hamilton retired from Columbia, and, still actively writing, he now divides his time between South Africa and New York. Through his teaching, books, and speeches, Hamilton has provided a platform from which to debate the great issues of the post–civil rights era. Whether broadening the discussion or challenging his colleagues regarding the direction of the struggle for equality, Hamilton has generated some of the most thoughtful scholarship on race in the twentieth century.

CHAPTER 24

The Developing Science
and Art of Anthropology

—⚬⚬⚬—

Virginia Heyer Young and Rosalind Rosenberg
with a Reminiscence by Fritz Stern

In the first essay below the anthropologist Virginia Heyer Young focuses on the striking contributions of Ruth Benedict and Margaret Mead to the developing science and art of anthropology. Young treats the subject at greater depth in her most recent book, Ruth Benedict: Beyond Relativity, Beyond Pattern, *published by the University of Nebraska Press in 2005. To this story two promising young students from the 1940s who later became University Professors—Donald Keene and Fritz Stern— have agreed to add their own personal tributes to Benedict as writer and teacher.*

These more personal accounts are followed by Rosalind Rosenberg's essay on three "daughters" of the anthropologist Franz Boas, women who through their personal interactions with the New York cultural scene (especially in literary circles and psychology) abetted each other's emancipation as scholars in the vanguard of feminism and studies of sexuality. The third member of the trio, along with Benedict and Mead, is the writer Zora Neale Hurston.

Rosalind Rosenberg, Ann Whitney Olin professor of history at Barnard College, has also written for Living Legacies about Virginia Gildersleeve as dean and president of Barnard. Her publications include Divided Lives: American Women in the Twentieth Century *(1992) and her major contribution to the university's 250th anniversary,* Changing the Subject: How the Women of Columbia Shaped the Way We Think about Sex and Politics *(2004), where the present subject is treated in greater depth.*

—Wm. Theodore de Bary

Benedict and Mead at Columbia:
A Student Looks Back

—〜〜—

Virginia Heyer Young

Although Ruth Benedict and Margaret Mead were parallel figures in many ways, they were of different generations intellectually, with different frames of reference and approaches to fieldwork. Benedict was concerned with classic problems and with applying comparatively the vast ethnographic literature onward from Herodotus and Bernardino de Sahagun, the Spanish priest who observed the conquest of the Aztecs. She had read in minute detail the whole European and American ethnographic record and sent her students for new types of data, drawing her innovative concepts from whole-culture comparisons using this material. Benedict conducted fieldwork in five southwestern Indian cultures, in some for only a month or two and with repeated trips to the pueblo of Zuni. Because of her partial deafness and dependence on lipreading, new languages and participant observation were difficult for her; she devoted much of her fieldwork to transcribing the texts of myths, folk tales, ritual poetry, and ritual procedures.

Mead carried out extensive participant observation in her own fieldwork, studying the learning of culture along with cultural values and structure. She conducted lengthy studies in seven cultures, a number seldom matched, and she worked in remote places where travel and living conditions were difficult. She had adequate command of these seven languages, interviewing and recording details of interpersonal behavior. She borrowed from behavioral psychology and psychiatry to develop more precise methods of field observation and recording, seeking to open the way to interdisciplinarity.

During Mead's field trips she and Benedict wrote each other often, sometimes every few days. The letters, archived with Mead's papers in the Library of Congress, give much insight into their friendship and their collaboration, their shared ideas and their intellectual differences. During the summer of 1925 before Mead left for her field trip to Samoa, she and Benedict had been lovers in a relationship that their letters indicate was close and passionate for both of them. Their correspondence suggests they had only one later erotic tryst, in the summer of 1941, but in all their communications there is an underlying sense of esteem and engagement in a cooperative mission. They had an acknowledged division of labor between the field and the university. From the field Mead asked Benedict for help of many kinds, from sending books, film, and food supplies, to handling insurance and banking transactions, to providing editing on manuscripts Mead wrote in the field and advice about her interchanges with colleagues. Benedict responded to all these requests and clearly felt an obligation to keep up Mead's spirits and to reassure her of the value of her fieldwork for the problems both of them considered fundamental in anthropology. Mead was greatly stimulated by fieldwork, and she felt personally close to her subjects. She was confident of her particular talent for careful and thorough observation. Mead's letters contain many keenly analyzed passages about the day's field observations along with related theoretical reflections.

Benedict became acting chair of the Department of Anthropology in 1931, when Franz Boas's health declined. She gained recognition for this role as well as for her influential book *Patterns of Culture* (1934). Sociologists Robert MacIver and Robert Lynd, along with other key faculty and administrators who served on committees to find a successor to Boas, indicated that she was the best qualified person for this position; but they could not overcome the resistance among top administrators to appointing a woman as department head. Benedict wrote Mead about her seesawing prospects with irony and humor and of her chances for appointment, "I know the difficulties."

Most student recollections of Benedict from this period expressed admiration, but some represented her as aloof and snobbish. She herself identified similar qualities, writing in her journal in 1934, "The great reward that my temperament has given me is detachment and unconcern." This was a protection against her feeling, at times, that she was a misfit, "a stranger in this land," as her biographer Margaret Caffrey put it. Benedict and her husband had separated in 1930, and soon after that she began a very happy lesbian relationship. She defended homosexuality in lectures and writings and, unlike Mead, did not attempt to conceal her own companionship with a woman. While homophobic attitudes were an undercurrent among some students and colleagues, her prestige as a scholar and her public reputation appear to have countered these opinions quite effectively. Male students have written that she was beautiful and intriguing. David McAllester recalled "that elegant figure and white hair that reminded me somewhat of a heron." I studied with Ruth Benedict from 1946 until her death in 1948, and I found she was easily approachable and indeed kind. She had a close interest in students' work, in our questions, in our financial needs, and in us as individuals. At sixty, when I knew her, a sense of self-confidence, not attributed to her in her early years, was in her manner. The trait some have called shyness was more accurately perceived by her colleague Cora

Ruth Benedict

DuBois as "profound modesty without a trace of self-derogation."

The influence of *Patterns of Culture* extended far beyond anthropology to the social sciences and humanities and to a general readership. "Frequently reprinted and translated into fourteen languages, it remains today the single most influential work by a twentieth-century American anthropologist," wrote historian George W. Stocking Jr. forty years after its publication. When Nazi persecution of German Jews became extreme, Benedict responded with *Race: Science and Politics* (1940). She lectured to diverse audiences and published in many forums on racism in American society. Her last book, *The Chrysanthemum and the Sword: Patterns of Japanese Culture* (1946), was a first for her discipline, portraying an encompassing cultural pattern in a large and socially complex nation. It is credited with helping to reverse war-generated American hatred of the Japanese among both government personnel and the public. The Japanese discussed her book widely, with some commentators critical but most considering it deeply insightful.

Benedict's and Mead's differences were reflected in their teaching. Benedict had the main responsibility in the department for graduate training in cultural anthropology from the late 1920s, when Boas began turning this over to her, to the time of her leave to work for the Office of War Information in 1943. She taught the classic subjects—social organization, religions of primitive peoples, mythology, history of theory—and area courses, usually on Australia and Melanesia. In 1935–36, a year when Mead was home from the field, Benedict engaged her to teach two innovative courses. One was on cooperation and competition in thirteen preliterate cultures. The other course was the Individual and Society, the first presentation at Columbia of the topic later called Personality and Culture.

After Benedict's death in 1948, Mead taught regularly as an adjunct professor. Rather than taking over Benedict's subject matter in teaching, she taught her own research methods developed over many years of fieldwork. She and Gregory

BENEDICT HERSELF

In the spring semester of 1948, my last term in graduate school, I signed up for Ruth Benedict's course in anthropology. I remember her, a stately, beautiful, physically attractive woman; I don't remember the title of the course. But then, the title didn't matter: the course was Benedict herself, her wisdom and humanity. I still have my class notes. She didn't lecture in any formal manner, but moved naturally from generality to particulars, from an introduction to the field of anthropology to all manner of subjects, ending with a discussion of child rearing. It all seemed unsystematic but ever so compelling. I once encountered her on the way to class and told her how as a history student I had been especially impressed by the warmth with which she had spoken of Tocqueville and R. H. Tawney; she admired these writers, she said, adding that history and anthropology were, after all, cognate fields. I don't think of her as a social scientist, but as a humanist, a traveler in the cultures of the world, a poet in prose.

She dealt with themes like personality and culture, childhood and society, always in comparative terms. Much of the course touched on "IoC," as she put it: In our Culture. And what insights, what fearlessness! "IoC children have center stage," my notes read. "Child is exhibitionist . . . Father and mother are spectators. That's what Europeans call bad manners." Or, "In many cultures, women are so secure as to make men *insecure*." Was this meant as a comment, perhaps a cautionary comment, on feminism? And yet she was so magnificently feminine—in appearance, voice, solicitude for women, especially mothers.

Her last class that term, I believe, was no different in style or substance from all the others: no flourish, only imaginative rumination. In those days, it was customary to clap at the end of the semester; we did, but I suddenly saw myself standing up and clapping, the class followed, and we gave Ruth Benedict a standing ovation. It turned out to be her last class; a few weeks later she died, unexpectedly. I see her still.

—Fritz Stern

Bateson had made major advances in ethnographic filming techniques, and their extraordinary film footage from Bali was used as a teaching tool in her classes. She oversaw small student projects in interviewing and observation techniques. Mead continued to be an important influence on students in a period when the anthropology department was dominated by ecological and materialist points of view that were highly critical of the fields of personality, culture, and national character in which she worked.

The seven Oceanic cultures Mead had interpreted made up her comparative table of cultural variation. It was her unique tool for weighing the big questions that she then took up: culture versus biology in gender differences in *Male and Female* (1949); culture change in a period of rapid ideological and institutional change in a society where fieldwork was not possible in *Soviet Attitudes Toward Authority* (1951); and a related problem, the collective adoption of new values and forms of interpersonal behavior in *New Lives for Old* (1956), her restudy of the Manus of New Guinea after their area had been under the wartime control of the naval forces of Japan and the United States. The small village society of the Manus, which twenty years earlier had been driven by objectives of self-gain, changed itself quite purposefully into a more communal, more hospitable society with a sense of place in a larger polity. *New Lives for Old* was about leadership as well, a subject seldom studied in depth. In *Continuities in Cultural Evolution* (1964), she applied her fine-grained perceptions about learning to the question of how advances in human adaptation came about during early human evolution. Learning during a period of rapid change was again her framework in *Culture and Commitment* (1970), a study of the generation gap in America in the Vietnam War period. In these books written after her early field studies and in her mature role as a public intellectual, Mead accomplished a feat that few anthropologists other than her mentor Ruth Benedict have matched, transposing knowledge of a vast range of human cultural behavior into comparative formats with which to view problems of modern societies.

Few have contributed more to the social sciences than either Ruth Benedict or Margaret Mead. Teacher and student, then collaborators for twenty-five years, they changed the discipline of anthropology. They were listened to by colleagues in sister disciplines, by the American public, and by governmental agencies in World War II, and they trained many scholars to carry on and refine their work. They had style as writers, brilliant minds, concern for the public problems of their day, and the personal courage to step out of conventional women's roles, to bear hostility for doing so, and to make enlightenment through social science their paramount priority.

Cats

2702 Yale Station
New Haven, Conn.
July 8, 1947

Dear Professor Benedict,

When I read you book "The Sword and the Chrysanthemum"
I was most impressed with it, for it was the first book which I
had seen that agreed with and even proved the theories that I had
unsystematically evolved while serving during the war as an interpreter and translator of Japanese. I used to interrogate prisoners
for purposes of psychological warfare, and my specialty was reading
Japanese diaries (I must certainly hold the record in this class),
with more or less the same purpose. I was surprised to learn that
some reviewers had said of your book that it was "very interesting
but no longer true in view of Japan's defeat". Nothing I had seen
in Japan after the war made me think that any profound changes had
actually taken place. That people now rioted for rice or were dis-
orderly in ration lines did not seem any proof to me that there had
been a breakdown of the system of obedience.

Today I received a letter from a Japanese friend of
mine living in Tokyo which I thought might interest you, as it illustrates perfectly one of the ideas in your book, that of the
Japanese attitude toward debt obligations. I have been sending this
friend packages of food and clothing about once every two weeks. In
the letters I have received from him he has often written of "bowing
his head with shame" because he was forced to ask for certain things,
or because he was unable to repay me in any way for my kindness. In
today's letter he wrote (in part), "Not only has the expense to you
been farm from inconsiderable, but the trouble involved in deciding
what to put into each of the packages, and in going out to buy all
those things has certainly been exceptional. I am sure that the
nuisance of getting together the packages and sending them all the
way from America has proved a great hindrance to your studies.
"My wife is also very grateful for your repeated kindnesses,
but says that it will not do for us to go on accepting such favors. I
know that it would be extremely impolite to refuse your presents, but
to tell the truth, my exceeding pleasure on receiving a present from
you is accompanied by worries as to whether it is a good thing to
accept too much of your generosity. I shall never forget your generosity, but I must beg you to discontinue sending the packages at this
point, or at least to send very few of them."

The writer is a university graduate and a person of considerable culture. He has three small children, and has by no means
adequate food or clothing for his family. Like most Japanese he is
living in crowded quarters now. For him to request me not to send any
more packages, although he must need them very much, would seem to
me to be clear enough proof that the necessities of life in Japan
today have not been able to destroy traditional Japanese attitudes. I
have had no training in anthropology, and perhaps am mistaken in my
conclusions, but thought you might like to learn about my friend. I
have sent the letter excerpt for your information only, and would appreciate it if you would not use it in any way, as I naturally do not
want him ever to find out that I have revealed this personal matter.

Yours very truly,

Donald L. Keene

*Letter from Donald
Keene to Ruth
Benedict, 1947*

The "Daughters" of Papa Franz:
Benedict, Mead, and Hurston

Rosalind Rosenberg

I have had a curious experience in graduate work in the last few years," Columbia anthropologist and department chairman, Franz Boas, wrote a colleague at the Chicago Field Museum in 1920. "All my best students are women." In common with other fields, anthropology had lost male students to the military during World War I, but the loss in Boas's department had been exacerbated by the chairman's strong antiwar views, which he expressed with some passion both in his classes and in the press. When Ralph Linton, who left the department to join the army in 1917, returned in full military attire two years later, Boas made him feel so uncomfortable that he finished his training at Harvard. Boas's antimilitarism had significant consequences for the gendering of anthropology at Columbia. As of 1920, not only were Boas's best students women, his only students were women. He addressed them by their first names. Behind his back, they called him "Papa Franz."[1]

In the years that followed, men returned to anthropology at Columbia, but only after World War II did they again constitute more than half the students in the department. And none of Boas's male students ever achieved the level of influence in the wider world that the most prominent of Boas's "daughters" did.[2] Two of those women—Ruth Benedict and Margaret Mead—became the most famous anthropologists of their time, and a third—Zora Neale Hurston—became the country's leading folklorist as well as America's most important black female novelist. Together, these three women carried on Boas's long-standing battle against racism in American society, but they also pushed in new directions, posing a collective challenge to some of American culture's most deeply entrenched prejudices about gender and sexual behavior, prejudices from which even Boas—liberal though he prided himself to be—never fully emancipated himself.

Their challenge can be seen most clearly in a series of books they published in the mid-thirties—Benedict's *Patterns of Culture* (1934), Mead's *Sex and Temperament* (1935), and Hurston's *Their Eyes Were Watching God* (1937). These three works constituted the culmination of a conversation that had begun in the twenties. Each author was a cultural relativist interested in deviance and the ways that a person shunned in one culture might be accepted in another. Each rejected the conventional belief that biology determined what it meant to be a man or a woman. And each drew inspiration from the ethnic and racial as well as the sexual complexities of New York City in their day. Although they differed from one another in important respects, they provided an intellectual framework for the study of race, gender, and sexuality that was to gain wide influence.[3]

A HAVEN FOR FEMALE SCHOLARS

A fourth woman proved critical to Benedict, Mead, and Hurston's success. She was Elsie Clews Parsons, the daughter of a wealthy banker, a graduate of Barnard College (1896), with a doctorate in sociology from Columbia (1899), who had gone on to a career as a leading feminist, public intellectual, and pacifist. During World War I, Parsons saw in anthropological fieldwork a refuge from the politics of war. When Boas lost much of his funding during World War I because of his antimilitarism, Parsons stepped into the breach. Committing her personal wealth to Boas's work, she not only contributed significantly to Boas's success in rebuilding anthropology at Columbia after the war, she also helped create a haven for female scholars.[4]

Parsons's most important recruit was Ruth Fulton Benedict. Born in 1887 in New York City, the first of two daughters of a doctor and a Vassar-trained teacher, Ruth Fulton grew up within a privileged community of Anglo-Saxon Protestants whose roots stretched back to the American Revolution. But she never enjoyed the sense of belonging that privilege should have brought. Her family regarded her as a moody child, given to violent tantrums. Ruth later attributed her behavior to the loss of her father, who died when she was two, and the quarreling in the household of her maternal grandparents in which she subsequently spent her childhood. Ruth's withdrawal from family life and her tantrums may have stemmed from these childhood experiences, but they may also have been the result of partial deafness, the product of a bout of measles when she was three that was discovered only when she entered school.[5] Whatever the reason, Ruth experienced life as an outsider. Preoccupied by death, frequently depressed, she retreated into an imaginary world and, as she grew older, sought refuge in literature and writing. Ruth's mother supported her daughters, first as a teacher, later as a librarian, and sent them both to Vassar, where the sisters entered an intensely intellectual community populated by strong, ambitious women. Majoring in English, she immersed herself in Shakespeare and the vast body of literary criticism that had grown up around his work.[6]

Following college, Ruth became, briefly, a social worker and then a teacher. Finding satisfaction in neither vocation, she accepted, with some misgivings, the

Franz Boas

marriage proposal of a young chemist, Stanley Benedict, and sought, without success, to have children. Tensions grew between them. Stanley wanted his wife to take care of him; Ruth needed meaningful work of her own. At thirty-one, her father's age when he died, she resolved to return to school. She learned of the New School for Social Research, a school founded by Columbia faculty disenchanted with their university's drift toward militarism, and she enrolled in a course entitled "Sex in Ethnology," offered by Parsons. Recognizing Benedict's brilliance, Parsons personally escorted her to an interview with Boas, who admitted her to graduate work at Columbia.[7] Boas had long worked to make anthropology a discipline that married art and science, but for him science had always predominated. What the world most needed, he believed, was the careful recording of the cultural practices of so-called primitive peoples before they disappeared. Benedict, steeped in literary criticism, viewed art as more significant. For Benedict, cultures, like literary works, had themes, larger meanings. Intrigued by irrational, dissonant, seemingly dysfunctional ideas, she resolved to specialize in the study of mythology as a way of understanding culture, how it worked, and how it changed. In her dissertation, *The Concept of the Guardian Spirit in North America* (1923), she brought her interpretive vision to the center of the anthropological enterprise at Columbia. Individuals, she believed, were products of culture but also creators of it, as myth-tellers and visionaries.[8]

In 1923, the year Benedict completed her thesis, she met Margaret Mead, a Barnard student fourteen years her junior who enrolled in a class with Franz Boas for which Benedict was the teaching assistant. Born in 1901, one of five children of Emily Fogg Mead, a sociologist, and Edward Mead, an economist at the Wharton School, Mead was as sunny and outgoing as Benedict was tormented and shy. Largely home-schooled by her paternal grandmother at the family's home in Pennsylvania, Mead set off for De Pauw University, her father's alma mater, in 1919, but feeling out of place in the midwestern setting, she transferred to the more cosmopolitan Barnard College the following year. Mead loved to write poetry and initially planned to major in English but soon concluded that she was not gifted enough to make a career as a writer and decided to follow her parents into the social sciences.[9] She tried sociology, economics, and psychology, but Boas and Benedict soon converted her to anthropology. Here was a discipline that seemed more open to the insights of the poet and literary critic than any of the other social sciences. Benedict and Mead shared their poems with each other and with Edward Sapir, another Boas student then teaching at Ottawa but a frequent visitor to New York. Benedict persuaded Mead that in anthropology the vision of the artist mattered. Moreover, as Benedict insisted, anthropology had to be "done now" since "primitive" cultures all over the world were disappearing under the assault of Western expansion.[10]

Turning to anthropology did not mean abandoning the other social sciences. Indeed, psychology, in particular, assumed a much more important place within anthropological research in the 1920s than it had previously enjoyed. Franz Boas, outraged over what he believed to be the misuse of psychological tests by those who wanted to close America's doors to further immigration, encouraged his students to conduct research in psychology as well as anthropology to challenge prevailing prejudices and policies. Ignoring department boundaries, Boas assigned Mead a topic in psychology for her master's essay. She was to administer standard psychological tests to Italian-American children in the New Jersey community where her family spent its summers and where her mother had been conducting research for her thesis in sociology for many years. Believing that these tests discriminated in particular against those whose first language was not English, he set as many of his students as he could to testing children in cross-cultural settings to see whether performance varied depending on how long their families had lived in this country. As predicted, Mead found that the children she tested varied in their performance depending on the social status of their families, how long they had been in this country, and how much English was spoken in the home. Other students working in Harlem found similarly that the longer African-American children who had migrated from the South lived in the North the better they scored on IQ tests.[11]

Mead employed psychological tests in fieldwork for the rest of her career, and psychoanalytic concepts informed much of her writing, especially in the 1950s. But the psychological approach that most influenced her was that offered by Kurt Koffka, whose work on Gestalt psychology, *The Growth of the Mind*, appeared in English as she was completing her study of Italian-American children. Excitedly passing the new book along to Ruth Benedict, she knew immediately that this was what they needed to make sense of culture. Testing was useful but limited. Psychoanalysis was fascinating but universalizing and static. Koffka wrote about psychological configurations—the notion that people respond to some stimuli and not others depending on the larger patterns to which they have become accustomed. The world would be a meaningless blur to anyone who had not learned from infancy to organize visual, auditory, and other stimuli into meaningful patterns.

Ruth Benedict was the first to make use of Gestalt psychology in her work. For years, Boas had urged his students to study the diffusion of practices and beliefs from one culture to the next as a way of critiquing the evolutionists' belief that all societies evolve by going through a fixed series of cultural stages. Boas and his students showed that people did not invent ideas according to their particular cultural stage; they simply borrowed them from neighboring peoples. The attention given to diffusion tended to blind investigators, however, to evidence of sharp differences between adjacent cultures. On a trip to the Southwest in 1925, Benedict noticed something that had escaped earlier researchers. Two adjacent peoples, the Zunis and the Pimas, while sharing much, were strikingly different as cultural totalities. The Zunis were methodical, orderly, controlled, rational—Apollonian—in their approach to life. The neighboring Pimas were emotional, violent, irrational—Dionysian—in theirs. Already interested in myths, Benedict began to see culture was more than a dispersion of ideas and behaviors across time and place; it occurred as a pattern—what later came to be known as a personality writ large.[12]

Benedict's deafness and her training in linguistics gave her an additional insight. Borrowing from phonology—the study of sound—she posited that culture was much like hearing. Just as any individual can pick up on only a limited range of auditory stimuli, so too any culture, to be coherent, must limit the possible range of psychological types that it honors. Benedict invented the metaphor of the "arc" of human potential, only part of which any given culture could incorporate.[13] She posited that a culture's particular personality gave it direction and purpose; the basic pattern of the culture served as an ideal, providing a standard or norm of acceptable thought and behavior and mediating change. These norms fundamentally shaped individual development. Each person had the capacity, for instance, to be passive or aggressive. Whether a person developed these traits depended, in large part, on what the cultural pattern into which he or she was born called forth.[14]

The idea of cultural patterning captured the imagination of Zora Neale Hurston almost from the time she enrolled at Barnard in 1925. Born in 1891 in the all-black town of Notasulga, Alabama, Hurston lost her mother when she was thirteen and left home soon after her father remarried. Supporting herself at odd jobs and writing short stories and plays, she picked up what education she could, including some courses at Howard University, where she earned a few high marks. Her record, however, was on the whole not good. "Ordinarily we would not admit a transfer with this record," Barnard's Dean Virginia Gildersleeve told Annie Nathan Meyer, the Barnard founder and trustee who discovered Hurston at an awards ceremony for promising black authors and recommended her for admission to Barnard. Notwithstanding Hurston's spotty record, the dean made an exception on the strength of the prize-winning short story she submitted as evidence of her talent.[15]

Hurston was Barnard's first black student; she also was likely the oldest student Barnard had ever enrolled. Blessed with a youthful appearance and abetted by a peripatetic past, Hurston had shaved seven years off her real age—thirty-

Zora Neale Hurston

three—by the time she reached New York City.[16] It says much about how difficult it was for a black woman to win admission to Barnard that the first one to succeed was an award-winning author, with the maturity and confidence of someone more than a decade older than the typical student.

Intent on developing as a writer, Hurston majored in English, but her adviser urged her to round out her education by exploring other fields. Intrigued by the idea of studying anthropology, she enrolled in a course with Barnard professor Gladys Reichard, who showed the paper she wrote for the course to Boas. Recognizing Hurston's talent and ability to relate to the black community, Boas admitted her to graduate work following her graduation in 1928, taught her the methods of anthropological fieldwork, and sent her to Florida to collect folklore for her doctoral thesis. Like Boas's other students, Hurston revered her mentor and adopted the female students' nickname for him. One day she burst into his office, asking for "Papa Franz." Boas's secretary shushed her, warning that she had better not let the professor hear her say that. "Of course, I knew better," Hurston later recalled, "but at a social gathering of the Department of Anthropology at his house a few nights later, I brought it up. 'Of course, Zora is my daughter. Certainly!' he said with a smile. 'Just one of my missteps, that's all.'"[17]

Though Hurston never completed a dissertation, she made important contributions to anthropology through her study of folklore, both in the vast material she collected and the insights she provided. She credited her academic training with Gladys Reichard, Ruth Benedict, and Franz Boas, "the king of kings," for giving her the perspective to "see my people as they really are."[18]

SEXUAL TABOOS

Boas's female students were as experimental in their personal lives as in their academic careers. In her memoir *Blackberry Winter* (1972), Mead recalled that her friends, half Jewish and half Gentile, were linked by a common love of poetry and a sense of being part of the cultural avant-garde. Together they explored Greenwich Village, paid homage to the bisexual Edna St. Vincent Millay, and studied theater with Barnard's lesbian theater director Minor W. Latham, who dubbed them the Ash Can Cats after a group of painters they admired. According to Mead, the group debated the theories of Freud and "learned about the existence of homosexuality . . . mainly through the occasional covert stories that drifted down to us through our more sophisticated friends and through upper classmen who were close to some members of the faculty."[19] In fact, Mead quickly became a sophisticate herself, embracing free love with women and men alike.[20]

The course of anthropology was most greatly influenced by her relationship with Benedict, who lived near Columbia in a rented room during the week and returned to Bedford Hills to Stanley (from whom she was increasingly estranged) on the weekends. As Lois Banner has shown in her study of Mead and Benedict's friendship, Mead awakened in Benedict sexual possibilities she seemed to have been struggling against much of her life.[21] For Mead the relationship proved to be one in a series of love affairs with women and men she engaged in throughout her life. Married three times, she later reported finding greater physical fulfillment with men, but greater spiritual fulfillment with women, most especially Benedict.[22] Mead had affairs with lesbians but did not think of herself as one. Nor did she regard herself as a bisexual; she simply thought that everyone had the capacity, under the right circumstance, to feel either same-sex or cross-sex attraction. For Benedict, the affair with Mead had a different meaning, an acceptance of homosexual feelings she had long denied. Fundamentally monogamous, she was deeply hurt by Mead's inconstancy. And yet, the relationship with Mead helped her sepa-

Mead in New Guinea,
1928

rate from Stanley in 1930 and find love with another woman, Natalie Raymond, the following year.[23]

Mead and Benedict's sexual experimentation carried real risks. Even in the Columbia anthropology department, where the valuing of human difference was a point of honor, tolerance did not extend to include the concept—much less the reality —of homosexuality. Boas characterized homosexuality as one of the "abnormal sexual habits." Edward Sapir, among Mead and Benedict's closest friends, judged homosexuality to be "unnatural," adding "the cult of the 'naturalness' of homosexuality fools no one but those who need a rationalization of their personal sex problems."[24] Though there were other lesbians in anthropology, including Gladys Reichard at Barnard, their sexual identity remained carefully concealed. So anxious was Mead about the danger her personal life posed to her career that she never revealed her many-sided love life even to the daughter, Mary Catherine Bateson, she bore in 1939. In fact, once when Mary Catherine confessed to a brief lesbian encounter, Mead upbraided her for not having considered the damage to her mother's career the relationship might have caused if news of it had become public.[25]

Zora Neale Hurston was just as secretive about her sexual liaisons as Mead and Benedict, but she had a reputation for being very much a part of Harlem's sexually experimental culture, with its nightclubs and "buffet flats," which catered to sexually

Zora Neale Hurston

diverse crowds. While lesbianism was regarded as deviant in Harlem, bisexuality suggested an abundant sexuality, and Zora was nothing if not abundant where sex was concerned. "Zora would go anywhere, you know—one time at least," her friend Arna Bontemps observed. She was so close to singer Ethel Waters, widely known to be bisexual, that Hurston believed they could speak for each other. "I am her friend and her tongue is in my mouth," Zora described their friendship in classic double entendre. At the same time that she made her way in sexually emancipated Harlem, Hurston conducted a long-distance relationship with Herbert Sheen, a man she had met at Howard. In 1927, on a field trip to Florida, she married him, but the marriage proved short-lived. She left him a few days later and divorced him in 1931. Four years later, she fell in love with Percy Punter, a Columbia graduate student twenty years her junior. Punter was "the real love affair of my life," she later recalled, the figure on whom the romantic hero in *Their Eyes Were Watching God* appears to have been modeled. But Punter wanted her to give up her career, something she could not do, and so that relationship ended, too. Self-sufficiency was Hurston's lodestar. She refused to be shackled by mere convention.[26]

THREE STUDIES OF SEX, GENDER, AND RACE

Following graduate work at Columbia, Benedict remained as an assistant, lecturer, instructor, and eventually assistant professor in the Columbia department; Mead took a job as a curator at the Museum of Natural History and divided her time between curatorial work and field trips to the South Pacific; Hurston supported herself as a writer and a folklorist. Though their careers diverged, they remained in contact and in the mid-thirties each wrote a book that challenged prevailing assumptions about the fixity of sexuality, gender, and race.

Each author adopted a tripartite structure to demonstrate that much of what Americans took to be natural—for instance, heterosexuality, feminine passivity, masculine aggression, and racial inequality—was, in fact, a creation of culture. Benedict and Mead chose three tribes. Hurston imagined three differently situated African-American communities. Benedict's chapters on the Dobu and the Kwakiutl in *Patterns of Culture* (1934), like Mead's chapters on the Mundugumor and Tchambuli in *Sex and Temperament* (1935), and Hurston's early chapters in *Their Eyes Were Watching God* (1937) caricatured aspects of American life—the cutthroat individualism, conspicuous consumption, and unequal gender relations that had assumed central importance under American capitalism. Benedict's chapter on the Zuni, Mead's on the Arapesh, and Hurston's on the all-black migrant labor camps of Florida, in pointed contrast, emphasized the possibility of more varied, cooperative, and equitable interpersonal relations. All three authors dealt with themes of sexual identity, gender, and race, but each emphasized one theme over the other two in her work.

Benedict was preoccupied by the issue of sexual identity. By the time she wrote *Patterns of Culture*, she had come to accept her homosexual orientation and to understand homosexuality as the product of "congenial drives." Western civilization, she wrote, "tends to regard even the mild homosexual as an abnormal," and in doing so makes it difficult for them to achieve their full potential. Cultures that honor sexual difference, however, as the ancient Greeks did, often benefit from the talents of their "deviants." She praised the Zuni not only because they accorded women real authority, but also because they created an honorable place for homosexuals, many of who made important contributions to communal life.[27]

Mead rejected the concept of sexual identity. She viewed sexuality as fluid and believed that every person has the capacity to respond to both sexes. Homosexuality, like masculinity and femininity, she insisted in *Sex and Temperament*, is a cultural creation. Only temperament, she argued, is innate. Some people are—by nature—more outgoing, assertive, or energetic than others. Mead did not believe, however, that any of these qualities is more likely to be found among males or females. Among the Mundugumor, for example, both males and females are aggressive. Among the Arapesh both are passive. And among the Tchambuli, women are the economic producers and men are the decorative objects. Mead never used the term gender, in part because it was not then in common use, but also because she saw no difference between the cultural construction of sexuality and the cultural construction of feminine and masculine behavior. In her view, all sex is socially con-structed, and homosexuality is more likely the result of imbalances of power between men and women than innate drives. She insisted that there were no homo-sexuals among either the Mundugumor or the Arapesh, because aggressiveness was valued for both men and women among the former, and passivity was valued for both among the latter. In America, by contrast, many men with passive tempera-ments are pushed into a homosexual behavior, in her view, because society rejects their submissive natures as not masculine. Homosexuality is therefore not innate, but rather the result of social pressure.[28]

Hurston shared Mead's view that sexuality is highly fluid, but her principal inter-est was in race and how groups use racial difference as a means of establishing gen-der and sexual dominance. In *Their Eyes Were Watching God*, she followed the devel-opment of Janie, her black protagonist, through three communities. The first is the racially and sexually violent community to which Janie's grandmother, Nanny, a woman raped as a slave by her white owner, is consigned. The female mulatto off-spring of this union, Janie's mother, grows up to be raped in turn by a white school-teacher and to produce Janie, whom she abandons to Nanny's care. In an effort to halt the cycle of rape and abandonment, Nanny marries Janie off to an older black farmer, whom Janie detests. Seeking a better world, Janie flees to the all-black town of Eatonville to become the wife of the town's mayor. While Janie's husband gains a powerful voice in a setting removed from the dominant white culture, Janie must settle for life on a pedestal, a mute trophy of male achievement. Only by escaping to the more egalitarian world of black migrant laborers, does she discover true love and gender equality. But the white world intrudes here as well, in the form of a real estate scheme to recover a swamp for farmland to be worked by mostly black laborers. When a violent storm destroys a flimsily built dam, unleashes floodwaters, and leads to ravaging disease, this egalitarianism breaks down. Bitten by a rabid dog, Janie's lover turns violent; Janie kills him in self-defense. In contrast to Benedict and Mead, Hurston suggested that gender equality cannot be sustained in a racially unequal world. Sadly, Janie returns to Eatonville, where among the black women of the town, she discovers her own voice. Telling her tale to her best friend, she authorizes her to speak to the others: "Dat's just de same as me 'cause mah tongue is in mah friend's mouf."[29] In Hurston's telling, same-sex friendship (and, perhaps, eroticism) could free one from the gender oppression that seemed inevitable in a world of racial inequality.

Benedict with two
Blackfoot men, 1939

Although Benedict, Mead, and Hurston all advanced the case for cultural relativism, only Hurston examined the ways in which gender relations varied depending on one's position within a larger racial hierarchy. To Mead and Benedict, race was a category that people of goodwill should ignore once anthropologists could demonstrate that it was socially constructed. To Hurston race was an embodied and historically potent reality, something that must stand at the center of any analysis of gender or sexuality. Only by examining the dominance of whites over blacks in American society could one understand the sexual oppression of all women.

Though each of their books reached large audiences, only the themes of gender and race attracted significant attention at the time. Mead was charged, by her husband and collaborator Reo Fortune, among others, with misrepresenting the

Arapesh as more peaceful than they in fact were. Benedict was charged with understating conflict among the Zuni. And Hurston was criticized for glorifying the folk and minimizing the economic oppression that blacks faced. Indeed, those who did not criticize these women's cultural relativism often criticized their failure to take economic structures of oppression sufficiently into account. So tabooed was the topic of homosexuality that critics avoided mentioning it.

DEFEAT AND VICTORY

In 1936, when Columbia President Nicholas Murray Butler forced seventy-eight-year-old Franz Boas into retirement, his obvious successor as department chair appeared to be Benedict, who had been running the department for several years. But a search committee, formed by Butler, hired Ralph Linton—the graduate student who had famously returned to Columbia after World War I dressed in uniform, now a professor at Wisconsin.[30] Boas was furious, but there was nothing he could do. Benedict won promotion to the tenured position of associate professor in 1937—the first woman in the university to reach that rank—and she continued to attract students, especially women, until her untimely death from heart disease at the age of sixty-one in 1948. But in the years that followed, the proportion of female graduate students in the department, about half during Benedict's leadership, quickly declined.[31] No other woman won tenure in anthropology until the 1970s.[32]

In the meantime, the bridge that Benedict had struggled to build between the humanities and the sciences was badly damaged, and Hurston's portrait of gender relations as a function of racial hierarchy was largely forgotten. The study of culture went into eclipse, in anthropology and elsewhere in the university, as World War II and the Cold War gave science a new importance in university life. In the social sciences historical materialism, functionalism, evolutionary biology, and empiricism competed for control. In the humanities, a new emphasis on structure eclipsed earlier interest in cultural context.

Only with the resurgence of feminism in the 1970s, the emergence of cultural studies in the 1980s, and the founding of queer studies in the 1990s, did the study of race, gender, and "deviant" sexuality attract new interest. By the end of the century these topics, so long discussed, if at all, in isolation, became the framework for study throughout the social sciences and humanities, not just at Columbia, but throughout the country and, indeed, around the world.

PART FOUR

HISTORY AND ECONOMICS

PHILOSOPHY

CHAPTER 25

Reminiscences of the Columbia History Department: 1923–75

—⟋⟍—

Jacques Barzun

In this essay, first published in the fall 2000 issue of Columbia *magazine, it was our extraordinary good fortune to be able to present Jacques Barzun's recollections of history at Columbia in his own time (1923–75). Jacques (if I may speak so familiarly as a former student of his who also had the privilege of working with him later as a scholarly colleague and administrator) graduated from Columbia College in 1927 and received his Ph.D. in history in 1932. His long and distinguished career at Columbia, the scholarly products of which are well known to the world at large, found unique expression in works reflecting his career as teacher and administrator—books such as* Teacher in America *(1948),* The House of Intellect *(1959), and* The American University *(1968).*

A longtime New Yorker, Jacques now lives "in retirement" in San Antonio, Texas, where in 2000 he published a book entitled From Dawn to Decadence: 500 Years of Western Cultural Life. *It is typical of Jacques's loyalty and long, generous service to the university that he also readily agreed to give us his personal observations on the Department of History, with which he was associated for so many years as student, scholar, and teacher.*

—Wm. Theodore de Bary

—⟋⟍—

The rotunda of Low Memorial Library, ca. 1920, when it still functioned as the university's reading room

One of the silliest things done today in the world of higher education is to publish an annual ranking of the leading universities. The weeklies that conduct such surveys pretend that the public wants to know which are best: it knows this about teams in professional sports, why not about colleges? The answer that is given is about departments, not institutions, so it is no guide to choosing a college. And the ranking is done by asking the members of departments to judge their colleagues elsewhere, so it yields very shaky estimates. They are based on the kind and amount of scholarly publication, so that added to the unconscious bias of personal connections there is that of agreement on doctrine and overvaluation of work done on the topic in fashion. In a word, the ranking procedure is the very negation of scholarly method. It tells the public nothing about college education.

To know the quality of a department, college, or university calls for residence within it in some working capacity, together with academic experience and the judicial mind. And even then, the most that can be ascertained is whether, on the whole, the performance is outstanding, competent, or substandard. When the testimony is detailed and abundant, as it was in the late eighteenth century about the universities of Scotland, one may conclude that as a group they attained excellence, and wisdom adds that some were better than others.

This preamble is to make clear the character of what follows, namely, how the Columbia history department appeared in the second and third quarters of this century, first to a student, next to a young colleague, then to a senior member, and finally to an academic administrator. These four witnesses are myself.

In 1923, when I entered Columbia College, it was in the fifth year of its influential innovation, the required course called Introduction to Contemporary Civilization in the West. It had replaced History 1, which had also been required. Contemporary Civilization (CC) was an amalgam of the political, economic, and intellectual history of Europe and America from A.D. 1200 to the 1920s. It was taught in small sections by instructors drawn from the departments indicated by the list of the subjects combined. To many observers it seemed strange at the time that instructors should be teaching matters "outside their field"; but if the student mind was capable of grasping the expanded offering, it was reasonable to suppose that the teacher's could stretch to a like extent.

This departure and the argument about it arose from a fact of history itself. In the preceding two decades, leading thinkers in every Western country had redefined the scope of the social sciences and of history in particular. A generation before them, the English historian E. A. Freeman had said: "History is past politics," and it was understood that to be complete a book-length piece of research could cover no more than a few years. The revolt at the turn of the century was against this narrow conception. When Karl Lamprecht came from Germany to the International Congress that met in St. Louis in 1904 to celebrate (a little tardily) the Louisiana Purchase, he declared that history must now make use of findings in the new sociology and psychology. A little later at Columbia, James Harvey Robinson gave the program of a "new history" that must take into account the life and force of ideas. In France, Henri Berr, responding to the worldwide spirit of Populism, called on scholars to replace the history of statesmen and warriors with that of "the people," which meant a sociological concern with the past. Simultaneously, interpreters of Karl Marx wanted to show economic facts as the engine of history. Wilhelm Dilthey in Germany saw on the contrary that cultural forms and styles made up a Zeitgeist that the historian ignored at his peril. Meanwhile in England, Lord Acton, who had just completed his editorship of the largely political *Cambridge Modern History* in twelve volumes, urged the young to "study a problem, not a period."

This wind of doctrine blowing from all quarters was what swept History 1 out of the Columbia College curriculum in 1919 and put Contemporary Civilization in its place. The declared purpose of the course was to equip the student with a sum of knowledge enabling him to understand what had led Europe to the war of 1914–18 and to the present civilization transformed by that worldwide event.

Indeed, by the mid-1920s at Columbia, the atmosphere of the university, and not alone that of the College, was permeated by ideas and feelings born of the war. Three members of the history department—James T. Shotwell, Carlton J. H. Hayes, and Parker T. Moon—had been involved in official work related in one way or another to treaty-making at Versailles; several of the younger members had been in the armed services; and the undergraduate body itself included an influential group of "veterans," who were completing their interrupted education or beginning it after postponement. Their presence lent a touch of maturity to class work in history: they had been to Europe and had *seen* the war.

—ɯ—

Like other departments of instruction at Columbia, history was divided into a College and a graduate branch. The latter, housed in Kent Hall, was composed of the senior members, who taught only graduate courses. The juniors across the road in Hamilton Hall taught the College boys under the direction of a full professor designated as head. He maintained the liaison with the other half as regarded appointments, promotions, and salaries. As for the curriculum, it was decided upon in a way that required him to be an able negotiator. After gauging the abilities of his young team, he proposed and the graduate branch disposed—except that the interdepartmental Committee on Instruction of the College, led by the dean, had ideas of its own. Not only did it not rubber-stamp everything that came from the departments, it also proposed. The College faculty, which was the entire College teaching staff, had final say.

It was the dean and his committee that organized Contemporary Civilization, and they took on the fight with its opponents wherever found. In general, the objection was not to the new course itself, but to assigning as teachers those at the instructor rank. These young men were doctoral candidates who were supposed to be writing their dissertations. Now they would be expected to learn a good deal that was "outside their field" while carrying a heavy schedule: two sections of CC and a third course—fourteen hours a week; it would be (and was) grueling. The students benefited from the small sections and from their mentor's freshly acquired knowledge, but the instructor was delayed in his progress toward the degree.

For him, too, the geographical division of the department was unfortunate. It deprived the young scholar of daily contact with his seasoned elders, and these had no chance to guide or judge the work of the juniors. In more than one instance, a senior member, voting on promotions, confused the identities of two juniors until his retirement and beyond. The annual dinner (blacktie) of the entire group, friendly enough, did not erase misconceptions.

For the College students, the gap between branches was bridged by the opportunity in their third year to take any first-year graduate course and count it toward the B.A.

In 1922 the survey given in Contemporary Civilization was supplemented by a second required year—CC-B—that explained the nature and the ways of economics, sociology, anthropology, and psychology. As a result, a student who emerged from the two CCs with a passing mark was capable of following with profit a specific course in any of the seven "sciences of man in society."

In history, the course most likely to be chosen first was Carlton Hayes's offering of the year in Modern European History. He varied the span from time to time, which often made it possible to take a second course with him the following year. Everybody knew that he was an enthralling lecturer. As he strode back and forth behind the wide counter of the large lecture room, he conveyed the drama of some decisive moment in the French Revolution or that of Bismarck's triumph when proclaiming Germany an empire. It was not bombast but history felt as well as recalled. Hayes's style had been abundantly sampled in CC through the assigned readings

from his two-volume *Political and Social History of Europe*, the leading textbook throughout the country. In 1934 Hayes reworked it into a *Political and Cultural History* of corresponding scope.

The former College Study in Hamilton Hall, early 1920s

An alternative was to sign up for Parker T. Moon's course on International Relations, also varied in span, but most attractive when it was entitled Imperialism and World Politics and covered the years 1870–1914. The causes of the Great War (as it was then called) were an inexhaustible topic in the profession and not less so among serious students. Moon also lectured out of abundant knowledge and with flamboyance when suitable. A graduate course was given in two lectures a week, followed by a third hour with an assistant for discussion, quizzes, and a term paper. Parker Moon quite often took the third hour himself and was uncommonly kind to the overawed youngsters who asked questions, mispronounced proper names, and did deep "research" in prewar diplomacy. His early death was an irreparable loss to them and the department.

Close to these two luminaries was the coming man, Edward Mead Earle. He also taught European diplomatic history, with a strong economic component. His recent dissertation on the Berlin-to-Baghdad Railway had been published as a regular trade book, a stunning event in the eyes of mere students and proof of his capacity. Earle's bright prospects were soon dimmed by the onset of tuberculosis. After a long recovery in Saranac, he was appointed the first head of the history section in the new Institute for Advanced Studies at Princeton.

A Columbia undergraduate's program in his last two years might show a straightforward concentration or "major," but owing to the CC spirit, the requirement was broadly interpreted. Advanced courses in economics, sociology, or anthropology were not alien subjects for a history major. And then there was General Honors. This was the two-year sequence created by John Erskine, of the English department, on a suggestion by George Edward Woodberry. It was designed to give a selected group of students the chance to read whole books instead of snippets. This innovation was the start of the Great Books movement and the cause of the continuing debate about "the canon" of Western classics.

Since as a collection these great works disregard the academic cutting up of thought into subjects, taking General Honors was really to fulfill the demands of the New Historians for an ecumenical outlook on the past. The reading list for Honors took the student from Homer to William James, the encounters along the way being with Thomas Aquinas, Machiavelli, Hobbes, Locke, Rousseau, Voltaire, and J. S. Mill, among others. This "mini-canon" varied according to the preferences of the two instructors of each small group. Every book had to be read in one week and well enough to outfit the student with ideas for two hours of conversational discussion.

General Honors was renamed The Colloquium when the mood of the day became hostile to indications of superiority, but the course remained the same in purpose, content, and method. Out of it came in 1937 the Humanities course, required in the freshman year and different from Honors only in the layout of the syllabus. It was later supplemented by Oriental Humanities, which introduced students to classics of India, China, and Japan. All this cutting across former subjects of instruction embodied the rediscovery that a culture is an intradependent whole It cannot be studied all in one piece, but the divisions made for convenience should not leave the student believing that they are intrinsic or permanent.

—⁓⁓—

Imbued with these ideas, a student going from the College to the graduate department of history found it an easy transition. A newcomer from another institution might at first sight think that the old separations were still in force. He was told that for the master's degree he was expected to take four or five lecture courses and one seminar "in his field," and on turning to the catalogue he would find courses listed as being in American or European history, Ancient or Medieval, English or some other national category, each limited in span and taught by a specialist. Only two bore the broad title of Thought and Culture: one given by Lynn Thorndike, From the Renaissance to the French Encyclopedists; the other by David Saville Muzzey, on the period 1750 to 1900 in Europe and the United States. There was besides a course in the history of science, and one requirement: historiography. The display looked very much like the standard curriculum at any other university.

But catalogue labels failed as usual to convey the spirit of the contents. To start with the course in the history of science so as to forget it promptly, it was in the hands of an ill-prepared man suffering from several disabilities, and it consisted exclusively of names and dates coupled with repetitious praise of the scientific method and derision of older beliefs. It gave the subject a bad name and did not survive the early retirement of its proprietor.

Again, the course in historiography was a misnomer, being what used to be called a "vaudeville course": each week for two hours straight one of the distinguished figures in the department, and occasionally a visitor, would come and do his turn by describing the range of his concern or the work of a great historian of the past. The lectures were well prepared; one learned miscellaneous facts, but not the technique of historiography. That omission was remedied thirty years later when Professor Henry Graff and I designed and gave a course that fitted the label.

At the earlier time, the remainder of the offering was of superior quality and nearly every course embraced more than was forecast in the description. For example, William R. Shepherd's Expansion of Europe was a vast panorama of social and cultural exchanges among four continents following the discovery of the New World. Gathering facts never before assembled had entailed wide-ranging research that Shepherd consigned to his written lectures, and these expanded each year like Europe itself. Full of his subject, he delivered them as if from memory, and every listener looked forward to the published volume. Alas, it never found a posthumous editor and publisher. On Shepherd's retirement the work in Latin American history was ably taken up by Professor Frank Tannenbaum, who was equally competent in the history of labor relations.

Muzzey's course in thought and culture had the merit of interweaving the ideas and movements originating from either side of the Atlantic and relating intellectual differences of temper to social conditions. As for Lynn Thorndike's, it was at first a cause of dismay. Though a lecture course, not a seminar, it was a study in the bibliography of the subject. Yet one learned a good deal of the substance as well, because in pointing out the scope of each of the sources, Thorndike gave thumbnail sketches of men and events; but it took synthetic power to organize the pieces into a history of the period. He was of course famous for his part in the rehabilitation of the Middle Ages, especially its scientific accomplishments. Volume after volume of his *History of Magic and Experimental Science* came out, full of facts newly dug out of the Vatican library or elsewhere and so detailed that reading him was a form of research in itself. On the other hand, his single volume on the history of civilization is a model of narrative speed and clarity.

The subject Hayes made his own was Nationalism. It had of course no geographical boundaries and took the student beyond politics and into all forms of literature as well as into music and the fine arts. His seminar on the subject could thus be taken twice, in successive years; the members would bring to it ever fresh reports on the manifestations of the ubiquitous *ism*.

The other seminar in Modern European History, Charles Downer Hazen's, was exactly the opposite: it repeated, year after year, and was none the less indispensable, because it taught method. The topics were not chosen by the student but assigned. One called for delving into the voluminous Clarke Papers for seventeenth-century radicals, another compelled one to master the figures in one of Disraeli's budgets, and so on—each as it were featured a type of difficulty. Hazen had every item at his fingertips, and the omission of a single essential point in the report to the class brought the question, "Did you not find, Mr. X (or Miss Y), that . . . ?" Known as "the Chevalier" on account of his Legion of Honor for work in France, Hazen was gentle but implacable; an amended paper must be turned in with the lacuna filled. It was no surprise that his two-volume history of the French Revolution was vivid and memorable—no textbook—by virtue of the skillful use of the small detail; and it was characteristic of his unacademic conception of history that he said he reread Carlyle's *French Revolution* once a year.

Austin Evans's courses in medieval history were less entrancing but solid also and, the subject being culturally remote, it was necessarily broader than a chronicle of politics. Scholarship on the Middle Ages has by now moved far from his understanding of it, but the substance has changed less than the inferences and interpretations. The Ph.D. candidate who must choose for his oral examination a major subject and two minors could readily build on the Evans course for one of the minors. The difference between major and minor was that questions on the latter would not touch on the bibliography.

The second minor might be in American history and there the array of courses was especially rich. In colonial history, Evarts Boutell Greene, the first American born in Japan, was supreme. Though not a facile lecturer, his charm in seminar

*Harry Carman at bat
on South Field, 1950*

induced an interest equal to his own in—everything; for example, the ethos of
Puritan New England compared with Hawthorne's view of it in *The Scarlet Letter*. It
involved a study of church records for confessions of fornication before marriage—
so frequent that it often appears on the books as FBM—and a brief inquiry into the
worldwide practice of bundling. At every point, the department showed by its
breadth of interest that it was indeed committed to the "new history."

Other scholars in American history—David Muzzey, Dixon Ryan Fox, John
Krout, Allan Nevins—each had his enthusiastic band of followers who would recommend to the neophyte this or that course as an absolute obligation before it was
too late. For—hard to believe—there would come a time in life when one would
cease to sit and listen, notebook in hand.

Particularly attractive was Nevins's fluent style, characteristic also of his biographies—Grover Cleveland, Henry Ford, Hamilton Fish—of which the last received
the Pulitzer Prize. He had had a prominent career in journalism and wanted to
entice the public to read history. He spurred the founding of the history magazine
American Heritage and created a new genre: oral history on tape. He organized the
Society of American Historians and established the annual Bancroft Prize for the
three leading works in the subject.

The story of the British Isles and empire was in the hands of Robert
Montgomery Schuyler and J. Bartlet Brebner, the one a gentle, multicompetent
New Yorker, the other a cheerful Canadian, who made the "North Atlantic

Triangle" an important historical subject. His *Explorers of North America* is a classic. The quiet humorist Schuyler dealt with English constitutional matters and the limited sway of free trade ideas; he edited the *Political Science Quarterly*, and he wrote an early paper on the supposed relevance to causation in history of Heisenberg's indeterminacy principle.

A gentleman from Virginia, Geroid Tanquaray Robinson had the daunting task of handling all by himself the whole of Russian history and, after a time, the growing number of students energized by Sputnik.

Meanwhile, the formidable William Linn Westermann, who deciphered the stacks of Greek papyri found near the Nile delta, was the drill master of the small band of seekers after ancient history. He inspired more admiring wonder for his expertise than affection for his person, because his attitude toward students (and some colleagues) was on the German model. Rigorous scholarship requires frigorous human relations.

—⟋⟍⟍—

Enough has been said so far to show that, unlike today, students in the late 1920s had immense respect for their teachers and noted their foibles as part of the common lot, rather than as a warrant for assuming equality and acting as customers. Asking for a better grade would have been a sign of delirium. There was great courtesy on both sides and no bandying of first names, but it was not unusual for a seminar leader to invite his students to an evening buffet at his house or for an outing in the country. Nor had learning as yet been discovered to be a cover for an oppressive social system. The result was pleasure in the hard work of ascertaining and interpreting fact and joy in the knowledge that one was an apprentice in a worthy guild. The young and their elders were alike "members of the University."

Apprenticeship was nonetheless exacting. After obtaining the B.A., which should not exceed four years, the M.A. took one year of courses, a day-long written examination, and a substantial essay. The Ph.D. called for two more years of course work, an oral examination in subject matter, and a dissertation examined on the galleys of a book, whether accepted for publication or to be privately printed at the author's expense. The orals were conducted very formally, in the Trustees' Room, by a committee of at least five professors flanked by two more from cognate departments serving as observers.

To the candidate preparing for the ordeal, the history major seemed a boundless expanse: modern European history stretched from 1500 to the present and from the Azores to Vladivostock. After the Second World War, perhaps as a concession to the returning veterans who were married and had children, the demand was greatly reduced: one could choose a single century, Russia was left out of Europe, and the examinee was often asked at the outset what he knew best. The dissertation was in typescript, and its examination was little more than copyediting.

But both in the earlier period and under this relaxed scheme, Columbia maintained strictness, whereas—again in both periods—some of the leading universities were content to test the candidate through an informal conversation in the sponsor's office with two or three other faculty members. The rationale was that they knew his or her quality from acquaintance during the preparatory years.

Unless already a full professor at another university, a new appointee to the department was assigned to teach in the College. As mentioned before, this meant two sections of Contemporary Civilization and one more, usually as assistant in one of the first-year graduate courses. On occasion the third course might be History 1 in "Extension," the division of evening courses for adults that later became the School of General Studies.

The head of the College history staff in those years was Harry J. Carman. Reared on a farm in upstate New York, he had made himself a specialist in the relation of successive American social and political conditions to the varying types of the contemporary agriculture. His introductory course in American history was a universal favorite, partly on its own merits, partly owing to the character of the teacher. Harry Carman possessed all the attributes of the paternal saint. He understood every mental and moral difficulty, sympathized with every trouble, and did something about it. The novice bewildered in his first year of teaching CC went to him for advice and a recharge of energy; the doctoral candidate consulted him about the tactics of examinations; his entire staff of instructors and assistant professors relied on him for support when the executive committee of the department annually debated reappointment and promotion. Carman became dean of the College, had influence in the city as conciliator in labor and race relations, and was a member of its Board of Higher Education—all this without neglecting his regular and self-imposed duties within the university.

"Harry's boys," as we came to be known to the executive committee across the street, consisted of aspirants whose promise was largely fulfilled. Charles Woolsey Cole, an economic historian who wrote the classic work on the theory and practice of French mercantilism before and under Colbert, became president of Amherst College and ambassador to Chile. Walter Langsam, specialist in colonialism,

James T. Shotwell

became president of the University of Cincinnati. Dwight Miner wrote the definitive book on the politics preceding the seizure of Panama for the Canal and was Carman's successor as the most popular interpreter of American history to college generations. Shepard Bancroft Clough, whose dissertation research in Flemish nationalism landed him in jail on the very spot of his inquiries, went on to write about economics and the fate of civilizations. Samuel McKee, who steadfastly declined to write a dissertation and was never promoted, was nonetheless an original and learned scholar, as well as a well-liked instructor in the history of the American West. All of us, in addition to fitful toiling at our dissertation topics, did our best, year after year, for the prosperity of Contemporary Civilization.

It was year after year, because promotions were postponed *sine die*. The Great Depression had struck, and it was our lot to remain at the instructor rank for a decade. Nobody thought of complaining; on the contrary we were all grateful to President Butler, who had decreed that nobody should be dismissed—or advanced in grade or salary.

By the time of my elevation to the professorial branch, in 1937, its quarters had been moved from Kent Hall to Fayerweather; and while I continued to teach in the College and also to participate in the design of the new Humanities courses, a group of new faces had appeared among the full professors—and kept appearing. They pursued the tradition of straddling barriers and combining fields. Henry Steele Commager was a specialist in American constitutional history, but he ranged freely over American social and intellectual history; so, a few years later, did Richard Hofstadter, who before his all-too-early death did pioneer work on the Reform Movement and on American thought and twice received the Pulitzer Prize. Salo Baron worked at his monumental social and religious history of the Jews. Richard Morris, a protégé of Professor Greene's in colonial history, was also interested in American law and made a study of notable cases under the title of *Fair Trial*. He went on to edit an *Encyclopedia of American History*, which by its completeness and accuracy has been standard ever since.

The unmistakable Southerner, Dumas Malone, after serving as editor-in-chief of the twenty-volume *Dictionary of American Biography*, came to Columbia and devoted his talents to writing the most detailed life of Jefferson, in four volumes. Carrying lightly his eminence from Ohio State, Walter Dorn was master of the cosmopolitan period of the Enlightened Despots and lectured about it with an abundance of telling incidents.

Early modern history was the province of Garret Mattingly, whose great gift of exposition made his biography of Katharine of Aragon, his pathbreaking study of Renaissance diplomacy, and his account of the Great Armada entrancing books that reached the general educated public. For *The Great Armada*, the Pulitzer Prize committee made an exception to its strictly American purview and bestowed on Mattingly a special prize never duplicated.

Equally original and publicly recognized, the work of Fritz Stern in German history also received an uncommon recognition. He first attracted notice by a masterly work on the friend and financier of Bismarck's schemes, Bleichroeder, and went on to take part in Germany's current self-questioning about its national history and character. His strongly buttressed yet temperate views brought him an invitation to address the Reichstag, which he did to general satisfaction. It was the same historico-political sense that later made him a capable provost of the university and for several months a resident adviser in Bonn to a new American ambassador. His subsequent studies were in the history of Einstein's career.

Multicompetent in a similar way, a much earlier appointee, James T. Shotwell, appears here out of chronological order as an a emblem of the past and a portent of the future. He could boast of having been the first instructor assigned to carry out at Columbia the precepts of Robinson's "new history." He showed his versatility by producing works on the history of the Eucharist and then on ideas related to the Industrial Revolution; afterwards an *Introduction to the History of History* and some 250 articles for the famous eleventh edition of the *Encyclopedia Britannica*, of which he was moreover the assistant editor. He founded at Columbia the series called Records of Civilization. These were little-known but significant works in the rise of Western culture, Christian and Islamic, that had never been translated or edited in English.

The editorship passed to Austin Evans after Shotwell's radical shift of scholarly concern, occasioned by the war in 1917. The Carnegie Endowment for International Peace had sought Shotwell for its executive post, but he chose to remain at Columbia, only to be drafted—so to speak—as a member of the historical commission that went to Versailles with President Wilson. From then on, Shotwell led a life of international endeavor that reduced his teaching to one intermittent course, of which the chief interest lay in the anecdotes about contemporary events and figures. Shotwell's very full career culminated in his editorship of *The Economic and Social History of the World War* in dozens of volumes that took eight years to publish.

Professor Shotwell was not the first academic in the country to be drawn away from the classroom and into the world of affairs, but his was a most conspicuous case in the early history of the flight from teaching. The invitation from Carnegie had caused deep concern to all the department heads of the Faculty of Political Science; they wrote a memorandum to President Butler, asking plaintively whether scholarship in the future would be divorced from its ancestral link with teaching the next generation and whether the university would or could resist the pulling power of wealth lodged in foundations. The questioners—and Butler too—were all for resistance. Everybody knows that it proved vain.

—m—

During the first decade and a half after my admission to the circle of seniors, the head of the history department (commonly called chairman and officially "executive officer") was, with a short interval, Carlton Hayes. It was an elective post with a three-year term, and everybody in the department had a vote, the latest assistant included. Hayes was an admirable executive, calm, not intrusive, seeing to it that meetings were short and fruitful, a good judge of talent in appointments and promotions, and above all a fine tactician in the annual battle with the university budget committee.

By the time of my becoming dean, in 1955, the chairmanship had passed to John H. Wuorinen, a native of Finland, competent in the several Baltic languages, whose first two books dealt respectively with nationalism and with prohibition in that country. A third described the settlement of Finns in Delaware. Wuorinen made an excellent chairman, even calmer than Hayes, and gifted with humor of much the same subrisive kind.

One of his departmental concerns was also one of mine: the time it took for the Ph.D. dissertation to be written after the orals had been passed. I enlisted the help of the university admissions officer, Dr. Hans Rosenhaupt, himself an able scholar-refugee, to make a study of the lists of candidates in the five departments of the Faculty of Political Science—History, Public Law and Government, Sociology, Anthropology, and Mathematical Statistics. It turned out that some unfinished degrees went back sixteen years and a large number between eight and twelve. These former students now held teaching positions and were so burdened with work and family life that they had no time to do research and write. Throughout the academic world, the ABD (All But Dissertation) was an unofficial but popular degree.

One cause was the vagueness that attached to the word dissertation. Many students and sponsors took it to mean the ultimate book on the subject—a life's work for one who could not devote his whole time to it. Another cause was the diffident attitude of sponsors, coupled with their accepting all who asked for their sponsorship. No reminders or inquiries were sent out to the delinquents, and some sponsors accumulated a crowd of unpromising applicants. The hospitable Allan Nevins was credited with at least a hundred. When he retired he vainly offered them in small platoons to his colleagues in American history.

The situation called for a pair of rules: one strongly suggesting a limit of 250 pages for the dissertation, and a second restricting to seven years the completion of the degree. An additional year would be granted to women for pregnancy. These proposals ran into some opposition at the faculty meeting: what if a student presented a masterpiece of 1,000 pages? It was decided to let that embarrassment be taken care of when it arose. With subjects better circumscribed, seven years proved workable, and the dissertation regained part of its original purpose, which was not to write a definitive work, but to show competence in research and writing. Students tend to be excellent researchers, full of good ideas, and they also tend to turn sponsors into unpaid copy editors.

Since the time of that reform, the coercive "Publish or Perish" has made the journal article the unit of scholarship and thus has helped to keep the length of the dissertation down—without improving the contents. The impression is abroad that the supply of desirable subjects has been exhausted, so that repetition is unavoidable. It may be so. What the reader finds in many an article is one or two fresh points, led up to and concluded by wrappings of well-known information.

Already a quarter century ago, the procedures for appointment and promotion felt the strain of this drift in scholarship. The committees were impatient with the "supporting material" that was submitted, and they were tempted to weigh the bulk of it rather than to look inside. They also fretted at the requirement to attend dissertation examinations as observers. As dean of faculties it was my duty to persuade the reluctant that until the rules were changed, they should be followed.

These complaints, this attitude, suggested not so much indifference or laziness as too many obligations. Many departments, and history notably, included members who belonged also to one or another of the institutes and centers for regional studies that had been set up at the behest of foundations. This double citizenship doubled the responsibilities—reports, students, meetings, paperwork, essays and dissertations to read—and quite naturally spurred the urge to whittle them down. It was not the flight from teaching, but it was akin to it by stemming from the same cause—the worldly demands on academics at the expense of teaching and of freely chosen scholarship.

At Columbia more than elsewhere, circumstances helped to augment this centrifugal force. Being in the city and exposed to contacts with every person and
agency pursuing worldly interests, the academic expert found it difficult to resist
offers that seemed compatible with his work at the university, especially if they wore
the guise of public service. The Second World War made yielding virtually a duty.
Well before that, it was "the community" that gave license to neglect students and
teaching, which in the end set off the 1968 student uprisings. A faculty in a small
town or on a hillside was protected from temptations by its being itself the community and isolated from the traffic of world organizations and potentates.

What is more, at Columbia an old tradition favored "outreach." The School of
Political Science, founded by John W. Burgess in 1880, was intended by him to perform a public service. Age seventeen and fighting on the Union side in the Civil
War, he reflected one night that minds better trained than the politicians on either
side of the struggle would have known how to avert it. A school should be established to provide that training. This idea possessed his mind and made him a scholar
and an educational promoter. His study of German and French higher education
supplied elements for his plan of a school specializing in history and the social sciences. The time was ripe. Columbia, Yale, Harvard, Johns Hopkins, each with a special bent, established graduate schools simultaneously, this top layer of instruction
turning colleges into universities.

Of course, Burgess expected that it would be the graduates, not the teachers of
his school, who would lead the world into better paths. But if learning is to guide
the reckless world, the mature scholar is surely better qualified than the fresh graduate. The logic is inescapable and as we saw, some members of the Columbia history
department gave in to it at least from the First World War onward. But it is equally
evident that with the single exception of Professor Shotwell, none of them became
an academic prodigal son, roaming the world while keeping a fitful connection with
his students and his chair. When Carlton Hayes was sent by President Roosevelt as
ambassador to Spain at a critical moment of the Second World War, he and Mrs.
Hayes occupied the dangerous post as a duty. The war over, Hayes resumed his
teaching for another half-dozen years. Fritz Stern showed the same native resistance
to the lures of the big world, particularly that of tramping about in the corridors of
power.

More than these examples could be cited, and I think that this integrity is somehow linked (as I shall suggest in a moment) to another of the departmental traditions, that of brilliant scholarly lecturing. I have mentioned Hayes and Moon; I
should add John Krout, whose course in American history was virtuoso public

speaking. So was Dwight Miner's in the College. Henry Graff on American diplomacy was another renowned performer, and Fritz Stern, Charles Cole, Walter Langsam, Dixon Fox, and Harry Carman were all accomplished lecturers, giving without notes an organized presentation of a topic in fifty minutes and covering—not truncating by lack of just proportions—the subject of the course.

Before closing, one lecture, unscheduled and unrepeated, must be mentioned for the record. During General Eisenhower's presidency of the university he was brought, on the spur of the moment, to the department's annual dinner. Robert Schuyler had assured him that no speech was expected, only conviviality with the group. In the middle of general conversation the question came up of Winston Churchill's war proposal to attack "the soft underbelly of Europe." The phrase sparked something like anger in Eisenhower, who proceeded to give with not a single hesitation a superb lecture on the military campaigns in the Balkans from the Peloponnesian War down to the present. It was a stunning performance, and from a man reputed to be without learning or readiness of speech. No one who heard him ever forgot it.

Why, among academics, speaking well should go with fidelity to teaching and a sense of responsibility to students may perhaps be referred to a simple habit expected of the profession: preparation. At any rate, the Columbia history department has been steadfast when elsewhere, and in other fields, the call for public service has been damaging to the institution and still more to the students. A partial list of recent or current members of the Columbia group is enough to support the generality.

Robert Paxton, Eric Foner, Alan Brinkley, Kenneth Jackson, William Harris, Eugene Rice, Elias Bickerman, John Mundy, Morton Smith, Ainslie Embree, John Garraty, Eric McKitrick, Walter Metzger, Graham Irwin, and Caroline Bynum stand high in the profession and have been faithful teachers. Not a few are also well known to the public that reads about the perspective of history on current events. Kenneth Jackson's acclaimed *Encyclopedia of New York City* is but one more sign that the principles of the "new history" are still at work.

CHAPTER 26

Jacques Barzun: Cultural Historian, Cheerful Pessimist, Columbia Avatar

—m—

Thomas Vinciguerra

For most of a century, Jacques Barzun has embodied Columbia. Despite his modesty and reserve, Barzun's brilliance as college student, teacher, historian, educator, cultural critic,` and university administrator has illuminated much of Columbia's twentieth-century history. As a longtime New Yorker, from youth to vigorous old age, he has been very much the urban and urbane intellectual and beyond that a scholar of national importance. In 2003 he was awarded the Presidential Medal of Freedom.

Thomas Vinciguerra has been a chronicler of Columbia as a former editor of Columbia College Today *and now as the curator of the unique Columbia tradition represented by the Philolexian Society, to which Barzun was a youthful contributor. He is currently deputy editor of the news magazine* The Week *and editor of* Conversations with Elie Wiesel *(Schocken, Random House 2001), written with Richard D. Heffner.*

—Wm. Theodore de Bary

—m—

On a rain-swept afternoon in November of 1996, Jacques Barzun returned to the Columbia campus to say good-bye. He had first set foot on Morningside Heights as a freshman in 1923. Now, almost three-quarters of a century later, the legendary historian and university icon was decamping with his wife, Marguerite, to her home city of San Antonio. It was a singular occasion, almost as if Alma Mater herself were preparing to abandon her throne.

The farewell reception that greeted Barzun in the Faculty Room of Low Memorial Library was graced by colleagues, former students, and myriad well-wishers. Some

*The face of American
intellectualism, 1956*

effusions were heartfelt. "You've been our inspiration and our role model," said University Professor Emeritus Fritz Stern. Other remarks were more jocose. "I wonder if Texas is ready for him," said Kenneth Jackson, the holder of Barzun's namesake chair in history. "I wonder if it's *big* enough for him."

For his part, Barzun responded with well-wrought self-deprecation. "I'm grateful that so many of you came on such a wretched day to hear so many comments made with such poetic license, and such disregard of the truth," he said. Then, as the laughter died, he offered quiet reassurance. Nothing as trivial as mere physical distance from New York, Barzun promised, would stifle him or sever his connection with alma mater. "We are not," he declared, "going into exile."

Three years later, at age ninety-two, Barzun kept his word by publishing *From Dawn to Decadence: 500 Years of Western Cultural Life, 1500 to the Present*. Rarely in recent years has a scholarly volume resonated so broadly with a receptive public, reaching number five on *The New York Times* best-seller list. *Newsweek* called it Barzun's "masterwork" and predicted, "*From Dawn to Decadence* will go down in history as one of the great one-man shows of Western letters." In *The New Criterion*, Roger Kimball called it "an exhilarating experience," allaying the fears of those who might be intimidated by its nearly nine hundred pages: "As the end approaches, one finds oneself madly trying to prolong the experience and delay coming to the final page."

It was only appropriate that in the twilight of his broad-ranging career, the former Seth Low Professor of History and University Professor had chosen to survey nothing less than half a millennium of Western civilization. For Barzun has been one of the last century's premier chroniclers and critics of our modern world—a pioneering cultural historian whose broader métier is, as he once characterized it, deeply humanistic:

> The use of history is for the person. History is formative. Its spectacle
> of continuity in chaos, of attainment in the heart of disorder, of purpose
> in the world is what nothing else provides: science denies it, art only
> invents it. Reading history remakes the mind by feeding primitive pleas-
> ure in story, exercising thought and feeling, satisfying curiosity, and
> promoting the serenity of contemplation. It is a spiritual transformation.

Barzun's scholarly passions are vast and varied. He has given us overviews of entire eras and movements, appreciations of figures as diverse as Hazlitt and Shaw, ruminations on the beauties and difficulties of the English language, and classic reflections on baseball and detective literature. As Arthur Krystal put it in *The New Yorker*, "Barzun is someone to whom experts turn for help in *their* fields." Such is the sheer scope of his *oeuvre* that when, in 1956, *Time* devoted a major story to the intellectual in American life, it was Barzun's visage that graced the magazine's famous red-bordered cover.

The *Austin Chronicle* felt similarly. In a profile coinciding with the release of *From Dawn to Decadence*, the newspaper's headline read simply, "The Man Who Knew Too Much."

The son of the noted literary scholar Henri Martin Barzun, he was born in 1907 and grew up in Créteil, a suburb of Paris, where the household seemed custom-made for the life of the mind. "It was a seedbed of modernism," he recalled. "I was surrounded by the young poets, painters, musicians, and sculptors who made Cubism, concrete poetry, atonality and the rest. Varèse, Apollinaire, Ezra Pound, Léger, Gleizes, Severini, Villon, Duchamp, Duchamp-Villon, Marie Laurencin, Cocteau and many others were to me household names in the literal sense—names of familiar figures around the house."

He got his first taste of teaching at the Lycée Janson de Sailly when he was only nine years old. With instructors being siphoned off by World War I, the school applied the Lancaster system, whereby older students taught the younger ones. Outside of the classroom, Barzun ranged through the family library. One of his favorite subjects was the American West. When, following the war, he joined his father on what came to be a permanent diplomatic mission to the United States, he fully expected to "come here and see Indians galloping across the plains."

It was not Indians, but urban bustle that greeted him in New York. Barzun's arrival at Columbia coincided with both the economic boom of the 1920s and the university-building boom under Columbia's towering president, Nicholas Murray Butler. In the company of such future colleagues as Meyer Schapiro, Lionel Trilling, William York Tindall, and Dwight Miner, Barzun quickly made his mark on the vibrant campus. He was president of the Philolexian Society, drama critic of *Spectator*, and author of the 1928 varsity show *Zuleika, or the Sultan Insulted*. Even then, his celebrated penchant for elegance was in evidence. Robert Schnitzer, his classmate and compatriot in Philo and the varsity show, recalls his typing out theater reviews for *Spec* while still dressed in black tie and opera gloves.

Academically, Columbia was in the midst of a golden age. John Dewey, John Erskine, Mark Van Doren, Irwin Edman, and Mortimer Adler were some of Barzun's classroom influences. Perhaps the most important was historian Carlton J. H.

Hayes, who specialized in the study of nationalism. After graduating the College as valedictorian, Barzun became Hayes's research assistant and helped him revise his widely used two-volume textbook, *The Political and Social History of Modern Europe*. For the second edition in 1934, the "Social History" of the title was replaced by "Cultural History," and Barzun had entered upon his academic specialty.

But what, precisely, was this new and novel discipline? Edward Rothstein explained in *The New York Times*: "Cultural history creates a web of interrelationships. Understanding the past does not just mean, say, tracing a philosophical idea through time, but seeing how that idea is woven into a cultural fabric. And cultural history, as Mr. Barzun thinks of it, traces the evolution of that fabric through time. It creates a coherent view of the past and its relationship to the present. By showing continuities and transformations in a tradition, it makes sense of the idea of a civilization."

As it happened, Barzun's early attempts to make sense of civilization coincided with its near-destruction during the calamitous 1930s. His Ph.D. thesis, published as *The French Race: Theories of Its Origins and Their Social and Political Implications Prior to the Revolution* (1932), countered the notion, fiercely held by the old French nobility, that they were a special ethnic strain, the heirs to Germans who had conquered the Gauls and Romans. Instead, Barzun found that his countrymen had no particular claim to purity; they were—in his tart phrase—"a hopeless mixture of not only Romans, but Iberians, Syrians, [and] Phoenicians."

Five years later, with *Race: A Study in Modern Superstition* (1937), he broadened his purview to survey notions of the title subject over the 150 years since the French Revolution. What he found was disturbing. "The race question," he wrote, "appears a much bigger affair than a trumped-up excuse for local persecution. It becomes rather a mode of thought endemic in Western civilization. It defaces every type of mental activity—history, art, politics, science, and social reform." Thus, in *Race* and in subsequent works like *Of Human Freedom* (1939), Barzun found himself grappling with philosophies that were then reaching their dark, perverted nadir in Nazi Germany. In *Darwin, Marx, Wagner: Critique of a Heritage* (1941), he further explored the "machine thinking" and pseudoscientific doctrines of the nineteenth century that helped undergird the Fascist, Communist, and totalitarian movements of the twentieth.

It was with *Romanticism and the Modern Ego* (1943) that Barzun found his most deeply held subject. The Romantics, he argued, were not merely sentimental escapists who had turned their backs on eighteenth-century classicism. Rather, they were idealists and individualists, struggling to create a new world in the aftermath of Napoleon. He returned to the theme in his two-volume *Berlioz and the Romantic Century* (1950). More than a biography of the composer, it addressed timeless questions of aesthetics. In *The Atlantic Monthly*, Charles J. Rolo hailed Barzun's "monumental scholarship" and declared that the study bore "the pervasive imprint of a deeply civilized mind."

Barzun's friend and student, Pulitzer Prize–winning historian Carl Schorske, echoes that opinion. "It brings into play the special nature of Jacques' own character," he observed recently. "His is a profoundly classical and cool temperament, and yet he has a deep affinity for the Romantics. Theirs are views that he doesn't necessarily agree with, but he applies his analytic cool to illustrate them splendidly."

This concern with duality has informed Barzun's other great fascination, William James. "Romanticism," Barzun has written, "implies not only risk, effort, energy; it implies also creation, diversity, and individual genius. This is why America is the land of romanticism par excellence, and why her greatest philosopher, William James, asserted the doctrine in its fullness against all absolute, classical limits." James's philosophy of pragmatism deeply influenced Barzun's entire way of perceiving and interpreting the world around him. *A Stroll With William James* (1983) is Barzun's tribute to his mentor—"a record of an intellectual debt."

The Barzun canon hardly ends there. *Pleasures of Music* (1951), *Music in American Life* (1956), *The Energies of Art* (1956), *Classic, Romantic, and Modern* (1961), *Science: The Glorious Entertainment* (1964), and *Clio and the Doctors* (1974) are just a few of the more than forty books he has written, edited, or translated. Beyond his scholarly paper trail, however, Barzun has uniquely shaped Columbia as an institution. Nowhere is his academic imprint stamped more clearly than on the College's general education curriculum.

Barzun was one of the minds behind Humanities A, now known as Literature Humanities. In 1937, when "Lit Hum" was launched, undergraduates were already being exposed to classics of Western literature and philosophy through Contemporary Civilization and the General Honors course. (The latter offering later became the Colloquium, which Barzun originally helped sponsor.) With Lit Hum, Barzun carried these "great books" efforts even further. He did more than help devise the course goals and syllabus; he won over graduate faculty who were loath to squander their time and expertise on mere undergrads.

Group of Artists, 1908, by Marie Laurencin. From left: Picasso, Fernande Olivier, Apollinaire, and Laurencin. Apollinaire and Laurencin were among the "household names" Barzun saw in his childhood home.

His powers of persuasion proved especially helpful when Art and Music Humanities were added to the College curriculum in 1938. Professor of Music Douglas Moore had argued, "We don't want freshmen wiping their feet on Bach." Barzun replied, "Doug, freshmen have been wiping their feet on Shakespeare for untold numbers of years." Moore immediately withdrew his objection.

In time, of course, Columbia's approach to general education would become a model for universities around the nation. In 1946, Barzun and Professor of English Harrison Ross Steeves reviewed the fledgling enterprise in *A College Program in Action*. Their evaluation remains as forceful a defense of the Core Curriculum as any ever written:

> The course rests on a series of related assumptions. First, that a college granting the Bachelor of Arts degree should not merely pave the way for professional training, but should try to produce educated men. Second, that if educated men are those who possess an inner life of sufficient richness to understand the slings and arrows of fortune, they must have learned to feed their souls upon good books, pictures, and music. Third, that the memorizing of labels, catchwords, and secondhand judgments about art and books is not educative in any real sense. And lastly, that to know and be at home with books a man must at some time or other read them for the first time.

When, in 1994, to celebrate the seventy-fifth anniversary of Contemporary Civilization, the Columbia College Alumni Association awarded the Alexander Hamilton Medal to the tenured teachers of the Core, it was Barzun who accepted on their behalf.

And yet Barzun's proudest contribution to the curriculum may have been his famed graduate seminar with Lionel Trilling. Conducted from 1946 to 1972, and formally titled Historical Bases of English Literature, the course was an intellectual immersion at the hands of two of the university's foremost humanists. The late Professor Emeritus of English Carolyn Heilbrun was among those who never forgot the Barzun-Trilling experience. Of a certain paper she had submitted, she later wrote,

> They discussed it as though my opinions and ideas mattered. Even more astonishing, they each annotated each paper, making comments in the margin, as no other paper I wrote in graduate school was ever marked, perhaps ever read. The respect they showed for us was invigorating, and full of the promise of what an academic life might afford.

For Heilbrun, it was a rare oasis in an academic environment that she had found distinctly misogynistic.

The course eventually became as renowned as its teachers. "We began to get letters and questions from all over the place because word got around that it was a good preparation for candidates for the Ph.D.," Barzun recalled modestly. Fred Friendly, later the director of the Journalism School's Media and Society Seminars, even wanted to air the joint offering as an interactive course on CBS television.

Barzun's other great curricular achievement was Methods of Research and Writing in History. Though this seminar was required only of first-year graduate history students, it formed the basis of *The Modern Researcher*, now generally acknowledged as one of the indispensable guides for all writers of nonfiction. Written with Professor Emeritus of History Henry F. Graff, it recently entered its sixth edition.

Barzun has long been a member of Columbia's pantheon of great teachers. He was, however, also a formidable, even overwhelming, figure to many of his charges. "I have known history students for the first time in their lives," wrote Carolyn Heilbrun, "to plagiarize a paper because they could not imagine themselves writing anything that would not affront his critical eye, let alone satisfy him."

It's not that Barzun cannot brook anything less than perfection. But he is wholly, even ruthlessly, exacting:

> I once had occasion to tell a group of graduate students that any of them would be lucky to achieve the fifth or sixth rank among historians. The remark was prompted by their dissatisfaction with all they knew: Gibbon was a bore, Macaulay a stuffed shirt, Hegel and Michelet were fools, Carlyle and Buckle frauds—this from students who could not write ten pages of readable and properly documented narrative. Pointing out that even second- and third-rate men, such as Milman, Bancroft, or Grote, were the superiors of these students' own instructors, who were by definition superior to the students themselves, was a sobering thought quite foreign to their experience.

Eventually, his persona became almost legendary. Allen Ginsberg once quipped that Barzun's true forte was not history, but "politeness." In the 1960s, when Columbia's tiny Monarchist Union called for the return of the university to the British crown, they insisted that Barzun be appointed royal governor "since he's the last aristocrat left."

The eminent psychologist Kenneth Clark, later a great admirer, was cowed by their first encounter. "Jacques Barzun, the person, fitted all too perfectly with Jacques Barzun, the name and the writer," he wrote. "He looked like his name. He personified prestige, authority, and self-confidence. The severity of his standards and his unapologetic insistence upon excellence in academic pursuits dominated all aspects of his person."

But Barzun's many friends know that this Olympian demeanor is but the outward mark of the man. "He is a man of truly great kindness," recalled the noted conductor Richard Franko Goldman in *The American Scholar,* "going out of his way to advise, encourage, and support a variety of people, and doing favors endlessly. . . . Conversation with Jacques Barzun is indeed one of the delights of life. For it, one needs all of one's resources, and one must stay honest. Jacques is an expert at puncturing pretension, and he never commits the misdemeanor of quoting himself. The fresh, free flow of ideas, comments, opinions, paradoxes, witticisms, and questions brings cheer to the soul and encourages response."

These qualities of spirit and mind characterize Barzun's prose as well. "The style is rich and complex," continued Goldman, "but it is always lucid and precise. . . . Barzun is never ponderous in the style of scholarly journals; his tone never appears 'earnest'; it is light, fast-moving, and as serious as Mozart, who also appreciated comedy." A fine example is this delightful reflection on our modern, materialistic times from *God's Country and Mine* (1954):

Many of us affect a tone of irony about gadgets, as if we lived always in realms above and dealt with trifles only during rare descents from sublime thoughts. The truth is that more and more of the important things in life turn on pinpoints. Our frustrations begin in trivialities— a telephone out of order, a car that will not start, a claim check whose number has been misread. The thing in cellophane that cannot be got at—plain to the sight but sealed like an egg—is the modern version of the torture of Tantalus. Catastrophes we will deal with like heroes, but the bottle top that defies us saps our morale, like the tiny arrows of the Lilliputians that maddened Gulliver and set his strength at naught.

When Barzun described Diderot's prose as "rapid, trenchant, sinewy," he knew whereof he wrote.

For many years, Barzun was literary adviser to Charles Scribner's Sons, and he has published several essential guides to writing, notably *On Writing, Editing, and Publishing* (1971), *Simple & Direct* (1975), and *A Word or Two Before You Go . . .* (1986), as well as revised editions of *Follett's Modern American Usage* (1966, 1974). In an age when impenetrable academic jargonizing has become all too common, Barzun remains a purveyor and advocate of clear expression. Strunk, White, Fowler & Co. would undoubtedly have approved of this passage from *Simple and Direct*:

The writer, consciously or not, writes for someone. He begins by being his own audience, in the sense of having to act toward himself like a demanding reader. His perpetual question is: Do these words, does this paragraph, does the entire piece, suit my present purpose? The purpose at large is always the same: it is to be understood aright. Reader and writer have both wasted their time if mental darkness is the only result of their separate efforts.

From 1957 to 1967, at the request of University President Grayson Kirk, Barzun served as Columbia's dean of faculties and provost. "It was clear," he recently recalled, "that in the previous dozen years, certain deans and heads of departments had become quasi-independent powers." As Barzun saw it, his job was "to recapture the university from past neglect and the several 'warlords.'" Among many other things, that meant centralizing the budget process, redirecting many school-oriented donations to the university, and establishing uniform rules for such matters as sabbaticals and promotions. To smooth over bruised egos, Barzun held a series of dinner meetings with members of the relevant departments. "Academic persons en masse think and act like any group of employees or protesters on the street," he noted wryly. "They believe in wild rumors and attribute sinister motives. But when talked to individually or in small groups they are as reasonable as one could wish."

As with his scholarship, Barzun cast a wide administrative net. His innovations are too many to enumerate, but among the best were establishing the university's Office of Art Properties and *The Columbia Forum*, an all-too-short-lived journal on academic and intellectual topics by members of the university community. What he called his "most revolutionary deed," however, was redesigning Columbia's academic robes, recasting them in their present familiar slate-gray, complete with twin Columbia crowns at chest level. The old black bombazine, he explained, "made our two-hour outdoor commencement under a hot sun an annual ordeal."

Barzun's experience in Low Library cemented his authority as a surveyor of the American educational landscape. In books like *Teacher in America* (1945), *The American University: How It Runs, Where It Is Going* (1968), and *Begin Here: The Forgotten Conditions of Teaching and Learning* (1991), he has inveighed against lapsed standards, the inflation of pedagogic goals and rhetoric, innovation to no end and, in his memorable phrase, "the educational nonsense." For millions of parents who wonder why Johnny still can't read, Barzun has many answers, most of which can be traced to the abandonment of first principles. "Schools are not intended to moralize a wicked world," he has written, "but to impart knowledge and develop intelligence, with only two social aims in mind: prepare to take on one's share in the world's work and, perhaps in addition, lend a hand in improving society, *after* schooling is done. Anything else is the nonsense we have been living with."

The nonsense, Barzun has found, flourishes not only at the primary and secondary levels, but in education's upper echelons. While defending the idea of the modern university as "a great engine of public service," he is ever mindful of its postwar tendency to lose sight of its main goal—scholarship—amid the encroachment of bureaucracy from within and government from without. Barzun has long cautioned against commodified learning, equating advanced degrees with credentials, and regarding the university as just another business. "The best colleges today," he said in 1963, "are being invaded, not to say dispossessed, by the advance agents of the professions, by men who want to seize upon the young recruit . . . and train him in a 'tangible skill.'"

But Barzun is not content to simply curse the darkness. He is a tireless supporter of the liberal arts and of the notion that the pursuit of truth may literally set one free. His defense of the study of Western culture—at a time when frivolity and what he

The staff of the Columbia Varsity, 1927, for which Barzun (front row, center) was editor in chief.

calls "the gangrene of specialism" threaten to consume college classrooms—is unapologetic, vigorous, and affirmative, as he wrote in "Of What Use the Classics Today?" in 1987:

> The need for a body of common knowledge and common reference does not disappear when a society is pluralistic. On the contrary, it grows more necessary, so that people of different origins and occupation may quickly find familiar ground and as we say, speak a common language. It not only saves time and embarrassment, but it also ensures a kind of mutual confidence and goodwill. One is not addressing an alien, as blank as a stone wall, but a responsive creature whose mind is filled with the same images, memories, and vocabulary as oneself. Otherwise, with the unstoppable march of specialization, the individual mind is doomed to solitude and the individual heart to drying up.

Yet even as he has argued for a shared cultural heritage, Barzun has been aware of the forces conspiring against it. In *The House of Intellect* (1959), he regrets the erosion of "concentration, continuity, articulate precision, and self-awareness"—all conditions necessary for intellectual life to flourish. The result, he notes acerbically, is "the rapid lowering of the logical pulse." *The Use and Abuse of Art* (1974) and *The Culture We Deserve* (1989) remain particularly pungent assessments of artistic, aesthetic, and moral degradation.

Indeed, the very title of *From Dawn to Decadence* makes clear Barzun's take on the present state of culture in general. "What we are witnessing in all the arts and in all that the arts refer to," he writes, "is the liquidation of 500 years of civilization—the entire modern age dating from the Renaissance." As his biographer Michael Murray put it, "He sees as tokens of decay the decline of manners and of conversation; the neglect by institutions of their original purpose or their inability to continue to fulfill it; the turning of debate into a classifying of motives rather than a meeting of arguments; and the all-encompassing shift from the democratic to the demotic."

Barzun's critics are quick to insist that things aren't nearly as bad as he would have us believe—that naysayers have been heralding the decline of the West ever since Oswald Spengler. Some have also written him off as a conservative ideologue or oversimplified his beliefs—claiming, for instance, that he thinks that the decline of jackets and ties as everyday wear necessarily portends the onset of a new Dark Ages.

These detractors might want to consider that Barzun himself believes that chaos, be it in life or art, brings with it the possibility of redemption. "In the past," he told the Independent Women's Forum in 2000, "decadence of this sort has come to an end often because of a sudden twist in the course of events. The fifteenth-century decadence was reversed, you might say, by the discovery of America, which opened up all sorts of possibilities and turned peoples' minds away from what they felt were hopeless ways of life." Barzun refuses to guess what might supplant the current decadence ("I'm an historian, not a prophet"), but he has an abiding faith in humanity's talent for muddling through: "I have always been—I think any student of history almost inevitably is—a cheerful pessimist."

Today, as he nears his century mark, Jacques Barzun resides quietly in San Antonio, where he visits the local theater and orchestra, keeps in touch with friends and colleagues, and stays busy working on what he mysteriously calls "a very short book about aspects of contemporary culture." A chevalier of the Legion of Honor and the recipient of the Gold Medal for Criticism of the American Academy of Arts and Letters—of which he was twice president—he continues to accrue accolades. In 2003, he received the Presidential Medal of Freedom, the nation's highest civilian honor. "Few academics of the last century," said President George W. Bush at the White House ceremony, "have equaled his output and his influence."

No doubt Barzun would be embarrassed to have this essay conclude merely with a catalogue of his laurels. These remarks, from a 2002 interview with *The American Educator*, might stand as a more appropriate coda. In the present context of a nation in conflict with itself and indeed with much of the globe, they reflect the enduring value of Clio in a way that only one of that Muse's masters can express:

> The student who reads history will unconsciously develop what is the
> highest value of history: judgment in world affairs. This is a permanent
> good, not because history repeats—we can never exactly match past

and present situations—but because the "tendency of things" shows an amazing uniformity within any given civilization. The great historian Jacob Burckhardt said of historical knowledge, it is not "to make us more clever the next time, but wiser for all time."

Plus, a person endowed with the knowledge of history reacts a good deal more serenely and temperately to the things that he encounters both in his own life and in the life of the country in which he lives. Besides which, history is a story—full of color and dramatic events and persons, of triumphs and dreadful actions, which must be known in order to form a true notion of humankind.

CHAPTER 27

Salo Wittmayer Baron: Demystifying Jewish History

—∽∭∾—

Michael Stanislawski

Born into a well-to-do Jewish family in Austrian Galicia, Salo Baron had a polyglot upbringing that provided him with a knowledge of German, Yiddish, Polish, and the Hebrew that came with a thoroughly traditional Jewish education. With these multicultural resources he entered the sophisticated culture of Vienna, where he added the multidisciplinary learning that came with three doctorates at the university—in philosophy, political science, and law—as well as with his ordination as a rabbi.

Michael Stanislawski, Nathan J. Miller Professor of Jewish History, traces Baron's spiritual and scholarly odyssey from Vienna to New York, where, first at the Jewish Institute of Religion and then at Columbia from 1930, the young scholar was able to pursue his ambition to become a professor of Jewish history.

With his many linguistic and disciplinary competencies and his early record of scholarly accomplishment, it is perhaps not surprising that Baron's sense of Jewish history would incline him more to emphasize the manifold achievements of his people than the dismal record of persecution and oppression that had dominated that history up to his time. Indications of this more positive and optimistic approach is the title of a groundbreaking 1928 article of Baron's, "Ghetto and Emancipation," which prefigures his monumental lifework, the Social and Religious History of the Jews, *eventually coming to eighteen volumes.*

During his years at Columbia, Baron opened up a field of scholarly endeavor whose distinguished resources include not only the current holder of the Salo Baron Chair, Yosef Yerushalmi, but also the author of the essay below.

—Wm. Theodore de Bary

—∽∭∾—

For nearly sixty years, Professor Salo Baron could be seen daily in the stacks of Butler Library, researching his epoch-making *Social and Religious History of the Jews*. When he was in his late eighties, and the *History* was in its sixteenth or seventeenth volume but had reached only the early modern period, Baron was often asked if he would get to the twentieth century. He always responded that he had a deal with the Creator: he would not be taken from this world before his life's work was completed.

ROOTED IN TRADITION

Salo Wittmayer Baron was the most important Jewish historian of his generation and a compelling presence at Columbia for much of the twentieth century. He came to Morningside Heights in 1930 to hold the Miller Chair in Jewish History, the first such professorship at a secular Western university. His voluminous scholarship—based on a novel conception of the nature of Jewish history and how to study it professionally—remade his field in the United States and worldwide.

Baron was born in 1895 to a wealthy and educated traditional Jewish family in the city of Tarnow, then in Austrian Galicia, the part of Poland absorbed into the Habsburg Empire in the late eighteenth century. In line with the cultural, linguistic, and political mores of the Jewish upper middle classes of this region, the Baron family spoke German, not the Yiddish of the impoverished Jewish masses of Eastern Europe, though the young Baron imbibed that language from his elders. He learned Polish as well and received a thorough Hebraic and traditional Jewish education. Baron continued both his secular and Jewish studies in Vienna starting in 1914 and ultimately—and amazingly—earned three doctorates from the University of Vienna, in philosophy (1917), political science (1922), and law (1923). During this period he also received his rabbinic ordination from Vienna's modern Israelitisch-Theologische Lehranstalt rabbinical seminary.

It was likely that Baron aspired to become a university professor of Jewish history, but this was unrealistic in interwar Austria. So for seven years he taught history at the city's Jewish Teachers College. At the same time, in New York, the charismatic Reform rabbi Stephen S. Wise was establishing the Jewish Institute for Religion (JIR), an innovative rabbinic seminary with a distinguished faculty that aimed to overcome the already fractious denominational differences among Jews and to produce Judaic scholarship at the highest levels. (Tellingly, after Wise's death in 1949 this ecumenical goal was no longer feasible, and the Jewish Institute for Religion merged with the Hebrew Union College, the Reform seminary in Cincinnati where

Wise himself was trained.) Wise was well connected with the Viennese community, and, on one of his frequent trips to Europe to recruit faculty, he learned about the young historian with the remarkable breadth of knowledge. In 1925, Wise invited Baron to come teach in New York. In his short time at the JIR, Baron taught a series of innovative and demanding courses—and outside the classroom he began to produce works of scholarship that revolutionized the study, and the conception, of Jewish history for decades to come.

Baron's work revealed a more nuanced reading of Jewish history than the "lachrymose" image of the suffering Jew— as depicted in Samuel Hirszenberg's 1905 painting, The Black Banner.

WOE, BEGONE

Most important was his June 1928 article in the influential publication *Menorah Journal* entitled "Ghetto and Emancipation: Shall We Revise the Traditional View?" The essay challenged head-on some of the cardinal premises of his predecessors by arguing that the history of the Jews was not, as Heinrich Graetz, the greatest Jewish historian of the nineteenth century, had memorably put it, a *Leidens- und- Gelehrtengeschichte*—a history of suffering and scholarship. In fact, Baron insisted, the notion that the Jews were persecuted more than any other group throughout history was simply wrong. During the Middle Ages, for example, the Jews were far better off than the peasants who made up the bulk of the population, he argued. The periodic pogroms and persecutions that did indeed afflict the Jews were horrific, but not constitutive of Jewish history or Jewish self-consciousness. On the other hand, the emancipation that began after the French Revolution was won at a price—the loss of the millennia-long autonomy of the Jewish communities.

The determinant forces in Jewish history, Baron claimed, were rather the Jews' idiosyncratic and hence often misunderstood amalgam of nationality and religion;

Dr. Salo Baron speaking at the podium in the Schiff building library reading room; Mordecai Kaplan is seated behind him.

their pervasive if perplexing—but ultimately self-perpetuating—ability to survive and flourish without a state or a territory and seemingly removed as well from nature; and an intense yearning for normalization through redemption. In order to understand the history of the Jews in any age or place, it was essential first to study what the Jews were doing between attacks. What were they thinking, writing, creating, selling, buying? "Surely," he wrote, "it is time to break with the lachrymose theory of pre-Revolutionary woe, and to adopt a view more in accord with historic truth." That sentence, with which he famously concluded his *Menorah* article, was a charge to the new generation of Jewish historians. He was arguing for a conception of Jewish history that took into account a complex mix of social, cultural, religious, and economic history. Moreover, any period of Jewish history, he insisted, always had to be studied both horizontally and vertically—that is, as part of the long experience of the Jews and in the context of the specific non-Jewish society in which they were living. This anti-lachrymose and "integrationist" approach heralded a rethinking of Jewish history and was regarded with great suspicion by many traditional historians, both within and outside the academy.

MUSICAL CHAIRS

Coincidentally, only a month before Baron's article was published, Linda Miller, a widow with strong ties to New York City's Reform Temple Emanu-El, approached Columbia University, offering to fund a chair in Jewish history. (Richard Gottheil, who had graduated from Columbia College in 1881 and was the son of the late rabbi of Temple Emanu-El, had been serving as instructor and professor of Semitic languages at Columbia since 1886.) Letters in Columbia's archives reveal an intriguing dance between Mrs. Miller and President Nicholas Murray Butler. Miller wanted a majority vote in the appointment while Butler explained, tactfully and more than once, that the university welcomed her suggestions but that they could be no more than suggestions. Baron's name was raised after other candidates were rejected or declined the post. Miller was leery about the thirty-four–year-old and unknown— and Eastern European!—scholar. Butler respectfully held his ground, and, in 1930, Baron came to Columbia to serve on the Nathan J. Miller Endowment, in memory of Mrs. Miller's late husband.

This was the first chair in Jewish history at any secular Western university. Its location within Columbia's Department of History, rather than a department of Semitics or a separate Judaica department, suited Baron's idea of Jewish history as a crucial piece of world history, to be studied neutrally with the professional tools that the historian of any civilization would use. At the time of Baron's appointment and for decades thereafter, the only other chair in Jewish studies at a major secular American university was the Littauer Chair at Harvard, held by the eminent philosopher Harry Austryn Wolfson. Together, Baron and Wolfson essentially founded the academic field of Jewish studies in the American academy.

Baron's influence on the field of Jewish history was enormous, both through his numerous publications and through his teaching at Columbia, where he trained most of the significant Jewish historians of the next generation, including his first successor in the Miller Chair, Gerson D. Cohen, who later became the chancellor of the Jewish Theological Seminary of America. Thanks to his exceptionally careful and far-reaching scholarship and through his teaching and mentoring of students, Baron slowly but eventually won acceptance for his conception of Jewish history. His interpretation became the reigning approach within the field throughout the United States and had major influence in European and Israeli academic circles as well. In time, any serious professional Jewish historian would be intimately acquainted with Baron's writings, and most would accept his critique of the previous conception of Jewish history.

This is all the more remarkable given that the anti-lachrymose philosophy predated the most lachrymose chapter in all of Jewish experience—the Holocaust, in which Baron's own parents were murdered. Baron continued to insist that Jewish history was not primarily a history of persecution but of creative intellectual, spiritual, and economic responses to the challenges—and at times the horrors—the Jews faced as a people. It's a testament to the solidity and depth of Baron's scholarship, and his commitment to it, that this new conception could survive a period that a third of the world's Jews did not.

MARRIED TO THE MUSE

Baron always claimed that he had only one research assistant, his wife, Jeannette Meisel Baron, whom he met when she was a graduate student in economics at Columbia,and married in 1934. Baron dictated his work to her, and she collaborated so meticulously in the writing, typing, and proofreading of his manuscripts that the published volumes were renowned for their lack of errors.

For decades the couple was a fixture on Claremont Avenue, Baron taking his daily walk in Riverside Park, Jeannette serving as the hostess of a European-flavored salon in their home. Their circle of intimate friends included Hannah Arendt, and the Barons were in her apartment when she died in 1975.

After World War II, Baron organized and headed the Commission for Jewish Cultural Reconstruction, which tried to salvage the remains of Jewish cultural artifacts in Europe after the Holocaust. In 1961 the Israeli government prosecutor called on Baron to testify at the trial of Adolf Eichmann about the nature of Jewish history and the Jewish community before World War II.

Within the academy, Baron's influence was extended through his creation of the journal *Jewish Social Studies*, which attempted to use the methods of the social sciences to examine Jewish society through the ages. In 1950 Baron established the Center for Israel and Jewish Studies at Columbia, which he directed until his retirement, and later the University Seminar in Israel and Jewish Studies, which he led and then participated in until his death.

But it was Baron's scholarship that was most important to him and particularly his *Social and Religious History of the Jews*, which was his bold attempt to emulate his nineteenth- and early twentieth-century predecessors, Heinrich Graetz and Simon Dubnow, and write an up-to-date, methodologically sophisticated world history of the Jewish people. He differed from these historians chiefly in studying Jewish history in its larger political, religious, and social context with the understanding that the Jews existed within other societies in spite of their own particularities. Beyond its remarkable range, from the biblical to the early modern periods, and its eloquent prose, Baron's *Social and Religious History* was remarkable for the rigor of its scholarly apparatus. Baron seemed to have read everything, and in every language, having remotely to do with Jewish history.

Alas, Baron's presumptive deal with the Creator did not hold, and his capacity for writing was severely diminished in his last years, especially after his beloved and younger wife, Jeannette, died in 1985, leaving him without the fastidious hand that had transcribed and recorded his thoughts. Beyond the eighteen volumes of the

Social and Religious History that were published, Baron wrote and edited some two dozen other books, including the crucial two-volume *The Jewish Community*, histories of the Jewish communities of Russia and of the United States, and more theoretical works both on the nature of history writing in general and on the relationship between modern nationalism and religion.

In 1979, a group of friends of the Barons established a chair at Columbia in his honor, and one of his star students, Yosef Hayim Yerushalmi, then at Harvard, moved back to Columbia to become the first Salo Wittmayer Baron Professor of Jewish History and the director of the Center for Israel and Jewish Studies. Soon thereafter, an anonymous donor gave $4.3 million to Columbia to establish an endowment for the Center for Israel and Jewish Studies and new chairs in modern Hebrew literature and American Jewish history, both lifelong passions of Baron. These professorships solidified Columbia as a world-class center of Jewish studies in all the disciplines, an eminence that Baron himself had more quietly established in the 1940s and 1950s. Before their deaths, the Barons themselves endowed the Salo and Jeannette Baron Prize in Jewish Studies, which is given every five years to the author of the best dissertation in Jewish studies throughout the university.

Sadly, Baron's attempt to write an all-encompassing history of the Jews from antiquity to the present was not realized, and it is unlikely, given the scope of knowledge and linguistic skills such a task entails, that another historian will attempt it again—particularly in our age of hyperspecialization. So Baron's lifework will doubtless remain not only the best global history of the Jews, but also the last.

CHAPTER 28

Richard Hofstadter: Columbia's Evolutionary Historian

Eric Foner

—⟋⟍—

Richard Hofstadter's stature, as not only a leading American historian but as a public intellectual who represented Columbia at its best in his time, is shown by the extraordinary honor done him when he was asked to give the commencement address in the spring of 1968. It is a long tradition at Columbia that the president, not an invited speaker, always gives this address himself. The sole exception was made in favor of Hofstadter, who in that year of radical challenge to the values of the university, stood firmly and spoke eloquently in their defense.

The story of the dominant figure in American historical writing in the post–World War II years is told by his successor to the distinguished Dewitt Clinton Professorship of American History, Eric Foner, who received his doctorate at Columbia under Hofstadter. Foner's publications have focused on the intersections of intellectual, social, and political history with special regard to race relations. The latest of his many award-winning books are Who Owns History? Rethinking the Past in a Changing World, *and* Give Me Liberty! An American History. *A winner of the Great Teacher Award from the Society of Columbia Graduates, Foner is an elected member of the American Academy of Arts and Sciences and of the British Academy. He has served as president of the Organization of American Historians and as president of the American Historical Association.*

—Wm. Theodore de Bary

—⟋⟍—

A remarkable number of prominent historians have taught at Columbia over the years, but probably none can match Richard Hofstadter in the enduring impact of his scholarship. A child of the Great Depression, he earned his master's and doctoral degrees and then taught here from 1946 until his untimely death in 1970. Despite the brevity of his career, Hofstadter left a prolific body of work, remarkable for its range, originality, and readability. Because of his penetrating intellect and sparkling literary style, Hofstadter's writings continue to exert a powerful influence on how scholars and general readers alike understand the American past.

"All my books," Hofstadter wrote in the 1960s, "have been, in a certain sense, topical in their inspiration. That is to say, I have always begun with a concern with some present reality." Although often identified as the chief practitioner of the "consensus" history of the 1950s, Hofstadter, in fact, exhibits, no single approach or fixed ideology in his writings. His approach to the American past changed several times during his career, reflecting his evolving encounter with the turbulent times in which he lived.

Richard Hofstadter was born in 1916 in Buffalo, New York, the son of a Jewish father and a mother of German Lutheran descent. As for so many others of his generation, Hofstadter's formative intellectual and political experience was the Great Depression. Buffalo, a major industrial center, was hard hit by unemployment and social dislocation. The Depression, he later recalled, "started me thinking about the world. . . . It was as clear as day that something had to change. . . . You had to decide, in the first instance, whether you were a Marxist or an American liberal." As an undergraduate at the University of Buffalo, Hofstadter gravitated toward a group of left-wing students including the brilliant Felice Swados, whom he later married.

The Hofstadter who arrived in New York City in 1936 was, as Alfred Kazin later recalled, "the All-American collegian just in from Buffalo with that unmistakable flat accent." At his father's insistence he first enrolled in a law school but soon transferred to the Columbia history department. For a time, the Hofstadters became part of New York's broad radical political culture in the era of the Popular Front. He was briefly a member of the Communist Party, although he "eased himself out" early in 1939. There followed a rapid and deep disillusionment—with the party (run by "glorified clerks"), the Soviet Union ("essentially undemocratic"), and eventually with Marxism itself.

Although Hofstadter mostly abandoned active politics after 1939, his earliest work as a historian reflected his continuing intellectual engagement with radicalism. His Columbia master's thesis, completed in 1938, showed how the benefits of New Deal agricultural policies in the South flowed to large landowners, while the conditions of sharecroppers—black and white—only worsened. The essay's critical evaluation of FDR, a common attitude among New York radicals, would persist in Hofstadter's writings long after the political impulse that inspired the thesis had faded.

As with many others who came of age in the 1930s, Marxism framed Hofstadter's general intellectual approach, but in application to the American past the iconoclastic materialism of Charles A. Beard was his greatest inspiration. Beard taught that American history had been shaped by the struggle of competing economic groups, primarily farmers, industrialists, and workers. A dialogue with the Beardian tradition shaped much of Hofstadter's subsequent career.

The young Hofstadter's thinking was deeply affected by the Great Depression.

While Beard devoted little attention to political ideas, however, Hofstadter soon became attracted to the study of American social thought. He once identified himself as "a political historian mainly interested in the role of ideas in politics, an historian of political culture." His interest was encouraged by Merle Curti, a Columbia professor with whom Hofstadter by 1939 had formed, according to his wife, a "mutual admiration society." Aside from his relationship with Curti, however, Hofstadter was not particularly happy at Columbia. For three years running, he was refused financial aid and was gripped by a sense of unfair treatment. Nonetheless, under Curti's direction, Hofstadter completed his dissertation, *Social Darwinism in American Thought*, published by the University of Pennsylvania Press in 1944. The book focuses on the late nineteenth century and ends in 1915, the year before Hofstadter's birth. But, as he later observed, the "emotional resonances" that shaped its approach were those of his own youth, when conservatives used such Darwinian ideas as natural selection, survival of the fittest, and the struggle for existence to reinforce conservative, laissez-faire individualism. Hofstadter made no effort to disguise his distaste for the Social Darwinists or his sympathy for the critics, especially the sociologists and philosophers who believed intellectuals could guide social progress (views extremely congenial to Hofstadter at the time he was writing). His heroes were early-twentieth-century philosophers like John Dewey, whom he presented as a model of the socially responsible intellectual, an architect of a "new collectivism" in which an activist state would improve society.

LIVELY AND LUCID

Hofstadter's first book displayed qualities that would remain hallmarks of his subsequent writing—among them an amazing lucidity in presenting complex ideas, the ability to sprinkle his text with apt quotes that make precisely the right point, and the capacity to bring past individuals to life in vivid, telling portraits. To the end of his life, Hofstadter's writings would center on *Social Darwinism*'s underlying themes— the social context of ideologies and the role of ideas in politics.

If *Social Darwinism* announced Hofstadter as one of the most promising scholars of his generation, his second book, *The American Political Tradition*, published in 1948, propelled him to the very forefront of his profession. He began writing this brilliant series of portraits of prominent Americans in 1943, while teaching at the University of Maryland. In 1946, a year after his wife's death from cancer, he returned to Columbia's history department as an assistant professor. An enduring classic of American historical writing, *The American Political Tradition* remains today a standard work in college and high school history classes and has been read by millions outside the academy. The writing is energetic, ironic, and aphoristic. Hofstadter's brilliant chapter titles remain in one's memory even after the specifics of his argument have faded: "The Aristocrat as Democrat" (Jefferson), "The Marx of the Master Class" (Calhoun), "The Patrician as Opportunist" (FDR).

Providing unity to the individual portraits was Hofstadter's insight that his subjects held essentially the same underlying beliefs. Instead of persistent conflict between agrarians and industrialists, capital and labor, or Democrats and Republicans, broad agreement on fundamentals, particularly the values of individual liberty, private property, and capitalist enterprise, marked American history. "The fierceness of the political struggle," he wrote, "has often been misleading; for the range of vision embraced by the primary contestants . . . has always been bounded by the horizons of property and enterprise."

With its emphasis on the ways an ideological consensus had shaped American development, *The American Political Tradition* marked Hofstadter's break with the Beardian and Marxist traditions. Along with Daniel Boorstin's *The Genius of American Politics* and Louis Hartz's *The Liberal Tradition in America* (both published a few years afterward), Hofstadter's second book came to be seen as the foundation of the "consensus history" of the 1950s. But Hofstadter's writing never devolved into the uncritical celebration of the American experience that characterized much "consensus" writing. As Arthur Schlesinger Jr. observed, there was a basic difference between *The American Political Tradition* and works like Boorstin's: "For Hofstadter perceived the consensus from a radical perspective, from the outside, and deplored it; while Boorstin perceived it from the inside and celebrated it."

In Hofstadter's account, the domination of individualism and capitalism in American life produced not a benign freedom from European ideological conflicts, but a form of intellectual and political bankruptcy, an inability on the part of political leaders to think in original ways about the modern world. If the book has a hero, it is Wendell Phillips. Alone among Hofstadter's subjects in never holding public office, Phillips was an engaged intellectual who used his talents first to mobilize opposition to slavery and then to combat the exploitation of labor in the Gilded Age. It is indeed ironic that Hofstadter's devastating indictment of American political culture should have become the introduction to American history for generations of students.

If his first two books reflected "the experiences of the Depression era and the New Deal," in the 1950s a different reality shaped Hofstadter's writing—the Cold War and McCarthyism. At Columbia, Hofstadter found himself part of the world of the New York intellectuals. But this world had changed dramatically since the radical days of the 1930s. He had "grown a great deal more conservative in the past few years," Hofstadter wrote in 1953. Hofstadter was repelled by McCarthyism and in the early 1950s spoke at meetings and signed petitions against it. Hofstadter's understanding of McCarthyism as the outgrowth of a deep-seated American anti-intellectualism and provincialism reinforced a distrust of mass politics that had been simmering ever since he left the Communist Party in 1939. After supporting with "immense enthusiasm" Adlai Stevenson's campaign for the White House in 1952, Hofstadter retreated altogether from politics. "I can no longer describe myself as a radical, though I don't consider myself to be a conservative either," he later wrote. "I suppose the truth is, although my interests are still very political, I none the less have no politics."

What Hofstadter did have was a growing sense of the fragility of intellectual freedom and social comity and the conviction that historians needed new intellectual tools to explain political ideas and behavior. The Columbia environment powerfully shaped his intellectual development. Hofstadter became more and more interested in how insights from other disciplines could enrich historical interpretation. Three colleagues in particular influenced him. Lionel Trilling's writing on the symbolic interpretation of literary texts suggested a new approach to understanding historical writings. Robert K. Merton's work explored the distinction between the "manifest" and "latent" functions of political ideas and institutions. And C. Wright Mills explored the status anxieties of the middle class in modern society. Hofstadter and Mills shared an improbable friendship—temperamentally and politically the Texas-born radical populist and the disillusioned New York intellectual could not have been more different.

These influences helped to make Hofstadter more and more sensitive to what he called the "complexities in our history which our conventional images of the past have not yet caught." Reared on the assumption that politics essentially reflects economic interests, he now became fascinated with alternative explanations of political conduct: unconscious motivations, status anxieties, irrational hatreds, paranoia.

Hofstadter applied these insights to the history of American political culture in a remarkable series of books that made plain his growing sense of alienation from what he called America's periodic "fits of moral crusading." Having come of age in a political culture that glorified "the people" as the wellspring of democracy and decency in American life, he now portrayed politics as a realm of fears, symbols, and nostalgia, and ordinary Americans as beset by bigotry, xenophobia, and paranoid delusions. *The Age of Reform* (1955) offered an interpretation of Populism and Progressivism "from the perspective of our own time." The South's downtrodden small farmers who had evoked sympathy in his master's essay on sharecroppers under the New Deal now, as Populists of the late nineteenth century, appeared as prisoners of a nostalgic agrarian myth who lashed out against imagined enemies from British bankers to Jews in a precursor to "modern authoritarian movements." He depicted the Progressives as a displaced bourgeoisie seeking in political reform a way to overcome their decline in status.

A similar sensibility informed Hofstadter's next two books. *Anti-Intellectualism in American Life* (1963), written, Hofstadter wrote, as a "response to the political and intellectual conditions of the 1950s," described an American heartland "filled with people who are often fundamentalist in religion, nativist in prejudice, isolationist in foreign policy, and conservative in economics" as a persistent danger to intellectual life. Frightened by the Goldwater campaign of 1964, Hofstadter brought together a group of essays in *The Paranoid Style in American Politics* (1965), which suggested that belief in vast conspiracies, apocalyptic fantasies, and heated exaggerations characterized popular enthusiasms of both the right and the left.

TWO, TOO MUCH

The Age of Reform and *Anti-Intellectualism* won Hofstadter his two Pulitzer Prizes. Ironically, however, both books today seem more dated than his earlier books. Their deep distrust of mass politics and their apparent dismissal of the substantive basis of reform movements strike the reader, even in today's conservative climate, as exaggerated and elitist. Historians have shown the Populists to be far more perceptive in their critique of late-nineteenth-century capitalism than Hofstadter allowed, and they have expanded the portrait of Progressivism to encompass labor unions, women's suffrage activists, and others far beyond the displaced urban professionals on whom Hofstadter concentrated. Nonetheless, as the historian Robert Kelley has written, these works had a powerful influence on the study of American political history: "They taught us to think not only of socioeconomic class, but of specific cultural milieux in which particular moods and world views are generated. Out of this came a new sensitivity to the power of the irrational, to tendencies among political groups to be swayed by concerns over status and by paranoid beliefs."

As social turmoil engulfed the country in the mid-1960s, Hofstadter remained as prolific as ever, but his underlying assumptions shifted again. In *The Progressive*

While Hofstadter delivered the commencement address to the class of 1968 inside the Cathedral of St. John the Divine, some graduates walked out in protest and staged a "counter-commencement."

Historians (1968), he attempted to come to terms once and for all with Beard and his generation. Their portrait of an America racked by perennial conflict, he noted, was overdrawn, but by the same token the consensus outlook could hardly explain the American Revolution, Civil War, or other key periods of discord in the nation's past (including, by implication, the 1960s). *American Violence* (1970), a documentary volume edited with his graduate student Michael Wallace, offered a chilling record of political and social turbulence that utterly contradicted the consensus vision of a nation placidly evolving without serious disagreements. Finally, in *America at 1750*, Hofstadter offered a bittersweet portrait that brilliantly took account of the paradoxical coexistence of individual freedom and widespread social injustice in the Colonial era. In this work, an unacknowledged pioneer of what came to be called the "new social history," Hofstadter's canvas now included slaves and indentured servants as well as the political leaders, small farmers, professionals, and businessmen on whom he has previously concentrated. The book remained unfinished at the time of his death from leukemia in 1970. *American at 1750* was to have been the first in a three-volume general history of the United States.

HISTORY WRIT SMALL

It was during the 1960s that I came to know Richard Hofstadter. He supervised my senior thesis at Columbia College in 1963 and later directed my dissertation. At this time, the history department was still divided into a graduate and an undergraduate branch, the former with offices in Fayerweather, the latter in Hamilton. Hofstadter taught mainly graduate courses but chose to keep his office in Hamilton (perhaps, as one of his former colleagues recently speculated, because there had been opposition to his receiving tenure and he was grateful for the strong support of Harry J. Carman, dean of the College).

For all his accomplishments, Hofstadter was utterly without pretension. Nor did he try to impose his own interests or views on his students. If no Hofstadter school emerged from Columbia, it is because he had no desire to create one. Indeed, it often seemed during the 1960s that his graduate students, many of whom were actively involved in the civil rights and antiwar movements, were having as much influence on his evolving outlook as he on theirs.

Among the department's American historians at this time were some brilliant lecturers—the witty, incisive William Leuchtenberg, the deeply thoughtful Eric L. McKitrick, the spellbinding Walter P. Metzger, and the legendary James P. Shenton, beloved by generations of undergraduates. Hofstadter was not a great lecturer—writing was his passion. He was at his best in small seminars and individual consultations.

Devoted to the idea of the university as a haven of scholarly discourse in a culture beset by irrationality and threats to academic freedom, Hofstadter was shaken by the upheaval of 1968, although he remained close to those of his graduate students who were involved. When asked to deliver the commencement address in place of President Grayson Kirk in May of that fateful year, he agreed. He knew that some of his students would sharply criticize him for lending his name to what we considered a discredited administration. "If I don't do it," Hofstadter told me, "someone far worse will." The ceremony was held in the Cathedral of St. John the Divine. When Hofstadter rose to speak, many of the graduating seniors departed for a "countercommencement" on Low plaza. Those who remained heard a short, eloquent speech reaffirming the university's commitment to "certain basic values of freedom, rationality, inquiry, and discussion." He ended by asking whether the university could go on. "I can only answer: how can it not go on? What kind of people would we be if we allowed this center of our culture and our hope to languish and fail?"

Shortly before his death, *Newsweek* published an interview with Hofstadter, a melancholy reflection on a society confronting a "crisis of the spirit." Young people, he said, had no sense of vocation, no aspirations for the future. Yet the causes of their alienation were real: "You have a major urban crisis. You have the question of race, and you have a cruel and unnecessary war." He rejected students' stance of "moral indignation" as a kind of "elitism" on the part of those who did not have to face the day-to-day task of earning a living. Yet ultimately, he went on, it was American society itself, not just its children, that had to change. "I think that part of our trouble is that our sense of ourselves hasn't diminished as much as it ought to." The United States, he seemed to be saying, would have to accept limitations on its power to shape the world. The stultifying official consensus he had explored in *The American Political Tradition* would finally have to end.

From *Social Darwinism* to *America at 1750*, all Hofstadter's books reflected not only a humane historical intelligence, but an engagement with the concerns of the times in which he wrote. It is impossible to say what his intellectual trajectory might have been had be not died so young. As C. Vann Woodward said at the memorial service, "It seems almost unkind to speak of Richard Hofstadter as a fulfilled historian—when he was cut down so cruelly in his prime." But his writings remain a model of what historical scholarship at its finest can aspire to achieve.

CHAPTER 29

Columbia and the Great Empirical Tradition of American Economics

—〰—

Gerald Friedman

As a Columbia undergraduate, Gerald Friedman studied economic history under Stuart Bruchey and Jacob Smit, macroeconomics under Philip Cagan, and labor economics under Aaron Warner. "Warner was truly inspiring," says Friedman. "In his quiet and (in the classroom) somewhat disorganized way, he changed my life by showing the connection between scholarship and social action."

Friedman pursues this theme here by showing how the empirical approach championed by Edwin R. A. Seligman, a founder of economics at Columbia, and his successors demonstrates the complexity and variety of economic and social institutions and thereby their susceptibility to change and reform. Seligman's successors in this tradition include John Bates Clark, Wesley Clair Mitchell, and John Maurice Clark, who supplied Franklin Roosevelt's New Deal with some of its most prominent "braintrusters," including the economist Rexford Guy Tugwell and his Columbia colleagues Adolph Berle and Raymond Moley.

Friedman is professor of economics at the University of Massachusetts, Amherst. Among his many publications is State-Making and Labor Movements: The United States and France, 1876–1914 *(1998).*

—Wm. Theodore de Bary

—〰—

Today's economists focus on the problems of individuals maximizing their welfare within an unchanging social environment, an effort depending on three conditions: technology, individual preferences, and the distribution of land, labor, and capital. They have nothing to say about broader issues of social change or the origins of property or the distribution of wealth. Indeed, modern economics has become a discipline whose claims as a science rest on finding definitive answers rather than asking important questions.

There was a time, however, not so long ago, when economics was a social science—when economists studied society and asked important questions about how society was organized and how it could be changed. After 1880 a new generation of university-trained economists rejected the individualism of English classical economics and studied the economy as part of a broader society. This made them natural reformers: Because it viewed society as a product of individual choice, the English classical tradition discouraged social reform to change economic outcomes. By rejecting this individualist assumption and viewing the economic system as a product of historical accident or interest-group power, the new economists opened the door to social reform. And nowhere did the new economists so well marry social reform to academic study as at Columbia University, where they created America's leading school of economics.

Among the first colleges to teach the subject, Columbia would attract leading scholars like Edwin Seligman, Wesley Clair Mitchell, John Bates Clark, and John Maurice Clark. "Institutionalism," a distinctive American approach emphasizing the importance of history and social institutions in economic affairs, developed at Columbia and its offspring, the New School of Social Research and the National Bureau of Economic Research. But in the Cold War years after World War II, too many economists came to define economic models by definitive answers, cultivating abstract models and forsaking social relevance and the tradition of empirical research.

EDWIN SELIGMAN AND THE CREATION OF THE COLUMBIA ECONOMICS DEPARTMENT

The study of economics began with the first classes at King's College as part of students' training in moral philosophy. Alexander Hamilton and John Jay, for example, prepared to found the United States by studying political economy there. Economics was first taught as an independent discipline at Columbia in the 1820s by the Reverend John McVickar. Stuck in what Columbia's Alvin Johnson called "the ruts of English classical orthodoxy," McVickar had little use for empirical analysis or the study of social institutions. Moreover, his theory of political economy was fundamentally conservative, opposing any public interference with the choices individuals make freely.

The true founder of Columbia's economics department was Edwin Robert Anderson Seligman. After receiving his B.A. (with high honors) from Columbia in 1879 and studying in Europe for three years, Seligman returned to receive one of the university's first Ph.D. degrees in 1885. He never left. He was made professor of political economy and finance in 1891 and McVickar Professor of Political Economy in 1904, retiring from that post in 1931.

In addition to promoting economics as an independent discipline, Seligman challenged the classical approach with its universal laws of individual maximization, insisting that economic activity was shaped and guided by history and the institutional environment. He taught generations of Columbia students and his colleagues that economic theories are time and place specific, describing behavior only within particular institutional structures. In place of the universal constants of deductive theory, Seligman urged economists to substitute historical and statistical treatments reflecting the institutional and historical determination of economic life.

John Bates Clark

Institutions made Seligman's economics an historical discipline because behavior depends on structures established by past experience and past conflict. "Economic life deals with man as existing in society," he wrote, and therefore can be defined only within specific institutional contexts that vary widely in time and place. This approach made Seligman the first institutionalist economist and a natural choice to edit the *Encyclopedia of the Social Sciences*. It also had political implications. "Men," he insisted, "are the product of history, but history is made by men" who can reshape their society to achieve different ends.

An active member of the university community, Seligman promoted economics, the social sciences, and research in general. In his debt are users of the Columbia libraries, to which Seligman donated his collection of 50,000 volumes and pamphlets on economics. For decades, he campaigned to raise faculty salaries and to provide for time and facilities for research. Seligman also fought to establish and edited the Columbia University Series in History, Economics, and Public Law to provide a wider audience for Columbia dissertations. But perhaps his greatest contribution was as a teacher. One colleague, Alvin Johnson, reported that his influence "upon the younger economists growing up around him was profound . . . the catholicity and generosity of Professor Seligman's approach to the works of other men influenced the whole current of economic discussion."

STATICS AND DYNAMICS: JOHN BATES CLARK'S IMPACT ON COLUMBIA ECONOMICS

Seligman attracted to Morningside Heights some of the country's most important economists, beginning with his friend John Bates Clark, whom he recruited from Amherst College in 1895. The most famous American economic theorist of his time and one of the most important Anglo-Saxon economic theorists of any time, Clark had already developed the neoclassical theory of income distribution in the 1880s. He demonstrated that under free competition and conditions of static equilibrium, productive inputs will be paid according to their individual contribution to output. "Where natural laws have their way," he wrote in *The Distribution of Wealth* (1899), "each productive function is paid for according to the amount of its product, then each man gets what he himself produces."

Clark's "marginal productivity" theory of distribution could lead to the very conservative conclusion that "[i]f wages, interest and profits, in themselves considered are fixed according to a sound principle, then the different classes of men who combine their forces in industry have no grievance against each other." But Clark was quick to acknowledge that his model was developed in total abstraction, by analyzing the static economic problem facing a kind of Robinson Crusoe living alone in an unchanging world, without history or any social intercourse. To be sure, this approach made Clark an odd companion to Seligman, and it explains why his type of theorizing had little impact at Columbia until decades after his death. His main contribution to Columbia's program in economics was his support of colleagues and students in their research into the limits of static competition, into collusion, monopoly, and economic dynamics. As America's premier economic theorist, he lent legitimacy to Columbia's growing band of institutionalists.

INSTITUTIONALISM AND WESLEY CLAIR MITCHELL

Clark withdrew from Columbia in 1910 to direct the History and Economics section of the Carnegie Endowment for International Peace. Once again charged with finding a department leader, Seligman found Wesley Clair Mitchell, the man who would set the pace for economics not only at Columbia but for the United States over the next forty years.

Mitchell was born in 1874 in the small Illinois town of Rushville; he attended the University of Chicago, planning to study classics. But he was distracted by courses in philosophy and in economics with John Dewey and Thorstein Veblen, iconoclasts who would influence Mitchell throughout his life. They led him to the social sciences as a way to effect and guide constructive social change. Mitchell received his Ph.D. and his first academic appointment from Chicago, from there moving on to the University of California at Berkeley, where he met his wife, Lucy Sprague Mitchell, Berkeley's first dean of women and founder of New York's Bank Street School of Education. He moved on to Columbia in 1914, where he remained (with one interruption in the early 1920s) until his retirement in 1944.

It was at Berkeley that Mitchell wrote *Business Cycles* (1913), a work that, according to the economist Arthur Burns, "marks an epoch of the business cycle . . . a landmark in the progress of inductive methods of economic study." Burns declared the book a masterpiece "in the world's economic literature . . . a landmark in the development of economics. No other work between Marshall's *Principles* and Keynes's *General Theory* has had as big an influence on the economic thought of the Western World."

Wesley Clair Mitchell

Business Cycles made innovative use of statistics and quantitative analysis to show how business cycles develop as cumulative and dynamic processes. Over the course of 600 pages, Mitchell relied on observation and data, consciously rejecting abstract theorizing. Economics, he explained, had made little progress because of its reliance on a "type of theory which has tried to progress by arbitrarily simplifying the problems and applying mathematical methods of analysis." Such methods, he continued, have produced "many formally correct results. . . . But I am not able to see that this work is a solution or even helps toward the solution of the problems which are of vital interest. It is a game of intellectual interest solely; and those who play it could have more fun with pure mathematics. My present inclination is to look for advancement along the line of more realistic study."

But Mitchell was never a naive empiricist. Instead, he cast his economic theory in a mold of evolutionary concepts focused on cumulative change. Economic affairs, like business cycles, should be understood as historical products because human behavior is governed by institutions and social values resulting from social change. In his famous Columbia graduate course Types of Economic Theories, Mitchell urged students to emulate natural scientists by using observations, experimental methods, and statistics but not to forget that, unlike the natural sciences, "economics deals with a subject matter that undergoes changes varying in pace and cumulative in character," without necessarily ever returning to any past equilibrium. The primary object of Mitchell's course, then, was "to help students to become better constructive workers by understanding more clearly the relation between cumulative economic changes and economic theory."

Mitchell never discounted the importance of individuals or individual rationality but stressed that individuals must be studied as social products. "Intelligence," Mitchell wrote in a critique of orthodox neoclassical utility theory, "is a social product developed in the individual through the exercise of his inherited propensities, and its special character depends upon the society into which the individual is born." As with Seligman, this approach made for reformist politics. If historically determined institutions shape economic behavior and cause poverty and unemployment, then society could choose different, better institutions. Mitchell's passion for social science research came from his deep concern for social reform. "We putter with philanthropy and coquette with reform," he complained to Lucy Sprague, "when we would fain find a definite method of realizing the demand for social justice which is so strong an element in human nature . . . and try to do what little we may to alleviate at retail the suffering and deprivation which our social organization creates at wholesale." He saw his research as a road map for constructive social reform: "What we need as a guide for all this expenditure of energy is sure knowledge of the causal interconnections between social phenomena."

In 1920, Mitchell joined Edwin Gay, dean of Harvard Business School; Malcolm Rorty, a statistician at AT&T; and N. I. Stone, a conservative socialist from the War Labor Board and the Brookings Institution, to form the National Bureau of Economic Research (NBER). The first NBER studies measured price levels, unemployment, and national income and its distribution. Solid, careful empirical studies with a minimum of open theorizing, these works were cast in Mitchell's mode and came to underpin the later explosion in macroeconomic research. By providing a neutral review body, Mitchell's NBER would insulate social science research from political controversy. Even more, it would promote social reform by providing a middle way between statist collectivism and laissez-faire individualism through the public exercise of private authority grounded in social science research.

Beyond his research, Mitchell shaped twentieth-century economics by personal example, balancing scholarship with respect for others working to advance empirical social science. These qualities allowed him to lead research projects extending far beyond his own work and encompassing many of the finest scholars of his time. Still, in the words of his colleague Alvin Johnson, "Wesley Mitchell by his own modest self constituted a great epoch in the economic thinking of our time."

THE NEW DEAL AND JOHN MAURICE CLARK

Seligman and Mitchell brought Columbia to preeminence among American economics departments. From 1904 to 1940, Columbia had twice as many graduate students as its orthodox neoclassical rival, Harvard, and its faculty and Ph.D.'s contributed more articles to the *American Economic Review*. Together, Mitchell and Seligman recruited a remarkable faculty, including Rexford Tugwell, Leo Wolman, Harold Hotelling, Carter Goodrich, Joseph Dorfman, Robert Hale, and John Maurice Clark.

When Tugwell went to New Deal Washington to join Columbia professors Adolf Berle and Raymond Moley in President Franklin Roosevelt's Brain Trust, he left behind the last of the great Columbia institutionalists, John Maurice Clark. Son of John Bates Clark, Maurice graduated from Amherst and earned his Ph.D. from Columbia in 1910. He began teaching at Columbia in 1926 and remained until his retirement in 1952.

As a child, John Maurice Clark learned statics from his father but sought "to proceed from static to dynamic economics," a study of "processes which do not visibly tend to any complete and definable static equilibrium." Maurice Clark showed that this was more than an intellectual problem. He would use dynamic economics to build a theory of economic institutions that would reincorporate ethics into economics.

Maurice Clark began with a dilemma. Economists distinguish between variable costs that depend on the amount of output and fixed, or "overhead," costs—such as rent, equipment, and management—that are independent of output. Maurice Clark observed that the growing use of machinery, financial capital, and professional management in early twentieth-century business increased overhead costs. In his classic 1923 volume *Studies in the Economics of Overhead Costs*, he demonstrated the implications of this finding for economic theory. Orthodox economists assume perfectly competitive markets in which producers will compete to sell their output at any price that covers the immediate costs of production. But when prices fall to marginal variable cost—the variable cost of producing one more unit of output— firms have no margin for their overhead costs. The orthodox assumption of competition will bankrupt firms with overhead costs under these conditions. Maurice Clark thus showed that firms survive only because they can charge prices above marginal variable costs, which occurs only in markets that are not perfectly competitive. He showed that monopoly and other noncompetitive markets are not exceptions but the norm; indeed, they are necessary for business survival in modern economic conditions.

As a matter of economic theory, "overhead costs" undermine the claim for a single static equilibrium price based on marginal variable costs. But if prices are not set in perfectly competitive markets, then we cannot assume any particular relationship between prices and variable costs. Maurice Clark noted that public utility regulators were ahead of economic theorists because they recognized overhead costs by allowing for prices above variable costs. But economists had not yet assimilated solutions like these into general models or established "any coherent principle" behind regulation policies.

Overhead costs are more than a problem for price theorists. Maurice Clark went further to demonstrate how overhead costs require a new approach to economic dynamics. The delineation of variable or overhead costs depends on laws, social conventions, and management strategies. Middle management or skilled labor, for example, can be counted as variable or overhead costs depending on policy and legal form. Here, Maurice Clark's work explicitly complements Mitchell's because his analysis of overhead costs showed the importance of the social institutions that determine prices, but which are ignored by narrowly individualist economic policies. "Costs that are 'direct' or 'variable' . . . from the standpoint of the employer," Maurice Clark argued, "are overhead costs from the point of view of society." "Every laborer," for example, "is his own 'overhead' and has his constant costs to meet whether he is working or not." Under slavery, these costs are borne by the enterprise; under free-labor capitalism they are borne by the workers whether or not they are employed. Labor costs vary with production under free-labor capitalism "because the terms of the wage contract are drawn in that way."

Thus, Maurice Clark uses a logical dilemma in price theory to overturn orthodox neoclassical microeconomics that ignores social institutions to conclude that perfect competition will lead to economic efficiency. "Overhead costs are seen to be a universal fact," he says, but who bears them and how they are allocated is socially determined, the product of a society's history and its politics. In practice, if never in name, Maurice Clark rejected his father's static equilibrium theory, replacing it with an economic model in which prices and distribution are determined in a dynamic process of social construction. "I have a theory of competition," Maurice Clark wrote Mitchell, "which argues that any fixed schematic laws must be misleading, because competition is an evolving thing." Complementing Mitchell's analysis of processes of cumulative change, Maurice Clark distinguishes his dynamic approach from the standard static equilibrium approach because his dynamism has no equilibrium point. "The distinguishing characteristics of economic forces of the supply and demand variety," Maurice Clark wrote, "as usually analyzed in economic theory, is that they are self-limiting." But "the business cycle shows unmistakably that the forces at work there are . . . self-reinforcing." Previous institutional theory, Maurice Clark argued, was static because it assumed that institutions smoothly adapt, taking the most efficient form to facilitate exchange and production. Instead, Maurice

Clark urged economists to recognize the independent standing of institutions, following the path of Seligman and Mitchell.

But evolutionary institutional economics also raises problems that the static view leaves out of sight. If institutions are important and malleable, then social scientists and other citizens must choose which institutions and which social groups they favor, "weighing the interests protected by one definition of rights as against the interests protected by another." Economists cannot, Maurice Clark argued, avoid ethical decisions. Here he completely abandons the conservative implications of his father's static theory and moves beyond even Mitchell's technocratic liberalism. The current treatment of overhead costs and unemployment, Maurice Clark warns, privileges machines over human labor. "The unemployment due to business fluctuations is, in its present form, unnecessary and fair social accounting would place a major part of the burden on industry, rather than all of it on those classes of labor least able to bear it successfully." He asks, "Is the argument here presented becoming dangerously socialistic?" That depends entirely on the reader's preconceptions. It does no more than make concrete a proposition that most people would admit at once in the abstract: namely, that there is waste and dislocation in private industry.

COLUMBIA AND THE DECLINE OF AMERICAN ECONOMICS

Supported by New Deal Washington, institutionalism dominated economics at Columbia after the 1930s. For a time, it was also well received in the broader economics profession. When the American Economic Association established the Francis A. Walker prize to be given every five years "to the living economist who . . . has during his career made the greatest contribution to economics," the first winner, in 1947, was Wesley Clair Mitchell; the second, in 1952, was John Maurice Clark. The Columbia tradition was also well recognized in the Nobel Prize in economic science. One of Mitchell's students Simon Kuznets was awarded the prize in 1971 for his "empirically founded interpretation of economic growth," and another Mitchell student Milton Friedman won the prize in 1976 for, among other work, his achievements in monetary history. Later winners included Robert Fogel, a Kuznets student (trained at Johns Hopkins), who shared the Prize with Douglass North in 1993 for "research in economic history" and use of quantitative methods "to explain economic and institutional change."

Columbia's institutionalist tradition was recognized again in 1996, when William Vickrey (Columbia's McVickar Professor of Political Economy) shared the Nobel Prize with Britain's James Mirrlees. Honored for his early work on the eco-

*William Vickrey,
1996 Nobel laureate.
The major work of his
later years followed
squarely in the
Mitchell tradition.*

nomic theory of incentives and asymmetric information, Vickrey did the major work of his later years—the economic study of institutions that influence the unemployment rate—squarely in the Mitchell tradition. Even as many other economists forsook past concerns, Vickrey continued to campaign to persuade governments to do more to reduce unemployment and devoted his research to studying how social institutions could be reorganized to reduce unemployment. Pursuing economic research designed to guide reform, Vickrey was a proper heir to Seligman, Mitchell, and the Clarks.

Kuznets, Fogel, and Vickrey notwithstanding, Columbia's emphasis on institutional history and the social determination of economic activity lost favor in the early 1950s. In an era of anti-Communist repression, some feared the reform agenda implicit in institutional economics. Perhaps equally important, economists were attracted to the mathematical elegance and definitive solutions offered by both neoclassical static theory and Keynesian economics. Even while sympathetic to much of John Maynard Keynes's work, Mitchell hoped that "our successors will attach a higher value to works that rest upon a fuller knowledge of actual conditions." But already in 1947, the American Economic Association passed over young Columbia-trained institutionalists like Mitchell's protégé Arthur Burns to award the new John Bates Clark prize—for the "American economist under the age of forty who is adjudged to have made a significant contribution to economic thought and knowledge"—to Paul Samuelson for his early mastery of both mathematics and economic theory. Mitchell, by contrast, was awarded the Francis A. Walker prize for his untiring labors as a master of the inductive method.

Perhaps institutionalism lost favor with economists because the empirical work was too hard, required too much modesty and acknowledgment of ignorance, and lacked any pretense of scientific precision in its answers. Institutionalist economists admit that their models cannot predict beyond current institutions and may not work so well even there. Calling on economists to admit that they cannot perfectly predict prices, Maurice Clark urged them to offer "bands" of possible prices. Worse, institutionalists like Mitchell and Maurice Clark urged economists to explore problems beyond their models' range, relying not on abstract mathematical models, but on the research of other social scientists, anthropologists, sociologists, and historians. Scientific economics, to Maurice Clark, "should be governed by the need for light rather than by the amenability of the materials to workmanlike manipulation." Economics was a science because of its empirical and experimental method rather than because of the rigid finality of its findings.

Sensitive to charges that his work lacked rigor and scientific validity because it did not give simple, definitive, and universal answers, Maurice Clark wrote Mitchell defensively that

> I have a theory of human nature which can't be used as a basis for deductive theorizing, because it includes too many various elements and leaves too much room for personal and group differences in values and behavior. But I had an idea that I spent a good deal of systematic thought in reaching that position. I also had an idea that it wasn't so very different from yours. And part of my systematic thought consists of methodological reasoning . . . and supports the conclusion that method represents the nearest thing to "scientific objectivity" in that matter which is humanly practicable.
>
> Anyhow, I hope sometime to be able to turn out a work that will be more systematic than this one.

This is the modesty, the humility that American economists rejected in renewing the search for simple, universal laws, turning inward to focus their mathematical tools on small, static problems. Narrowing their inquiry to individual behavior in circumstances of static equilibrium, Samuelson and his followers reached definitive answers but to trivial questions. Forsaking institutional studies, economists abandoned the pressing social questions that engaged Seligman, Mitchell, and John Maurice Clark. This has made Columbia's a lost tradition for the moment, but—let us hope—not for too long.

CHAPTER 30

Benjamin Graham:
Father of Value Investing

—ɯ—

Bruce C. Greenwald

Benjamin Graham's career is partly a story of connections between Columbia and New York City—in this case between a Columbia College graduate in mathematics and the dynamic financial markets for which the city has long been the world center.

Although Graham attributed much of his success in securities analysis to the liberal education he got in the College, it was his early employment in a New York investment firm that enabled him to learn the business firsthand and to develop the principles of investing by which he transformed a highly intuitive and speculative enterprise into something approaching a science. Subsequently, on the basis of this practical experience as well as his talent for identifying relevant, publicly available data, he was able to return to Columbia and incorporate his newly developed skills into formal academic instruction of the kind that attracted Warren Buffett in the early 1950s, at the onset of the latter's own amazing career as an investor. Indeed Buffett reversed the process of Graham's own development—from hands-on experience to academic instruction—by studying first under Graham and working as his assistant before launching his own famous investment firm.

Graham's legacy is captured here by one of his successors at the Graduate School of Business, Bruce C. Greenwald: "In this world of practical investment management, Graham's general contributions have been so completely absorbed that they are bred into the bone of basic investment practice." Greenwald, the Robert Heilbrunn Professor of Finance and Asset Management, has specialized in market mechanics, corporate finance, and managerial economics, and his current research centers on asymmetric information problems in equity pricing and value investing strategies. He teaches the core course Corporate Finance, the Elective Economics of Strategic Behavior, and an advanced seminar on value investing. Greenwald received the 1997 Margaret Chandler Award for Commitment to Excellence in teaching and in 2000 became the first professor from the Columbia Business School to win the university's Presidential Teaching Award.

—Wm. Theodore de Bary

—ɯ—

A brilliant investor and magnetic teacher, Benjamin Graham contributed more to the development of modern professional investment practices than any other single individual. He created an approach to analyzing securities that even today, seventy years after his pioneering work, is the basis for the success of a strikingly large fraction of outstanding investors.

The idea that business practices, even in agriculture, should be the object of professional study and continuous improvement is a surprisingly recent one. From Roman times until roughly 1800, there appears to have been no significant increase in economic productivity and hence no measurable improvement in average global standards of living. From 1800 to 1850, economic growth began at a relatively slow but steady pace in Europe and North America. Relatively rapid improvements in living standards only arrived in the latter half of the nineteenth century. Adjusting for inflation, the wages of American workers rose by about 70 percent in the forty years between 1850 and 1890, doubled between 1890 and 1930, and, despite the Depression, tripled between 1930 and 1970. Life expectancy over this period rose from forty-one to seventy years. Since 1970, modern standards of living have begun to spread beyond Europe and North America, most notably to Japan, China, India, and other parts of Asia.

Although scientific progress provided the basis for these changes, it is notable that the relevant developments in science preceded the rise in living standards by many years. The proximate cause of rising productivity appears to have been the systematic application of technology through sustained attention to improving business (including agricultural) practices. The acceleration in economic growth in the late nineteenth century coincided with the emergence of "scientific" management and its dissemination through universities and other institutions, like the Agricultural Extension Service in the United States.

Formal business education in the United States arrived in 1824, when James Gordon Bennett established his "Permanent Commercial School" in New York. He taught reading, elocution, penmanship, basic math and science, history, geography, and languages. Specific business training consisted of commercial law and political economy. Although Bennett's school soon disappeared, similar institutions flourished, producing notable graduates like Henry Ford (Detroit Business University), John D. Rockefeller (Dyke College of Cleveland), Thomas Watson (Elmira School of Commerce), and even Herbert Hoover (Capital College of Business, before Stanford).

Focused college-level business education did not arrive until 1881, when the University of Pennsylvania began to offer undergraduate business courses through its Wharton School, followed by the University of Chicago and the University of

California in 1898. Graduate business school courses were first available in 1900, when the Tuck School opened at Dartmouth. Harvard Business School was established in 1908, and Columbia Business School in 1916.

This latter period from the 1880s through the early 1900s also saw the developments of "scientific management" associated with Frederick W. Taylor. Taylor introduced systematic time-and-motion studies and other pioneering innovations at the Midvale Steel Company in the 1880s, doubling productivity within a decade. His approach, known as Taylorism, was widely disseminated, although controversial, throughout the 1890s. It led ultimately to a number of broadly based disciplines devoted to improvements in business operations, including statistical production control, organizational theory, linear programming, and other mathematically based optimization techniques.

However, when Benjamin Graham, aged seventeen, enrolled at Columbia in 1911, very little of this had penetrated the College curriculum. He majored in mathematics but took an eclectic mix of courses, notably in philosophy, foreign languages, and English (but not Latin, which Graham felt he had mastered sufficiently at Townsend Harris High School in New York). He did so well at Columbia that when he graduated in 1914, he was offered the opportunity to stay and teach not only mathematics but also, separately, English and philosophy.

Despite the strong appeal of an academic career, Graham took a job on Wall Street. This was partly a matter of economic necessity. Graham had worked steadily throughout his college years, providing an important source of income for the household of his widowed mother and brothers, and graduation did not relieve him of this financial responsibility. But the influence of Dean Frederick Keppel, who felt that educated Columbians had a great deal to offer America's important business institutions, also figured in Graham's decision. Keppel also helped arrange a job for Graham at the firm of Newberger, Henderson and Loeb as a bond salesman.

When Graham arrived on Wall Street in 1914, speculation was the dominant factor in securities markets. "In 1914, [the] mass of financial information [about companies] was largely going to waste." Graham wrote. "What counted most was inside information of various kinds, some of it relating to business operations . . . but more of it to the current activities and plans of market manipulators, the famous 'They' who were responsible for all significant moves, up and down."

Financial analysis of company operations was relatively rare, superficial, and largely limited to bonds rather than stocks. The available guidance for fledgling investors consisted chiefly of a standard text, *The Principles of Bond Investment*, by Laurence Chamberlain. Nothing like today's range of books, courses, and academic literature on investing existed.

*David Dodd,
Graham's collaborator
on the Security
Analysis course and
book of the same name*

What Graham did have increasingly available was published financial information on the companies whose securities were for sale. This was issued by the companies themselves and disseminated in standard formats by firms like Standard and Poor's. It was also reported to regulatory bodies, like the Interstate Commerce Commission, where it could be examined by the investing public, although few investors chose to do so. Graham, with his academic orientation, was naturally drawn to these data. His "school training had made (him) searching, reflective and critical," he recalled later, and that enabled him to "respond readily to the new forces that were beginning to enter the financial scene."

Graham began by looking at situations where the intrinsic value of a stock could be calculated with some precision. In 1915, the Guggenheim Exploration Company planned to dissolve and distribute its holdings to shareholders. These holdings consisted of shares in other copper mining companies, which, like Guggenheim shares, were quoted on the New York Stock Exchange. Graham calculated that the value of such non-Guggenheim shares held by Guggenheim exceeded the value of Guggenheim stock. As a result, buying Guggenheim represented an advantageous purchase of known assets—in Graham's terms an "investment," not a "speculation." Furthermore, by selling appropriate amounts of the shares of the constituent holdings (this could be done even if one did not currently own the stock, a practice known as "shorting") Graham could lock in this gain. When the Guggenheim Company dissolved and distributed the constituent shares, these shares could be delivered to satisfy the earlier purchases. The success of this operation contributed both to Graham's reputation and his emerging investment philosophy.

Graham developed methods for identifying the intrinsic value of the securities that he bought or sold. In the Guggenheim case, this was a matter of simple arithmetic. In other situations, Graham would examine in detail the individual assets on a company's published balance sheet, assigning values to them based on the accounting numbers. To cash, accounts receivable, and other current assets, he assigned values close to the officially published figures. To plant, equipment, and less tangible assets, he assigned conservative values below the published figures, using his carefully developed knowledge of the industry in question. From this asset value, he would subtract the full published value of liabilities to arrive at a "net" asset value. Then Graham would compare his calculated value for a company to the price at which it was selling in the stock market (the number of shares outstanding times the price per share). He found wide variations in the relationship between his calculated values and the market prices of essentially similar enterprises. Sometimes the stock market price of a company (e.g., a railroad) would exceed its calculated "net" asset value by two or more times. A similar company (e.g., another nearby railroad) would trade at half or less of its calculated value. Graham, of course, concentrated his stock (and bond) purchases on the latter companies with striking success.

Later Graham learned to cross-check these asset-based valuations with valuations derived from a company's potential earnings. Thus, he not only looked at whether a company's assets could be acquired in the stock market at a discount, but also verified that the returns these assets were likely to earn in the future justified his basic judgment of intrinsic value. For example, if Graham thought a company's net assets were worth $8 million and an appropriate return on those assets was 10 percent (based on what investors were earning in other comparable investments), then he looked at the company's published income statements to verify that future earnings were likely to exceed $800,000 per annum.

If the earnings picture satisfied this criterion, then when the company was selling in the stock market for $4 million (e.g., one million shares outstanding at $4 per share), Graham would buy its stock with redoubled confidence. Graham's basic approach was to look at the underlying economic reality and assiduously collect the relevant information from as many perspectives as possible. It was a natural outgrowth of his broad and rigorous education at Columbia.

The wonder of all this was that such a commonsensical approach should be so revolutionary. But as Graham noted, market prices of stocks were anything but rationally determined. In a memorable passage he wrote,

> Imagine that in some private business you own a small share. One of your partners, named Mr. Market, is very obliging. Everyday he tells you what he thinks your interest is worth and offers either to buy you out or to sell to you an additional interest on that basis. Sometimes his idea of value appears plausible. Often, on the other hand, Mr. Market lets his enthusiasm or his fears run away with him and the value he proposes seems to you a little short of silly. If you are a prudent investor will you let Mr. Market's daily communication determine your view of

the value of the enterprise? You may be happy to sell out to him when he quotes a ridiculously high price and equally happy to buy from him when his price is low. But the rest of the time you will be wiser to value your holdings based on full reports from the company about its operations and financial position.

In financial markets, where speculative fever dominated investor behavior, the benefits of Graham's scientific approach were manifest.

One of the earliest beneficiaries was Graham himself and not just in his personal investments. Graham embodied his insights in written reports to investors that circulated on Wall Street. One such report on the Missouri Pacific Railroad reached a partner at J. S. Bache soon after Graham's arrival at Newberger. Impressed by this work, Bache offered Graham a job in the "statistical" department at $18 per week, a 50 percent increase over his salary as a rookie bond salesman. In response, Newberger offered Graham a raise to $15 per week and the opportunity to establish a "statistical" department at the firm specializing in Graham's new approach to investment analysis. Graham gratefully accepted this counteroffer, beginning what he describes as his "real and definitive career as a security analyst." He later learned that if he had gone to Bache, Newberger would have resolved never to hire another "college man."

By the beginning of 1920, Graham had become a junior partner at Newberger, Henderson and Loeb. He had expanded the statistical department, now known as the "research" department, to include an assistant, another Columbia graduate two years his junior. In addition, he had achieved a significant reputation as an investor and was managing discretionary accounts for family, friends, and favored customers.

However, all this activity failed to occupy Graham fully. In 1917, he had become a partner in a phonograph shop with his brother, had trained actively with the U.S. Army Reserve in the hope of participating in World War I, and had published an article in the *American Mathematical Monthly*. In 1918, he began a flourishing career as a financial writer, contributing technical material regularly to the *Magazine of Wall Street*, at the time a leading financial publication.

In 1923, Graham left Newberger to work for a series of financial partnerships in which he received a share of the profits for managing contributed funds. These efforts culminated in 1926 in a partnership with Jerome Newman (a graduate of both Columbia College and the Law School) in what subsequently became the Graham-Newman Corporation, where he worked until his retirement until 1956. During this period, while accumulating substantial personal wealth, Graham remained dedicated to the task of professionalizing investment practices. In the fall of 1927, he taught a course called "Security Analysis" at the Extension Division of Columbia. It was heavily oversubscribed, including an assistant professor at Columbia Business School named David Dodd. Beginning in the fall of 1928, Graham and Dodd offered Security Analysis together at the Columbia Business School. Taught continuously until 1954, the course was enormously popular, spawning the book *Security Analysis* (1934) by Graham and Dodd.

Security Analysis was Graham's masterpiece. There were four more editions, in 1940, 1951, 1962, and 1988. Copies of the first edition now sell for up to $20,000. Still in print today, it remains an important text for modern investment analysts. The book articulated the basic approach to security valuation and investment decisions developed by Graham with Dodd's help. As important, it showed with constantly updated examples how those principles could be applied by creatively seeking and systematically analyzing relevant company data. Together, the book and the course trained generations of remarkable investors whose loyalty to Graham's ideas and subsequent investment success constitute a major part of his legacy. The list is led by Warren Buffett, the most successful investor in financial history, who was drawn to Columbia by Graham's book, took Graham's course in the early 1950s, and later worked for Graham before establishing his own notable investment partnership. Other investors on the list are Walter Schloss, Irving Kahn, William Ruane, Charles Munger, David "Sandy" Gottesman, Tom Knapp, Robert Heilbrunn, Ed Anderson, Jack Alexander, and Max Heine, all of whom were either direct disciples of Graham's or became closely connected to him after reading *Security Analysis*. Later generations of Graham and Dodd investors, including Mario Gabelli, Charles Royce, Robert Bruce, John Neff, Michael Price, and Seth Klarman, either were students of Roger Murray, Graham and Dodd's successor at Columbia and coauthor of a later edition of *Security Analysis*, or were influenced strongly by Graham's writings. Their extraordinary record of investment success over decades (in defiance of the laws of simple probability) is an enduring tribute to the value of Graham's work.

On the heels of the publication of *Security Analysis*, Graham was a major force behind the formation of the New York Society of Security Analysts (NYSSA). Established in 1935 by an informal group of like-minded investment research analysts, the society was dedicated to the development of professional standards in security research and investment practices. To that end, Graham proposed in 1942 that a board of qualifiers of the NYSSA certify financial analysts who met prescribed requirements. This proposal was later adopted by the Institute of Chartered Financial Analysts (another group Graham nurtured) and survives today as the widely respected CFA certification process. Graham was also an important early contributor to the *Financial Analyst's Journal* (then called the *Analyst's Journal*), which is still a respected vehicle for disseminating financial and security analysis research. The current organizational structure of the modern financial analysis profession owes an enormous debt to Graham.

In 1949, urged to produce a book for serious nonprofessional investors, Graham wrote *The Intelligent Investor*, his best-known work. Reissued in 1954, 1959, and 1973 editions, *The Intelligent Investor* more than fifty years after its initial publication is still one of the best-selling books for serious investors. Graham had a gift not only for clear thinking but also for effective exposition. With its distinction between investing and speculating, its use of comparative investment choices to clarify the underlying concept of intrinsic value, its focus on controlling risk by seeking a margin of safety between price and value, and its compelling metaphor of Mr. Market (see above), *The Intelligent Investor* is a classic of financial exposition. As a description of sound investment practices for nonprofessionals, the book has rarely, if ever, been equaled. Recently reissued in a fifth edition, it continues to sell over 30,000 copies per year.

Graham's career was not limited to Wall Street. After his formal retirement in 1956 and move to California, he taught for fifteen years as a Regents professor at UCLA's business school. He was a continuing source of advice to his former students. In 1968, at the initiative of Warren Buffett, who was troubled by contemporary stock market conditions, a distinguished group met with Graham (then seventy-four years old) in San Diego to seek his advice. The experience was so valuable that the group continued to meet with Graham on a regular basis until the end of his life. Graham also enjoyed a distinguished career as an expert consultant on economic and financial matters that ran parallel to his career in investments. In 1937, he published *Storage and Stability*, which presented an innovative system of general commodity (as opposed to gold and silver) backing for U.S. currency. Graham's proposal, which he advocated further in *World Commodities and World Currency* (1944), was never adopted but received respectful attention from the economic policy community. Finally, Graham wrote a number of plays; one of them, *Baby Pompadour*, opened on Broadway in December 1934 (it closed after four performances). Graham attributed the breadth of his interests in great measure to his Columbia education.

After Graham's death in 1976 at the age of eighty-two, his approach to investment analysis was for a time eclipsed by modern portfolio theory, which emphasized the unpredictability of individual stock returns. However, more recent statistical work on stock price behavior in the United States and around the world has tended to confirm his original insights, contrary to academic orthodoxy. And applications

of behavioral psychology to economic decision making, for which Daniel Kahneman won the Nobel Prize in 2002, have provided strong support for Graham's approach. The behavioral finance literature offers an explanation of the mystery of why all investors don't follow an approach like Graham's, with simple statistical decision rules that would outperform portfolios constructed by 95 percent of investment professionals, a rate verified by worldwide, long-term statistical studies. The reason may be that deep-seated psychological drives rule investors' decisions, overriding financial fundamentals.

In the world of practical investment management, Graham's general contributions have been so completely absorbed that they are bred into the bone of basic investment practice. At the same time, his more particular followers who practice "Graham-and-Dodd-style value investing" continue to perform significantly better than average investors.

Even after retirement, Graham was a continuing source of advice to his former students, including Warren Buffett.

CHAPTER 31

Eli Ginzberg: Skeptical Economist, Conservator of Manpower

—₪—

James W. Kuhn

I first learned of Eli Ginzberg's reputation as a maverick economist and public figure in Washington, D.C., in 1949, at the start of my faculty career. It was only later that I learned of his collegial other side—his readiness as a loyal Columbia graduate to join the messy political struggle needed to save the university when it came under siege in 1968. He volunteered to serve on the Executive Committee of the Faculty, which eventually brought some semblance of order and authority to the campus. It was there that I first met this legendary figure and came to appreciate him in his less spectacular role as a dedicated citizen of the university community, who endured long hours of committee meetings, political harangues, and negotiations to help save the day for Columbia.

This episode does not figure in James Kuhn's tribute to Eli Ginzberg's professional career. But no one is in a better position than Professor Kuhn, a close associate of Ginzberg for nearly half a century, to tell his story. Now Courtney Brown Professor Emeritus in the Graduate School of Business, Kuhn served as a staff associate in Ginzberg's Conservation of Human Resources program from 1966 to 1976. He was vice dean of the Business School from 1974 to 1976 and director of its business ethics program from 1989 to 1995. Nationally he has served as a senior staff economist on the Council of Economic Advisers (1968–69). Among his many books are Beyond Success: Business and Its Critics in the Nineties *(1991, with Donald W. Shriver) and* Values in a Business Society: Principles and Issues *(1968, with Ivar E. Berg).*

—Wm. Theodore de Bary

—₪—

Ginzberg (center) with the 1997–1998 Revson Fellows. The Charles H. Revson Fellowship, for which Ginzberg served as director from 1979 to 2002, assists urban leaders who have made a substantial contribution to New York City.

Eli Ginzberg once confessed that he had a lifelong "love affair" with New York City, his home for all of his ninety-one-plus years. He enjoyed its excitement, its continually changing population, and vibrant cultures. Though both his parents were immigrants and religious, he said he always "felt totally at home on its streets and subways and in its schools." In its brash and confident nature, he recognized his own. In 1934 Wesley Clair Mitchell offered to recommend him for an assistant professorship at the University of Wisconsin, working with the famed John R. Commons. During a yearlong trip around the United States, he stopped by Madison. Years later he said, "I wouldn't have been happy there. It was way out in the sticks, where from the college campus you could see cows grazing."

He had already decided that, even without immediate job prospects, Columbia "would at least in theory provide me with an ideal working environment." His keen, wide-ranging intellect contrasted with his parochial geographical preferences, which were "not so much New York as Manhattan; not so much Manhattan as the West Side; not so much the West Side as Washington Heights during my youth and Morningside Heights during most of my adulthood."

Ginzberg recognized that both of his parents, in different ways, greatly influenced his style of life and approach to his scholarly work. At the time of Eli's birth, in 1911, his father, Louis, was already a preeminent Jewish scholar in both the United States and Europe. While the intricacies of Judaica did not appeal to him, Ginzberg learned from the paternal example that deep satisfaction in work depended upon using one's time effectively. Many years later, he admitted that though he had pursued an area of expertise distant from his father's, "I have probably been competing in terms of scholarly output these many decades."

From his mother, Adele, he learned that one did not need to respect authority or convention. She went her own way and spoke her mind, not caring whether family, friends, or strangers thought her too brash. Ginzberg went his own way too, always challenging accepted economic doctrines. His mother was not an intellectual but an activist. In later years, when he presented her with inscribed copies of one book or study after another, she always asked whether it would "be of any use or help to those who need to be helped . . . [Why would anybody] spend the time and effort required to write a book unless it could do somebody else some good?" Ginzberg recognized that he owed his "policy orientation—which has dominated my work— to my mother, who always sought to make the world a little better."

Too bright to be challenged by the first six years of public school, Ginzberg attended an accelerated junior high school. There he showed ability in his "reading" classes, but not particularly in mathematics, science, or foreign languages.

Nevertheless, he had already decided that he would attend Columbia. Despite quotas for Jewish students from the New York area, he easily gained admission. As a volunteer subject, he had become an expert test-taker in Professor E. L. Thorndike's testing laboratory at Teachers College. In the admissions tests he ranked at the mean level of the second-year class at the Yale Law School! Some of his later skepticism about "objective" selection techniques in hiring "the best" candidate may have originated in this experience.

A precocious student, he earned his B.A. at twenty and his Ph.D. three years later, in 1934. His teachers already were or would soon become outstanding economists: Wesley C. Mitchell, John Maurice Clark, Fred C. Mills, and Arthur F. Burns. An important course for Ginzberg was Mitchell's Current Types of Economic Theory, which encouraged students to examine the historical setting and doctrinal background of the eighteenth- and nineteenth-century economists. They began with Adam Smith and the sociopolitical issues that shaped *The Wealth of Nations*. Much later Ginzberg recalled

> I could not possibly reconstruct the sense of excitement that I experienced as I read [the book] for the first time. Nor could I reconstruct the intensity of my feelings as I saw the possibility of correcting a major historic misinterpretation and revealing Adam Smith for what he was, a liberal reformer, instead of as so many wished him to be, a rigid defender of free enterprise.

Conventional economic analysis, as presented in 1930s textbooks and taught in Eli's classes, explained the unprecedented Depression that had befallen the United States and other advanced countries by focusing on markets and their presumed equilibrating influence through supply and demand. Ginzberg found such explanatory variables too simple to explain the complex causes of economic failure. Smith's close examination of wealth creation offered him a far more congenial and compelling analysis.

Not surprisingly, he chose to reexamine Smith's *The Wealth of Nations* in his doctoral dissertation. He was impressed that Smith described the key to a nation's wealth as the

> "skill, dexterity and judgment with which its labour is generally applied." He then includes in his analysis not only the market forces that influence the demand and supply of labor, but also the circumstances that govern the development of skill, the institutions that

facilitate or retard the proper distribution of the labor force, the manner in which the values that people hold help to determine the investments which they make in the training of their children, and a great many other aspects of the complex process involved in the development and utilization of human resources.

Smith's approach to economics would become Eli's own, not only the focus on human resources and the preference for empirical observation—in all its complexity and ambiguity—over theory, but also the habit of evaluating policies by their contributions to people's lives, a natural preoccupation for Smith, who was best known during his lifetime as a moral philosopher. These elements are present in the published version of Eli's dissertation, *The House of Adam Smith*, some of whose characterizations of Smith may be taken as Eli's maxims, guiding his own future research:

> Adam Smith did not preach the doctrine of economic freedom for its own sake; he was much too critical of fanatics to be guilty of any fanaticism himself.
>
> Smith did not object to the interference of the state with certain economic forces and, in the case of labor argued strongly in favor of such action. In his opinion, public interest could best be served by the education of the populace, and he proposed the use of public monies for this purpose.
>
> Life interested this man [Adam Smith].
>
> Smith was interested in production in a dynamic society, [while mainline economics is] . . . full of intricate and delicate analyses of many and difficult problems, but the historical, sociological, and political discussions which fill the *Wealth of Nations* are missing.
>
> The classical economists made the great mistake of undertaking investigations at a specific time, within a specific cultural scheme, and projecting their results until they became independent of both time and place. This approach enabled them to disregard the prospects of institutional change and hence to avoid the moralistic implications of Scottish economics.
>
> *The Wealth of Nations* is permeated with the view that all economic analysis must be concerned with the benefit or harm which the public derives from the institutional structure . . . a preoccupation with the public welfare.

Throughout his career Ginzberg retained his esteem for Adam Smith. Toward the end, in his memoir *The Eye of Illusion* (1993), he predicted that Smith, alone among economists with major reputations, would retain his standing in the twenty-first century, adding, "But young economists earn their doctorates these days without ever having read a single page of *Wealth of Nations.*"

During a postdoctoral year as a Cutting Travel Fellow, Ginzberg decided to see America and set out on a cross-country automobile trip to examine the impact of the Depression firsthand, in the spirit of Adam Smith. He questioned corporate executives, managers, and workers to find how they were responding to their practical daily problems—particularly the effects of declining production and massive unemployment. Contrary to the common assumption of economists at the time that the market would impose a rational order on pay scales across an industry, Ginzberg found that higher-paid workers—or employers—were not necessarily more able than the lower-paid. Throughout corporate ranks, only a few were brilliant, many were smart, some were dull and even stupid. He concluded that

> If economists see their task as figuring out what is happening in the production and distribution of goods and services, I cannot imagine why they spend almost all of their time reading, criticizing, and extending the work of their colleagues rather than directing more effort to becoming better acquainted with the decision-making processes of the world of business.

Starting in 1935, while working on his analysis of the data gathered during his trip, he was also in the classroom, testing his talents as an instructor in the Business School. He probably approached his first courses much as he did in later years, "once over lightly." Self-confident, articulate and drawing freely on his wide reading and acute personal observations of "how things actually work," he lectured fluently without extensive preparation. He seldom examined his students but required term papers, which he read closely but quickly. In later years, he often assigned term papers to trusted staff members to grade. He declared that he enjoyed teaching, and he must have, for he never took a sabbatical and once calculated that he taught each semester for fifty-three years, with a total enrollment of about 10,000. He taught his last class December 3, 2002, a week before his death at the age of ninety-one and a half.

A colleague, reading Eli's autobiography, notes that he never described the courses he taught. What he offered was essentially "Ginzberg's economics." He respected but displayed little allegiance to the courses or curricula of his colleagues. Many found him a challenging teacher, but some complained that they learned little in the way of "hard" theory. Instead he offered no more than rules of thumb. Though he did not dismiss analytic techniques, he maintained that "scholarly refinements in methodology far outdistance the pool of relevant information we need about how the economy and society operate. We need alternative models, beyond Adam Smith's great contribution of the efficiency of the competitive market." He was willing to use his talents to search for the secrets of the unknown and to give students a vision of possible improvements in the operations of the economy and the society. Of course, he knew that in such an endeavor "the odds of failing far outdistance the likelihood of success." But they did not dissuade him. Like other creative researchers, he was still able, over his long career, to spend much of his time on his other activities, creating for himself a new, emerging role—the entrepreneurial professor.

In 1935, he did not yet understand the kind of researcher he would become; he was taking his first step in pragmatic policy analysis. With a grant from the University Council for Research in the Social Sciences, he could devote most of his time to making sense of the complex empirical data he had gathered during his fellowship—a task for which he found his doctoral studies had not prepared him. Wrestling with, categorizing, and giving shape to the wealth of data, impressions, and undigested stories proved more difficult and time-consuming than he had appreciated. So did the work of creating a rigorous analytic framework that would allow convincing confirmation of a thesis. These lessons, requiring four years of hard work, resulted in the book *The Illusion of Economic Stability* (1939).

Ginzberg read Keynes's *General Theory of Employment, Interest, and Money* (1936) but rejected its explanation of the economic collapse and his remedy of compensatory government spending. Keynes "sought to explain too much, too simply," Ginzberg wrote. "Movements of the economy were in my opinion more than epiphenomena and were rooted in such real factors as the size and competencies of the labor force, industrial capacity, and the speed and direction of technological change." His firsthand interviews with business managers had convinced him that markets were inherently unstable as technology, institutions, social behavior, and values waxed and waned. The self-regulating marketplace was always in peril, subject to manipulation by the powerful and needing government intervention. Eras of boom might be labeled "New Eras," but if they were based on financial speculating that fed on itself, depression was sure to follow, though timing depended upon chance.

Eli's first research study did not receive public acclaim, but taught him valuable lessons. It showed him that economic policies should

Ginzberg (center) with Columbia colleagues, circa 1950

seek equity; that a self-regulatory economy is an oxymoron; that government played a critical role in regulating the economy and the society; that racism was an unsolved problem; that our continental dimensions had an important impact; and finally that we could no longer be an island unto ourselves, if ever we had been—these were the convictions that I held in 1939, when my initial learning years came to an end.

Ginzberg found great satisfaction in completing the first of his empirical studies. Ever after, he declared, the fitting closure to all his varied research projects was first to commit his ideas to paper and then to publish them. He had this experience eighty-four times, according to *Who's Who,* and colleagues have estimated that a complete list of his published books would be larger by at least a fifth.

The next project, prompted by a suggestion from Eli's mentor Wesley Clair Mitchell, was a three-part study of unemployment, starting with the responses of workers of different religious and ethnic groups in New York City. The second part focused on labor mobility in South Wales and the third on the new role of labor leaders as social activists. Unfortunately for the project, the first two unemployment studies were published in the midst of World War II, when the problem was no longer a shortage of jobs, but of workers.[1] Nevertheless, Eli Ginzberg was gaining a reputation in manpower studies, with a pioneering approach based on the conviction that interdisciplinary research, using the insights of both psychology and economics, could explain more of the intricacies of labor markets than economic analysis alone.

After the declaration of war in December 1941, the military needed manpower experts as it began to mobilize millions of volunteers and draftees for the Armed Forces. In September 1942, Ginzberg reported for duty in Washington, D.C., as a civilian, a status he maintained throughout the war. His first assignment was to the Control Division, Services of Supply (SOS). Later it became the Army Service Forces (ASF)—the largest organization ever put together in the United States, with some 2 million military and civilian employees—twice the size of AT&T at its peak. During his four years in the federal government, Ginzberg learned, firsthand, the skills and strategies of working within huge bureaucracies. Assigned to work on the manpower aspects of the Army's health and medical problems, he could hardly have realized at the time how much his hectic experience in the wartime Pentagon would enable him to contribute later to the shaping of public policies on one of the largest sectors in the American economy.

He learned fast. His first assignment was to recommend reforms in the organization's planning and execution of its personnel missions. After three weeks of intensive research, he submitted a forty-page report. The commanding officer, Major General Clinton F. Robinson, returned it with such comments as "ridiculous!" "stupid!" or "impossible!" on almost every page. Shocked, Ginzberg realized that he had

> failed to take account of the political elements in the equation: namely,
> the time and other costs involved in altering the existing organizations;
> the risks attached to putting reforms in place and finding that many of
> them worked no better than the systems they had superseded; and still
> other basics that I had overlooked or minimized.

His academic perspective had ignored the practical realities of operating in a large bureaucracy. His reports after this harsh lesson recommended only changes that the commander could implement, with reasonable promise of improving outcomes. Robinson found him, thereafter, a useful and valued analyst. It was a lesson

Ginzberg would apply to all subsequent policy recommendations.

He learned as well that numbers can be slippery, hardly objective indicators of the real state of affairs. He learned, for example, that though Congress had set manpower limits of 7.7 million, the sum total of all men and women already inducted was 8.3 million, about 9 percent above the ceiling. Though the excess enlistments entailed billions of dollars of costs, the Army was more concerned about the need to retain all personnel already in service. The commanding staff knew that soon enough it would need even more personnel but did not want to be called to task by Congress. General Robinson told Ginzberg to devise a reconciliation between the facts and the Congressional ceiling. Ginzberg set to work:

> I knew, without having to be told, that the Army had no intention of reducing its numbers by 600,000 not many months before launching the invasion of Europe. My solution postulated that the congressional ceiling referred to 7.7 million active duty soldiers. Accordingly I developed a sufficient number of categories of inactive soldiers—in basic training, in hospitals, in transit, in confinement—to account for the 600,000 overage.

No member of Congress ever detected the sleight of hand.

Eli's monthly analytical reports of personnel use in various departments and technical services highlighted both over- and under-performers. The standout in the latter category was the Medical Department. After several such reports, General Raymond Bliss, assistant surgeon general in charge of Medical's operations, tracked down the author to discuss the matter. He then sent Ginzberg on a tour of selected hospitals across the country. Ginzberg found that personnel use was even worse than the data had revealed. Thereupon, Bliss assigned Ginzberg to design a new organizational structure to ensure more effective control from Washington.

Pleased with Ginzberg's proposal for a new control division, Bliss offered him the directorship. He accepted the challenge, but not without maintaining his ties to the existing Control Division until he was sure that he would be allowed to set up the new division as he wished. He selected an expert staff of about twenty but ran afoul of bureaucratic rules of the Civil Service Commission, which would not approve the new division unless his three highly paid top appointees supervised not just twenty, but seventy or eighty subordinates. For the first time in his career, Ginzberg threatened to take the matter to the press, laying the blame for inadequate facilities for battle casualties at the door of the Commission. The threat worked and for the rest of the war, he directed the Resources Analysis Division for the Surgeon General's Office with the small staff of his own choosing.

Manpower planning, he found, was both chancy and difficult. For example, before the invasion of Europe (D-day), his division was asked to prepare hospital facilities to handle battle casualties. Resources Analysis predicted 181,000 patients in available general hospitals by day D + 6, a forecast that turned out to be only a thousand patients off. But on checking further, Ginzberg found that the staff had seriously *overestimated* casualty rates while grossly *underestimating* the lengths of hospital stays. By luck, the two errors had compensated for each other.

His wartime experience revealed to Ginzberg how political pressures affect medical and health policies. Through the early months of 1945, he testified before congressional committees, defending the reluctance of the surgeon general—Norman Kirk—to demobilize military doctors. With the European war coming to an end, Resources Analysis estimated that the surgeon general would need enough doctors to handle 500,000 serious casualties in the first month after an expected invasion of the Japanese home islands.

But political forces had been set in motion by a public expecting a quick end to the war. With 40 percent of all doctors in the country commissioned, many rural communities had managed with no (or few) doctors during the war and now demanded the immediate return of doctors who had accumulated enough "service points." The surgeon general understood the popular desire "to get their doctors back," but he knew from reliable health indices that the booming war economy, with its higher incomes, over-full employment, ample food, and good morale had significantly improved general civilian health during the war years—far more than additional visits to physicians could have accomplished. One intemperate congressman from Michigan rejected this argument and conducted a bitter, browbeating altercation with Eli. The surgeon general concluded that he could not ignore such public feelings and changed his policy. As it turned out, the swift end to the Pacific war reduced the need for medical personnel. The demobilization of doctors proceeded.

With the war's end in both Europe and the Pacific, Ginzberg was asked to prepare his division for the transition to peace. In May 1946 he carried out his last wartime task, representing the United States, on behalf of the Department of State, at the Five-Power Conference on Reparations for Non-Repatriable Refugees. His return in June marked the end of a hitch of three years and ten months of full-time work with the military.

Back at Columbia, Ginzberg resumed his research. By the late forties he had published the study of new labor leaders that he had begun before the war. Drawing upon his experience with the Surgeon General's Office, he wrote and published *A Pattern for Hospital Care* (1949). Returning to another subject he had studied before the war, he produced *Occupational Choice: An Approach to a General Theory* (1951). He considered it a breakthrough work, providing a theoretical structure for the messy and confused field of vocational guidance. The study suggested that the process of "choosing" may extend over many years, from the preteens, when people first begin to recognize their interests, through the maturing years, as they discover the limits of their capacities and constraints of their interests and values. Further, the researchers found that people are also guided by objective realities, such as the years of affordable and/or desired education.

In early 1947 Major General Howard Snyder, who became Dwight D. Eisenhower's personal physician and who as Assistant Inspector General (Medical) had worked with Ginzberg during the war, arranged a luncheon at the Pentagon with Eisenhower, to whom the Columbia University trustees had offered the presidency. Eisenhower had been mulling over problems that had arisen during the nation's mobilization of young people for wartime training and service and wanted to find out why, of the 18 million youths examined, nearly a tenth (1.75 million) were rejected for service or prematurely separated during the war. The causes and remedies of such a waste, he thought, would be useful information to the nation, particularly its military and business leaders. Snyder urged Eisenhower to discuss these issues with Eli, who responded warmly.

After the General's arrival on Morningside Heights on May 2, 1948, Ginzberg recalled, "I saw him at least twice a week, frequently for an hour and a half or two hours in his office." Eisenhower asked Ginzberg to draft a research proposal and then helped raise funds for an initial multiyear study. Ginzberg prepared a research agenda, entitled *Adjustment to Work*, with a strategy for financing; Eisenhower contributed many emendations, corrections, and suggestions. He noted, for example, that Ginzberg had not consulted with any labor leaders. The omission was quickly remedied.

Walter Reuther, the able, prominent leader of the United Auto Workers, commented on the draft that he found the project's title carried with it a manipulative connotation, unsuited to a project studying human beings. Ginzberg took the point and searched for another title:

> At the time, I was reading a book about Theodore Roosevelt and discovered that while he was a great advocate of conserving the nation's natural resources, his original formulation encompassed both human and natural resources. Accordingly I suggested to Eisenhower that we

use Roosevelt's term, the Conservation of Human Resources, which he accepted.

Within a few months, the renamed Conservation of Human Resources project gathered a number of corporate sponsors. Rowan Gaither, on behalf of the Ford Foundation, asked if the university would sponsor and direct a "National Manpower Council, with a distinguished national membership." It would conduct studies of "priority manpower problems and report to the public on how they might best be resolved." President Eisenhower approved the university's responsibility for the Council, and Ginzberg agreed not only to chair the NMC but also to direct the CHR.

Under Dean Philip Young, Columbia's Business School had assumed administrative responsibility for both the NMC and the CHR. Ginzberg was by now a regular faculty member, and the dean found both research groups compatible with the School's mission and services. However, Eisenhower left Columbia in 1953, and Young left with him. The new dean, Courtney C. Brown, quickly became unhappy with the CHR and the NMC. First, he had no direct control over either, and second, he believed their fund-raising competed with his own efforts. Ginzberg persuaded John A. Krout, the provost, to assume administrative responsibility for the two projects, enabling Ginzberg to operate autonomously within the university. Looking back in 1993, he characterized his management of CHR as "a benign dictatorship, in which for decades I exercised sole responsibility and raised all the required funding."

Through the 1950s, Ginzberg and his CHR researchers pursued the Eisenhower-initiated studies of wartime uses of manpower. Constructing a database of more than 70,000 soldiers from the records of the Selective Service System, the Armed Forces, and the Veterans Administration, they published their findings in 1959 as a three-volume work, *The Ineffective Soldier: Lessons for Management and the Nation*.[2]

The studies revealed that Army personnel policies varied widely, sometimes rejecting capable servicemen and at other periods retaining totally unfit persons. Professional specialists, such as psychiatrists, often went "far beyond their knowledge base and recommended rejection or premature separations" to accommodate "strong preferences of the military." Personal capabilities vary, not only among people, but also over time. "Many recruits," they concluded, "did better or worse than their earlier records suggested," partly because most people are remarkably adaptable and trainable. For example, the 300,000 illiterates accepted for service in World War II performed satisfactorily (based on their records) after up to ninety days of remedial education. Selection processes might, thus, wisely be designed to consider such obvious and "knowable" guides as the ability to hold a job, stay out of trouble with the criminal justice system, marry, and support dependents. Obviously government could help by enhancing the educational system. Illiteracy and poor schooling in an economy based on ever more advanced technology would impose ever higher costs on society. The research suggested that wise manpower policies required both public and private programs to offer second-choice opportunities for the young who encounter displacement or difficulties in finding a place in the world of work. The study's conclusions were hardly surprising or pathbreaking, offering sensible, practical approaches to managing human resources.

Ginzberg and the CHR researchers also published five other studies during the 1950s, all of which appeared before *The Ineffective Soldier*.[3] The most important was *The Negro Potential* (1955), which presented new data about the performance of black men in both military and civilian life. It highlighted the high costs of continuing segregation and discrimination not only for the men themselves and the black community, but for all sectors of American life. Advances would come only with "more and better schooling."

Ginzberg later remarked that "even with President Eisenhower's interest and support our carefully crafted research effort . . . as well as related efforts in military manpower research, never made much of a mark on the Pentagon." On the other hand, he reported to Dr. Howard Snyder in mid-1957 that while "it is very difficult for me to assess the cumulative impact of our work to date on business . . . there is evidence to show that . . . we have opened up some new ways of thinking and acting with respect to the human resource factor." CHR had also called attention to the importance of industry's dipping down into the noncollege group, where much talent resides, and pointed out how managers, in effectively using "Negroes, women and . . . [the] handicapped," act to their own advantage and contribute to "American democracy by broadening opportunities for the individual citizen." As early as the mid-1950s the CHR staff also examined the problems of working women and returned to this theme in *Educated American Women: Self Portraits* (1966). Asked to summarize the book's message, Ginzberg tartly replied, "American industry operates on the principle that it prefers dumb men to smart women."

Over the last thirty years of Ginzberg's research, CHR's manpower studies challenged the conventional two-sector model of the American economy—the private, for-profit sector and the government. Ginzberg insisted on the importance of a growing nonprofit sector, accurately predicting in the mid-1960s that nonprofit employment at the turn of the twenty-first century would account for more than a third of the total, led by health and medical services.[4] Ginzberg and his collaborators focused more and more on the need for informed policies both in the uses of human resources and the delivery of medical aid to those in need.

CHR's studies were evidently widely read by doctors and hospital administrators. Of some 900 citations of Eli's published works since 1965, about 90 percent were in medical and public health journals and books. His major findings were, first, that "the competitive market model could not be relied upon for efficient resource allocation or policy guidance"; second, that "many of the poor faced a greater need for food than medicines"; third, that "physicians are willing to practice only in locations where they can make a satisfactory living—i.e., in large metropolitan communities," a situation that implies grossly uneven regional and area distribution of health resources; and fourth, that "modern hospitals cannot be built and maintained in isolated low-income areas." He concluded that challenges facing the American health system "are easier to formulate than to resolve."

As a participant in many commissions, advisory committees, conferences, and councils—and faculty meetings beyond counting—he developed another rare talent, identified by Professor Robert M. MacIver, a colleague and former student: Ginzberg listened unobtrusively and observed intently, noting other members' enthusiasms, passions, or indifference. When discussions wandered into irrelevancies, he would quietly recall the question at issue. He never forced his own opinions, but he could persuasively summarize an inchoate group discussion (conveniently ignoring dismissible opinions) and then offer a "sense of the meeting" or his perception of "the consensus," which often so artfully presented majority preferences that his formulation carried the day.

In addition to his research and publications, Ginzberg put a high priority on his many Washington ties—as consultant, lecturer, and adviser. While he had benefited greatly from his experience with the large bureaucracies of the federal government during World War II, he also acknowledged the good fortune of his relationship with Eisenhower: "It is not often that an academic researcher is sponsored by a national hero who within a few years enters the White House."

Near the close of his career, Ginzberg asked himself, "How, with the benefit of hindsight, do I evaluate these many decades of research that my colleagues and I devoted to the policy arena, both in deepening analysis and in formulating plans for reform?" His modest answer was "a mixed bag, with a few successes, some contributions, and many efforts that resulted in few if any positive results." He recognized that he had gone his own way, aiming to identify and analyze major social problems "in the hope of focusing attention and pointing directions for remedial interventions. . . . the researcher's influence is difficult to trace and policy successes are at best likely to be few and far between."

George Schultz, who held three cabinet posts, including secretary of labor, characterized Eli's contributions more generously, noting his involvement in key developments in the manpower field: "The list of original ideas which came from his thinking is long and important."

Professor Victor R. Fuchs found that despite Eli's cautions about policymaking, he "never lost his empathy for the poor, for the chronically ill, and for the health problems of minorities—especially Blacks and Hispanics." He approached all issues "with a hard-headed view, not seeking villains or imagining that there are easy solutions to difficult problems . . . [He believes] that a combination of clear thinking and compassion could bring us closer to the best of all possible worlds—but he is not sure that it will."

Eli Ginzberg enjoyed the honors and praise he received. He was well aware that few scholars receive even one Festschrift; he was awarded two, in related areas of manpower studies.[5] But he remained at heart a skeptic and a realist, with more modesty than colleagues might have suspected. Almost a decade before his death, he wrote:

> The conclusion that I have arrived at and must live with is that policy research, like discipline-focused research, is subject to many vicissitudes in formulation, implementation, and obsolescence. And the odds are against the survivability and significance of most research, discipline-based or policy oriented.

PART FIVE

COLUMBIA AS A UNIVERSITY

CHAPTER 32

John W. Burgess and the Birth of the University

—⁓—

Roger Bagnall

Many alumni know "Burgess" as a section of Butler Library. Less familiar is the vital role that John W. Burgess (1844–1931) played in the transformation of Columbia from a college to a university. Burgess helped to realize Columbia president Frederick A. P. Barnard's dreams of a university and built graduate faculties that would fulfill the ambitions of Barnard's successor, Nicholas Murray Butler, for a truly international university.

Burgess's original model was the German university of the late nineteenth century, but what evolved out of his modest graduate program (initially a School of Political Science attached to the Law School) was a complete graduate school with a broad international reach. This was well suited to the global vision of Butler himself and of later colleagues like James T. Shotwell (active in the Carnegie Endowment for International Peace) and the distinguished international lawyer Philip Jessup. Indeed, as Roger Bagnall tells the story, Burgess's vision reveals the lineaments not only of a graduate school especially strong in the social sciences and public affairs, but also something much like our present School of International and Public Affairs. To all this one could well add Burgess's role in building a small college library into a major university library, which itself became a monument to Butler.

For some in Burgess's day who identified strongly with the original undergraduate school (the School of Arts, as it was then known), this major expansion into the graduate arena appeared to be a real threat—a university taking over what had been cherished as an intimate liberal arts college for young New York gentlemen. But the College faculty met this challenge with a new development of its own in the early twentieth century: a program of undergraduate liberal education (known today as the Core Curriculum) that became a living legacy in its own right.

Roger Bagnall, an expert in classics, ancient history, and archaeology, has served as one of Burgess's successors in the role of dean of the Graduate School of Arts and Sciences (1989–93) and deputy vice president for Arts and Sciences (1992–93). A graduate of Yale (B.A. 1968) and the

University of Toronto (Ph.D. 1972), Bagnall chaired Columbia's classics department in 1985 and 1986 and again from 1994 to 2000. He was elected to the American Academy of Arts and Sciences in 2000 and the American Philosophical Society in 2001.

—Wm. Theodore de Bary

———————

Thank God, the university is born. Go ahead." The most celebrated eight words of Columbia's history were this telegram from trustee Samuel B. Ruggles, for which Professor John W. Burgess was roused from his sleep in Paris on June 8, 1880. They marked trustee approval for the start of the School of Political Science, the first part of what was to become the Graduate Faculties and later the Graduate School of Arts and Sciences. With them, Columbia stepped boldly forward into the small circle of universities in the vanguard of graduate education and research in the United States and laid the foundations for decades of preeminence as a doctoral institution. The decision was recognized at the time by some of the principal actors for the historic move that it was. In later years, Burgess was, as Columbia's first graduate dean and one of the best-known figures in American social science, to place these events squarely at the center of a foundation legend, with himself as the hero. His memoirs, written in old age but in a still firm hand a half-century later, are constructed around those stirring days of 1880, when he was just thirty-five years old. At President Eisenhower's Columbia inauguration in 1948, Professor Robert Livingston Schuyler was still describing Burgess as a "great Founding Father of Columbia."

The route to the trustees' meeting of June 7 was a complicated one. Burgess described it in his reminiscences, but he never understood some of the most interesting detours and potholes. The actual story has remarkable significance for the university of today and much of its most recent history. Although Burgess worked closely with some of the trustees and lobbied them to a degree scarcely conceivable to today's faculty, he was not privy to their discussions or their minutes. From these we can see that the form taken by the Graduate School was as much the child of Ruggles and of President Frederick A. P. Barnard as it was of Burgess.

Samuel Ruggles, nearing eighty at the moment of his triumph (he died a year later), was a successful businessman and economist, a Yale graduate but for many years a Columbia trustee. He was part of the group of trustees who had sought since the early 1850s to transform a sleepy undergraduate college into a real university, with only partial success. The Law School (launched in 1858) was narrowly professional and functioned practically as a private, for-profit venture of its sole professor, Theodore Dwight. Other ambitions had to be set aside, except for the School of Mines (founded in 1864), the ancestor of today's School of Engineering and Applied Science and an early model of every-tub-on-its-own-bottom budgeting. (The College of Physicians and Surgeons was a separate institution in this period.) Jurisprudence and public law were taught by Francis Lieber but to tiny audiences, because they were not required. After Lieber's death in 1872, it took four years to find and attract a replacement—Burgess.

John Burgess was born in 1844 to a well-off Tennessee family with Union loyalties. His first college experience at Cumberland University was cut short by the Civil War, and he narrowly escaped conscription into the Confederate army by enlisting in the Union forces. He later traced his interest in law and political science back to his horrific war experiences, which led him to devote his life to the search for peaceful means of resolving conflict. (Late in life this staunch Republican used the phrase "an institution for genuine pacifist propaganda" for the School of Political Science). After his discharge, he used his accumulated military pay to go to Amherst College, which remained the center of his affections to the end of his life, although in his time it—like almost all colleges—lacked practically all of the subjects to which he was to devote his career. He wanted to follow it with law school at Columbia, attracted by Francis Lieber's courses in public law. However, three months of typhoid caused him to miss the start of the school year, and he did his legal training in a law office instead. After a stint teaching at Knox College, he took all his savings and went off to Germany in 1871 for two years of advanced study, accompanied by his wife, Augusta, and his Amherst friend Elihu Root.

German universities were a revelation to Burgess, as they were to so many young Americans seeking advanced education in the late nineteenth century. His stays in Göttingen, Leipzig, and Berlin gave him opportunities to study Roman law and history, philosophy, European constitutional history and law, and economics and statistics with some of the most eminent scholars of the century, including Wilhelm Roscher, Ernst Curtius, Johann Gustav Droysen, and the great Theodor Mommsen. In these years Burgess formed his ideas not only of what a university should be but also of the connection between university and world. As a protégé of the American ambassador, George Bancroft, he met Bismarck, von Moltke, and other political notables and saw how they formed part of the same social world as the eminent professors—some of whom had political careers of their own. Although Burgess eventually saw that the German model could not be taken over unaltered in a newer, democratic country like the United States, he embraced its main features and eventually impressed them on graduate study at Columbia. His affection for Germany never diminished, and he was vehemently opposed to American involvement in World War I.

But in 1873 he returned to America with no job in hand. Theodore Dwight soon offered him a part-time position at the Columbia Law School, to replace Lieber, but Burgess used this to spur Amherst to create a regular post for him, and he returned to his beloved alma mater full of dreams of adding a graduate program in historical and political studies. The faculty showed no signs of support for this idea, but a group of exceptional students from the class of 1874 volunteered to stay on with their charismatic teacher (whom they nicknamed *Weltgeist,* "World Spirit") for an additional year, entirely outside the formal structures of the college. Burgess's colleagues, now actively hostile, added to his teaching load to punish him for this sign of independence. The students after their year went off to Germany for graduate study, and Burgess began to think that perhaps Amherst, with its pious hostility to research, was not the ideal spot for his dream school.

Theodore Dwight did not give up easily. Burgess was invited to give a series of lectures at Columbia in January 1876. Samuel Ruggles was in the audience throughout, and at the end, Burgess recorded, Ruggles came up and said, "You are the man we have been looking for ever since Lieber's death. You must come to Columbia." The courtship was protracted and Burgess's agony at leaving Amherst figures prominently in his account, but when the trustees elected him to a professorship both in the College and in Law, at an annual salary of $7,500 (the equivalent today of some $125,000 tax-free—what all of the College's professors got in 1876), he accepted.

He recorded in old age his discouragement on arriving at Columbia: "I found the institution to consist of a small old-fashioned college, or rather school, for teaching Latin, Greek, and mathematics and a little metaphysics, and a very little natural science, and called the School of Arts; a School of Mines for teaching a little more natural science and educating mining and civil engineers; and a School of Law of a quasi-proprietary nature." Classes were held only from ten o'clock to one o'clock, all of the students commuted, and the library was a mere 25,000 volumes in a firetrap, kept open about ninety minutes a day by a librarian whose chief pleasure was underspending his acquisitions budget. It was not a promising setting for the creation of a great university on the German model.

There were two saving graces, to Burgess's eyes. One was the group of trustees led by Ruggles; the other was President Barnard. They figure as the other agents for good in the saga of the founding. Burgess may not have known just how committed Barnard was to the creation of a real university. Already in his 1866 report, a year after arriving, the president had argued that Columbia had a duty to become a university and to raise money for this purpose. But the path hardly ran smoothly, and the years from 1876 to 1880 were a period of complex maneuvering that would take many pages to recount. Burgess's main goal was to get a required third year in Law devoted to public law and political science, which all LL.B. students would take. Dwight was opposed to this plan, believing that the extra year would cause him to lose students (and thus, as Burgess pointed out, income). He wanted it to be an optional postbaccalaureate year, leading to a master's degree. But Burgess, who saw Dwight teaching hundreds while he had a few dozen for his electives, found that proposal unacceptable. In his

John W. Burgess became Columbia's first graduate dean and one of the best known figures in American social science in the late nineteenth and early twentieth centuries.

account, Dwight's unwillingness to make Roman law, administrative law, and constitutional law and history required parts of the legal curriculum—and to hire candidates of Burgess's choice to teach them, one might add—was the determining cause of the founding of the new school.

What Burgess did not know, apparently, was that it was not Dwight but the treasurer, Gouverneur Morris Ogden, who made the decisive move to put aside the plans for a third year at the Law School. Indeed, the reminiscences show that Burgess thought that his attentions had won the treasurer to his way of thinking. But there had been bad blood between the frugal Ogden and the visionary Ruggles for a quarter-century, with public pamphleteering on both sides as early as 1854. The young professor was simply deceiving himself if he thought anything fundamental had changed. Ogden was opposed to both the additional year for the bachelor of laws and the optional master's year. Either would have cost money, and to the treasurer's mind the College was a zero-sum game. There was widespread hostility to Barnard's idea of fund-raising, and tuition was still comparatively cheap: even after a rise from $100 to $150, it took fifty students to pay Burgess's salary. Today it would take five.

Samuel Ruggles (1800–1881) was a strong trustee supporter of Columbia's transformation into a university.

These four years between Burgess's arrival and the vote of 1880 were not without progress. In 1877 he got the trustees to hire Richmond Mayo-Smith (Amherst 1875) as his assistant for teaching history and economics in the College. And the Faculty of Arts moved during 1879–80 to add M.A. courses in a number of subjects, a development of which Burgess, with his low opinion of his collegiate colleagues, thought little. He formulated instead a proposal for a separate "department," ostensibly aimed at the formation of civil servants, to embrace his courses, those of Mayo-Smith, and Roman and administrative law in addition. In its original formulation, the plan sounds far more like the School of International and Public Affairs (SIPA) of today than like a graduate school of arts and sciences. But President Barnard recognized (or redirected) what was really at stake, transformed the proposed unit from department to school, and the trustee resolution called it a "School of Political Science." (Barnard was usually ahead of everyone; in 1879 he expressed the view that Columbia College would eventually admit women, and even though in the short term this goal was diverted—against his wishes but in line with Burgess's preference—to a separate women's college named after him, he saw the future more clearly even than Burgess.)

There was opposition from the College faculty, and—more importantly—from many trustees who were graduates in Arts and saw the project as a threat to the institution as they had always known it. The emblematic figure is undoubtedly Hamilton Fish, chair of the trustees and former secretary of state. Burgess always saw him as an ally, but his position was complicated. Unable to bring himself either to support the proposal that would so radically change the College he loved or to oppose what he knew was demanded by the times, when at last the time came for the question to be debated, he dramatically handed the gavel to another trustee, Morgan Dix, and left the room and the trustees. Ruggles, Barnard, and their supporters carried the day.

Much more was to follow in the next decade, and Burgess was at the center of it all. "The ten years from 1880 to 1890 were filled with committees, conferences, boards, reports," he said in 1930. Within five years Columbia developed the largest graduate program in the country, and the late 1880s and 1890s saw it radically reorganized under Seth Low's leadership, with the founding of faculties in philosophy (the humanities) and pure science, the creation of more professional schools, the institution of deanships—Burgess was the first dean of political science (1890) and later of the unified Graduate Faculties (1909)—the renaming of the institution itself as Columbia University, and the move to Morningside Heights. Burgess's genius as a teacher served him in good stead, for one of his earliest undergraduate pupils at Columbia was Nicholas Murray Butler, who was as faculty member, dean, and president a forceful exponent of the kind of university Burgess sought. Butler described Burgess as "the most brilliant and interesting teacher it has ever been my good fortune to hear." Their mutual admiration society is unmistakable.

The early founding and independence of the School of Political Science gave Columbia an extraordinary lead in the development of research and graduate education in the social sciences. Burgess founded not merely a school, but most of the infrastructure of a profession, as he had planned from the start. The early graduates of the School included some of the most distinguished social scientists of the next generation. From being behind the times, Columbia rocketed to a dominant position. But the School was not purely academic in character, and in 1893 Burgess pointed out that Harvard and Hopkins, with more fellowship money available, dominated the market for prospective university teachers. Columbia, by contrast, kept the practical goal of professional service in mind, stressing "the philosophical development of professional study." The relationship with the School of Law, in particular, turned out to be close and lasting, leading to a fruitful connection of pure and applied scholarship over many decades and helping to make Law a far more academic institution than it was in the 1870s. Munroe Smith, whom Burgess hired to teach the Roman law he valued so much in his German education, was to play an important role in the Law School for more than four decades.

The founding of the School of Political Science transformed Columbia as well, and not only by starting its development into a research university. Burgess's strong international bent—the closest model for the school was in fact not the German university but the Ecole Libre des Sciences Politiques in Paris—helped to make the university part of a transatlantic scholarly community from the start. Burgess was also the first great advocate of creating an important library at Columbia, and it was he who brought his former student Melvil Dewey (Amherst 1874) to New York as chief librarian in 1883. The libraries exploded in size under Dewey and his successors, and Burgess devoted considerable energy to buying books in history, law, and the social sciences to help create a collection that would sustain research and graduate education.

Heroic deeds are rarely accomplished without significant cost. From the perspective of Columbia in the year 2005, it is hard to not to notice two ways in which the process that led to the foundation of the School of Political Science bequeathed a more mixed legacy to the university than has usually been recognized. First is the fact that it was done in the teeth of opposition from the School of Arts—Columbia College, as we would call it now. Although Columbia did not go as far as Johns Hopkins (newly founded in 1876) in becoming a graduate institution, neither did it follow the path of Harvard and Yale in making graduate study an organic part of the existing departments in the undergraduate schools. The separatist path was at the root of much of the College's opposition to Burgess's proposals. It is not obvious that the "university party" of the trustees had much choice in the matter; Burgess's path was probably the only way open to them of avoiding Columbia's decline into irrelevancy in an era of rapid change in higher education. That was certainly Nicholas Murray Butler's view, expressed publicly at the festivities at the fiftieth anniversary of the founding in 1930. But this path left a legacy of College alienation from the Graduate Faculties, as shown in a later reference by Burgess to "the idea that the university was hostile to the interests of the School of Arts." As Burgess indeed remarked in 1913, President Seth Low knew that a private university depended on the alumni of the College for its financial support, not on those of the graduate school. But only in the 1990s did the old divisions truly start to fade and the graduate and undergraduate schools begin to see and pursue their common interest.

What is equally striking from a modern perspective is the activist role of the trustees and president. Columbia was exceptional even by the standards of the 1870s in this respect. Today, the majority of the faculty have probably never met a trustee, let alone witnessed the trustees choosing new members of the teaching staff. And the president's time is to a large degree consumed with development and other external roles. But the fact that a university could be created and run from the top down was surely not lost on the young Nicholas Murray Butler, who was to become by far the most dominant president Columbia has ever known. The submersion of the wishes of the faculty in 1880 has in this way, I believe, contributed to Columbia's comparatively weak traditions in faculty governance, especially in the arts and sciences.

But hindsight is easy. What Columbia's best minds saw in the late 1870s was a combination of opportunity and obstacles, and they seized the one by steamrollering the other. From the remarkable partnership of professor, president, and trustee, Columbia gained a leading role in the remaking of American higher education and an incomparable distinction in the nascent social sciences. That legacy, along with some of its costs, is still very much part of today's university.

CHAPTER 33

Virginia Gildersleeve: Opening the Gates

—⁙—

Rosalind Rosenberg

To most Columbia College undergraduates in the years between the two world wars, Virginia Crocheron Gildersleeve was an even more remote figure than was President Nicholas Murray Butler—both were much occupied with extracurricular activities higher even than top-level university administration. As a pioneer of the feminist movement and as a leader in what she called "Many a Good Crusade" on the national and international levels, Gildersleeve had other things to do than wait for bumptious Columbia students, charging across Broadway in their annual rituals of burning down the Barnard fence and storming the Brooks/Hewitt dormitories raucously, to claim her condign attention.

Rosalind Rosenberg, who has provided an intimate view into the life of this distinguished stateswoman, is Ann Whitney Olin Professor of History at Barnard College and the author of Beyond Separate Spheres: The Intellectual Roots of Modern Feminism *(1982);* Divided Lives: American Women in the Twentieth Century *(1992); and* Changing the Subject: How the Women of Columbia Shaped the Way We Think About Sex and Politics *(2004).*

Wm. Theodore de Bary

—⁙—

Virginia Crocheron Gildersleeve, dean of Barnard College and adviser to Columbia Women Graduate Students from 1911 to 1947, did more to advance the cause of women at Columbia University than any other person of her time.

In 1911 undergraduate education for women had been available for only two decades, and many graduate courses and professional schools remained closed to them. By the time Gildersleeve retired thirty-six years later, Columbia was granting more advanced degrees to women and hiring more female faculty than any other university in the United States. This achievement had much to do with Columbia's situation in New York City, long the country's most ethnically diverse metropolis, its economic heart, its media capital, and its principal haven for ambitious, rebellious, heterodox women. New York's opportunities enabled women to make important advances in all of the city's colleges and universities. Their achievements were greatest at Columbia, and Gildersleeve's successful use of Barnard College as a staging ground for her campaign on behalf of female graduate students and faculty goes a long way toward explaining why.

Born in 1877, the daughter of Judge Henry Alger Gildersleeve and Virginia Crocheron, Gildersleeve grew up in a town house on West Forty-eighth Street near Fifth Avenue. "We . . . were not 'in society' exactly," Gildersleeve later recalled, "we were professional people." She prepared for college at the Brearley School and upon graduation in 1895 thought of attending Bryn Mawr, but her mother preferred that she stay closer to home. Her father had attended Columbia Law School, and her older brother Harry graduated from the College in 1890. She had once accompanied Harry to the College's library on 49th Street, where the shaded green lights and rows of books had deeply impressed her. So she enrolled at Barnard, which had just opened its doors a few blocks away on Madison Avenue. Gildersleeve followed the College when it moved uptown to elegant new quarters alongside Columbia on Morningside Heights a couple of years later, and there she studied European history with James Harvey Robinson, sociology with Franklin Giddings, and history of philosophy with Nicholas Murray Butler. She graduated first in her class in 1899, and the offer of a graduate fellowship prompted her to stay on at Columbia, where she received a master's degree in history in 1900. After five years of teaching first-year composition at Barnard, she returned to Columbia for a Ph.D. in English, which she earned in 1908. Her dissertation, "Government Regulation of Elizabethan Drama," signaled a lifelong interest in interdisciplinary studies. Not wanting to leave home, she turned down an associate professorship in English at the University of Wisconsin, despite being warned that academic advancement required a willingness to move from school to school at the beginning of one's career. Instead, she pieced together teaching assignments at Barnard and in Columbia's graduate program in English, until an assistant professorship in English opened at Barnard in 1910. She assumed the position of dean of Barnard College and adviser to women graduate students at Columbia in 1911.

WOMEN AND POLITICS

When Gildersleeve took over the stewardship of Barnard College, the woman's movement was in full flower and both parents and trustees were anxious about the movement's possible corrupting effects on young women. Gildersleeve had barely settled into her new office when the distraught mother of a student arrived at her door. The mother implored her to forbid Barnard students from participating in a planned suffrage parade down Fifth Avenue. To "march in a parade would be a shocking and shameful thing" for the students to do and would "injure the college greatly," the distressed mother warned. Nor was this mother alone in opposing student support for woman suffrage. At Vassar College administrators so feared adverse publicity should their students become involved in the unladylike world of political activism that student supporters of the suffrage movement had to hold organizational meetings in the local graveyard to avoid detection. And at Barnard itself, members of the Board of Trustees opposed Barnard students having anything to do with woman suffrage. Foremost among these opponents was trustee Annie Nathan Meyer. Although Meyer had led the campaign to open Barnard College in the late 1880s, she opposed woman suffrage on the grounds that it fostered sex antagonism. Notwithstanding Meyer's outspoken views, Gildersleeve refused to interfere with student suffragists; indeed, she encouraged faculty and students to engage freely, not only in the fight for suffrage, but in all the political movements of the day. In contrast to Vassar, with its ban on all suffrage activity, Gildersleeve's Barnard boasted a chapter of the New York State Woman Suffrage League and an openly acknowledged Socialist League. And in the area of campus known as the Jungle (where Lehman Hall now stands) many a stump speaker defended a controversial cause.

For all Gildersleeve's openness to heterodox political views, she had ambivalent feelings toward feminism. She rejected the confrontational tactics of those like Alice Paul and her followers who, following the example of British suffragists, courted arrest as they castigated public officials for not supporting women's right to vote. British-born Barnard English professor Caroline Spurgeon, who became Gildersleeve's companion in the 1920s, once chided the Barnard dean that she "did not appreciate the need of militant feminism because she had not been trampled upon enough." Gildersleeve countered that she "was not battering at the doors from without but working from within." To be effective she thought it essential "to avoid as far as possible creating antagonisms" for, as she later recalled, "most of my colleagues outside of Barnard had to be handled rather gently."

New York in the 1910s fairly burst with political, cultural, and economic energy. For women this energy produced unprecedented opportunities in journalism, publishing, education, retailing, law, medicine, and social work. Determined that her students should be prepared to take advantage of whatever chance might become available, Gildersleeve organized a Committee on Women Graduate Students, to which she recruited Barnard Professor of Geology Ida H. Ogilvie and two male colleagues, James Harvey Robinson from Barnard and John Dewey from Columbia. Together they worked to advance women's interests in the graduate faculties and open Columbia's professional schools. The School of Journalism admitted women when it opened in 1912, and the School of Business did the same when it opened in 1916. Winning entry sometimes took more, however, than a simple decree that women might take classes. The School of Journalism, for instance, required a course in government as a prerequisite. Barnard did not at that time offer any such course, government being a subject thought suitable only for the male students at Columbia. But taking advantage of the Board of Trustees' desire to win admission for Barnard women to Columbia professional schools whenever possible, Gildersleeve quietly hired one of Robinson's students, Charles Beard, to teach Barnard's first course in American government.

Addressing the men of Phi Beta Kappa, Gildersleeve saw a chance to press her case further in 1915, when the Columbia Chapter of Phi Beta Kappa asked her to be the first woman ever to speak them at their annual convocation. In welcoming her as that year's speaker, Professor Harold Webb of the Columbia physics department sent her a list of the subjects of prior addresses to serve as a guide. These subjects included "Competition in College," "New Humanities for Old," and, most recently, "The College Man's Opportunity in Public Life." Having reviewed these titles, Gildersleeve selected her own: "Some Guides for Feminine Energy." Gildersleeve's address was a genteel, but nonetheless clear, declaration of war on the male-led university. She began by pointing out that 1915 was not only the year of the Great War in Europe, but also the year of the twenty-fifth anniversary of Barnard's founding. And therefore, she declared, "Speaking . . . as a representative of a feminine college on a feminine anniversary, I feel committed to a feminine subject, and for this I crave your indulgence."

As most of her listeners would have been aware, "feminine energy" had been a matter of obsessive concern among academics for many years. Back in 1873, Dr. Edward Clarke of the Harvard Medical School had published a book in which he claimed that the higher education of women would kill off the middle class. Basing his dark prophecy on a view, widely held among physicians at the time, that the

Barnard's Class of 1899—the college's seventh graduating class. Gildersleeve is in the second row from the front, third from the left.

body is a closed energy system, he explained that energy available for one task—the development of a woman's mind—would not be available for another: the development of her reproductive organs. In short, the mental strain of higher education would inevitably render women students infertile. The prospect of infertility raised, in turn, the specter of "race suicide," which was the belief that middle-class, white, Anglo-Saxon Protestants were marching toward extinction as a consequence of their declining birth rate. According to President Theodore Roosevelt, there would soon not be enough sons to go to Harvard. Angry, but undaunted, talented young women had been flooding the colleges ever since, distinguishing themselves academically and, in due course, maternally. However, concern about the limits of feminine energy lingered, especially in the minds of male academics. Could women really be expected to excel academically, given the reproductive and domestic demands on their energies? This was the question that Gildersleeve was implicitly addressing in her speech.

Her answer was a simple *yes*: women had plenty of energy; indeed, their energy sought new outlets, since the technological change of the previous generation had removed the great bulk of domestic work from the home. A learned woman could read by an electric light, rather than having to devote winter afternoons to making candles. A learned woman could even, with a clear conscience, abjure motherhood now that improved public health and declining infant mortality made it unnecessary to breed as many children as once had been the case. In the modern world

women could have the same ambitions as men. Having laid down the gauntlet in her
Phi Beta Kappa address, Gildersleeve began to move on several fronts: scheming
first to open the remaining professional schools to women, second to create opportunities on the faculty, and finally to press for broader opportunities in the world.

LAW AND MEDICINE

As a member of the University Council, Gildersleeve met regularly with the
deans of all the schools that composed the university, and at every opportunity she
mentioned the importance of extending greater educational advantages to Barnard
students. The dean of the College of Physicians and Surgeons, Dr. Samuel Lambert,
seemed sympathetic but insisted that change must await the school's move to larger
quarters. New York women had been pressing the medical school to open its doors
ever since 1873, when suffrage leader Lillie Devereux Blake petitioned the Columbia
trustees on behalf of a group of women, including one who wanted to attend the
medical school, that Columbia's charter made the institution available to the "youth
of the city," a group that should be read to include women. Unwilling to wait any
longer, Gildersleeve told the dean in 1917 that "a brilliant young Swedish woman,
Gulli Lindh," was about to graduate from Barnard and attend the Johns Hopkins
Medical School but that she would rather stay in New York. The dean responded
that he would be happy to have her and others but that, at a minimum, he had to
provide additional laboratory space and a woman's restroom. Gildersleeve, assisted
by the American Women's Medical Association, offered to raise the necessary
$50,000, and the medical school took Lindh as well as five others to keep her com-
pany. Four years later, Lindh graduated first in the class, and two of the other women
graduated third and fifth.

Dean Harlan Stone and his law school faculty proved more resistant to
Gildersleeve's blandishments. In 1915 President Butler lent Gildersleeve his support
by calling a meeting at his home of the educational committee of the Columbia
trustees and several of the more senior members of the law school to discuss the matter of women's admission. Butler and the trustees favored the change, but the law
faculty, fearful that admitting women would cause their best male students to flee to
all-male Harvard, flatly refused. Gildersleeve's wry suggestion that the two schools
hold hands and take the dangerous step toward coeducation together did not
receive a favorable reply. Indeed, in a letter the following week Stone advised her
that the majority of his faculty viewed coeducation as "unwise" and warned against
further "agitation" on the matter. Although Yale Law School's decision to admit

women in 1917 drew positive notices from the press, Columbia Law School refused to follow its example. By 1924, the year Gildersleeve lay the cornerstone of a dormitory to help house Columbia's exploding female graduate population, women's enrollment at the university outpaced men's by 18,000 to 15,194. But still Columbia Law School refused to open its doors.

It took another two years of determined effort, including a Barnard faculty petition appealing to the law faculty's sense of justice, before Columbia Law School grudgingly and narrowly agreed in December 1926 to admit not women in general but only those Barnard students who were particularly recommended by the dean of Barnard College. Law School Dean Huger Jervey warned Gildersleeve against giving any publicity to her victory. He did not want "the appearance created that the law school had determined at this time generally to admit women equally with men." Gildersleeve complied and sent only her best graduate, Helen Robinson, for admission in the fall of 1927. But word of the law school's action got out, and two female Columbia graduate students, one with a master's degree, the other with a doctorate, sought admission. Jervey found them too well qualified to turn away. Margaret Spahr, who already had received master's and doctoral degrees from Columbia, was the first woman to graduate from the Law School. She did so in two years and in the process became the first woman to serve as an editor of the *Columbia Law Review*. In 1942, the last professional school holdout, the School of Engineering, succumbed to the Gildersleeve treatment and admitted female students.

CREATING THE WAVES

Scholars have written a great deal in the past two decades on the importance of World War II in opening up jobs in war industries to women; this was the era of Rosie the Riveter. Much more important in the long run, though, was the chance created by the war to open science to women. Predictably, Gildersleeve played an important role in that effort. In articles, radio broadcasts, and speeches she hammered away at her favorite wartime theme: to win the war the nation needed "trained brains"; to have enough, the country would have to turn to its women.

Gildersleeve did everything she could to keep her students in school, to dissuade them from quitting to take a job in a factory—no matter how glamorous wartime propaganda made the job seem. She also did everything she could to keep from losing her students to marriage. She seems to have accepted the fact that, given the wartime pressures, marriage to departing soldiers would occur; she simply drew the line at students following their new husbands to wherever they might be sent. In

Gildersleeve in 1945 with members of the WAVES, the Navy's female reserve corps, at the U.S. Naval Training School in the Bronx. Gildersleeve helped found the WAVES, winning a place for women in the Armed Forces, and later served as president of its advisory board.

her view young wives were far better off at Barnard, completing their education, than they were staying near some military camp on the other side of the country.

The war offered Barnard an unprecedented chance to turn out physicists, chemists, and mathematicians who could have their pick of good jobs. Gildersleeve was aware of the Manhattan Project across the street at Columbia and the fact that women were being hired to work on it. She knew that there was a pressing need for engineers, and she used this knowledge to win women admission to Columbia's School of Engineering. She housed one of the country's foremost code-breaking programs at Barnard. She found jobs for anthropologists with the Army and Navy, which were desperately seeking specialists who could advise their aviators how to get along with the peoples of the South Pacific. She established one of the country's first programs in international relations to prepare women for the Foreign Service. And she won a place for women in the Armed Forces by helping to found the WAVES, the Navy's female reserve corps. The WAVES, under Gildersleeve's leadership, became a military branch of the Seven Sisters. Gildersleeve served as president of its advisory board. Its highest-ranking officer was the much younger president of Wellesley, Mildred McAfee; its second in command was Gildersleeve's close friend, English Professor Elizabeth Reynard; its officers—8,500 at one time—were all college graduates or had at least two years of college with two more years of professional or business experience.

Gildersleeve had no illusions about what would happen to women's opportunities after the war: they would shrink, perhaps even disappear. But, she insisted, where opportunity remained, her students were going to have as big a competitive advantage as she and the educational resources at her command could assure.

"WE THE PEOPLES OF THE UNITED NATIONS"

The opportunity to build on the accomplishments of the war came in February 1945 when Franklin Roosevelt named Gildersleeve to the U.S. delegation to write the United Nations Charter. The only woman named to the delegation, Gildersleeve won her spot through both her war work and her reputation as an internationalist. That reputation dated back to 1916 when, influenced by Nicholas Murray Butler, Gildersleeve had begun speaking to Barnard students about establishing an international organization, even before America entered World War I. A "league to enforce peace," she called it. She thought it should include an international court, but she also advocated establishing an organization that would foster contact among nations, even when there were no outstanding disputes. Many women leaders of her day, including most notably Jane Addams, were pacifists. Gildersleeve was not. But she strongly supported the League of Nations and worked on postwar committees to lobby the American public on its behalf. That work failed, but Gildersleeve enjoyed greater success within academia.

When the war ended, a delegation of British educators came to the United States in search of innovations that might be usefully transplanted to England. One of these educators was Caroline Spurgeon, a Shakespeare scholar. Meeting Spurgeon allowed Gildersleeve to broach the topic most on her mind: the need to establish an organization that would foster international cooperation among like-minded academic women. Gildersleeve imagined an organization built on the model of the American Association of Collegiate Alumnae; Spurgeon had in mind her own British Federation of University Women. In 1919 they created the International Federation of University Women (IFUW), housing it in London with a second home in Paris at Reid Hall.

For two decades, between World War I and World War II, Gildersleeve worked through the IFUW to keep alive the spirit of international understanding, even as isolationism gripped her country. She twice served as president of the IFUW, became a trustee of the American College for Girls in Turkey as well as the Near East College Association, and traveled throughout Europe and the Middle East. When war came again, Gildersleeve joined the Commission to Study the Organization of the Peace, headed by Barnard history professor James T. Shotwell. Longtime colleagues and friends, Shotwell and Gildersleeve had taken the same seminar on medieval Europe taught by James Harvey Robinson in 1900. During World War II they met once a month with fellow commissioners, who included

Owen Lattimore, an Asia specialist for the Office of War Information who would later be falsely charged by Joseph McCarthy as a Russian spy; John Foster Dulles, a Wall Street lawyer who would go on to be Dwight D. Eisenhower's secretary of state; and Max Lerner, a syndicated columnist for the *New York Post*, to plan America's participation in a world organization following the war. The commission's recommendations influenced the work undertaken at Dumbarton Oaks in 1944, which in turn became the basis of the UN Charter proposals she and the world's delegates took up in 1945.

Shortly before Gildersleeve was to leave for San Francisco, a celebration was held in her honor at the Commodore Hotel. There she was feted by, among others, William Allan Neilson, who had been her dissertation adviser at Columbia and was the past president of Smith College. Neilson noted that Gildersleeve's appointment gave recognition to the increasing importance of academically trained experts in politics and the increasing influence of women in world affairs. Neilson regretted that Gildersleeve would be the only woman on the U.S. delegation, "but that will not matter," he concluded, "if only the men will listen."

The delegates were charged with writing a charter that addressed two issues: to prevent future wars through the creation of a Security Council and to enhance human welfare through the establishment of an Economic and Social Council. Gildersleeve was assigned to the committee responsible for creating this second council—the one, as she put it, in charge of doing things rather than preventing things from being done. She took particular pride in helping insert into the charter's statement of purpose the following goals for people around the world: "higher standards of living, full employment, and conditions of economic and social progress and development." Moreover, she persuaded the delegates to adopt the following aim for the UN: "universal respect for human rights and fundamental freedoms for all without distinction as to race, sex, language, or religion." Gildersleeve endorsed these goals not only for their importance to the enhancement of human welfare, but also because she saw them as providing job opportunities for all the women who had been training to be health professionals, research scientists, lawyers, teachers, and social workers. She was advocating an international Works Progress Administration for educated women. To carry out its work, the council was given the power to appoint whatever commissions it deemed necessary, but Gildersleeve insisted that the charter require the appointment of one in particular: the Commission on Human Rights. This commission, under the direction of Eleanor Roosevelt, would write the Universal Declaration of Human Rights three years later. This declaration, in turn, was to serve as the basis for all of the UN's work on behalf of women throughout the world over the next two generations.

Gildersleeve shaking hands with U.S. President Harry Truman after she signed the United Nations Charter in San Francisco in 1945. She was the only woman on the U.S. delegation, a sign of the small but increasing influence of women in world affairs.

Establishing the Commission on Human Rights may have been Gildersleeve's most enduring accomplishment at the conference, but the achievement that most cheered her English professor's heart was her success, with her aide, Barnard English Professor Elizabeth Reynard, in drafting the opening lines of the United Nations Charter's Preamble. In place of the version suggested by Field Marshal Jan Smuts of South Africa, which read "The High Contracting Parties, determined to prevent a recurrence of the fratricidal strife which twice in our generation has brought untold sorrow and loss upon mankind. . . ." she offered the simpler, more democratic, and more American, "We the peoples of the United Nations, determined to save succeeding generations from the scourge of war, which in our time has brought untold sorrow to mankind. . . ." The Smuts version rounded off the preamble, much to Gildersleeve's distress, but at least she and Reynard had succeeded in crafting the opening lines.

Gildersleeve's contributions to women's rights and international peace owed much to her experience on Morningside Heights. Though born and raised in the comfortable confines of New York's Episcopalian upper crust, she gained a far broader perspective on the world as a student. She later credited her mentor, historian James Harvey Robinson, for teaching her tolerance and the capacity through careful scholarship to put herself in the place of others from very different cultural backgrounds. Robinson's influence shaped her career.

SIGNS OF THE TIMES

While opportunities for women blossomed during Gildersleeve's administration, minority admission figures at Barnard continued to reflect the wider realities of her time. Barnard had only a few black students while Gildersleeve served as dean, most notably novelist Zora Neale Hurston, who entered Barnard in 1925 on a full scholarship arranged by Annie Nathan Meyer. Pauli Murray, who would go on to be one of the outstanding civil rights lawyers and feminist leaders of her generation, was turned away in 1927 for want of funds and the inadequate preparation she had received in the segregated schools of Durham, North Carolina. In the 1930s, civil rights activists apparently convinced Gildersleeve of the need both to recruit talented black students and to provide full scholarships to enable them to attend. Pressed by students in the early 1940s to do more, Gildersleeve paid for the full scholarship of at least one black student from Harlem out of her own pocket. But by the time Gildersleeve retired, still only eight of Barnard's 1,400 students were black.

Jews played a central role at Barnard from the beginning. Annie Nathan Meyer led the campaign to found Barnard, and banker Jacob Schiff served as the first treasurer of the Board of Trustees. Barnard students, led by future *Nation* editor Freda Kirchwey, abolished sororities on campus in 1915 because of their undemocratic spirit, secrecy, and attitude toward Hebrew members. Gildersleeve herself disdained religious exclusivity and refused to categorize her students in any explicit way. Nonetheless, an implicit categorization, one based on class, clearly existed at Barnard. Sephardic and German Jews who had attended private schools won admission to Barnard without difficulty. But the daughters of Eastern European immigrants who had attended New York City's public schools encountered greater resistance, especially as their numbers began to rise. Compared to most of the other elite women's colleges of the time, Barnard appears to have been relatively open; by World War I the proportion of Jews was roughly 20 percent compared to 6 to 10 percent at most other women's colleges At that point, both Columbia and Barnard began recruiting students from outside New York City and by evaluating all applicants on the basis of psychological tests, interviews, and letters of recommendation, as well as academic criteria. In the two decades before World War II, this process of selective admissions kept the percentage of Jewish students at both Columbia and Barnard from rising any higher.

MAKING COLUMBIA A VANGUARD FOR WOMEN

However uneven Gildersleeve's record may have been with respect to advancing the interests of minorities, she deserves much of the credit for the fact that, during her tenure as dean of Barnard College, Columbia dramatically outpaced other universities in the advanced degrees it awarded to women, both in raw numbers and in the percentage of degrees awarded. Under her leadership, Barnard had one of the highest ratios of female to total faculty in the country, and that faculty prided itself on offering opportunity to talented women not available even at most other women's colleges. This concentration of women scholars gave many Barnard students the confidence to think that they too might pursue academic careers. To keep faculty standards high, a 1922 agreement reiterated the right of Barnard professors to teach in the graduate faculties and gave Columbia departments an important say in Barnard tenure decisions. This policy increased the status of those women professors on the Barnard faculty who won promotion to tenured positions but at a price. Gildersleeve was perfectly frank in keeping women relegated, disproportionately, to the lower ranks. To maintain close relations with Columbia she needed to be able to attract top-flight male scholars and pay them more. She knew that given Barnard's situation in New York City she would always have an ample pool of talented women to fill the lower ranks. Sociologist Mirra Komarovsky, a Russian immigrant, had published two books before she could persuade Gildersleeve to promote her to assistant professor.

At the same time, however, Gildersleeve was entirely supportive when it came to marriage and motherhood. In the 1910s, when the New York Public Schools still barred married women from teaching, Gildersleeve insisted that a woman's marital status was entirely her own business. This had not always been the case. When Barnard Dean Emily James Smith had married in 1900, the Board of Trustees had encouraged her to continue her work; but under her successor, Laura Drake Gill, who served as dean from 1901 until 1911, married women were not so fortunate. In 1906 Gill demanded the resignation of physicist Harriet Brooks over the vehement protest of Brooks's department chair, Margaret Maltby, when Brooks announced her intention to marry. In contrast, married female faculty members became common under Gildersleeve's tenure. Some were even mothers, and in 1931 Gildersleeve began to consider ways of helping women to balance family and career. At about the same time that she agreed to grant a paid leave of absence to a male professor who was in the hospital, a female member of the staff asked for the usual leave of absence without salary because she was going to have a child. "It suddenly struck me as unfair that you should receive full salary if you went to the hospital because of illness but that if you went in order to provide another citizen for the community, you should lose all your pay." She raised the matter with President Butler, who "looked a little startled." But when Gildersleeve mentioned to him that France was providing such a benefit to its female teachers, Butler readily agreed. "We should have women teachers with fuller lives and richer experience, not so many dried-up old maids," he opined. Gildersleeve recorded this remark in her memoir without comment, her victory evidently having trumped the implicit insult from her boss and old friend. With the help of Barnard trustees and staunch feminists Helen Rogers Reid and Alice Duer Miller, Gildersleeve persuaded the Barnard Board of Trustees to enact a maternity policy that provided one term off at full pay or a year off at half pay for all new faculty mothers. In the first year three women took advantage of this new policy.

Curiously, the policy was reduced in 1953 under the leadership of Millicent McIntosh, the mother of five, in one of Barnard's periodic budget reduction efforts. The revised policy allowed for leave at half pay, with the time off to be determined in consultation with the dean of the faculty. Although students later remembered McIntosh, rather than Gildersleeve, as the champion of the working mother, Gildersleeve deserves the greater credit for initiating policies that helped make the combination work. By the 1970s, faculty women who gave birth in those years later recalled, the pattern was ten days leave with one course reduction. But even so, Barnard remained rare among institutions of higher education in acknowledging that it had faculty who might be mothers and who had special needs.

A NEW GENERATION OF AMERICAN WOMEN

Barnard's relationship with Columbia, together with Columbia's situation in New York, helped produce an unusually high concentration of female academics on Morningside Heights, compared to the numbers of faculty elsewhere in the country. This concentration helped fuel a revolution of rising expectations that insured that Columbia women would play a pivotal role in the 1960s movement to protest the limits on the opportunity available to them both at the university and in the society beyond. The concentration of women at Columbia also facilitated research over many decades that was then considered outside the mainstream of scholarly endeavor: research on women, families, and children as well as interdisciplinary research on a wide variety of fields. This research created the distinctive point of view from which the modern women's movement would eventually develop at the same time as it gave women academics fields of research in which they encountered virtually no competition from men.

When Gildersleeve began her academic career at the turn of the twentieth century, American women had barely established a toehold in higher education, and that toehold was by no means secure. By insisting that women could succeed at the very pinnacle of academic and professional life, she swam against powerful currents of public prejudice. Many parents sent their daughters to women's colleges like Barnard with the expectation that they would be sheltered from such corrupting influences as feminist ideas. But Gildersleeve did not see herself as a surrogate mother. She aspired to be a leader of a new generation of American women— women who deserved to be prepared for every opportunity that they might be able to claim.

Through her work Gildersleeve and other pioneers like her provided the essential conditions necessary to winning for women full equality with men in American society and throughout the world. In gaining for women access to Columbia's medical school, she helped change the face of American, and later world, health care. In gaining for women access to Columbia Law School, she helped open the way for women's full participation in politics, a calling for which a law degree, if not essential, has nonetheless become the single most important qualification. In broadening women's scholarly horizons, Gildersleeve laid the groundwork for some of the most innovative scholarship of the twentieth century. And in helping to draft the charter of the UN, Gildersleeve assured that the issues to which she had devoted her career on Morningside Heights would be addressed throughout the world in the decades that followed. By insisting that women have the right to every educational opportunity open to men and by fighting her whole life to secure that opportunity, she helped establish the bedrock on which feminists have been building ever since.

CHAPTER 34

Carl W. Ackerman:
The Journalism School's
Other Founder

—◁‖▷—

James Boylan

The story of Carl Ackerman as the key figure in the rise of the School of Journalism during the twentieth century—indeed, a living legend as dean of the school in its first century of life—may also be considered problematic as part of the Living Legacies series. After all, Ackerman did not see his vision of the J-school, based on a two-year program, become more fully realized in his own time.

The school owes its founding in 1903 to the enterprising publisher Joseph Pulitzer, after whom the prizes were named that became almost synonymous with the school, as well as to his collaboration with the no less enterprising Columbia president Nicholas Murray Butler. But after a rather desultory start in its early years, the school began to take definite shape with the appointment of Ackerman, a graduate of its first class, as the first actual dean (not just a "director") in 1931. Ackerman then proceeded to sharpen and focus its mission on training in the skills that most counted in the newsrooms of metropolitan newspapers.

Ackerman's original concept of a two-year graduate program drew more heavily on Columbia's rich academic resources than Butler thought the university could afford; hence the persistence, instead, of the existing one-year program. It was thus left to a later president, Lee Bollinger, and a new dean, Nicholas Lemann, to implement a twenty-first-century version of Ackerman's original two-year professional program. In James Boylan's account of Ackerman's long tenure as dean, his reputation, if not notoriety, came not from any close, hands-on administration of the program itself, but from his more public role, as he became involved in extracurricular activities of a controversial nature and global scope.

—Wm. Theodore de Bary

—◁‖▷—

Columbia University's School of Journalism (now the Graduate School of Journalism) is properly considered the creation of the publisher Joseph Pulitzer. But the school had what amounted to a second founder: its first dean, Carl W. Ackerman—not only because he stuck around for twenty-five years, but because he cast the school in a format that almost seventy years of successors were unable to dislodge.

Ackerman is largely forgotten; even those who attended the school in his era did not know him well. We in the class of 1951 recall seeing him perhaps three times in our year: at an opening reception, maybe at a holiday party (but maybe not), and at graduation—those few of us who chose to attend. He did not teach, and I suspect he was rarely glimpsed even peeking into a classroom.

He looked a little like a bespectacled Buddha and was formal, even fussy, in his dealings with colleagues. His papers at the Library of Congress reveal a man much concerned over personal status and real or imagined slights. He thrived on ceremonies and honors. This is not the profile of an ideal, or typical, journalism dean. So why remember him? Primarily because the steps he took early in his tenure determined into the indefinite future the nature of the curriculum and instruction at the school.

How did such an unlikely figure come to be named dean in the first place? To explain, it is necessary to reach back to the school's origins. The agreement that created the School of Journalism in 1903 melded the idealism of Pulitzer, a wealthy magnate of the yellow press, and the practicality of Nicholas Murray Butler, the university's president, then at the start of his long tenure. Pulitzer envisioned a school that would foster a new breed of practitioners who would turn journalism into a "great and intellectual profession"—a vision indeed, because newspaper journalism at that time could scarcely be considered either intellectual or a profession. For his part, Butler accepted Pulitzer's proffered $2 million endowment, which became available after Pulitzer's death in 1911, and turned it into brick, stone, faculty, and a student body.

When the school opened in 1912 Butler made a good-faith effort to carry out Pulitzer's vision of an encyclopedic education for omnicompetent journalists. He lent leading scholars from other divisions to teach the students government, law, history, languages, science, fine arts, and, of course, journalism history, ethics, and skills. Students who took to this backbreaking load cherished it. But many dropped out, and others felt so oppressed that the school was several times on the verge of a strike.

More significantly, Butler soon realized that the scheme was too expensive to be covered by the Pulitzer endowment. Sizable chunks of the money had gone, of

Ackerman (back to camera) in the 1930s, making one of his rare appearances in the classroom

course, to construct the journalism building on the corner of 116th Street and Broadway and to create the prizes in arts, letters, and journalism that bore Pulitzer's name and have been administered at the school ever since.

To make ends meet, the four-year program was cut back to its two final undergraduate years, and the scholars from other faculties were summoned home. The remaining teachers were primarily retread newspapermen.

The school suffered from unsteady leadership. The first director, Talcott Williams, was a garrulous elder statesman of the press, worn out by the time he retired in 1919. His successor was a pipe-smoking professor of literature, John W. Cunliffe. The school spent the 1920s in the doldrums, fortunate enough to attract talented students but falling far short of giving them the education Pulitzer had envisioned.

Butler took decisive steps in 1931 to restore the school's reputation. First, he found, or rediscovered, Carl W. Ackerman. A graduate of Earlham College in Indiana, Ackerman had entered the school as a fourth-year student and had earned a degree in 1913 with the school's first graduating class. In the First World War, Ackerman made a name as a foreign correspondent, initially with United Press, covering the conflict from both sides, and was one of the first on the scene of the execution of the tsar and his family in the Bolshevik Revolution. In the early 1920s his stature was such that he became an extraordinary intermediary in negotiations between the Irish and British governments. Then he switched to public relations, wrote an admiring biography of his employer, George Eastman of Eastman Kodak, and was just starting a new job at General Motors when Butler called him back to Columbia.

At the announcement of Ackerman's appointment as the school's third director (he soon became the first dean), the GM connection played badly. Ackerman was attacked in the professional press as representing the calling—public relations—that was destroying honest journalism, and one of Pulitzer's sons denounced the appointment. Butler, however, himself a master of publicity, regarded Ackerman's PR experience as an advantage. In fact, Ackerman was far from alone among the school's early graduates in having left low-paying pure journalism for corporate money.

Ackerman took charge in the fall of 1931 and, carrying out Butler's mandate, began steps designed to win the school respect without overburdening its parent institution.

Even before he was in office, Ackerman made it clear that the school would no longer welcome all comers. He said he would exclude those who, he believed, dulled the school's professional reputation and sense of purpose: would-be novelists, would-be playwrights, drifters, and women. Women had been admitted since the school's first days, but under Ackerman their numbers were reduced to single digits in each class; they didn't gain numerical equality until 1977, long after Ackerman was gone.

He tightened the curriculum by tossing out such frivolities as playwriting and fiction, and he focused instruction on newsroom skills. The school's bulletin was stripped of Pulitzer's idealistic words about public service and referred instead to the duty of journalists to make the news business prosper.

Ackerman found his formula for the future in a call by the leading professional association, the American Society of Newspaper Editors, for journalism education on the graduate level. In 1934 he proposed, and the faculty approved, that the two-year program become a graduate school requiring a bachelor's degree for admission. The proposal came back from Low Library stripped of its second year, so the program became a one-year capsule leading to a master of science—"science" because Butler did not want to attach the prestige of an arts degree to so humble a calling as journalism. (A second year was not restored until 2004, under Dean Nicholas Lemann.)

The new scheme had the advantage of focus: students pursued an almost lock-step course of study and had to finish in one academic year or not at all. It had the advantage, budgetwise, of demanding few tenured professors—the bulk of the instruction could be offered by part-timers hired from the downtown press.

At the start of each year, the entire class of sixty-five or so was caged in a single newsroom and subjected to boot-camp training. As the year went on, instruction gradually eased off into benign neglect, to the point that students in effect did a lot of self-teaching, fanning out from the 116th Street IRT station to cover stories anywhere in the city, sometimes not seeing an instructor all day. Laboratory news pages, edited by students, displayed their work in the format of a New York afternoon newspaper.

Within its limits, it worked well. In general, students emerged feeling they knew the ways of metropolitan journalism; just as important, they shared a lasting sense of collegiality. No matter that critics called the curriculum merely undergraduate training transferred to graduate level, the graduates regarded themselves as an elite.

The man who shaped this prosaic new version of Pulitzer's dream seemed, curiously, not to take much interest in how it was executed. Ackerman, as is minutely revealed in his papers, continually looked for diversion, political or otherwise. He had an itch to play on grander stages than the tiny institution he headed.

In 1934, when the American Newspaper Publishers Association got into a spat with President Franklin D. Roosevelt over an effort to enlist newspapers in a recovery program, Ackerman pitched in on the side of the publishers, coming close to accusing the president of plotting a Fascist state. In a similar dispute four years later, he again joined with the publishers, who were trying vainly to avoid paying overtime under the new Wages and Hours Act. He saw himself as a spokesman for the American press—at least for that part of it that owned the presses—and in return his declarations in his annual reports were treated in the press as holy writ.

Ackerman also tried to expand his on-campus visibility. In 1938 he reached an agreement with the wealthy Godfrey Lowell Cabot and his diplomat son to establish awards to journalists for promoting "inter-American understanding." The Maria Moors Cabot Prizes, named for the senior Cabot's late wife, were troubled in their early years. Candidates were customarily scrutinized by the U.S. State Department; even so (or perhaps inevitably), journalists touched with Fascism made the list—with one awardee so suspect that Jews invited to the prize dinner boycotted it. But Ackerman never wavered in his determination to continue the prizes, and he treasured the trips he took to Latin America and the Caribbean to vet candidates. But in setting up the Cabot Prizes Ackerman created the first real competitor under the same roof to the Pulitzers, which he also administered, and opened the door to a plethora of awards that turned the school into a prize-giving machine.

His neglect of the daily operation of the school earned Ackerman a written rebuke from President Butler in 1939, and he promised to do better—to meet with the faculty regularly, to pay closer attention to instruction, and to create opportunities for journalism students to draw on the resources of the university. But none of this happened. Instead, he continued to search for new fields to conquer, and World War II gave him a unique opportunity. One of Ackerman's classmates in the journalism class of 1913 had been Hollington K. Tong, who was then a minister in the government of Nationalist China under Generalissimo Chiang Kai-shek. Tong proposed to Ackerman that Columbia establish a school of journalism in the wartime capital, then known as Chungking.

Ackerman was taken with the idea. In Washington, he gained secret funding from the Office of Strategic Services, the predecessor of the CIA. After recruiting his associate dean, Harold R. Cross, and a group of young graduates, he sent them off to China in 1943, by slow boat and by plane over the Hump. Only when the instructors arrived did they find that the school would be under the direction of the Kuomintang, the ruling political party. Moreover, although the American instructors did their best to teach straight-ahead American journalism, it was clear that the party had in mind the training of secret agents and propagandists. Cross fumed and fussed at the situation and left after a year. The school closed at the end of the war, and Ackerman subsequently received an award from the Nationalist government.

After World War II, President Butler retired and died, and the university searched for a successor. Ackerman, Butler's protégé, favored Butler's deputy, Frank D. Fackenthal, and was distinctly chilly toward the name that rose to the top of the list, General Dwight D. Eisenhower. Ackerman had nothing good to say about Eisenhower during the search or during the general's relatively brief tenure in Low Library.

He carried this dislike over into the election campaign of 1952, after he became irritated because Eisenhower, long since away as NATO commander, continued to claim the Columbia President's House as his residence. When Columbia spokesmen hinted that all of Columbia stood behind Eisenhower, Ackerman loudly proclaimed that he supported the general's opponent, Adlai E. Stevenson—this from a man whose politics had apparently always been to the right of Stevenson's, and Eisenhower's, for that matter.

Ackerman knew he was nearing the end of his career and could afford to be independent. In 1953 he took an even bolder political position. While most American institutions, including universities, were bowing to the demands of the McCarthyite inquisition, Ackerman abruptly declared the files of the Journalism School closed to investigators without subpoenas. Earlier, he had let the FBI see the files of the wife

of Alger Hiss, a chief target of postwar investiga-
tions. She had attended
the school briefly in the
1920s. Now he changed
his mind, asserting that
McCarthyism was placing
a damper on free expres-
sion. The university's head
of public relations begged
him to grovel before the
FBI or at least back off,
but Ackerman felt no
need to make such com-
promises. Invoking the
Pulitzer tradition of inde-

pendence, he dramatically made his stand public. (This apparent conversion may in reality have been a last expression of his deep conservatism, a rooted distrust of state power.)

In 1951, the Journalism School conducted an experimental fax broadcast. Ackerman checks out the final product.

Ackerman no longer wished to continue, especially after the death of his wife, so in 1954 told the administration he wanted to leave. He had to wait two years, though, until Columbia found a successor, just as he completed his twenty-five years in the dean's office. He accepted a few honors as he departed and then retreated into isolation in his apartment not far from the campus, visiting the school rarely and only by invitation.

To the students who passed through the school during his tenure, he was a distant personage. Among his colleagues, if not loved, he was certainly respected for his expansive vision and administrative tenacity. And to his successors, the one-year graduate program remained a rock in the middle of a stream, an obstacle to be dealt with, tinkered with, reshaped, and incrementally improved into something resembling a challenging graduate education; and never, in the twentieth century at least, was it entirely overcome.

CHAPTER 35

Frank Tannenbaum and Collegial Learning in the University Seminars

—ᴍ—

Robert L. Belknap
with a Reminiscence by Robert Alexander

Even those old enough to remember Frank Tannenbaum as the inspired founder and benign ruler of the University Seminars were not around when young Tannenbaum made his entry to Columbia College on the recommendation of the warden of Sing Sing Penitentiary. This was after the young anarchist and political activist had paid with a short stretch in prison for his illegal occupation of a church in New York's Lower East Side along with fellow First World War "Wobblies" and a number of homeless people. Tannenbaum did not lose his radical ideals when he came to college, but they became considerably softened under the influence of the historian Carlton J. H. Hayes, the economist Edwin R. A. Seligman, and the philosopher John Dewey. From these learning experiences Tannenbaum emerged as a strong advocate, no longer of class warfare, but of the trade union movement and also as a pioneer historian of labor, slavery, and penology. Several of these interests, moreover, led him to Latin America and to a close association with left-wing and labor movements there.

It was Tannenbaum's fundamental belief in communitarian movements as the most authentic and indeed practicable means of human improvement that inspired him in the founding of the University Seminars: they would serve as the capstone to the scholarly learning process, engaging public intellectuals from Columbia and elsewhere in informed discussion of contemporary issues.

The story of how Tannenbaum enlisted some of the best minds in the university in this process is a collegial one, told here by Robert L. Belknap, who comes to the subject by a quite different academic route, via Dostoevsky and Russian literature. He too has had a long involvement with collegial learning and teaching, first in the College's Humanities program, which he chaired for several years, then in the university-wide General Education Seminars held in the seventies, and finally in the University Seminars themselves, whose faculty advisory committee he chaired before succeeding Aaron Warner as director in 2000.

Robert Alexander, professor emeritus of economics at Rutgers University, was an early student of Tannenbaum's and has carried on the latter's work as a Latin Americanist, with prime attention to left-wing and labor movements. From close personal association with Tannenbaum, he manages to open up in a brief note a wide vista of the latter's off-campus involvement in the political life of Latin America. As it happens, Alexander himself carries on a Columbia family tradition: his father, Ralph, was a well-known professor of marketing in the School of Business.

—*Wm. Theodore de Bary*

Frank Tannenbaum wrote more than a dozen books, on penology, on slavery, and on Latin America, grounding his scholarship on energetic research and on direct experience with the greatest leaders and also with the most abased populations in many countries. His greatest contribution to the intellectual world, though, may be a unique Columbia enterprise: the University Seminars. These seminars continue the education of the Columbia faculty, which is also the unpublicized purpose of two other Columbia inventions, the Core Curriculum and the regional institutes. The seventy-five seminars meet about once a month. Some 600 to 700 Columbia professors and twice that many from other institutions attend as members, and about 1,000 others, sometimes including graduate students, attend as guests. Each seminar selects its own members and speakers—or may have no speakers, simply gathering once a month to fight about a practical or intellectual problem.

Unlike a university department, no university policy or plan governs seminar subject matter. The director's boss is the assembly of seminar chairs, and the seminars' diversity of interests runs counter to the uniformity and coherence of purpose all good administrations need. University departments thrive when they can focus their energies, and they aspire to be at the cutting edge, alert to the latest important development. But the cutting edge by definition is narrow, whereas all University Seminars are required to be interdisciplinary and many aspire to involvement in the next important development or the one after that. Such aspirations are risky, but Tannenbaum believed in the value of making mistakes. A great university should make as few mistakes as possible, but a very great university should have a little corner where mistakes are not avoided but are combated, laughed at, and occasionally corrected. In the University Seminars, Tannenbaum's adventurous generosity of spirit gave Columbia such a home for the spontaneous interaction between error and its unpredictable antidotes.

The seminars emerged naturally from Tannenbaum's career and his character. He was one of the few Columbia undergraduates to be a conspicuous public figure before he was admitted as a freshman. In his teens, he had joined the Wobblies, or International Workers of the World, whose tactics and doctrines of class struggle had struck fear into the hearts of many American industrialists. In the cruel winter of 1913–14, he led groups of the homeless to stage what later generations would call sit-ins in New York churches. Like most such demonstrations, Tannenbaum's had both an immediate and a long-range purpose. He wanted a night's lodging for his hundred followers, and he wanted to call society's attention to the plight of the unemployed. Several churches responded in Christian fashion and paid the price of a night's lodging, and the *Times* obliged with front-page indignation over Tannenbaum's effrontery. Eventually, the church of St. Alphonsus on the Lower East Side asserted its civil rights and on March 4, 1914, called the police. The *Times* headline read, "I.W.W. Invaders Seized in Church . . . Tannenbaum Is Held in $5,000 Bail." Tannenbaum was sentenced to a year in the penitentiary on Blackwell's Island. He said later that he gave the police a date of birth designed not to represent reality, but to guarantee a stay in jail rather than the more sheltered experience of a boy's reformatory.

At any rate, the record we have shows that Frank Tannenbaum was born in 1893 in Brod, a city then in Austrian Galicia, now in Poland. In 1905, his family moved to the United States and settled in Massachusetts on a farm near Great Barrington. In 1906, he left alone for New York, lived with relatives, ran elevators, waited on tables, and went to the Ferrer School, at 63 West 107th Street, whose president boasted that it was "the first institution devoted to the constructive side of anarchism." Lincoln Steffens and Emma Goldman taught there. With this background, Tannenbaum used his time in jail not to explore the riches of self-pity, but to learn about the penal system and the recurrent frustrating efforts to make it just and redemptive. He met Thomas Mott Osborne, the warden of Sing Sing, and acquired a sense of prison life that led him later on to write three scholarly books on penology. Two of his chief proposals in these studies have become standard doctrine by now: parole when a convict is judged ready for release, which is widely practiced, and education in preparation for release, which is honored more in the breach than in the observance. His third proposal remains a rarity in the prison world. Tannenbaum believed that our humanity rests in large part on our active participation in social groups. He felt that prisons dehumanized their inmates by depriving them of organized social action and the responsibility that goes with it. He therefore advocated the kind of self-government that Osborne had instituted for the inmates of Sing Sing. Years later, he arranged to be incarcerated in Sing Sing to see this system actually at work.

Osborne recommended Tannenbaum to Dean Frederick P. Keppel at Columbia, and he was admitted to the College in 1914. At Columbia he studied history with Carlton J. H. Hayes and economics with Edwin R. A. Seligman, establishing the professional background for his scholarly career; but John Dewey's philosophy courses and personal interactions did the most to give Tannenbaum's radicalism a substrate of Jamesian pragmatism. This body of understanding rests on experience more than on abstractions, and Tannenbaum gave up the idea of class warfare partly from experience but also because, as time went on, he began to question the abstract idea of class. Indeed, in his 1950 book *A Philosophy of Labor*, he wrote, "The whole concept of 'class' is a hindrance to social analysis." But he also questioned social class on a moral basis. Membership in a class is thrust upon us, and for Tannenbaum, a world where we do not make our own relationships is as dehumanizing as a prison. He therefore rejected Marxism and felt that Soviet Russia had made two mutually contradictory decisions: it aspired to centralized control of all important actions and also

> to a higher material well-being for the mass of its people. It cannot pro-
> vide it without becoming a great industrial society and cannot become
> a great industrial society without freedom of private judgment in infi-
> nitely variable instances. If such freedom comes into being, as it must if
> industry is to develop, then the freedom will destroy the present police
> state.

This analysis was about thirty years ahead of that of the CIA or most political science departments.

Tannenbaum dedicated his first book to Dewey: *The Labor Movement: Its Conservative Functions and Social Consequences* (1921). In this book, he stated, "Trade-unionism is a repudiation of Marxism because its ends are moral rather than economic. It is a social and ethical system, not merely an economic one . . . The values implicit in trade-unionism are those of an older day . . . security, justice, freedom, and faith." He treasured the union movement because it restored social meaning to the lives of workers who had surrendered their active membership in villages or guilds or other human groupings to serve an industrial master. Tannenbaum valued the economic achievements of labor unions, but their central meaning for him was their participatory nature. He saw them as the antithesis of utopian constructs. They were always changing, unfinished, imperfect, and evolving. His involvement in labor history antedated his life at Columbia, but he felt grateful to Columbia all his life for giving

A young Tannenbaum (left) with his brother and their dog

him the intellectual resources to place the history of labor unions in the history of the world and a vision of society.

Tannenbaum's scholarly reputation as a labor historian and a penologist has its origins in his experiences before he came to Columbia. The other two chief components of his scholarship took shape soon after. Dean Keppel formed a small group whose undergraduate members included Tannenbaum, Albert Redpath (a future Columbia general counsel and trustee), and three men who later became major scholars at Columbia—Horace Friess, James Gutmann, and John Herman Randall. Their charge was to meet regularly at the Faculty Club to discuss serious problems. They continued to do so for fifty years, strengthening Tannenbaum's belief that important ideas emerge from ongoing face-to-face discussions. These meetings were interrupted only for reasons like Tannenbaum's year of service in the army in 1917. He spent much of that year in the deep South and encountered the subject of his third great body of scholarship, the American black and the underlying history of slavery. In his 1946 book *Slave and Citizen* he compared the destinies of blacks in Latin America and in the British colonies. Spaniards and Portuguese came to slavery in a context dating back to ancient Rome, where it had no connection with race but came simply from being on the losing side of a war. There was also a long tradition of manumission, and in some Latin American countries slaves could buy their liberty on the installment plan, paying one twenty-fourth of their appraised value and borrowing the rest of themselves, paying interest on their outstanding value until they had amortized the whole. These and many other elaborate legalities gave slaves a moral identity in the state, and the Catholic Church reinforced this humanity by refusing to exclude them from its sacraments or sanction the dissolution of marriages by the master. Every Latin American knew many blacks who were not slaves, and many knew slaves who were not black.

England had no such tradition, and English colonies on the islands and in North America excluded blacks from the legal world. They might be the only witnesses to a murder but could not testify, and neither the Protestant churches nor the legal system moved to protect marriages and other sacraments against the property rights of owners. In several states, a freed slave had to leave the state within ninety days, so that being black meant being a slave. Tannenbaum linked the moral status of a human being with that person's ability to enter responsibly into relationships, and he felt that blacks in Latin America had emerged from slavery with this moral status intact. In the north, the British lack of experience with slavery had left the blacks and, even more, their white oppressors crippled morally, so that the "emancipation may have legally freed the Negro, but it failed to free the white man, and by that failure it denied to the Negro the moral status requisite for effective legal freedom." This delay, due to the relatively brief tradition of slavery in the English-speaking world, meant that it would take much longer in our country and the British West Indies than in Latin America before

> physical proximity, slow cultural intertwining, the growth of a middle group that stands in experience and equipment between the lower and the upper class, and the slow process of moral identification work their way against all seemingly absolute systems of values and prejudices. Society is essentially dynamic, and while the mills of God grind slow, they grind exceeding sure. Time—the long time—will draw a veil over the white and black in this hemisphere, and future generations will look back upon the record of strife as it stands revealed in the history of the people of this New World of ours with wonder and incredulity. For they will not understand the issues that the quarrel was about.

Tannenbaum's long view of the Soviet system has been proven right. This much longer view of the outcome for blacks and whites and others in the Americas

TANNENBAUM AS LATIN AMERICANIST

As a teacher and adviser at Columbia, Frank Tannenbaum was best known as a Latin Americanist.

Although his first acquaintance was with Mexico, about which he wrote several books, Frank's knowledge of Latin America was comprehensive. At that time, he had probably traveled more widely than any other scholar of the area and was in close touch with both leaders and rank-and-file citizens. These contacts he maintained to the end. His office bookshelves were filled with volumes bearing handwritten dedications from a wide range of literary and public figures.

One measure of his reputation both here and in Latin America was the graduate seminar he gave in his later years at Columbia. It had a limited number of students and met in his large office. Maté was served to all those present who had a taste for it. A different person lectured each week, usually a Latin American or Caribbean literary or political figure who was visiting New York at that time and had been invited, through the agency of the State Department, to appear in Frank's office that afternoon.

Frank Tannenbaum took great pleasure in this seminar and was proud of the list of guest lecturers. His greatest coup was the occasion when three successive presidents of Venezuela appeared at the same time—General Lopez Contreras, his handpicked successor General Medina Angarita, and Romulo Betancourt, who had overthrown Medina and been conspired against by Lopez Contreras. According to Tannenbaum, all three were civil to one another at the meeting and engaged in more give-and-take than ever before or since.

Tannenbaum was also a most conscientious dissertation adviser, as I learned when he served as the "outside" from history on the dissertation committee for my Ph.D. in economics. Its subject was labor relations in Chile. Tannenbaum read the thesis with great care, and there was hardly a page on which he did not offer a criticism or suggestion. Later he confided to me that he was sure the chairman of my Ph.D. dissertation committee had not read a single page of the document, and he wanted to be sure that someone read it carefully.

It was that kind of care and concern that won for Frank Tannenbaum so many "disciples" who were proud to claim him as the inspiration for their lifelong interest in the study of Latin America.

—Robert Alexander

remains unrealized but shows how he thought history works.

Tannenbaum's career as a scholar and a teacher centered not on penology, labor history, or racial history, but on an area where all three of these interests shed light on innumerable complexities—Latin America. He went to Mexico in 1922 as a journalist for the *Century Magazine,* in the aftermath of the Revolution of 1910 and the Constitution of 1917. He distrusted most revolutions but felt that the Mexican one had served two important ends. It had disrupted the *hacienda* system, which he regarded as combining the evils of the American mill town and cotton plantation: centralized decision-making, an enclosed culture, a caste system, and the impossibility of those participatory institutions that for Tannenbaum constituted the means to moral humanity. The Mexican revolution had also begun the process of restoring to the Native Americans some part of the self-determination that the Spaniards and later the mixed breeds had been trying to destroy since the fifteenth century. Decades later he would contrast this revolution in a subsistence economy with Castro's in Cuba. Cuba had virtually no Native Americans and was a comparatively rich industrialized country with an export economy based on sugar and tobacco. In order to destroy a corrupt and oppressive government, Castro had disabled a promising society. Tannenbaum predicted in 1959 that Castro would be unable to carry through his early dream of relinquishing power to a democracy and would be entrapped into the lifelong status of just another Latin American *caudillo*, since his power was personal, not derived through a participatory organization that people joined freely.

Tannenbaum's books draw on a broad range of available scholarship, usually for hard facts not for opinions to support or oppose, but he always tried to go to the real source of information. At times, this would mean reading archival materials from Simón Bolívar or early chronicles of the Spanish conquest, but he relied centrally on his contacts with the people directly involved. He traveled for two years through Mexico on donkey back with a handful of Native American companions. He hiked the length of Puerto Rico, canoed the length of the Amazon, and knew much of upland South America in the only way it was accessible, on foot. But his friendships with the disempowered that he met on such expeditions reinforced his friendships with and usefulness to the movers and shakers of Latin America. While Lázaro Cárdenas was president of Mexico and on until Tannenbaum's death, the two were in frequent contact, sharing their awarenesses and experiences.

The idea for the University Seminars evolved naturally out of Tannenbaum's gradual discovery that scholarly and practical problems have interlocking solutions that can best be arrived at in ongoing unstructured discussion. In the 1940s, Nicholas Murray Butler liked the idea as a way of mobilizing the immense intellectual resources of the university to treat national problems too new and pressing to have evolved into a university department or a scholarly tradition. Butler had retired by March 8, 1944, when professors William Westermann, Harry Carman, James Shotwell, Horatio Smith, Robert Schuyler, Horace Friess, Herbert Schneider, John Krout, Schuyler Wallace, Frank Tannenbaum, Wesley Mitchell, Arthur Macmahon, John H. Randall, James Gutmann, Philip Jessup, Leo Wolman, Joseph Chamberlain, and Frederick Mills proposed that Acting President Frank Fackenthal establish a group of permanent seminars. The guiding spirit of this movement was Tannenbaum. The proposal said in part that the university should

> announce the establishment of perhaps no more than half a dozen sem-
> inars devoted to the study of some of the basic institutions continuous
> in human society, such, for instance, as the state, war, the organization

of labor including the history of slavery, crime, or such ever-present issues as conflict between church and state, friction between urban and rural areas, or the human family. . . . These institutions are more comprehensive than any course or any department and reach beyond the present organization of any faculty.

. . . Most important . . . is the essential condition of *permanent association.* . . . It is essential that associates may be free to hesitate, fumble, retract and make many new starts. . . . Time is the essence of the matter, and, given time enough, the group will grow into a true intellectual fellowship . . . facets of the question must be presented and considered, not once, but over and over again. . . .

The group must feel completely free to follow its own bent, it must be responsible only to its own academic conscience, and it must be untrammeled in organization, method, and membership.

It must be based upon voluntary association, where membership is a privilege, and where the only compensation is the sense of intellectual growth, and the esteem of one's equals in a common intellectual endeavor. (Frank Tannenbaum, "The University Seminar Movement at Columbia University," *Political Science Quarterly* 68, no. 2, June 1953)

Fackenthal accepted this proposal, whose main intentions have persisted in the University Seminars until the present day. Any group of Columbia professors may propose a seminar, provided that they do not come from a single department and that they include experts from outside Columbia. If a committee of their fellow professors finds their purpose intellectually serious and their plan sound, the operation Tannenbaum started gives them a room to meet in, a rapporteur to record their discussions, and some travel money for a visitor or two, and they start meeting once a month to work on their problem; only then, perhaps, do they need to begin to worry about grant proposals, budget allocations, departmental involvements, and the other truths of academic life.

By 1945, five seminars were operating: The State, Peace, Religion, Rural Life, and The Renaissance. Tannenbaum provided guidance, inspiration, and cash, which he raised from foundations, corporations, and individuals, including himself. Alice Maier provided the full office support for the seminars, and until Tannenbaum's retirement as a professor in 1964, there was no director, no Seminar office, and no charter or constitution for the seminar movement, which Tannenbaum in his grandiose moments hoped would eventually replace the university. Over the next two years, needing a title and a university office to work from after his retirement, Tannenbaum regularized his own position into a directorship. With a clear sense of his own mortality, he debated whether to incorporate the Seminars as a separate entity or to keep them as a part of Columbia. With the help of Lawrence Chamberlain, vice president of the university, and his old friend Albert Redpath, its counsel, he negotiated a charter that he felt would protect the "creative spontaneity" of the Seminars from an "unstructured situation [where] interference is inevitable—because the desire for general rules and uniformity is irresistible," as he wrote in a letter to Chamberlain on March 23, 1964. The University Council approved Tannenbaum's draft of the constitution on April 19, 1966, and it stands with slight revisions as the basic rule for the Seminars today.

When Tannenbaum died in 1969, there were fifty seminars, and for the past quarter century, there have been seventy or eighty, with up to 3,000 participants. To support this movement he had initiated, fostered, and chartered, Tannenbaum and his wife left the Seminars more than $1.5 million in their wills, and others made major additions to this endowment in the 1970s and 1980s. The seminar participants and speakers continue to be not only Columbia professors but also professors and other experts of every sort from all over the world who have been invited to join or speak. Some seminars also invite graduate students, but 30 percent follow the lead of "a distinguished member of the faculty, with a national reputation as a teacher, [who] threw up his hands and said, 'Mercy, no. We don't want them to see us flounder.'"

Tannenbaum believed that fruitful initiatives came from the bottom up.

The seminars are no longer all permanent. While three of the first five have survived, half of those established in the next fifty years have either merged or dissolved. And the Seminars have come to accept the dissolution of a seminar as a proper corollary of their voluntary nature and even to encourage the formation of seminars to study a particular problem over a finite period, but Tannenbaum's basic vision remains intact.

The University Seminars reflect Tannenbaum's cast of mind, his sense that even insoluble problems demand understanding, that the practical and the intellectual worlds cannot be dealt with separately, that joining a participatory organization defines one's moral and social humanity, and, most of all, that simple problems in simple economies and societies can be handled by fiat from authority but that the intricate problems of modern life demand private judgments in infinitely variable instances, the kind of judgments that emerge in long, freewheeling discussion in voluntary groups.

The University Seminars, however, are also very much a product of New York City and Columbia University in the 1940s. New York had a wealth of academic, cultural, business, and governmental institutions that made it in many ways the center of the postwar world, and Columbia was a central institution of New York. Today the city and the university are richer and more varied than they were then, but neither is as central, since more and more cities have skylines, banks of world importance, corporate headquarters, great museums, and splendid symphonies and more and more universities have celebrated faculties; many even have institutes and core curricula borrowed from Columbia.

Within the university especially, the environment in the 1940s encouraged the founding of the University Seminars. The undergraduate requirement that all students take a program in general education alongside their majors and electives had shaped the minds of two generations of students. More important and less noted in a university that tended to promote its most eminent scholars from within, these Core courses had shaped the minds of a large part of the faculty. Columbia professors had had to function in the rough and tumble of discussion classes dealing with texts far from their departmental specialties. Their teaching experience made them more receptive to a scholarly life of face-to-face disputation on issues to which they brought expertise from outside the departmental framework. This fertile ground for interdepartmental studies, coupled with the New York location, also made 1940s Columbia the natural place to invent area studies institutes, something new in the academic world, called into existence by the need to staff the United States' new international obligations with specialists in a region as well as an academic department. But like the general education courses, and more self-consciously, these institutes also were instruments for the education of the faculty. The need was national, but Columbia's academic milieu and geographic location enabled it to take the initiative in this innovation, as it did in the University Seminars, whose primary function was the education of the faculty and its exploitation for the solution of fresh or age-old problems.

Tannenbaum loved Columbia as the institution that had opened up the world to him. He expressed his gratitude by giving his university an enterprise that opens up the world to 3,000 Columbians and others every month and—through their teaching, writing, and discussion—to innumerable others everywhere. He believed that important and fruitful initiatives came from the bottom up, taking the form of a movement rather than an organization, and he therefore rigorously abjured control of the individual seminars, just as he composed a charter in which Columbia renounced direct control of the seminar movement. Columbia had the administrative courage to abide by that restriction.

Today, we call the Seminars an enterprise more often than a movement, but Columbia continues to use them in the spirit of the film *Fast, Cheap, and Out of Control,* which proposes hundreds of little robots to explore Mars, rather than one large one that can only answer questions already established as important. The Seminars remain the place for Columbia to take its administrative and intellectual risks.

Today the academic milieu remains cordial to interdepartmental studies. The Core Curriculum for undergraduates remains healthy; the regional studies institutes that Columbia pioneered have become deeply established at Columbia and widely imitated around the world; and the university has fostered an array of other interdepartmental undertakings in the natural and social sciences. These developments legitimize the enterprise of the University Seminars and at the same time offer competition. The Seminars are no longer the only game in town for those who want to cross departmental boundaries. At the same time, they make a good incubator for projects that want to bypass the administrative, personal, and financial costs of obtaining large grants and incurring large responsibilities for their tentative initial steps. When a university seminar turns into an institute, we feel that it has done its job very well. When it dissolves after a few years and a dozen good articles by various members, we feel that it has served a different purpose just as well. If we are faithful to the spirit of adventure that Frank Tannenbaum brought to Columbia, we neither prescribe nor rank these purposes but simply bring our intellects together to explore the widest range of experience we can encounter.

CHAPTER 36

The Core Curriculum: Van Doren, Erskine, and the Great Books Legacy

—⟶⟶—

John Van Doren and Carl Hovde
with Reminiscences by John D. Rosenberg and John Hollander

Mark Van Doren was already a living legend when I arrived on campus in 1937. He was not only the talk of literary-minded folks on the fourth floor of John Jay Hall—he was even the toast of the drinking crowd at the Gold Rail and the West End. Close friends of mine managed to squeeze into his overcrowded classes, and although my own luck as a Chinese history major was not that good, under the influence of my upperclass betters (among them Thomas Merton and Robert Gerdy, later an editor at The New Yorker*) I made an extracurricular point of reading Van Doren's* Shakespeare *and subsequently his* Noble Voice. *Later I also caught up with his* Liberal Education, *which became a landmark on the subject. It is full of perennial wisdom, some of it even—believe it or not— on the Asian humanities.*

The essays below give us a sense of Van Doren as well as his legacy in the College's Core Curriculum. Included are reminiscences of two prominent former students. John Rosenberg, who graduated in 1950, was a student of Van Doren's, and he re-creates here something of the magic woven by Van Doren during his inspirational classes. Rosenberg himself has been a veteran teacher of the Humanities course (of which Van Doren was a founding father) and of nineteenth-century English literature. A recipient of the Mark Van Doren Great Teacher Award as well as of the Heyman Center Award for Distinguished Service to the Core Curriculum, John is very much a part of the living legacy that comes down from Van Doren.

Van Doren probably thought of himself mostly as a poet, and this side of him is addressed by another former student, John Hollander, the Sterling Professor of English at Yale University, who is himself not only one of America's leading poets but an essayist, anthologist, and a much-honored teacher who carries on the ideals of liberal education that characterize the Core.

In addition to his role as teacher and poet, Mark Van Doren was a major figure in the Great Books movement, which reached out to the University of Chicago, St. John's College in Annapolis and Santa Fe, and many other American campuses. We are fortunate to have Mark's son John, long executive editor of The Great Ideas Today *(a companion to the Great Books program), to give us a first-hand account of how that program developed. Carl Hovde, former dean of the College and a prominent leader of the Humanities program, tells us something of how the program has developed in more recent years, still as an integral part of the Core Curriculum in the College.*

Wm. Theodore de Bary

The Beginnings of the Great Books Movement at Columbia

John Van Doren

It is generally agreed that what became the Great Books movement in American higher education (if "movement" will serve as a general term) began at Columbia College in 1920 with the offering of a course known as General Honors. This was the conception of John Erskine of the English department, who thought all students should have as part of their education the experience of reading and discussing what he called great books. He believed that could best be done in a class that would not be taught in the ordinary sense by an instructor but would consist of a conversation among the students over which the instructor would merely preside—asking questions, helping the talk along, disentangling it when necessary, but in no sense serving as an authority on the work being considered. Actually there were two leaders of this kind for each section of the class, a requirement that Erskine in an inspired moment laid down and which was designed to prevent, as apparently it did prevent—at least when the leaders were of approximately equal stature—any one person from dominating the conversation, directing all the talk to himself.

There was never a very large enrollment in the course, which against Erskine's wishes was restricted to upperclassmen, but there were enough takers so that he could not himself teach all the sections even with the help of a colleague. He found many of the senior faculty at the College were unwilling, or perhaps they had not the courage, to take sections (they gave various excuses), so he turned to younger members for discussion leaders. Among these was Mark Van Doren, who in 1923 was joined by Mortimer Adler, with whom he led a section of the course until it was discontinued in 1928. (It was later reconstituted.) There were also, among others, Raymond Weaver, Herbert Schneider, Rexford G. Tugwell, Irwin Edman, John Bartlet Brebner, and, later, Moses Hadas. In 1929 Adler left the College for the University of Chicago, where he wrote trenchantly and often about great books and where he also led an annual great books seminar with the university president, Robert M. Hutchins. Van Doren subsequently helped to design what became Humanities A at Columbia in 1937, a course designed for freshmen that has since evolved into Literature Humanities. By then, great books were being taught not merely at Columbia and Chicago but at St. John's College in Annapolis, where, with the addition of scientific and mathematical classics examined in tutorials and laboratories, they constituted the entire course of study for the students and still do. Without such additions, they have since been more or less established also in courses at numerous other colleges and universities around the country, as well as dis-established, lately, at some of them.

THE CHALLENGES

What was the thinking of those who instituted the study of these books in the college curriculum? Why did they hold that this study should be undertaken, not just by some students, but by all? How could they maintain, as they did, that as all students should read such books, so the whole faculty of a college should teach them, irrespective of the disciplines which as professors they represented? How could they ignore, or at least put aside, questions of language, history, and criticism, which were regarded in some quarters as insuperable obstacles to the kind of study they proposed? For most of the great books had to be encountered in translation, none was considered as a product of the age in which it appeared, and no scholarly or critical interpretation of them was allowed to preempt the students' own.

Erskine himself thought that such study should be commenced because most students were simply not "well read." His list of about eighty works, to be taken up over two years, was designed to cure that defect, and while some of his titles have since disappeared from such courses, most are still encountered in them wherever they exist. Erskine defended the readings he chose, against his opponents on the College faculty of the time, in terms that are still used everywhere to justify their

MY GREAT FRIENDS

My great friends do not know me.
Hamlet in the halls,
Achilles by the river, and Don Quixote
Feasting with the Duke see no one there
Like me, like Mark Van Doren, who grows daily
Older while they look not, change not,
Die not save the deaths their masters made.

Those, yes, over and over.
And Bottom stands tremendous,
And Sancho rubs his head, half comprehending
Knighthood, and Malvolio's cold voice
Invites the madhouse hour. These neither die
Nor rise again. They look not, change not,
Only as folly, wonderful, lasts on.

Still my great friends ignore me,
Momently grown older
And dying in the west. They will be there
Forever, gods of the world, my own immortals
Who will not go along. Nor do I ask them.
Let them forever look not, change not,
Die not save as mortals may behold.

—Mark Van Doren

presence: that such books were not addressed to the specialists; that they could be read at least the first time through with a decent swiftness rather than with perfect comprehension (General Honors read one book a week); that they should be encountered so far as possible in the whole rather than through excerpts; that they were not just literary works—General Honors read Homer and Shakespeare, but it also read Plato, Aristotle, St. Augustine, and Spinoza; and that those who led the discussion of these authors should not stifle it with scholarship.

No one claimed that the kind of reading that satisfied General Honors was good enough. Erskine maintained that a lifetime was required for that. "We do not expect the students to get what they should from the readings," Jacques Barzun said (he was speaking of the later Humanities course), "but what they can."

The propositions underlying what Erskine himself first conceived as a kind of gentlemanly acculturation became clear with practice. They may be sought not only in his writings but in those of Adler and Van Doren, who wrote of them at length in his *Liberal Education* (1944), and of course a number of others, among them Hutchins. Scott Buchanan, dean of St. John's and the author of the college catalogue of 1937 in which its program was set forth, was a source of ideas for all of them. Adler and Van Doren taught with Buchanan at the People's Institute of Cooper Union in New York in the 1920s, where classes in the great books for adults were offered to immigrants and native laborers who were eager to acquire the education that circumstances had deprived them of. Buchanan thought such classes were really the forge on which much of his understanding of how great books might best be used to teach and learn—how instructive they really could be—was hammered out.

Of these propositions on which the study of such books was thought to stand, not all were adhered to by Erskine himself, at least not to the same extent that others did. Two that were essentially the same, and which everyone held to, were, first, that there is something common to us as human beings, whatever divides us, which the great books may be said to address; and second, that there exists what might be called a permanent present in which books of this kind may be found—they are "contemporary to every age," Hutchins said—and in which they can always be profitably read. The first of those assumptions has lately been challenged by those who find our differences—of culture and gender—more important than our similarities, and doubtless such differences deserve more consideration than they were likely to have had in 1920: They have been recognized partly by the addition of an Asian Humanities requirement at Columbia and, at St. John's, Santa Fe, a faculty study group for Asian great books. On the other hand, the notion of a permanent present has always been rejected by those who insist that the great books are products of history, that what we have from that source is intelligible only as an expression of it, and that to consider any writing without reference to this, through the learning that conveys it, is hopelessly misleading.

THE TEST OF TRUTH

A third proposition, that the great books are not without defects—more, that their contentions are sometimes wrong—and that the business of their students is to recognize the first fault and correct the second for the sake of their own understanding—was equally important to Van Doren and Adler, particularly the latter, who said that Erskine, "though a naturally great teacher in his day," treated all such books "as if they were *belles lettres*" and sought only the recognition of them as literary works—fine art like painting or sculpture, which it would be presumptuous to question. Adler thought philosophical and other expository works, at least, should stand the test of truth. If Aristotle, for instance, says that some men are natural slaves, we must reject the argument not because we do not like it but because it leads to the impossible conclusion that there are two species of human being: We may suppose that Aristotle was misled by the limitations of the slaves he saw about him and "mistook their nurture for their nature," as Rousseau observed, but we cannot call him right. Van Doren thought even works of poetry had better be as true as possible. He noted that *Paradise Lost,* seeking as it does to explain why things are as they are, is weakened by its Ptolemaic scheme of heaven, which Milton knew was false (as Dante, who also used it, did not) but which he thought more suitable for his purposes than the Copernican one; and by a theology we can't believe, which allows Christ to be reassured by his Father, before his earthly career begins, that he need fear nothing because he will be taken back to his throne after his sufferings are over—as if the world would have found itself in a savior who never had to doubt the salvation of his soul. By comparison, Erskine could only explain his dislike of *Othello,* which he thought "full of splendid verse," as a latter-day refusal to accept that "in the supposed circumstances of the play, [Desdemona] just naturally had to be smothered"—a judgment that seems not so much a claim of truth as an expression of taste.

Both Adler and Van Doren paid a price for taking positions of this sort. Adler, who thought much philosophy was false and said so, was routinely dismissed as doctrinaire by colleagues who did not recognize the doctrine implicit in their own belief that their discipline does not comprehend truth at all, but deals only with opinion. Van Doren was taken to task for presuming to argue, in *The Noble Voice* (1946), that whatever their virtues, Wordsworth and Byron, like Milton and Vergil, were unsuccessful when it came to writing narrative poems, as compared with Homer, Dante, and Chaucer. The reviewer of the book in *The New Yorker* complained that "Mr. Van Doren cites no authorities." "It didn't seem to have occurred to her," he said, "that I was trying to be one."

IN CLASS WITH MARK VAN DOREN: A REMINISCENCE

I sat in Mark Van Doren's classes in the late 1940s, a dazzling time for an English major in Columbia College. The fourth floor of Hamilton Hall comprised at that time perhaps the most brilliant configuration of teacher-critics of literature ever assembled in a single English department. The most remarkable presence in that distinguished company belonged to Mark Van Doren.

No other teacher I have ever known conveyed so abundantly or freshly the actual feel of an idea caught in flight. He did not teach a particular body of knowledge; rather he appeared to embody the act of thinking itself. He had a powerful athleticism of mind and loved to wrestle in public with paradox. Indeed, paradox was his pedagogic medium. The irony of inquiry played over his handsome features as he spoke, and his resonant voice was transfixing. He never taught a conclusion, and once he had explored a subject, he left its further elaboration to others. He wrote a superb book on all of Shakespeare's poems and plays, then gave his famous Shakespeare course to a gifted junior colleague, Andrew Chiappe. Instinctively gracious and generous, he knew that the best teaching is not the exhibition of mastery but a joint and joyous inquiry, a shared quest. Only the very best of teachers—Moses Hadas also comes to mind—can reach all of those who have ears to hear; Van Doren stretched the minds of athletes and future engineers, not only of aspiring poets and English professors.

I arrived on the College scene too late for Van Doren's Shakespeare lectures but not for his new classes on narrative art, including Cervantes. None of us who attended those classes will forget certain moments, for they have entered the very fabric of our thought. I still hear echoes from them more than half a century later, a scarcely audible music that accompanies me when I walk into my Humanities class and we talk about Don Quixote's dreams of reality and the reality of his dreams.

In 1958, almost a decade after graduating, I heard Van Doren give his farewell lecture, which happened also to be on *Don Quixote.* I sat on the floor in the aisle of an overcrowded amphitheater. I had never seen so many students crowded into a single room or been witness to such absolute attentiveness. At the very end, with the courtesy of the Don himself, he thanked us all for the quality of our attention.

—*John D. Rosenberg*

Mark Van Doren
teaching his last class
at Columbia, 1958

AN ACT OF INTELLECTUAL COURAGE

One further proposition, regarded by these figures as fundamental to the study of the great books, was that such books are their own teachers, as distinct from the instructors who conduct classes in them. This is true of any book taken in and for itself, rather than as a window through which we look at a "subject" it may be said to reveal. But other books have less to say for themselves, do not raise so well the questions implicit in the ideas they contain or the actions they render. It is because the great books do both of these things, Erskine sensed at the beginning, that they are best considered round a table of which they may be said to occupy the center, equidistant from everyone present. General Honors had such a table, as does the St. John's seminar. A defect of Columbia's Lit Hum is arguably that it does not and that instructors must resist a temptation to direct the talk toward the front of the room.

What were the students supposed to learn from such books? Erskine said that they would derive a sense of the culture in which they lived and the tradition from which, whether they knew it or not, they came. This is less persuasive if you come, say, from Korea. Van Doren contended merely that "the common possession" of the great books "would civilize any society that had it." But he and Adler and Buchanan insisted also that what the books would give any student who read them seriously was a grasp of the liberal arts—the arts of grammar, rhetoric, and logic, or reading, writing, and thinking—which, they pointed out, was after all the aim of the liberal education the student was trying to acquire. On any subject, what terms are proper to what we wish to say? What is the best way to say it? How can this be structured so as to be both intelligible and defensible? That most of us tend to feel helpless when we must respond to these questions is a sign that we are not very competent in the liberal arts. The authors of the great books can be seen as good practitioners of them. What they say may strike any reader as wrong in a given case rather than right, but it will be in large measure his familiarity with the sort of books they wrote that teaches him to know the difference. So armed, he or she will have a fair chance of arriving at a better view of that subject along with a just judgment of the book's attempt to deal with it. This is what led Adler to define the liberal arts as "the basic skills of learning."

Implicit in the phrase "liberal arts" is the idea that such arts in fact are liberating, and if the authors of the great books were and are good liberal artists, then it is freedom in some basic sense that they help us to attain. The figures remembered here who urged their study deeply believed that this was so and would have been skeptical of those among us now who seek the study of such books from a conviction that they provide us with a canon or tradition or culture by which we may be safely anchored. There is nothing safe about the great books. Even Marx's "Manifesto," the doctrine of which we dismiss, must shake our capitalist complacencies. In political terms—and the freedom such arts aim at is partly political—what is to be sought, Buchanan argued, is the ability envisioned by the Founders of the Republic to create and maintain a government of free human beings. This is far beyond what is usually perceived as provided by the Bill of Rights. "Civil Liberties are permissive," Buchanan said, "but they are not enabling." To recognize the forces that contest the present world, to sort out the claims made for and against them, and to decide between their encouragement or restraint, is the hard task of a citizenry that cannot make good choices without the arts, whose object is to free it from ignorance, gullibility, and confusion.

Irwin Edman, one of the first Columbia instructors to lead a General Honors seminar

A priori freedom is intellectual, and the weakness of the liberal arts among us is still more radically indicated by the fact that our minds are shackled by the very education that is supposed to deliver them. So at least Buchanan, again, believed, pointing out that this education has led us to suppose that our intellects are incapable of arriving at the truth of most things, certainly those outside the area of specialization in which we have undertaken to train them. We think we cannot grasp mathematics or science or philosophy or poetry, as the case may be. Thus we allow ourselves—*will* ourselves—to become "cripples in our minds and fractions of men in our lives," Buchanan said. "Some of us," he added, "are willing to crush the Socratic formula ('I know what—or that—I do not know') and say 'I know nothing.'"

The reading of the great books, each of which may be said to constitute an act of intellectual courage on the part of its author—a willingness to try to state what had not been stated, or stated so well, before—was intended by the figures recollected here as in some degree an antidote to this self-inflicted poison. Was that good medicine? Those who urged their study believed that such books address us as if we could see the truth in them or recognize its absence, not as if this were beyond our capabilities. For anyone, from whatever cause, that may prove not always to be the case. To the extent that it is, however, such books would seem to demonstrate, as their protagonists believed they would, that each of us has an intellectual faculty, and that, while its strength varies, its nature is the same in us all—that we are all capable of what Socrates called "following the argument."

There are many who doubt this, denying the presence of the intellect, at least in most of us, beyond what may serve to store the lessons of those who, somehow provided, impress them upon us, whereby we are in a manner stamped—informed, if you prefer. This may be so sometimes. Perhaps that is all that be achieved in certain cases. But such a credo seems better suited to a zoo than to a college, let alone a commonwealth. At any rate the conviction of those who instituted the great books, and of those who still teach them, was of a different kind, and is. Perhaps we have to leave it there.

MARK VAN DOREN AS POET AND TEACHER

One of the reasons I came to Columbia was to study with Mark Van Doren. I'd heard his name frequently as an important figure in the American literary world; my mother spoke of him with literary reverence; he had received what was for me at sixteen, at least, the imprimatur of T. S. Eliot's praise for his book on John Dryden. I had also read some poems of his in Conrad Aiken's wonderful 1944 Modern Library anthology of *Twentieth-Century American Poetry* (so influential, I believe, for many writers of the generation after World War II); I remember particularly liking "The Whisperer" and recognizing the kinship of its closing turn with that of some contemporary short stories I was immersed in (but not, at the time, its kinship with Hardy). Similarly, "Axle Song," very Emersonian in some ways—something that I wouldn't really grasp for many years:

> That anything should be
> Place, time, earth, error—
> Or a round eye in man to see:
> That is the terror.

> And a true mind to try
> Cube, sphere, deep, short and long—
> That as the burden of the sky's
> Hoarse axle-song. . . .

And taking up further the agenda in his splendid short poems of over a decade earlier, "Segments" and "Circumstances," with their relation to Emerson's great essay, "Circles." Mark's poems kept company with the poetry of modernity—of Hardy, Robinson, Frost—that I now admire more and more but could least appreciate at the time (being attracted to the more sensational modernism of Eliot, Stevens, and Williams).

It was only after I had begun to study with him that I first read a poem that became a favorite of his among my literary friends, the widely anthologized poem that starts:

This amber sunstream, with an hour to live,
Flows carelessly, and does not save itself;
Nor recognizes any entered room—
This room; nor hears the clock upon a shelf,
Declaring the lone hour; for where it goes
All space in a great silence ever flows.

Later on I came to "And did the Animals?" about the consciousness of being in the ark among the animals that Noah had preserved and a preface for me to all his disturbingly sensitive poetry about animals.

I started at Columbia after he had turned over his Shakespeare course to another of my great teachers, Andrew Chiappe. But I was electrified by his Verse, a mini-course (meeting once a week) with forty to fifty students but with the tone and procedure of a seminar rather than a lecture. Short poems or passages from longer ones, mimeographed, read aloud by Van Doren, were then examined, sometimes with his opening commentary, sometimes only through his shrewdly framed questions to the class.

We were led through a number of texts that have continued to stay with me, and whose selection itself I have continued to consider, among them: the ballade from Chaucer's *The Legend of Good Women*; Hart Crane's "Praise for an Urn"; the first two stanzas of Wordsworth's "Resolution and Independence" (and getting me to notice how in the second line, *"The rain came heavily, and fell in floods"*); the opening stanzas of George Meredith's "Love in the Valley"; "The Second Coming" of Yeats, but also his "The Cat and the Moon"; Matthew Prior's brilliant "The merchant, to secure his treasure, / Conveys it in a borrowed name"; Hardy's "The Convergence of the Twain"; Frost's "The Oven-Bird"; Dryden's "In Memory of John Oldham"; as well as that staple of introduction to modern poetics, Sir Thomas Wyatt's "They Flee from Me," in both the original version and that rendered more smooth by his editor, Tottel (one had, of course, to prefer the more metrically and rhetorically awkward original).

Mark would range in his interpretive concerns from putting a line under a microscope to the widest of digression. And in the very conjunction of those, his teaching voice was the same as that in his poems however differently pitched. Students of all kinds—not just future writers—can learn more from a poet teaching great literature to them than from a "workshop." Van Doren's kind of teaching was, one always felt, part of his poetic discourse.

—*John Hollander*

What Columbia College Is Known For

Carl Hovde

Every undergraduate college has its own identity produced by a combination of location, physical plant, curriculum, and the styles of instruction and administration. For a good many colleges it is hard to say what is most important in the mix, but for Columbia College the answer is clear: The required courses largely create its basic nature. It is not only that at Columbia there are courses that students must take, for many colleges have distribution requirements; students must take so many credits in science, in literature, and so on, but the choice of particular courses is up to them. Columbia students make two choices of this kind—they can (and must) choose from a limited number of sciences and, by the time they graduate, they must have taken two terms from a list of courses intended to give them some experience beyond the dominant cultures of the West.

With the exception of these electives, the Columbia requirements are designed to be a set of courses taught in small sections where students are for the most part studying the same things at the same time as all the other classes in each course. They take composition, a year each in two courses that concentrate on literature and on public policy and governance respectively, and finally one term each of music and the visual arts.

The oldest of these courses, called Introduction to Contemporary Civilization, developed from a requirement introduced in 1919, the faculty having decided that the origins and implications of World War I were issues that all students should ponder. Requirements in music and art were added to literature and social sciences courses in 1947. These six courses, particularly the last four, are called the Core program.

LITERATURE HUMANITIES

The yearlong Humanities course, now called Literature Humanities, does two things. It introduces students to some major literary, historical, and philosophical works in the Western tradition, and it does so in small classes through discussion intended to make students think actively from moment to moment rather than listen to lectures. Though the course was introduced in 1937, coming out of the background described by John Van Doren, it and other courses in the Great Books movement have a history going back to major changes in the college curriculum that began to develop a hundred years earlier.

Well into the nineteenth century, a college education in the liberal arts at Columbia and similar schools was still shaped toward an elite male population and was still based on a classical curriculum. Columbia had entrance requirements in both Greek and Latin; students continued these studies in college, and the texts studied were sometimes looked at more for their historical settings and philological character than for their artistic natures and the issues they embodied. With the increasing importance of the sciences and technology, however, together with the rise of the social sciences, the curriculum began to get crowded. Modern studies and the modern languages in which they had in part developed began to diminish the emphasis on the classics, except for those students who wanted to concentrate there.

As the new learning continued to develop into the twentieth century, some at Columbia began to look on undergraduate work primarily as initial training for further professional study, something that could be done in less than the traditional four years. The "preprofessional option" became more available, allowing many students into specialized training after two or three years. For the faculty members and administrators who encouraged this, the traditional college experience had become something of an obstacle, and they looked on the College as tangential to the central task of the university.

The defenders of the College prevailed in the long run, however, asserting that the traditional four years were important to the development of a well-educated person who had interests nourishing both private and public life. Most though not all of the teachers on this side of the argument were understandably from the language departments and the other humanistic disciplines. They sometimes spoke of the "whole man," and if that rhetoric now sounds old-fashioned, what they meant has not changed: the desire to provide students with humanistic experience that will long resonate, the better to make the mind more interesting because more resourceful in knowledge and imagination.

As the older curriculum came under greater pressure, the College faculty began to think about how to preserve for the students an exposure to the humanistic past while making room for the studies indispensable to the modern world.

As John Van Doren's essay points out, John Erskine was a central figure in what developed. A graduate of both Columbia College and the graduate school, he joined the faculty in 1909 after teaching at Amherst. He was a graceful and urbane man well versed in music as well as literature. After teaching at Columbia for many years, he served as pres-

Among the extraordinary group of instructors to lead the first pioneering General Honors courses at Columbia were (from left) Raymond M. Weaver, J. Bartlet Brebner, and Rexford G. Tugwell.

ident of The Juilliard School and was much involved in the city's music scene.

Erskine became an educational reformer, and part of his impulse came from his mixed experience as an undergraduate in the College. He loved the Latin classics but felt that except for one or two teachers they were badly served. In a memoir, he recalled a young, untenured teacher with whom he took two fine courses in Horace and Catullus, saying that this young man had all the virtues that a particular (unnamed) professor lacked, observing, "Perhaps that is why the Latin department did not make a stronger effort to keep him." He went on to say that "Latin and Greek are not dead languages unless we assassinate them. But many professors of the classics are conservatives of the worst kind; they conserve the wrong thing. Aware that they have a precious thing in their keeping, they hate to admit that the precious thing is merely life."

It is a sign of how much literary instruction was done in the early twentieth century and of Erskine's motivations that he caused a fuss when in a 1908 essay he maintained that "the teachers of literature should say as little as possible about the background of a poem or about the biography of the poet, these matters belonging rather to history than to literature; he should rather point out the admirable things in the poem. . . ." This opinion brought him a few letters of praise but a lot more denouncing him as "an idiot on the way to be a nuisance." Forty years later his view would be a basic assumption in the high tide of the literary attitudes called the New Criticism, but near the turn of the century it was by no means taken for granted.

In the years before World War I, Erskine began to think about a course that might answer these concerns, and, after the interruption of the war years and Erskine's own educational service abroad for the military, he returned to Columbia. After playing an important role in the founding of what came to be called Introduction to Contemporary Civilization, he developed the course to which the

John Erskine

faculty gave the name General Honors; it began in 1920 and was the first of the "great books" courses in this country. Four assumptions were important in the design. First, the works read should be major ones as a means to continue the humanistic curriculum of an earlier time. Second, most of them would have to be read in translation, given the diminished attention to the ancient languages. Third, students should approach the works directly, not through secondary articles and books about them. And fourth, the classes should be conducted as discussions, not lectures, to ensure that students would be thinking for themselves.

As Erskine looked back on his efforts to establish this course, he remembered feeling rather embattled. "Most of my colleagues were still hostile to the idea," he reported, "and they tried to protect the students—and themselves—from it by decreeing that my course should be open only to the specially qualified, who would take it as an extra, or as they liked to say, as 'honors.' The registration the first year was not large. We divided the class into small sections so that discussion might be easier. All the sections met at the same time, on Wednesday evenings, and over each section two of my younger colleagues presided. From the beginning it was the young teachers who made the class possible."

Judged against the later history of the General Honors course, the enrollment that first year was not so small. There were six semester sections over the year, and the "younger colleagues" who joined him make in hindsight an impressive list: Mortimer J. Adler, J. Bartlett Brebner, Irwin Edman, Clifton Fadiman, C. W. Keyes, Emery E. Neff, Henry Morton Robinson, H. W. Schneider, Rexford Tugwell, Mark Van Doren, Raymond M. Weaver, and Arnold Whitridge.

In 1929 the course was suspended for three years as the College concentrated on staffing the new second-year requirement, Introduction to Contemporary Civilization, but was reborn in 1932 with the title Colloquium in Important Books. The course has been in the Curriculum ever since, though in recent years it has not been offered every term because of staffing problems. Also, fewer students take it than in earlier years because they can now choose among more varied cultural courses in the junior and senior years than were then available.

The success of Erskine's General Honors was the background for the 1937 expansion of that idea into the required course now called Literature Humanities. It is so named to distinguish it from the courses Music Humanities and Art Humanities, but the title is rather misleading since a number of religious, philosophical, and historical works are on the reading list in addition to the more numerous works in epic, drama, and fiction.

Though Erskine himself was not much involved in the discussions that established the 1937 humanities requirement for all students, the faculty's reaction showed that most teachers had been won over to his view that students should approach rich and often difficult texts directly, not through some advanced explanation, whether in an article, textbook, or lecture. Erskine had earlier heard many objections from colleagues that one could not expect much from the weekly interaction of a young student and a major work, and when one hears reservations about the course in our own day, eighty years later, it is still the same view that one hears—that the treatment of these major works is so brief and sketchy that it is better to read nothing than to do so in this way.

But is this a serious argument? Erskine, remembering the old debates, wrote about the matter with energy:

> How often was I told by angry colleagues that a great book couldn't be read in a week, not intelligently! And how often have I retorted, with my own degree of heat, that when the great books were first published, they were popular, which was the first step toward their permanent fame, and the public who first liked them read them quickly, perhaps overnight, without waiting to hear scholarly lectures about them. I wanted the boys to read great books, the best sellers of ancient times, as spontaneously and humanly as they would read current best sellers, and having read the books, I wanted them to form their opinions at once in a free-for-all discussion. It would take two years of Wednesday evenings to discuss all the books on my list. Even by the end of the first year all the boys in the class would have in common a remarkable store of information, ideas about literature and life, and perhaps an equal wealth of aesthetic emotions, which they shared in common. Here would be, I believed, the true scholarly and cultural basis for human understanding and communication. Compared with this result, what a waste of time it seemed to spend a term on mastering one book or one author in detail, and acquiring the mastery by yourself as it were, in solitude.

If one were to take that last sentence literally, most of us would disagree, since one of the purposes of college is to make one at least aware of what mastery might mean, even though the young student is not likely to achieve it. In context, however, it is clear what Erskine intended to say—that a narrow focus of study to the exclusion of all else is not an adequate experience.

One can't really argue with Erskine's answer to the charge of superficiality—that though all of the works on the Humanities list are worthy of study in great depth (and have received it), everyone who studies a work in great detail has at some time read it for the first time. Except for the professional student of literature, one is more likely after college to read *The Iliad* if one is reading it again, and the student's encounter with the works on the Humanities list has a benefit going beyond those particular titles.

One of the intentions of the course is to destroy the aura of difficulty often attached to the titles of famous works, to make a person comfortable picking up a book no matter how formidable its reputation. If one has spent some time with Homer and Virgil, one is more likely to read, say, Spenser's *The Faerie Queen* later on one's own. It is good to remember that *Paradise Lost* is after all just a poem that can be read, and that *War and Peace* is a good story, however intermittently charged with meditations on military psychology and the fate of nations. The Humanities course tries to make the famous look like the familiar, to make the classics thought of as works that one can simply pick up and read or reread at any stage of life. Is it useful to read a good book of criticism about Dante? Of course, but it is not worth doing unless one has read some Dante first. Only a small number of college graduates become full-time literary people, and it is likely that if a college student is asked to think about a few essays of Montaigne, the probability is greater that the student who has read him will come back to him later in life.

THE WORKS

The desire to provide modern students with something of the older humanistic culture explains why the first term's readings are so heavily Greek and Roman, along with the Bible, recently given more time on the syllabus; they are the foundation works of Western civilization. The second term's readings are less coherent, since they range from Hellenistic times to the nineteenth or even the twentieth centuries—but these too are Western works.

One of the lively issues in recent years at Columbia and elsewhere concerns the wisdom of concentrating on the Western tradition in a course of this kind. In our age of multiculturalism and the praise of diversity, the comment is sometimes made that in doing so the Humanities course enshrines a fixed canon, and hence a set of harmonious assumptions and "hegemonic beliefs" reflecting a narrow and now provincial complacency. But while it is true that the reading list is made up of Western works, this is done because our country developed in the Western tradition, and if students are to understand other world cultures in some measure, they cannot sensibly do so without initial grounding in their own. It is of course true that students should be asked to study cultures outside of the dominant Western ones (and at Columbia they are required to do so), but if Humanities were to become a sampling of the world's diverse traditions, it would be a cafeteria of confusion.

More to the point, it is nonsense to think that there is some kind of self-satisfied harmony within the Western tradition. The works on the Humanities list contradict and struggle with one another more often than not and are typically more efficient in unsettling the unexamined beliefs with which the students approach them rather than imposing a set of new ones. The aim of the course, as with all good education, is to equip and encourage students to think for themselves, not to indoctrinate them with a set of convictions derived from some imagined and fictitious harmony of minds. This is not to say, of course, that diverse national or ethnic cultures don't warrant the serious attention of our students: The days are long gone when one could assume the universal superiority of Western European culture and hence ignore other traditions with a quiet conscience. The issue is not if such studies should be in the undergraduate curriculum, but how and when they should be undertaken.

Does such work belong in the first-year Humanities course? The faculty doesn't think so, but not because they hold such work to be unimportant. The point is that one cannot learn everything at once and that up to a point there is a sensible sequence in which things are to be done. A student who has no initial grounding in the major traditions of the West is ill equipped to understand unfamiliar cultures because there are no foundations from which to draw contrasts and comparisons. Just as a Chinese student should have some familiarity with China before turning attention to the West, so the American student should have at least an introductory knowledge of where the country comes from before studying other traditions. First things first.

Humanities concentrates on major Western works because that is the history out of which the country developed. After initial experience of this kind, Columbia College students are asked to study cultures other than those dominant in the West. In this major cultures requirement, they are invited to take Asian Humanities and Asian Civilization, which are parallel to the Western-oriented basic courses. The requirement also allows for the study of African and Latin American cultures, as well as a minority culture within the United States. The point is that students must broaden their knowledge beyond the major traditions that shaped western Europe and in large measure formed the United States as well.

Those who are critical of the Humanities reading list sometimes speak of a "canon" of enshrined works beyond which nothing may be read, but when thinking about the course it is well to avoid the term, with its possible implication of a fixed list beyond which nothing is acceptable. The works are chosen by the teachers every two years; a small committee makes the initial recommendation, which is then vetted by the full staff. Over the life of the course (now sixty-two years old), well over 100 titles have been taught. The hardest thing for the staff to resist is adding a new title without making room for it by dropping a work already on the list. These discussions are always intense; teachers have their favorite books, but there are limits to what the students can be asked to read in a course that already makes large demands.

The only criterion for a work to be admitted is that it be rich enough to provoke the interest of undergraduates. It is that much better if it has issues that relate it to other books on the list, but there is a good chance of that if the work is a substantial one. Every teacher has personal interests and develops ideas that are to be followed through in the class discussions; the appropriate work is one diverse enough to answer to both individual interests and to the large, general issues that every attentive reader must find in it.

THE SHIFTING CORE

If one examines the reading lists over the life of the course with an eye to how often works are taught, there are four groups. First, there are a few that have remained on the syllabus from the beginning: *The Iliad* and Dante's *Inferno*, for example. Then there are authors, Herodotus and Ovid among them, who are often though not always present. Third, there are a number who come in less often, as Apuleius or Jonathan Swift. Finally, there are works that are tried for a time but that seem not to lend themselves as well as others to this kind of course. *Paradise Lost* seemed to require too much external knowledge to work well in a short time, and Madame de La Fayette's *The Princess of Clèves* appeared not to have enough resonance with other works on the list. From time to time, of course, a work is unsuccessful with a given class because the teacher has not yet found a way to make it interesting. For this reason the Humanities teachers like to talk with one another about what they do in their classrooms.

It sometimes happens, of course, that works are added to the list in response to fresh cultural issues represented in the staff. For many years there was no work by a woman on the Humanities list, and this changed as one of the benefits of feminism. That did not mean, of course, that women's issues had not been talked about in the course before Jane Austen and Virginia Woolf entered the reading list. No one could read or teach *The Odyssey* or the Greek dramatists, let alone Boccaccio, without treating the role of women in a central way. But it was high time that works not only about women, but by them, were adopted; and by no means only because the College became coeducational in 1983. However a text comes to be on the reading list, there is a firm rule for the teachers: When the list has been approved by the majority of the teachers, all of them must teach the books agreed upon. Anyone unwilling to do this should not be in a Humanities classroom since this commonality is at the heart of the enterprise.

The fact that all students are talking about the same works at the same time encourages serious conversation outside of the classroom. Students from different sections often talk about the works they have all read and are thinking about, comparing different angles of interpretation that naturally occur in the different groups led by independent instructors. This common experience is even more important at Columbia than it might be at some other schools, because it provides a unifying experience on an urban campus where the pressures of space and of New York City itself make it harder to create a sense of college community. That comes more easily at some schools that have much larger campuses with more diverse facilities and a traditional house system where a relatively small number of students come to know one another well by virtue of separate residence halls and dining rooms. Too, it is an obvious benefit that this common experience at Columbia is an intellectual one: Students educate one another outside of class as well as in it.

As one thinks about the particular texts used in the course over the years, it is clear that in one way the course is better than it used to be because we have been living in an age of great translations. Fifty years ago there were a fair number of translations so inadequate that one had to accept much of a work's reputation on faith because the artistic character of the original had almost entirely disappeared. While it is true that "poetry is what is lost in translation," it is now much less true because a good many excellent scholar-poets in our day have both an expert knowledge of the original text and the fine linguistic taste in English that allows a good deal of the tone and temper of the original to come through. Only a few of the translations used fifty years ago are still in use. A teacher can now point to more of the artistic qualities in *The Iliad* even in English translation, qualities that were simply not on the page some decades ago.

This happy change is not only because each age makes its own translations, though this is substantially true—Alexander Pope's eighteenth-century version of *The Iliad* is a great one, though clearly not appropriate for use in Humanities now. It has come about in the last few decades that translation has come to be valued and studied as an art in itself. There are seminars and workshops that hone the skills of people who would not earlier have found such help, and while no instruction can repair a tin ear, there are more competent translators now than there were earlier.

That better translations give students closer access to the original languages reinforces another obvious reason for the course's impact—the books are powerful quite apart from what happens in the classroom. This is not to undervalue the teacher's role, of course, for that is of the greatest importance. Students will better understand what they are reading—and themselves—as a good teacher shapes the content and style of the discussions. But even in the rare case of a weak instructor, the students read works of such interest that poor teaching can't do as much damage as it otherwise might. While Humanities is not "instructor-proof," the teacher builds upon complex and resonant works that have become well known because of these very qualities. When good teaching makes the most of such books, the experience is unforgettable.

THE STAFF

Though there is an occasional problem with the instruction in a particular class, something inevitable in a course that now has fifty-five independent sections, those in charge of Humanities take pains to field the best staff possible. The instructors are made up of three groups: senior faculty, nontenured but full-time junior faculty, and graduate students who have had earlier experience in the classroom, most often in teaching the required composition course given in the freshman year. The academic departments that provide teachers for the course must supply a certain number depending on their size and history, and the proportions between the three groups will vary from one year to another depending on the need for departmental courses and the pattern of faculty leaves.

Those who teach meet every week during the academic year in sessions organized by the senior faculty member directing the course—a position normally held for three years. The sessions are informal, designed to help teachers prepare the work that the students have read. There is typically a faculty speaker expert or at least one comfortable with the work at hand, and after a talk lasting half an hour or so, staff members weigh in with questions or comments about the substance of the work or about how best to approach it with students. Attendance at these meetings is not required, but it is usually good because even the senior faculty, who may have taught the course repeatedly, find the discussion helpful as they begin to think about the work again.

For the graduate students teaching the course for the first time, there is an additional weekly session normally conducted by the director of the course. Here the new teachers learn more about the work to be taught the following week, and there is more emphasis on effective presentation of the material than is true of the sessions for the full staff. The graduate students who teach Humanities are selected by recommendation and interviews from a large group of applicants, and the special guidance for them continues through the year and includes reports and class visits that often produce helpful advice.

In the sessions for the full staff, it sometimes happens that a faculty member not currently teaching the course will attend for the pleasures offered by what is a rather rare occasion—an interdisciplinary faculty seminar in which there are no distinctions of rank. Senior faculty, junior faculty, and graduate students are in this context simply colleagues with the same problems and opportunities, and they are all there to get what help they can in preparing to teach a work in which only a few of them may be specially trained. Those who have taught the course before often make comments based on their own experience, and these are often helpful to others near the beginning of their careers.

Given this interaction, the meetings provide a useful apprenticeship for those starting out; the atmosphere is collegial since the younger teachers are in full charge of their classes just as the old hands are—no one serves as a "discussion leader" for a senior lecturer. This gives everyone a large responsibility, and many younger teachers have pointed to service in Humanities or Introduction to Contemporary Civilization as shaping experiences in their careers. It would be good for the course if funding could be found to allow a larger number of graduate students to teach these courses for a third year in addition to the two now usual, and also to allow some graduate students to continue teaching them for a time after they complete their doctorates. Many young teachers do very well even in their first year, but whether a teacher is young or old, the course makes very large demands, and one is better at it after some seasoning.

THE TEACHING CHALLENGE

There are three reasons why teachers find Humanities arduous no matter what their age or experience. It covers a wide range of material most or all of which is outside the expert knowledge of any one person. It moves with great speed, typically allowing only a week even for a work of much complexity. And most of all, it is conducted by discussion, not as a lecture course. Given this combination, if teachers are conscientious, they spend more time preparing Humanities than an offering in their own disciplines. Each week the teacher rereads (or occasionally reads for the first time) the next work on the schedule and learns more about it both by private reading and attendance at the meetings. Finally, the teacher must work out a series of questions that will both interest the students and lead the discussion toward the major themes in the work at hand and its relation to others.

Any teacher who has taught a course through discussion knows that it is a process both interesting and unpredictable: The challenge is to see that coherent intellectual work gets done rather than a random scattering of thoughts that may be fun but doesn't go anywhere. One can never be sure what is going to happen in class. Sometimes the teacher's plan works out beautifully; on other days, the discussion doesn't seem to jell; and on still other occasions it may take a direction entirely unplanned but be effective nonetheless. To manage all this takes a degree of concentration and flexibility never involved in a lecture course, and these are qualities rarely called upon even in a seminar when one is treating material with which one is professionally at home. The discussion format is crucial to the purposes and success of both Humanities and CC; without it these courses would be entirely different, and for those who teach them as they are now taught, not worth carrying on.

In the history of Humanities, the teachers have always thought that each instructor should be in complete charge of a particular class and have resisted suggestions that the students be required to attend lectures by experts on the various works. This stress on the teacher's independence is not a matter of the teacher's pride, or nervousness that the students might discover that their teacher is not an authority on every work on the reading list—the students soon become aware of this in any case. The teacher's proper autonomy rests on the basic assumption of the course—that intelligent people, no one of whom may be a specialist in the matter at hand, can read and talk about it to their mutual benefit. This common discussion is central to seeing the classics as works that any educated person can enjoy. The teachers want full control of their classes because if students were distanced from their instructor at this stage by an intervening expert, whether in print or in person, this would encourage the view that people shouldn't pick up these books at all without expert help.

During the 1960s, for example, the Humanities staff rejected a recommendation by a faculty committee that a mandatory series of lectures be established at which both students and teachers would hear an expert talk about the work to be read each week. Many of the faculty who supported this idea had either never taught the course or had not done so for quite a long time, and they found it hard to understand why the Humanities staff was so strongly opposed. The teachers, on the other hand, felt that such a system would turn them into discussion leaders subordinate to the official authorities who would lay down the basic lines of inquiry and hence reduce the independence of the classroom teachers.

The teaching staff never objected, on the other hand, to the students' occasional and successful efforts to establish a series of weekly lectures by precisely the same experts. Why the difference? Because the student-run series was an additional and optional hour that did not officially establish a secondary status for the teacher. This might seem a trivial cavil on the part of the staff: Why should they object to their students' hearing an expert talk about the work? The answer is that they did not but felt only that within the agreed-upon commonality of the reading list and the final examination, their own independence in the classroom was crucial to the course. When the students organized a series of well-attended lectures, many of the teachers were there as well, happy to learn something more about the work at hand and to be aware of what the students might raise in the classroom discussion coming up. This was a very different matter from the use of a formal class hour, reducing the teacher's time from four hours a week to three, and the creation of an atmosphere in which the teacher would often be expected to take off from the specialist's explanation of the work.

The instruction in Humanities thus exists in a careful balance between the common character of the enterprise and the autonomy of the individual on the other. It would be an exaggeration to say that each of the fifty-five classrooms in Humanities offers a unique course on the same texts, but there is a measure of truth to this. The particular teacher's interests and knowledge will shape that section's discussion differently from all the others, but this independence operates within the context of common understanding that over time has been shown to work well.

Humanities has served the College's students well in a number of ways. For some it has been so alluring that they have pursued further studies in the humanities and have themselves become teachers in schools throughout the country. For the great majority of students, whatever they may do after graduation, it has provided an experience calculated to whet the appetite for further reading of a serious kind, making life more interesting. Humanities remains one of the most popular of the Core courses, and as long as the administration is solidly behind it and the teaching staff remains properly balanced and deeply engaged, the course should have a long future and a bright one.

CHAPTER 37

The Core Curriculum:
Wisdom, Training, and
Contemporary Civilization

—⁓—

J. W. Smit

Introduction to Contemporary Civilization has been described as "probably the most famous course ever in the American curriculum." Here J. W. Smit, Queen Wilhelmina Professor of the History of the Low Countries, tackles the original course in the College's signature Core Curriculum, from the forces that encouraged its creation in 1919 through its many evolutions across the past eight decades.

Wim Smit is well suited to the task. A Dutch native, Smit studied at the University of Utrecht, where he received his doctorate in 1958. He taught at Utrecht until 1965, when he joined the Columbia faculty. A specialist in the social, cultural, and economic history of early modern Europe, especially the Low Countries, he was hired to teach in the Graduate School of Arts and Sciences. Yet, he gravitated toward the Core, teaching CC since the 1970s and twice serving as chair of the course (1978–82, 1989–92). He served on the Commission on the Core Curriculum (1988–89) and was the first chair of the Standing Committee on the Core Curriculum (1990–93). Smit received the Mark Van Doren Award for Great Teaching in 1984 and was a corecipient (with James Mirollo) of the first award for Distinguished Service to the Core Curriculum in 1993. A polymath with wide scholarly interests, Smit holds the unique distinction of being the only teacher to have taught all four basic Core courses—CC, Literature Humanities, Music Humanities, and Art Humanities.

Wm. Theodore de Bary

—⁓—

O ne wonders whether the small band of Columbia professors who, just after World War I's end, produced yet another proposal for reforming the College's curriculum could ever have imagined that their creation would be celebrated close to a century later as part of Columbia's legacy to American higher education. Yet we who celebrate Contemporary Civilization and also are aware of its history can just as easily wonder if that band would see the course we know today as its own. For the founders might view CC's current syllabus as the victory of something they had fought against. And I would like to suggest that such a first impression would be at the same time right and wrong.

When the College faculty voted in January 1919 to require Contemporary Civilization, they were giving their support to an original, albeit precarious, alternative to two sides in a long-standing debate. Starting in the 1870s, university faculties across America engaged in sometimes heated discussions about traditional higher education and its relevance to modern society. What was more important? The "wisdom" and character-building supposedly provided by the old classics-based humanities curriculum, or the more specialized, technical professional training central to the modern natural and social scientific disciplines, engineering, medicine, and law?

At Columbia, the debate was as heated as anywhere. And at the risk of caricaturing the main camps, on one side stood the advocates of a deeply entrenched, largely classical (and highly prestigious) humanities curriculum with an emphasis on general education—a curriculum designed to create cultured, polished gentlemen. On the other stood their critics—primarily professors in newer, more specialized research-based disciplines that did not yet have a firm place in the College curriculum—who argued for greater academic freedom, disciplinary diversity, and more focused professional training. In short, general education linked to the traditional humanities was pitted against specialization linked to the professions and the sciences. While it cannot be denied that the newcomers had their own professional interests in mind when they opposed the traditional curriculum, it is just as easy to argue that their very choice of academic specialty embodied a true concern with the real-world civic problems posed by the "second industrial revolution" of the late nineteenth century. And however much we might rightly sympathize with staunch advocates of humanistic training, it is hard not to concede that in their heyday, before they became the academic underdogs, they easily could create an atmosphere that was downright hostile to talk of professional training and real-world "practicality." And it's equally hard not to understand their critics' puzzlement at how the capacity to quote Horace or Virgil could help one understand the modern world.

In their argument with what I'll call the "wisdom" camp, advocates of the "training" camp did not work in an intellectual void. Their model for reform also came from Europe, more specifically from Germany, the home of the prestigious and highly successful new-style research university, with its emphasis on specialized, research-based training and high standards of scholarship in the natural and the social sciences. Many American scholars who had earned their degrees abroad sought to reform their own schools along German lines. At Columbia, one such German-trained professor was John W. Burgess, whose proposals for reorganizing the government department's curriculum had the enthusiastic support of President Frederick A. P. Barnard and his successor, Nicholas Murray Butler.

In a blow to the wisdom camp's case for general—or perhaps "liberal" would be better—undergraduate education, Butler, who during his presidency said that many at the College were engaged in mere "intellectual dawdling," floated the so-called Columbia Plan (1905) that would shepherd students who wished to work at a more rapid tempo into graduate or professional school right after the sophomore year. Motivated individuals would be free to rush ahead professionally, but general, liberal education and a common curriculum would fall by the wayside.

The advocates of "dawdling" fought back but with weapons that were too antiquated to be effective—so much so that, on reading their rhetoric, the committed humanist yearns to put other words in their mouths, words that reflect the very basic fact that the wisdom camp's curriculum had been the standard introduction into real-world problems for hundreds and hundreds of years. But, seemingly oblivious to that line of argument, Dean of the College John Howard Van Amringe stubbornly insisted that the purpose of a college education was, as he somewhat quaintly put it, "to make men" (not professional specialists) by shaping students' characters through the contemplation of ancient wisdom contained in the Greek and Latin classics. His argument reflected Columbia's old self-image as a sort of cultural finishing school for the sons of the New York elite, and it is perhaps too easy for us now, in a very different world, to mock it. But it is also apparent that Van Amringe's rhetoric was no answer to the concerns of Burgess, Barnard, and Butler, who could not ignore the need to prepare Columbia's students for a changing, and increasingly powerful, America.

It was to be expected that at the beginning of the twentieth century, the trend against liberal education, then linked almost exclusively with the traditional humanities, would begin to gather steam. It was a trend that was powerfully supported by the waves of first- and second-generation immigrants who began to seek admission to American colleges and universities. For men like Butler, it was those institutions' responsibility to turn the most intelligent and driven of those new citizens into managers, engineers, scientists, technicians, and teachers. But however gifted, the new sort of student generally had not received the classics-based high school training that was common among the old elite and that was a virtual prerequisite for the old-style curriculum.

So too Columbia, which had educated so many of the New York establishment, was going to face a quite different student population. How suddenly the immigrant pressure surfaced and how strong it became is not exactly clear, but it was probably gradual. But change eventually came: The 1916 abolition of Latin as an admissions requirement was the first formal adaptation to the new reality. It was a signal that, in the battle against the old ideal of general education, the newcomers and the advocates of professional schooling were allies. But the fight had a long way to go. Against this background, the easy acceptance in 1919 of something as radical as CC might seem to be just short of a miracle. It was a reversal of sorts, the general education idea in a new and very different key. And to make any sense of it, we must first understand the sea change in American life that preceded it.

In 1914, World War I began, with America as only an interested bystander. But in 1917, the United States had become actively involved. While "The Great War" hardly deserves its global moniker when compared with World War II, contemporaries perceived that this war was not simply the old-fashioned Clausewitzian pursuit of diplomacy by military means. Certainly after the Russian revolution, during the same year that the United States entered the war, it began to look more like a tectonic shift, long in preparation, that was going to change the face of the world. It also seemed that clashing ideologies played as much a role as clashing interests or at least clashing interests easily translated into ideological rhetoric.

Universities, which supposedly specialized in understanding the wedded worlds of interests and ideas, were expected to give more than just technical support to the war effort. Columbia's contribution was the 1917 creation of a course in war issues, with the purpose, in the words of later Dean of the College Herbert Hawkes, of "understanding the worth of the cause for which one is fighting." Because the war ended just a year later, the course did not have a long life. But the work put into creating it ironically bore fruit in the idea of creating something similar, a course devoted instead to peace issues, which were—again in Hawkes's words—"far more important as a field of instruction of our college youth" than the issues of war.

So, the initial thinking about CC took place in the exhilarating atmosphere of the first months of peace, marked by a mix of idealistic and realistic anticipation of a new world waiting to be built. The experience of the war had produced a sense of national community, but one also knew (or simply feared) that powerful forces within the country made consensus precarious. Among those forces were ignorance and lack of interest. As the historian (and later dean) Harry Carman—soon one of the main forces behind CC—put it somewhat later, "the vast majority of Americans never critically examine our existing social standards." And that could mean trouble.

It was no doubt in part this sense of civic responsibility and a felt need to improve each Columbian's ability to "understand the civilization of his own day and participate effectively in it," as CC's first syllabus put it, that pushed some creative faculty members away from the extremes of the two prewar camps toward a new synthesis: general education that aimed at a different sort of wisdom, one bound up not only with the old history of ideas, but also with the methods and the more contemporary focus of the newer, more specialized social science disciplines.

On January 20, 1919, the College faculty, after but a few scant weeks of discussion, resolved to accept those innovators' ideas and voted to replace the required introductions to philosophy and history, so central to the traditional curriculum, with something entirely different. The new required course, which would meet five days a week for one-hour classes, would place new demands not only on students but also on the faculty, who would be charged with teaching something that neither they nor anyone else had ever taught. As it was a new concept, a committee was created and charged with the daunting task of composing a syllabus. The committee managed to have an elaborate document printed before the fall semester and complete yet another in time for the spring.

Certainly, the unusual speed of these events and the absence of strong opposition to a new general education requirement that cut back the power of older, more established departments demand explanation. Part of it, no doubt, was Butler's support. Even before the war, this longtime opponent of general education had begun to soften his stance. But now he showed almost a convert's enthusiasm, which prompted a *Jester* cartoon portraying the new course as Butler's weapon against the Bolshevik threat. (Perhaps there is something to that.) Whatever its source, that no-doubt contagious enthusiasm, combined with a general mind shift induced by the war, cannot in itself account for such a quick and large leap over an old faculty divide.

Indeed, the advocates of specialized professional and graduate-style education may have been placated because this attempt at general education was fundamentally different from what Van Amringe had promoted. The syllabus offered students

J. W. Smit, Queen Wilhelmina Professor of History, is the only person to have taught all four of the basic Core courses: Contemporary Civilization, Literature Humanities, Art Humanities, and Music Humanities.

an interesting mix of the varied disciplines of its principal proponents: John C. Coss, the first chairman, was a philosopher; Rexford Tugwell, an economist (and later a prominent member of FDR's Brain Trust); and Harry Carman, a historian. The course they put together essentially was a comprehensive introduction to a social scientific and historical analysis of what they called the "insistent problems of the present world."

Although some grumbled about alleged superficiality, the people who took the initiative wanted rigorous scholarship, and the course syllabus reflected that intention. But they also wanted their scholarship to serve ethical and civic goals. Their philosophy was similar to that of philosopher John Dewey—a member of the Columbia faculty who did not participate directly in developing the course, but who looked on it with a sympathetic eye—for whom education was meaningless if disconnected from the experience of civic life. As their softer, more humanities-based ethical concerns crept into a primarily social-science based syllabus, the language of the old traditionalists was fused with that of their opponents. One early participant, Professor Cassius Keyser, called for an education that would instill in students "a certain wisdom about the world." Butler found perhaps the most felicitous use for this old and un- (or at least non-) scientific language when, in his address to the university in September 1919, he spoke of the need to give students a firmer message about the realities of life—"to get knowledge and translate it into wisdom." Wisdom as the ultimate end of the pursuit of knowledge: Was that not the perfect summary of what the founders of CC were aiming at? Perhaps unaware, Butler had paraphrased one of Jacob Burkhardt's best aphorisms about the study of history. Its purpose, he wrote, was to teach you "not to be clever the next time, but to be wiser forever."

How then did CC's trajectory shift from a course grounded in the social sciences, with their focus on the problems of the present, to one based on the "great books" of the past?

The best place to start is the official 1919 course syllabus, which is not, of course, in any way an ordinary syllabus. A far cry from the one-page-per-semester photocopied book list that we now find in the CC office, it might seem to us today almost too centralized, even tyrannical, for it outlines specifically—session after session, week after week—precisely the issues to be discussed and the pages to be read. But more than a centralized schedule of assignments, it was itself an intellectual document, an admirable achievement of concentrated, systematic thought about man in nature and society. It was not so much a syllabus as the detailed outline of a book.

It was, indeed, first printed as a booklet, and one that became thicker and thicker over the years, as the likes of maps and essays (sometimes written by the staff) were added. But though the booklet's content expanded, its conceptual structure remained unchanged for more than a decade: A survey of geography and the physical environment (hence the maps), Part I was called The World of Nature; Part II, The World of Human Nature, stressed social psychology, ethics and forms of human behavior, with an emphasis on "individual traits that are socially significant"; Part III was a more historical treatment of the socioeconomic and intellectual history of the United States and Europe; and Part IV tackled the insistent contemporary problems. Titled National States of Today, the course's final section covered such things, according to Carman's notes, as "nationalism, imperialism, industrialization and economic growth" and "imperialism in its relation to backward peoples" (problems, it is interesting to note, that—without the judgmental term "backwardness," of course—more modern versions of CC have been accused of neglecting).

When it comes to course readings, one thing in particular might strike the present-day Columbian as odd: Not surprisingly for a course that began as a modern, real-world alternative to the general education of the prewar traditionalists, its readings included no "great books" nor any primary sources. The material students had to digest was, as it were, predigested for them in texts often written especially for the course by their own Columbia professors: J. H. Randall's *Making of the Modern Mind* provided a challenging overview of Western philosophy; Irwin Edman's *Human Traits and Their Social Significance*, though written by a philosopher, served as an introduction to social anthropology; and the titles of John Dewey's *How We Think* and Carleton J. H. Hayes's *Economic and Political History of Modern Europe* speak for themselves.

Though not "great books," these texts were not easy reading. The first CC students worked hard. The sheer mass of problems thrown at them was daunting, involving much more than a passing acquaintance with European and American history, social psychology, world geography, philosophy, economics, and politics.

What actually went on in those first CC classrooms cannot, alas, ever be recovered, so we will never really know how much of the syllabus (given time constraints) was addressed, how much the students absorbed, or how well the class discussions functioned. But from the little available evidence, it seems that the students viewed their experience very positively and were willing to sustain the heavy workload. The teaching staff made it a point to stay close to them, invite their reactions, and take their ideas seriously—things that might not have been students' daily experience in less experimental courses.

A sampling of texts from the current Contemporary Civilization syllabus

To anyone familiar with academic life, it can all sound almost unreal: eager, happy students in a demanding required course and a cooperative faculty from different departments imbued with a joint sense of purpose. But though the picture of CC's earliest years has no doubt been touched up by time, it is clear that consensus and a sense of shared mission were real.

Curiosity as to how that consensus was achieved makes us wish we had a record of what went on in the weekly staff lunches where continuous adaptations of—and to—the syllabus were hammered out. Those discussions would no doubt provide some significant insights into an important phase in American intellectual life, to the thinking of a diverse group of characters bound together by what might seem to us a naïve, but nonetheless attractive, coupling of scientific beliefs with educational and political idealism. For they had an enviable trust that science could solve society's most urgent problems.

Until the early 1940s, it seems, that consensus more or less endured, even through inevitable challenges. Perhaps the biggest problem was something anyone who has taught CC even recently can all too well understand: Even now, with our abbreviated book list and our much welcomed flexibility, it's hard when you must link texts with life (and through discussion, not straight lecture, at that) to avoid an unceasing struggle with time. In those days, things were in some ways harder, for everything was written into the syllabus and the reach of the required material was more vast; but things were easier, as well. Since the course was not yet part of a "core," much less an "extended core," the staff could simply make CC longer. Which they did.

In 1928, unable to telescope the mass of required material into the space of one year, the College created CC-*B*, which essentially was Part IV of the original syllabus—the crucial contemporary issues—while CC-*A* kept Parts I–III. For this new yearlong course, government and economics professors sacrificed *their* required introductory courses to make CC a reality, just as their historian and philosopher colleagues had done a decade before.

If nothing else, this unusual willingness to forgo departmental independence suggests that in the 1920s and 1930s, the new program generally was accepted by the faculty, even in those disciplines most inclined to prefer German-style specialization and training. Despite tensions and conflicting interests, the consensus behind CC was strong. And for a good many years, both courses, taught by an assortment of professors from across the faculty, thrived.

But as is the world's wont, things did not remain rosy. Thirty years after CC-B's birth, it was dead, and CC-A was radically transformed. By the time of the turmoil of 1968, the consensus seems to have broken.

—⟋⟍⟋—

From the little that has been written about the great change in CC that took place in the 1960s, just what happened is not exactly clear. (It would certainly be useful, while there are still people alive who actually participated in, or simply witnessed, CC-A's transformation and CC-B's death, for someone to write the story.) What we do know is that, though an inkling of the difficulties appeared in the 1940s, only in the late 1950s did those problems become intense.

Between 1957 and 1968, four committees were set up to make sense of the travails of both halves of CC (but especially of the more troubled CC-B, which never achieved its partner's organization and unity of purpose) and suggest solutions. Those reports reveal low staff morale and an unwillingness of tenured faculty to participate—signals of a changed attitude toward general education.

The attitude of the faculty—tenured and untenured, across disciplines—had indeed changed, shifting toward something very familiar: For the individual professor, the need to survive professionally in increasingly research-focused disciplines made CC's teaching load seem much more onerous, and departments, pressed to meet internal staffing needs, were more and more reluctant to share faculty with CC. In a more general manner, the expansion and increasing specialization of the faculty had watered down the old *esprit de corps*. The MacMahon Committee report of 1957, which deemed faculty recruitment to be among CC's most crucial weakness, made valuable suggestions for increasing faculty participation, but later committees saw little chance for CC-B's survival. In 1968, after several attempts at reorganization, a course that had basically been dead for several years finally was given its funeral.

CC-A, which had faced many of the same challenges that its defunct other half had confronted, was allowed to live, in part, because it still breathed. For no matter what staffing problems it might have had, it enjoyed a cadre of faithful senior professors and young instructors. Professor Peter Gay recalled his experience: "When I first began teaching CC, it was with something of a Deweyite (or shall I say dewey-eyed) common faith." And he remembers how the instructors wouldn't have missed one of the staff's weekly lunch meetings, where course material and pedagogy were the main topics on the table.

But after 1968, those meetings would be about a different course. No longer able to rely on CC-*B* to handle Part IV of the original curriculum, the staff, if they wanted to be true to the course's title, would have to reincorporate the contemporary. And they would have to squeeze it back into a two-semester format with a very different syllabus. For the new CC, it was decreed in 1968, was to be based not on the old social sciences and history but on classic texts that students would read in their entirety.

A shade from 1919 might not recognize the course that was supposed to be his legacy. Now that specialized, research-based training and scholarship had prevailed in academe, he might wonder if what had once been a refuge *from* the old-style humanities had become instead a refuge *for* it? How had a social science-based course with a focus on the present—and built around secondary sources—become a humanities course based on primary texts dear to the students of the past? Had the whole focus on the present and its "insistent problems" been lost?

Professor of Economics Harold Barger, perhaps the last from his discipline to teach CC, certainly thought so. In an interview with *Spectator,* he announced his refusal to teach what he pejoratively described as just a "great books course." What he probably meant was that the "great books" are read because they are great in themselves, not because they naturally fall into place around themes appropriate for a course focused on contemporary issues. Was there not a risk that CC would become a book- and author-centric literature course, a philosophy-based equivalent of Literature Humanities? Given CC's origins and history and the considerable energy that social scientists had put into it, his disappointment was understandable. And he was probably not the only old-time CC instructor to share these worries.

But without filling in some more details of the life of CC-*A* following its split from CC-*B* in the 1920s, we risk exaggerating the changes of the 1960s. For starting as early as the 1930s, CC-*A* had slowly but surely transformed from a course that relied solely on secondary sources to one based heavily on excerpts from primary documents in social, political, and economic thought. Clearly, the staff had grown to believe that to merely read modern texts that commented on Aristotle, Aquinas, or Mill (among the few white males on the original syllabus who were dead) was not sufficient. Students ought rather to read and comment on actual works.

This was the beginning of the so-called Red Books, the two volumes of *Introduction to Contemporary Civilization in the West,* the first edition of which was published in 1946 (with revised editions in 1954 and 1960). It was a publication that would be used in colleges all over America; its excellence made the name of

Columbia stand for the very idea of general education of a modern sort—a twentieth-century alternative to the classics-centered curriculum of the pre–World War I opponents of specialization. The Red Books represented the last large-scale collective efforts of the CC staff, and as a legacy, their importance is second only to that of CC itself.

The change in the reading list that the Red Books marked did not mean a change in CC's purpose, though not everyone, of course, believed that. The transition was, not surprisingly, criticized by some fundamentalist 1919ers, who were uncomfortable with the shift to what they called "ideological-literary texts" alone. But a mere glance at the two volumes' table of contents refutes the charge: along with the "ideological-literary texts" (those primary sources in civic and moral thought), the volumes contained historical documents illustrating real-world social, political, and economic issues of the past (e.g., constitutions or labor contracts, manorial records, parliamentary debates, and popular manifestos). The section "Early Modern Capitalism and the Expansion of Europe," for example, included texts from Jacob Fugger (the great early modern banker), rebellious German peasants, and Christopher Columbus. Under "The Elaboration of the Sovereign State," a student could find, along with Jacques Bossuet's defense of absolutism, government documents penned by Cardinal Richelieu and Jean-Baptiste Colbert, and the British Hat Act of 1732.

Though the secondhand social analysis found in the earliest syllabi had for the most part been deleted from the Red Books, like their predecessors, they had an explicit topical and thematic structure. The shift toward "literature" had not eliminated the goal of helping students develop the mental tools they would need to analyze civic reality in all its complexity and study the past to learn the sorts of questions they might ask of the present. In the days before the social sciences began taking over the study of the civic—before knowledge, training, and specialization began to triumph over "wisdom"—it was, after all, on historical-literary texts that people relied to learn about the civic world. There was, in short, no necessary incompatibility between the course's new material and its goals. And, should CC-A's teachers cut back on the explicitly contemporary, they had their CC-B partners, in theory, waiting to fill it all in.

The Red Books' 1960–61 edition was nonetheless their swan song. It would be only eight years before they joined the ranks of the booklet-length CC syllabi of the 1920s; their approach, short documents and excerpts selected around major themes, would be rejected in favor of that of Literature Humanities, with its emphasis on reading whole books. And though today's reality, for the most part, is excerpts, not whole books, chosen by individual instructors, the official syllabus is still based on the model of 1968.

No more than the introduction of the Red Books decades earlier did the transition to great books (in theory read whole) require a change either in the course's substance or in its teachers' will to include the contemporary. But it could. For it did increase the danger that the course would lose some coherence and unity of purpose. Without the formal conceptual framework that, albeit in different forms, had provided CC with structure from 1919 through 1968, it would be trickier to fulfill the course's original mandate.

The so-called great books, often vilified as a dead and even an oppressive "canon," are equal and often superior to more recent analysis of civilization. And they are easy to use as pedagogical tools to help students look more lucidly at the present's "insistent problems." It's hard, for example, to think of a better way to understand the centripetal and centrifugal forces in all societies that can make what seemed so steady fall apart than by reading Thucydides' account of the breakdown of social order during the Peloponnesian War. But Thucydides also can be read from many angles—from the point of view of historiography, for example, or naval history, or Greek tragedy—not all of them related to CC's themes. And if you have less than two hours to devote to him, where do you start? The complication, in short, is that—in the context of a thematic course where the books are less the end than the means—the greatness of great books makes it crucial that teachers learn how to use them to suit the course's purpose. Beginners, who have not yet run through the reading with a class, understandably need help.

In the end, the survival of CC as conceived by that small band of post–World War I professors depends not so much on what sources are read as on how those sources are taught. In this area, there is reason for concern. Because of the expansion of the College, CC now has more than twice the number of sections than when it started, exacerbating the old and potentially threatening problems of faculty recruitment and *esprit de corps* as well as leading to the loss of the "common faith" of which Peter Gay spoke with amusement but also affection that kept CC-A alive in the 1960s.

As graduate student preceptors with mere two-year appointments (giving them neither time to acquire experience nor wiser fellow students to turn to for help) increasingly become the cork upon which CC must be kept afloat, there is a real danger that it will become what people like Harold Barger feared—a mere great books course. This is not due, of course, to the preceptors' lack of intellectual capacity nor determination. It is due, rather, to CC's difficulty. It's a tough place in which to begin to learn a professor's most basic skills: inventing exam and paper topics, grading, guiding individual students, and learning to steer between the twin temptations of letting discussion drift according to the proclivities of the loudest students and lecturing to keep coherence and beat the clock. For in CC, you're not teaching your specialty, and the texts you're working with don't automatically serve your goal of balancing present with past and theory with practice and keeping your eye steadily on themes. Graduate students, whose careers depend on the ability to focus on their own narrow specialty—nineteenth-century German philosophy or medieval Islam or early modern Russia or Church history—may succumb to the expedient of delivering an "it's September, so it must be the Greeks" textbook overview of Plato and Aristotle and sitting back to listen while the class bully or ideologue goes on and on.

So, then, does the legacy of the past live on in present-day CC? In general, yes, with the proviso that, as its purpose and themes are not automatically built into the official syllabus—which brings the advantage of freedom and flexibility—it needs continuous vigilance on the part of the administration and faculty. But vigilance alone will not do. It also will require more teacher training and other forms of support.

Today's CC is not a replica of that of 1919 (see the Notes section for the CC syllabus for 2004–05, pp. 663–65). In some ways, it is worse; in some ways, it is better. But the most important thing is this: CC still gives a precious coherence to the student body and can do the same for faculty lucky enough to be involved. It challenges the students to contemplate extraordinary thinking, to read and write more carefully, and to reflect upon themselves. And—one hopes—it makes them humble before the power of genius.

CHAPTER 38

The Core Curriculum:
Asia in the Core Curriculum

—⟡—

Wm. Theodore de Bary

The post–World War II incorporation of Asia in the College's Core Curriculum was an unprecedented development but a natural extension of Columbia's prewar initiatives in general education, anticipated in the 1930s by the founding fathers of Contemporary Civilization and Humanities like Harry J. Carman and Mark Van Doren. This essay lays out the story of Asia in the Core in several dimensions, including curricular development, the philosophy and practice of multicultural education, and major contributions to the translation and publication of classic Asian texts.

Wm. Theodore de Bary

—⟡—

Columbia's course in Contemporary Civilization, begun in 1919, had led the way to a new curriculum, and the parallel Humanities course had just been added in 1937, when Columbia teachers began thinking about the inclusion of Asia in the Core Curriculum. Professor (and later dean of the College) Harry Carman (American history), Mark Van Doren and Raymond Weaver (English literature), Burdette Kinne (French), Moses Hadas (Greek and Latin), and James Gutmann and Charles Frankel (philosophy) were among those who foresaw this need as early as the mid-1930s.

Thus, like CC and Lit Hum, Columbia's Asian Humanities and Civilizations courses were the outgrowth of an educational vision that went beyond the academic specialties of its early proponents. These scholars thought of themselves as responsible, not only for scholarship in their own fields, but also for the broader education of young people at a formative stage in their lives as citizens and more broadly as human beings.

Though Asia came into focus for many with World War II, academia's preoccupation with the war actually delayed implementation of the early vision. Thus, it was only in 1948–49 that Hadas and Herbert Deane (political science) could give a pilot Oriental Colloquium. That neither instructor was an "Orientalist" (or Asia specialist) demonstrates scholars' willingness in those days to venture beyond their own fields—a venturesomeness already shown by the CC and Humanities staffs, who were drawn from many fields.

College students in that experimental colloquium also were nonspecialists. They included John Hollander, a poet and later Sterling Professor of English at Yale; John Rosenberg, later Trent Professor of English and Comparative Literature; and Jason Epstein, who became a writer, editor, and publisher at Random House.

In 1949–50, Oriental Humanities (later called Asian Humanities) followed and, in 1950–51, Oriental Civilizations. Traditional "Orientalism," which had been dominated by language study on the graduate level, was at a low ebb in those days, so the aims and methods of the new program derived from the educational philosophy and practice of general education in the College, which emphasized the reading and discussion of source materials in small classes. In the 1960s, Columbia added Asian Art Humanities and Asian Music Humanities, so that the Asian Core program included a full complement parallel to the required Western Core courses.

While the number and variety of Asian Core courses grew, Columbia began to recruit and train additional staff so that the number of sections could be increased. Militating against this, however, was the increasing trend toward academic specialization and departmentalization of instruction. Though designed along the lines of the Core Curriculum, the Asian courses lacked the staff necessary to make them a required part of the Core. Without a large pool of scholars, expansion of the staff and sections for the Asian program was limited and slow. Nevertheless, with the arrival of Ainslie Embree in Indian studies and the extension of the program at Barnard under John Meskill, gradual progress was made. Provost Jacques Barzun and Deans Lawrence Chamberlain of the College and Millicent McIntosh of Barnard were instrumental in supporting these efforts. Barbara Miller, a Barnard student who came up through the program, became a distinguished addition to the staff in Sanskrit studies and contributed many translations, and Irene Bloom, who succeeded Meskill at Barnard, became a leader in the joint Barnard-Columbia program after the 1990s.

The 1990s presented both fresh opportunities and more problems. One opportunity resulted from a recommendation of the College's 1988 Commission on the

Core Curriculum that all students satisfy a "Major Cultures" requirement; that is, study outside the scope of the Western Core. Asian Civilizations and Humanities courses are among the options offered. This, and the subsequent expansion of the College enrollment, have created greater demands for additional sections of the basic Asian courses—demands exceeding the staff availability.

In response, the University Committee on Asia and the Middle East (successor to an earlier Committee on Oriental Studies) set up a 1998 summer workshop to train graduate student preceptors and raised funds for two postdoctoral teaching fellowships. These have enabled a few more sections, though far short of what is needed.

The term "general education," as it gained currency in the mid-twentieth century, originally referred to the reform of university education, which had become dominated by departmental specialization and by the elective system that lent itself to the same trend. The history of these movements tells us something about why "general education," whether as a term or as a practice, is somewhat anachronistic and should be replaced with "core curriculum." At the same time, however, the recent rise of "multicultural education" underscores the need for equipping that central "core" with multicultural dimensions.

The original educational challenge arose from the sense of both civilizational crisis and a new intellectual opportunity following World War I. The great aim (or at least the great ideological slogan) of that war had been "to make the world safe for democracy," yet the devastation of Western Europe, the high cost to Britain, and unsolved postwar problems left many people wondering whether civilization itself, much less democracy, could survive.

One response to these twin challenges was the development at the College of the War Issues course (soon reconceived as Peace Issues) course that addressed the civilizational crisis against the background of historical developments that shaped the issues. (John Herman Randall 's *The Making of the Modern Mind*, a basic CC text in the 1920s and 1930s that placed modern problems in a historical context, became widely used in courses modeled on CC that proliferated in American colleges.) Given the focus of the War and Peace Issues courses on contemporary problems in relation to basic civilizational values, it is hardly surprising that the course was rechristened Contemporary Civilization. Moreover, with its hope and concern for the establishment of a new world order based on the peaceful resolution of human problems, it is not stretching things to say that this central concern of the course was "civility" in its broadest sense.

Ainslie T. Embree brought Indian studies into the Humanities program

The topical treatment, the concern for values and ideas, the contemporary interest combined with historical background, and, above all, the use of challenging source readings as the basis for class discussion became defining characteristics of Contemporary Civilization. Another defining characteristic was that it was required of all students, a break from the dominant elective system.

The justification was civic. Along with the inescapable trend toward academic specialization, the College believed it should educate students to deal in an informed way with problems of contemporary society. Preparation for leadership and citizenship was undoubtedly among the course's aims, but the method of personal engagement with urgent contemporary problems through active class discussion (rather than just lectures) was almost an end in itself. In other words, the discussion method promoted active civil discourse on civility—learning by doing.

These shared moral and social concerns, along with a sense of corporate responsibility, justified limiting students' freedom of election—while also, it is important to add, limiting the faculty's freedom to teach their own specialties. In the interests of education, the faculty had to subordinate their personal research interests to the needs of a common curriculum, taught in a collegial fashion.

Subsequently, the idea of having a "required core" spread widely, but one hardly need mention today that the original sense of corporate responsibility and faculty *esprit de corps* has proved difficult to sustain. Thus the true *esprit de* <u>core</u> has often been dissipated, and today "core" at many places means only "what is required," though few remember why. Usually a "core" amounts only to a distribution requirement— at best a methodological smorgasbord—and not a genuinely collegial effort to bring a range of disciplines to focus on questions of common concern.

This is what happened at the University of Chicago and Harvard, both of which embraced the idea of general education in the 1930s and 1940s with much fanfare. At Chicago, the program was identified initially with the Great Books program promoted by Robert Hutchins and Mortimer Adler, but with the Great Books program spun off as a separate adult education foundation, the university shifted to a divisional structure tailored more to traditional disciplinary groupings (humanities, social sciences, etc.) and a common core became dissipated. At Harvard, the so-called "general education program" quickly became departmentalized, and Dean Henry Rosovsky's reforms did little to arrest a gradual fragmentation. In effect, academic specialization reasserted itself at both schools, "general education" became converted into distribution requirements, and the idea of core concerns, key issues, and classic texts addressed by all students became less central.

In retrospect, one can see that the very generality and flexibility of "general education" bent too readily before academia's centrifugal tendencies. From this one may draw an important lesson concerning the concept of a "core." Difficult though it is to sustain against academic departmentalization and specialization, a "core" goes to the heart of the educational enterprise—the notion of a common humanity. Though "a common humanity" may itself be a difficult philosophical question, if it ceases to be a question and a key issue for shared discussion, we are in deep trouble, exposed to the divisiveness of ethnic and political conflicts.

Practically speaking, this is the real problem facing the Core Curriculum today, not the dead hand of Eurocentric tradition or the stolid resistance of a WASP establishment. For change has been taking place all along, and if not all of it has been for the good, by no means has all of it been for the worse, either.

—⚏—

The first important change in the Columbia Core came in the 1930s with the addition of the Humanities sequence, which consisted of the reading and discussion of major Western literary and philosophical works as well as parallel courses in art and music. There were always more masterworks than could be included in any course, and more than enough to command attention and provoke argument. The important thing was to have a common reading list, a shared discourse, and collegial discussion. This ongoing, open-ended dialogue between past and present is sometimes referred to as "The Great Conversation," because the great minds speak to each other, comment on their forebears, and argue with them. Another way of putting it, with more intellectual bite, is "disputatious learning."

Both the original Core courses and the Asian courses modeled on them make use of major works, not just to learn from the past but to put before students models that challenge, stretch the intellect, and exercise the moral imagination. Thus, the true greatness of "great books," from this educational point of view, lies not in their perfection but rather in their pivotal quality—their ability to focus on key issues and expose the mind to crucial alternatives. Far from settling things, they are unsettling, always open to reinterpretation. They encourage reflective thinking, critical analysis, and the formulation of the student's own arguments. The canon (if such it be) and the questioning of it have proceeded together. There should be questioning *and* something of value that has stood the test of time, worthy of serious consideration. Contrary to a common academic conceit, questioning alone is not enough: questioning without affirmation is sterile; affirmation without questioning can be stultifying.[1]

A "core" in this sense refers not just to content or canon but also to process and method—to a well-tested body of challenging material, cultivated habits of critical discourse, and procedures for reexamination and redefinition. A viable core can neither be slave to the past nor captive to the preoccupations, pressures, or fashions of the moment. It should serve rather to advance students' intellectual growth and self-awareness, cultivate their powers of thought and expression, and prepare them to take a responsible part in society. The focus has differed in the two kinds of courses: on society and civility in the Civilization courses; more on the individual and on a shared, but at the same time diverse, humanity in the Humanities courses. In either case the method has emphasized practice in civil discourse in a collegial setting.

—m—

Almost from the beginning, proponents of the Core Curriculum were conscious of its initial Western focus and anxious to extend its horizons. This consciousness is reflected in the title, Introduction to Contemporary Civilization in the West, and the original syllabus of the honors course, Classics of the Western World. "West" in the original Core courses signified an acknowledgment of inadequacy and limitation, not an affirmation of Eurocentrism. And no sooner had the Humanities course been added to the Core in 1937 than leaders of the movement (e.g., Carman and Gutmann, though neither was an Asianist) began to agitate and plan for counterpart courses in Asian civilizations and humanities, which were added as soon as practicable after World War II.

The way in which this was done is highly significant for today's debate on multiculturalism. Its focus was on core concerns, humanity and civility, and the method of instruction put a premium on collegial discussion (that is, civil discourse). It did not assume the superiority of Western ways or values or the primacy of a European canon, but rather acknowledged the presence of other major civilizations of great depth, complexity, and longevity as well as comparable discourses on perennial human concerns.

This assumption of parallel discourses had no difficulty gaining confirmation from the Asian works themselves, but without a single "Asian tradition" (in the sense of "pan-Asian"), some judgment had to be exercised in identifying major traditions

for a one-year course; in our case, we identified Islamic, Indian (including both
Buddhist and Hindu), Chinese, Japanese,
and, later, Korean civilizations. That judgment, however, was almost made for us,
given our prior and most fundamental
assumption concerning the nature of any
tradition or canon: that it be self-defining
and self-confirming. Thus it was not for us
to find Asian counterparts to Western classics, but only to identify what Asians themselves had recognized as works commanding special respect, either through enduring
appeal or irrepressible challenge.

*Chinese philosophy
scholar Irene Bloom,
circa 1993*

Within each major tradition, this is primarily an internal dialogue, independent
of external involvement (except to the
extent that, from at least the seventeenth century onward, many Western writers
have embraced what the Islamic, Indian, Chinese, and Japanese traditions have long
esteemed). Thus, in the Islamic tradition, Al Ghazali and Ibn Khaldun have based
themselves on the Qur'an and commented on the great Sufis, while European writers since the Middle Ages also have recognized the stature of Al Ghazali and, more
recently, Ibn Khaldun. In the Indian tradition, the *Upanishads* and Ramayana take up
the discourse from the *Vedas*, the *Gita* from the *Upanishads*, and Shankara from both.
And in China, Mencius draws on Confucius, Xunzi comments on both Confucius
and Mencius, the Laozi and Zhuangzi confront the Confucians, and so on. Almost
all Asian classics relate to each other as major players in their own league, members
(even if competitors) of their own discursive company.

Enough of the original discourse must be reproduced for this internal dialogue
to be recognized and evaluated meaningfully. To recognize and judge the adequacy
of one writer's representation of another requires familiarity with the other. The
same is true of the literary form. Indeed, in any domain, the genre, voice, and medium
of expression enter strongly into the judgment of what is a classic or canonical.

The Asian Core includes courses in humanities, civilizations, music, and art, so
Columbia's overall program is less bibliocentric than the discussion thus far might
lead one to believe. But it is in the discussion of classic texts that one can most easily observe the kind of internal give-and-take that should be incorporated in the

Donald Keene (left) and Burton Watson in 2001

larger discussion of a core. Including one or two such Asian classics in a world civilization, history, or literature course is almost worse than including nothing at all. It is tokenism, and even if such a course is equally and uniformly sparing in its representation of all cultural artifacts, it is only tokenism on a grander and more dangerous scale. If one's initial framework is a Western civilization or humanities course, the addition of just one or two Islamic, Indian, or Chinese works will almost always be prejudicial, no matter how innocently intended, for the work, bereft of context, will inevitably be read in a Western frame of reference. Even if the instructor compensates by lecturing about the breadth and variety of the non-Western culture, the information still comes second-hand, and the student must depend on the instructor's word.

No one can prescribe a fixed or minimum number of classics for such a multicultural program. Nevertheless, one could offer as a rule of thumb that at least five or six such works are necessary to establish the context of any particular discourse, assuming that the works are well chosen and suggest not only a tradition's range of possibilities but also how it has grown and developed. For unless a discourse's cumulative nature—its continuities, discontinuities, and mature syntheses—are adequately represented, a reader's tendency is to see individual works as embodying some static cultural essence rather than being landmarks along the way.

In a multicultural education that serves human commonality as well as cultural diversity, both content and method may vary. A core program, however, should give priority to the repossession (both sympathetic and critical) of a given society's main cultural traditions and then move on to a similar treatment of other major cultures. To the extent that time and resources allow, it would consider still other cultures that, for a variety of reasons, have not played such a dominant role in world history so far. (In the East Asian context, I would certainly point to Korea in this respect.)

At least two other general principles seem applicable to this educational approach. One is that it is best, if possible, for the process to extend to more than one other culture, so that there is always some cultural triangulation. Such a multi-

READINGS IN ASIAN HUMANITIES AND CIVILIZATIONS

A main feature of Contemporary Civilization and the Humanities courses is the reading and discussion of source materials. To provide these for the major Asian traditions was a challenge, eventually met by myself (the chair of the program) and collaborators in two book series: a *Sources* series (for use in Asian Civilizations courses) and *Translations from the Asian Classics* (for Asian Humanities courses), all published by Columbia University Press.

The first series includes *The Sources of Japanese Tradition* (1958, revised 2005), *The Sources of Chinese Tradition* (1960, revised 1999), *The Sources of Indian Tradition* (1958, revised 1988), and *The Sources of Korean Tradition* (1997). These two-volume sets, originally intended for Columbia students, now are used on campuses across the United States and abroad; they are among the longest and best-selling titles in the Columbia University Press catalogue. In the 1990s, the Committee on Asia and the Middle East (successor to an earlier Committee on Oriental Studies) began a major revision and expansion of all eight volumes of the *Sources* series, including the two on the Korean tradition.

With assistance from the Carnegie Corporation and in the 1960s from the United States Office of Education, the *Translations* series were expanded, so that to date more than 150 titles have been published for use in general education on Asia. Donald Keene and Burton Watson were major contributors to this effort.

An essential part of the Asian Humanities and Civilizations instructional program from its inception has been the committee's publication of translations and teaching aids conducted under the direction of its Publication Committee. Royalties from the Sources and Translations series have been returned to the Oriental Studies Fund, which has continued to support publications of use to the teaching of Asia in the Core Curriculum.

cultural perspective can then predominate over simplistic we/they, self/other, East/West comparisons. Thus, Columbia's Asian Humanities course includes readings from several major Asian traditions, which allows for significant cross-cultural comparisons quite apart from those students naturally make between their own and any single Asian tradition.

A second principle is that any such treatment should give priority to identifying central concerns. I have suggested "civility" and "humanity" (to which "the common good" or "commonality" could well be added) as basic categories or core concepts. A main reason for using original texts has been to proceed inductively—to ask what are the primary questions being addressed in each reading, what are the defining concepts and values, and in what key terms are proximate and ultimate concerns expressed? Such questions may well be open-ended, but at this stage of learning— and for purposes of cross-cultural discussion—we should be looking for centers of gravity, points of convergence, common denominators.[2] Why? Because as a matter of educational coherence, it is best to work from some center, however tentatively constructed, to the outer reaches of human possibility. For purposes of establishing civil discourse, some working consensus, initially tradition-based but increasingly multicultural, is needed.

The priorities and sequence just proposed would, it seems to me, be applicable to almost any cultural situation. Other peoples set their own priorities, so one naturally expects each tradition to confront its own classics first, and then move on to ingest others. Indeed, one would concede this as a right—that in China's schools, for instance, Chinese civilization would have priority; in India, Indian; and so forth. Starting from the premise that every person and people needs its own self-respect, as well as a minimum of respect from others, each must have a proper self-understanding—to come to terms with its own past. This is essential not only to its own cultural health but to healthy relations all around.

The key to success in such an endeavor is how well one identifies core human issues and how one selects texts that illuminate them. This requires constant reflection, reexamination, and dialogue among world traditions. But as each tradition participates in this multicultural discourse, we can hope to expand gradually the horizons of civil discourse and the scope of shared values, which will be key to the solution of our common global concerns about the environment, human rights, and world peace.

—m—

Although Columbia pioneered in the development of courses in Asian Civilizations and Humanities specifically designed for the Core, many students and faculty have felt the need to integrate better multicultural elements in upper-level courses that would build on the basic courses—in much the same way that the earlier honors colloquia did as an extension of CC and Humanities—but now including Asian materials alongside Western.

To this end a series of workshops has been conducted that aims at the incorporation of East-West materials in senior-level colloquia or capstone courses, building on core courses introductory to Western and Asian civilizations. Its purpose is primarily educational, that is, the continuation of a learning process that broadens the horizons and perspectives an educated person brings to the understanding of problems, one's own and those of other societies. But this continuing process of liberal learning can also serve as an accompaniment on the upper College level to work on one's major and give an added dimension to senior seminar projects.

Because we are working in the context of a well-defined, sequential Core Curriculum, these workshops face severe time constraints, both with regard to the limits imposed by course requirements on students and to the time faculty can devote to any new venture on top of the already heavy demands of a general education program. Thus the achievement of a broad, multicultural perspective (spanning several major traditions) requires great selectivity and intense focus on key texts that speak to the chosen theme. One risks being charged with superficiality either in ignoring some relevant texts or not going as deeply into the chosen ones as their inherent depth might call for. This however is not an unfamiliar dilemma in liberal education, the practice of which is always a delicate balancing act for generalists and always exposed to the complaints of purists and specialists.

In the four-tiered staging of the current series of workshops and colloquia, moreover, we have recognized that one must deal with major traditions in stages—not as static, timeless entities to be represented only by a few classic texts, but as civilizational traditions that have undergone historical development. The idea here is to track their trajectories in the course of some historical vicissitudes and try to identify, not timeless essences, but perennial human concerns, marked by shared commonalities in the midst of cultural and historical differences.

As examples of these concerns or perennial issues one may consider the following:

1. Nobility and Civility (Leadership and Citizenship)
2. Religion and the State
3. The Self and the Dignity of the Individual
4. Law and Constitutionalism
5. The Good Life

If this exercise has started with the theme of Nobility and Civility, it has reversed the usual approach of looking in the East for something like the ideas, concepts, or issues that are discussed in the Western traditions—like Mortimer Adler's *Hundred Great Ideas in the Hundred Great Books*—and instead has taken issues prominent in the Asian classics at the dawn of civilization, when earlier concepts of status nobility, the warrior (samurai) ethic, and class behavior were subject to the test of universalizing civilizational values; and then it has asked whether the Western classics have something to say on the same issues.

The details of our readings and interdisciplinary participation, for both our fac-

*Mark Van Doren
believed a real
classic could
survive translation.*

ulty workshops and the subsequent courses offered to college juniors and seniors (who would already have taken "core courses" in the traditions represented) are available on the Internet through the Heyman Center for the Humanities. Details of the syllabi and workshop faculty may also be found in the Notes section of this volume (see pp. 665–67). We have learned much from these experimental efforts about what it is practicable to do in such courses, and we have compiled the results in syllabi and workbooks that can be shared with others, from whose own experiments we shall be glad to learn.

Translation has been an issue for the Core Curriculum from the beginning, whether the works translated were referred to as "classics," "important books," "Great Books," or "major texts." Under whatever rubric they were offered, these books, it was said, were ones any educated person ought to have read—as if what it meant to be "educated" could be taken for granted in those days, even though education itself was undergoing rapid change.

—⁂—

In the early twentieth century, the elimination of Western classical languages—Greek, Latin, and Hebrew—from college requirements was followed by a widespread desire to continue reading of the "classics," still thought essential for educated "gentlemen," in translation. When this change occurred, defenders of the classical languages objected that something would inevitably be lost if the classics were not read in the original. That there would indeed be some loss could hardly be doubted, but John Erskine (Class of 1900), an early proponent of reading the classics in translation, didn't consider the loss overwhelming. "How many people read the Bible in the original?" he asked.

Indeed, Mark Van Doren, who subsequently became a leading proponent of the Humanities curriculum, insisted that one test of a real classic was that it could survive translation. He meant, of course, that such a work dealt importantly with issues, concerns, and values so pertinent to, and so perennial in, human life that any work addressing them in a challenging way would not become obsolete. This is true of Latin and Greek classics translated into English, French, or German, and it is no less true of the quick ascent and commanding position of Shakespeare in non-English literatures and cultures.

Nor is this true only of the West. "Classics" of several Asian traditions have survived translation within Asia. Chinese works translated into Korean and Japanese have become accepted as "classics" in their adoptive lands, just as Greek and Latin works became "classics" within many European cultures. The same, of course, has been true of Indian works translated into South and East Asian languages and, now, Western works esteemed as classics in Asia.

To say this, however, is not to dismiss translation as a minor issue. The standing of classics in one tradition may compel our attention, but the availability and quality of translations have clearly influenced Humanities courses. To a degree greater than most people today are aware, enough have been translated from Asian languages so that major works, already well known in the nineteenth- and early twentieth-century West, had long since challenged Western thinkers.

Indian and Sanskrit scholar Barbara Stoler Miller, circa 1986

Nevertheless, Asian translations were not complete or satisfactory for our purposes when Asian Humanities and Civilizations was inaugurated in the late 1940s. Enough good translations were available to launch a worthwhile program, but there were many gaps. A major problem also faced the extension of the program beyond a select few in an honors colloquium—the lack of accessible translations, not heavily burdened with scholarly annotation, that were suited to the general reader.

Fortunately, help was forthcoming from young scholars whose translations were to establish a new standard, not only for scholarly excellence, but also for accessibility. First, Donald Keene compiled his *Anthology of Japanese Literature* (1955), which made Japanese classic writings available in a convenient, low cost form, albeit at the cost of abridgement of works better read in whole. Keene later made up for this limitation by translating whole works only partly translated in the *Anthology.* Most notable has been his translation of Kenkō's *Tsurezuregusa,* published as *Essays in Idleness* in the Translations from the Asian Classics series, which was launched specifically to meet the needs of the Asian Humanities course. Next came his translation of *Major Plays of Chikamatsu* and subsequently the drama *Chōshingura.* With follow-up work from Keene's students, Royall Tyler and Karen Brazell, Keene's translations of Noh plays in his *Anthology* have been substantially supplemented by competent, inexpensive paperback translations. Ivan Morris, before his untimely death a teacher of Asian Humanities, translated the *Pillow Book* of Sei Shōnagon, a Japanese classic only excerpted in Keene's *Anthology*. These translations have become standard works and virtual classics of the translator's art.

Although many Chinese classics already had been translated, most notably by James Legge and Arthur Waley, and were indispensable to the Asian Core program, many other Chinese classics remained either untranslated or unavailable in a form suitable for students. In response, Burton Watson's translations of Chinese classics convey the diversity and range of the Chinese—and what subsequently became the East Asian—tradition. Watson's early versions of alternative ancient Chinese "classics"—Mo Zi (Mo Tzu), Xun Zi (Hsün Tzu), Zhuangzi (Chuang Tzu), and Han Feizi—quickly made available in paperback by Columbia University Press, became standard items on Humanities reading lists and indeed set a new standard for Chinese translations for the general reader. Watson's translating range, versatility, and virtuosity also were apparent in his renderings of the *Records of the Grand Historian* by Sima Qian (Ssu-ma Ch'ien), the *Vimalakirti* and *Lotus* sutras, and his anthology, the *Columbia Book of Chinese Poetry*—all of which made their way onto the Asian Humanities reading list.

The biggest translating challenge came with the neo-Confucian tradition, which was a response to the challenge of Buddhism and Daoism. The key texts are mostly the commentaries of Zhu Xi (Chu Hsi) on the Confucian classics, and commentaries often are far more difficult reading than the original works. For this reason, many instructors avoid the neo-Confucian texts in favor of more literary works (of which there is an almost unlimited supply). But these neo-Confucian texts were the operative "classics" that shaped intellectual and ethical traditions of China, Japan, and Korea from the thirteenth to the twentieth centuries, and avoiding them is like ignoring everything in the West from Dante on.

A similar problem presented itself with medieval Islamic and Indian traditions. It is not an easy dilemma to resolve, considering, for example, the lack of a suitable translation of Shankara-charya's commentaries on the *Brahma Sutras*. To some extent, excerpts can address this deficiency. Students have access to Shankara in the *Sources of Indian Tradition*, and to Zhu Xi in new translations included in the second edition of the *Sources of Chinese Tradition*. Still this is a compromise—better than nothing but less than satisfactory.

The Asian Core program has produced a major translator of Indian thought and literature. Barbara Miller, who began as a Barnard undergraduate taking Oriental Humanities, went on to graduate studies in Sanskrit. She composed accessible translations of the *Bhagavad Gita*, the *Shakuntala* of Kalidasa, *The Love Song of the Dark Lord* (*Gita Govinda*), and the lyric poetry of Bhartrihari. Before her premature death, Barbara established herself as not only a prime contributor to the Asian Humanities program but also a leading figure in Indian and Sanskrit studies.

Thus, while an Asian Humanities program can rely on the inherent greatness of certain works recognized as "classics," still their ability to "survive translation" (in Van Doren's terms) depends on having skilled translators able to convey their contents in terms meaningful enough to new audiences in changing times and different cultures.

Yet, there will never come a time when all translation is finished for all eligible texts, since there will never be a complete, definitive, and final rendering of the "original" meaning of such texts. Dealing as they do with pivotal issues, subject to different interpretations and expressing themselves in highly suggestive, expandable ways, these works may always be brought to life in new renderings. Readers who wonder how much of a gap may exist between the original and translation can look at alternative translations to get a sense of common ground and lines of difference. They have recourse, too, to scholarly expertise, but, since specialists differ among themselves as much as translations do, this is not a perfect solution.

It remains true, however, that, though any translator is welcome to take up the challenge and offer his own interpretation, not all translations meet the need equally well. We in the Asian Core can count ourselves fortunate in having had an especially able group of translators, whose great translations almost match the great works themselves.

CHAPTER 39

Hall of Fame: Lou Gehrig, Columbia Legend and American Hero

—⚬—

Ray Robinson

Before he was the Iron Horse, he was Columbia Lou. Lou Gehrig attended Columbia College from 1921 to 1923, playing both football and baseball before signing with the Yankees and embarking on a legendary major league career. Despite his somewhat rocky encounters with campus social life, described by Ray Robinson in the essay below, Gehrig always remained true blue: he returned to Morningside in the late 1930s as a guest lecturer at a Teachers College physical education course. ("Bat Used as Textbook," The New York Times reported, noting that the audience consisted of forty registered students and 110 ringers and autograph seekers.) He also served on an Alumni Federation recruitment committee. To the end of his abbreviated life he remained an avid fan of the Lions and followed the football team's progress on the radio.

Ray Robinson has carried on a Columbia legacy from his father, Louis Robinson. He has been an editor at Pageant, Coronet, Good Housekeeping, *and* Seventeen, *and has written biographies of Lou Gehrig, Christy Mathewson, Will Rogers, and Knute Rockne. Robinson has also contributed many articles to* The New York Times, The Washington Post, *the* New York Daily News, TV Guide, *and* American Heritage.

Wm. Theodore de Bary

—⚬—

Not too many years ago, when I was a guest at a forum about Lou Gehrig at the National Baseball Hall of Fame in Cooperstown, New York, a questioner asked me what kind of a man Gehrig was. The answer is not as simple as it may seem at first glance, for Gehrig, a professional athlete, was more complex than most modern-day baseball players. What I told him was that Gehrig had to be judged by the totality of his tragically short life and not just by his batting statistics. I pointed out that Gehrig was shy and pursued by insecurity. I also volunteered that he was a person of quiet dignity who departed life with exemplary grace. But above all, I emphasized that he was a person who always believed in striving to do his best, no matter what the circumstances. It is that last characteristic that made Gehrig such a dynamic force on the baseball diamond—and also made him into a figure who transcended his sport. It is remarkable that even today many young people regard him as an icon and valuable role model.

Gehrig's words of hope, grace, and humility on July 4, 1939, as he bid farewell to baseball and his team, the New York Yankees, have often been referred to without sarcasm as the game's Gettysburg Address. The speech is included in William Safire's *Lend Me Your Ears*, a collection of the world's greatest speeches throughout history.

I was one of the celebrants that melancholy afternoon, sitting in the right-field bleachers where he had deposited so many home runs on behalf of his team. I was an eighteen-year-old admirer, and like so many there that day, I sat teary-eyed as I listened to the man who was called "the Iron Horse" deliver his valedictory. Most of us present were not aware that Gehrig was dying of amyotrophic lateral sclerosis (a disease ultimately named after him). But we did suspect that this man, who had played in a record 2,130 consecutive games, all with the Yankees, from 1925 to 1939, would never put his spikes on again.

In writing about Gehrig's speech, author Wilfrid Sheed said that "all present in Yankee Stadium that day had been given a license to love a fellow human to the limit, without qualification, and to root for that person as they'd never rooted for themselves. . . . If the Stadium had emptied out suddenly, and he had been left standing there alone, Gehrig would have felt no less lucky, because the appearance merely confirmed what he already knew, that he was having a very good day. . . . A day like that was worth a thousand of the old ones."

In the early days of the Great Depression, I lived across the street from Columbia. I never got to see Gehrig hit his legendary home run off the dial outside of South Field or off the steps of Low Library ("He gave his Alma Mater many a nervous moment," wrote Bill Corum, a New York sports columnist who was also a graduate of Columbia's School of Journalism). In fact, by the late 1920s Columbia had stopped playing its ball games on South Field altogether.

Columbia's most eminent dropout since Alexander Hamilton

But as a ten-year-old grammar school kid I had composed a letter, with the help of a friend, asking Gehrig if we could come to Yankee Stadium for an interview on behalf of our school paper. We never expected a response, for we thought Gehrig would have little time to speak to such tiny hero-worshippers. But our certainty of failure was soon proved wrong when a handwritten letter from Gehrig arrived several days later. We were struck by the careful, graceful penmanship, considering the size and strength of the writer. Yes, Gehrig had written, "I'll be happy to talk to you. Just use this letter to come to the clubhouse."

Unfortunately, when we went to Yankee Stadium the next day, the policeman guarding the clubhouse door denied us entrance. We were invited to wait—and that's what we did. Games started in those days at 3:30 p.m. (the Yankees were celebrated as the team of the "five o'clock lightning" in recognition of their propensity for late rallies), so we had a long wait. We kept listening for crowd noises that might hint how the Yankees were doing, and once, when we heard a swelling roar, we were convinced it must have been a Gehrig homer. Finally, the game was over, and within a short time, Gehrig appeared. He was hatless, coatless, and tieless, and his thick brown hair—no blow-dry in those simpler times—was still damp from the shower. He had the kind of deep tan that today's players have forfeited to night games.

As he walked by us at a fast pace, we set out after him, calling out his name. He stopped and looked at us, and we waved his letter at him. He took a quick look at his letter and then asked if we had enjoyed the game. When we answered that we weren't able to get in, he appeared genuinely sorry. Then, when we brought up the interview, he said he was in a hurry to get home, but maybe we could do it another day. Then he took two crumpled tickets from his pocket and handed them over. "Did you really wait all afternoon?" he asked as he stepped into his car. "Yes, we did," I answered, hoping he'd reverse himself and grant us an interview on the spot. But that wasn't to be the case. Waving his hand at us in a friendly gesture, Gehrig said, "I'm really sorry." Then he was gone.

I never forgot Gehrig's kindness and manner and over sixty years later wrote what I hoped was a fair-minded biography of him.

THE EARLY DAYS

Henry Louis Gehrig was born on June 19, 1903, at 103rd Street and Second Avenue in the lower-middle-class section of Manhattan's Yorkville. His parents were Heinrich Gehrig and Christina Fack, part of the large number of German immigrants who had come to America at the turn of the century. Of the four children born to Christina, Lou was the only one who survived infancy. He was raised in a poor household, close to the poverty level, but when Lou became famous his mother always insisted that he was not "a product of the slums."

As a shabbily dressed Yorkville youngster and later when his family moved to Washington Heights, Lou played in the streets and schoolyards and swam in nearby rivers. His father was often ill and sometimes drank too much. He had some skills as a metal worker but often found it hard to obtain employment. Christina, on the other hand, worked almost constantly. She cleaned floors, cooked for others (including a job at the Columbia Sigma Nu fraternity house), and worked as a laundress—anything to bring money into the house.

Gehrig attended Commerce High School, where he became proficient at football and baseball. As a Commerce senior in 1920, he hit a ninth-inning home run with the bases loaded in an intercity game at Chicago's Wrigley Field. The feat earned him his first newspaper kudos, including some comparisons to Babe Ruth—rather a crushing burden to impose on a young ballplayer off the streets of New York. In the process of hailing his achievement, one newspaper misspelled his last name.

Impressed by Gehrig's skills and with his eye mainly on the young man's football talents, Bobby Watt, graduate manager of athletics at Columbia, encouraged Lou to enroll at Columbia. At the time, Christina Gehrig was convinced that her son might wind up as an engineer or architect. But even as he played on the line and in the backfield for Columbia's footballers (where he joined Wally Koppisch, a running back with All-American credentials), Gehrig's destiny turned out to be baseball.

Gehrig spent two years on Morningside Heights, which later won him the nickname of "Columbia Lou" in the nation's press. That was far preferable to "Biscuit Pants," which he was also called on occasion. By leaving Columbia in his junior year, Gehrig became Columbia's most eminent dropout since Alexander Hamilton. On one level, Gehrig's time at Columbia was quite productive. It was on the Lion campus that he apprenticed for stardom in major league baseball, and it was where he gained the friendship and advice of baseball coach Andy Coakley, a former big league pitcher, who recognized and nursed Lou's large talents.

On the other hand, Gehrig felt that he never gained full acceptance from his fellow students at Columbia. At Phi Delta Theta fraternity, where he was pledged, he waited on tables and often performed other tasks. In an era when many fraternities emphasized the social backgrounds and bank accounts of their members, Gehrig lacked such credentials. He had to rely on his athletic prowess to win the condescending approval of his fellow students. His family background, with two parents who had difficulty with English, plus his own meager interpersonal skills and clumsiness, exposed him to frequent ridicule. He was often disparaged for his awkwardness and lack of social polish. He ran up a small debt to the fraternity, which he was reluctant to repay even in his halcyon years. Such treatment by his associates gnawed at his own sense of unworthiness too much to forget the snobbery he confronted, although he did appear as a guest lecturer at Columbia's Teachers College

Though Gehrig was recruited to play football at Columbia, his powerhouse home runs wowed Yankee scout Paul Krichell, and before long Gehrig was on his way from South Field to Yankee Stadium.

in the 1930s, an indication that he held no grudge against the school itself. Also, in conversations with his wife, Eleanor, whom he married in 1933, he commented on the role that his Columbia education had played in his learning to appreciate reading, good books, and classical music.

FROM COLUMBIA TO THE BIG TIME

On April 18, 1923, when Yankee Stadium opened for the first time, Babe Ruth fittingly christened the spectacular new edifice with a home run. On the same afternoon at Columbia, pitcher Gehrig struck out seventeen Williams batters for a team record. Somehow, Columbia still managed to lose the game. Only a handful of collegians were at South Field that day, but more significant was the presence of the bowlegged Yankee scout, Paul Krichell, who had been trailing Gehrig for some time. However, it wasn't Gehrig's pitching that particularly impressed him. Instead, it was Gehrig's powerful hitting from the left side of the plate. During the time

Krichell had been watching Gehrig, the bulky Columbian had hit some of the longest home runs ever seen on various Eastern campuses.

Within two months Gehrig had signed his name to a Yankee contract. A bonus of $1,500, a veritable fortune for Gehrig and his family, was enough to get him to leave his studies. Two years later Gehrig would become part of a symbiotic slugging relationship with Ruth in the heart of the vaunted Yankees lineup. Batting fourth as the cleanup man behind the Babe, Gehrig became half of the most devastating one-two punch in the game's history. His consecutive game streak began in June 1925, when he appeared as a pinch hitter for Peewee Wanninger. The next day, Gehrig replaced Wally Pipp at first base and stayed there for fourteen years. Ultimately, he became the all-time player at that position, which he played unfailingly through broken bones, split fingers, aches, pains, and menacing beanballs.

Gehrig accumulated 493 home runs, had a lifetime batting average of .340 (only two points behind the Babe), and batted in 175, 174, and 184 runs in the years between 1926 and 1930. To this day his twenty-three home runs with the bases loaded surpass all players in history. In a 1932 game at Philadelphia, he became the first player in the twentieth century to hit four home runs in one game.

Yet, through the years of the Roaring Twenties, Prohibition, the Jazz Age, the Great Depression, and the New Deal, Gehrig constantly played in the bulging shadow of his Rabelaisian teammate, Ruth. The Babe outhit, outhomered, outate, and outpublicized Lou. Even in the 1928 World Series against St. Louis, in which Gehrig knocked out four home runs and batted in nine runs, the Babe hit .625, an all-time high in a four-game series. When a fatigued Ruth left the Yankees after the 1934 season, along came the San Francisco phenom, Joseph Paul DiMaggio, in 1936, to deprive Gehrig of the press attention he so richly deserved.

It's hard to know exactly how Gehrig felt about all of this. On the surface he seems to have been content being the Yankees captain—essentially a symbolic role. But what also seems clear is that he had a profound sense of himself as a public figure, with a self-designated role as a loyal team player, a loyal son, a loyal citizen, and a loyal employee. Such an unquestioning commitment may have placed a heavy burden on him, at times costing him dearly in human relationships. For example, he assigned himself the role of preserving, certifying, and codifying all rules of Yankee behavior. On a ball club with more than a few rogues and rapscallions on the premises, such a posture was hardly designed to win him great popularity. Gehrig's relationship with the Babe was a case in point. In the early years, Gehrig had expressed great admiration for Ruth, but as time went by the two men barely spoke to each other, on or off the field.

TWILIGHT

In the spring of 1939, after a relatively mediocre season in 1938, Gehrig's sturdy body started to fail him. He wasn't connecting solidly with the ball, nor was he fielding his position properly. He even had trouble tying his shoelaces. Disturbed by his inadequacies, Gehrig informed Manager Joe McCarthy that he was going to step down for the good of the team. McCarthy, who was tremendously fond of Gehrig, had difficulty accepting his decision. He was convinced something was terribly wrong with Gehrig but encouraged him nonetheless to keep trying. Gehrig thought otherwise. Within a short period of time the Mayo Clinic, where Gehrig had seen physicians for a physical examination, issued a chilling report indicating that he was suffering from amyotrophic lateral sclerosis, an incurable disease. Only a few, including Eleanor Gehrig, knew that Lou was a dying man. It is possible that Gehrig himself didn't know, although some things he said in the last two years of his life sounded as if he had such suspicions.

The depth of Lou's feeling toward Eleanor was underlined by a handwritten letter he sent from Detroit the day after he terminated his active career. In part, this is what he wrote:

> My sweetheart—and please grant that we may ever be such—for what the hell else matters—that thing yesterday I believe and hope was the turning point in my life for the future as far as taking life too seriously is concerned. It was inevitable, although I dreaded the day, and my thoughts were with you constantly—how the thing would affect you and I—that was the big question and the most important thought underlying everything. I broke before the game because I thought so much of you. Not because I didn't know you are the bravest kind of partner but because my inferiority grabbed me and made me wonder and ponder if I could possibly prove myself worthy of you. As for me, the road may come to a dead end here, but why should it? Seems like our back is to the wall now, but there usually comes a way out. Where and what, I know not, but who can tell that it might not lead to greater things. Time will tell. . .

On the special day in his honor on July 4, 1939, Gehrig spoke his farewell words without a hitch and with no notes in his hand. This was surprising, since slurred speech is often characteristic of ALS victims. After that day Gehrig chose to remain with the team, even as he found it increasingly difficult to walk the few feet out to the home plate umpire to deliver the Yankees lineup. That year the Yankees won the pennant, then defeated Cincinnati in the World Series. On the trip to Cincinnati, New York's mayor, Fiorello La Guardia, sat next to Gehrig on the train and spoke to him about joining the New York City Parole Commission. When La Guardia told Gehrig that he could be an inspiration to many youngsters in trouble, Gehrig reminded the mayor that he knew little about the law or the workings of the Parole Commission. But the mayor was insistent. "All you need is common sense, and you have that," he told Gehrig. La Guardia followed up his proposal by sending Gehrig a number of books on criminology, sociology, and psychology. Gehrig diligently read them and then informed the mayor he would accept his offer. Before arriving at this decision, Gehrig consulted Eleanor, who told him, "It is a fine chance to do something good for the old hometown."

LAST DAYS

Prior to joining the Parole Board, Gehrig was unanimously voted into the National Baseball Hall of Fame by the Baseball Writers' Association in December 1939. A rule was waived that would have required him to have been retired for one year. At the same time, the Yankees retired Gehrig's uniform, making him the first major leaguer to be honored in such a way.

Gehrig was sworn in to his new civic role on January 2, 1940, for a ten-year term, with the mayor on hand to give the inductee his official blessing. Gehrig's primary duty was to render judgments about the time of release for prisoners in the city's penal institutions. The commission's caseload more than 6,000 a year, and Gehrig was assigned his share of cases.

For one year, while he was still physically able to travel downtown to lower Manhattan by car, with Eleanor doing the driving, Gehrig maintained a regular schedule. He had almost daily contact with street criminals, hoodlums, vagabonds, pimps, prostitutes, and con artists, a rung of society he had hardly known anything about in his years as an athlete.

In reflecting on his role, Gehrig said that "only a small percentage of men have to go back to prison. I think that many convicted fellows deserve another chance. However, we not only have to play fair with the fellow who's gotten bad breaks, but we must also consider the rights of taxpayers and our duties towards them. We don't want anyone in jail who can make good."

By the spring of 1941, Gehrig had become too ill to pursue his parole tasks, and he requested from the mayor a leave of absence. Until then La Guardia had not been aware of how frail he had become. By that time it had become difficult for Gehrig to even sign his name or to lift a piece of paper.

As his body wasted away, Gehrig's mind remained active and untouched by the disease. When friends came to visit, he rarely complained. A good deal of the time he listened to music and opera. On June 2, 1941, seventeen days before his thirty-eighth birthday, Lou Gehrig died in his sleep at home.

Tributes poured in from everywhere, from President Franklin D. Roosevelt, who sent flowers, to New York's Governor Herbert Lehman, to the redcaps at Grand Central Terminal. More than 1,500 telegrams and messages flooded his home in Riverdale. One of his mourners, Bill Dickey, a former teammate who had once roomed with him, said, "He doesn't need tributes from anyone. His life and the way he lived were tribute enough. He just went out and did his job every day."

PART SIX

COLUMBIA AND THE WORLD

CHAPTER 40

James T. Shotwell: A Life Devoted to Organizing Peace

—◊◊◊—

Lisa Anderson

During an age in which President Nicholas Murray Butler himself played a spectacular public role on a world stage, James T. Shotwell (1881–1965), though perhaps less in the limelight, was inti-mately involved in such international developments as the signing of the Treaty of Paris in 1919, the organizing of the League of Nations and the International Labor Organization, and the creation of the United Nations in 1945, while also planting the seeds of international studies at Columbia in ways that could later bear more varied fruits in the School of International and Public Affairs.

The author of our essay on Shotwell is Lisa Anderson, currently dean of the school and someone who recognizes in Shotwell's life work an anticipation of many of today's most redoubtable challenges in world affairs as the school tries to meet them. Anderson is chair of the board of the Social Science Research Council and a member of the Council on Foreign Relations, two bodies Shotwell helped to found. She notes that dozens of alumni of the School of International and Public Affairs are active at the United Nations and the head of the International Labor Organization is a SIPA parent. Thus Shotwell's legacy is being handed on to new generations here and abroad.

Wm. Theodore de Bary

—◊◊◊—

In the Hall of Mirrors at Versailles, a small, dapper, mustachioed man stood "close to the front and over by the wall" for the signing of the Treaty of Paris in 1919 and "saw everything close at hand." The historian of the American delega-tion and author of the provisions establishing the International Labor Organization, he had been intimately involved in the negotiations that ended the Great War and created the League of Nations; he certainly deserved a good view of the ceremonies. In 1945, at the San Francisco Conference that established the

United Nations, the same man, now portly and his trademark mustache completely white, chaired the semiofficial American group "chiefly responsible," he wrote, "for the economic and social provisions of the charter." Although pneumonia cut short his stay in San Francisco, he later wrote that he had "never had a more inspiring experience" than in this effort to "weld the aspirations to peace into a worldwide organization."

James T. Shotwell, Bryce Professor of the History of International Relations at Columbia University, devoted most of his life, as he put it, "to the organization of peace." Considering the period his life spanned—he died at ninety in 1965, having studied and taught at Columbia for nearly fifty years—this was no small project. He was present at, indeed instrumental in, the creation of some of the most important international institutions of the twentieth century. He believed that his was the beginning of a new era, a time in which rapid technological advances demanded new conceptions of how states resolved their differences. Both in his scholarship and in his constant, restless buttonholing of the rich and powerful around the world, he argued that in the modern world peace is not merely the absence of war, but something that needs to be planned and organized. He did all he could to encourage that organization, and in doing so he helped provoke an entirely new academic field—international relations—and proposed many of the policies and instruments by which governments today approach management of their common affairs.

Born in Ontario to American Quakers, Shotwell received a B.A. from the University of Toronto in 1898 before coming to New York to study under Columbia historian James Harvey Robinson. At Columbia he encountered a lively intellectual community, seized with debates about the "New History." He quickly adopted his adviser's view that the increasingly influential "scientific" methods of studying society might be applied to the practice of history, and he applied them in his dissertation in medieval history, "A Study of the History of the Eucharist." He would later observe that although he took "a semester on the history of international law, by the distinguished jurist John Basset Moore, later a judge on the World Court, . . . this was the only course that had any bearing on international relations in the faculty of Political Science, a subject . . . on which most of my later life was spent." Nonetheless, he seems to have been quite content in the department, and by 1903 he had been appointed an instructor. As he recalled:

Next to Robinson, my closest friend in Columbia was Charles Beard . . . Our offices were close together—Robinson's, Beard's and mine. At the end of the day, we generally got together and talked over the state of the world and of our souls, and were very frank about both. Beard was a lovely spirit—one of the most likeable men I have ever known . . . Beard and I later differed very much in outlook. He became an isolationist and I went into the field of international relations. Our differences were never minimized in our talks with each other. I am happy to say, though, that they never created a moment's difference in our personal feeling toward each other.

Reflecting the still-powerful influence of European intellectual life in American universities at the end of the nineteenth century, Robinson told Shotwell that if he wanted a permanent position at Columbia, he should spend some time in Europe. This he did, spending more than a year visiting a variety of universities on the Continent and improving his fluency in several European languages. To subsidize his journey, he contracted to write articles and soon became the managing editor of the enormously influential eleventh edition of the *Encyclopædia Britannica.* This not only provided a handsome salary and honed his organizational skills, but afforded him the company, or at least the acquaintance, of some of the best-known figures of the day, from Bertrand Russell to Henry Ford, both of whom were contributors. Shotwell himself wrote nearly 250 articles—including the article on "History"—and commissioned hundreds more, capturing the publishers' intention to make the *Encyclopædia* "a real mirror of the intellectual life of the present."

For the next decade or so, Shotwell honed his scholarly writing and teaching back at Columbia; by 1908 he had been appointed a full professor. He was particularly intrigued by the influence of science and technology on historical change, a theme that would later shape his work in international relations. Like many of his Progressive Era colleagues, he saw a direct link between scientific innovation, including the practice of modern scientific scholarship, with its constant testing of theories and questioning of authority, and the dissemination of liberal values like the rule of law and republican government. He was a popular and dedicated instructor, publishing syllabi and curricula in journals like *History Teacher's Magazine.* Still, the opportunity to extend the influence of his research beyond the classroom was evidently an early temptation. In 1917 the new Carnegie Endowment for International Peace—founded by Andrew Carnegie at the beginning of that decade with the mission to "hasten the abolition of international war, the foulest blot upon our civilization"—invited him to serve as director of research. The Faculty

Committee on Instruction conveyed its concern about the prospect of losing one of its "most talented investigators" to University President Nicholas Murray Butler (who was, not coincidentally, also the president of the Endowment).

> Is the university to be superseded by other institutions in that function which has hitherto been considered peculiarly its own—the enlargement of the bounds of human knowledge? Is research to be severed from its wonted and most helpful association with the training of the on-coming generation?

This plea foreshadowed tensions between teaching and research, universities and independent research organizations, that would only grow through the twentieth century. For the moment, however, Shotwell elected to stay at Columbia.

The outbreak of World War I and America's entry into the war created new possibilities and priorities. Woodrow Wilson captured Shotwell's imagination in his call for mobilization: "In the sense in which we have been wont to think of armies there are no armies in this struggle," said Wilson. "There are entire nations armed . . . The whole Nation must be a team in which each man shall play the part for which he is best fitted." For Shotwell, this was an irresistible challenge to use his professional skills in the public interest. As he put it:

> Almost immediately after the United States declared war in April 1917, I went to Washington to see what historians could do by way of national service. . . . I found myself chairman of a National Board for Historical Service. Although it was a voluntary body, it was a branch of the wartime Committee on Public Information . . . [which] became the propaganda organ of the Government for the war.

Many of his colleagues felt that the work of historians should not be deployed so directly to public purposes, since serving as propagandists, even in a good cause, risked compromising their scholarly integrity. Shotwell seems to have been entirely comfortable with the project, however, seeing himself merely as equipping the government and citizenry with the "scientific facts" they needed to support the war effort.

Indeed, Shotwell soon went a step further. Arguing that the conscientious scholar "must think in terms of constructive statesmanship, rather than the mere question of fighting the war," he began looking toward planning the new world order that would

follow the war. This was a job for which university professors were well equipped but for the constraints on their time; in the July 1918 issue of *Columbia University Quarterly*, he argued that teaching was not always the most effective use of the time and talents of the faculty; instead the university should "make scientific research careers possible for young men, instead of throwing upon them a crushing burden of instructional work."

Shotwell himself had been on leave since the beginning of the war effort and was available for "a telephone message that [President Wilson's adviser] Colonel House wanted to see me . . . in connection with preparations for the Peace Conference which would sooner or later have to be called at the end of the World War." Shotwell was soon deeply involved in a quasi-secret group called "The Inquiry," housed first at the offices of the American Geographical Society on Broadway and 115th Street and then in the university library. This group was

Allied military officers stand on furniture to see the peace treaty being signed at Versailles in 1919. James T. Shotwell, inside the Hall of Mirrors, had a much better view.

Howard Chandler Christy's painting of the U.S. delegation signing the UN Charter. The lone woman in the painting is Virginia C. Gildersleeve, former dean of Barnard College. Presiding at the 1954 unveiling ceremony were (from left) Wesley F. Rennie, representing the Carnegie Endowment's NGO conference group; David Vaughan, representing the United Nations; Joseph E. Johnson, president of the Carnegie Endowment; and Shotwell, president emeritus of the Endowment.

charged with studying, as he put it, "the political, economic, legal and historical elements of the problems which would have to be faced in the treaty of peace."

Although a contemporary journalist called this group "Colonel House's troupe of performing professors," the members themselves—and they included columnist Walter Lippmann—were convinced that they were social engineers, tasked with designing the institutional architecture of the entire postwar world on the basis of modern social science. As Shotwell himself conceded, "some of this work was academic and unusable in the rapid hours of the Peace Conference, and the career diplomats in Paris ridiculed the mass of reference books and documents of which I had charge," but he reported with satisfaction that "they soon found that even some of the more obscure studies were of real importance in the making of a treaty which was recasting the structure of political and economic life in Europe." Shotwell was assigned issues of "social justice" and international labor, arenas he considered especially crucial after the Bolshevik Revolution in Russia. His work led directly to the establishment of the International Labor Organization in 1919.

Soon after the ILO was launched, Shotwell turned back to history but once again with characteristic ambition. After the Peace Conference was over, he accepted an assignment from the Carnegie Endowment to edit a history of the impact of the World War on the economic and social life of nations, "not merely," he said "a study of its cost but of the way in which it had affected the life and thought of a generation."

For the next several years he lived most of the time in Europe, and within a decade there were 150 volumes covering fifteen countries.

Although the influence of this comprehensive effort to chronicle the causes and consequences of the Great War was not as broad as Shotwell had hoped, he continued to advocate an active public role for scholars. The war had allowed university-based researchers to participate in addressing the political, social, and economic problems of the day, and Shotwell fervently believed that this involvement in public affairs on the part of faculty should outlast the war itself. Like most of the reformist intellectuals of his generation, he believed that the modern social sciences, with their empiricism, attachment to laws and regularities, and challenge to authority and tradition, supported the great causes of the day, including efforts to end war and secure peace.

His documentation of the impact of the Great War had been intended to demonstrate that war was no longer a feasible instrument of national policy and, in that same spirit, he was instrumental in launching several institutions that would shape the foreign policy and international affairs landscape for the rest of the century, including the Royal Institute of International Affairs in London and the Council on Foreign Relations in New York. He was also active in the then-new Social Science Research Council, serving in 1927 as the first chair of its Advisory Committee on International Relations and then director of planning and research in international relations, shaping the contours of the Council's work in this new field.

During the 1920s he worked on drafting and promoting the proposal made by French Foreign Minister Aristide Briand that the United States and France "renounce the use of war." Shotwell was disappointed by the final version of the Kellogg-Briand Pact of 1928 since, as he put it, "in the last analysis the establishment of international peace is not a negative but a positive act—not mere renunciation of an outworn technique but the acceptance of peacetime methods in international relations. It will mean more, not less, of these relations in the future." In order to truly secure peace, in Shotwell's view, these relations required organization and management, and in that opinion, he was expressing the views liberal theorists of international relations continue to espouse today.

By 1930, Shotwell was back at Columbia full time; in 1937 he was named to the Bryce Professorship. He spent the decade elaborating his arguments that modern war was too destructive to serve as an instrument of policy. He viewed the Great Depression as the last battle of World War I and was a vocal advocate of free trade. "It is a short-sighted view," he said, "which would keep the backward nations in a

Shotwell (left) inspecting the battlefield near Passchendaele in April 1919, with General Sir Arthur Currie (pointing with his cane), a childhood friend and commander in chief of the Canadian forces during the war.

condition of economic dependence upon any one nation or group of nations. . . . There is only one way by which prosperity can continue to meet the increasing demands of increasing organized industry, and that is by a parallel increase of the buying power of the common man the world over." Similarly, he argued that Americans needed to look beyond their parochial experience. "The French," he declared, "have long been trying to teach us the simple lesson that there must be security before there can be disarmament, but it is a lesson which we find hard to learn, simply because we have security and do not need to arm, at least by land, to maintain it. All we need to do is to make sure that the Atlantic and Pacific Oceans are not dried up."

Shotwell was of course deeply dismayed by the outbreak of World War II, but by 1943, the year after he formally retired from his faculty post at Columbia—he continued to offer courses for several more years—he was once again deeply involved in planning for peace. In May 1944, he and a group of colleagues published a "Design for the Charter of the General International Organization" to succeed the ruined League of Nations. Although it got little formal response from the State Department, the United States, Britain, the Soviet Union, and China issued proposals after the Dumbarton Oaks conference in October of that year that closely paralleled those of the Shotwell Commission. Shotwell himself was active in organizing an educational campaign to support the United Nations, and he went to San Francisco in April 1945 as a consultant, representing the Carnegie Endowment. He was elected by the forty-two U.S. consultants there to lead their delegation.

In 1948, having resigned from almost all of his professional activities and planning his retirement, Shotwell was again drafted into service at the Carnegie Endowment. When then president Alger Hiss was granted a leave of absence to fight his court battle against Whittaker Chambers, Shotwell was elected president, a position he held for two years. During the 1950s, he continued to travel and write; his last book, *The Faith of a Historian*, was published only months before his death.

James T. Shotwell represented the first generation of genuinely cosmopolitan American policy intellectuals. His obituary in *The New York Times* observed that he was "among the most respected and dedicated protagonists of internationalism in the United States," a man who saw "the world as a whole." In many respects, this vision was to remain a minority view in the United States, particularly as the Cold War consumed the second half of the twentieth century, and Shotwell was well aware of the obstacles to its realization. Reflecting on the impact of what he called "the great communist controversy" on the United Nations, he wrote that "the full and adequate implementation of the revolutionary concept in the Charter may be long delayed." He was, however, at heart an irredeemable optimist: "The success or failure of that organization is a measure of civilization itself. There can be no surer guarantee of its ultimate success."

Shotwell's combination of scholarly enthusiasm, pragmatic engagement in the world, and abiding optimism, his conviction that social scientists should deploy their learning to public purposes, his faith that human intervention might improve the human condition, and his ability to "see the world as a whole" became hallmarks of Columbia's study of international relations.

Friedrich Rohde helped with the research for this essay.

CHAPTER 41

Louis Henkin and the
Age of Rights

—⚏—

J. Paul Martin

The human rights movement as a subject of both academic study and active advocacy on an international scale was already a vision in the mind of constitutional lawyer Louis Henkin when he was asked to present his ideas, hopes, and plans to the university-wide general education seminars being held in the Kellogg Center of the School of International and Public Affairs during the 1970s. The timing was right. Human rights issues were a logical follow-up to the American civil rights movement of the fifties and sixties, and the field was gaining new support on the national level from the election of Jimmy Carter in 1976. In this wider context Henkin established his Center for the Study of Human Rights as a base from which to instigate and coordinate a broad range of human rights courses and programs. These would soon extend beyond Columbia's liberal arts departments and professional schools to develop into a worldwide network of training programs.

The historic significance of this movement has only increased with spreading globalization in many areas of contemporary economic, social, and cultural life, which presents new challenges of threatening dehumanization vis-à-vis the traditional values of diverse civilizations.

From the inception of the Center in 1977, Paul Martin has been a key associate of Louis Henkin's in the direction and administration of its programs. With advanced degrees in theology, education, and history, Martin has sought to broaden the disciplinary base of human rights at Columbia in order to meet the intellectual challenges facing human rights and international law in a world dominated by political realism and pragmatism. Prior to coming to Columbia, Martin taught at the University of Botswana, Lesotho, and Swaziland; studied theology in Rome; and was an officer in the British Army. A key emphasis of his current work is helping to build the human rights capacity of NGOs and universities in Africa, Asia, and Latin America.

Wm. Theodore de Bary

—⚏—

Louis Henkin (right) with his childhood friend George Gottlieb, in the 1930s

"Ours is the age of rights. Human rights is the idea of our time, the only political-moral idea that has received universal acceptance . . . Human rights is the subject of numerous international agreements, the daily grist of the mills of international politics, and a bone of continuing contention among superpowers."

Henkin and his family arrived in the U.S. in 1923.

These challenging words are drawn from the preface of Columbia Law School Professor Louis Henkin's classic *The Age of Rights*, published in 1990 as the world was witnessing the end of both the Cold War and apartheid. But some fifteen years later, what seemed to be a new dawn now appears as only a brief change in scenery. Encouragingly, though, interest in human rights education and research continues to expand at Columbia. Henkin has been at the heart of that growth.

Henkin would join the Columbia Law School faculty in 1962, but only after he had completed a four-year military career during World War II, a clerkship with Supreme Court Justice Felix Frankfurter from 1945 to 1946, and then appointments at the U.S. Department of State, brief service as a consultant to the UN Legal Department, and five years as a professor of law at the University of Pennsylvania.

THROUGH ELLIS ISLAND

Henkin was born in Russia in 1917 and was called Lazer, short for Eliezer, his actual name. When he and his family arrived at Ellis Island in 1923 they needed a Yiddish-English interpreter to explain to the immigration officers why they should be admitted. Lazer was so shy he would not speak. His father feared the authorities might assume the boy was disabled and send the whole family back. Thinking fast, he asked him what four times seven was. Lazer answered correctly, and the Henkins were let in.

Henkin's father, Rabbi Yosef Eliahu Henkin (1880–1973), took them to the Lower East Side, where Henkin studied in Jewish schools and later at Yeshiva University. Rabbi Henkin was a major figure in the Orthodox Jewish world, revered both in New York and later in Israel for his leadership of the charitable organization

Ezras Torah as well as for his scholarship. He exemplified an ethic later described by his son as "piety, probity, and poverty." Henkin inherited both the intellect and the religious convictions. For many years Jewish students and faculty members at Columbia knew they could find an afternoon minyan, or prayer group, in his office.

While he was studying at Yeshiva University, Louis Henkin, as he had come to be called, saw his roommate filling out an application for Harvard Law School. Henkin decided to apply as well. He was accepted—with a full scholarship. Henkin was eventually elected to the editorial board of the *Harvard Law Review* and upon graduation in 1940 was offered a coveted clerkship with the famous Judge Learned Hand. The winds of war blew his plans off course.

Henkin was drafted into the U.S. Army in 1940, and, as a soldier with mathematical—as well as legal—expertise, he found himself serving with an artillery observation unit, seeing combat in Tunisia, Sicily, and southern Italy. He later moved up through the Rhône valley to the German border.

In August 1944, during the invasion of France, Henkin and twelve other U.S. soldiers were near Toulon when they surprised a German colonel and two other officers. After a brief standoff with arms drawn, Henkin, the Jewish immigrant from Russia and former Harvard Law student who spoke "re-Teutonized Yiddish," initiated a negotiation that led to his meeting with the local German company commander. Eventually he persuaded him and his seven officers and sixty-seven men to surrender to the thirteen Americans. For his daring and persuasiveness, the soon-to-be-demobilized soldier received the Silver Star for gallantry in action.

LAW AND RIGHTS

Throughout his career as a professor and legal scholar, Henkin has divided his time and interests among constitutional law, law and diplomacy, and human rights. He has been particularly influential in the law of U.S. foreign relations and international and comparative human rights, both as a scholar and as a practitioner. In 1950–51, as an officer in the U.S. Department of State, he was assigned to the UN Bureau of the State Department to monitor the progress of the Korean armistice negotiations. More than fifty years later, he was back at the UN serving on its Human Rights Committee charged with monitoring the implementation of the Covenant on Civil and Political Rights. Above all he has been professor, author, and mentor, beloved by experts and by the thousands of students who have sat in his classes during his forty-two years at Columbia. In 1981 the university designated him University Professor.

Henkin (front row, right) with the First Field Artillery Observation Unit, U.S. Army, circa 1940

One of the fundamental themes of Henkin's scholarship has been the links among international law, international human rights, constitutionalism, and the U.S. Constitution. His retirement resolution, recorded in the minutes of the Law faculty, outlines the scope of his thinking: "Both Constitutional law and International law are relevant to the adherence of our own government to the commands of our Constitution and to international norms, in its treatment of the rights of aliens as well as citizens, outside as well as within our borders, and in the shaping of our foreign policy to reflect the importance of fostering respect for human rights wherever they are threatened."

Most recently he has turned his attention to war and terrorism, arguing, in a May 2005 speech at the University of Santa Clara, that with the adoption of the UN Charter in 1945 "the traditional concept and status of war was intended to end" and that in the contexts of Afghanistan and Iraq, it is not "clear whether the invocations and references to 'war' are rhetorical, metaphorical, constitutional, legal or a combination of these." This leads him to conclude that "it would contribute to clarity and understanding if we could do away with that 'W' word, eliminating it from contemporary legal discourse." The speech illustrates one more time his ability to identify the abuse and misuse of terms and concepts in international law and in the constitutional law of foreign affairs, typically through their conversion into metaphors. Earlier in his career he had pointed to the same abuse, misuse, and careless use of the term sovereignty. He saw this "S" word as a weapon against the international human rights movement by those who argued that the international law of human rights unduly restricted national sovereignty.

As his writings and speeches have reverberated around the world, the world has come to seek advice from him. In the 1980s, for example, national delegations from Nepal, Indonesia, Sudan, and Uganda visited Columbia to study with Henkin how rights might be best incorporated into their constitutions. In each case, Henkin would explore themes associated with his core position that "a constitution that is authentically constitutionalist must secure constitutional legitimacy and constitutional review, authentic democracy, accountable government; and one that will respect and ensure individual human rights and secure basic human needs." One of Henkin's seminal and most accessible works, *How Nations Behave,* was inspired by his debates with colleagues from political science as well as by his perception of the need to reinforce international law as real and as a necessary foundation for human rights. According to Yale Law Professor Harold Koh, the book launched a thousand articles about compliance with international law. "In my case," said Koh, "it has pushed me toward both the intellectual and the political enquiry that I expect will occupy the rest of my days: the study of why nations obey international law." The current debates about torture and the treatment of prisoners of war illustrate only too vividly how important Henkin's scholarship remains today as one of the accepted foundations of contemporary scholarship in international law and particularly the role of human rights in foreign policy.

Important though his international influence has been, it is his role as beloved professor and educator that has consumed the greater part of his energies. His classes have inspired a new generation of legal scholars and professors focusing on international law and human rights after studying with Henkin. Among them are Carlos Vasquez of Georgetown, Sean Murphy at George Washington, Barbara Stark at Hofstra, Penelope Mathew at Australian National University, Martin Flaherty at Fordham, Oscar Vieira at Getulio Vargas School of Law in São Paulo, Brad Roth at Wayne State, and Mary Ellen O'Connell at Ohio State. Lee Bollinger, Columbia's president, also studied with him. Among Henkin's students at SIPA, where he also taught, were Madeleine Albright, the former U.S. secretary of state, and Ibrahim Gambari, a former foreign minister of Nigeria and for ten years its ambassador to the UN.

Martin Flaherty remembers his first meeting with Henkin when he was still a student. "Henkin decided to take me out to lunch. He bounded down seven flights of stairs, leaving me in his wake. He was over seventy at the time." He also found Henkin's teaching more stimulating than that of others. "Frustrated with my own class in constitutional law, I sat in on Lou's, since he covered at least ten cases compared to the other professor's one." Many of his students recall Henkin's personal and professional support as they sought to find careers in human rights advocacy.

Henkin's human rights work at Columbia took on a special dimension in 1977. Just after Jimmy Carter was elected, Provost Wm. Theodore de Bary set up a committee out of which grew the Center for the Study of Human Rights. The first activities of the Center were directed by an executive committee composed of Mitchell Ginsberg, then dean of the School of Social Work, Arthur Danto, Johnsonian Professor of Philosophy and art critic of *The Nation,* and Henkin. Paul

Martin, who was then the director of Columbia's Earl Hall Center, was administrator and later became its executive director. The following twenty-five years saw the steady growth of human rights studies across the university.

In 1978 human rights were simply not a subject of study outside international law. Columbia was, however, the home of two major scholars in international law and human rights, Henkin and Oscar Schachter, one of the major legal architects of the first forty years of the UN. While both were then teaching courses on human rights, Henkin believed that human rights were not just for lawyers—so the new Center's executive committee included a philosopher and a social worker as well as Henkin, a lawyer. (Martin was trained as a historian.) The Center's first project was a monthly University Seminar on human rights, which quickly became a forum where scholars from different disciplines could debate such topics as the role of human rights in U.S. foreign policy. The seminar still meets seven or eight times a year.

In the early 1980s Henkin led a yearlong seminar on human rights teaching for Columbia faculty members from the humanities and social sciences. Faculty discussed the works of John Locke and Immanuel Kant and the modern writings of thinkers such as Susan Okin, Michael Sandel, and Herbert Marcuse. In addition to learning about international law, participants were exposed to the emerging fields of economic and social rights, the human rights of women, and the implications of human rights for development aid. The seminar sowed the seeds for the current range of course offerings at Columbia. Graduates and undergraduates can now choose from more than forty-four courses in nine schools.

Law remains at the core of Columbia's multidisciplinary approach to human rights studies, and the Law School has always offered the largest number of courses, most of which are open to students from across the university. In 1998 the Law School created the Human Rights Institute. Henkin is the chair of its executive committee, and Catherine Powell was the faculty director for its first four years. The Institute has developed three main program areas: transitional justice, human rights in the United States, and the Human Rights Teaching Fellows Program.

Henkin continues to encourage faculty members from other departments to contribute to human rights studies at Columbia. The Department of English and Comparative Literature, for example, has long offered courses on race, ethnicity, and gender issues from a rights perspective. Law professors have taught courses in the College curriculum, and leading figures in the New York human rights community have taught throughout the university. The recent expansion at the undergraduate level has been energized especially by professors Andrew Nathan, Julie Peters, Thomas Pogge, and Michael Stanislawski in Columbia College and by professors Irene Bloom and Peter Juviler at Barnard.

Henkin also saw to it that from its beginnings in 1978 the Center would be committed to training and supporting activists from developing countries. In the early years this took the form of summer training programs at Columbia for scholars and NGO activists from Africa, Asia, and the Americas who were just beginning to appear as leaders in their still embryonic movements. The Center was able to obtain grants to welcome teachers and potential teachers of human rights studies from the United States and other countries, especially those with little in the way of a human rights culture, enabling them to spend a year at Columbia as visiting scholars. In the late 1980s the Center inaugurated its renowned Human Rights Advocates Training Program, which continues to bring a remarkable group of NGO

Henkin's door remains open to scholars and activists from the United States and overseas.

leaders and teachers to the university each year for four months. These advocates describe in classrooms, seminars, and conferences their often dangerous and always challenging experience on the front lines. The participation of these visitors adds a vividness and depth to the study of human rights at Columbia. After all, a discussion about poverty is very different when two or three of the participants have experienced it and have seen children die because of it. Their presence creates an atmosphere of honesty and humility and brings home the fact that to make a difference one needs real blueprints, not just bright ideas and infusions of funds. Scholars are forced to go beyond saying why rights might help to showing how they really can. Program alumni have gone on to play important roles in their own countries and in the international movement. Hina Jilani, for example, besides being a courageous advocate for women's rights in Pakistan, is the UN special representative for human rights defenders and this year received the Millennium Peace Prize.

Henkin with human rights advocate K. R. Renuka of India

The realization that scholars might be too complacent in their thinking led directly to a new course entitled Rethinking Human Rights. Its purpose is to raise all the most challenging questions and read the most provocative publications. This course is taught by five faculty volunteers to address the most debated topics, analyses, and critiques, especially those that have broad implications for the way scholars, practitioners, and policy makers think about human rights in the modern world. Among lawyers working on human rights who have recently joined the Columbia faculty are Mary Robinson, the former UN high commissioner for human rights and former president of Ireland, and Michael Doyle, an expert on the UN and on peacekeeping.

One of the most exciting outcomes of human rights studies at Columbia has been the creation of a worldwide network of advocates, experts, and scholars. Henkin has talked about the importance of building bridges between the human rights community and the civil rights movement, the world of religion, the activist world, and the media. He and his wife, Alice, have both served as active members on the boards of numerous human rights organizations. He is a charter member of Human Rights First, which was founded in 1978 as the Lawyers Committee for Human Rights. Similarly, he has long encouraged Columbia graduates and student interns to work with large and small human rights organizations and in the United Nations. In the 1980s and 1990s he participated in projects in Africa where the Center had received grants to help countries like Egypt, Sudan, and Uganda to incorporate human rights into their national constitutions and legal systems.

Columbia human rights graduates are in hot spots from Iraq and Afghanistan to the Congo and Indonesia. The Center is in contact with them daily, passing along information on jobs, conferences, and educational opportunities, and helping NGOs and universities seeking to promote human rights studies overseas. Today, for example, in São Paulo, Professor Oscar Vieira has worked with the city's two major universities and helped to create two international NGOs that promote human rights and human rights teaching in Latin America, Africa, and Asia.

These networks can be lifesaving. Two years ago one former advocate had been put in a Liberian prison, was being tortured, and was in danger of death. Key to his release—which saved his life—was the intervention of the Uruguayan government at the insistence of another former advocate who is a member of its parliament. Even then, the Liberian lawyer needed two months of hospitalization to recover. Today, the former advocate, Tiawan Songloe, is attorney general in the new Liberian government. Felipe Michelini is now deputy minister of education in Uruguay.

WORLDWIDE REPUTATION

Columbia enjoys a worldwide reputation for human rights studies. This year 165 individuals applied to the Human Rights Advocates Training Program for the ten places it offers each year. Human rights courses are among the most successful of all courses in attracting students during the summer session. In the Liberal Studies Master of Arts program, the human rights concentration attracts more students than any other specialization, including American Studies. Columbia faculty members and the staff of the Center continue to help establish human rights research and education programs at universities around the world. Columbia graduates run programs in places as diverse as Iowa, Australia, Brazil, Guatemala, Japan, South Africa, Switzerland, and Zimbabwe.

Over the years the Center and its associated faculty and students have wrestled with many practical and intellectual challenges. In the 1990s, with a major grant from The Pew Charitable Trusts, the Center worked on religious freedom in Eastern Europe, bringing religious and other figures from the region for study and exchanges at Columbia. Today this program works with religious professionals and scholars around the world to find ways in which the international human rights community can improve relations among people of different religions. Another topic of interest has been human rights and corporate social responsibility. This program has promoted debates between industry leaders and critics on campus. Interestingly, the issue of the role of human rights in U.S. foreign policy and especially in external aid programs is again moving to center stage. Europeans feel that there is a big gap between the United States and the EU. In September 2004, the Center sponsored an EU-U.S. dialogue on the place of human rights in the foreign affairs of the two continents.

Henkin's door is open to scholars and activists from the United States and from overseas, and he unfailingly seeks to engage his visitor, both to challenge and to learn. In discussions that have taken place in his office and around the world, he especially enjoys examining how the idea of human rights can best be incorporated into and enforced by domestic institutions. He has the ability to focus on the most sensitive questions and on the heart of a given debate without alienating those who disagree with him. He can, however, be blunt. Harold Koh recounts the story about Henkin at a meeting in Washington, D.C., defending his position on the expropriation of property in U.S. foreign relations law, saying to one highly paid lawyer, "That may be what your clients pay you to advocate, but that's not the law and I am not going to say that."

The promotion of human rights around the world still has a long way to go. At Columbia an immediate need is to make the most of the university's multidisciplinary resources to expand faculty research on such key questions as the role of a human rights approach in alleviating poverty and improving the protection of especially abused groups—such as forced and illegal migrants and refugees, trafficked and enslaved persons, prisoners, and certain abused populations of women and children. The input of the various disciplines is necessary because the solutions are complex. It is not enough to feed a hungry person and prevent a young boy from being forced into sweatshop labor; one has to be able to build an environment where families can provide for themselves and their dependents and have access to a minimum of education and health care. As Henkin continually reminds his students, the ensuring of human rights is a legal obligation on all governments.

Yet human rights remains a controversial issue. Some members of the international business community, for example, see human rights advocacy as antithetical to American business interests overseas. On the other hand, activists in other countries claim that human rights efforts are being used as a cover for Western economic imperialism and as a way to impose secular values and individualism on their religious societies. Confronted with these challenges, the university is looking for new ways and new resources to promote faculty research in the field.

In his late eighties, Henkin still teaches two courses each semester. The Louis Henkin Professorship of Human and Constitutional Rights has been created and endowed in his honor at the Law School. He remains a source of intellectual and moral support, a giant of the human rights movement since the Second World War.

If today so many of Columbia's faculty members and students are committed to being active contributors as researchers, teachers, trainers, and advocates to the many challenges that constitute the modern human rights movement, it is because Louis Henkin showed them how intellectual stature and moral commitment, academic excellence, and humanitarianism could and indeed must stand together and demand the respect and support of the academy and the world at large. In 1999 Columbia University recognized his enormous contributions with an honorary doctorate in law:

> We hail you as America's leading scholar of international law, as a brilliant teacher, as the creator of the interdisciplinary subject of Human Rights. Since your early days with Hand and Frankfurter, you have enlivened classrooms, authored prophetic books, codirected our Center for the Study of Human Rights, and attained our highest rank, University Professor. In urging America to be faithful to its founding truths, you are an exemplar of fidelity to the values of this university.

Now in his late eighties, Henkin continues to inspire and guide the study of human rights at Columbia.

New York
June 28, 1901

President
Columbia University.

Sir,
I send you herewith a
deposit check for $12,000. as a
contribution to the fund for
Chinese Learning in your
University.

Respectfully
Dean Lung
"a Chinese Person"

CHAPTER 42

East Asian Studies at Columbia

—m—

Wm. Theodore de Bary and Donald Keene

Columbia's early start in East Asian studies is attributable to the initiatives of two Asian émigrés—one from China and one from Japan. Both men, dedicated to their home cultures, sought to encourage their study in an adopted land. Dean Lung ("Dean" is a family name) was the servant of Horace Walpole Carpentier, a Columbia trustee at the turn of the last century. From his modest means, Dean Lung presented the university with $12,000 in support of Chinese studies, and General Carpentier quickly augmented the gift.

Ryūsaku Tsunoda, who came to the United States from Japan in 1917, fulfilled a great ambition when he rallied the support necessary to create a library and a center for Japanese studies—which became the Japanese Collection at Columbia. Though he himself held no advanced degrees, for decades he served as a dedicated mentor to Columbia students and faculty, among them George Sansom, the eminent British historian of Japan who would eventually become the first director of Columbia's East Asian Institute.

Along with University Professor Emeritus Donald Keene, I was both a pre– and post–World War II student of Tsunoda's and Sansom's and also of L. Carrington Goodrich's, whose leadership of the Chinese program in the thirties and forties established a firm footing for Chinese studies in fulfillment of Dean Lung's early ambition. Asian studies expanded greatly at Columbia in the fifties and sixties, especially in connection with the undergraduate program of core courses in Asian studies and with the graduate program at the East Asian Institute. In these essays Donald and I honor those whose early, seminal contributions were relatively inconspicuous on campus at that time and whose careers were somewhat less celebrated in their own time than those of the famous figures otherwise featured in Living Legacies.

Wm. Theodore de Bary

Dean Lung, whose devotion to learning helped inspire Columbia's early start in Asian Studies

East Asian Studies at Columbia: The Early Years

Wm. Theodore de Bary

Not least among the things that got Columbia off to an early start in Chinese studies was the letter sent in 1901 by Dean Lung to President Seth Low, who was about to become mayor of New York that year. Lung enclosed a check for $12,000 for the "fund for Chinese learning."

Some have supposed that the "Dean" in this name was an academic title, a thought perhaps stemming from the widespread belief in the West that learning in China had been the preserve, if not almost a monopoly, of an educated Confucian elite. Actually, however, "Dean" was just an ordinary Chinese surname (usually rendered "Ding" or "Ting"), and it belonged to the manservant of a Columbia trustee— a personal valet whose relatively humble status did not preclude his testifying to the deep respect for learning that Confucianism had engendered in most Chinese.

Whatever the fund for Chinese learning amounted to at Columbia in those days, it could not have been much. The first contribution to Chinese studies had been made only the year before by alumnus and trustee William Barclay Parsons in the form of a gift of Chinese books to the library. That same year the eminent scholar in Indo-Iranian studies, Abraham Valentine Williams Jackson, urged President Low to set up instruction in Chinese studies, but it was clearly the initiative of Dean Lung and the deep respect held for him by the trustee General Horace Walpole Carpentier that led the latter to contribute the substantial sum (for those days) of $226,000 to set up an endowment for Chinese studies. The endowment was established in memory of Dean Lung, as a tribute to this "Chinese person" who was not just his valet but also a friend, admired for his personal qualities and love of learning.

Prompted in part by this action, the noted Columbia anthropologist Franz Boas made a powerful plea in 1902 for Columbia and the American Museum of Natural History together to establish "a great Oriental School" that would "imbue the public with a greater respect for the achievements of Chinese civilization." In "A Plea for a Great Oriental School," Boas, referring to the collections being acquired for the museum by Berthold Laufer, said, "We hope by means of these collections to bring out the complexity of Chinese culture, the high degree of technical development achieved by the people, the love of art which pervades their whole life, and the strong social ties that bind the people together. . . ."

Then, expressing a view often repeated later in the century, he added, "Under present conditions a more extended knowledge of East Asiatic cultures is a matter of great national importance . . . and in order to deal intelligently with the problems arising in this area we require a better knowledge of the people and of the countries with which we are dealing. . . . It was hoped that the establishment of these collections [at the Museum] would give an impetus for the universities of our city, particularly Columbia University, to take up the establishment of an East Asian Department. This hope has been fulfilled at an unexpectedly early date. Through the gift of General Carpentier a Department of Chinese has been established at Columbia University. . . ."

EARLY SCHOLARS

Even with this endowment, however, the new department was slow getting started. Chinese studies of any kind hardly existed in America, and almost no qualified scholars were available. Instead Columbia turned to distinguished professors from Europe. Herbert Allen Giles from Cambridge University inaugurated the program with a series of lectures in 1902. He was followed by Friedrich Hirth, a German authority on ancient China, who occupied the Dean Lung chair until 1917. Thereafter a tenuous program was carried on by the short-term incumbency of scholars, mostly from a China missionary background, and by inviting professors who represented the leading sinological studies in Europe, including Paul Pelliot of Paris (1926), William E. Soothill of Oxford (1928), and Jan J. L. Duyvendak of Leiden, who visited six times between 1929 and 1946.

Meanwhile, other developments were taking place that would have a profound effect on Chinese-American relations. After the fiasco of the antiforeign Boxer Rebellion in 1900, the Manchu government of China adopted more progressive policies emphasizing cooperation with the West and Japan, including an expanded program of study abroad for promising young scholars, some of them supported by funds from the indemnity payable to the United States as part of the Boxer peace settlement. Many came to study at Columbia and later became major figures in Chinese government, diplomacy, education, and academic life.

Outstanding among these was Hu Shih, a student of John Dewey's, who became a leader of the literary renaissance in Republican China; Chinese ambassador to the United States; president of China's premier university, Beijing University; and subsequently president of the Academia Sinica in Taiwan. Following in Hu's footsteps was Fung Yu-lan, another student of Dewey's, who became the leading figure in

Chinese philosophy down to 1949. V. K. Wellington Koo contributed greatly to the development of a modern Chinese foreign service, later becoming Chinese ambassador to the United States, foreign minister, acting prime minister of the Republic of China, and vice president of the International Court of Justice, The Hague; T. F. Tsiang, a graduate of the Department of Public Law and Government, served as China's permanent representative at the United Nations. Also at the UN was another of the many students of John Dewey's, P. C. Chang, who was to play a leading part in the formulation of the Universal Declaration of Human Rights (1948). Chi Ch'ao-ting in economics became a major figure in the development of the social sciences in Republican China.

These are just a few members of a Columbia-educated generation who served importantly in the development of Chinese American cultural and diplomatic relations during a period when the serious study of China at Columbia was just getting under way.

In 1902, concurrent with the founding of the chair in Chinese studies, the Manchu government, as part of its new opening to the West, made a substantial gift of books to the fledgling Chinese collection, a set of the encyclopedic collection *Tu-shu chi-ch'eng*, which included copies of much of the Chinese historical and literary legacy—a monument to the finest of classical scholarship that had been patronized by the Manchu regime, handsomely printed in an old-style, fine rice-paper edition. The acquisition of additional library materials went on through the twenties and thirties, with the support of the American Council of Learned Societies and the Rockefeller Foundation, to the point where Columbia's Chinese collection became a major American resource along with the collections at the Library of Congress and Harvard. Needless to say, no serious study of China could be carried on without such a collection, the existence of which itself attracted both scholars and students. Fung Yu-lan, who became China's leading philosophical historian and chair of the Department of Philosophy at Beijing University, recalled fondly his early days "on the banks of the mighty Hudson," when he worked his way through graduate study with Dewey as a library attendant of this new Chinese collection (then housed in Low Library).

The collection proved also to be a magnet for other East Asian collections—Japanese and Korean—that naturally found their place alongside the Chinese. In 1929, through the generosity of the Japanese Imperial Household and Baron Iwasaki (of the Mitsubishi interests), a Japanese collection was brought to the university and put in the care of Ryūsaku Tsunoda, who too had come to study with Dewey. While curator of the collection, Tsunoda sidelined as a lecturer in Japanese

Wellington Koo (left), an early student from China, went on to become Chinese ambassador to the United States, foreign minister, and acting prime minister of the Republic of China.
Sir George Sansom, who began teaching Japanese history at Columbia in the late 1930s, became the first director of the East Asian Institute.

cultural history, and, without ever being named as a formal member of the tenured faculty, became the father of many later American scholars of great distinction. Soon after Tsunoda arrived in 1934, Sir George Sansom, a noted British diplomat and scholar, began his lectures at Columbia on Japanese history.

L. CARRINGTON GOODRICH

By this time the department had been renamed the Department of Chinese and Japanese and came under the leadership of L. Carrington Goodrich, who was to provide the stability and continuity of direction for the program (hitherto lacking) in the thirties, forties, and fifties. Goodrich, from a New England missionary family, had grown up in China before attending Williams College and then served in the developmental work of the Rockefeller-supported China Medical Board until he decided in 1926 to pursue an academic career in the new program at Columbia. After making his way through a succession of teachers and visiting professors to the Ph.D. in 1934, he led in the assembling both of a growing China collection and a gradually expanded staff, including Chi-chen Wang in Chinese literature, Hugh Borton in modern Japanese history, and Cyrus Peake in modern Chinese history. Both Borton and Peake had studied in Columbia's history department and served in the government during World War II.

Nevertheless, before and during World War II, the department remained small, the offerings in languages and history were limited, and typically classes were offered to only a handful of students—in the late thirties usually no more than half a dozen. The present writer started elementary Chinese under Goodrich as an undergraduate in 1938. I recall that the second-year class included myself; a classmate who did not continue with Chinese but later became a distinguished microbiologist; a couple of would-be China missionaries; Paul Robeson, who had become enamored of the Chinese Communist cause and wanted to sing militant Chinese songs; and a German woman, who turned out to be a spy for Hitler, using her studies at Columbia as a cover for espionage activities. As one can imagine, the work of the class was quite a mix, responding to such diverse interests, backgrounds, and levels; though serious enough, it was anything but the systematic, highly focused, intensive study that came to characterize postwar language study. But few in numbers though they were, students were highly motivated, very bright, or both, and so things somehow worked out.

Wang taught classical language and literature. As a liberated child of the Revolution and alienated from much of traditional culture, he tended to be somewhat cynical and less than inspiring as a lecturer. His forte was as a translator of modern literature, and though allergic to all talk of grammar, he would spend long hours in virtually tutorial sessions with those determined enough to benefit from his fine command of both Chinese and English.

As a scholar, Goodrich was a down-to-earth, careful historian with broad interests in material culture, cultural exchanges with Europe, and in both early and later periods of Chinese history. But—perhaps on the rebound from his culturally conflicted early life as a "missionary kid" in a China riven by revolution and civil war—he largely disqualified himself from engagement with the religious and political issues that so roiled the modern scene. He was given to meticulous scholarship on concrete, factual matters but also had a gift for clear, straightforward, unadorned prose that served him well in his best-known work: *A Short History of the Chinese People* (1943). The most famous Chinese scholar of the day, the aforementioned Hu Shih, called this book "the best history of China ever published in any European language."

A kindly, generous, and courtly person, Goodrich was respected as the evenhanded and conscientious administrator of the program in Chinese studies and became recognized at home and abroad as one of the founding fathers of Chinese studies in America. He was early elected president of the American Oriental Society and the Association of Asian Studies, and for a long time was head of the New York Oriental Club.

A major adjunct and accessory to Goodrich's career as scholar, teacher, and administrator was his wife of sixty-five years, Anne S. Goodrich, who managed to combine roles as caring mother of a large family, a warm-hearted hostess in their Riverdale home to Goodrich's students and colleagues, and a scholar in her own right, with published accounts of Chinese Daoist temples and monasteries in the Beijing area.

A FLOURISHING PROGRAM

Thus far is the history, in very brief, of the early years of Chinese studies at Columbia. The next stage in this development was the major expansion of the program in the fifties and sixties—a considerable enlargement in the staff, courses, and students of the department as well as of companion programs in the professional schools. Much of this was attendant upon the development in the fifties of the College's general education program in Oriental (now Asian) studies, which established a much broader base for Asian studies and with which I myself was much involved. I was involved, too, with the strengthening of the language program through support from the National Defense Education Act. On the graduate level, new programs benefited substantially from Ford Foundation grants. This is all another story, but it should be noted that in the course of these developments came the addition of Korean studies—another pioneering venture that warranted a change from the name of the Department of Chinese and Japanese to East Asian Languages and Cultures and which gave a significant new dimension to the work of the East Asian Institute.

Before concluding this brief account of the early phase in East Asian studies, I want to mention two episodes that provide a striking counterpoint to the foregoing—which might otherwise appear to have followed a smooth and steady pattern of unproblematical growth.

The first comes to mind in connection with the 250th anniversary of Columbia, which recalls the bicentennial celebration of 1954. On that occasion I was asked to mount a special convocation relating the bicentennial theme—"Man's Right to Knowledge and the Free Use Thereof"—to East Asia. For this I invited Hu Shih and Daisetz T. Suzuki as representatives of the Chinese and Japanese traditions respectively. By now Hu needs no further introduction to readers of this essay, but something should be said about Suzuki.

Earlier, Tsunoda and I had joined Professor Horace Friess, chair of the religion department, in inviting Suzuki to give a series of special lectures at Columbia on Zen Buddhism. By this time (1954), Suzuki was already something of a celebrity, an early

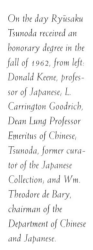

On the day Ryūsaku Tsunoda received an honorary degree in the fall of 1962, from left: Donald Keene, professor of Japanese; L. Carrington Goodrich, Dean Lung Professor Emeritus of Chinese; Tsunoda, former curator of the Japanese Collection; and Wm. Theodore de Bary, chairman of the Department of Chinese and Japanese.

and well-known cult figure for the Beats at Columbia. Tsunoda (less well-known outside of Columbia and even to local Beats such as Allen Ginsberg and Jack Kerouac) had for some years been teaching a wide range of courses on Japanese history, religion, and literature. As one who took a broad approach to Japanese thought and especially to Buddhism, he had reservations about Suzuki's special promotion of Zen at the expense of other aspects of Buddhism and Japanese thought overall. Nevertheless, Tsunoda joined in the invitation to Suzuki, and the series went well. In fact, Suzuki's Columbia lectures came to be regarded as a significant launching pad for the academic study of Zen.

Now to the bicentennial convocation. As a young reformer in Republican China, Hu had been identified with the New Culture and popular literature movements, generally antitraditional and often anti-Confucian. But Hu's American mentor, John Dewey, who lectured to enthusiastic audiences in China during the late teens, was by no means unappreciative of Confucianism, and by the time of this convocation Hu himself had mellowed greatly on the subject. To no one's surprise on this occasion, he spoke appreciatively of knowledge and learning in the Confucian tradition, and, against the background of the current Chinese Communist repression of intellectuals, eloquently endorsed the bicentennial theme of "Man's Right to Knowledge." Contrary to a widespread misinterpretation of Confucianism as authoritarian and thus a long-term cultural factor conducive to the intellectual repressions of the Mao regime, Hu acclaimed Confucius and later Confucians as defenders of intellectual freedom and independent scholarly inquiry.

This was not the first time that Hu and Suzuki had squared off on scholarly issues, and the latter gave no quarter here to Hu. He challenged the very basis of scholarly learning, contending that man's right to knowledge was an illusion unless it was predicated first on man's need for enlightenment (*satori*). In Suzuki's view, the need for a higher spiritual freedom would take priority over any advocacy of intellectual freedom.

In the ensuing discussion it was not to be expected that Hu and Suzuki would come to agreement on an issue defined in such disparate terms. The result was pretty much a standoff, but not of the kind commonly expressed in the cliché: "East is East, West is West, and never the twain shall meet." Hu stood for both East and West and for the commonality of human values; if Suzuki stood for any commonality, it would be one that came through the East, with few, if any, concessions to the modern, liberal West.

THE CHINESE HISTORY PROJECT

The second episode involves another high-level intellectual engagement on a global horizon, but this time in the arena of politics and the social sciences. Today hardly anyone remembers that there existed at Columbia from 1939 to 1951 a major scholarly research project, of international dimensions and involvements, called the "Chinese History Project." It was initiated by Karl August Wittfogel and George Taylor (neither of them Columbians) and, with the support of the Institute of Pacific Relations and Rockefeller Foundation, was housed at Columbia to take advantage of its strong Chinese collections, essential for any in-depth research. No doubt the location was also Wittfogel's choice; as a refugee scholar from Hitler's Germany, he, like many others at Columbia and the New School, preferred the challenging intellectual environment of New York, especially its émigré scholars, to a place such as the University of Washington, Taylor's base.

The Chinese History Project was nothing less than an ambitious attempt to rewrite the whole dynastic history of China, with special attention to its institutions and systemic features. For this purpose outstanding scholars from China, as well as others already in the United States, were recruited and brought to New York to assist in the work on individual periods (dynasties). Wittfogel was to provide the overall theoretical and methodological guidance. In Germany he had been associated with the famous Frankfurt school of left-wing social scientists, and he thought of himself as following up on the work of Marx and Max Weber in the analysis of Asian societies. An active Communist intellectual, he engaged in dialogue with the likes of Bertolt Brecht, Thomas Mann, and Georg Lukács. Jailed by Hitler for his opposition to Nazism and distrusted by Moscow for his intellectual independence, he escaped into exile in China and then the United States. By 1939 (the year the project was started at Columbia but also a watershed year for those disillusioned by the sudden agreement between Hitler and Stalin [the Molotov-Ribbentrop Pact of 1939] to divide up Europe between them), Wittfogel had already begun to distance himself from Communism, a tortuous and painful process for someone quickly stigmatized as a "renegade" and "traitor to the cause" and one estranged from friends with whom he had been associated either in the Party or the Institute of Pacific Relations.

Despite these political complications and those involved in the evolution of Wittfogel's own theoretical and ideological position, the Chinese History Project continued through the war years and eventually produced a substantial volume dealing with the history of the Liao Dynasty (907–1119). Others dealing with the Han and Ching dynasties (much larger projects) were under way when the Cold War brought new complications for the project. Wittfogel was called to testify before the Senate Internal Security Subcommittee, chaired by Senator Pat McCarran, investigating the Institute of Pacific Relations as a research organization allegedly influenced by Communists, and his testimony implicated Owen Lattimore as well as other writers or scholars said to be aligned with the Communists. As if he had thereby broken some unwritten law against informing on his colleagues, Wittfogel was soon ostracized by many scholars in the field—becoming virtually an academic pariah. His grant support evaporated, his staff dispersed elsewhere, and he was asked to vacate the space he occupied in Low Library. In the midst of this turmoil, Wittfogel did manage to complete his own major work, *Oriental Despotism, A Comparative Study of Total Power* (completed in 1954, published in 1957), in which he set forth his mature views on Marx's concept of the Asiatic mode of production, the hydraulic economy and society, the agro-managerial state, and Communist totalitarianism. Given the author's international reputation and the political nature of the issues he addressed, it is not surprising that the book aroused enormous controversy, pro and con, all over the world. What is surprising is that as late as 1999 some pundits included it among the hundred great books of the twentieth century. Recently, too, Jonathan Spence, the China historian at Yale, has drawn renewed attention to the importance of Wittfogel's contribution to Western perceptions of China and to the incisiveness of his analysis of the uses of power both in traditional China and by Mao Zedong.

There was not, however, to be any revival of the Chinese History Project or any reclaiming of a place for Wittfogel in Chinese studies at Columbia—which is our subject here. He continued to live on Riverside Drive, where he kept up a kind of cosmopolitan salon for New York intellectuals (mainly of a Social Democratic persuasion, identified with the *New Leader* magazine) and also kept up correspondence and activities on a global scale (one of them a celebratory homecoming in Germany where in Dusseldorf he was welcomed by political and scholarly figures, including "Red Rudy" Dutschke of the so-called New Left, once of dubious fame in the European student revolt of the late 1960s but later greatly mellowed). Wittfogel's involvements at Columbia, however, were largely limited to a group of anthropologists (principally professors Marvin Harris and Morton Fried) and occasional appearances at special seminars on Asia in world history conducted by Professor of Indian History Ainslie Embree.

Many early Chinese scholars at Columbia went on to become major figures in government, diplomacy, and academic life. Pictured here at a 1955 reception are Chinese ambassador to the United States Wellington Koo and former ambassador Hu Shih.

In the present context, the question naturally arises: Where did Goodrich stand in all this? The answer is that he stood pretty much apart. Wittfogel could never have been lodged in Low Library in the first place without Goodrich's approval, nor could he have been removed later except as Goodrich allowed or caused it to happen. Yet almost from the beginning there was a world of intellectual and ideological difference between the two scholars working in the same building. Again East may be East, and West West, but it was the twain on either side of the same building that did not meet—the down-to-earth factual and largely nonpolitical scholarship of the practical, plain-spoken American scholar Goodrich, standing worlds apart from the ideologically intense, theoretically driven, macroscopic analyses of the sophisticated European scholar, washed up on the banks of the Hudson by the political storms and tides of the twentieth century.

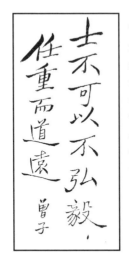

"The Scholar must be stout-hearted and perseverant, for his burden is heavy and his journey is long." The calligraphic inscription was written by Dr. Hu Shih in 1952 when he was raising funds to aid Chinese intellectuals who had become refugees from Communist China. The quotation is from *The Analects of Confucius*, where it is attributed to Confucius's disciple Tseng Tzu. As capitalized by Hu, "Scholar" has the special significance of a man of learning and noble character who must endure great hardships in the service of Heaven and humankind.

—*Wm. Theodore de Bary*

There is, however, something of a happy ending to all of this. In the 1960s, as Goodrich's successor in the chairmanship of the department, I organized a project to compile the *Dictionary of Ming Biography*. Goodrich came out of retirement to head it up editorially, and two of Wittfogel's former colleagues in the Chinese History Project, Fang Chao-ying and Tu Lien-che, came back (all the way from Australia!) to constitute the backbone of the research staff. The large, encyclopedic, two-volume work, completed in 1976, was not the dynastic history envisaged by Wittfogel, but it stands as a monument to collaborative Sino-American scholarship and remains the single most important reference work on the Ming Dynasty (1368–1644). At the time of publication, Fang and Tu received honorary degrees from Columbia, East finally meeting West, and, after all, at a convocation held in Low Library—named after the very president, Seth Low, to whom Dean Lung had sent his check in 1901 to get Chinese studies going at Columbia.

Ryūsaku Tsunoda: Pioneer of Japanese Studies at Columbia

Donald Keene

Donald Keene's reminiscences of Tsunoda were written after Tsunoda's retirement from Columbia in 1955. They were first published in Japanese by the leading cultural review Bungei Shunju *in 1962 to acquaint the Japanese public with the life of an expatriate scholar few of them had heard about in the period of estrangement between the United States and Japan during and just after World War II.*
—Wm. Theodore de Bary

At Columbia University, when people say *sensei* they are certain to be referring to Ryūsaku Tsunoda *Sensei*, "teacher." But when we call him *Sensei*, it is not merely an expression of the respect due to a senior scholar and mentor but a mark of our special affection.

Sir George Sansom, for many years his colleague at Columbia, once called *Sensei* the father of Japanese studies in America and stated that he was proud to be his disciple. But however much he may be called *Sensei*, the most remarkable thing about Tsunoda *Sensei* is his amazing youthfulness. He was born in 1877, but he looks like a well-preserved gentleman of sixty, and his heart is that of a young man. The retirement age at Columbia is sixty-five, but sometimes for special reasons this is extended to sixty-eight; Tsunoda *Sensei* must surely be the first ever to deliver lectures on a regular basis at the age of eighty-five, and he will probably be the last.

I first met Tsunoda *Sensei* twenty years ago. No doubt because it was just on the eve of the outbreak of the Pacific War, I was the only student officially enrolled for his course on the history of Japanese thought. It must surely have been a nuisance to prepare and deliver lectures on such difficult subjects as Buddhism and Neo-Confucianism, all for the sake of one student, but Tsunoda *Sensei*, as I came to expect of him, spared no pains in his teaching. He would cover the blackboard until it was white with quotations in Chinese and would pile stacks of books on the classroom table, bringing home to me the breadth and depth of Japanese studies.

On December 5, 1941, *Sensei*'s lecture took place as usual, but three days later *Sensei* was taken into custody as an enemy alien. Two months later I joined the Navy. It was not for another four years that I again heard *Sensei*'s lectures. *Sensei*, after two or three months of detention, was brought to trial, where he was asked among other things if, in view of the fact that he lived near the George Washington Bridge, there wasn't a possibility that he might blow up the bridge. Such a foolish question was asked because of the general dread of all Japanese during the war.

As *Sensei* talked of the duties and responsibilities of any foreigner who had lived for many years in America, he spoke with such sincerity in his voice that the judge was moved. Finally, the judge asked, "Mr. Tsunoda, are you a poet?" He was quite serious, and his question, far from being foolish, showed a real understanding of *Sensei*'s character.

Sensei seldom talks about himself and is absolutely silent on the subject of his family, but after twenty years' acquaintance I have learned the main facts of his life. He was born in Gumma Prefecture in 1877 and after going up to Tokyo studied English literature under Tsubouchi Shoyo (known especially for his studies of Shakespeare) at the Tokyo Senmon Gakko, the predecessor of Waseda University. Deeply interested in social questions, Tsunoda went to Kyoto intending to work for the betterment of the *eta* (outcaste class). He was so horrified to see the filth in the hovels and the wretched condition of people eating with their hands that he felt utterly powerless, and when he discovered that his *geta* (shoes) were imbedded so deeply in the muddy street that he could not move, this seemed a symbol of his own helplessness. This must have been a severe blow to the young idealist.

In 1897, at the age of twenty, he published his book on Ihara Saikaku, the first book ever to have been written about the great seventeenth-century novelist. In 1899 appeared his translation of *Social Evolution* by Benjamin Kidd, and in 1904 a translation of *The History of Ethics* by Wilhelm Wundt.

Sensei first heard about America from an American teacher at Tokyo Senmon Gakko, and full of the spirit of adventure appropriate in a man of the Meiji era, *Sensei* apparently decided at this time to journey to the New World. In 1909 he went to Hawaii on the invitation of the Buddhist Mission. He seems to have enjoyed his stay in Hawaii but moved on to New York and began studying at Columbia University, taking courses with John Dewey and others in philosophy. At first *Sensei* thought it was hopeless attempting to study philosophy in a noisy place like New York, but gradually he came to feel the strange attraction of the human melting pot that New York is and in the end came to make it his permanent home.

At the time (about forty years ago) the Chinese language and Chinese civilization were taught in a few American universities, but the study of Japanese civilization was limited to Japanese art. There were almost no collections of Japanese books, and Americans who wished to study about Japan in an academic manner (there were extremely few of them) had no choice but to go abroad to Europe or Japan. In America Far Eastern studies meant the study of Chinese. Professors of Chinese tended to dismiss Japan as a nation of imitators; needless to say, they knew no Japanese. *Sensei*, deploring this situation, returned to Japan and gathered funds and books so as to establish a center of Japanese studies in America. The center he envisaged was eventually founded at Columbia, and *Sensei* was appointed director of the center and lecturer in Japanese civilization. From about 1928 to 1941 *Sensei* taught Japanese thought, history, and classical literature at Columbia. I myself studied under *Sensei* for three months before the war, and no sooner was I released from military duty in February 1946 than I returned to Columbia as a graduate student, eager to hear *Sensei's*

Tsunoda was interested in every period of Japanese intellectual history.

lectures again. At the time his advanced class consisted of five or six students, all people like myself who had studied Japanese during the war in the Armed Forces and all desperately anxious to return to the academic world. We begged *Sensei* for additional lectures, and in the end he was teaching two hours a day of classical literature alone. In three semesters, as I recall, we read the Suma and Akashi chapters of *The Tale of Genji*, much of *Tsurezuregusa* and *The Pillow Book* of Sei Shonagon, the Noh plays *Matsukaze* and *Sotoba Komachi*, and the whole of *Five Women Who Loved Love*

Sir George Sansom (left), widely known as the premier Western historian of Japan, and Ryūsaku Tsunoda, called Tsunoda Sensei (right), the father of Japanese studies in America.

and *The Narrow Road of Oku*. I imagine that this must have been a record amount of Japanese classical literature for any class outside Japan to have read in so short a time.

Several things in *Sensei's* lectures attracted us. First of all, there was our discovery on being led into an unfamiliar, distant world that, surprisingly enough, shared many intellectual and emotional problems with our own world. *Sensei* never attempted to "modernize" the thought of the writers of the past but pointed out instead their essential points and their perennial, universal qualities. His students realized that whatever he discussed—whether Shingon Buddhism, the Chu Hsi school of Confucianism, or the Shinto of Motoori Norinaga—was necessary information for the understanding of modern Japan; at the same time, they realized that these topics marked important stages in the history of mankind as a whole, and they felt the narrowness of the traditional Western-oriented education they had hitherto received. His classes gave students the pleasure of participating in an intellectual adventure.

His lectures, despite his advanced years, were full of enthusiasm, and his opinions were not only original but poetic. *Sensei*'s first lecture in his course on the history of Japanese thought was unforgettable. It dealt with the importance of the sun, mountains, and the water at the dawn of Japanese civilization. He gave numerous examples and analyzed psychological characteristics of the Japanese still surviving to this day that stem from these three factors. The lecture captured the imagination of the students with its tone, at once pragmatic and poetic. When *Sensei* lectured about the yin-yang system of thought, he did not dismiss it as mere superstition in the manner of some scholars, but discussed it as an attempt to classify the phenomena of the universe and made us respect the men of ancient times who had devised it.

Sensei was interested in every period of Japanese intellectual history, but the independent thinkers of the Tokugawa period seem to have attracted him most. Immediately after the end of the war the young people who were attempting to build a new, democratic Japan preached the necessity of making a clean sweep of the old traditions as feudalistic, but Sensei, who believed deeply in democracy, wondered if there were not a connection between Japanese tradition and modern men, and if there was nothing in tradition that might prove of use to the Japan of the future.

Whatever work *Sensei* discussed, he was able with surprising skill to make us understand its literary value, and even as we haltingly read the difficult classics before us, we were struck by the beauty of the style. *Sensei* must surely have read such a work as *Tsurezuregusa* (*Essays in Idleness*) many times before he taught it to us, but he communicated the wonder of its style by the excitement and delight in his voice, which suggested that he had discovered Yoshida Kenko's masterpiece for the first time.

For the past forty years *Sensei* has lived in the ultramodern city of New York and seems very fond of his life here. *Sensei* is, after all, imbued with the spirit of enlightenment of the early Meiji period and is fond of anything new. (It is by no means accidental that he should now be plunged in a study of Benjamin Franklin.) He lives in a modern apartment, and when visitors come, he is likely to serve them a steak, his proudest accomplishment as a chef. He is always dressed in well-fitting suits and looks rather like a retired diplomat.

Among *Sensei*'s pleasures in New York, watching baseball games occupies an important place. He was a longtime, fanatical devotee of the New York Giants, and the Giants' move to San Francisco came as a great shock. Probably he is now forced to watch the Yankees play, though for years he detested them.

Another pleasure of *Sensei*'s life in New York is the Hudson River and Fort Tryon Park facing it. *Sensei* loves the mighty Hudson, so much so that his long walks along its banks before the war seemed to have started rumors that he was a spy. One evening, just as the war was ending, *Sensei* saw the sun sinking above the Hudson and imagined it was symbolic of the future of Japan. When he writes in the Japanese-language newspaper published in New York he often uses a pen name based on the names of the Hudson River and Fort Tryon Park.

But probably *Sensei*'s deepest attachments in New York are to Columbia University. Probably no one has ever taught as long at Columbia as *Sensei*, and he is well acquainted with the history of the university. He has frequently attended lectures given during the past thirty years by famous professors of history, philosophy, and religion and can tell interesting anecdotes about the great teachers of former days.

Sensei seems to have become a New Yorker through and through, but this is not the case: sometimes, when apologizing to Japanese guests for the inadequacy of the hospitality he has offered he even says, "It's the best I can do, considering I'm away from home." *Sensei* is beyond any doubt a Japanese, and no matter how long he may live abroad, it is unlikely that there will be any change. *Sensei* sometimes travels in

Tsunoda Sensei wrote this poem—his last—in 1964, shortly before leaving New York to return to Japan.
Always loyal both to the land of his birth and his adopted country, he comforted himself with the thought that modern air travel made a return trip possible almost overnight. He never reached his destination; on November 29, 1964, he died en route in Hawaii.

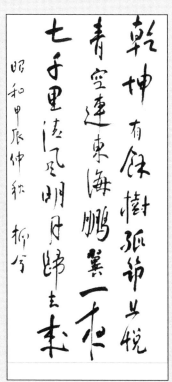

POEM, FALL 1964

Kenkon wa Kokyō o tatsuru ni amari ari
Katsu yorokobu
Seikū tōkai ni tsuranaru o
Hōyoku ichiya shichisen ri
Seifū meigetsu iza kaerinan.

In this world
There still is room
For this solitary walking-cane—
And I rejoice.
Azure skies stretch
Across the Eastern seas.
But one night on phoenix' wings
Can span
Seven thousand *ri*.
With fresh winds and a bright moon
I may return.

America, and he is apt to say on seeing the home of Thomas Jefferson or the region of Lake Champlain where John Dewey was born that he would like to retire to such a place. But no matter how attracted he may be to the scenery or atmosphere of a place, anywhere that is not Japan is likely always to remain "away from home." It is precisely because he is so completely Japanese that he has been able to exert so strong an influence on generations of American students.

But the point on which *Sensei* and his disciples differ the most is the question of his fame. We would like to see our beloved, wonderful teacher recognized throughout the world, but *Sensei* seems utterly indifferent on this matter. Not only is he absolutely opposed to any self-propagandizing, but he rarely refers to his private life and seems reluctant to answer any questions. It is a real question in my mind whether or not *Sensei* will be pleased to read this article about him. Perhaps he may be outraged at this invasion of his privacy—though I cannot recall ever having seen him outraged—but I cannot refrain from wishing to spread word about him. I have had the privilege of being taught by many splendid teachers, but none his superior.

CHAPTER 43

A Cycle of Cathay and Columbia

—⚭—

A Memoir by Donald Keene

—⚭—

Although Donald Keene and I, one year apart at Columbia College, must have been almost the only undergraduates who ventured into Chinese language studies in the late thirties and might have been expected to run into each other in the process, we only met for the first time when we both showed up in January 1942 at the Naval Japanese Language School in Berkeley. Donald had been a commuter from Brooklyn, more a habitué of New York cultural life than I, heavily occupied as I was in campus affairs. But what made us instantly recognizable to each other on the distant ground of Berkeley was our common intellectual foundation in the Humanities and CC courses and in the Honors Colloquium at Columbia and our admiration for many of the same teachers. This shared experience marked us as kindred souls, and despite the divergent course of our later careers, it has been the basis for a close Columbia friendship for more than sixty years.

Wm. Theodore de Bary

—⚭—

I was born in Brooklyn and attended neighborhood public schools, graduating from James Madison High School and entering Columbia in 1938 at the age of sixteen. I was sure I was receiving a good education and never envied those who attended famous private schools, perhaps because I didn't know anybody who had attended one. I had reason for confidence. Even at Seth Low Junior High School the teachers of foreign languages were almost all native speakers of French, Spanish, or German, and the English teachers taught us British pronunciation. But although I enjoyed school, my childhood was overcast first by the Depression and later by discord at home.

My father, after various business ventures that failed because of the Depression, finally established a successful import-export company in Spain and decided to move the family—my mother and myself—to Barcelona in the autumn of 1936. The outbreak of the Spanish Civil War that summer put an end to these plans. If this war had not occurred, I would certainly never have become a scholar of Japan.

Soon after I realized we would not be going to Spain, my parents separated under circumstances that are still painful to recall. This, too, changed my life. I had dreamt of going to college in some beautiful or at least rustic place, but my mother's dependence made it impossible even to consider leaving New York. Fortunately, a high school teacher (who knew nothing of my family situation) persuaded me that Columbia was the best place for me. On June 18, 1938, my sixteenth birthday, I received word that I had won a Pulitzer Scholarship, awarded to ten New York City high school graduates a year. I would be exempt from tuition expenses for four years, and there was an allowance for food and other expenses.

The same high school teacher had also decided that while at Columbia I should study languages—Greek, Latin, French, and German—and if possible, nothing else. I discovered, however, that as a freshman I was required to study Humanities and Contemporary Civilization. I gave up Latin and German with regret, but the Humanities course, taught by Mark Van Doren, was one of the most important experiences of my life, and I am grateful to Columbia for having had this requirement.

While in high school I had read some of the great books, but as the result of the enormous reading assignments of the Humanities course, I soon left behind all I had previously read. Because I still lived in Brooklyn, over an hour away by subway, the time was too precious to waste, and I ruined my eyes reading the Everyman Classics in badly lit subway cars. But I had no regrets. To be present four days a week as Mark Van Doren, speaking without lecture notes, brought out the meaning of the great works of the Greeks, the Romans, and the later writers was a joy each time. Most of the works I read at that time have remained with me. Whenever I discuss the Noh plays of Japan, for example, Aristotle's *Poetics* inevitably comes to mind.

I remember one book I disliked, the *Confessions* of St. Augustine. I parodied it to friends, making fun of Augustine's guilty feelings over having stolen a pear. Then in class Van Doren spoke so movingly about the work that, although I had virtually no free time, I reread the *Confessions*, ashamed of my immaturity.

Mark Van Doren's class had another, totally unpredictable influence on my life. His section of the nine o'clock Humanities class contained students whose last names began with K, L, M, and N. My seat was directly in front of one occupied by a Chinese student named Lee. We exchanged casual greetings, and once in a while

Keene with Japanese novelist Ryotaro Shiba

I asked him something about China. I never before had been much interested in China. I had supposed that a knowledge of English and other European languages would give me the qualifications of a cultured man. I had read most of Balzac in French and the major works of Russian literature in Constance Garnett's translation, but I had never asked myself if India or China or Japan had a literature.

The next summer Lee and I went to the World's Fair in Flushing Meadows and were given a glimpse into the future. We saw television for the first time and a car that ran on electricity. We gradually became close friends, and at the beginning of our sophomore year we agreed to meet each day for lunch at the East Asia Restaurant on Broadway. The lunch special, usually fried rice or egg foo yung, cost twenty-five cents. After lunch Lee would give me a Chinese lesson. He did not feel confident of his Mandarin pronunciation, so he taught me only the meanings of the characters, not their sounds. The text he used was a novel he happened to have picked up in Chinatown, by no means a suitable textbook, and I learned very little. I was fascinated all the same with the language, and in my junior year took a class in Chinese language with Professor L. Carrington Goodrich and in Chinese literature with Professor Chi-chen Wang.

At this time there were probably fewer than a dozen American universities where Chinese was taught, and I felt lucky to be at Columbia. The Chinese texts we read were mainly about filial sons who look after their aged parents, and the pace of instruction was slow. Once in a while I listened to Linguaphone records in a corner of the library stacks. I imitated the conversational practice, but I had no hope of actually speaking Chinese.

One day, by accident, I put on a Japanese record. This was the first time in my life I had ever heard the language. Unlike the sleepy voice of the Chinese man on the records, the Japanese man seemed to be barking out orders. I took this as proof that the Japanese were basically militaristic. It did not occur to me that if the recording had been made by a Japanese woman, the language might have sounded melodic and even beautiful.

One day in the late spring of 1941, as I was studying in the East Asiatic Library (now the Faculty Room) in Low Library, a man came up to me and said he had often seen me eating at the East Asia. He asked if I would have dinner with him. I gladly agreed, though eating out twice in one day was an extravagance.

My new friend, George Kerr, had taught English in Taiwan for several years. He regretted that he had never learned Japanese (the island was then a Japanese possession), but a former student, who was an American citizen, had returned to this country, and Kerr had decided to ask him to tutor him in Japanese at his place in the country. However, Kerr reasoned, if he studied all by himself he would probably desert his books whenever the weather was fine. He was therefore looking for a few others to spend a month or two learning Japanese with him in the mountains of North Carolina. I hesitated, fearing that Lee would be upset if I studied Japanese, the language of his country's enemy, but the chance to leave New York in the summer was too good to permit matters of conscience to intervene.

The Japanese textbook we used, designed for six-year-olds, opened with an exclamation of delight over the blooming of the cherry trees. The following lessons were also given over to appreciation of nature with no mention (contrary to my expectation) of the glory of serving as a soldier in the Emperor's army. Japanese seemed more difficult than Chinese, but it had a recognizable grammar, and the pronunciation was simple.

When I returned to Columbia in the fall of 1941 I signed up for a course in Chinese language, another in Japanese language, and, at Kerr's suggestion, one on the history of Japanese thought. I discovered on the first day of class that I was the only person who had registered for the course in Japanese thought. I offered to switch to some other course, but the teacher, Ryūsaku Tsunoda, answered, "One is enough." A couple of weeks later two other students, both Japanese, joined the class, but at first the lectures were only for me. They were prepared as carefully as for a seminar of graduate students. When I arrived in the classroom the blackboard would already be covered with passages in Chinese and Japanese, quite beyond my comprehension of either language. Tsunoda would also bring to class a pile of books, just in case I asked a question that required a detailed answer. I was overcome by admiration for the man and for his love of his subject. He was a true *sensei*, my teacher of a lifetime.

On December 7, 1941, I went hiking in Staten Island with my Japanese tutor of the preceding summer. When the return ferry reached the Battery, a boy was selling *The Enquirer,* the only newspaper published on Sunday afternoons. The headline read "Japs Attack U.S., Hawaii, Philippines Bombed by Airmen!" I laughed, remembering headlines in this scandal sheet that predicted New York would be wiped out by an earthquake or a flood, but for once *The Enquirer* had told the truth, as I discovered from the radio on returning home. My friend spent that night in an all-night movie, afraid to be seen.

The next day at Columbia, students gossiped about how many ships were actually sunk in Pearl Harbor. Lionel Trilling, whose course in nineteenth-century English literature I was taking that semester, told us in his ironic manner that if we were drafted we would not be required to turn in a term paper. However, if he was also drafted and attached to the same unit, the requirement would stand.

Tsunoda *Sensei* did not appear that day. He had already been arrested as an enemy alien and sent to Ellis Island. He was released after a trial and went back to Columbia, where he taught throughout the war years. He had refused to be repatriated to Japan because he detested the military clique that ran the country. By the time *Sensei* was released, a couple of months later, I was in the Navy Language School, then at the University of California in Berkeley. I had already earned enough credits to graduate, though my diploma was awarded the following June. George Kerr because an officer in Naval Intelligence. Suey Ling Lee, my Chinese friend, could not graduate with his classmates in the spring of 1942. He was unable to fulfill an engineering requirement of a summer of work in a factory, because prejudice against Chinese was so strong at the time that no factory would take him on.

The course was supposed to take eighteen months but, because of the urgent need of translators and interpreters, we finished in eleven months and were then sent overseas. When I entered the school I knew some Japanese but could not say a sentence with confidence; by the time we graduated I could read texts of considerable difficulty, write a letter, and even give an address in Japanese at the graduation ceremony.

My fellow students at the school included men who would become leaders of East Asian studies in America. Among them there was no one I admired more and felt closer to than Ted de Bary. I had not known him as an undergraduate, but I knew his name as a "big man on campus." We not only became friends, but, as I remember distinctly, we made plans for returning to Columbia and working together when the war was over. But of course we had no idea how long the war might last. Quite by chance we were sent on the same operations, to the Aleutians and later to Okinawa. In the immediate postwar era, however, Ted was in Japan and I

Keene in Japan: "A devoted missionary of Japanese culture"

was in China. At his suggestion, we saved our letters (and made them more literary, no doubt) in the hopes of publishing them. The book that resulted, *From a Ruined Empire,* has gone through several printings and has been translated into Japanese.

We returned as graduate students to Columbia and were in the classes taught by Tsunoda *Sensei* in Japanese literature, thought, and history. (Almost all of the American teachers of Japanese subjects were still in the military and Tsunoda took on their various tasks.) We read works of classical literature of various periods including Saikaku's novel *Five Women Who Loved Love.* This was undoubtedly the first time in American history that a class had read this entire work, which was in extremely difficult Japanese and was also widely mistaken for a work of pornography. Ted's translation, made in connection with the lectures, itself ranks as a classic.

Ted went to China to study, and in 1948, about the time he returned to Columbia, I left for England with a fellowship to study Arabic and Persian at Cambridge University. Luckily for me, the concerned professors decided I could not possibly learn two difficult languages in the one year provided by my fellowship. But I discovered that a teacher was needed for conversational Japanese, and I gladly took advantage of this opportunity. I later became a lecturer in Japanese with the equivalent of tenure and expected to spend the rest of my life in England.

In 1953 I had a year's leave from Cambridge to study in Japan. I was extremely fortunate in making friends with people who made it possible for me to know Japanese intellectual life in a way uncommon for foreigners at that time. I enjoyed my life in Japan so much that I asked Cambridge to allow me to remain there another year, but this request was refused. Just at this time I had word from Columbia offering me an assistant professorship. I was reluctant to leave Cambridge, the most beautiful place I have ever lived, but when I was told I might spend another year in Japan, that settled matters. During the second year in Japan I compiled the two anthologies of Japanese literature that, I suppose, have been my most widely read books. I also began writing in Japanese for magazines and newspapers, quite a different experience from the classroom.

I began teaching at Columbia in 1955. At first I taught not only language and literature, but also history. I was extremely busy with preparations, but I found time somehow to make a translation of Dazai's novel *The Setting Sun* and for the first time enjoyed some of the pleasures of social life in New York. Where did I ever find the time?

I have always enjoyed teaching, but at one point during the 1970s I thought of giving up my job. Having undertaken to write single-handedly a history of Japanese literature, I feared that I could not complete it if I continued to teach full time. I told Ted de Bary, then provost of the university, of my intention, but he suggested instead that I teach only one of the two semesters. I followed this suggestion, and it worked out well. It took about twenty-five years to complete the four volumes of my history, and I went on to publish thirty or forty other books in both English and Japanese. I have generally spent up to two-thirds of each year in Japan but have always taught one semester at Columbia. I had assumed that when I was eligible to retire I would go to Japan for the rest of my life, but when the time came I discovered that I was not ready to lose my friends in New York or to give up teaching entirely. I retired in 1992, but I still teach one class. As a devoted missionary of Japanese culture, it gives me pleasure to think I have passed on my enthusiasms to several generations of students, and I am grateful to the teachers and friends who have made this possible.

CHAPTER 44

Columbia's Russian Institute:
The Formative Years

—⟋⟋⟍—

Catharine Theimer Nepomnyashchy

The Soviet Union lasted a little less than seventy-five years. For the last forty-five of those it was the focus of study of Columbia's Russian Institute, from the onset of the Cold War in 1946 through the collapse of the Gorbachev regime in 1991. Since then the Harriman Institute, as it is now called, has concentrated on the Soviet Union's successor states and former satellites.

The academic mission of the Russian Institute—the first interdisciplinary effort to study the Soviet Union at a major American university—faced special challenges from the start. As the Cold War quickly grew more adversarial, the Institute encountered antagonism not only from Soviet government agencies and publications but also in an increasingly oppressive political climate at home, where Senator Joseph McCarthy identified two of the Institute's founding professors as members of the "Communist conspiracy." Even after the anti-Communist fever of the early 1950s subsided, the challenge of maintaining intellectual autonomy in the midst of the Cold War remained, particularly in the new discipline of Sovietology.

Catharine Theimer Nepomnyashchy, the Ann Whitney Olin Professor of Russian Literature at Barnard College and current director of the Institute, has told an important part of this story here, focusing on the background and early years of the Institute mainly through the experiences of its founders and first students.

—Tom Mathewson

—⟋⟋⟍—

The Russian Institute opened its doors to students on September 25, 1946, inaugurating a bold pedagogical and scholarly initiative, the first of its kind in the United States, designed to respond to the threat and promise of the

At the Moscow Conference of August 1942. From left to right: Winston Churchill, W. Averell Harriman, Joseph Stalin, and Vyacheslav M. Molotov.

new world into which the country had emerged from the Second World War. Not only had the war thrust an isolationist and reluctant nation onto the international stage as victor and power broker, but it had transported thousands of young men from Main Street, USA, into contact with exotic peoples and places on the other side of the world. Clearly the United States would need specialists in the regions that would dominate international politics in the postwar world. In June 1945, just as the war was ending, Columbia University President Nicholas Murray Butler announced plans to establish the Russian Institute with a generous grant from the Rockefeller Foundation. It was to be the first of six regional institutes "for the study of the life and thought of principal areas of the modern world." The same press release announced the establishment of the School of International Affairs, which was to "function in close association with the institutes." Butler did not downplay the significance of the endeavor: "I regard this whole undertaking as one of outstanding importance not only in the history of Columbia University and its worldwide relationships, but in the history of higher education generally," he said. "It is constructive and forward-facing, and points the way to what will soon be recognized as a dominant worldwide interest in the field[s] of government, economics, and the intellectual life."

It was appropriate that the Russian Institute was the first of the area institutes, since no territory presented a more urgent challenge than the Soviet Union, our wartime ally and ideological rival, also poised by its triumph over Hitler to assert itself more forcefully in the world. Perhaps equally important, the USSR seemed particularly well suited to study founded on the "integration of disciplines," a fundamental tenet of the area studies approach. As Philip E. Mosely, then director of the Institute, explained in 1954, "The Soviet ideology and system of control assume that all aspects of life must be closely interrelated and directed by a central purpose. This assumption, even if fulfilled imperfectly, challenges workers in many disciplines to combine their efforts to study a regime which attempts to control or direct all human activities on the basis of explicitly defined programs."

THE FORMATIVE WARTIME EXPERIENCE

The concept of "area studies" (routinely enclosed in scare quotes in the early days, even after the founding of the Institute) had been a subject of discussion before the war, and one of the directors of the Russian Institute would later point to classics as the original model of transdisciplinary studies. Nonetheless, the wartime experiences of those who would become the core faculty of the institute unquestionably gave shape and urgency to the project, just as military service redirected many young men toward careers in what would later come to be known as Sovietology.

In particular, academics were recruited to the Office of Strategic Services (OSS) and the Office of War Information (OWI). At least indirectly, the work of such anthropologists as Margaret Mead and Ruth Benedict, especially Benedict's study of Japanese culture for the OWI, *The Chrysanthemum and the Sword*, sensitized policymakers to the value of studying regional cultures. As for Soviet studies, it was the OSS—and specifically the USSR Division of its Research and Analysis Branch, headed by Columbia professor Geroid Tanqueray Robinson—that served as incubator.

Robinson, the founding director of the Russian Institute, was a leading member of the rare breed of prewar Russia specialists. As a Columbia graduate student, he was one of the few American scholars who conducted research in the Soviet Union before World War II. He completed his doctorate and joined the Columbia faculty in 1924. Robinson's dissertation, published in 1932 as *Rural Russia under the Old Regime*, established him as one of the foremost authorities on the region. He was promoted to full professor in the history department in 1938.

Robinson was summoned to Washington on September 1, 1941, to assemble a team of American-born researchers—it was assumed that any Russian émigré volunteers would compromise the scientific objectivity of the project—to penetrate the veil of secrecy that had fallen between the Soviet Union and the West in the prewar years. Given the scarcity of established experts, the Division culled its personnel largely from talented younger scholars without previous specialization in Eastern Europe. Their experiences in the OSS would transform them into the first postwar generation of Sovietologists, among them Robert C. Tucker and Barrington Moore, Jr. (both originally trained as classicists), and the newly minted Ph.D. in economics Abram Bergson. The Division could also call on an impressive cadre of consultants, like Philip E. Mosely, a Balkans specialist then on the Cornell faculty, and John Newboldt Hazard, who spent the war years in Washington as deputy director of the USSR branch of the office responsible for Lend-Lease. Hazard also came to Washington with unusual experience. After what he later recalled as a brief stop in "gloomy" Russia "with its communist inefficiency and even brutality" on a round-the-world trip following graduation from college, he hardly expected to go back. But while studying at Harvard Law School, Hazard was offered a fellowship to continue his studies in the USSR, where he spent three years studying law at Moscow University, finishing at the height of the Stalin purges in 1937. Bergson, Mosely, and Hazard would join Robinson on the original Russian Institute faculty.

Geroid T. Robinson (left), founding director of the Russian Institute; Philip E. Mosely (right), a Balkan specialist who came to Columbia from Cornell

Not only did this wartime experience provide the core personnel of postwar Soviet studies, but it fundamentally shaped the newly emerging field. Even during the wartime alliance, American information gatherers had to develop ingenious strategies for teasing out usable data on the Soviets, often finding reliable statistics on the German enemy easier to come by. Certainly more important in the long term, however, was the lesson of the effectiveness of collaboration across disciplinary boundaries in solving problems requiring regional expertise—the model that would become the basis of area studies.

Like the faculty, the students in the first classes of the Russian Institute were forged by their service in the war. One of the Institute's most illustrious graduates, Marshall Shulman—who would go on to direct the Institute and to serve three secretaries of state—arrived in the inaugural class with a wealth of experience. A literature major at the University of Michigan, Shulman had begun a career as a journalist when he volunteered for the military at the start of the war. He was recruited away from his posting as a glider pilot to serve in Burma in the OWI's first psychological warfare unit. There he flew missions dropping leaflets encouraging Japanese soldiers to surrender. This program became the model for similar operations throughout the Pacific. Like Robinson's group half a world away in Washington, Shulman learned the value of teams with a variety of skills working together to solve problems resulting from a clash of alien cultures.

William Korey, another member of the Institute's first graduating class, was called up with the Enlisted Reserve Corps in 1943. Having studied some Russian as a history major at the University of Chicago, he was assigned to the Army Specialized Training Program and ended up serving in Berlin in May 1945. The final division of the city had not yet taken place, and Korey found himself in frequent contact with his Russian counterparts, reinforcing his earlier fascination with the USSR. His experience rescuing Jews in DP camps in Berlin helped to shape his career as a prominent human rights activist and scholar. Their wartime experience left the first Institute classes serious, politically engaged, and idealistic. In Korey's words, "A new world was aborning," and the roughly fifty students who began their studies at the Russian Institute in 1946 were convinced they were going to conquer it.

WHY COLUMBIA?

Columbia's role in this pioneering initiative in Soviet studies was in a sense overdetermined. Situated in a great metropolis that had just been chosen as the site for the newly founded United Nations, Columbia was also one of a handful of American academic institutions to boast significant resources in Russian studies dating back well before the Second World War. Russian had been taught briefly at Columbia for the first time in 1909, but it took the extraordinarily gifted linguist John Dyneley Prince, originally hired at Columbia as a professor of Semitic languages, to found the Department of Slavonic Languages at Columbia in 1915. By 1920, in line with Prince's commitment to a range of Slavic languages and literatures, the university offered instruction not only in Russian, but in Polish, Czecho-Slovak, Serbo-Croat, and Comparative Slavonic. By the time of the founding of the Russian Institute, Columbia could boast strong library resources on the Russian region as well. Having begun modestly with the purchase of collections of revolutionary pamphlets, Columbia in the 1930s joined a handful of American institutions with sizable collections in Russian history and literature. The importance of the collection was underscored with the hiring of Semen Akimovich Bolan, the first Russian bibliographer in the Columbia University libraries, in conjunction with the founding of the Russian Institute in 1946. Yet Columbia's strength in Russian studies before the war lay almost exclusively in the humanities. The challenge in creating a truly multidisciplinary program was to add social science faculty with expertise in the Soviet Union.

The first step was to win over the Arts and Sciences disciplinary departments. Together with Schuyler C. Wallace of Political Science, who was to become the first dean of the School of International Affairs, Geroid Robinson put together a proposal designed to respect departmental boundaries and standards. All Institute faculty were to be housed in departments, and all students were to be required to complete requirements for disciplinary degrees as well as for the Russian Institute Certificate. In John Hazard's words:

> Their scheme took into consideration what they knew to be the hostility of men and women in each traditional discipline for the granting of interdisciplinary degrees. Their plan did not call, therefore, for a new Columbia degree. It was to create a coordinating body for interdisciplinary study, not a new department of Russian studies. Each member of this coordinating body would have to meet the scholarly tests of his fellows in the department with which he would be concerned. In short, a political scientist teaching about the Soviet system of government would have to pass the tests for appointments to the political science department, and so on around the circle of departments. . . . If a department had no specialist in its field who could qualify also as a knowledgeable person about the U.S.S.R., Robinson would recommend one, and urge his or her appointment. Hopefully, the candidate would pass muster.

Once this hurdle was cleared, the next order of business was to fund the ambitious endeavor. The Rockefeller Foundation came through with a $250,000 grant to be disbursed over a five-year period. This enabled Robinson to recruit the Institute's core faculty, who were all new to Columbia: John Hazard was appointed to the Department of Public Law and Government, Philip Mosely was recruited from Cornell in International Relations, and Abram Bergson was housed in Economics. The fifth member, the literature specialist Ernest Simmons, had spent the war years implementing the pilot Program in Soviet Civilization at Cornell with Rockefeller Foundation support; his Columbia appointment was in the Department of Slavic Languages.

For all the promise of the new endeavor, a threat hung over the Institute from the very beginning. The founders realized that the Russian Institute, as the first and only academic organization of its kind in the United States, might render Columbia vulnerable to red-baiters, even in the pre-McCarthy years. Robinson and Wallace appealed to William Langer—the Harvard historian who, as chief of the Research and Analysis Branch of the OSS, had originally brought Robinson to Washington—

Harriman Institute for Soviet Studies Founded

Harrimans Give CU $10 Million

To meet the critical need for greater Western understanding of the Soviet Union, the University announced last Thurs., Oct. 21, the creation of the W. Averell Harriman Institute for Advanced Study of the Soviet Union with a gift of $10 million from Gov. and Mrs. Harriman.

Declaring that "there is no greater threat to our future than ignorance of the Soviet Union," President Sovern made the announcement at a ceremony on the Morningside Heights campus honoring Harriman. Former Secretary of State Cyrus R. Vance and Harriman addressed the convocation.

Sovern also announced the additional gift of $1.5 million from the Gladys and Roland Harriman Foundation to create a professorial chair in Soviet economics at Columbia named for W. Averell Harriman's late brother and his widow (story page 6).

"Through the foresight and generosity of the Harrimans, we will be able to develop and train a generation of younger specialists, ensuring the future availability in America of a cadre of highly trained diplomats, scholars, political leaders, journalists and researchers with expertise on the Soviet Union," said Sovern. "We have dangerously few experts on the Soviet

Pamela and Averell Harriman with President Sovern on the steps of Low Library before the Oct. 21 convocation at which the W. Averell Harriman Institute for Advanced Study of the Soviet Union was announced. The Harrimans gave Columbia $10 million to create the institute.

and he agreed to found the Russian Research Center (now the Davis Center), for which he obtained funds from the Carnegie Corporation. The Harvard Russian Research Center, although never as integrated into the student life of the university as its Columbia counterpart, would, in Hazard's words, "pace Columbia for decades as a training ground for specialists." The two centers have cooperated closely, as in their joint sponsorship for over a quarter-century of the annual Arden House conference on U.S.-Russian relations.

DETECTIVES AND SPIES: THE EARLY LIFE OF THE INSTITUTE

Reminiscences of the Institute's first years convey a palpable sense of mission and excitement. A mature entering class, seasoned by the war years, took on the

Marshall D. Shulman served as director of the Harriman Institute in the 1960s, 1970s, and 1980s.

Institute's daunting requirements with a sense of purpose. The capstone experience was a seminar in the second year in which students researched topics for their Institute certificate essays. Once a month all of the seminars met together, and students in all disciplines presented their research.

The distinct personal styles of the core faculty members left a strong imprint on the students' experience of the Institute. Robinson—who dressed in wing collars and always sported a vest, a lorgnette, and his Phi Beta Kappa key—was aloof and a harsh taskmaster, including in his seminars meticulous lectures on how to organize note cards and writing copious comments on students' papers, sometimes longer than the papers themselves. Hazard and Mosely were the most approachable. Robert Belknap, who began studying in the Institute in 1951 and went on to join the Slavic department faculty and direct the Institute in later years, recalled of Hazard, "He was so gentle and casual that you didn't realize how much to the point he was." Elizabeth Valkenier, who worked closely with Mosely when she studied at the Institute in the 1960s and went on to teach political science and art history at Columbia, speaks warmly to this day of his dedication to his students, recalling one incident in particular: "At one point, and that I know for a fact, President Johnson had invited him for lunch at the White House and he said . . . 'I have a seminar.' Can you imagine someone doing that? That 'I have a seminar' meant more than meeting with Johnson."

As in the OSS during the war, the faculty at the Institute were training their students in research methodologies tailored to penetrate Soviet obfuscation about everything from production statistics to the rigors of everyday life in the USSR. Belknap, describing himself as a "post-adolescent literary type" at the time, found himself drawn into the courses in the social sciences: "Abe Bergson was busy inventing matrix economics as a form of detective work. . . . and he made economics effective in a way that was quite exciting. . . . the Institute was seductive. It got you interested in those things." By the same token, Ernest Simmons trained his students to mine contemporary Soviet literature for clues about the daily life of Soviet citizens and the vagaries of the official party line. A June 1953 *Collier's* article entitled "They Know More about Russia Than Anybody," about the Russian Institute faculty and their counterparts at the Harvard Russian Research Center, conveys something of the fascination of early Sovietology even for the general public:

> Who are these experts who can so easily pierce the Iron Curtain? What
> magic X-ray eyes do they possess?
>   They are ordinary Americans whose only magic is brain power.
> Their X-ray eyes are nothing more than the proven methods of good
> scholarship.

Yet not all reviews of the Institute's work were so positive. On July 24, 1951, *Pravda* attacked the Russian Institute as a "hotbed of American slanderers" where "ignorant professors drivel to young listeners selected on the basis of the greatest mental defectiveness and the least moral decency." The Soviet newspaper *Trud* described the Institute in even blunter terms, as a "mass production factory for spies, saboteurs, and murderers." Mosely's response to such Soviet assaults was philosophical: "It was then that we knew we were getting at the truth about Russia."

More disturbingly, during the McCarthy years there were difficulties with the delivery of Soviet periodicals to the library, and the Institute faculty found itself under assault by the conservative press and under scrutiny by the House Un-American Activities Committee. Hazard and Simmons were each labeled "a member of the Communist conspiracy" by Senator Joseph McCarthy himself. Belknap recalls Simmons "standing up in class and saying, 'Yesterday was an extraordinary day for me. I was roundly attacked on the front page of *Pravda* and on the floor of the United States Senate.'" Moreover, when Hazard was called to testify before HUAC on Lend-Lease activities during the war, he instead found himself being interrogated about why he had gone to the Soviet Union in the 1930s to study. In order to obtain a new passport, he was forced to submit an affidavit, prepared by a Columbia University lawyer, avowing that he had never been a Communist. The noted scholar and Russian Institute graduate Stephen Cohen has described a "poisonous atmosphere of witch-hunt in the educational profession" at the time. This certainly took a toll on the Institute community. Marshall Shulman recalls that students became more circumspect out of concern that open expression of political opinions might affect their recommendation letters and job prospects. "There were a lot of passions raised in that period," he says. "Some were raised in ignorance and . . . over-excitement, given the political context." Shulman nonetheless concludes that "the good thing about the environment of Columbia is that I came to feel that it protected me. . . . The university did, for the most part, protect students so they weren't subject to undue political pressures."

THE LEGACY OF THE EARLY YEARS

Despite the renown of its early faculty members, the institute was never a "think tank" with a strict research program, largely because the faculty were too involved in teaching and curriculum development. Nonetheless, the "Studies of the Russian Institute" series, initially funded by the second major grant from the Rockefeller Foundation and continuing to the present day as "Studies of the Harriman Institute," has sponsored over 130 volumes by Institute faculty, alumni, and fellows. Throughout its six decades, the Institute has played a leading role in shaping U.S.-Russia relations and area studies in the United States primarily through its graduates, who have included U.S. ambassadors to Moscow Walter Stoessel, Jack Matlock, and Alexander Vershbow, Secretary of State Madeline Albright, and Marshall Shulman, who served as special assistant to Secretary of State Dean Acheson in the early 1950s and as special adviser to his successors Cyrus Vance and Edmund Muskie in the late 1970s, with the rank of ambassador. The Institute has also produced human rights activists, business leaders, and, last but hardly least, many of the foremost academic specialists in the region across the disciplinary spectrum, including the Slavists Edward J. Brown, Victor Erlich, Rufus W. Mathewson Jr., and Robert A. Maguire, the social scientists Stephen Cohen, Alexander Dallin, Ronald Grigor Suny, and the Central Asia specialist Edward Allworth.

AFTER THE FALL

In 1982, in gratitude for a generous gift from Ambassador Averell Harriman and his wife, Pamela, the institute was renamed the W. Averell Harriman Institute for

Mikhail Gorbachev

Advanced Study of the Soviet Union. By the end of the *glasnost* period, the Institute's reputation under its new name was so well established that, upon the collapse of the Soviet Union, the faculty decided to shorten the name to the Harriman Institute. With the demise of the enormous empire it was established to study and the consequent end of the Cold War, the Institute faced—and, over a decade later, continues to face—the greatest challenge in its history: how to retool the original model of area studies to serve in a globalizing world? Rather than retreating to the study of Russia narrowly conceived, the Institute reaffirmed its commitment to the study of the entire area occupied by the former Soviet republics and in 1997 merged with the Institute for East Central Europe. The Institute continues to fund courses, conferences, and lectures devoted to its ever more diverse region.

In an address at the annual dinner of the Russian Institute in 1954, Columbia's bicentennial year, Ambassador Harriman cautioned that, "Some of the greatest mistakes of judgment have been made by experts in a single field who do not see or know the wider problems—experts in one area of the world or one aspect of life. Mistakes can also result from undue concentration on one element of the many-sided problem we face or on one means of handling it." For all the changes the Institute, its region, and its constituent disciplines have undergone in the intervening years, the commitment to an integrated method of study remains unaltered. Reaching across the boundaries of nations, cultures, and fields of study, this interdisciplinary and comparative approach will underlie the Institute's response in the years ahead.

A Communitarian at Large

—ɱ—

Wm. Theodore de Bary

Without question the last word in Living Legacies *at Columbia rightly belongs to Wm. Theodore de Bary. His inspiration has given the project its life over the past seven years, and his lens—intellectual, academic, and personal—has provided its focus. Many of the distinguished authors in this volume are his personal colleagues and friends, and it was his command of twentieth-century Columbia and his intellectual ambition that brought the number of essays in the series to more than fifty ("What about Eli Ginzberg? . . . Surely we need Dewey!").*

But surely we need de Bary! The story of Columbia's provost emeritus, an alumnus of the College and faculty member for over fifty-five years, is quintessential Columbia.

*First, we think of his scholarship. As author, editor, and teacher, de Bary has introduced the field of Asian humanities to the United States. His editions of classic Asian masterworks in translation (*Sources of Chinese Tradition, Sources of Japanese Tradition, *and analogous volumes for Korea and India) have reached generations of Western students and scholars, even as his critical interpretations have placed Asian ideals in a comparative perspective. Throughout, his scholarly focus has remained the development of neo-Confucianism in China, Japan, and Korea in a distant age when, as in our own, public intellectuals and civic culture played a major role. In his own odyssey through the twentieth century and its conflicts—Depression-era radicalism, World War II, the Vietnam War era, the culture wars—de Bary has epitomized the humanist scholar as citizen—erudite, engaged, and committed to truth over ideology. A lecture title from the 1960s, "Education for a World Community," captures his humanist world view, one that avoids the stridencies of partisanship and nationalism and emphasizes both the particulars defining the world's cultures and the universals connecting them. It is a stance more timely than ever today as American universities and American society adapt to global change.*

Next, there is his citizenship. Columbia has been this communitarian's academic community since the 1930s, when he arrived on campus from Leonia, New Jersey, with dorm-room linens sewn by Mrs. Harold Urey, a neighbor and the wife of Columbia's Nobel laureate chemist. In the account below we follow de Bary through nearly seventy years on Morningside, from Butler to Bollinger. There's the student shaped by campus encounters with Harry Carman and Raymond Weaver and Harlem encounters with Louis Armstrong and Father Divine. We see him introducing East Asia to the Core Curriculum as a junior professor, serving as chair of East Asian Languages and Cultures, and then assuming a broader administrative role—in the University Senate in Columbia's reconstruction period after the campus wars of the late 1960s, as provost during the 1970s, and—in a calmer time—as the director of the Heyman Center and founder of the Society of Senior Scholars. This program continues to bring some of Columbia's most distinguished faculty emeriti into the undergraduate classroom each semester. Throughout the decades, de Bary has passionately and thoughtfully upheld the place of general education at the undergraduate level within the research university.

The idyll at the end of "A Communitarian at Large" should not be taken too literally. Emeritus or not, de Bary still teaches more classes than most on the active faculty, and in 2004 Harvard University Press published his Nobility and Civility: Asian Ideals of Leadership and the Common Good.

Here, then, is de Bary on de Bary, the coda to his latest anthology, which could well have been called Sources of Columbia Tradition.

—*Jerry Kisslinger*

—॥—

I f I speak of myself here as a communitarian, it owes much, I believe, to the town I grew up in and later to the larger world communities I grew into. Leonia, New Jersey, where I got my start, was sometimes called a bedroom community for Columbia faculty, across the Hudson from Morningside Heights. It was, however, more than just a commuter town. Leonia had a strong civic sense and many community organizations—church, school, cultural, political, charitable—as well as a lively consumer cooperative supported by volunteer activity. As a boy I took much of this for granted and did not fully appreciate, until leaving it for other parts, how much this very civic community had contributed to my formation.

What I did realize at the time was the difference such a setting could make to a family in straitened circumstances like my own. My mother, a former newspaperwoman, had become a single parent and sole support not only of her own five children but of three of her sister's. She did this, besides fulfilling her strong role as a parent, by working as a local correspondent for the county newspaper and then as editor of the hometown paper. She did it also, however, with the help of many good neighbors, including Columbia families, and some contribution from the odd jobs we children took on—in my case lawn mowing, gardening, car washing, paper delivery, and assisting a milkman delivering from an old-style horse-drawn wagon. We were a tight-knit family. Nothing I might say here could express how much my older brother and younger sisters meant to me.

We all worked hard, but this did not interfere with a normal childhood and schooling, including for me a wide range of extracurriculars (baseball manager, head of the debating club, student council). But in those Depression years (1929–1937), I also became exposed to political currents of the time and susceptible to socialist ideas and pacifism. Together with a neighbor, Bob Alexander, I carried on a local branch (or perhaps I should say a "two-boy twig") of the Young People's Socialist League, associated with the American Socialist Party of Eugene Debs and Norman Thomas. (See Alexander's recollection of Frank Tanenbaum on p. 495.) I remember, at age thirteen, attending a campaign rally for Thomas's presidential candidacy in 1932; marching up Seventh Avenue in an antiwar parade in New York; visiting the headquarters of left wing (IWW) and labor movements off Union Square; and meeting with Carlo Tresca, the Italian syndicalist in exile and editor of *Il Martello* (later assassinated, it was said, by an agent of either Mussolini or Stalin). We also rented out for the night an empty storefront room for meetings to which we invited speakers from the city like Bayard Rustin, the black labor and political leader; the socialist economist Harry Laidler; the theologian Reinhold Niebuhr; the early environmentalist Scott Nearing; and an IRA revolutionary whom I remember especially for his brogue and frequent incantation "comes the rewolt." Ours was distinctly a penurious project, however, and that we could carry it on at all testified to the personal generosity of the speakers and also, no doubt, to their amusement at the political precocity and jejune idealism of the boys who invited them.

This rather offbeat activity did not interfere with a more conventional life in school and community. When it came time for me to deliver a valedictory address on graduation from high school, instead of pushing my own political agenda, I chose a more middle-of-the-road theme dealing with foreign policy and the need for a competent foreign service. (If this sounds a bit stuffy, I should note that the evening before at Class Night I had impersonated Ella Fitzgerald singing "Shine.") Still, my choice of topic gives an early intimation of the broader world outlook that I would carry with me to college.

COLLEGE YEARS AT COLUMBIA

When I was offered a virtually full scholarship to Columbia, I quickly accepted it. In fact I applied nowhere else, disdaining other Ivy League colleges as "elitist" or as "country club" schools, in which a young "proletarian" like myself would be a misfit. When I went off to college, however, I was made at home in the new community by friends from the old: Mrs. Harold Urey, wife of the Nobel Prize–winning chemist at Columbia, whose lawn and gardens I had taken care of, made a matching set of curtains and bedcover for my dorm room in John Jay Hall.

The eagerness with which I embraced the new learning opportunity at Columbia is shown by my response to the challenge issued by my teacher Harry Carman in my first Contemporary Civilization class. "You realize," he said, "that we are just dealing here with civilization in the West. What we need are young people who will prepare themselves to include Asia in this program." Columbia being one of the very few schools offering Chinese language courses at that time, I could take up Carman's challenge by starting the study of Chinese and subsequently directing my history major toward East Asia. For most of my fellow students, however, who had not heard Carman on the subject, my going off on this Chinese and Asian tangent seemed distinctly odd.

Fortunately for me the College did not require a strict major but had a "maturity credit" system that allowed one to range widely over the humanities and social sciences. Thus I benefited from fine teachers like Raymond Weaver and Moses Hadas (in the honors course known as the Colloquium), Ernest Nagel in philosophy, and Carlton Hayes and Jacques Barzun in European history. Others whose courses I did not take were also my teachers in a broader sense: I read Mark Van Doren, Lionel Trilling, and Joseph Wood Krutch (nature writer as well as drama critic) simply because they were part of the College culture.

A distinct part of that culture for me in the late thirties was Harlem. I had a summer job at Lenox Avenue and 124th Street, and spent much time at the Apollo Theater and Savoy Ballroom, listening to Louis Armstrong, Count Basie, Duke Ellington, and the like. At other times I went with the Catholic chaplain, Father George B. Ford, who used to take students to visit the revival meetings at the Harlem church of Father Divine.

Again there was time in college for extracurriculars, as comanager of the Debate Council (which conducted a radio program, *Public Discussion Forum*, Saturdays on WOR), as president of a campus service society, and eventually as chairman of the student government in 1940 and 1941. I was also involved with the humor magazine *Jester*, or perhaps I should say with a succession of *Jester* editors from Edward Rice and Robert Gerdy (later a *New Yorker* editor) to the poets Robert Lax and Thomas Merton (a few years older, but still part of the "Jester crowd" on campus). Our common interests ranged from jazz to the literary and religious (in Merton's case, to Dorothy Day, the Catholic Worker movement, and pacifism).

*From left to right: de
Bary, Otis Cary, and
Donald Keene, at
Nuuanu Valley,
Honolulu, Hawaii,
1943.*

Political developments overtook most of these cultural activities. During the civil
war in Spain, most socialists and many liberals joined the United Front movement in
support of the Loyalists, only to be left, as George Orwell was, with a bitter experience of collaboration with the Communists. But the great shock for us came in 1939
with the Molotov-Ribbentrop Pact, the agreement between the Soviets and the Nazis
that left Hitler free to concentrate on attacking Britain and the Jews. Overnight the
student movement "against war and Fascism" was turned by the Communists into one
of disengagement from "Imperialist Britain," a move allied on the far right to America
First isolationism. The question of Britain's survival, standing alone under Hitler's
attack in the Battle for Britain, gave "antiwar" people something to think about. Some
of my most admired teachers, like Carlton Hayes, Allen Nevins, and Reinhold
Niebuhr, became leaders in the Committee to Defend America by Aiding the Allies,
and I too became persuaded of the need actively to resist Hitler. I should note also
that as a regular reader of *The Partisan Review* and *The Nation*, I followed a similar evolution in the thinking of the Trillings, both Lionel and Diana.

De Bary and his future wife, Fanny Brett (left), with unidentified fellow revellers, Dean's Drag, 1940

At this juncture Eleanor Roosevelt, who had long been close to the student movement, sent Joseph Lash, a junior associate of hers and former student antiwar leader at City College, to visit me as chairman of the College student government and enlist me in the cause of organizing student support for aid to Britain (the Lend-Lease Act). At her invitation I attended a meeting at the White House and joined in that effort.

Just as I was about to graduate, the situation changed again when Hitler turned on Stalin and directed his armies eastward. At that point I received a traveling fellowship from Columbia normally used for study at Oxford or Cambridge, obviously not feasible at the time. When I reconciled myself to graduate study at Harvard instead, in the fall of 1941, I did not realize how much I would benefit from the teaching of a young scholar there in Japanese studies, Edwin Reischauer. Up to that time my work had been mostly on the China side (with strong pro-Chinese, anti-Japanese prejudices on my part), but Reischauer, from a family of missionaries to Japan, was aware of the great contribution Japanese scholars had made to the study of China and taught a general course embracing all of East Asia. This was my introduction to the idea of an East Asian community as a larger context in which to study

China, and when I was asked much later (1982) to inaugurate the Reischauer Lectureship at Harvard, I was glad to acknowledge my debt to its namesake.

WORLD WAR II IN THE PACIFIC

Before the end of my first semester at Harvard, the Japanese attacked Pearl Harbor (December 7, 1941). I was recruited into Naval Intelligence and went on to further study of the Japanese language at Berkeley. It was in Berkeley that I first met Donald Keene, but it was on the move of the language school to Boulder that I married my college sweetheart, the most beautiful and charming girl I had ever seen when I first met her at a Barnard tea dance in the fall of 1939. I am glad to report now that we celebrated our sixtieth wedding anniversary at St. Paul's Chapel in June 2002, with our four children and ten grandchildren.

From Boulder, Keene and I were shipped out to Pearl Harbor, which remained our permanent station for almost three years while we were sent on different campaigns to the Aleutians, mid-Pacific, and Okinawa. These experiences again broadened my experience of Asia. Our unexpected involvement with Korean labor forces serving the Japanese in the mid-Pacific prompted me to start the study of Korean (and thus include Korea in my growing conception of an East Asian community). Also fateful was my discovery of a Japanese book, knocked off the shelves of a wrecked Okinawan home, entitled *The Culture of the Ryukyu Islands (Ryukyu no bunka)* and edited by Yanagi Soetsu, head of the Japanese Folk Art Museum, who opened my eyes in that book to the distinctive culture and crafts of the Ryukyus and also to the folk arts of Japan, which became a lifelong interest.

After the Japanese surrender, ironically enough, Donald (the specialist par excellence in Japanese) was sent with the Marines to Tsingdao and Beijing, while I went to Sasebo, Japan, and Tokyo with a technical survey mission. We agreed to keep a file of our letters recording our firsthand experiences of China and Japan. The project was later expanded to include letters from other friends in similar situations. Eventually one of them, Otis Cary at Amherst House in Kyoto, had them translated and published in Japanese, and the success of that project prompted Kodansha to publish the original English version under the title of *War-Wasted Asia* (1975, later changed to *Letters from a Ruined Empire*). Anyone now interested in my observations on the occupation of Japan in the fall of 1945 can find them there.

From Tokyo I was reassigned to the Office of Naval Intelligence in Washington, where I served as head of the Far Eastern desk in the spring and summer of 1946. On demobilization I was given to believe that I could transfer to the State

Department at a rank roughly equivalent to my Navy one (lieutenant commander), which would have meant a much more comfortable life for Fanny and our new family. But she supported my earlier aim of an academic career, so I returned to graduate study at Columbia on a $1,500 fellowship and the GI Bill. During this period (1946–1951) we lived in a converted army barracks at Camp Shanks in Orangeburg, New York, a community of young veterans' families, where much of the life was shared, including a very active consumer cooperative, a cooperative garden, a community association, and a car pool to Morningside Heights.

GRADUATE STUDIES

My graduate studies were mainly directed toward a Ph.D. in Chinese, but the influence of Ryūsaku Tsunoda further expanded the East Asian dimensions of my work. As a product of Meiji-period Japan, Tsunoda had a deep knowledge not only of Japanese history, literature, and religion, but also of the classical Chinese studies that were still a part of Japanese education in the late nineteenth century (as they were not of my post-1911-Revolution teachers in Chinese history and literature). His influence led me to take a master's degree in Japanese studies, especially in thought and religion as well as literature, and greatly expanded my awareness of Japanese studies in Chinese philosophy and Buddhism.

This in turn strengthened my desire to get inside the Chinese tradition in the same way. I had already become highly skeptical of the prevailing Marxist (or pseudo-Marxist) views of Chinese history and society based on a unilinear Western model and was determined to suspend all Western preconceptions of the same until I could see things from the inside, from a mature, premodern, Chinese perspective. This I found, first of all, in my study of Huang Zongxi's *Waiting for the Dawn* (*Mingyi daifanglu*, 1662), which offered a critique of Chinese dynastic history from the Confucian point of view, and secondly from Huang's work as an intellectual historian of the period from 1000 to 1650 in China. In the process I had to do much reading in the original sources of neo-Confucianism as well as in the institutional histories of China essential to understanding *Waiting for the Dawn*.

From 1948 to 1949 I continued my doctoral research in Beijing; this gave me a matchless opportunity to observe what was left of the old China and to make the acquaintance of leading Chinese scholars, like Hu Shih, Fung Yu-lan (both former students of John Dewey's), and, later in Canton, Chien Mu, Liang Fangzhong, Tang Zhunyi, and Wing-tsit Chan. This experience made it possible for me to "exile" myself from Western preconceptions about China and Asia and to become much more self-conscious about Western, especially "modernist," assumptions implicitly accepted by many Marxists and neo-Marxists (as well as "postmodernists").

A senior Chinese associate of mine at Columbia in the fifties and sixties, Chiang Yee, wrote a series of books on life in the West as seen by an exile from China. Yee called himself "The Silent Traveler"—a way of registering the cultural distance he felt, as a classically educated poet and artist, from the Western cities he was viewing and appreciating with some interior reserve. I thought of myself in much the same way vis-à-vis both the West and Asia and once hoped to write a book, "The Silent Traveler at Home," to convey the sense of interior distance I felt from my own culture, my own place and time in the West, observing them from an Asian standpoint. Such a project would not, however, have been at the expense of my remaining humanist, religious, communitarian, and ecological views, any more than Chiang Yee, in his books, had divested himself of his classical Chinese sensibilities.

ASIA IN THE COLUMBIA CURRICULUM

I had hardly returned from China in 1949 when Harry Carman, now dean of the College, asked me (even before I had finished my dissertation) to lead a new program to incorporate Asia in the College's Core Curriculum. I agreed and undertook to teach Asian parallels to the Western Civilization and Humanities courses and to develop suitable texts and translations. Thus began a ten-year program to compile six volumes (now ten and still counting) of source readings: *Sources of Japanese Tradition, Sources of Chinese Traditions,* and *Sources of Indian Traditions* (eventually extended to include Korean and Tibetan sources). Although designed for general education, these pioneering efforts quickly came into wide use on even advanced levels of education.

This series was soon supplemented by another, *Translations from the Asian Classics,* providing whole works for use in the Humanities course. These eventually came to more than fifty volumes, along with several parallel texts on the history of Asian traditions. Conferences in the fifties and sixties, sponsored by the Carnegie Corporation and the Association of American Colleges, introduced these materials to American college presidents and deans. At the inception of the National Defense Education Act, I gave a keynote speech at a Princeton conference that emphasized that the larger interests of the United States would be better served by a broad humanities approach to other civilizations than by the narrower "language and area studies" approach. My speech, entitled "Education for a World Community," was later published in *Liberal Education* (December 1964). In contrast to the original "national defense" emphasis, the early development of the NDEA program under Donald Bigelow was, I believe, influenced by this humanistic perspective, which also contrasted with the strategic area studies approach favored by the Ford Foundation in its support of foreign policy and security-oriented area studies at other major universities.[1]

These same humanistic aims informed my administration as chairman of the Department of Chinese and Japanese (later extended to East Asian Languages and Cultures) in the 1960s. This period saw the relocation of the department and East Asian Library to more spacious quarters in Kent Hall, my initiatives to establish the University Seminars on Asian Thought and Religion and on neo-Confucianism, and the project to compile the *Dictionary of Ming Biography* (edited by L. Carrington Goodrich and Chao-ying Fang).

In all of these activities on behalf of general education—which is necessarily a collegial enterprise, a matter of teamwork—I incurred obligations to many coworkers and collaborators, too numerous to mention here. Among them, however, no one was more important than Donald Keene. By the mid-fifties he had already established himself as a leading scholar of Japanese literature and teacher at Cambridge University, but when I asked him to return to Columbia he readily agreed to join me in these new ventures. We have been close colleagues and even closer friends ever since.

At the end of this period (the 1960s) I was elected president of the Association of Asian Studies and gave an address dealing with the political role and responsibilities of a scholarly membership organization at the height of the "Vietnam crisis." In the face of demands that the Association itself take an official stand against the war, I pointed out that the group's charter identified it as a nonpolitical organization and argued that the Association should be "nonpolitical but not unconcerned," that is, it should serve proactively as an open forum for the expression of different scholarly views on major political issues (*Journal of Asian Studies* 39, no. 4, August 1970).

In 1966 to 1967 I spent a long-deferred sabbatical leave doing research in Kyoto and Taipei, to follow up on the work started in Beijing and Canton much earlier, which could only be pursued part-time in the above-mentioned seminars and in scholarly conferences that I arranged as chair of the Committee on Chinese Thought of the American Council of Learned Societies. The published outcome of these efforts was the volumes *Self and Society in Ming Thought* (1970), *The Unfolding of Neo-Confucianism* (1975), and *Principle and Practicality* (1979), all of them centered on issues of the self, community, and the state in different phases of the neo-Confucian movement in China and Japan.

CRISIS IN THE COLUMBIA COMMUNITY

Hardly had I returned from my sabbatical in the fall of 1967 when I was asked to serve as dean of the College. No administrative position would have meant more to me than this, but having spent so much of my time on program administration in the fifties and sixties, I declined lest my own scholarly work be put off again indefinitely. The subsequent course of political events, however, made me wonder if I had not made a mistake. The riots of the spring of 1968 forced me out of my study and into a much larger university involvement. I participated in numerous faculty meetings attempting to deal with the political crisis and negotiate a peaceful resolution of the issues. At one meeting of the entire university faculty, an executive committee was established to represent the faculty vis-à-vis the students and administration, and I was asked to accept nomination as representative of the Faculty of Philosophy. I reluctantly agreed, thinking that there would be few other volunteers in such a politically charged atmosphere; put simply, I thought "someone had to do it." To my surprise, when the ballot reached me I found that Lionel Trilling was also listed as a candidate—someone I would certainly have deferred to had I known in advance. But since I fully expected him to win, it relieved me to think of this as a reprieve. Unfortunately, in the final count I was elected and thus was launched on a new career.

The executive committee of the faculty brought some stability to the campus, but its principal function became to draw up, in consultation with the trustees, a plan for a new university senate. A main feature of the plan, and one which I strongly backed, was that this senate would represent not just faculty but all the main constituencies of the university: administration, faculty (tenured and nontenured), students, staff, and alumni. This plan was adopted and the University Senate came into being in 1969. I was elected to it as a faculty member and then chosen as chairman of the executive committee—in effect the responsible leader of the senate.

The main work of this new body during my chairmanship (1969–71) was to restore order to the university and act on demands for reform put forward during the crisis. One of these was for a new set of rules of university conduct and discipline that would be backed by the authority of faculty and students, and not just by a reputedly "repressive" administration (which by this time had been largely discredited in the eyes of all, left and right). Another action was the adoption of a new university calendar, henceforth to break over the Christmas and New Year holidays, instead of at the end of January—a system that has remained substantially in effect ever since. Still another step was the adoption of a new set of rules and procedures for tenuring faculty—a key issue in regard to academic freedom.

Students occupy a building during the campus unrest of 1968.

Among the many issues addressed in my 1971 report on the senate's first two years was the question of the status of the university chaplain (traditionally an Episcopalian priest) of St. Paul's Chapel and of the Earl Hall headquarters of the religious counselors. During the disturbances, radicals had occupied the chapel and Earl Hall, and the chaplain himself had walked off the job. We appointed a committee to decide what to do with the radical squatters and how to reorganize religious activities on campus. The committee's recommendation was for a nondenominational directorship of Earl Hall, with a policy-making board representing the various religious counselors. As to the question of what to do with St. Paul's Chapel, the recommendation to restore it to its religious functions, rather than let it go on as the headquarters of a political underground, came at a climactic meeting of the committee in which the anthropologist Margaret Mead made the decisive statement: "Every community needs a sacred space." This authoritative judgment from the reigning culture guru, respected by young and old alike, cleared the way for senate passage of a recommendation to restore the chapel to its religious functions.

The significance of these "peace-keeping" efforts on the campus may be lost on anyone who did not live through those violent days—a violence inflicted on Columbia not only by a small minority of its own students but by revolutionaries from other campuses who converged on Morningside Heights to occupy buildings and disrupt all normal academic functions. Because I continued to meet with my classes during a strike that was euphemistically called "a moratorium on classes," I was attacked as a "liberal Fascist" and my office in Kent Hall was ransacked. My daughter Catherine, a student at Barnard, was roughed up by bullies (often referred to more benignly as "picketers") when she tried to come and see me. Other faculty, both senior and junior, were subject to similar intimidation (see Robert Ball's essay on Gilbert Highet). Often we were lucky just to complete a meeting of the University Senate without disruption. One who has not witnessed the fragility of academic institutions—the soft underbelly of democracy so dependent on the restraints of ordinary civility and rational discourse—would have difficulty understanding what it took to survive all this. But eventually, by the patient, unspectacular work of committed faculty, students, and staff, order was restored.

By this time the struggle to save the university had so engaged me that despite my aversion to more administrative work, I agreed in 1971 to serve as vice president for academic affairs and provost. I need not dwell on the challenge the chief academic officer faced: the unprecedentedly large deficit the university was running, the intense competition for scarce resources, the political problems attaching to our dependence on state and federal funding, the disaffection of many alumni from what they saw as a weak-willed administration and self-indulgent faculty, and so on.

Here I would rather speak of a few good things that my colleagues and I tried to do. First of all was the prompt, efficient conduct of ordinary business, including budgeting, fund-raising, and faculty recruitment, appointments, and promotions. A matter I gave special attention to was faculty meetings that would actually face up to the responsibilities of educational policymaking (as compared to airing petty grievances or sitting through long-winded political speeches). Simply to preside at so many meetings, uptown and downtown, was a great burden on my time, but I considered it essential to responsible university governance. One could not defend academic freedom on any front, left or right, if faculty members did not take responsibility for stating publicly the educational standards, policies, and program priorities they were ready to uphold. This could not be left to administrative decision.

Among the responsibilities reserved for the provost were difficult decisions about the future of several schools and programs. Dire as the university's financial situation had become by 1970, my predecessor as vice president and provost, Polykarp Kusch, concluded that Columbia was overstrained in its academic commitments, and he proposed a rigorous policy of excision in the name of "selective excellence." One school that he wanted to eliminate—Library Service—was already in trouble when I took over, though it hung on for two more decades. Another was International Affairs, a decision that would have meant abandoning Columbia's long-standing commitment to this broad field, so distinguished by the earlier leadership in world affairs of Nicholas Murray Butler, James T. Shotwell, and Philip Jessup. This was to me unthinkable, and I thought instead of how the School of International Affairs might be strengthened (as in time it certainly was). The School of the Arts was more problematical, but I asked my old mentor Jacques Barzun to head up a review committee, which concluded that the School of the Arts should be kept and that the arts should have a prominent place at Columbia.

Reid Hall in Paris was something else again—literally. It was the off-campus site of Columbia's only junior-year-abroad program but had been neglected during the years of crisis on Morningside, running a deficit the trustees felt the university could not afford. It was nevertheless a beautiful mansion and courtyard in a most desirable quarter of Paris, the sale of which the trustees thought could help offset Columbia's own deficit. Against this, I rallied faculty support for Reid Hall's retention and redevelopment, which was accomplished mainly through the superior management of a new director, Professor Danielle Haase-Dubosc of Barnard. It has since thrived as a major center for language study and research of many kinds—a great resource for students and faculty alike.

Two other programs presented different dilemmas. One was the fate of the Lamont-Doherty Geological Observatory in Palisades, New York, whose founding director, Maurice Ewing, had resigned after a bitter dispute with my predecessors. I spent much time with the scientists there and their foundation supporters, discussing the future of their work, and helped to keep the staff intact as a base for future development. Poignantly enough Ewing himself, the master builder, returned not long after; his dying request was to be buried on a slope across from the Observatory, in an old cemetery facing the Hudson.

Barnard was another case. Some of our deans thought that incorporating it more fully into the university would be a way to deal with demands for more coeducation and to streamline faculty deployment and student services. President McGill himself was inclined that way (favoring a Harvard/Radcliffe model), and my resistance to the idea did not help our personal relationship. Even talk of a takeover tended to poison our working relations with Barnard. To me it was politically impracticable, and, quite apart from my personal involvements (my wife and two daughters were alumnae), I believed that there was a place for a woman's college with its own history and autonomy. So indeed it has remained.

Even in that difficult climate there were opportunities for innovative educational programs. In the early 1970s the provost's office assisted University Professor Louis Henkin in developing a pioneering program in studies in human rights. The Society of Fellows in the Humanities, a new program for postdoctoral teaching fellows with major support from the Mellon Foundation, was closely tied to instruction in the interdisciplinary Core Curriculum. The General Education Seminars, a series of weekly luncheon sessions at the Kellogg Center, were based on the idea that core curricula should not be confined to the early undergraduate years, but should be carried on into graduate and professional school programs.

Other administrative offices reporting to the provost faced different challenges. In 1971 to 1972 we were threatened with a cutoff of all federal funds if we did not have an officially approved affirmative action program. Thanks to skillful negotiations with Washington conducted by deputy provost James Young, we succeeded in meeting the federal requirements without adopting a numerical quota system or compromising any academic standards. Essentially the same system has remained in effect ever since. And at the request of Athletic Director Al Paul, I formulated a statement of university policy affirming the educational and cocurricular values of physical education, intramural sports, varsity athletics, and club sports. It is my understanding that good use is still made of this statement, thirty years later, by the staff and coaches of the program, through good seasons and bad. My final academic budget was in balance. A more complete account of this period can be found in my final report as provost (August 19, 1978).

I had been conscious throughout my provostship of the danger it held for my primary work as a scholar and teacher. Aware that only one of my predecessors (Barzun) had succeeded in returning to the classroom and to productive scholarship, I kept my hand in by continuing to teach one course (alternating Chinese Thought and Japanese Thought) first thing Monday morning. The rest of the week was mostly downhill. Nevertheless my retirement proved somewhat bittersweet. I had enjoyed working with many fine people and could not help feeling a certain nostalgia, wondering how things would work out for the projects we had launched together.

BACK TO TEACHING AND RESEARCH

Immediately on leaving the provostship I spent a year in research at Kyoto University and the National Central Library in Taiwan. By the end of 1979 China had opened up again, after a long stretch, dating back to 1949, during which I had been persona non grata to Beijing because of my criticism of Mao and, later, the Cultural Revolution. Now I was able to revisit my old haunts but unfortunately found that few of my old friends had survived "anti-rightist" attacks on "bourgeois" scholars.

My scholarly work for the next ten years (1979–89) focused mostly on issues I had addressed earlier: the nature of the self, self-cultivation, and personhood in neo-Confucianism, especially the forms of spirituality and religious dimensions, long ignored, and the relation of these to ecology, public philosophy, and civil society. Apart from the specific studies I produced,[2] my general conclusions were published in endowed lectureships that I was invited to give at other universities and later were translated into Chinese, Japanese, and Korean. I was the first Westerner invited to give the Chien Mu Lectureship at the Chinese University of Hong Kong, honoring a distinguished Chinese scholar who had kept Confucian studies alive at the New Asia College (a university in exile, somewhat like the New School in New York) during the same period when I had been trying to develop them at Columbia; his studies in Song-Ming intellectual history had been a great help to me. My lectures there were published under the title *The Liberal Tradition in China*—an idea shocking to many who had thought of Confucianism only as conservative, failing to recognize the potential for self-criticism, self-renewal, and regeneration within the tradition.

I broadened this line of thought further when I inaugurated the Reischauer Lectureship at Harvard, offering an overall conspectus on the major stages in the development of East Asian civilization that was published by Harvard University Press as *East Asian Civilizations* and extended it again in the 1988 Tanner Lectures at the University of California, Berkeley. These were published as *The Trouble with Confucianism* (Harvard 1991), by which I meant to suggest the conflicted character of Confucian reformist ideals as they became distorted, misappropriated, or vitiated in unfavorable historical circumstances. I elaborated still further on this theme in *Asian Values and Human Rights, A Confucian Communitarian Perspective*, a book based on my Wing-tsit Chan Lectures at the University of Hawaii, 1997, and on a paper delivered at a conference on civil society sponsored by Pope John Paul II at Castel Gandolfo, 1989, which discussed the Confucians' difficulties in developing a mid-level civil infrastructure linking family-based local communities vertically to the higher levels of imperial bureaucratic rule. The last stage in this series of general

essays is *Nobility and Civility: Asian Ideals of Leadership and the Common Good* (Harvard, 2004), which ranges broadly over Indian, Chinese, and Japanese civilizations (ancient, medieval, and modern) and considers how these ideal values became contested and conflicted in the course of history.

In the midst of all this I managed, at long last, to revise my original doctoral dissertation on Huang Zongxi's critique of China's dynastic rule, translated by me under the title *Waiting for the Dawn*. The dissertation was finally published in 1993, forty years after I had defended it.

COLUMBIA'S CORE CURRICULUM

During the late eighties the dean of Columbia College, Robert Pollack, asked me to chair a commission to review what had come to be known as the general education program, a term co-opted by Daniel Bell in the title of his 1967 book, *The Reform of General Education*. After a year's intensive discussion of the matter, this blue-ribbon committee of the College faculty reaffirmed the importance of the basic program and recommended strengthening it by adding courses in civilizations other than the Western. It also adopted the term "Core Curriculum" instead of "General Education," so as to emphasize the primary focus on central human concerns and avoid the generality and looseness that had become identified with the Harvard version of general education. By this time most academic disciplines were far out on the limbs of specialized research, aiming always to "go beyond" the beyond, with little attention to the educational trunk of the tree and its life-nourishing core.

Although our recommendations were approved by a formal vote of the College faculty that was never rescinded, what emerged later as the Major Cultures requirement offers a wide variety of courses, only one of which need be "a broad introductory course." It is essentially a distribution requirement without any core—a smorgasbord similar to the Harvard system. However the term "Core Curriculum" itself has stuck and is now the standard.

From 1979 to 1989 I continued to teach four courses per semester, two undergraduate Core courses and two graduate, plus evening colloquia for alumni. This has continued since my formal retirement in 1989 until the present. This pro bono volunteer work suggested to me the possibility of organizing a corps of other professors emeriti who would render this service through a Society of Senior Scholars at the Heyman Center for the Humanities. The Center had been launched while I was provost, initially to provide a home for the Society of Fellows in the Humanities, postdoctoral fellows who were teaching in the Core. But if there were retired professors who had long taught in Core courses, still able and willing to do this on a reduced, part-time schedule, it would make sense to organize and house them with the new postdoctoral fellows. This way the postdocs would benefit from the experience and established expertise of the senior scholars while the latter would enjoy the stimulation of working with young people. This idea particularly appealed to John Sawyer, president of the Mellon Foundation, who helped set up an endowment to support the program. Later, when an external review committee (Professors Jerome Schneewind of Johns Hopkins and David Bromwich of Yale) came to evaluate the work of the Heyman Center, they particularly noted the success of the program in bringing together scholars and students on several levels of age and experience.

When the Heyman Center was built in the late seventies, the combination of public rooms (designed for seminars and colloquia, not large lectures) surrounded by individual scholars' offices was admirably suited to the intimate discussion emphasized in the Columbia Core. But the architects' preferred materials were glass and steel (the "signature" of Gwathmey, Siegel), and I thought something was needed to offset their cold severity. I asked my old friend George Nakashima to design and make furniture in warm unfinished wood marked by the Japanese taste for the color and texture of natural grain and a simplicity matching but also balancing the architects' own chaste design. George was not then as famous as he became when discovered by wealthy connoisseurs like Nelson Rockefeller and the Metropolitan

Museum of Art, but his monumental seminar tables and graceful chairs, together with the *Peace Altar* that his studio produced for the second incarnation of St. Paul's Chapel, have made Columbia a major collector of Nakashima's work.

The Center's common room has proven to be a congenial setting for the fifty to sixty scholars assembled in the early summer of 2002, 2003, and 2004 for workshops on new multicultural approaches to the Core Curriculum, courses in which classics from the major world traditions, East and West, are discussed in relation to perennial themes of human civilization. These courses are intended for the junior/senior level of general education—i.e., for the Core extending beyond the first college years—and eventually for graduate and adult education. Already three semesters of such colloquia have been conducted with excellent results and warm enthusiasm on the part of all—college seniors, regular faculty, senior scholars, and postdoctoral fellows.

THE SILENT TRAVELER NOW AT HOME

As I write this final paragraph, having recently retired from the directorship of the Heyman Center, I expect to limit myself to part-time teaching of Asian humanities, especially in the company of old friends in the alumni colloquia. I should be spending more time at home, in the cooperative community Fanny and I joined more than fifty years ago in Rockland County and in the home that we named Hotokudō, the Japanese version of a Confucian concept that conveys the sense of "requiting kindness" or "blessings shared" (i.e., blessings received from one's forebears and shared with family, neighbors, and friends). This will give me more time to tend to my garden, cultivated over the years according to the natural and organic methods learned long ago from the Nearings and others. I look forward to continuing Sunday afternoon visits from Donald Keene. God willing, and the Buddha perhaps smiling on us as we sit in the garden, enjoying the glories of unspoiled nature in that sylvan setting, we may reminisce again about times past.

ABOUT THE EDITORS

—⚏—

In more than five decades on the Columbia University faculty, **Wm. Theodore de Bary,** John Mitchell Mason Professor Emeritus and provost emeritus of Columbia University, has won international regard as a scholar, author, and teacher who has introduced generations of Western students to Asian humanities. His scholarly work has focused on the major religions and intellectual traditions of East Asia, especially Confucianism in China, Japan, and Korea. He is widely credited with introducing the field of neo-Confucian studies to the United States while championing an entirely new vision of the place of Asia in a general education, including Columbia College's renowned Core Curriculum. The seminal series of readers (*Sources of Chinese Tradition, Sources of Japanese Tradition, Sources of Indian Tradition,* and *Sources of Korean Tradition*), for which he served as editor, have seen wide use in colleges and universities throughout the United States and abroad. Formally retired since 1989, as a volunteer teacher he continues to carry a full load of courses and seminars at Columbia University. In all he is the author or editor of more than twenty-five books, the most recent being *Nobility and Civility: Asian Ideals of Leadership and the Common Good* (Harvard University Press, 2004). Among his many honors and awards for teaching and scholarship was election to the American Academy of Arts and Sciences in 1974 and in 1999 to the American Philosophical Association.

Jerry Kisslinger is executive director of communications for development and alumni relations, Columbia University, and author of *The Serbian Americans.*

Tom Mathewson is manager of the Columbia University Senate and a freelance editor.

NOTES AND BIBLIOGRAPHIES

CHAPTER 2: GILBERT HIGHET AND CLASSICS AT COLUMBIA: BIBLIOGRAPHY

In general I have benefited from the Gilbert Highet Papers, in Columbia's Rare Book and Manuscript Library. The following bibliography consists of publications primarily by people who knew Highet and/or studied his work:

Ball, R. J., ed. *The Classical Papers of Gilbert Highet*. New York: Columbia University Press, 1983. See especially 13–14 for a full list of articles about Highet, and 349–78, for a full bibliography of his publications.

———. *The Unpublished Lectures of Gilbert Highet*. New York: Peter Lang Publishing, 1998.

Calder, W. M., III. "Gilbert Highet, Anthon Professor of Latin, Emeritus." *Classical World* 66 (1973): 385–87.

———. "Gilbert Highet," *Gnomon* 50 (1978): 430–32.

Campbell, B. "Gilbert Highet, Scholar and Poet, Dies of Cancer at the Age of 71." *The New York Times* (January 21, 1978): 24.

Crosby, J. "Mr. Highet Talks on Books." *The New York Herald Tribune* (May 21, 1952): 25.

Fadiman, C. "The Most Exclusive Lunch Club in Town." *Book-of-the-Month Club News* (April 1976): 6–8 (Special Fiftieth Anniversary Supplement).

Highet, Keith. "The Military Career of Gilbert Highet." *Classical World* 95 (2002): 386–409.

Stephenson, W., ed. *British Security Coordination: The Secret History of British Intelligence in the Americas, 1940–1945.* New York: Fromm International, 1999, especially x–xi, for Highet's role in this project.

Suits, T. A. "Gilbert Highet." In *Classical Scholarship: A Biographical Encyclopedia*, ed. W. W. Briggs and W. M. Calder III. New York: Garland, 1990, 183–91.

———. "Gilbert Highet." In *American National Biography*, ed. J. A. Garraty and M. C. Carnes. New York: Oxford University Press, 1999, vol. 10, pp. 760–61.

Wilson, Elena, ed. *Edmund Wilson: Letters on Literature and Politics (1912–1972)*. New York: Farrar Straus and Giroux, 1977, especially 456–60, on *The Classical Tradition*, and 505, on the radio lecture about Wilson.

CHAPTER 8: THE MANY LIVES OF PAUL OSKAR KRISTELLER: NOTES

1. The typescript survives in the Paul Oskar Kristeller Collection in Columbia's Rare Book and Manuscript Library.

2. His practicing is mentioned in the *Pisaner Tagebuch*, ed. P. E. Hübinger (Heidelberg-Darmstadt, 1961), pp. 22–23, of the brilliant young German student of Romance literature Karl Eugen Gass, destined to die on the Russian front, who spent some time at the Scuola Normale Superiore: "The German instructor is Chr. [Gass's code name for Kristeller to circumvent the Nazi censors]. At midday one finds him upstairs playing the piano . . . Only one window shutter is open and through it a bright beam of sunlight falls on the wall and on the piano at which the solitary player sits. He plays quite well even if faultily every now and then. But he played this midday Bach's Fugues and Preludes with astonishing power and clarity and a feel for the melodic lines. The next day, he played Mozart."

3. *Reminiscences of Paul Oskar Kristeller (1981–1982)*, 66, in the Oral History Collection of Columbia University.

4. Kristeller had also once toyed with the idea of becoming a professional mathematician. See his *Life of Learning*, (New York: American Council of Learned Societies, 1990), 5–6, for an amusing account of how he was disabused of this idea by his experience in a mathematics seminar at Heidelberg.

5. I owe this anecdote to Robert Somerville of Columbia's history and religion departments. The only published

specimens of Kristeller's poetry that I know of appear at the start of the first two volumes of his *Iter Italicum*.

6. See the frontispiece of *Supplementum Festivum: Studies in Honor of Paul Oskar Kristeller*, ed. J. Hankins, J. Monfasani, and F. Purnell Jr. (Binghamton, NY: Medieval & Renaissance Texts & Studies, 1987). See also the photographs in Paul Oskar Kristeller and Margaret L. King, "Iter Kristellerianum: The European Journey (1905–1939)," *Renaissance Quarterly* 47 (1994): 907–29. Only in the picture of him with his glasses on at the Scuola Normale Superiore in Pisa would his American students easily recognize their maestro. See also *Rifugio precario. Zuflucht auf Widerruf: Artisti e intellettuali tedeschi in Italia 1933–1945. Deutsche Künstler und Wissenschaftler in Italien* (Milan, 1995), 187, Plates 129–131.

7. Eugene F. Rice Jr. in the pamphlet "Paul Oskar Kristeller at Ninety, May 22–23, 1995" (New York: Columbia University, 1995), 12. The pamphlet commemorates Columbia's award of the Nicholas Murray Butler Medal in Gold to Kristeller.

8. I thank Marion Kuntz of Georgia State University for this information.

9. Bainton had never heard of Kristeller before he received a letter from Gentile's protégé Delio Cantimori asking for help. See *The Correspondence of Roland H. Bainton and Delio Cantimori 1932–1966: An Enduring Transatlantic Friendship between Two Historians of Religious Toleration*, ed. John Tedeschi (Florence, 2002), pp. 89–99, and passim.

10. Years ago, the classicist Berthe Marti told me a touching story about that day. The Yale professor of German literature Hermann Weigand and his wife met Kristeller at the pier and drove him to their home outside of New Haven, where he would stay while teaching the seminar. During the trip, Kristeller remained noncommunicative. When they opened the door to the house, he saw their piano, headed straight for it, played for two hours, and then, with the trauma of the experience assuaged, began to talk freely.

11. An even earlier work, his 1928 dissertation, also received good reviews and is still respectfully cited in the literature on Plotinus.

12. Reprinted several times, "The Modern System of the Arts" traced the emergence of the modern system of the five fine arts, ending with Kant, "the first major philosopher who included aesthetics and the philosophical theory of the arts as an integral part of his system."

13. A complete bibliography by a young German scholar, Thomas Gilbhard, is now in preparation.

14. The fifty-seven boxes of correspondence in the Kristeller Collection in Columbia's Rare Book and Manuscript Library certainly contain evidence of how much and often Kristeller assisted students and colleagues.

15. "Recollections of My Life," *European Legacy, Toward New Paradigms: Journal of the International Society for the Study of European Ideas* 1 (1996): 1863–78, 1866 (with the assistance of David Hollander).

16. *Reminiscences*, 654–55.

17. Frederick Purnell Jr. of Queens College relayed this comment to me.

18. This turn of phrase belonged to Kristeller's old friend Ronald Bainton, who used it to describe someone else in his *Roly: Chronicle of a Stubborn Non-Conformist*, (New Haven: Yale University Divinity School, [1988]), 13.

CHAPTER 10: THE "CONSCIENCE OF COLUMBIA": REMEMBERING MARJORIE HOPE NICOLSON, SCHOLAR AND TEACHER: NOTES

1. E. H. Wright to President Nicholas Murray Butler, January 12, 1940, Ernest Wright Central Files, University Records and Archives, Columbia University, New York (hereafter cited as Wright Central Files). For a useful bibliography, see *In Honor of Marjorie Hope Nicolson*, printed by Columbia University, February 17, 1962. The main source of information on Nicolson's life is an oral history. See "The

Reminiscences of Marjorie Hope Nicolson" (1975) in the Columbia University Oral History Collection (hereafter cited as MHN Oral History, CUOHROC). For a more detailed portrait of Nicolson's career and views on academic women, see Andrea Walton, "'Scholar,' 'Lady,' 'Best Man in the English Department'?: Recalling the Career of Marjorie Hope Nicolson", *History of Education Quarterly* 40 (Summer 2000): 169–200. The author would like to thank the *History of Education Quarterly* for permission to draw on material and reuse passages from this earlier article. Also, thank you to Professor Edward Tayler, who provided feedback on a late version of this essay.

2. For a complete bibliography, see *In Honor of Marjorie Hope Nicolson.*

3. Marjorie Hope Nicolson, "Scholars and Ladies," *Yale Review* 19 (June 1930): 794.

4. Marjorie Hope Nicolson, "The Romance of Scholarship," in *The Humanities at Scripps College* (Los Angeles: Ward Ritchie, 1952), 47–59; idem, "The Rights and Privileges Pertaining Thereto . . ." in *A University between Two Centuries*, ed. Wilfred B. Shaw, 403–26 (Ann Arbor: University of Michigan Press, 1937). See also MHN Oral History I, #1, 3, CUOHROC.

5. Edward W. Tayler, "In Memoriam: Marjorie Hope Nicolson (1894–1981)," *Journal of the History of Ideas* 42 (October–December 1981): 666. For student admiration of Nicolson's erudition, see AAUW award announcement, Box 952, Marjorie Hope Nicolson Papers, Smith College Archives (hereafter cited as Nicolson Papers).

6. See MHN Oral History I, #3, 83, CUOHROC. See also 83–84.

7. Tayler, "In Memoriam," 665. See also MHN Oral History, I, #3, 95, CUOHROC.

8. G. S. Rousseau, "Éloge," *Isis* 73 (March 1982): 98.

9. MHN Oral History II, #6, 178, CUOHROC.

10. Nicolson, "A Generous Education," *PMLA* 74 (March 1964): 6.

11. Marjorie Hope Nicolson to Mrs. Neilson, n.d., "Saturday evening" (October 1946), Folder 16, Box 982, Nicolson Papers. For a general overview, see Margaret Farrand Thorp, *Neilson of Smith* (New York: Oxford University Press, 1956).

12. Nicolson, "Rights and Privileges," 416.

13. Nicolson, "Scholars and Ladies," 788.

14. Nicolson, "Scholars and Ladies," 793–95.

15. Nicolson, "Scholars and Ladies," 789, 791; idem, "Experiments of Light," review of *Madame Curie: A Biography*, by Eve Curie, in *Essays of Three Decades*, ed. Arno L. Bader and Carlton F. Well, 469 (New York: Harper & Brothers, 1939). See also "We Need More Research," May 1, 1938, clipping, Box 382, Records of the Office of the President, Smith College Archives.

16. Nicolson, "Scholars and Ladies," 792, 793.

17. Nicolson, "Rights and Privileges," 414. The reference is to William Wordsworth's "Ode: Intimations of Immortality," stanza v.

18. *Smith College News,* March 10, 1981.

19. For a discussion of Columbia's resistance to coeducation and to the advancement of faculty women, see Andrea Walton, "Women at Columbia: A Study of Power and Empowerment in the Lives of Six Scholars" (Columbia University, Ph.D. diss., 1995); and idem, "The Dynamics of Mission and Market in the Coeducation Debates at Columbia University in 1889 and 1983," *History of Education* 31 (November 2002): 589–610.

20. For a discussion of Benedict's circumstances, see Margaret Caffrey, *Ruth Benedict: Stranger in the Land* (Austin: University of Texas, 1989), 276–278, quote at 276.

21. Marjorie Hope Nicolson to President Nicholas Murray Butler, April 7, 1940, Wright Central Files.

22. Nicolson's letter acknowledged the university's generosity when it informed her that it planned to double her salary raise. Nicolson to Frank Fackenthal, April 7, 1947, Nicolson Central Files, University Records and Archives, Columbia University, New York (hereafter cited as Nicolson Central Files).

23. Remarks delivered by Professor Alice Fredman, Memorial Service for Marjorie Hope Nicolson, April 29,1981 (in author's possession); Marjorie Hope Nicolson, "The Professor and the Detective," *Atlantic Monthly* 1511 (April 1929): 483–93.

24. See Nicolson's review of Mortimer Adler's *How to Read a Book* in *Yale Review* 30 (September 1940): 180.

25. Nicolson, "Merchants of Lights," 356. In the early 1940s Nicolson served along with Teachers College's critic of progressive education Isaac Kandel and Columbia's Oscar J. Campbell and Horatio Smith as a member of the MLA's Commission on Trends in Education. See Nicolson, "Literature in American Education," *American Scholar* 13 (Winter 1943–44): 122–25.

26. Marjorie Hope Nicolson, "Education in America," *Yale Review* 35 (March 1946): 537, 538.

27. Marjorie Hope Nicolson, *Newton Demands the Muse: Newton's Opticks and the Eighteenth-Century Poets* (Princeton: Princeton University Press, 1946), 22.

28. See Richard Bevis, "Eternal Snows: Pope's Temple of Fame and the Aesthetics of the Infinite," *Eighteenth-Century Life* (October 1986): 44–58. Literary interest in Nicolson seems to be increasing: see note 51 and Marjorie Hope Nicolson, *Mountain Gloom and Mountain Glory: The Development of the Aesthetics of the Infinite*, with a foreword by William Cronon (Seattle: University of Washington, 1997).

29. By the late 1940s, Columbia's English department had established itself as the nation's premier group of university literary scholars and teachers (AAU rating number 1). See Oscar James Campbell, "The Department of English and Comparative Literature," in *A History of the Faculty of Philosophy*, ed. Jacques Barzun (New York: Columbia University Press, 1957), 95.

30. Campbell, "The Department of English and Comparative Literature," 97.

31. See Tributes to Adele Mendelson, Department of English and Comparative Literature Folder, Columbiana Collection, Columbia University, New York.

32. The Columbia-educated literary scholar Carolyn G. Heilbrun offers her perspective on her student years in the department, where both Nicolson and Susanne Nobbe taught, in Carolyn G. Heilbrun, "The Profession and Society, 1958–83," *PMLA* 99 (May 1989): 411.

33. Rosalie Colie, "O quam te Memorem, Marjorie Hope Nicolson!" *The American Scholar* 34 (Summer 1965): 469.

34. Nicolson's earlier association with Lovejoy and Neilson, both prominent figures in the early years of the AAUP, nurtured and strengthened her commitment to the integrity of the academic profession. Nicolson, for example, joined John Dewey, William Allen Neilson, Morris Raphael Cohen, and Robert Sproul in sponsoring the Academic Freedom–Bertrand Russell Committee. See clipping, Folder 30, Box 982. 1, Nicolson Papers.

35. Nicolson to Vice President John A. Krout, November 24, 1954; report December 15, 1954; report January 12, 1955, Nicolson Central Files.

36. See note 1.

37. Nicolson, "A Generous Education," 12.

38. Quoted in *The New York Times*, December 29, 1963; Nicolson, "A Generous Education," 6.

CHAPTER 12: EDMUND BEECHER WILSON: AMERICA'S FIRST CELL BIOLOGIST: REFERENCES

Much of the information in this article has been obtained from the following sources:

Baxter, A. L. "Edmund Beecher Wilson and the Problem of Development: From the Germ Layer Theory to the Chromosome Theory of Inheritance." Ph.D. diss., Yale University, 1974.

Gilbert, S. F. "The Embryological Origins of the Gene Theory." *Journal of the History of Biology* 11 (1978): 307–51.

Gilbert, S. F. *Developmental Biology*. 6th ed. Sunderland, MA: Sinauer Associates, 2000.

Gilbert, S. F. "In Friendly Disagreement: Wilson, Morgan, and the Embryological Origins of the Gene Theory." *American Zoologist* 27 (1987): 797–806.

Harrison, R. G. "E. B. Wilson." *Science* 84 (1936): 565.

Lillie, F. R. *The Woods Hole Marine Biological Laboratory*. Chicago: University of Chicago Press, 1944.

Morgan, T. H. "Edmund Beecher Wilson." *Biographical Memoirs*, vol. 21, 315–42. National Academy of Sciences. Washington DC: The National Academy Press, 1940.

Muller, H. J. "Edmund B. Wilson—An Appreciation." *American Naturalist* 77:5–37 (1943): 142–72.

Maienschein, J. "Old Wine in New Bottles." *Nature* 407 (2000): 21.

———. *Transforming Traditions in American Biology, 1880–1915*. Baltimore: Johns Hopkins University Press, 1991.

Sedgwick, W. T., and E. B. Wilson. *General Biology*. New York: H. Holt and Co., 1886.

Sturtevant, A. H. "Thomas Hunt Morgan." *Biographical Memoirs*. Series by the National Academy of Sciences, 33 (1959): 284–325.

CHAPTER 13: THOMAS HUNT MORGAN AT COLUMBIA UNIVERSITY: NOTE

1. As pointed out by Harriet Zuckerman, this view was not shared by Muller, who stood further away from the group than the rest and thought that his own contributions had not been fully recognized: see Zuckerman, 1977, 141–43; see also Allen, 1978, 201–8.

BIBLIOGRAPHY

Allen, G. E. *Thomas Hunt Morgan: The Man and His Science*. Princeton, NJ: Princeton University Press, 1978.

Goldschmidt, R. B. "The Impact of Genetics Upon Science." In *Genetics in the Twentieth Century, Essays on the Progress of Genetics in Its First Fifty Years*, edited by L. C. Dunn. New York: Macmillan, 1950, 1–23.

Harrison, R. G. "Embryology and Its Relations." *Science* 85 (1937): 369–74.

Jaffe, B. *Men of Science in America: The Story of American Scientists Told Through the Lives and Achievements of Twenty Outstanding Men from Earliest Colonial Times to the Present Day*. Rev. ed. Chapter 16. New York: Simon & Schuster, 1958.

Judson, H. F. *The Eighth Day of Creation: The Makers of the Revolution in Biology*. New York: Simon & Schuster, 1979.

Kohler, R. E. *Lords of the Fly: Drosophila Genetics and the Experimental Life*. Chicago: University of Chicago Press, 1994.

Morgan, T. H. *Embryology and Genetics*. New York: Columbia University Press, 1934.

———. *The Theory of the Gene*. New Haven: Yale University Press, 1938.

——— et al. *The Mechanism of Mendelian Heredity*. New York: Holt Rinehart & Winston, 1915. Reprinted. by Johnson Reprint Corporation, with an introduction by Garland E. Allen, 1978.

Shine, I., and S. Wrobel. *Thomas Hunt Morgan: Pioneer of Genetics*. Lexington: University of Kentucky Press, 1976.

Sturtevant, A. H. *Thomas Hunt Morgan. Biographical Memoirs*, vol. 33, 295. Washington DC: The National Academy Press, 1959.

———. Unpublished interview (1965) with G. E. Allen. Pasadena, Caltech Archives, p. 28.

———. *A History of Genetics*. New York: Harper & Row, 1965.

Watson, J. D. *The Double Helix: A Personal Account of the Discovery of the Structure of DNA*. New York: New American Library, 1968.

Zuckerman, Harriet *Scientific Elite: Nobel Laureates in the United States*. New York: Free Press, 1977.

CHAPTER 13: AN AMERICAN CENTURY OF BIOLOGY: BIBLIOGRAPHY

Beadle, G. "Biochemical Genetics." In *Recollections in Phage and the Origins of Molecular Biology*. Edited by J. Cairns, G. S. Stent, and J. D. Watson. Cold Spring, NY: Cold Spring Harbor Laboratory, 1966.

Carlson, E. A., and Herman Joseph Muller. *Yearbook*, American Philosophical Society, 137–42.

Judson, H. F. *The Eighth Day of Creation: The Makers of the Revolution in Biology*. New York: Simon & Schuster 1979.

Kevene, H., L. Ehrman, and R. Richmond. "Theodosius Dobzhansky Up to Now." In *Essays in Evolution and Genetics in Honor of Theodosius Dobzhansky*, edited by Max K. Hecht and William C. Steere. New York: Appleton-Century-Crofts, 1970, 1–41.

Lederberg, J. "Francis J. Ryan." In *University on the Heights*, edited by Wesley First. Garden City: Doubleday and Co., Inc., 1969.

———. "Genetic Recombination in Bacteria: A Discovery Account." *Annual Review of Genetics* 21 (1987): 23–46.

Lewis, E. B. "The Bithorax Complex: The First Fifty Years." Reprinted from *Les Prix Nobel*, edited by T. Frängsmyr. Stockholm: Almqvist & Wiksell, 1995, 232–60.

Morgan, T. H., et al. *The Mechanism of Mendelian Heredity*. New York: Holt Rinehart & Winston, 1915. Reprinted by Johnson Reprint Corporation, with an introduction by Garland E. Allen, 1978.

Sturtevant, A. H. *A History of Genetics*. New York: Harper & Row, 1965.

Watson, J. D. *The Double Helix: A Personal Account of the Discovery of the Structure of DNA*. New York: New American Library, 1968.

CHAPTER 13: GENETICS, BIOLOGY, AND THE MYSTERIES OF THE MIND AT THE CUSP OF THE TWENTY-FIRST CENTURY: BIBLIOGRAPHY

Jacob, François. *The Logic of Life*. Translated by Betty E. Spillman. Princeton: Princeton University Press, 1981.

James, William. *Principles of Psychology*. New York: Henry Holt, 1890.

Kandel, Eric R., Thomas M. Jessell, and James H. Schwartz. *Principles of Neural Science*. 4th ed. New York: McGraw-Hill, 2000.

CHAPTER 20: EDWIN HOWARD ARMSTRONG: PIONEER OF THE AIRWAVES: REFERENCES

Burns, Ken. *Empire of the Air: The Men Who Made Radio*. Florentine Films, 1991; available from PBS Home Video.

Katzdorn, Mike. E. H. Armstrong Web Site, revised January 15, 2002, http://users.erols.com/oldradio/.

Lessing, Lawrence. *Man of High Fidelity: Edwin Howard Armstrong*. Philadelphia: Lippincott, 1956.

Lewis, T. S. *Empire of the Air: The Men Who Made Radio*. New York: HarperCollins, 1991.

CHAPTER 21: PAUL F. LAZARSFELD'S SCHOLARLY JOURNEY: NOTES

1. This is a version of a keynote address delivered at "An International Symposium in Honor of Paul Lazarsfeld," Brussels, Belgium, June 4–5, 2004.

2. Quoted in David Sills, "Paul F. Lazarsfeld 1901–1976," *Biographical Memoirs*, vol. 56, National Academy of Sciences (Washington DC: The National Academy Press, 1987), 254.

3. Paul F. Lazarsfeld, "An Episode in the History of Social Research: A Memoir," in *Intellectual Migration: Europe and America, 1930–1960*, ed. Donald Fleming and Bernard Bailyn (Cambridge, MA: The Belknap Press of Harvard University Press, 1969), 270–337.

4. Ibid., 272–73.

5. Ibid., 276.

6. For an essay on humanist scholars who migrated during this period, see Harry Levin, "Two *Romanisten* in America: Spitzer and Auerbach," in *Intellectual Migration*, ed. Fleming and Bailyn, 463–84.

7. One local fact provides fresh perspective on the importance of the flow of talent to the United States that began in earnest during the 1930s: Roughly one-third of Columbia University's current tenured faculty was born in nations other than the United States. In fact, the quality of American research universities today depends significantly on the ability to offer continued opportunities to talented students and scholars from abroad, especially in the science and engineering fields.

8. This follows closely the discussion in David L. Sills, "Paul F. Lazarsfeld 1901–1976," *Biographical Memoirs*.

9. This anecdote was told to John S. Reed by Lazarsfeld and is reported in John Shelton Reed, "A Research Assistant's Recollections." Presented at the Paul F. Lazarsfeld Centennial Celebration and Conference, Columbia University, September 29, 2001. Accessed from the Web on May 9, 2004, at: http://www.angelfire.com/blues/jsreed/pfl.html.

10. Seymour Martin Lipset, "The Academic Mind at the Top: The Political Behavior and Values of Faculty Elites," The Paul F. Lazarsfeld Lecture, Columbia University Center for the Social Sciences, February 12, 1982, published in *Public Opinion Quarterly* 46 (1982): 143–68; David L. Sills, "Paul F. Lazarsfeld 1901–1976," in *Biographical Memoirs*; Allen H. Barton, "Paul Lazarsfeld as Institutional Inventor," *International Journal of Public Opinion Research* 13, no. 3 (2001): 245–69.

11. Robert K. Merton, "Working with Lazarsfeld: Notes and Contexts," in *Paul Lazarsfeld (1901–1976): La Sociologie de Vienne à New York*, ed. Jacques Lautman and Bernard-Pierre Lécuyer (Paris: Editions L'Hartmann, 1998); based on a talk delivered at Colloque Paul F. Lazarsfeld 15–17 décembre 1994, Université de Paris-Sorbonne (Paris IV); Raymond Boudon, introduction to *On Social Research and Its Language/Paul F. Lazarsfeld*, ed. R. Boudon (Chicago: University of Chicago Press, 1993), 1–29.

12. James S. Coleman, "Paul F. Lazarsfeld: The Substance and Style of His Work," in *Sociological Traditions from Generation to Generation: Glimpses of the American Experience*, ed. Robert K. Merton and Matilda White Riley, (Norwood, NJ: Ablex, 1980), 153–74, at 155.

13. Ibid.

14. Quoted from John Shelton Reed, "A Research Assistant's Recollections."

15. Raymond Boudon, introduction to *On Social Research and Its Language/Paul F. Lazarsfeld*, 12.

16. Charles Tilly, "Event Catalogs as Theories," *Sociological Theory* 20, no. 2 (July 2002): 249. This is the published version of the paper that Tilly presented at the Columbia University Lazarsfeld Centennial Celebration in 2001. Merton's interest in the sociology and history of science led him, of course, to consider the "theory" that lies in the uses of scientific instruments and methods.

17. Robert K. Merton, "Working with Lazarsfeld," 193–99.

18. I want to thank Esther Shin, my assistant, who collected these data in May 2004.

19. When Lazarsfeld came to the United States, the only social research organization that was at all comparable and that predated the Bureau was the Institute for Research in Social Science, founded by Howard Odum in 1924 at the University of North Carolina.

   Lazarsfeld was also instrumental in obtaining Ford Foundation support to establish the renowned Center for Advanced Study in the Behavioral Sciences in 1954, even if, after the fact, he thought the Center was "a travesty"—an unfortunate deviation from his original idea of a professional school for advanced social research training.

20. Among other women collaborators were Marie Jahoda, Herta Herzog, Marjorie Fiske, Hazel Gaudet, and Patricia Kendall.

21. Paul F. Lazarsfeld and Robert K. Merton, "Friendship as a Social Process: A Substantive and Methodological Analysis," in *Freedom and Control in Modern Society*, ed. Morroe Berger, Theodore Abel, and Charles Page (New York: Van Nostrand, 1954),18–66, quoted at 56 .

22. I can recall as a graduate student seeing Paul late at night in his Fayerweather office with his loyal and able assistant Helen Houdeskova sitting in a chair taking dictation. This was before the age of computers: data were analyzed with the Bureau's famous "counter-sorter"; correlation coefficients were computed with adding machines; and drafts of papers had to be typed and retyped. On the night in question, he was composing a paper, referring to three-by-five index cards as he paced back and forth, then discarding them onto the floor. I never could capture this style of composition. It is perhaps no wonder that most of these drafts were offered up for Merton's editorial assistance.

CHAPTER 24: THE "DAUGHTERS" OF PAPA FRANZ: BENEDICT, MEAD, AND HURSTON: NOTES

1. Interview with Paula Rubel. To the end of his life, Boas addressed his male students as "Mr."

2. Boas had daughters of his own, and his namesake, Franziska, followed her father into anthropology. She specialized in dance.

3. Lois W. Banner, "Mannish Women, Passive Men, and Constitutional Types: Margaret Mead's *Sex and Temperament in Three Primitive Societies* as a Response to *Ruth Benedict's Patterns of Culture*," *Signs* 28, no. 3 (Spring 2003): 833–58. I agree with Lois Banner that Mead and Benedict's work constituted a conversation between them, but while Hurston was never an intimate of either, she was very much part of their circle, and her work spoke to a number of the issues they raised in theirs.

4. Desley Deacon, *Elsie Clews Parsons: Inventing a Life* (Chicago: University of Chicago Press, 1997), 243–78.

5. Lois W. Banner, *Intertwined Lives: Margaret Mead, Ruth Benedict, and Their Circle* (New York: Knopf, 2003), 43–65.

6. Margaret Mary Caffrey, *Ruth Benedict: Stranger in This Land* (Austin, TX: University of Texas Press, 1998), 44–50.

7. Judith Schachter Modell, *Ruth Benedict: Patterns of a Life* (Philadelphia: University of Pennsylvania Press, 1983), 1–113.

8. Ruth Benedict, "The Concept of the Guardian Spirit in North America" (Ph.D. diss., Columbia University, 1923). Published in *Memoirs of the American Anthropological Association*, vol. 29 (Monasha, WI, [1923]), 84.

9. Susan Ware, *Letter to the World: Seven Women Who Shaped the American Century* (Cambridge: Harvard University Press, 1998), 89; Jane Howard, *Margaret Mead: A Life* (New York: Fawcett, 1984), 42.

10. Margaret Mead, *Blackberry Winter: My Earlier Years* (New York: Touchstone, 1972), 111–12.

11. Daniel J. Kevles, *In the Name of Eugenics: Genetics and the Uses of Human Heredity* (New York: Knopf, 1985), 137–38.

12. Caffrey, *Ruth Benedict*, 154.

13. Clifford Geertz, *Works and Lives: The Anthropologist as Author* (Stanford, CA: Stanford University Press, 1988), 113.

14. Caffrey, *Ruth Benedict*, 153–55.

15. Gildersleeve to Meyer, June 9, 1925, Box 7, Folder 3, Meyer Papers.

16. Valerie Boyd, *Wrapped in Rainbows: The Life of Zora Neale Hurston* (New York: Scribner, 2002), 17.

17. Zora Neale Hurston, *Dust Tracks in the Road* (1942; reprint, New York: Harper Perennial, 1991), 123.

18. Graciela Hernandez, "Multiple Subjectivities and Strategic Positionality: Zora Neale Hurston's Experimental Ethnographies," in *Women Writing Culture*, ed. Ruth Behar and Deborah A. Gordon (Berkeley: University of California Press, 1995) 160–62; Hurston, *Dust Tracks*, 123.

19. Margaret Mead, *Blackberry Winter*, 103.

20. Hilary Lapsley, *Margaret Mead and Ruth Benedict: The Kinship of Women* (Amherst: University of

Massachusetts Press, 1999), 30–31, 76, 158, 308; Banner, *Intertwined Lives*, 195–98.

21. Banner, *Intertwined Lives*, 181, 185, 187, 225, 233.

22. Lapsley, *Margaret Mead and Ruth Benedict*, 75–76.

23. Banner, *Intertwined Lives*, pp. 251, 304. As Lois Banner has found in examining the scores of letters Mead and Benedict wrote to one another from the 1920s through the 1940s, they never used the term "lesbian" in referring to one another, although Mead referred to other women they knew as lesbians. Today Mead would be regarded as bisexual and Benedict as a lesbian.

24. Franz Boas, "Anthropology," in *Encyclopedia of the Social Sciences*, vol. 2, ed. Edwin R. A. Seligman (New York: MacMillan, 1930), 85; Edward Sapir, "The Discipline of Sex," *American Mercury* 16 (1929): 417, as quoted in Caffrey, *Ruth Benedict*, 198.

25. Mary Catherine Bateson, *With a Daughter's Eye: A Memoir of Margaret Mead and Gregory Bateson* (New York: William Morrow, 1984), 124.

26. Boyd, *Wrapped in Rainbows*, 127–31, 161, 224–25, 271–75.

27. Banner, "Mannish Women, Passive Men, and Constitutional Types," 833–56; Ruth Benedict, *Patterns of Culture* (New York: Houghton Mifflin, 1934), 262–65.

28. Mead, *Sex and Temperament in Three Primitive Societies* (New York: Morrow, 1935), 293, 296–97, 305–6.

29. Zora Neale Hurston, *Their Eyes Were Watching God* (1937; reprint Urbana: University of Illinois Press, 1978), 17.

30. H. E. Hawkes, "Report of the Committee on Anthropology," January 18, 1937, Hawkes Papers, Columbiana. Lapsley, *Margaret Mead and Ruth Benedict*, p. 257. According to Lapsley, Dean Howard McBain wanted Columbia to be the first university to have a female head of a department; Mead thought Benedict did not have the temperament for the job; Parsons disapproved because Benedict had never finished the Southwest concordance. For an excellent discussion of the problems that female anthropologists faced in trying to advance in the profession, see Deacon, *Elsie Clews Parsons*, 262–72.

31. Virginia Heyer Young, *Ruth Benedict: Beyond Relativity, Beyond Pattern* (Lincoln, NE: University of Nebraska, 2005).

32. Paula Rubel, of the Barnard College Department of Anthropology, won tenure in the university in 1972. The next female anthropologist to win tenure (and the first in the Columbia department since Benedict to do so) was Katherine Newman in 1989.

CHAPTER 31: ELI GINZBERG: SKEPTICAL ECONOMIST, CONSERVATOR OF MANPOWER: NOTES

1. *Grass on the Slag Heaps: The Story of the Welsh Miners* appeared in 1942; *The Unemployed* in 1943, and the third study, *The Labor Leader*, was published after the war, in 1948.

2. Volume 1: Eli Ginzberg, James K. Anderson, Sol W. Ginsburg, M.D., and John L. Herma, *The Lost Divisions*; volume 2: Eli Ginzberg, John B. Miner, James K. Anderson, Sol W. Ginsburg, M.D., and John L. Herma, *Breakdown and Recovery*; volume 3: Eli Ginzberg, James K. Anderson, Sol W. Ginsburg, M.D., John L. Herma, Douglas W. Bray, William Jordan, and Major Francis J. Ryan, *Patterns of Performance*. All were published by Columbia University Press, 1959.

3. Eli Ginzberg, Sol W. Ginsburg, M.D., and John L. Herma, *Psychiatry and Military Manpower Policy: A Reappraisal of the Experience of World War II* (New York: Columbia University Press, 1953); Eli Ginzberg, chair, *What Makes an Executive? Report of a Round Table on Executive Potential and Performance* (New York: Columbia University Press, 1955); Eli Ginzberg, assisted by James K. Anderson, Douglas W. Bray, and Robert W. Smuts, *The Negro Potential* (New York: Columbia University Press, 1955); Eli Ginzberg and Ewing W. Reilley, assisted by Douglas W. Bray and John L. Herma, *Effecting Change in Large Organizations* (New York: Columbia University Press, 1956); Eli Ginzberg, *The Wealth of a Nation* (New York: Simon & Schuster, 1958).

4. Eli Ginzberg, Dale L. Hiestand, and Beatrice G. Reubens, *The Pluralistic Economy* (New York: McGraw-

Hill, 1965).

5. Ivar Berg, ed., *Human Resources and Economic Welfare. Essays in Honor of Eli Ginzberg* (New York: Columbia University Press, 1972); Irving Louis Horowitz, ed., *Eli Ginzberg: The Economist as a Public Intellectual* (New Brunswick: Transaction Publishers, 2002).

CHAPTER 37: THE CORE CURRICULUM: WISDOM, TRAINING, AND CONTEMPORARY CIVILIZATION

Current Contemporary Civilization Syllabus

Below is a list of required readings for all sections of Contemporary Civilization during 2004–05. The number following each reading indicates the minimum number of class sessions that an instructor is expected to devote to it. Instructors may excerpt longer readings unless otherwise indicated. While paperbacks still form the backbone of the course, many readings are available to students via the Contemporary Civilization Web site.

Even with seventeen sessions devoted to mandatory readings in the fall (sixteen in the spring) instructors still have at least eight sessions in each semester for readings assigned at their discretion. These readings can take the form of additional texts to be purchased, packets of photocopies, or texts drawn from the Internet.

CC 1101 (FALL 2004) REQUIRED READINGS
Plato, *Republic* (complete) (2)
Aristotle, *The Nicomachean Ethics* (1)
Aristotle, *Politics* (1)
The Old Testament: Exodus, Deuteronomy (1)
Cicero, *On Duties* (1)
The New Testament: Matthew, Romans, Galatians (complete) (1)
Augustine, *City of God* (1)
The Qur'an (1)

Medieval Philosophy (1)
Averröes, *On the Harmony of Religion and Philosophy* (selections)
Aquinas, *The Summa Against the Gentiles* and *The Summa of Theology* (selections)
Maimonides, *The Guide of the Perplexed* (selections)

Machiavelli, *The Prince* (complete) (1)

The New World (1)
Sepúlveda, *Democrates Alter; Or, On the Just Causes for War Against the Indians*
Las Casas, *Apologetic History of the Indies and Thirty Very Juridical Propositions*

Selections from *The Protestant Reformation* (1)

The Scientific Revolution (1)
Galileo, "Letter to Madame Christina of Lorraine, Grand Duchess of Tuscany" AND
Descartes, *Discourse on Method for Conducting One's Reason Well and for Seeking Truth in the Sciences* (complete) OR
Newton, *The Principia* (selections)

Descartes, *Meditations on First Philosophy* (1)

Hobbes, *Leviathan* (1)

Locke, *Second Treatise of Government* (1)

Assignment over Break: Kant, "What is Enlightenment?"

Texts:
Plato, *Republic* (Hackett)
Aristotle, *The Nicomachean Ethics* (Oxford)
Aristotle, *Politics* (Hackett)
The Holy Bible: Revised Standard Version (Meridian)
Cicero, *On Duties* (Cambridge)
Augustine, *City of God* (Penguin)
The Meaning of the Holy Qur'an (Amana)
Machiavelli, *Selected Political Writings* (Hackett)
The Protestant Reformation (Harper & Row)
Descartes, *Discourse on Method and Meditations on First Philosophy* (Hackett)
Hobbes, *Leviathan* (Oxford)
Locke, *Second Treatise of Government* (Hackett)

CC 1102 (SPRING 2005) REQUIRED READINGS
Hume, *An Enquiry Concerning the Principles of Morals* (1)
Rousseau, *Discourse on the Origin and Foundations of Inequality Among Men* (1)
Rousseau, *On the Social Contract, or Principles of Political Right* (1)

Kant, *Grounding for the Metaphysics of Morals* (1)
Smith, *Wealth of Nations* (1)

French Revolution (1)
Sieyès, "What is the Third Estate?"
The Declaration of the Rights of Man and of the Citizen
Preface to the French Constitution of 1793
Olympe de Gouges, "The Rights of Woman"

Counter-Revolution (1)
Burke, *Reflections on the Revolution in France*
Bentham, "Anarchical Fallacies" (selections)

Wollstonecraft, *A Vindication of the Rights of Woman* AND
Mill, *The Subjection of Women* (1)

Tocqueville, *Democracy in America* (selections) (1)

Mill, *On Liberty* OR *Utilitarianism* (1)

Marx, selections from *The Marx-Engels Reader* (1)

Darwin, *On the Origin of Species by Means of Natural Selection* (1)

Nietzsche, *On the Genealogy of Morals* (1)

Du Bois, *The Souls of Black Folk* AND "The Souls of White Folk" (1)

Freud, *Civilization and Its Discontents* (1)

Woolf, *Three Guineas* (1)

Modern Issues (any two from the following)
Arendt, *The Human Condition*
Fanon, *The Wretched of the Earth*
Foucault, *Discipline and Punish: The Birth of the Prison*

MacKinnon, *Towards a Feminist Theory of the State*
Rawls, *A Theory of Justice*

Texts:
Hume, *An Enquiry Concerning the Principles of Morals* (Hackett)
Rousseau, *The Basic Political Writings* (Hackett)
Kant, *Grounding for the Metaphysics of Morals* (Hackett)
Smith, *Wealth of Nations* (Modern Library)
Burke, *Reflections on the Revolution in France* (Hackett)
Wollstonecraft, *A Vindication of the Rights of Woman* (Dover)
Tocqueville, *Democracy in America* (Hackett)
Mill, *On Liberty and Other Essays* (Oxford)
The Marx-Engels Reader (Norton)
Darwin, *On the Origin of Species* (Broadview)
Nietzsche, *On the Genealogy of Morals/Ecco Homo* (Vintage)
Du Bois, *The Souls of Black Folk* (Dover)
Freud, *Civilization and Its Discontents* (Norton)
Woolf, *Three Guineas* (HBJ)
Arendt, *The Human Condition* (Chicago)
Fanon, *The Wretched of the Earth* (Grove)
Foucault, *Discipline and Punish: The Birth of the Prison* (Vintage)
Rawls, *A Theory of Justice* (Harvard)
MacKinnon, *Toward a Feminist Theory of the State* (Harvard)

CHAPTER 38: ASIA IN THE CORE CURRICULUM: NOTES

1. See *Eastern Canons: Approaches to the Asian Classics*, ed. Wm. Theodore de Bary and Irene Bloom (New York: Columbia University Press, 1990), 25–26.

2. See the topics for discussion suggested for each major work included in the *Guide to the Asian Classics*, 3rd edition (New York: Columbia University Press, 1989).

WORKSHOPS AND COLLOQUIA ON NOBILITY AND CIVILIZATION, EAST AND WEST

For the pilot program of workshops and colloquia for a multicultural approach to the Core Curriculum supported by the Mellon Foundation, the first series focused on the theme of nobility and civility, East and West, and proceeded in the following sequences:

Workshop on nobility and civility, classic antiquity	May 2002
Pilot colloquium/seminar	Spring 2003
Second phase workshop on medieval period	Fall 2003
Capstone colloquia or Major seminars	Fall/Spring 2003–04
Third phase workshop on modern period	May 2004
Capstone colloquia or Major seminars, senior level	Fall/Spring 2004–05
Fourth phase workshop on contemporary period	May/June 2005

I. Classical Antiquity

For the first faculty workshop (summer 2002) and the following student colloquium (spring 2003), the readings were taken from the following list of works representing the classical periods of the major world traditions.

Classical West: *Iliad* and *Odyssey*, Herodotus and Thucydides, Plato and Aristotle, Cicero and *Aeneid*, St. Augustine; **Middle East and India:** Al Farabi, Nizam al Mulk, Shah Nameh (Seyavash), Dhammapada and Buddhacarita, *Bhagavad Gita*, Artha Sastra and Kama Sutra; **China and Japan:** *Confucian Analects*, Mencius and Xunzi, Laozi and Hanfeizi, Shōtoku's Constitution, Saichō and Kukai.

II. For the second workshop and colloquium, the readings were taken from among:

Europe: Dante Alighieri, Chrétien de Troyes, Geoffrey Chaucer, Thomas More, Castiglione, Montaigne, Molière, Thomas Hobbes; **Middle East and India:** Al Ghazali, Maimonides, Usama Ibn Munkid, Ibn Tufayl, Averroes, Ibn Khaldun, Santideva, Visakhadatta, Ilanko Atikal, Manjhana, Sukraniti; **East Asia:** *Lotus Sutra, Golden Light Sutra,* Hui yuan, *Sutra of the Humane King,* Kenkō's *Essays in Idleness, Tale of the Heike,* Zhu Xi, Huang Zongxi, Yi T'oegye and Yi Yulgok, Kaibara Ekken, Yamaga Sokō and Muro Kyusō.

III. A third stage workshop entitled Leadership and citizenship and dealing with the modern period 1800–1930 C.E. was held in summer 2004, chaired by Pierre Force (chair of the French department) and Andrew Nathan (chair of political science). It included the following readings:

Europe and America: John Locke, Bernard Mandeville, Charles de S. Montesquieu, Jean-Jacques Rousseau, Adam Smith, Heinrich von Kleist, G. W. F. Hegel, Ralph Waldo Emerson, Alexis de Tocqueville, Søren Kierkegaard, Walt Whitman, Fyodor Dostoevsky, Leo Tolstoy, Friedrich Nietzsche, Emile Durkheim, Max Weber; **Middle East and India:** Ziya Gokalp, Sadegh Hedayet, Naquib Mahfous, Jalal al-E Ahmad, Rabindranath Tagore, Mahatma Gandhi, Sri Aurobindo, Muhammad Iqbal, Jawaharlal Nehru, R. K. Narayan; **Japan and China:** Aizawa Seishisai, Yokoi Shōnan, Sakuma Shozan, Fukuzawa Yukichi, Asahi Heigo, Yoshino Sakuzo, Kang Youwei, Zhang Zhidong, Liang Qichao, Sun Yatsen, Liang Shuming.

IV. Contemporary Period (1930–present)

Europe and America: Norbert Elias, Vladimir Nabokov, Ortega y Gassett, Milovan Djilas, Hannah Arendt, James Joyce, John Rawls, Charles Taylor, Lionel Trilling, Virginia Woolf, Arthur Miller, Thomas Mann, Varlam Shalamov, Anna Akhmatova, Adam Michnik; **Middle East and India:** Naguib Mafouz, Forugh Farrokhzad, Baqir al-Sadr, Larbi Sadiki, Amartya Sen, Girish Karnad; **Japan and China:** Oe Kenzaburo, Mishima Yukio, Ueno Chizuko, Maruyama Masao, Tang Junyi, Fang Lizhi, Li Ziaojiang, Wei Jingsheng, Gu Mu.

Staff for the workshops and colloquia have been drawn from among the following faculty participants:

Ryuichi Abe, Chair, Department of Religion
Bradley Abrams, Associate Professor of History
Robert Belknap, Professor Emeritus of Slavic Languages; Director, University Seminars
Courtney Bender, Assistant Professor of Religion and Sociology
Akeel Bilgrami, Johnsonian Professor of Philosophy and Director of the Heyman Center for the
  Humanities
Irene Bloom, Ann Whitney Olin Professor Emeritus of the Humanities, Barnard College
Richard Bulliet, Professor of History; former Director of Middle East Institute
Charles Cameron, Associate Professor of Philosophy, Barnard College
Taylor Carman, Associate Professor of Philosophy, Barnard College
Rachel E. Chung, Adjunct Assistant Professor of Music; Instructor of East Asian Civilizations
Hamid Dabashi, Professor and Chair, Middle East Languages and Cultures
Dennis Dalton, Professor of Political Science, Barnard College
Jenny Davidson, Assistant Professor of English and Comparative Literature
Wm. Theodore de Bary, John Mitchell Mason Professor Emeritus of the University, Asian Studies
Wiebke Denecke, Society of Fellows, Chinese Intellectual History
Kathy Eden, Mark Van Doren Professor in Literature Humanities; Chair, Humanities Staff
Pierre Force, Singer Professor of CC/Core; Department Chair, French-Romance Philology
Julian Franklin, Professor Emeritus of Political Science
Ernesto V. Garcia, Teaching Fellow in Philosophy
Eileen Gillooly, Director of Core Curriculum, Columbia College

Carol Gluck, George Sansom Professor of Japanese History

Christopher Hill, Assistant Professor of Japanese Literature, Yale University

Carl Hovde, Professor Emeritus, English/Comparative Literature; Chair, Friends of the Heyman
    Center; former Dean of Columbia College

Andreas Huyssen, Villard Professor of German and Comparative Literature

Robert Hymes, Carpentier Professor of East Asian Studies; Chair, East Asian Languages and Cultures

David Johnston, Joseph Straus Professor of Political Philosophy

Matthew Jones, Associate Professor of History

Hossein Kamaly, Specialist in Area Studies (Middle East), School of International Affairs

Jinhong Kim, Associate Professor of History and Religion, Rutgers University

Young-kun Kim, Professor of Political Science, City University Graduate Center

Susan Landesman, Adjunct Professor, Committee on Asia and the Middle East

Deborah Martinsen, Adjunct Associate Professor of Slavic; Assistant to Director of the Core
    Curriculum

Rachel McDermott, Associate Professor of Asia and Middle East, Barnard College

Mary McGee, Adjunct Professor of Indian Religion; Dean of Students, General Studies

James Mirollo, Parr Professor Emeritus of English and Comparative Literature; Member of Society of
    Senior Scholars; former head of Literature Humanities

Scott Morrison, Society of Fellows in the Humanities, Political Science

Andrew Nathan, Class of 1919 Professor of Political Science; Chair of Political Science

Richard Norris, Professor Emeritus, Union Theological Seminary

Peter Pouncey, Professor Emeritus of Classics; former President of Amherst College

Wayne Proudfoot, Professor of Religion

George Saliba, Professor, Middle East Languages and Cultures; teacher of Islamic Civilization courses

Amiya Sen, Professor of Electrical Engineering and Applied Physics, Applied Mathematics; former
    Chair, Curriculum Committee, Electrical Engineering

Allan Silver, Professor of Sociology

W. J. Smit, Queen Wilhelmina Professor of History; former Chair of CC

Gary Tubb, Dharma Hinduja Senior Lecturer in Sanskrit, Department of Religion

Neguin Yavari, Assistant Professor, Department of Religion

Junior Participants

    Ari Borrell, EALAC, Barnard, Instructor in East Asian Humanities

    Rachel Chung, Music, EALAC, Preceptor in Asian Music Humanities

    Bonnie Kim, EALAC, Preceptor in Korean Civilization

    Chad Kia, MEALAC, Preceptor in Middle East Civilizations

    Jason Bahbak Mohaghegh, MEALAC, Preceptor in Middle East Civilizations

    Nerina Rustomji, History, CC Steering Committee

    Malena Takvorian, MEALAC, Preceptor in Middle East Civilizations

    Jaret Weisfogel, EALAC, Preceptor in East Asian Civilizations

    Selma Zecovic, MEALAC, Preceptor in Middle East Civilizations

All four of the spring workshops listed above and all six semesters of the colloquia have been conducted to the great satisfaction of both faculty and the student participants, and concluded with a
recommendation that the workshops and colloquia be continued on a regular basis.

CHAPTER 45: A COMMUNITARIAN AT LARGE: NOTES

1. This approach also anticipated many of the issues later raised by "Orientalism" and "Cultural Studies."

2. *Neo-Confucian Orthodoxy and the Learning of the Mind-and-Heart* (New York: Columbia University Press,
1981); *The Message of the Mind in Neo-Confucianism* (New York: Columbia University Press, 1988); and
Learning for One's Self (New York: Columbia University Press, 1991).

ILLUSTRATION CREDITS

INDEX

Page numbers for illustrations are in *italic*.